Thinking about the future
8,9,10 (→ some 11,12)
Consumer decision p

"CB is **clear, concise and conceptual."**

    – Craig Marty;
    University of Dubuque

"CB is a well written book, that has a **focused perspective on both practical and theoretical aspects of consumer behavior.** Students see *CB* as more relevant compared to some of the other texts out there."

    – Susan Myers;
    University of Central Arkansas

an innovative concept in teaching and learning solutions designed to best reach today's students

Stats pulled from the following sites:
- http://www.crunchgear.com/2009/02/10/how-do-you-compare-teens-spend-31-hours-a-week-online/.
- http://www.sfnblog.com/circulation_and_readership/2009/03/study_newspaper_readership_down_despite.php
- http://www.thnews.com/article.php?id=8761
- http://mediacrit.com/free-papers

"Using *CB* in my classes has been a very positive experience. I have found the content to be well written and grounded in traditional consumer behavior theory, while my students seem to relate particularly well with the timely examples provided by the authors."

    – Dr. C. David Shepherd;
    Georgia Southern University

SOUTH-WESTERN
CENGAGE Learning

CB2

Barry J. Babin, Louisiana Tech University
Eric G. Harris, Pittsburg State University

Executive Vice President and Publisher, Business & Computers: Jonathan Hulbert

Vice President of Editorial, Business: Jack W. Calhoun

Editor-in-Chief: Melissa S. Acuña

Director, 4LTR Press: Neil Marquardt

Executive Editor: Mike Roche

Developmental Editor: Julie Klooster

Editorial Assistant: Kayti Purkiss

Sr. Project Manager, 4LTR Press: Michelle Lockard

Executive Brand Marketing Manager, 4LTR Press: Robin Lucas

Vice President of Marketing, Business & Computers: Bill Hendee

Marketing Coordinator: Shanna Shelton

Sr. Marketing Communications Manager: Sarah Greber

Sr. Content Project Manager: Martha Conway

Media Editor: John Rich

Print Buyer: Miranda Klapper

Production House: Bill Smith Studio

Sr. Art Director: Stacy Jenkins Shirley

Internal & Cover Designer: Ke Design, Mason, Ohio

Cover Image: © Getty Images/Comstock Images

Title Page Images: Getty Images

Page iii Images:

1. © ISTOCKPHOTO.COM/SEAN LOCKE

2. © ROBERT STAINFORTH/ALAMY

3. © MIKE KEMP/RUBBERBALL/ JUPITERIMAGES

4. © MARK YAMAMOTO/ORANGE COUNTY REGISTER/NEWSCOM

5. © PICTURE PARTNERS/ALAMY

Sr. Image Rights Acquisitions Account Manager: Deanna Ettinger

Photo Researcher: Terri Miller

Sr. Text Rights Acquisitions Account Manager: Mardell Glinski Schultz

Text Permissions Researcher: Elaine Kosta

For product information and technology assistance, contact us at **Cengage Learning Customer & Sales Support, 1-800-354-9706**

For permission to use material from this text or product, submit all requests online at **cengage.com/permissions**
Further permissions questions can be emailed to **permissionrequest@cengage.com**

The names of all products mentioned herein are used for identification purposes only and may be trademarks or registered trademarks of their respective owners. South-Western disclaims any affiliation, association, connection with, sponsorship, or endorsement by such owners.

Library of Congress Control Number: 2009942945

Student Edition ISBN-13: 978-0-324-83000-2
Student Edition ISBN-10: 0-324-83000-9

Student Edition with PAC ISBN 13: 978-0-324-82999-0
Student Edition with PAC ISBN 10: 0-324-82999-X

South-Western Cengage Learning
5191 Natorp Boulevard
Mason, OH 45040
USA

Cengage Learning is a leading provider of customized learning solutions with office locations around the globe, including Singapore, the United Kingdom, Australia, Mexico, Brazil, and Japan. Locate your local office at: **international.cengage.com/region**

Cengage Learning products are represented in Canada by Nelson Education, Ltd.

To learn more about 4LTR Press, visit **4ltr.cengage.com/busn**

Purchase any of our products at your local college store or at our preferred online store **www.CengageBrain.com**

Printed in the United States of America
1 2 3 4 5 6 7 12 11 10 09

BRIEF CONTENTS

CONTENTS

© MIKE KEMP/RUBBERBALL/JUPITERIMAGES

WENN/NEWSCOM

PART TWO INTERNAL INFLUENCERS

3 Consumer Learning Starts Here: Perception   40

© TONY BAKER/PHOTOTANICA/GETTY IMAGES

4 Comprehension, Memory, and Cognitive Learning 60

5 Motivation and Emotion: Driving Consumer Behavior 82

6 Personality, Lifestyles, and the Self-Concept   102

© MIKE KEMP/RUBBERBALL/JUPITERIMAGES

7 Attitudes and Attitude Change   120

© STEFANO OPPO/PHOTONICA/GETTY IMAGES

PART THREE   EXTERNAL INFLUENCERS

8 Consumer Cul

©ISTOCKPHOTO.COM/BOLESLAW KUBICA

9 Group Influence   168

© ISTOCKPHOTO.COM/MINH TANG

PART FOUR   CONSUMPTION PROCESSES

10 Consumers in Situations   190

© CHUCK SAVAGE/CORBIS

11 Decision Making I: Need Recognition and Search 212

© VARIO IMAGES GMBH & CO. KG/ALAMY

12 Decision Making II: Alternative Evaluation and Choice 230

© TOSHIFUMI/KITAMURA/AFP/GETTY IMAGES

For my family and my mentors, especially Bill and Joe.
—Barry Babin

To my family, Tara, Christian, and Sydney.
—Eric Harris

what do you think?

In any business, the customer is truly the most important person.

1 2 3 4 5 6 7

strongly disagree   strongly agree

The marketer that

understands consumers will be able to design products that provide more value, and through this process, enhance the well-being of both the company and its customers.

1

What Is CB, and Why Should I Care?

After studying this chapter, the student should be able to:

LO1 Understand the meaning of *consumption* and *consumer behavior.*

LO2 Describe how consumers get treated differently in various types of exchange environments.

LO3 Explain the role of consumer behavior in business and society.

LO4 Be familiar with basic approaches to studying consumer behavior.

LO5 Describe why consumer behavior is so dynamic and how recent trends affect consumers.

Introduction

how many times a day does the typical college student act like a consumer? If we stop to think about it, we find that the entire day is filled with consumption and consumption decisions. What should I wear? What will I eat for breakfast? What music should I listen to? Will I go to class today? What am I going to do this weekend? Many questions like these are routinely answered within the first few moments of every day, with the answers ultimately turning the wheels of the economy and shaping the quality of life for the individual consumer.

How can simple decisions be so important to society? The answer to this question is one of the key points of this chapter and of this text. Indeed, the consumer answers these questions by choosing the options that offer the most value. Thus, consumer behavior is really all about value.

As long as time keeps moving, things happen. In the same way, as long as people keep consuming, things happen. To illustrate, think about the chain reaction that is set in place when a consumer purchases an electronic device like a BlackBerry® Curve™ smartphone. The store will have to replace the item in inventory. The manufacturer will have to replenish the stock. This means that raw materials will have to be purchased from suppliers. The raw materials and finished products will all need to be shipped by companies such as UPS or DHL. But that isn't all. The consumer will need a new service plan to take advantage of the device, and companies like AT&T will kindly oblige.

For the consumer, owning the BlackBerry will lead to greater access to the Internet, more opportunities to purchase things including MP3s and related accessories, and more opportunities to communicate with others. Most importantly, assuming all goes well, the consumer will have improved his or her quality of life!

Although some courses are titled simply "buyer behavior," this example illustrates that there is much more to *consuming* than simply *buying*. This does not diminish the importance of getting someone to buy something. But, consumption goes on long after purchase, and the story of consumption ultimately determines how much value is created.

As you can see, our behavior as consumers is critically important not just to ourselves, but to many other people. This is why so many people are interested in learning about the field of consumer behavior. The marketer who understands consumers will be able to design products that provide more value, and through this process, enhance the well-being of both the company and its customers. Policy makers who understand consumer behavior can make more effective public policy decisions. Certainly, last but not least, consumers who understand consumer behavior can make better decisions concerning how they allocate scarce resources. Thus, an understanding of consumer behavior can mean better business for companies, better public policy for governments, and a better life for individuals and households.

> The purchase of a product like this sets in motion a chain reaction with implications for the consumer and the economy.

© PRNEWSFOTO/VERIZON WIRELESS/NEWSCOM

LO1 Consumption and Consumer Behavior

Consumer behavior can be defined from two different perspectives. This is because the term refers to both

1. Human thought and action and

2. A field of study (human inquiry) that is developing an accumulated body of knowledge.

If we think of a consumer considering the purchase of a new PDA, consumer behavior can be thought of as the actions, reactions, and consequences that take place as the consumer goes through a decision-making process, reaches a decision, and then uses the product. Alternatively, if we consider the body of knowledge that researchers have accumulated that attempts to explain these types of thoughts and actions, we are approaching consumer behavior as a field of study. Thus, rather than choosing between the two alternative approaches, an understanding of the way the term *consumer behavior* is used is best gained by considering both approaches.

CONSUMER BEHAVIOR AS HUMAN BEHAVIOR

First, **consumer behavior** is the set of value-seeking activities that take place as people go about addressing realized needs. In other words, when a consumer comes to realize that something is needed, a chain reaction begins as the consumer sets out to find desirable ways to fill this need. The chain reaction involves psychological processes, including thoughts, feelings, and behavior, and the entire process culminates in value.

The Basic CB Process

Exhibit 1.1 illustrates the basic consumption process. Each step is discussed in detail in later chapters. However, the process is briefly illustrated here in the context of the BlackBerry Curve purchase. At some point, the consumer realizes a need for better communication with other people and access to outside media, including the Internet. This realization may be motivated by a desire to do better on the job or to have better access to friends and family. A **want** is simply a specific desire that spells out a way a consumer can go about addressing a recognized need. A

EXHIBIT 1.1
The Basic Consumption Process

- Need
- Want
- Exchange
- Costs and Benefits
- Reaction
- Value

© ISTOCKPHOTO.COM/JAROSLAW WOJCIK

consumer feels a need to belong and socialize, and this creates a desire for communication devices.

After weighing some options, the consumer decides to visit an AT&T store where communications devices are sold. After looking at several alternative devices, the consumer chooses a BlackBerry Curve. Next, the consumer participates in an exchange in which he or she gives up economic resources in return for receiving the product. An **exchange** is the acting out of a decision to give something up in return for something of greater value. Here, the consumer decides the BlackBerry will be worth at least the price of the product and the service plan that will be needed to make the device functional.

The consumer then uses the product and experiences all the associated costs and benefits. **Costs** can be thought of as negative results of consumption. The costs involve more than just the price of the product. Time is spent in both shopping for and learning how to use the Curve. It can take physical effort to visit retail stores during the process. Time and money that are spent cannot be allocated toward other activities or processes, resulting in high opportunity costs for the consumer. **Benefits** are positive results of consumption. The benefits are multifaceted, ranging from better job performance to more entertainment from the MP3 feature.

Over time, the consumer evaluates the costs and benefits and reacts to the purchase in some way. These reactions involve thoughts and feelings. The thoughts may involve reactions to features such as the ease of use. The feelings may sometimes include frustration if the features do not work correctly or conveniently. Ultimately, the process results in a perception of value. We will discuss value in more detail in Chapter 2.

Consumption

Another way to look at the basic consumer behavior process is to consider the steps that occur when consumption takes place. Obviously, a consumer consumes! Interestingly, very few consumer behavior books define consumption itself. **Consumption** represents the process by which goods, services, or ideas are used and transformed into value. Thus, the actions involved in acquiring and using a mobile communications device

> Consumption represents the process by which goods, services, or ideas are used and transformed into value.

like a BlackBerry will create value for a consumer. If the product performs well, a great deal of value may result. If the consumer is unhappy with the product, very little value or even a negative amount of value may result. As mentioned, this outcome affects consumer well-being by affecting quality of life.

CONSUMER BEHAVIOR AS A FIELD OF STUDY

Consumer behavior as a field of study represents the study of consumers as they go about the consumption

economics study of production and consumption

process. In this sense, consumer behavior is the science of studying how consumers seek value in an effort to address real needs. This book represents a collection of knowledge resulting as consumer behavior researchers go about studying consumers. Consumer behavior sometimes is known as buyer behavior. Even though the purchases consumers make are clearly important, the study of consumers goes beyond the point of purchase. For this reason, the term *consumer behavior* seems more appropriate.

Consumer behavior, as a field of study, is a very young field. The first books that discuss consumer behavior or buyer behavior date from the 1960s.[1] Thus, compared with older disciplines, researchers have had less time to develop the body of knowledge. Therefore, each decade the accumulated body of knowledge grows significantly. Clearly however, much uncertainty remains, and the body of theory that is accepted by researchers and practitioners is relatively small. This is one reason consumer behavior is so exciting to study. Consumer behavior research is quickly expanding the knowledge base.

Like other disciplines, consumer behavior has family roots in other disciplines. Exhibit 1.2 lists some related disciplines.

Economics and Consumer Behavior

Economics is often defined as the study of production and consumption.[2] Accordingly, it is easy to see that marketing has its origins in economics, particularly with respect to the production and distribution of goods. As the definition implies, economics also involves consumption. Therefore, consumer behavior and economics also have much in common. However, the economist's focus on consumer behavior is generally a broad or macro perspective. For example, economics studies often involve things like commodity consumption of nations over time. This may even involve tracking changes in consumption with different price levels enabling price elasticity to be determined. The data for a study like this may be taken from historical sales records. It's important to note that studies like these do not involve input from individual consumers.

To illustrate a macro perspective, we note that researchers and marketing managers are very interested in emerging markets like China and India. Although these places may seem like very distant lands with little relevance to most business students, nothing could be further from the truth. Within a decade, estimates suggest that China will surpass the United States as the leading country in terms of total consumer purchasing power. Thus, economists might be very interested in estimating the demand for consumer products like alco-

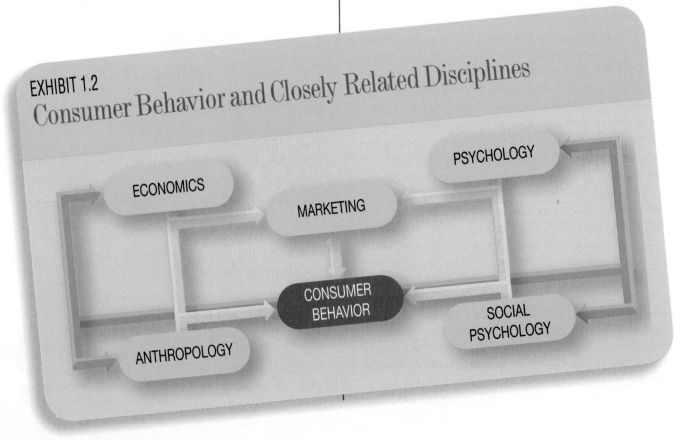

EXHIBIT 1.2
Consumer Behavior and Closely Related Disciplines

holic beverages in an emerging market like China. One study shows that Chinese consumers display greater price elasticity for wine coolers and wine than they do for beer.[3] In other words, changes in price do not affect overall beer consumption as much as they do consumption of wine or wine coolers. This pattern suggests beer is more of a staple good to Chinese consumers; thus, beer consumption should remain relatively stable compared to other beverages.

In contrast, consumer behavior researchers generally study consumer behavior at a more micro level, often focusing on individual consumer behavior. As such, consumer research often involves experiments or interviews involving responses from individual consumers. For example, consumer researchers examined the extent to which exposure to advertisements promoting alcoholic drink specials influences college student drinking. The study was conducted by getting responses to such ads from individual consumers. Results suggest that students have a more positive attitude toward the bar running the specials and intend to buy more because of the specials when they are exposed to the ad.[4]

Psychology and Social Psychology

Psychology is the study of human reactions to their environment.[5] Psychologists seek to explain the thoughts, feelings, and behaviors that represent human reaction. Psychology itself can be divided into several subdisciplines. Social psychology and cognitive psychology, in particular, are highly relevant to consumer behavior.[6] **Social psychology** focuses on the thoughts, feelings, and behaviors that people have as they interact with other people (group behavior). Consumer behavior most often takes place in some type of social setting; thus, social psychology and consumer behavior overlap significantly. **Cognitive psychology** deals with the intricacies of mental reactions involved in information processing. Every time a consumer evaluates a product, sees an advertisement, or reacts to product consumption, information is processed. Thus, cognitive psychology is also very relevant to consumer behavior.

Marketing

One doesn't have to look very hard to find different definitions of marketing.[7] Many of the older definitions focused heavily on physical products and profitability. Even though products and profits are very important aspects of marketing, these definitions are relatively narrow. **Marketing** involves the multitude of value-producing activities that facilitate *exchanges* between buyers and sellers. These activities include the production, promotion, pricing, distribution, and retailing of goods, services, ideas, and experiences that provide value for consumers and other stakeholders.

Consumer behavior and marketing are very closely related. Exchange is intimately involved in marketing and as can be seen from Exhibit 1.1, exchange is central to consumer behavior too. In fact, in some ways, consumer behavior involves "inverse" marketing as consumers operate at the other end of the exchange. Marketing actions are targeted at and affect consumers while consumer actions affect marketers. A marketer without customers won't be a marketer very long! In fact, without consumers, marketing is unnecessary.

Consumer Behavior and Other Disciplines

Marketing, as a recognized discipline, grew out of economics and psychology. Commerce increased tremendously with the industrial revolution and the coinciding political changes that fostered economic freedom in many countries. Businesses looked to the new field of marketing for practical advice initially about distribution and later about pricing, packaging, and advertising. Eventually, what some have called the "subdiscipline" of consumer behavior emerged as competition focused marketers on how consumers made decisions.[8] Thus, although marketing may have originally shared more in common with economics, the turn toward consumer research brought numerous psychologists into the field. Many of these psychologists became the first consumer researchers.

Today, consumer behavior and marketing remain closely tied. Consumer behavior research and marketing research overlap with each other more than they do with any other discipline. Thus, the double-headed arrow connecting the two disciplines in Exhibit 1.2 represents the fact that marketing and consumer research contribute strongly to each other. After marketing, consumer behavior research is most closely intertwined with psychology research.[9] Consumer research is based

sociology the study of groups of people within a society with relevance for consumer behavior because a great deal of consumption takes place within group settings or is affected by group behavior

anthropology study in which researchers interpret relationships between consumers and the things they purchase, the products they own, and the activities in which they participate

largely on psychology, and to some extent, psychology draws from consumer behavior research.

Other disciplines share things in common with consumer behavior. **Sociology** focuses on the study of groups of people within a society and thus has relevance for consumer behavior because consumption often takes place within group settings or is in one way or another affected by group behavior.

Anthropology has contributed to consumer behavior research by allowing researchers to interpret the relationships between consumers and the things they purchase, the products they own, and the activities in which they participate. Other disciplines such as geography and the medical sciences overlap with consumer behavior in that they draw from some of the same theories and/or research approaches. However, at least

based on how much the research in consumer behavior is connected with other disciplines, the connection consumer behavior shares with economics, marketing, and psychology (and social psychology) is quite strong.[10]

LO2 The Ways in Which Consumers Are Treated

the customer isn't always "king." Look at the list of familiar service environments:

- A typical driver's license bureau
- The registrar's office at a state university
- The line for cashing a check at a bank
- A university health clinic
- Cable television service
- A hair salon
- A New York City fine dining establishment

Think about the following questions. Does a consumer receive the same quality treatment at each of these places? What is the waiting environment like at each of these places? Is there a clean, comfortable waiting area with pleasant music? How dedicated are the employees to delivering a high-quality service experience? How likely are employees to view the customer as a nuisance? If you don't see the point of these questions yet, contrast the waiting area at a driver's license bureau with the elaborate lounge where customers wait while sipping a cocktail or aperitif before dining in a fine dining establishment in New York City.

Some organizations can survive while treating customers little better than dirt, and others need to pamper customers just to have a chance of surviving. Consider these two questions in order to understand how important serving customers well should be to any given organization:

1. How competitive is the marketing environment?
2. How dependent is the marketer on repeat business?

COMPETITION AND CONSUMER ORIENTATION

Where do consumers go if they don't like the service at the driver's license bureau? If the choice comes down to

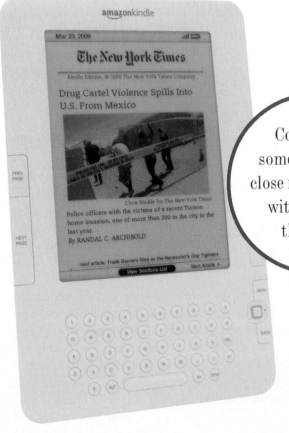

Consumers sometimes have close relationships with the stuff they own.

© JOSHUA KRISTAL/ALAMY

DMV *customers* can face long lines (sometimes over 100 people in some areas) and wait times counted in hours not minutes.[12] However, a few states have turned to technology and private outsourcing to improve service. Drivers can renew licenses online in some states or go to one of hundreds of companies who have been authorized to provide licensing services. As a result, consumers are now being served more conveniently, and states have better and more accurate information about drivers.

The realization that competition is important to protecting consumers is recognized by government. In the United States, many federal laws regulate the market to ensure business competition. The Robinson-Patman Act, the Sherman Act, and the Clayton Act are examples of such legislation. Practices such as price fixing, secret rebates, and customer coercion are governed by these acts.

Competition eventually drives companies toward a high degree of consumer orientation. **Consumer (customer) orientation** is a way of doing business in which the actions and decision making of the institution prioritize consumer value and satisfaction above all other concerns. A consumer orientation is a key component of a firm with a market-oriented culture. **Market orientation** is an organizational culture that embodies the importance of creating value for customers among all employees. In addition to understanding customers, a market orientation stresses the need to monitor and understand competitor actions in the marketplace and the need to communicate information about customers and competitors throughout the organization.[13] More profitable firms are usually market oriented with a few exceptions that will be discussed later.[14]

> **consumer (customer) orientation** way of doing business in which the actions and decision making of the institution prioritize consumer value and satisfaction above all other concerns
>
> **market orientation** organizational culture that embodies the importance of creating value for customers among all employees

Why do you get treated better in some environments than others? Perhaps competition is a clue.

visiting the bureau or not driving, nearly all consumers will put up with the less-than immaculate surroundings, long waits, and poor service that typically go along with getting a driver's license. Put yourself into the shoes of the service providers at the bureau. Is there any concern about doing something that would make a customer want to return to do business again? Is there any real incentive to provide a pleasant and valuable experience?

In essence, the driver's license bureau typifies a service organization that operates in a market with little or no competition and a captive audience. No matter how poor the service is, they know consumers will return to do more business when the term on their license expires. The incentive for better customer treatment remains small.

Contrast this with the restaurant. A dining consumer in New York City has over 6,000 full service restaurants to choose from. Customers do not have to tolerate poor treatment. They can simply go next door. A few exceptions exist; nevertheless, a highly competitive marketplace in which consumers have many alternatives practically ensures good customer service.

Unfortunately, public services provided by government institutions can often be notorious for poor service.[11] Unlike a restaurant, DMV management may not be so compelled to adjust workloads to demand.

RELATIONSHIP MARKETING AND CONSUMER BEHAVIOR

Let's go back to the list of service environments. Certainly, banks and restaurants are generally in very intense competition with rival businesses. Businesses are

relationship marketing activities based on the belief that the firm's performance is enhanced through repeat business

touchpoints direct contacts between the firm and a customer

challenged to get consumers to repeatedly purchase the goods or services offered. Even in a city with a population as great as that of New York, without repeat business, each restaurant would have fewer than ten customers per night. In addition, repeat customers are considered less costly to serve.[15] For instance, while a lot of advertising may be needed for every new customer to learn about a restaurant, old customers already know the place.

Thus, **relationship marketing** is based on the belief that firm performance is enhanced through repeat business. Relationship marketing is the recognition that customer desires are recurring and that a single purchase act may be only one touchpoint in an ongoing series of interactions with a customer. **Touchpoints** are direct contacts between the firm and a customer. Increasingly, multiple channels or ways of making this contact exist including phone, e-mail, text messaging, and face-to-face contact.[16] Every touchpoint, no matter the chan-

nel, should be considered as an opportunity to create value for the customer. Like any type of relationship, a customer–marketer relationship will continue only as long as both parties see the partnership as valuable.

Marketers are increasingly realizing the value of relationship marketing. Wait staff sometimes provide business cards to customers so that they can ask to be served by the same person or team on their next visit. Notice that with relationship marketing, the firm and its employees are very motivated to provide an outstanding overall experience. In sum, both a competitive marketplace and a relationship marketing orientation create exchange environments where customers are truly treated as "king."

LO3 Consumer Behavior's Role in Business and Society

WHY STUDY CONSUMER BEHAVIOR?

many students find studying consumer behavior interesting relative to many other courses. After all, everyone reading this book has years and years of experience as a consumer. Thus, students should come into the course with a greater sense of familiarity. Not only is the subject interesting, but consumer behavior is also an important topic to understand from multiple perspectives. Each perspective provides another opportunity to find interest in the subject matter. Consumer behavior (CB) is important in at least three ways:

1. CB provides an input to business/marketing strategy.
2. CB provides a force that shapes society.
3. CB provides an input to making responsible decisions as a consumer.

CONSUMER BEHAVIOR AND MARKETING STRATEGY

The ultimate hallmark of success for a business is long-term survival. One hundred years is not a long time in the course of history. But very few companies will survive for even 100 years. Exhibit 1.3 lists some famous

MassMutual
PlanSmart™
Simple. Sound. Smart.

Solutions to help maximize
retirement plan success

FOR PLAN SPONSOR USE ONLY

MassMutual
FINANCIAL GROUP

We'll help you get there.™   Retirement Services

What are some touchpoints for a company like Mass Mutual?

international companies, the products they are known for, and their age.

None of these companies are 100 years old! Each of these companies has beaten the odds, and even though we may think about them as lasting forever, chances are some of these "giants" will not be around 100 years from now. So, surviving is not a trivial goal, and the companies that do survive long-term do so by obtaining resources from consumers in return for the value they create. This is a basic tenet of **resource-advantage theory**, which is a theory explaining why companies succeed or fail.[17] Consumer research is needed to understand what makes a consumer give up scarce resources. Ultimately, consumers give up resources in the pursuit of value.

What Do People Buy?

When a consumer buys something, he or she gives up resources in the form of time, money, and energy in return for whatever is being sold. Consider a customer who purchases a Kindle. What does he or she really get? Well, the tangibles include mostly plastic and some integrated circuitry. These are the parts that make up the product. No reasonable consumer would trade any significant sum of money for plastic and circuitry. A consumer isn't really buying **attributes**, or the physical parts of a product. However, the plastic enables the product to be small and light and the integrated circuitry enables this small, light product to function as an electronic reader. Once again, we can ask, is this really what the consumer wants? The fact is, this function enables the consumer to enjoy the benefits of information availability in a very convenient package. Outcomes like these are

valuable and what the customer is ultimately buying.

Marketing firms often adopt poor strategies when they don't understand exactly what a product truly is because they don't understand exactly what they are selling. With this in mind, a **product** is a potentially valuable bundle of benefits. Theodore Levitt was one of the most famous marketing researchers. Among other things, he was famous for pointing out the fact that consumers don't really seek products. The Make-Up or Hope feature on the following page describes other situations where a company could easily misidentify exactly what it is they sell.

One consumer researcher studied why people bought milk shakes. In contrast to expectation, the largest share of milk shakes purchased in the study was bought before noon, many before 10 A.M., and many were consumed in a car. After studying many milk shake drinkers, one theme emerged. A milk shake is a good solution for consumers with long commutes. They satisfy one's hunger, they are neat, they can be consumed while using one hand, and they take about 20 minutes to finish—the better portion of the commute. The value provided by the milk shake is partly dealing with hunger but also partly dealing with boredom. Thus, the researcher suggested making shakes even thicker so

EXHIBIT 1.3
How Old Are These Companies?

COMPANY[18]	CORE PRODUCTS	YEAR OF "BIRTH"	PLACE
IBM	Computing, Tabulating, Recording	1911	New York
Home Depot	Building Supply and Retailing	1979	Georgia
Walmart	Mass Merchandising	1962	Arkansas
Microsoft	Computer Software	1975	California
Tesco	Food Retailing	1919	London, UK
Samsung	Electronics	1969	Seoul, South Korea
McDonald's	Fast Food	1956	Illinois
Toyota	Motor Cars	1937	Japan

they took even longer to finish as a way of improving the "product."[19]

Ultimately, companies need to understand why people buy their products in order to understand what business they are in. This is also how they identify their competitors. Let's look at the companies that produced buggies (horse-drawn carriages from 100 years ago) and slide rules (rulers used to do calculations). They did not go out of business because their products were flawed. The companies that did well producing those products went out of business because they failed to innovate and because they didn't understand that they were actually competing with Ford automobiles and Texas Instruments calculators, respectively. Products like VHS players, CD players, and tape recorders are all fast on the road to obsolescence as the technologies that provide the benefits of musical or video entertainment change. Thus, in this sense, technologies don't provide value directly; the activities and benefits associated with the technologies do.

Ways of Doing Business

Much of the discussion thus far presumes that a company is market oriented. That is, the presumption is that a company has prioritized understanding consumers, as would be the case if in a consumer-oriented corporate culture. This isn't always the case. Each company adopts a way of doing business that is epitomized in their corporate culture. Fortunately, corporate cultures fall roughly into one of several categories representing different ways of doing

Make-Up or Hope?

Theodore Levitt was a leader in the cause of getting managers to not allow their companies to become *myopic*. A myopic business view defines the business in terms of products that are sold and not in terms of the value that consumers receive. For instance, the National Radio Company was defined as a—guess what?—radio company! Up until the 1960s, the company was one of the leading names in the business and produced some of the finest radio receivers and transmitters. However, there is a good reason why you've probably never heard of this company! Things change!

Here are some examples of better ways to look at products.

CONSUMERS DO NOT WANT:	CONSUMERS DO WANT:
¼ inch B&D drill bits	¼ inch holes so they can hang things
Kodak film	Recorded memories
Lawn mowers	Pride that comes with a great looking lawn
Roach spray	Dead roaches
Dry cleaning service	Clothes that do not stink

What about a customer buying make-up or cosmetics? What is really being purchased? Charles Revson, founder of Revlon, said, "In the factory Revlon manufactures cosmetics, but in the store we sell hope." Revlon considers itself in the hope business! Thus, in Revlon's eyes, the "hope" helps provide the value as much as the cosmetics. Revlon's understanding of the way value is actually provided makes them see 20/20.

Sources: *Branding Ad Vice* (2004), "Needful Things," October 13, **http://brandingadvice.typepad.com/my_weblog/2004/10/index.html,** accessed January 14, 2007; Christenson, C. M., S. Cook, and T. Hall (2005), "Marketing Malpractice: The Cause and the Cure," *Harvard Business Review*, 83, 74–83; Kellog, D. (2006), "Hope and Agility: The Revlon Test," Mark Logic CEO Blog, **http://marklogic.blogspot.com/2006/07/hope-and-agility-revlon-test.html**, accessed December 7, 2007.

business. Exhibit 1.4 summarizes different business orientations. These orientations often guide a firm's market segmentation practices.

In **undifferentiated marketing**, the same basic product is offered to all customers. Mass merchandisers typify undifferentiated marketers in that they rely on selling high volume to be successful. As such, they focus on serving very large segments in which consumers do not have specific desires (are not picky). Undifferentiated marketers generally adopt a **production orientation**, wherein innovation is geared primarily toward making the production process as efficient and economic as possible. In other words, the emphasis is on serving customers while incurring minimum costs. Walmart typifies this approach with their Supercenters and their state-of-the-art distribution network, which ships massive quantities of products to stores around the world at the lowest possible cost.

Differentiated marketers serve multiple market segments each with a unique product offering. A market orientation usually serves a differentiated marketer well. The emphasis here is on matching a product with a segment.

Toyota (**www.toyota.com**), for example, has three business units each targeted toward a different automotive segment. Scion appeals to consumers interested in economy cars with a unique sense of style. Of course, Toyota operates under the Toyota name itself offering a more conservative line of autos for consumers seeking a blend of performance and reliability. Finally, Lexus provides luxury cars to those who want the most in performance, style, comfort, and reliability. Taking differentiated marketing even further, each Toyota line offers coupes, sedans, and SUVs. Thus, a Toyota product exists for practically any automobile consumer's taste. Without an understanding of consumers, Toyota would have a difficult time matching products to segments.

Differentiated marketing can be taken to the extreme with a practice known as **one-to-one marketing**. Here a different product is offered for each individual customer, and each customer is essentially treated as a segment of one. Computer-aided information processing, design, and production have helped make this a reality on a large scale. Many casinos, for example, develop promotional packages for individual customers based on information collected and stored about that customer's preferences.

Niche marketing is practiced by firms that specialize in serving one market segment with particularly unique demand characteristics. Firms that practice niche marketing may be consumer oriented. However, some niche marketers are product oriented and produce a product that has unique appeal within a segment. A clothing firm such as Talbot's provides fashions for the career-oriented woman. They don't have a "juniors" section because this is not a segment they choose to serve. Talbot's stays in touch with its market with a considerable amount of consumer research. Moreau et fils is a producer of high-quality Chablis (white wine from the northern Burgundy region of France). Moreau does little consumer research because they

undifferentiated marketing plan wherein the same basic product is offered to all customers

production orientation approach where innovation is geared primarily toward making the production process as efficient and economic as possible

differentiated marketers firms that serve multiple market segments each with a unique product offering

one-to-one marketing plan wherein a different product is offered for each individual customer so that each customer is treated as a segment of one

niche marketing plan wherein a firm specializes in serving one market segment with particularly unique demand characteristics

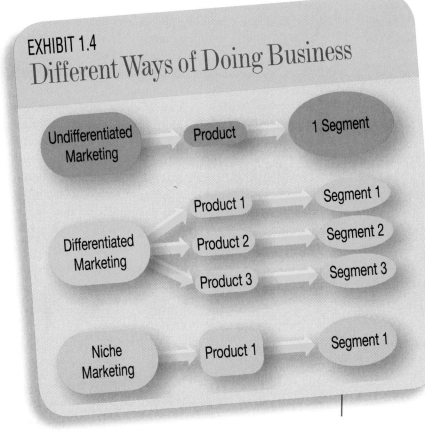

EXHIBIT 1.4
Different Ways of Doing Business

produce fine Chablis. They have little interest in changing the product because a change would mean marketing something other than chablis. Moreau wines are more expensive than mass-produced wines or high-production wines from companies like Chateau St. Michelle (which better typifies a differentiated marketer).

CONSUMER BEHAVIOR AND SOCIETY

The things that people buy and consume end up determining the type of society in which we live. Things like customs, manners, and rituals all involve consumption—value-producing activities. Certainly, not every society around the world is the same. Just think about the ways we eat and the types of food consumed around the world. Additionally, when governments create laws that govern the way we buy and consume products, consumer behavior is involved. Thus, consumer behavior creates the society in which we live and serves as an important source of input to public policy in a free society.

For example, how does society treat smoking? Interestingly, smoking used to be shown often in popular culture as an acceptable behavior. On the famous TV classic *The Andy Griffith Show*, produced in the 1960s, Andy Taylor, the likable sheriff and "Pa," was commonly depicted smoking a cigarette in the living room while talking to his young son, Opie. Cigarette advertisements made up a large chunk of all TV advertising. In the theater, James Bond smoked, and his image was certainly not harmed by the behavior. At home,

practically every room in the house included at least one ashtray. "No smoking" sections did not exist, and on airlines, flight attendants (or stewardesses) walked the aisles of the plane offering passengers "coffee, tea, or cigarettes."

My how things have changed! Smoking has become nearly taboo in the United States. Smoking inside any public building has been made practically impossible either due to laws restricting smoking or rules created by building owners prohibiting smoking. "No smoking" sections in restaurants are now also seen in many parts of Europe and in most cosmopolitan cities around the world. We should note that consumers ultimately created this change in society. Smoking, as a consumption activity, is increasingly looked upon as a non-value-producing activity. Furthermore, politicians realize political advantage in creating more restrictions as consumer opinion continues to turn against the behavior. Such decisions should be made with a thorough understanding of the consumer behavior issues involved.

Another current public policy issue concerns the use of mobile phones. Consider how much consumers' widespread adoption of the mobile phone has changed, and continues to change, society. In Europe and North America alone, consumers account for over 1 billion—that's 1,000 million—mobile phones! Consumers in Asia and Africa are adopting mobile phones at an even faster rate so that today, just about ½ of all consumers in the world have a mobile phone. This means a total of about 4.5 billion mobile phones![19a] That's not bad for a product that did not exist as we know it 25 years ago. Certainly, the mobile phone has been a discontinuous innovation and has altered our behaviors and communications in many significant ways. The Hold the Phone feature raises some interesting questions about consumers' behavior with their mobile phones.

I miss my lung, Bob.

California Department Of Health Services. Funded By The Tobacco Tax Initiative

As this billboard shows, attitudes toward smoking have certainly changed over the last few decades. Smoking isn't so cool.

Hold the Phone! Consumers and Their Phones around the World

Even though "car phones" have provided value to consumers for many years, the mobile phone that we know today really traces back to the Motorola "Brick" of the 1980s. We can safely say that practically all readers of this book own a mobile phone of some type. In fact, the most popular "handy," as mobiles are known in parts of Europe, now provides high-speed Internet access, serves as an MP3 player, functions as a camera, and contains many other cool features.

In the United States, 40% of children 12–14 years of age have their own cell phone. A recent study in the United Kingdom suggested that 80% of children have a mobile phone, including over 1,000,000 kids under the age of 10. As a result, the British government is allowing public schools to create rules governing mobile phone usage in school.

Restrictions on the use of mobile phones in cars are also being enacted or considered in the interest of public safety. However, will we see greater restrictions such as "no phone" sections in restaurants? Consider the following list. Do any of these behaviors violate acceptable mobile phone etiquette?

1. Having a mobile phone conversation at the dinner table
2. Using the mobile while seated on an airplane
3. Using profanity on the phone
4. Using the phone in a movie theater
5. Using the phone in a public bathroom toilet stall
6. Speaking so loudly that your phone conversation is easily overheard by others
7. Browsing your PDA or texting while involved in a group conversation

The majority of Americans consider mobile phone users to be rude. This is interesting considering that the vast majority of Americans are mobile phone users! Should public restrictions on mobile phone usage be created that govern when, where, and how a phone can be used? Studies of consumer behavior help provide input into public policy decisions on issues like these.

Sources: Speer, Pat (2006), "Commentary: Industry Observations and Opinion from the Staff," *Insurance Networking and Data Management*, 10, 4; Cairns, W. (2006), "Child Culture; Kid Consumers and Growing Pains," *Brand Strategy*, (December 18), 46; Heller, Laura (2005), "Back-to-School: Pencils, Homework . . . Cell Phones?" *DSN Retailing Today*, 44 (April 25), 42.

© CORBIS/SUPERSTOCK

CONSUMER BEHAVIOR AND PERSONAL GROWTH

We face many important decisions as consumers. Among these include choices that will affect our professional careers, our quality of life, and the very fiber of our families. By this point in your life, you have already experienced many of these decisions. Some decisions are good; some are not. All consumers make dumb decisions occasionally. For instance, modern consumers often carry incredibly high debt relative to our ancestors. Total American consumer debt exceeded $900 billion in 2007. That's about $10,000 per family.[20] American consumers are not alone. In the United Kingdom, the typical young consumer (18–24 years of age) also has credit card debt totaling nearly $10,000 US.[21] College students are prime targets for credit cards and as can be seen on many college campuses, students are quite willing to apply for cards in exchange for something as mundane as a new t-shirt. As a result of the debt they amass, many consumers continue to have negative net worth years into their professional life.[22]

The decisions that lead to high levels of debt do not seem to be wise as bankruptcy, financial stress, and lower self-esteem often result. Although often overlooked, decisions about budget allocation are very relevant

What's the best way to study consumer behavior?

© ISTOCKPHOTO.COM/COGAL

aspects of consumer behavior. There are many other avenues that can lead consumers to make poor decisions.

Thus, when consumers study consumer behavior, they should come to make better decisions. Several topics can be particularly helpful in enlightening consumers, including

1. Consequences associated with poor budget allocation
2. The role of emotions in consumer decision making
3. Avenues for seeking redress for unsatisfactory purchases
4. Social influences on decision making, including peer pressure
5. The effect of the environment on consumer behavior

LO4 Different Approaches to Studying Consumer Behavior

Consumer researchers have many tools and approaches with which to study consumer behavior, and researchers don't always agree on which approach is best. In reality, the consumer researcher should realize that no single best way of studying consumer behavior exists. Rather, different types of research settings may call for different approaches and the use of different tools. Thus, we provide a brief overview of two basic approaches for studying consumer behavior. The pur-

pose is to provide the reader with an idea of how the knowledge found in this book was obtained. For a more detailed view of the different research approaches, the reader is referred elsewhere.[23]

INTERPRETIVE RESEARCH

One consumer's music is just noise to another consumer. What creates value in the musical experience? What does music mean and how much does the meaning shape the value of the experience? These are questions that evoke very abstract comments and thoughts from consumers. They are questions that lend themselves well to interpretive research.[24] **Interpretive research** seeks to explain the inner meanings and motivations associated with specific consumption experiences. These interpretations are generally made through the words that consumers use to describe events or through observations of social interactions. Consumer data are interpreted to derive meaning rather than analyzed to draw firm conclusions.

Interpretive research generally falls into the category of qualitative research. **Qualitative research tools** include things such as case analyses, clinical interviews, focus group interviews, and other tools in which data are gathered in a relatively unstructured way. In other words, consumer respondents are usually free to respond in their own words or simply through their own behavior. Data of this type requires that the researcher interprets its meaning. Therefore, the data are considered **researcher dependent**.

The roots of interpretive consumer research go back over 50 years to the earliest days of consumer research. The focus was on identifying the motivations that lie behind all manners of consumer behavior including mundane things such as coffee drinking or taking an aspirin, to more elaborate issues such as what "drives" one to buy a Ford versus a Chevy.[25] The motivational research era in consumer research, which lasted through the early 1960s, generally proved disappointing in providing satisfying explanations for consumer behavior on a large scale. Unfortunately, many interpretive research tools were scarcely applied for years afterwards. However, these approaches have made a recent comeback and are now commonly applied to many aspects of the field.

Interpretive researchers adopt one of several orientations. Two common interpretative orientations are phenomenology and ethnography. **Phenomenology** represents the study of consumption as a "lived experience." The phenomenological researcher relies on casual interviews with consumers with whom the researcher has won confidence and trust. This may be supplemented with various other ways that the consumer can tell a story. **Ethnography** has roots in anthropology and often involves analyzing the artifacts associated with consumption. An ethnographer may decide to go through trash or ask to see the inside of a consumer's refrigerator in an effort to learn about the consumer. These approaches represent viable options for consumer researchers.

QUANTITATIVE CONSUMER RESEARCH

Which consumer group is most likely to listen to rap music? Statistical models can be applied to retail sales data to identify clusters of music consumers based on their likelihood of buying specific types of music.[26] For example, these tools can be used to help explain how a 45-year-old consumer who buys Bob Seger music belongs to a segment that is also likely to buy a Faith Hill recording. Similarly, another segment of consumers likes the music of Nirvana and Green Day. These two segments may be differentiated on factors such as age, income, and possibly even education.

Instead of buying music, a researcher might ask which consumers are most likely to pirate music via the Internet.[27] This issue illustrates the interplay between ethics and consumer behavior. The researcher can design a questionnaire and ask consumers to respond to questions using 10-point scales. The questions seek answers to things like the risk of being prosecuted, the extent to which music stars are idolized by the consumer, and the perceived social acceptability of music pirating. Responses can be used to explain how likely a consumer is to illegally pirate music. The researcher may find that one segment of music consumers is more likely to pirate than is another segment.

Credit Card Crazy

© ISTOCKPHOTO.COM/SLAVOLJUB PANTELIC

The topic of consumer debt illustrates the reasons why consumer behavior is important to study. Credit card usage has implications for marketing, society, and for personal growth. It can also be studied using any of the consumer behavior research approaches.

The Consumer Credit Protection Act addresses the problem. Among other things, it focuses on requiring companies to give ample notice before increasing interest rates, and enforcing effective rates on outstanding debt if a consumer chooses to cancel a card. It also provides some relief for consumers facing bankruptcy.

Supporters argue that many consumers need help with dealing with debt and that more regulation is needed. Others fear that the Act will further restrict lending and weaken the economy at a time when commerce should be encouraged rather than discouraged.

Research reveals that if consumers become more aware of the negative outcomes of excessive debt, they will be less likely to purchase more than they can afford. Qualitative research also delves into the feelings that consumers have about their cards. These feelings can be altered by using affinity cards in which donations are given to causes proportionate to a purchase amount.

Sources: Nenkov, G., J. J. Inman and J. Hulland (2008), "Considering the Future: The Conceptualization and Measurement of Elaboration on Potential Outcomes," Journal of Consumer Research, 35 (June), 126-141. Mekonnen, A., F. Harris, and A. Laing (2008), "Linking Products to a Cause or Affinity Group: Does this Really Make them more Attractive to Consumers?" European Journal of Marketing, 42 (1/2), 135-153.

These studies typify quantitative research. **Quantitative research** addresses questions about consumer behavior using numerical measurement and analysis tools. The measurement is usually structured, meaning that the consumer will simply choose a response from among alternatives supplied by the researcher. In other words, structured questionnaires typically involve multiple-choice-type questions. Alternatively, quantitative research might analyze sales data tracked via the Internet or with point-of-sale scanners.

Unlike qualitative research, the data are not researcher dependent. This is because the numbers are the same no matter who the researcher may be. Typically, quantitative research better enables researchers to test hypotheses as compared to interpretive research. Similarly, quantitative research is more likely to stand on its own and does not require deep interpretation. For example, if consumers have an average attitude score of 50 for brand A and 75 for brand B, we can objectively say that consumers tend to prefer brand B. Exhibit 1.5 summarizes some key differences between quantitative and qualitative research.[28]

LO5 Consumer Behavior Is Dynamic

all one has to do is examine the differences in standards of living between today's consumers and the consumers living just 40, 80, or 100 years ago to gain an appreciation of how consumer behavior has changed over time. As an overall statement, we can say that consumers are never completely satisfied. Actually, this is a good thing because as companies strive to meet consumer demands, increasingly innovative products are offered, and companies grow in response to increased sales. As a result, they hire more people and raise the income levels throughout the economy.

The way marketers respond to consumers is changing dramatically. Marketers have historically used advances in technology to provide consumers with greater opportunities to communicate with companies. Today, billions of consumers around the world have 24-hour, seven-day-a-week access to markets via the Internet. Consumers do not need to wait to go to a retail store to purchase music. They can download their favorite new tunes while walking down the street with a PDA or other mobile device. Here are some of the trends that are shaping the value received by consumers today.

INTERNATIONALIZATION

When Starbucks opened its first store in 1971, the thought may not have occurred that the concept could spread to other parts of the state of Washington or even other parts of the United States. In 1996, Starbucks opened its first store outside the United States in Tokyo, Japan. Today, Starbucks operates over 7,000 company-owned stores in over 40 countries.[28a] Whether one is on business in Guadalajara, Mexico; Seoul, South Korea; London, England; Nantes, France; or Ruston, Louisiana, he or she can start the morning off with a tall Sumatra or a venti latte. Almost anywhere the modern consumer travels, he or she can find a familiar place to eat or drink. An Outback Steakhouse, a Pizza Hut, or a McDonald's never seems far away!

EXHIBIT 1.5
Comparing Quantitative and Qualitative Research

Qualitative Research	Research Aspect	Quantitative Research
Discover Ideas, Used in Exploratory Research with General Research Objects	Common Purpose	Test Hypotheses or Specific Research Questions
Observe and Interpret	Approach	Measure and Test
Unstructured, Free-Forms	Data Collection Approach	Structured Response Categories Provided
Researcher Is Intimately Involved. Results Are Subjective.	Researcher Independence	Researcher Uninvolved Observer. Results Are Objective.
Small Samples—Often in Natural Settings	Samples	Large Samples to Produce Generalizable Results (Results that Apply to Other Situations)
Exploratory Research Designs	Most Often Used	Descriptive and Causal Research Designs

Obviously, the success of Starbucks shows that visiting a Starbucks provides many consumers with a high-value experience.

Although these chains can be found worldwide, consumers are not alike everywhere these firms operate. An Outback Steakhouse in Seoul will offer kimchi (fermented cabbage) on the menu, something neither American nor Australian. Companies must therefore deal with geographical distances as well as cultural distances. The international focus of today's modern company places a greater demand on consumer behavior research. Every culture's people will interpret products and behaviors differently. The meanings these consumers perceive will determine the success or failure of the product being offered.

TECHNOLOGICAL CHANGES

It is no secret that we are living in an age of ever-increasing technological advances. These advances seem to be coming at a faster and faster pace all the time. Upon reflection, we may realize that technology has influenced business practices since the advent of industry. Certainly, many retailers felt threatened by mail order technology that was practiced through the Sears Roebuck catalog and the telephone. In 1895, the Sears catalog contained 532 pages of products that enabled rural consumers to obtain things that would have been otherwise difficult to get.[29] Why would people go to a store when they could simply telephone and have products delivered to their door?

In the mid-20th century, television revolutionized consumer behavior. Not only did TV change advertising forever, but true home shopping became a possibility. Now, the consumer could actually see a product in use on television and then make a purchase either by picking up the phone or punching buttons on a cable device. Why would someone go to a store?

> Why would people go to a store when they could simply telephone and have products delivered to their door?

In the 2000s, a consumer now has 24/7 access to purchasing almost any type of product. The Internet has made geographical distance almost a nonissue. Additionally, the consumer can truly shop on his or her own schedule, not on a schedule determined by store hours. Communication technology has also advanced tremendously. Mobile communication devices continue to get smaller and smaller and now, one can access stores via the Internet using a Razr that is smaller than most wallets. The entire world is now truly the market for consumers in free countries. With this being said, total U.S. Internet retailing still accounts for less than 5% of all retailing. Internet retail sales continue to grow, but in 2005 these sales accounted for only $88 billion of the over $3 trillion in U.S. sales.[30] Interestingly, if travel agent services are included, the total rises to $133 billion.[31]

What types and amounts of value do consumers seek when shopping online? When a consumer needs an airline ticket, he or she is seeking a solution to a real problem. Buying an airline ticket isn't generally a fun thing to do. Thus, the consumer is primarily seeking "utilitarian" value. We discuss different types of value in the next chapter.

Although technology continues to change, the basic consumer desire for value hasn't changed. In fact, the dot.com failures of the late 1990s illustrated that companies that do not enhance the value consumers receive from the current ways of doing things fail. Today, web technologies are generally looked at as complementing

Shopping online can be a valuable experience, but are virtual shopping and "real" shopping equally gratifying?

the United States and Europe. In Europe, families are averaging less than one child per family. If this trend were to continue, these countries would experience declining populations. Exhibit 1.6 displays select birthrates.[32]

The combination of working couples and lower birthrates has led to greater levels of consumer affluence. As a result, many consumer segments have become targets for products once considered to be luxuries such as cruises and high-end automobiles. Furthermore, consumers have generally become less price sensitive in many categories. Families eat out more often and are more likely to own the latest electronic devices than were consumers of the past.

The right pane of Exhibit 1.6 displays the life expectancy for citizens of a number of different countries. If we consider life expectancy as a proxy for standard of living, we can see that as the birthrate declines, the standard of living increases. Thus, unfortunately, the countries with the highest birthrates in the world are among the poorest. In developed countries, more wealth is spread over fewer consumers. Further, the growth trends in population affect the consumer culture in many ways. One major issue in the United States today is the aging baby-boomer population. This segment of the consumer population is expected to dramatically affect business practices for many years to come.

traditional retailing more than competing with the bricks-and-mortar option. A dot.com retailer has a difficult time competing with a shopping adventure to Harrods of London because of the gratification offered by the experience itself.

CHANGING DEMOGRAPHICS

In most of the western world, notable demographic trends have shaped consumer behavior patterns greatly over the past quarter century or so. First, households increasingly include two primary income providers. In contrast to the stereotypical working dad and stay-at-home mom, families today include two parents with a career orientation. Second, family size is decreasing throughout

EXHIBIT 1.6
Projected Birthrates per Couple and Life Expectancies for Countries around the World (2010)

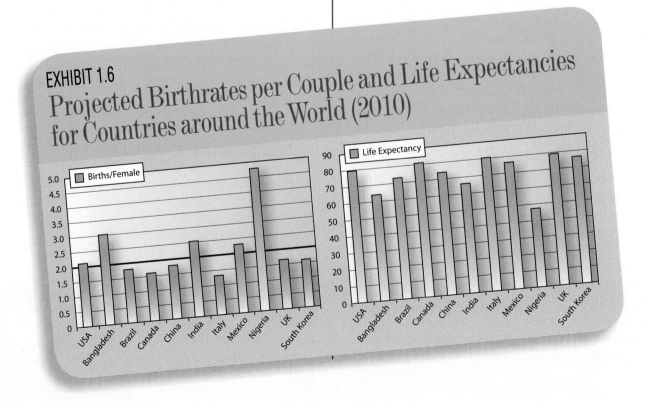

Chapter 1 Case

Blaire O'Neil is hiring staff for Vous Vois Vision. She purchased the failing optical retail store that formerly operated under the name York Opticians. York had always emphasized what they called value in their advertising and boasted that no glasses in the store were over $199. Blaire is taking a different approach. Her dad had tried to talk her out of getting into a "dying industry." However, Blaire believes the old positioning around low price was myopic and failed to recognize that things that offer value are the things that are worthy, special, and significant.[33] Glasses are no different.

Although more and more consumers are opting for corrective surgery to remedy impaired vision, she believes there are untapped market segments consisting of consumers sensitive to the ability to express one's true self with their eyewear. She attended an industry "market" (trade show) that emphasized the potential growth in designer frames and contact lenses that change the appearance of one's eyes. The trade show even boasted that some consumers with perfect vision still wish to purchase designer frames to capture specific moods or to accent their favorite outfits. Additionally, the average price for a pair of sunglasses has more than doubled in the last decade and more and more consumers are visiting optical stores for their sunglass needs. Although Blaire was nervous about this venture at first, a closer look at the market leaves her feeling confident she has found her niche—or niches!

Questions

1. Using the basic consumption process in Exhibit 1.1, illustrate how a consumer "consumes" eyewear.

2. Do you think Vous Vois Vision should adopt a product, production, or market orientation? Explain why.

3. Almost any business involves some ethical questions. In this case, discuss the ethics involved in potentially selling contact lenses or even designer glasses to a consumer who sees well enough not to actually "need" vision correction.

4. Why might Blaire be interested in hiring a researcher to do some interpretive research about consumers and eyewear?

I get a lot out of shopping even when I don't buy anything.

1 2 3 4 5 6 7

strongly disagree   strongly agree

Consumers are

sometimes willing to sacrifice quality and even satisfaction, but consumers never willingly sacrifice value.

2

Value and the Consumer Behavior Value Framework

After studying this chapter, the student should be able to:

LO1 Describe the consumer value framework, including its basic components.

LO2 Define consumer value and compare and contrast two key types of value.

LO3 Apply the concepts of marketing strategy and marketing tactics to describe the way firms go about creating value for consumers.

LO4 Explain the way market characteristics like market segmentation and product differentiation affect marketing strategy.

LO5 Analyze consumer markets using elementary perceptual maps.

LO6 Justify adopting the concept of consumers' lifetime value as an effective long-term orientation for many firms.

Introduction

Putting together a band is one thing; making a living by making music is another! Several college buddies, each majoring in business, are exploring a career in the music industry by starting and managing a band. Although they initially think the business courses they are taking seem to be removed from the music business, they eventually realize that many issues discussed in their marketing classes fit very well when promoting their band. As such, they begin to ask several questions about the market. One key question is what makes a consumer willing to pay to hear a band or buy a tune. They all agree that probably more than anything else they can think of, one consumer can absolutely love a song that another consumer absolutely hates. They want to play Emo, but is there money in Emo?

They come across the following data showing consumer preferences for different types of music in a newspaper story[1]:

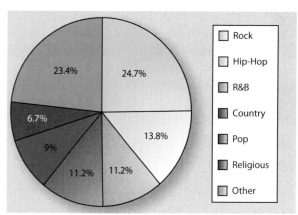

What is your favorite type of music?

Why do some consumers love one type of music and loathe another? This is a question the band cannot answer. But they wonder whether they should let the preferences of consumers shape the music they play. Would being consumer oriented in this way be a wise business decision? Are some customers worth more than others? These are all basic consumer behavior issues that ultimately tie back to value!

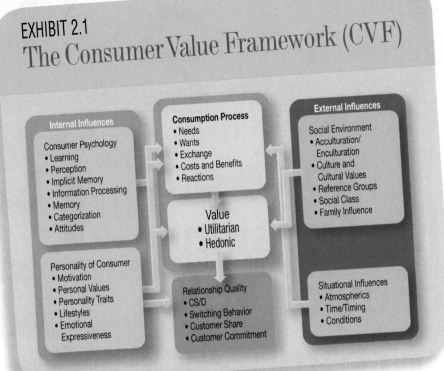

EXHIBIT 2.1
The Consumer Value Framework (CVF)

LO1 The Consumer Value Framework and Its Components

Consumer behavior is multifaceted. Not only does the study of consumer behavior involve multiple disciplines, but anyone who has ever made a major purchase like a house, an automobile, or an apartment knows that many factors can affect both the purchase decision and the way one feels after the purchase. This book covers many of these factors.

THE CONSUMER VALUE FRAMEWORK

Given the potential complexity involved in explaining consumption, a framework for studying consumer behavior is useful. Exhibit 2.1 displays the framework used in this book. The **Consumer Value Framework (CVF)** represents consumer behavior theory illustrating factors that shape consumption-related behaviors and ultimately determine the value associated with consumption. The different components shown with different colors roughly correspond to the different parts of this book. However, the student of consumer behavior must recognize and accept the fact that each aspect of the CVF is related in some way to other components of

the model. The arrows connecting the different components typify these connections.

VALUE AND THE CVF COMPONENTS

Value is at the heart of experiencing and understanding consumer behavior. Thus, we will never get too far from value in any chapter of this book. We'll expand more on value later in this chapter and throughout the book. In the rest of this section, we present the basic components of the CVF that either contribute to or are outcomes of value.

Relationship Quality

Over the past two decades or so, **Customer Relationship Management (CRM)** has become a popular catchphrase, not just in marketing but in all of business. A basic CRM premise is that customers form relationships with companies as opposed to companies conducting individual transactions with customers. A CRM system tracks detailed information about customers so more customer-oriented decisions can be made with these decisions hopefully leading to longer-lasting relationships.

A CRM orientation means each customer represents a potential stream of resources rather than just a single sale. **Relationship quality** reflects the connectedness between a consumer and a retailer, brand, or service provider.[2] In practice, a strong, or high-quality,

The Grocery Game

The heart of the CVF is value. Consumers around the U.S. are finding a lot of value by playing the Grocery Game (**www.grocerygame.com**). The game is really a process that allows consumers who are willing to put in the time and effort to stock up on groceries at dramatically discounted prices. Manufacturer coupons are one of the key game pieces. Select coupons can be tied to select retailer discounts to allow common grocery items to be purchased for less. "Green items" are free using the Grocery Game. Consumers then compete to see who can save the most money. Although buying groceries may not seem very glamorous, a lot of Grocery Game players get really excited about saving potentially hundreds of dollars each month.

The Grocery Game is not for everyone. It takes someone with a specific lifestyle and in a certain situation to be so strongly motivated to save money on grocery items. A family-oriented consumer with multiple children at home who enjoys activities that save money is more likely to play than is a single consumer living in a small flat. The Grocery Game clearly offers utilitarian and hedonic value.

Sources: **http://www.thegrocerygame.com/con__WhatIsTheGroceryGame.cfm?**

© ISTOCKPHOTO.COM/JANINE LAMONTAGNE

relationship is typified by a consumer who buys the same brand each time a need for that product arises. Businesses see loyal customers as being more profitable than customers who are prone to switch providers each time they make a purchase.

When a consumer realizes high value from an exchange with a company, relationship quality improves. Over time, a consumer who experiences high consumer satisfaction from dealing with one company may well become a loyal, committed customer. Restaurants like the Yard House, based in Irvine, California, have created high customer loyalty by carefully managing its beverage programs.[3] True to its name, the Yard House specialty remains draft beer poured into thin "half-yard" or "yard" sized glasses. However, the company soon realized that, by adding other creative offerings to the beverage menu, they could increase the amount of repeat business. Thus, the Yard House stays on top of beverage trends and today offers hundreds of beers, exotic nonalcoholic drinks, an extensive wine list, and multicolored martinis. Now, rather than advertising heavily to attract new customers, they can rely more on the same customers to return time and time again. International companies like Dell and Home Depot have also found success in delivering high relationship quality.[4]

Consumption Process

Consumers must decide to do something before they can receive value. This process involves deciding what is needed, what options for exchange are available, and the inevitable reaction to consumption. The consumption process can involve a great deal of decision making and thus represents a consumer decision-making process. Many factors influence this process, and these factors can be divided into different categories such as internal and external influences.

Internal Influences: The Psychology and Personality of the Consumer

The Psychology of the Consumer. "It's a small world after all! It's a small world . . . " Sorry! But, now that this song is stuck in your head, why do you think this happens? Is getting a song stuck in someone's head a good idea if you want to sell something? Will consumers react the same way to an increase in a price from $80 to $100 as they would to a price decrease for the same product from $120 to $100? Is there a good reason to sell a product for $69.99 rather than $70? All these questions involve the psychology of the consumer. In other words, these things are **internal influences**, things that go on inside of the consumer or that can be thought of as part of the consumer.

The psychology of the consumer involves both cognitive and affective processes. The term **cognition** refers to the thinking or mental processes that go on as we process and store things that can become knowledge. A child hears parents talk about smoking as a *nasty* thing to do. Smoking becomes associated with nastiness, and the child may develop a dislike of smoking. **Affect** refers to the feelings that are experienced during consumption activities or associated with specific objects. If the child continues to receive negative information about smoking, the belief about its being nasty may result in feelings of disgust.

Many people think of these types of things when they think of consumer behavior. Certainly, our perceptions help shape the desirability of products, which can influence decision processes and the value perceived from consuming something. Recall that value is a subjective assessment. Therefore, value is very much a matter of perception.

The Personality of the Consumer.
Every consumer has certain characteristics and traits that help define him or her as an individual. We refer to these traits generally as **individual differences**. Individual differences, which include personality and lifestyle, help determine consumer behavior. For example, a consumer with a

Stuck on Me!

Consumer research has suggested some songs that are most likely to get stuck "in your head." Once you hear one of these songs, perhaps even just a small part of the song, you can expect to have it with you, at least mentally, for quite some time. Nearly all consumers admit to experiencing this phenomenon, and many consumers say that songs often get stuck in their heads. Professor James Kellaris at the University of Cincinnati believes this happens because there is something that the brain perceives as inconsistent in the song and one is motivated to replay the song in an effort to satisfy the resulting curiosity. Yes, "It's a Small World" is one such song. Here is a list of some songs that will be stuck in your head after reading this; notice that several are songs created for an advertisement:

> "It's a Small World After All"
> "We Will Rock You!" by Queen
> Chili's Baby Back Rib song
> "YMCA" by the Village People
> Meow Mix jingle (Meow meow meow meow, meow meow meow, …)
> "The Sun will Come Out Tomorrow!"
> "Bohemian Rhapsody" by Queen (..easy come, easy go, little high, little low, hit me where the wind blows…)
> Free Credit Report .com

Sometimes, psychology can be difficult to explain.

Sources: Hoffman, Carey (2001), "Songs That Cause The Brain To 'Itch': UC Professor Investigating Why Certain Tunes Get Stuck in Our Heads," UC News, **http://www.uc.edu/news/kellaris.htm**, accessed January 10, 2007; *Advertising Age* (2004), "10 Songs Most Likely to Get Stuck in Your Head," 75 (12/20), 12. **www.keepersoflists.org/index.php?lid=1864**, accessed May 24, 2007.

lifestyle oriented toward spending time outdoors may be more likely to desire a convertible automobile than someone who is happier indoors.

Companies have spent vast amounts of money and time trying to harness individual differences in a way that would allow consumer choice to be predicted. They do so because individual differences like these include basic motivations, which trigger consumer desires. Also, individual differences shape the value experienced by consumers and the reaction consumers have to consumption.

External Influences

Why do some consumers like foods like sushi or habañero peppers while others wouldn't consider eating these things but instead prefer eating a hot dog? Why do consumers in different parts of the world have such different tastes for food? In Korea, a typical breakfast often includes a fish soup of some type. In Australia, one might smear a bit of vegemite (yeast extract made into something resembling peanut butter in texture but not taste) onto toast in the morning. In the United States, a bowl of frosted flakes with cold milk poured over the top is a common way to start the day. Each of these dishes is disgusting as a breakfast food to someone somewhere in the world and just fine to consumers in a different place. Even a simple thing like breakfast can cause quite different reactions in different consumers.

These types of events typify external influences on consumers. **External influences** include the social and cultural aspects of life as a consumer. They directly impact the value of activities although the influence comes from sources outside of the consumer. Thus, they are critical to a thorough understanding of consumer behavior.

Social Environment. Consumers learn a culture, including important things like rules about what types of food are appropriate for breakfast and how to greet people. In addition, any time a consumer chooses to do something to, at least in part, please or appeal to another consumer, he or she has been influenced by the **social environment**. The social environment includes the people and groups who help shape a consumer's everyday experiences. Reference group influence is one mechanism through which social influences work. A child's tastes for breakfast foods are shaped very much by what he or she learns from parents and an innate desire to conform to their wishes.

Situational Influences

External influences also include situational influences. **Situational influences** are unique to a time or place that can affect consumer decision making and the value received from consumption. Situational influences include the effect that the physical environment has on consumer behavior. For example, the presence of music in an environment may shape consumer behavior and even change buying patterns. Similarly, music can affect one's feelings when waiting for service. If so, a market for music that creates positive effects on consumers exists. Other characteristics such as the economic condition at a given time also affect the value of things. Factors like these are discussed further later.

Much of the remainder of the book will be organized around the Customer Value Framework. The CVF should be a valuable study aid particularly given that the different theoretical areas of consumer behavior are so closely related to each other. Additionally, the CVF is a good analysis tool for solving consumer behavior business problems. Lastly, the CVF is a valuable tool for businesses that are trying to understand the way consumers respond to their product offerings. Thus, the CVF is useful in developing and implementing marketing strategy.

external influences
social and cultural aspects of life as a consumer

social environment
elements that specifically deal with the way other people influence consumer decision making and value

situational influences
things unique to a time or place that can affect consumer decision making and the value received from consumption

COURTESY OF MÖVENPICK-HOLDING, SWITZERLAND

MÖVENPICK
OF SWITZERLAND

NEU

Am Ende glauben Sie noch,
Sie hätten es selbst gemacht.

MÖVENPICK
Birchermüesli

External influences determine the value of many things including what's for breakfast!

LO2 Value and Two Basic Types of Value

t he heart of the Consumer Value Framework, and *the* core concept of consumer behavior, is value. **Value** is a personal assessment of the *net worth* obtained from an activity. Value is what consumers ultimately pursue because valuable actions address motivations that manifest themselves in needs and desires. In this sense, value captures how much gratification a consumer receives from consumption.

When a consumer chooses a fast-food restaurant, chances are lower prices, greater convenience, or faster service have offset food quality. Consumers will also repeat behavior for which they have previously experienced low satisfaction. Interestingly, Walmart stores do not have a relatively high consumer satisfaction index, yet we need only drive by a Walmart store to know that many customers repeatedly visit Walmart. Walmart delivers value. In contrast to these examples, contriving a situation where consumers are not seeking value is virtually impossible. In fact, everything we do in life is done in the pursuit of value.

Value perceptions are derived from consumption after considering all costs and benefits associated with the consumption activity. In the everyday vernacular, people sometimes use *value* as a synonym for *price*, particularly *low price,* but this view is narrow-minded. We do use price to try to reflect value; however, price is in many ways a very poor proxy for value. Just think of the things that come to mind as of most value. How easily can one put a "price" on these most valued things?

THE VALUE EQUATION

Exhibit 2.2 reflects some components of value and how a consumer might put these together to determine the overall worth of something—or its value! Worth to a consumer is actually a function

This screen shot shows how different technologies can be used to provide value by delivering the same benefits—in this case, communication!

of much more than price. Value can be modeled by playing the "what you get" from dealing with a company against the "what you have to give" to get the product. Nearly all the components in the value equation come into play when a consumer buys a product like a car that requires multiple considerations.

Later in the book a chapter is devoted to describing value and other related concepts including expectations, satisfaction, and quality. However, because value is an essential part of consumer behavior, a basic overview is provided in this chapter.

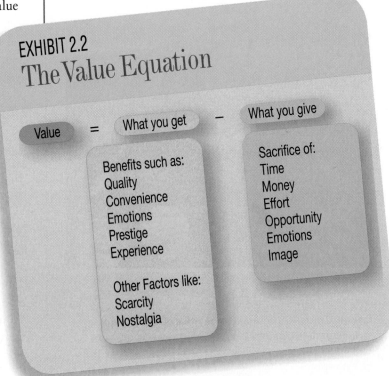

EXHIBIT 2.2
The Value Equation

$$\text{Value} = \text{What you get} - \text{What you give}$$

Benefits such as:
Quality
Convenience
Emotions
Prestige
Experience

Other Factors like:
Scarcity
Nostalgia

Sacrifice of:
Time
Money
Effort
Opportunity
Emotions
Image

Value can be understood better by looking at its types. While theoretically, one could probably break down value into many very specific types, a very useful value typology can be developed using only two types. Thus, we distinguish utilitarian value from hedonic value.

UTILITARIAN VALUE

Activities and objects that lead to high utilitarian value do so because they help the consumer accomplish some task. **Utilitarian value** is derived from a product that helps the consumer solve problems and accomplish tasks that are a part of being a consumer. A rational explanation can usually be given when somebody explains why something was purchased when utilitarian value is involved. For instance, when a consumer buys Clorox bleach, he or she undoubtedly will be cleaning something. Quite simply, the bleach enables something to become clean. Having something clean is gratifying to the consumer even if the actual process of cleaning is not. In this sense, utilitarian value is often thought of as a means to an end.[5] Value is provided because the object or activity allows something else to happen or be accomplished.

Bleach provides no benefit to consumers until it is used. Thus, consumers purchase it for utilitarian value.

HEDONIC VALUE

The second type of value is referred to in the consumer behavior literature as hedonic value. **Hedonic value** is the immediate gratification that comes from experienc-

Dining with Emeril is an experience high in hedonic value!

ing some activity. Seldom does one go to a horror film, ride Disney's Space Mountain, or read fiction in an effort to get a job done. With hedonic value, the value is provided entirely by the actual experience and emotions associated with consumption, not because some other end is or will be accomplished.

Conceptually, hedonic value differs from utilitarian value in several ways. First, hedonic value is an end in and of itself rather than a means to an end. Second, hedonic value is very emotional and subjective in nature. Third, when a consumer does something to obtain hedonic value, the action can sometimes be very difficult to explain objectively.

Rather than being viewed as opposites, utilitarian and hedonic value are not mutually exclusive. In other words, the same act of consumption can provide both utilitarian value and hedonic value. Dining in a nice

The very best consumer experiences are those that provide both high utilitarian value and high hedonic value.

restaurant like Emeril's is an event. One doesn't have to go there to eat, but dining there is a lot of fun—an experience—BAM! However, the consumer also accomplishes the task of having dinner—getting nourished. In fact, the very best consumer experiences are those that provide both high utilitarian value and high hedonic value.

Exhibit 2.3 illustrates the value possibilities associated with consumption. A marketer that provides low levels of both values is not likely to survive very long. Generally, a consumer goes to a fast-food restaurant to accomplish the task of getting something to eat, and doing this as quickly as possible. Food quality may take a back seat to convenience. When the fast-food experience becomes slow, the consumer receives little value of either type.

utilitarian value value derived from a product that helps the consumer with some task

hedonic value value derived from the immediate gratification that comes from some activity

EXHIBIT 2.3
Consumption Activities Can Fall into Any of These Categories

		Utilitarian Value	
		Low	High
Hedonic Value	Low	Bad Positioning – slow "fast" food	Okay Positioning – fast, "fast" food
	High	Okay Positioning – restaurant w/ nice atmosphere but poor food	Superior Positioning - restaurant w/ great atmosphere and great food

In contrast, restaurants can survive by specializing in providing one type of value or the other as would be the case in a place with a great atmosphere but perhaps less than the best food or service quality. The best experience comes when a restaurant can put everything together—high-quality food and impeccable service all packed in a memorable place with a great atmosphere. These are the types of experiences a consumer is most likely to want to repeat.

LO3 Marketing Strategy and Consumer Value

One way that a company can enhance the chance of long-run survival is to have an effective marketing strategy. To an army general, a strategy provides a way of winning a military conflict. Generally, a **strategy** is a planned way of doing something.

With hedonic value, the value is provided entirely by the actual experience and emotions associated with consumption, not because some other end is or will be accomplished.

MARKETING STRATEGY

If strategy is a way of doing something, given the purpose of business, a **marketing strategy** is the way a company goes about creating value for customers. The strategy also should provide an effective way of dealing with both competition and eventual technological obsolescence by making sure that value is delivered in a way that is not easily duplicated by other companies and not defined only in terms of the tangible product offered.

A complete understanding of the value consumers seek is needed to effectively develop and implement a strategy. AT&T may compete directly with Sprint, but AT&T also competes with companies like Skype, which provides local, long-distance, and even international calling via the Internet all for prices much lower than traditional telephone services. The consumer who uses Internet calling services like Skype no longer needs a telephone to receive the benefits of talking to friends and family who are far away. If AT&T laid out a marketing strategy that depended on people buying and owning "phones," technological obsolescence would represent a real threat. A better strategic orientation would focus on providing value by enabling and facilitating communication.

Strategies exist at several different levels. Exhibit 2.4 demonstrates this point. Basically, **corporate strategy** deals with how the firm will be defined and sets general goals. This strategy is usually associated with a specific corporate culture, which provides an operating orientation for the company. Marketing strategy then follows. Different business units within the firm may have different marketing strategies. In describing how value is created, the strategies tell why customers will choose to buy things from the company.

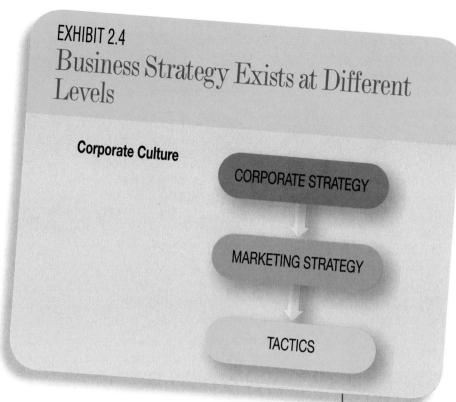

EXHIBIT 2.4
Business Strategy Exists at Different Levels

Corporate Culture

CORPORATE STRATEGY

MARKETING STRATEGY

TACTICS

palate accurate enough to be able to choose their favorite brand in a blind taste test. The fact of the matter is that Coke is more than colored, carbonated, flavored water. As ads have proclaimed, "Coke adds life!" If anyone doubts this, all they need to do is look back to the 1980s and see what happened when "old" Coke was pulled from the market in favor of "new" Coke. Consumers revolted and demanded that Coke be restored even though the "new" Coke was supported by millions of dollars of research that focused on flavor.

Other products require installation or other types of service before the benefits can be enjoyed. A GPS navigation system is in many ways a technological marvel. However, without a subscription to an information service, the consumer will never realize its benefits. Service

Strategies must eventually be implemented. Implementation deals with operational management. In marketing, this level includes activities known as tactics. **Marketing tactics**, which involve price, promotion, product, and distribution decisions, are ways marketing management is implemented. Together, marketing strategy and marketing tactics should maximize the total value received by its customers.

TOTAL VALUE CONCEPT

Products are multifaceted and can provide value in many ways. Even a simple product like a soft drink offers consumers more than a cold drink that addresses one's desire to quench a thirst. If a soft drink was a product that provided value only as a thirst quencher, the market share statistics for soft drink brands would certainly be different than they are today. Exhibit 2.5 shows U.S. market share data.[6]

As can be seen, Coca-Cola accounts for just less than half of all soft drinks sold. Taken together, the big-name companies represent nearly 90% of all soft drink sales. A quick visit to the supermarket will verify that Coke is far from a bargain product as soft drinks go. Brands such as Faygo and Shasta offer soft drinks at prices far lower on average than Coke. Yet, these brands have a fraction of the market share that Coke enjoys. Furthermore, consumers often do not have a

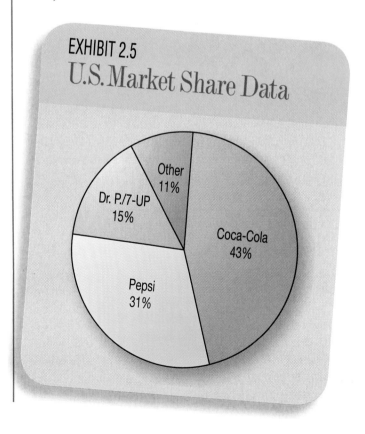

EXHIBIT 2.5
U.S. Market Share Data

Other 11%
Dr. P./7-UP 15%
Coca-Cola 43%
Pepsi 31%

elements like these and things such as installation, warranty, and product training make up the augmented product. The term **augmented product** means the extra things needed to fully obtain a product's benefits.

Thus, every product's value is made up of the basic benefits, plus the augmented product, plus the "feel" benefits. A company must try to understand all the ways a product offers value to its customers.

© WENN/NEWSCOM

How does the Ferrari provide value? If you understand this, you understand the total value concept.

> Every product's value is made up of the basic benefits, plus the augmented product, plus the "feel" benefits. A company must try to understand all the ways a product offers value to its customers.

The **total value concept** is practiced when companies operate with the understanding that products provide value in multiple ways. Many products and brands, for instance, provide some benefits that produce utilitarian value and some that provide hedonic value. The value that the product provides helps establish the meaning of the brand in the consumer psyche.

THE TOTAL VALUE CONCEPT ILLUSTRATED

Let's consider a consumer who purchases a 2008 Ferrari F430 Coupe. Does the consumer buy the car for its 483 horsepower V-8 engine, carbon-filament doors, bright red color, or semi-automatic gear box? No, the consumer buys the car because of the total value offered. How does the Ferrari F430 Coupe offer value? The answer may not be the same for all consumers, but here are some likely reasons:

1. **Transportation.** In other words, the Ferrari solves the job of getting a consumer from point A to point B. This is one way the Ferrari provides value—utilitarian value in this case.

2. **The Ferrari service plan.** A Ferrari needs TLC. Ferrari offers a 3-year warranty which means for at least 3 years, the problem of repairing the Ferrari is solved—utilitarian value added.

3. **The feelings associated with driving the car.** The car is very, very fast and handles well. Of course, the car will probably go above the speed limit, but how would we ever know that? The excitement that is the Ferrari driving experience provides hedonic value.

4. **The positive feelings that go along with ownership.** The Ferrari owner will certainly take pride in the car. He or she may also believe that social status comes from being seen as a Ferrari owner. He or she can also impress friends with a drive on Highway 1.

5. **The feelings of status and pride that come with ownership.** A Ferrari jacket and cap help make the statement, "I'm a Ferrari owner." The realization of ownership provides a hedonic value.

6. **The negative feelings that go along with ownership.** Hopefully, our Ferrari owner is independently wealthy. At a price tag of over $200,000 US, the car loan could be the size of a modest mortgage—not including insurance. If the Ferrari is a financial strain, then worry will result when the owner thinks about the car. In addition, the Ferrari needs servicing every 12,000 miles, servicing that is quite expensive and not covered in the warranty. Friends may have also suggested that Ferraris are unreliable. All of these feelings may distract from the hedonic value offered by the car.

Altogether, most readers would certainly like to own the Ferrari but probably not care to pay the high price. Thus, the Ferrari does not offer enough value for us to make the necessary sacrifice. A Honda Civic may do the trick although the hedonic to utilitarian value ratio may not be the same as with a Ferrari.

Automobile marketers sometimes miss the total value equation for their product. General Motors offered consumers a "total value promise." They hoped this would convey the idea of extended warranties, more standard equipment, and lower sticker prices. Are they missing something if they believe total value is confined to these tangible aspects?

A few years ago, GM created a discount program in which consumers received the employee discount on new car purchases. This program was wildly successfully in producing sales. Among other factors, GM's plan was increasing the value equation in the consumer's favor both by lowering the price and also by creating feelings that created positive emotions during the buying process. Consumers perceived themselves as getting a great deal and thus the program added hedonic value.[7] However, consumers also learned that GM cars can be sold at these low prices and that there was no need to pay a price premium for this brand. By 2009, GM had gone through bankruptcy and is surviving only with drastic government intervention. The reasons for their poor performance are many, but some claim that once the drastic discounting began, consumers were unreceptive to GM products at "non-employee" prices.

Thus, innovation is necessary if consumers are to provide high value. When a firm practices the total value concept, a full understanding of how value can be created from a product is necessary. Today, Ferrari might consider rolling routine service into the warranty plan as a way of enhancing value—particularly given the reliability of competitors like the Acura NSX. Total value is also affected by the technologies and infrastructures that exist. For instance, is Ferrari researching a way to provide value if gasoline-powered engines or high-speed highways become obsolete? What value would a Ferrari offer if you couldn't drive it?[8]

Marketing management involves managing the marketing mix and deciding to whom the effort will be directed. The **marketing mix** is simply the combination of product, pricing, promotion, and distribution strategies used to position some product offering or brand in the marketplace. The marketing mix represents the way a marketing strategy is implemented within a given market or exchange environment.

marketing mix combination of product, pricing, promotion, and distribution strategies used to implement a marketing strategy

target market identified segment or segments of a market that a company serves

market segmentation separation of a market into groups based on the different demand curves associated with each group

LO4 Market Characteristics: Market Segments and Product Differentiation

t he term **target market** is often used to signify which market segment a company will serve with a specific marketing mix. Thus, target marketing requires that market segments be identified and understood. But, what exactly is market segmentation?

> Groups of consumers that have similar tastes end up as part of a market segment.

MARKET SEGMENTATION

Market segmentation is the separation of a market into groups based on the different demand curves associated with each group. Market segmentation is a marketplace condition; numerous segments exist in some markets, but very few segments may exist in others. We can think of the total quantity of a product sold as a simple mathematical function (f) like this:[9]

$$Q = f(p, w, x, ...z)$$

where Q = total quantity sold, p = price, and w, x, and z are other characteristics of the particular product.

© HOLGER HILL/FSTOP/GETTY IMAGES

The function means that as price and the other characteristics are varied, the quantity demanded changes.

For example, as the price of HDTVs decreases, the quantity sold increases; in other words, there is a negative relationship between price and quantity sold. This type of relationship would represent the typical price–quantity relationship commonly shown in basic economics. As the length of the warranty increases (w in this case), more HDTVs would be sold. Thus, if we limit the demand equation to two characteristics (price p and warranty w in this case), the equation representing demand or total sales for HDTVs overall might be

$$Q = -3p + 2w$$

The numbers, or coefficients, preceding p and w, respectively, for each group represent the sensitivity of each segment to each characteristic. The greater the magnitude of the number, the more sensitive that group is to a change. In economics, this is referred to as **elasticity**. This equation suggests that consumers are more sensitive to price than warranty as indicated by the respective coefficients, -3 for price and $+2$ for warranty in this case.

However, this overall demand "curve" may not accurately reflect any particular consumer. Instead, the market may really consist of two groups of consumers that produce this particular demand curve when aggregated. In other words, the two groups may be of equal size and have demand functions that look something like this:

$$q_1 = -1p + 3w$$
$$q_2 = -5p + 1w$$

In this case, q_1 and q_2 represent the quantity that would be sold in groups one and two, respectively. Group one is more sensitive to the warranty, and group two is more sensitive to price. If we put all the segments together, we get total demand once again:

$$Q = q_1 + q_2$$

Thus, a market for any product is really the sum of the demand existing in individual groups or segments of consumers. The fast-food market may consist of many segments including a group most interested in low price, a group most interested in food quality, a group most interested in convenience, and perhaps a group that is not extremely sensitive to any of these characteristics. In this sense, market segmentation is not really a marketing tactic because the segments are created by consumers through their unique preferences. Market segmentation is critically important to effective marketing though, and the marketing researcher's job becomes identifying segments and describing the segment's members based on characteristics such as age, income, geography, and lifestyle.

Exhibit 2.6 depicts the market segmentation process. For simplicity, the quantity sold is considered only a function of price. The frame on the left depicts overall quantity demanded. Typically, as price goes up (moves right on the x-axis), the quantity sold goes down, meaning price is negatively related to quantity. The frame on the right breaks this market into three segments:

1. The orange line depicts a segment that is highly sensitive to price. Changes in price correspond to relatively large changes in sales. In this particular case, price increases reduce the quantity demanded.

2. The green line represents a segment also sensitive to price so that higher prices are demanded less, but this segment is not nearly as sensitive as the first segment. Changes in price are not associated with as large of a change in quantity sold.

3. The violet line turns out to be perhaps most interesting. Here, when price goes up, the quantity sold actually goes up, too. Thus, the group is sensitive to price but actually buys more at a higher price than at a lower price.

Actually, although a positive relationship between price and quantity may seem unusual, *backward*

EXHIBIT 2.6
Total Market Sales and Sales within Market Segments

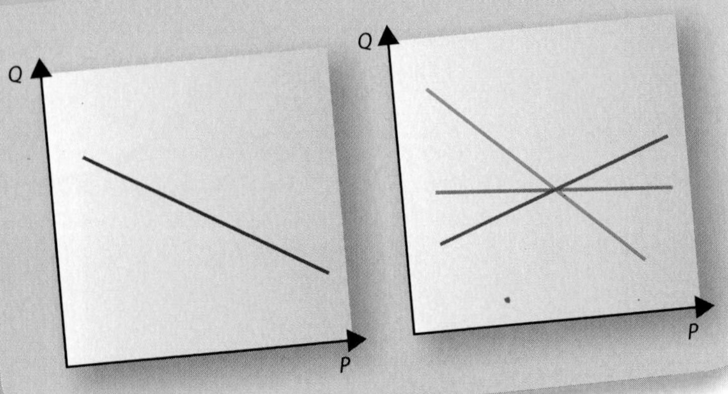

sloping demand, a term used in economics to refer to this situation, is hardly rare. When one considers product category demand, many products will display a positive price–quantity demanded relationship. For instance, how much perfume with a brand name Ce n'est pas Cher could be sold in a gallon container for $2? Probably not very much! However, Chanel No. 5 is highly demanded at about $250 an ounce!

Earlier, we discussed the soft drink market in the context of the total value concept and pointed out how higher-priced brands were the best sellers. Thus, if we think of the change in price as the difference in price between the bargain brands and Coke, most consumers seem to prefer higher-priced sodas. At the very least, soft drink consumers are insensitive to price. Although this may seem inconsistent with "rational" economics, consumer behavior theory can explain this. In fact, the answer is that the name brand soft drinks like Coke simply are worth more, meaning they are more valuable, than are the bargain soft drinks! This is a very important point to understand. Ultimately, consumer segments exist because different consumers do not value different alternatives the same way.[10]

Market segments are associated with unique value equations just as they are associated with unique demand equations. Thus, if each segment is offered a product that closely matches its particular sensitivities, all segments can receive high value. This brings us to product differentiation.

PRODUCT DIFFERENTIATION

Product differentiation is a marketplace condition in which consumers do not view all competing products as identical to one another. We refer to commodities very often as products that are not seen as different no matter who produced them or where they were produced. Regular gasoline approaches a commodity status, but even here some consumers will see certain brands as unique. In contrast, not very many consumers would view all music the same. Indeed, country music stands out clearly from rock, both of which are different from classical music, which is different from reggaeton or emo. Product differentiation affects consumer value because more consumers can find a product offering more closely matching their peculiar needs. The increased value is often reflected in decreased price sensitivity within markets characterized by much product differentiation.

> Cheaper products don't always outsell their higher-priced alternatives.

product differentiation marketplace condition in which consumers do not view all competing products as identical to one another

product positioning way a product is perceived by a consumer

perceptual map tool used to depict graphically the positioning of competing products

LO5 Analyzing Markets with Perceptual Maps

Product differentiation becomes the basis for **product positioning**. Positioning refers to the way a product is perceived by a consumer and can be represented by the number and types of characteristics that consumers perceive. A standard marketing tool is a perceptual map.

PERCEPTUAL MAPS

A **perceptual map** is used to depict graphically the positioning of competing products. When marketing analysts examine perceptual maps, they can identify competitors, identify opportunities for doing more business, and diagnose potential problems in the marketing mix. For instance, the analyst may realize that by changing the amount of some product characteristic, they can "move" closer to some segment's ideal point, and thus increase the competitiveness of the product. Alternatively, a new business may choose to position a product in a way that leaves it facing little direct competition. This can be done by "locating" the product as far away from other brands as possible.

ILLUSTRATING A PERCEPTUAL MAP

ideal points combination of product characteristics that provide the most value to an individual consumer or market segment

Exhibit 2.7 illustrates a perceptual map. Perceptual mapping is used throughout this book as a way to link differences in consumer behavior to changes in marketing strategy or tactics. In this case, the perceptual map has been generated by a consulting firm exploring the possibility of a new radio station in the Springdale market.

The researcher has collected data on nine radio stations and on the **ideal points**, meaning the combination of radio station characteristics providing the most value, of six Springdale consumer segments. These are indicated by stars. The *x*- and *y*-axes of this plane are dimensions used to separate competitors from low to high on a specific characteristic. Here, the *x*-axis separates radio stations based on the era of music they feature. Thus, stations feature music from the 1960s through today. The *y*-axis separates radio stations based on how much the format features news and talk versus music.[11] The analyst can draw several conclusions from the perceptual map including:

1. Stations playing contemporary music with very little news and talk experience the most intense competition. WEAK, WAKY, WOBL, and WYME all offer "late-model" music with very little news and talk. Thus, they compete rather directly.

2. The blue segment (indicated by the blue star) finds the most value in "late-model" music with little news and talk. Currently, WAKY has the highest share of this segment (the ideal point is very close to WAKY's location).

3. WATE, which plays 1980s music mixed with news and talk, appeals very strongly to the orange segment. This could be a very loyal market segment for WATE.

4. WXPC does not have a format similar to any ideal point.

5. The purple segment appears practically unserved.

After analyzing the perceptual map, the analyst draws several conclusions:

1. Because the station is a start-up without massive resources, an "oldies" format with nearly all music is recommended in an attempt to capitalize on the purple segment.

2. The highest demand quadrant appears to be quadrant 1, with contemporary music and little news/talk, but a lot of resources would be required to start here because of the entrenched competition. Thus, option 1 appears preferable.

3. A potential threat exists if WXPC were to decrease the amount of news and talk, thus moving them toward the purple ideal point; however, this appears unlikely. If WXPC were to undergo a format change, a move to more news and talk to try to capitalize on the red segment's ideal point appears easier because of the relative proximity.

USING CONSUMER BEHAVIOR THEORY IN MARKETING STRATEGY

Businesses are constantly using consumer behavior to make better strategic and operational marketing decisions. Therefore, we will focus on using consumer behavior in business decision making many times through the course of this book. Students, and practicing managers for that matter, sometimes struggle with the application aspect of consumer behavior. Essentially, this comes down to effective decision making. Checklists can be a useful aid to decision making as a way to effectively develop marketing strategy and tactics. Exhibit 2.8 displays a consumer behavior analysis checklist—the CB checklist.

The CB checklist is simply used by applying each question to the given situation. Ideas for improving the situation should emerge from the answers provided. In addition, even though an answer may not result directly, going through the checklist may generate some thoughts that would not have occurred otherwise.

EXHIBIT 2.7
A Perceptual Map for a Local Rock Music Radio Market

EXHIBIT 2.8
The CB Idea Checklist

Question	Idea
What specific consumer needs and desires are involved? • Is a specific product(s) involved in this situation? • Can something else provide the same value or address the same need or desire?	
How is the product positioned (types and amounts of value intended)? How is our position superior to competitors? • How can we move closer to desirable ideal points? How is our position inferior to competitors? • How can we isolate ourselves from competition?	
How does the consumer actually receive value from this company? • In the current situation, Has value been diminished? Can value be enhanced? • Can the product be modified to enhance value? • Can the company introduce a new product to enhance value? • Can the company add services to improve value for consumers? • Can communication be improved? • Is a competitor in a better position to provide superior value? • If so, how?	
Where is this product consumed? • Can value be enhanced by changing the consumption setting?	

Who?
• Is buying the product?
  1. Individual Consumers
  2. Groups of Consumers (Families)
  3. Business Consumers
• Is not buying the product?	

Why should a consumer? • Buy this product? • Avoid this product?	
When do consumers? • Find the product most valuable? • Find the product least valuable?	
What are the key CVF elements involved in understanding the consumption process in this case?	
Is additional consumer research needed? • Will the information be worth what it would cost to obtain it? • What type of research would be required?	

© IMAGE COURTESY OF THE ADVERTISING ARCHIVES (BOTH)

Both Versace and H & M specialize in clothing, but do they appeal to the same segment with the same type of design? The answer to this question determines how much they compete with each other.

LO6 Value Today and Tomorrow—Customer Lifetime Value

We defined marketing earlier as value-producing activities that facilitate exchange. In other words, marketing makes exchange more likely. Exchange is far from a one-way street. Consumers enter exchange-seeking value and marketers likewise enter exchange-seeking value. The value the company receives from exchange may be slightly easier to explain than is the value that a consumer receives. Obviously, when a consumer spends money for a product, the company receives economic resources in the form of revenue, which can be used to pay employees, cover costs, and help the firm grow. The company may also receive additional benefits if the consumer becomes a loyal customer who is an advocate for the firm's products.

Thus, not every customer is equally valuable to a firm. Firms increasingly want to know the customer lifetime value associated with a customer or customer segment.[12] **Customer Lifetime Value (CLV)** represents the approximate worth of a customer to a company in economic terms. Put another way, CLV is the overall, long-term profitability of an individual consumer. Although there is no generally accepted formula for the CLV, the basic idea is simple and can be represented as follows:

$$CLV = npv \text{ (sales } - \text{ costs)} + npv \text{ (equity)}$$

The customer lifetime value then is equal to the net present value (npv) of the stream of profits over a customer's lifetime plus the worth attributed to the equity a good customer can bring in the form of positive referrals and word of mouth. Consider a consumer shopping twice weekly at IKEA (see **www.ikea.com**). On average, this IKEA customer spends $200 per week, or $10,400 per year. If we assume a 5% operating margin, this customer yields IKEA a *net* $520 per year. Even if any potential positive word-of-mouth is not considered, the consumer is worth about $9,000 to IKEA today assuming a 30-year life span and a 4% annual interest rate.

Interestingly, until recently Walmart did not record customer level data. Thus, out of over 500 terabytes of data, they had no data on CLV.[13] In contrast, other firms, from convenience stores to Harrah's Casinos, have elaborate systems for tracking individual customer behavior and targeting these consumers with individualized promotions and products. This allows them to practice one-to-one marketing in a real sense and to identify segments of consumers containing a high proportion of very valuable

E-Segments

Practically everybody "surfs" the Internet these days. But some consumers are more likely to make purchases online than are others. Researchers have identified segments of consumers who have relatively different sensitivities to different characteristics of online shopping. At a simple level, consumers who make numerous purchases online tend to be more sensitive to the convenience perceived with online shopping and tend to be younger and wealthier and to spend more time on the Internet overall than the segment of online shopping avoiders. This latter segment is very sensitive to concerns about security.

Segments representing the heavy online shopper and those who avoid online shopping can both be broken down more specifically into categories. For online shoppers, there are those who see online shopping as providing high utilitarian value as evidenced by the predominance of purchases associated with the consumer's business or job. Conversely, other consumers simply enjoy the online shopping experience in its own right, meaning that online shopping provides a high hedonic value. Whether shopping is done in the store or online, shopping enjoyment remains important in understanding what people buy.

Source: Swinyard, William R., and Scott M. Smith (2003), "Why People (Don't) Shop Online: A Lifestyle Study of the Internet Consumer," *Psychology & Marketing*, 20, 567–597. Martin, C. (2009), "CONSUMPTION MOTIVATION AND PERCEPTIONS OF MALLS: A COMPARISON OF MOTHERS AND DAUGHTERS," Journal of Marketing Theory and Practice, 17 (Winter), 49-61.

customers. For instance, one retailer found that high CLV customers tended to have the following characteristics:[14]

- Female
- 30–50 years of age
- Married
- $90,000 income
- Loyalty card holder

In contrast, the low CLV customers tended to have quite different characteristics:

- Male
- 24–44 years of age
- Single
- Less than $70,000 income
- Single channel shopper (meaning only Internet or only stores)

Thus, marketers can maximize the value they receive from exchange by concentrating their marketing efforts on consumers with high CLVs. The E-Segments feature illustrates a way CLV analysis could be tied to market segmentation.

Chapter 2 Case

Headquartered in Woonsocket, Rhode Island, CVS Caremark is the number one provider of prescriptions in the United States with over 6,200 locations in forty-four states across America. CVS/pharmacy serves the health care needs of its customers by providing convenience and a high overall perceived value.[15]

Along with its pharmaceutical products, CVS "front store" retail sales include health and beauty products at affordable prices. CVS has a large selection of upscale cosmetics with the latest advances in skin care and has expert beauty consultants on staff.

In 2006, CVS launched their in-store Photo Centers, offering customers fast, convenient, and high-quality image processing. CVS/pharmacy now has the largest distributed photo printing network of any retailer in North America.

CASE

In 2001, CVS/pharmacy was financially strong, with number one market share positions in major drug store markets such as Boston (28.8%), Chicago (51%), and Houston (36.9%). Competition, however, was becoming increasingly fierce from rivals such as Walgreens, Osco, Rite Aid, Eckerd, and Kroger.[16]

Specifically, Walgreens posed a serious threat to CVS in 2001—aggressively expanding in key growth markets such as Houston and Chicago where CVS had enjoyed a leading market share.[17]

CVS's loyal customers were now being tempted to switch to the competition by Walgreens' low prices and 24-hour service. CVS needed to devise a new marketing strategy to retain its loyal customers.

CVS MAKES ITS MOVE

In February of 2001, CVS launched a new customer loyalty program called ExtraCare® in its 4,100 stores. Customers could sign up for a CVS ExtraCare card and receive 2% back on their purchases in the form of a coupon printed at the bottom of their receipt. It also rewards customers with $1.00 to spend on front store merchandise for every two prescriptions filled.

ExtraCare customers may choose to disclose personal information, such as their home address and phone number, but it is not required. A customer may still receive in-store discounts even if they have only provided a name. Customers who do provide an address receive mailings with special offers and coupons, and information about new products tailored to their shopping habits.

In August of 2001, year-to-date same store pharmacy sales increased by 14.7% and overall store sales increased 10.9%.[18]

SUMMARY AND CONCLUSIONS

In addition to the substantial investment in technology required by the ExtraCare program, CVS continues to invest in growth through acquisition. In 2005, CVS/pharmacy integrated 1,200 Eckerd drugstores in markets such as Texas and Florida. In 2007, CVS integrated 700 Sav-on and Osco drugstores in the California markets.

In 2008, ExtraCare has become a successful customer loyalty program, with more than 50 million cardholders in the United States. Through cardholder transactions, CVS has improved their ability to respond to customer needs, based on the information collected through card sales. The ExtraCare program also enabled CVS/pharmacy to maintain its market share, despite the discounting efforts and fierce rivalry of its competition.

Today, customer relationship management software and other improvements in information technology have enabled marketers to better understand the needs of customers on a one-to-one basis. Similar value card programs are evident in many different industries. Consumers receive rewards for purchasing virtually every type of product—from grocery stores to drive-through coffee retailers.

Questions

1. Visit the CVS/pharmacy website (**http://www.cvs.com**). What other benefits does CVS provide to ExtraCare customers? Provide examples of both utilitarian and hedonic value.
2. Suppose a major competitor launches its own customer value card program. How might CVS respond? What recommendations would you give CVS to improve the ExtraCare program?
3. What are the advantages and disadvantages of *not* requiring personal information from customers for participating in the ExtraCare program?
4. What ethical issues would CVS need to consider before changing their ExtraCare policy to require an address and phone number?

The communication

of value relies on consumer perception and learning.

what do you think?

My perceptions of advertisements are usually accurate.

1 2 3 4 5 6 7

strongly disagree   strongly agree

3

Consumer Learning Starts Here: Perception

After studying this chapter, the student should be able to:

LO1 Understand the elements of consumer perception.

LO2 Know the phases in the consumer perception process.

LO3 Be able to apply the concept of the JND.

LO4 Apply the concepts of implicit and explicit memory.

LO5 Know the ways in which a consumer's attention can be enhanced.

LO6 Know the difference between intentional and unintentional learning.

Introduction

marketing strategy represents the way a firm goes about creating a unique and valuable bundle of benefits for the consumer. As such, marketing strategy focuses on value creation. Unfortunately, many firms never fully understand the value they create, and this can lead to major problems. For example, the firm web van.com started amid the dot-com boom in the late 1990s. The idea was to deliver groceries directly to consumers. However, the firm failed to last even five years. The issue that marketers commonly face is that consumers don't always perceive the value being offered. Of course, if a consumer doesn't think that the product will deliver the value desired or doesn't perceive the product in the intended way, the purchase will not be made!

> **learning** change in behavior resulting from some interaction between a person and a stimulus
>
> **perception** consumer's awareness and interpretation of reality

The communication of value relies on consumer perception and learning. **Learning** refers to a change in behavior resulting from the interaction between a person and a stimulus. **Perception** refers to a consumer's awareness and interpretation of reality. Accordingly, perception serves as a foundation upon which consumer learning takes place. Stated simply, value involves learning, and consumer learning begins with perception. Although learning and perception are often treated as distinct subjects, a close inspection of the topics reveals that they are actually very closely related.

Sometimes, consumers set out to *intentionally* learn marketing-related information. Other times, consumers learn *unintentionally* (or incidentally) by simply being exposed to stimuli and by forming some kind of response to it. Both types of learning rely, to greater or lesser degrees, on perceptual processes.

This chapter focuses on issues that are central to understanding the learning process. Specifically, the

exposure process of bringing some stimulus within proximity of a consumer so that the consumer can sense it with one of the five human senses

sensation consumer's immediate response to a stimulus

attention purposeful allocation of information-processing capacity toward developing an understanding of some stimulus

chapter details the earliest phases of perception along with a number of issues related to unintentional learning. The chapter closes with a discussion of *conditioning,* which represents a well-known approach to unintentional learning. Intentional learning and the cognitive processes associated with it are discussed in a later chapter.

LO1 Consumer Perception

What's more important, perception or reality? This probably seems like a typical "academic" question, but the issue is very important to consumer researchers. Researchers expend a great deal of effort on trying to understand consumer perception because the way a message is perceived greatly influences how consumers learn.

Perception and reality are distinct concepts because the perceptions that consumers develop do not always match the real world. For example, we've probably all listened to a fanatical sports fan boast about his or her favorite team. The cliché "rose-colored glasses" is an accurate description because the favored team is rarely as good as the fan makes it out to be. Perception simply doesn't always match reality. Perception can also be ambiguous. Exhibit 3.1 illustrates this point.

As we have noted, perception can be thought of as a consumer's awareness and interpretation of reality. In this sense, perception represents a *subjective* reality, whereas the objective reality is represented by what actually exists in the environment. For example, when dinner is served, the objective reality is that a certain amount of food has been placed on a dinner plate. This food can be weighed so that the actual amount becomes known. However, the amount of food that is perceived by a consumer is a different issue. How can this be? The answer to this question illustrates the concept of subjective reality. In this case, subjective and objective reality may not be the same simply because the size of the plate affects the quantity of food a consumer perceives.

Exhibit 3.2 illustrates this effect by showing the same amount of food on three different plates. Placing food on a smaller plate may actually increase the chance that diners are satisfied with the portion because they perceive that they are getting more![1] With the smaller plate, they may perceive that they are full, but they may want to continue eating with the larger plate.

EXPOSURE, ATTENTION, AND COMPREHENSION

During the perceptual process, consumers are *exposed* to stimuli, devote *attention* to stimuli, and attempt to *comprehend* stimuli. **Exposure** refers to the process of bringing some stimulus within the proximity of a consumer so that it can be sensed by one of the five human senses (sight, smell, taste, touch, or sound). The term **sensation** is used to describe a consumer's immediate response to this information. McDonald's sends the message that "four bucks is dumb" with billboards exposing consumers to a not-so-subtle message about coffee.

Simply being exposed to stimuli does not guarantee that a consumer will pay attention. **Attention** is the purposeful allocation of information-processing capacity toward developing an understanding of some stimulus. Many times, consumers simply cannot pay attention to

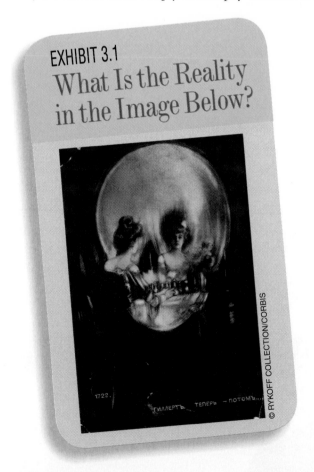

EXHIBIT 3.1
What Is the Reality in the Image Below?

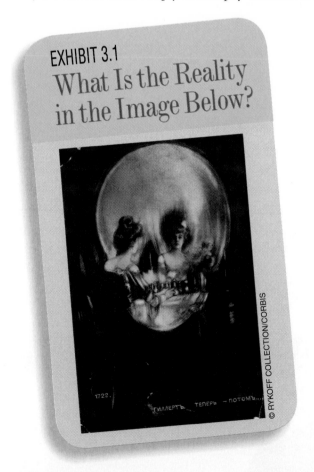

© RYKOFF COLLECTION/CORBIS

EXHIBIT 3.2
Objective and Subjective Reality Don't Always Match

Enough to Eat?
May look like more
than 500 grams

500 grams of food

Not Enough to Eat?
May look like less
than 500 grams

and interpret information in the way that has been intended, but this is not always the case. As a simple example, think of the various meanings assigned to words. For example, to one consumer *tight* might mean "cool" or "hip." To another, *tight* might relate to how well a product fits. Notice that consumers can be presented with the same stimuli and comprehend them in different ways.

all the stimuli to which they are exposed. As such, they are selective in the information to which they pay attention. Quite simply, there is just too much stimulation in the environment for consumers to pay attention to everything!

Comprehension occurs when consumers attempt to derive meaning from information they receive. Of course, marketers hope that consumers comprehend

LO2 Consumer Perception Process

i f a friend were to ask, "Do I look good in this outfit?" you would immediately draw upon your perceptions when determining how to respond to his or her question. (Whether or not you voice your true opinion is an entirely different subject!) As we have stated, in its most basic form, perception describes how consumers become aware of and interpret the environment. Accordingly, we can view consumer perception as including three phases. These phases include *sensing*, *organizing*, and *reacting*. This is shown in Exhibit 3.3 on the following page.

Notice that the phases of perception correspond to the elements of exposure, attention, and comprehension. That is, we sense the many stimuli to which we are exposed, we organize the stimuli as we attend and comprehend them, and we react to various stimuli by developing responses. This process is discussed next.

SENSING

Sensing occurs when one of the consumers' senses is exposed to an object. Sensing therefore represents an *immediate* response to stimuli that have come into contact with one of the consumer's five senses (sight,

© SCOTT EKLUND/RED BOX PICTURES

When consumers go by a billboard, they are provided with an opportunity to pay attention to the message.

cognitive organization process by which the human brain assembles sensory evidence into something recognizable

assimilation state that results when a stimulus has characteristics such that consumers readily recognize it as belonging to some specific category

smell, touch, taste, or sound). Thus, when a consumer enters a store, views a website, tastes food, encounters an advertisement, or tries on some clothes, the perceptual process is put into action. However, sensing alone does not allow a consumer to assign meaning. This leads to the second stage of the perceptual process.

ORGANIZING

Imagine being blindfolded and handed an unknown small object. How would you determine what the object might be? Of course, the object can be felt. Is it rough or smooth? Is it soft or hard? These answers may narrow down the alternatives. A consumer's brain is addressing questions like these every time something is encountered. Accordingly, this process takes place literally thousands of times each day. In fact, organization takes place so quickly in most cases that we are unaware of the process.

When we speak of **cognitive organization**, we refer to the process by which the human brain assembles the sensory evidence into something recognizable. This is an important part of perception. Exhibit 3.4 may help you visualize this process. The organization that takes place in your brain is analogous to someone performing a sorting task—like sorting mail. When an object is first picked up, the sorter has no clue concerning what slot the object belongs in. However, several pieces of information allow the sorter to place the object into progressively more specific categories.

When someone tries to decide if an outfit "looks" right, the perceptual process goes to work. Consider the clothing pictured in Exhibit 3.3. Is this outfit appropriate for Emilia, a professional consultant? At first we note that the outfit obviously is perceived as women's clothing. However, does the outfit represent proper business attire? If Emilia's brain sorts the object into this category, then she will perceive this as appropriate. Another consumer may perceive the outfit differently. Again we see the subjectivity of perception.

Consumers develop an interpretation during this stage of the perceptual process and begin to *comprehend* what the stimulus is. This interpretation provides

EXHIBIT 3.3
Sensing, Organizing, and Reacting

SENSING

ORGANIZING

REACTING

What will everyone else think?

Does this fit?

an initial cognitive and affective meaning. As we discussed in a previous chapter, the term *cognitive* refers to a mental or thinking process. Imagine you had taken part in a blind cola taste test (meaning you didn't know which cola you were tasting). After taking a sip, your first impression may be that you are tasting Coke, and you may like it. When we use the term *affective*, we refer to feelings that develop along with the understanding of the stimulus. If you are a loyal Coke drinker, the good feelings that go along with drinking Coke also will become active. Over a series of positive encounters with stimuli that you like, the result could even be an improved mood.[2]

Importantly, not every object is easily categorized. When a consumer encounters a stimulus that is not easily categorized, the brain instinctively continues processing in an effort to reconcile inconsistencies. When even this extra effort leaves a consumer uncertain, he or she will generally avoid the stimulus.

In general, however, depending on the extent to which a stimulus can be categorized, three possible reactions may occur.

1. **Assimilation. Assimilation** occurs when a stimulus has characteristics such that individuals readily recognize it as an example of a specific category. A light brown, slightly sticky, sweet, round food with a hole in the middle is easily recognized as a doughnut in nearly every part of the world.

accommodation state
that results when a stimulus
shares some but not all of the
characteristics that would
lead it to fit neatly in an existing category and consumers
must process exceptions to
rules about the category

contrast state that results
when a stimulus does not
share enough in common
with existing categories to
allow categorization

EXHIBIT 3.4
A Visual Image of the Organization Process

MAIL

© ISTOCKPHOTO.COM/PATTIE STEIB

2. **Accommodation.**
   Accommodation occurs when a stimulus shares some, but not all, of the
   characteristics that would lead it to fit
   neatly in an existing category. At
   this point, the consumer will
   begin processing, which
   allows exceptions to rules
   about the category. For
   example, in New Orleans,
   a tourist may encounter a
   beignet, which is a French
   doughnut. Because the
   beignet does not have a hole, the
   tourist's perceptual process may have
   to make an exception to the rule that all doughnuts
   have holes.

3. **Contrast. Contrast** occurs when a stimulus does not
   share enough in common with existing categories
   to allow categorization. For example, consumers
   in Kyrgyzstan routinely enjoy fermented mountain
   mare's milk. The only similarity to the milk that
   most western consumers know is the color. So, when
   a westerner tastes the milk, particularly if the taster
   doesn't know what is being consumed, contrast is a
   nearly certain outcome. People tend to not like things
   that are so completely unknown. Therefore, contrast
   is usually associated with negative feelings. Curiously,
   research indicates that stimuli that are mildly incongruent with expectations are actually preferred![3]

Categorization is discussed
in more detail in Chapter 4.

REACTING

The perceptual process ends with
some reaction. If an object is successfully recognized, chances are
some nearly automatic reaction
takes place. For example, when a
driver notices that the car in front
of her has its brake lights on, the
learned response is to apply brakes as well.
Here, the reaction occurs as a response or behavior. Note that reactions can include both physical and mental responses to the stimuli that we
encounter.

Applications to Consumer Behavior

The perceptual process has many implications for
consumer behavior. For example, think about how
the music playing in a store can affect one's perceptions of the store. Would a fine watch be perceived the
same way with AC/DC or Mozart in the background?[4]
Also, returning to the question "Do I look good in this
outfit?" Note that online retailers often use technology
to allow for more realistic depictions of clothing in an
attempt to improve consumer perceptions and retail performance.[5] If consumers perceive that a piece of clothing
will look good and be a good fit, they will be more likely
to purchase it.

SELECTIVE PERCEPTION

Consumers encounter thousands of stimuli each day.
If all stimuli were consciously processed, they would
truly be overloaded. Rather than processing all stimuli,

consumers practice selective perception. *Selective perception* includes selective exposure, selective attention, and selective distortion. That is, consumers are selective in what they expose themselves to, what they attend to, and what (and how) they comprehend. **Selective exposure** involves screening out most stimuli and exposing oneself to only a small portion of stimuli present. **Selective attention** involves paying attention to only certain stimuli.

Consider a consumer walking through downtown Seoul, South Korea. How can he or she possibly pay attention to all of this information? Marketers use the term *clutter* to describe the idea that consumers are often bombarded with too much information in their daily lives. Consumers can't possibly pay attention to all of this. Instead, they will choose something that stands out, or is personally relevant, and devote attention to that object.

Selective distortion is a process by which consumers interpret information in ways that are biased by their previously held beliefs. This process can be the result of either a conscious or unconscious effort. For exam-

ple, consumers with strongly held beliefs about a brand tend to comprehend messages about the brand either positively or negatively, depending on their initial attitudes. As we illustrated with the meaning of the word *tight*, two consumers can be exposed to the exact same stimuli and derive different meanings from them. Sports fans are great examples of the selective distortion topic. A fan from one team can become enraged when a "bad call" goes against his or her team. The fan from the other team can be thrilled. Note again that both fans see the exact same thing but comprehend the information differently.

We now discuss the exposure, attention, and comprehension concepts found in perception in more detail.

EXPOSURE

We need to discuss a number of issues pertaining to the exposure stage. Of course, it's obvious that marketers who want to inform consumers about their products must first expose them to information. As such, exposure represents a first step to learning. In fact, it's a vital component of both intentional and unintentional learning. As we have already discussed above, exposure occurs when some stimulus is brought within the proximity of a consumer so that it can be sensed. This is a very important part of perception.

Of course, consumers cannot be expected to learn from information to which they've never been exposed. If someone were to ask you "have seen the new Rock Band™ video game?" and you were to reply "no," then you probably haven't been exposed to it! Next, we discuss issues that pertain to exposure, beginning with subliminal processing, the absolute threshold, the just noticeable difference, and the mere exposure effect.

SUBLIMINAL PROCESSING

Subliminal processing refers to the way in which the human brain senses very low-strength stimuli, that is, stimuli that occur below the level of conscious awareness. These stimuli are said to be below the **absolute threshold** of perception. This type of "learning" is unintentional by definition because the stimuli fall below the absolute threshold. To illustrate effects occurring below the absolute threshold, consider what often happens when a mosquito lands on one's arm. Chances are

What would you pay attention to if you saw this?

© ED FREEMAN/THE IMAGE BANK/GETTY IMAGES

the mosquito is so small that the person will not be consciously aware of the sensation. Therefore, the mosquito is below the absolute threshold. Likewise, sounds often occur that are below the threshold. Images can also be displayed for such a short period of time, or at such a low level of intensity, that the brain cannot register what the image is.

If one is influenced by stimuli below the level of conscious awareness, the influence can be described as being *subliminal*. As we will see, although this type of learning is quite popular among consumers, the effectiveness of the process is highly questionable.

Subliminal persuasion has been a hot topic with consumers for many years. Many popular conceptions fuel this interest. For instance, consumers often believe that

- Marketers can somehow induce them to purchase products by using subliminal advertising.
- Products or packages can be subliminally altered to make them more appealing to consumers.
- Sexual imagery can be "hidden" in a product, its packaging, or its advertisement.
- Their own well-being can be enhanced by listening to subliminally embedded tapes of nature sounds and/or music.[6]

Notice that the belief is that consumers can learn, and that behavior can be changed, without the consumer trying to learn anything at all. That is, learning is purported to take place because of exposure to subliminal stimuli.

The most famous example of subliminal perception involved a researcher for an ad firm who claimed that he had embedded subliminal frames within the movie *Picnic* in a New Jersey movie theater several years ago. Exhibit 3.5 illustrates the way this process reportedly took place. Very brief embeds of the phrase "Drink Coke" and "Eat Popcorn" were supposedly placed in the movie. The researcher claimed that popcorn sales rose nearly 60 percent as a result and that Coke sales rose nearly 20 percent. This experiment is often called the "Vicary experiment."

> **subliminal persuasion** persuasion that results from subliminal processing

> Estimates suggest that over 60 percent of Americans believe that advertisers can exert subliminal influences strong enough to cause purchase behavior.

This so-called experiment grew in such popularity that researchers attempted to replicate the study. Interestingly, these replications failed to produce any increase in desire for popcorn or Coke. Consumer researchers have also conducted experiments that test the effectiveness of sexual embeds involving air-brushed genitalia, the word *sex,* or provocative nudity in advertisements. Results of these experiments generally indicate that these practices do nothing that would make a consumer more likely to buy the advertised product.[7]

As a general statement, it can be said that research examining subliminal processing is conclusive: Subliminal "persuasion" is ineffective.[8] This is not to completely dismiss subliminal processing as having no impact whatsoever on what consumers might learn or how they might behave, but any effects appear to be very small and have little chance of significantly influencing consumer attitude or choice.

Despite the evidence that reveals that subliminal advertising is ineffective, consumers are generally willing to believe that such powerful influences exist.[9] Estimates suggest that over 60 percent of Americans believe that advertisers can exert subliminal influences strong enough to cause purchase

EXHIBIT 3.5
The Vicary Subliminal Persuasion "Study"

The motion picture *Picnic* is run with a standard projector.

EAT POPCORN!!

A frame is replaced displaying a subliminal message for 1/2000 second.

The movie *Picnic* continues while the audience flocks to concession stand.

JND just noticeable difference; condition in which one stimulus is sufficiently stronger than another so that someone can actually notice that the two are not the same

behavior.[10] Over the years, books have fueled the controversy by promoting the idea that advertisers know about, and use, certain "hidden persuaders" that create an irresistible urge to buy.[11]

Interestingly, consumers are often willing to attribute their own behavior to some kind of "uncontrollable influence," especially when the consumption involves products like cigarettes or alcoholic beverages.[12] Thus, consumers' willingness to believe that subliminal persuasion tricks them into buying these products may simply be evidence of an attempt to downplay their own role in decision making.

As a final thought on subliminal perception research, it should be emphasized that the Vicary experiment was a *hoax*. Vicary never conducted the experiment. Rather, he fabricated the story completely in an effort to create positive publicity for the advertising firm.[13] Paradoxically, marketers sometimes make light of the entire subliminal persuasion topic by presenting images in advertisements that they know consumers will see!

LO3 Applying the JND Concept

We have discussed the concept of the absolute threshold as representing a level over which the strength of a stimulus must be greater in order to be perceived. A closely related concept deals with changes in the *strength* of stimuli. The **JND** (just noticeable difference)

Subliminal Groovin'!

Is the devil really hidden in the grooves of old rock LPs? Many rock artists have been accused of subliminally embedding messages within their music. Sometimes, according to the accusers, if you play the music backward, which made only slightly more sense back in the days of record players, you can actually hear the messages. Here are some examples from songs you may have heard:

- In "Another One Bites the Dust" by Queen, there is a hidden message that says: "It's fun to smoke marijuana!"
- In the Judas Priest album *Stained Class*, the repeated subliminal message "do it" occurs in an effort to encourage suicide.
- In "Stairway to Heaven" by Led Zeppelin, the hidden message includes "I live for Satan" and "Here's to my sweet Satan."

In nearly all cases, no support exists for the claims. On occasion, when the song is played backward, something audible may occur. These occurrences are more likely the result of phonetic accidents (accidental sounds) than intentional persuasive attempts. However, in the early 1980s, the rock band Styx included a "warning" sticker on the album *Kilroy* indicating that hidden messages were contained. This was Styx's attempt at poking fun at this belief.

Sources: Henry, W. A., and E. Pappa (1990), "Did the Music Say Do It?" *Time*, 136, 65; **http://www.secretsyoushouldknow.com/music.htm**, accessed February 6, 2007.

© COMSTOCK IMAGES/JUPITER IMAGES

represents how much stronger one stimulus has to be relative to another so that someone can notice that the two are not the same.

The JND concept may be best explained in terms of a physical example. How do people pick out one sound over another? For example, for consumers to be able to physically discern two sounds that originate from the same location, the two sounds must be separated by at least 0.3 second. Otherwise, the two sounds seem as one. Thus, separating them by only 0.1 second is likely to produce the perception of one sound. Separating them by 0.5 second or more is likely to produce the perception of two different sounds.[14] As another example, imagine you are staring at a light. How much difference must occur in the intensity of the light in order for you to be able to discern that the intensity has changed?

Haven't I Seen You Before?

Internet technology changes almost daily. New gadgets allow different ways to search for products, information and people on-line. Some of these techniques involve new ways of finding images of people. When these technologies involve changes in images, some subtle, perhaps even unnoticeable, changes in what people see may be possible.

Technologies exist which can change the pictures of individuals in very small ways (morphing) that can make one person look more similar to another. For instance, a political candidate's photograph could be changed to include 5 – 10 percent of the features of a particular consumer. Research shows that if this is done, even if the consumer doesn't notice the change, they show a tendency to like the candidate better. Why? The politician now looks more familiar! It may be comforting to know that any change due to an effect below Weber's law is canceled out by less subtle information about the candidate.

Sources: Bailenson, J.N., S. Iyengar, N. Yee, and N.A. Collins (2008), "Facial Similarity between Voters and Candidates Causes Influence," Public Opinion Quarterly, 72 (5), 935-961. Bulik, B.S. (2007), "Media Morph: People Search," Advertising Age, 78 (5/28), 18.

> **Weber's law** law stating that a consumer's ability to detect differences between two levels of the stimulus decreases as the intensity of the initial stimulus increases

- **Quantity.** Small differences in quantity are often not perceived as being different. For instance, if a toilet paper roll is reduced from 412 to 407 sheets, consumers are not likely to perceive a difference.

- **Quality.** Small improvements in quality may not have any impact on consumers. Thus, if a service provider promotes some improvement in quality such as faster service or better food quality, the difference must be large enough to create a true perceptual difference.

- **Add-on Purchases.** A small additional purchase tacked onto a large purchase may not create the perception of increased spending. For instance, a consumer buying a $125 pair of athletic shoes may be very receptive to the suggestion of adding a pair of $5 socks to the order. The total for the shoes is not perceived as being really different than the total for the shoes and socks together.

In general, the ability to detect differences between two levels of a stimulus is affected by the original intensity of the stimulus. This is known as **Weber's Law**. More specifically, the law states that as the intensity of the initial stimulus increases, a consumer's ability to detect differences between two levels of the stimulus decreases.[15] For example, if the decibel level at a rock concert decreases from 120 to 115 dB, the change likely won't be noticeable. Marketers sometimes need to understand if they should change things a little at a time, so that the changes are not noticed, or change things a lot at once, so they are noticed. The JND has numerous implications for marketers who attempt to provide value for consumers, including:

- **Pricing.** Consumers do not perceive very small differences in price as truly different.[16] A price of $19.95 is generally not perceived as being different from a price of $19.99. Thus, marketers may consider increasing prices in small increments as a way of avoiding a negative backlash from consumers. Conversely, a price reduction needs to be large enough so that consumers truly perceive the new price as representing significant savings.

Retailers commonly mark prices down during promotional events. But do consumers really notice the difference?

JMD just meaningful difference; smallest amount of change in a stimulus that would influence consumer consumption and choice

mere exposure effect effect that leads consumers to prefer a stimulus to which they've previously been exposed

In general, these examples highlight an important idea: When marketers consider making a "positive" change, such as a drop in price or an improvement in quality, they should make sure the difference is large enough to be perceived by consumers. Conversely, when they consider making a "negative" change, such as an increase in price or a reduction in quantity being offered, they should think about implementing the change in small increments so that a difference is not perceived. However, the marketer should make sure that changes are not perceived as being deceptive. Such action would be unethical.

JUST MEANINGFUL DIFFERENCE

A topic closely related to the JND is the **JMD** (just meaningful difference). The JMD represents the smallest amount of change in a stimulus that would influence consumer consumption and choice. The issue at hand is how much of a change in price is really needed to *influence* behavior and learning. For example, a consumer can surely "notice" the difference in the price of an automobile when it is dropped from $19,999 to $19,899. Clearly, this is a $100 difference. However, is this price drop really meaningful? Retailers generally follow a rule that states that price drops need to be at least 20 percent to be considered effective.[17]

MERE EXPOSURE EFFECT

The **mere exposure effect** represents another way that consumers can learn things unintentionally.[18] Specifically, the mere exposure effect refers to the finding that consumers will prefer an object to which they have been exposed compared to one to which they have not been exposed. This effect occurs even when recall of the stimulus does not exist! That is, the effect occurs even when consumers don't realize that they've been exposed to the stimulus.

Exhibit 3.6 illustrates a classical approach to studying the mere exposure effect. Suppose a group of consumers were shown the list of Norwegian words. Among these words, two were target terms representing potential name brands for a new energy food.

The experiment usually takes place by first exposing subjects to something they have little chance of knowing. In this case, Norwegian words are used. Realize that Norwegian words sometimes contain some extra letters that do not exist in the English alphabet. Thus, on January 10, subjects were exposed to the list of words on the left. Then, on May 10, the same subjects were exposed to the list on the right. If you look closely, you'll notice that two of the words on the May 10 list were also on the January 10 list.

The results of this type of experiment generally show that the two "familiar" words will be preferred even though subjects have no recall of having ever seen them before. Note that in this case consumers not only develop preferences for words, but they learn them as well. In fact, the learning process facilitates positive feelings that become associated with the stimuli.[19] The mere exposure effect therefore has applications in both consumer learning and attitude formation.

The mere exposure effect is very resilient. That is, the effect holds up for practically any kind of object being studied. If the Norwegian words are replaced with faces, names, Chinese characters, brand logos, web pages, or musical samples, the mere exposure effect still holds.[20] Theoretically, an explanation for the increased liking involves familiarity. Even though consumer can't "remember" seeing the stimuli, some degree of familiarity is created.

All things equal, consumers prefer familiar things to nonfamiliar things. Therefore, once someone has been exposed to an object, he or she will exhibit a preference for the familiar object over some-

EXHIBIT 3.6
The Mere Exposure Effect Illustrated

January 10	May 10
Agentur	baadsmand
Forfølgelse	Prestegård
alderdomssvakhet	prosti
Overvære	tidsperiode
Prestegård	anmerkning
brændevinsbrænderi	bryggeri
Amme	tjueseks
Nittiende	mindreårig
Disktriktslege	Forfølgelse
Bagermester	badedrakten

Ethical Dilemmas in Mere Exposure

Generally speaking in consumer behavior, we think of preattentive processing as illustrated by the mere exposure effect in terms of how the likelihood that a consumer would purchase something might change. However, perhaps the mere exposure effect can help explain why a consumer might steal something. Research suggests that once a consumer is merely exposed to some unethical act, he or she becomes more tolerant of that behavior. Thus, a consumer may be able to hear coworkers in the next cubicle talking about how to pirate music. Even though the consumer is paying no attention to the discussion, he or she may become more tolerant of music pirating and therefore become more likely to practice the behavior.

Source: Weeks, W. A., J. Longenecker, J. A. McKinney, and C.W. Moore (2005), "The Role of Mere Exposure Effect on Ethical Tolerance: A Two-Study Approach," *Journal of Business Ethics*, 38, 281–294.

© ISTOCKPHOTO.COM/DAN BRANDENBURG

sumer were less distracted from the stimulus.

Note on Subliminal and Mere Exposure Effects

Before moving on, we should distinguish the mere exposure effect from subliminal effects. A subliminal message is one that would be presented below the threshold of perception. In other words, if you can physically see the object, then the process is not subliminal. With the mere exposure effect, the objects can clearly be seen and someone could pay attention to them if a reason existed to do so. Just as with the Norwegian words, no attempt is really made to keep someone from seeing them. That is, the stimuli are presented with enough strength to be above the threshold of perception.

thing completely unfamiliar. Several relevant points can be made about the mere exposure effect.

- The mere exposure effect is created in the absence of attention. For this reason, the effect is considered **preattentive**.[21] That is, learning takes place simply from exposure (hence, the name!).

- The increased liking associated with the mere exposure effect is easy to elicit. Thus, marketers can use this effect to improve attitudes marginally.

- The mere exposure effect has the greatest effect on novel (previously unfamiliar) objects.

- The size of the effect (increased liking) is not very strong relative to an effect created by a strong cohesive argument. For example, a Notre Dame football fan might develop a preference for a face to which he's repeatedly been exposed, but if he finds that the face belongs to a USC fan, the preference will likely go away!

- The mere exposure effect works best when the consumer has lower involvement in processing the object, and indeed when a consumer is distracted from processing the focal stimulus. For example, if a small brand logo is displayed on a magazine page across from some very involving story, a greater increase in liking would be found than if the con-

LO4 Implicit and Explicit Memory

We just noted that one of the more interesting aspects of preattentive mere exposure effects is the finding that the learning that takes place with this process appears to be more effective when a consumer is distracted from processing the stimulus. An explanation for this apparently counterintuitive finding is that our brains actually have multiple processing or "memory" mechanisms.[22] Although memory is the subject of another chapter, we simply say here that preattentive effects (like the mere exposure effect) result in implicit memory. **Implicit memory** is memory for things that a person did not try to remember, as with things learned passively and unintentionally. In contrast, traditional information processing results in explicit memory. **Explicit memory** occurs when the person is indeed trying to remember the stimuli, such as when learning is intentional. Consumers respond favorably to stimuli to which they've been exposed even when they don't realize that they've learned material!

An interesting application of implicit memory and mere exposure involves brand placements in video games. Video games, quite simply, can be very captivating! This means the person playing the game will likely not be paying attention to things like innocuously embedded brand logos. So, when the logos are executed within a game in a way that creates implicit memory, the attitude for the brand improves.[23] Furthermore, the more involving the game is, the stronger is the preattentive effect!

Product placements represent another way that promotions can impart implicit memory among consumers. Product placements involve branded products being placed conspicuously in movies or television shows. These placements can result in implicit memory formation. For instance, researchers in the United Kingdom once demonstrated implicit memory learning by exposing children to the movie *Home Alone*. Half of the children saw the movie with a scene in which the actors consumed unbranded drinks. The other half saw the identical scene with the exception being that drinks were from Pepsi cans. After the movie, the children were given their choice of soft drink. Those who saw the unbranded drink scene chose Coke and Pepsi in similar proportion to the U.K. market share. However, those who saw the "branded" scene chose Pepsi over Coke by a wide margin.[24]

ATTENTION

Attention is the purposeful allocation of cognitive capacity toward understanding some stimulus. Intentional learning depends on attentive consumers. There are many types of attention, including the previously defined preattention and selective attention, as well as involuntary attention. **Involuntary attention** is a type of attention that is beyond the conscious control of the consumer and that occurs as the result of exposure to surprising or novel stimuli. For example, if you were to cut your finger, you would automatically direct attention to the injury due to its pain. When attention is devoted to a stimulus in this way, an orientation reflex is said to occur. An **orientation reflex** is a natural reflex that occurs as a response to a threat from the environment. Ultimately, the orientation reflex represents a protective behavior.

NASCAR offers brands exposure to a large consumer segment. Here, Nicorette sponsors NASCAR driver, J.J. Veley.

LO5 Enhancing Consumers' Attention

*a*s mentioned earlier, consumers are so bombarded by stimuli in the marketing environment that they simply cannot devote attention to all the stimulation. This presents a particularly difficult challenge to marketers trying to break through the clutter. What's more, consumers today have so many sources of information and entertainment (MP3 players, PCs, cell phones) that an entire other layer of clutter must be penetrated in order to

© TONY BAKER/PHOTONICA/GETTY IMAGES

> Getting a consumer's attention is even more difficult in today's multi-tasking society.

gain attention! Because of all the clutter in the marketing environment, marketers are constantly trying to capture a consumer's attention. Here are a few tools that marketers can use in order to do so.

- **Intensity of Stimuli.** All things equal, a consumer is more likely to pay attention to stronger stimuli than to weaker stimuli. For example, vivid colors can be used to capture a consumer's attention. Loud sounds capture more attention than do quieter sounds. A television commercial with a louder volume than the rest of the programming tends to get consumers' attention.

- **Contrast.** Contrasting stimuli are extremely effective in getting attention. Contrast occurs in several ways. In days past, a color photo in a newspaper was extremely effective in getting attention. However, today's newspapers are often filled with color, so a color advertisement stands out less. A black-and-white image in a magazine filled with color, however, can stand out. A period of silence in an otherwise noisy environment can attract attention.[25] Like loud television commercials, silent commercials also usually work in gaining consumer attention. Social

outcasts also create attention because of the contrast with social norms.[26] Marketers often show consumers who "stand out from the crowd" as a means of capturing attention for an ad.

- **Movement.** With electronic billboards or retail shelf tags, marketers attempt to capture consumer attention by the principle of movement. Items in movement simply gain attention. Flashing lights and "pointed" signage are particularly effective tools for gaining consumer attention.

- **Surprising Stimuli.** Stimuli that are not expected also get consumers' attention. Infomercials often contain surprising scenes. Recent infomercials showed a car running over a man's hand and putty holding things together even when pulling a "fully loaded 18-wheeler."

- **Size of Stimuli.** All else equal, larger items garner more attention than smaller ones. Marketers therefore often attempt to get their brands to appear large in advertisements as an attempt to gain attention. This is one reason why advertising copywriters frequently employ large headlines in their advertisements.

- **Involvement. Involvement** refers to the personal relevance toward, or interest in, a particular product. In general, the more personally relevant (and thus more involving) an object, the greater the chance that the object will be attended to. We discuss involvement in more detail in the cognitive learning chapter.

As we have noted, gaining consumer attention is an important task for any marketer. Of course, paying attention can be beneficial for consumers as well. In order to actively learn about products and services that offer value, consumers must devote cognitive capacity for the task. The next section deals with comprehension.

COMPREHENSION

As stated previously, consumers organize information and attempt to understand it in the comprehension stage. Accordingly, comprehension refers to the interpretation or understanding that a consumer develops about some attended stimulus. Comprehension is an especially important topic for marketers because they obviously want consumers to interpret messages in the intended way. It is important to again stress the difference between subjective and objective reality. It is during comprehension that biases enter into perception. So, a fan of Dodge trucks may comprehend a message from Chevy very differently than would a die-hard Chevy fan. Furthermore, personal factors such as intelligence and motivation affect comprehension. Comprehension is discussed in more detail in the chapter that covers cognitive learning and information processing.

LO6 The Difference between Intentional and Unintentional Learning

before moving on to cognitive learning and information processing, we want to discuss in more detail the distinction between the two types of consumer learning—intentional and unintentional learning. Both types of learning concern what cognitive psychologists refer to as perceptual processes; however, with **unintentional learning**, consumers simply sense and react (or respond) to the environment. Here, consumers "learn" without trying to learn. They do not attempt to mentally comprehend the information that is being presented. That is, they are exposed to stimuli and respond in some way. With **intentional learning**, consumers set out to specifically learn information devoted to a certain subject. To better explain intentional and unintentional learning, we examine two major theories in the psychology of learning.

BEHAVIORISM AND COGNITIVE LEARNING THEORIES

Recall that perception and learning are closely related topics. As the behavioral psychologist B. F. Skinner once wrote: "in order to respond effectively to the world around us, we must see, hear, smell, taste and feel it."[27]

Psychologists are often thought to follow one of two general theories of learning. One theory focuses on changes in behavior that occur through responses to stimuli without concern for the cognitive mechanics of the process. The other theory focuses on changes in thought and knowledge and how these precipitate behavioral changes. Those who follow the first approach follow a **behaviorism approach to learning** (also referred to as the behavioral learning perspective). This approach suggests that because the brain is a "black box," the focus of inquiry should be on behavior. In fact, B. F. Skinner, the thought leader in behaviorism, argued that no description of what happens inside the human body can adequately explain human behavior.[28] Thus, the brain is a black box, and we can't look inside.

From the behaviorism perspective, consumers are exposed to stimuli and directly respond in some way. Thus, the argument is that the focus should be on "stimulus and response." Those who follow behaviorism do not deny the existence of mental processes; rather, these processes are considered to be behaviors themselves. For example, thinking is an activity in the same way that walking is, and

Describe what is going on in this consumer's "mind." This consumer appears to be actively trying to learn.

© ISTOCKPHOTO.COM/SEAN LOCKE

all psychological processes are to be viewed as actions.[29] Note that the term "conditioning" is used in behavioral learning, as behavior becomes conditioned in some way by the external environment.

Those who follow the second approach are said to follow an **information processing (or cognitive) perspective**. With this approach, the focus is on the cognitive processes associated with comprehension that lead to consumer learning. The information processing perspective is taken with this perspective and the brain is thought to contain a "mind" that acts much like a computer.

In previous years, the behavioral learning and cognitive perspectives were viewed as competing against one another. However, we steer clear of the debate because on closer inspection, the two theories really share much in common. At the very least, both perspectives focus on changes in behavior as a person interacts with his or her environment. Here, we adopt an orientation perhaps more directly applicable to consumer learning by separating learning mechanisms into the intentional and unintentional groups that we have presented. The next section discusses unintentional learning and how consumers respond to stimuli to which they are exposed. Intentional learning is covered in the chapter that deals with cognitive learning processes and comprehension.

UNINTENTIONAL LEARNING

Unintentional learning occurs when behavior is modified through a consumer–stimulus interaction without any effortful allocation of cognitive processing toward that stimulus. With this type of learning, consumers respond to stimuli to which they are exposed without thinking about the information. Notice that the focus is on *reacting*. That is, the focus is on responses to stimuli without making any effort to engage in cognitive processing.

Unintentional learning can be approached from the behavioral learning perspective. Two major approaches found in behavioral learning theory that apply are *classical conditioning* and *instrumental conditioning*.

Classical Conditioning

Classical conditioning refers to a change in behavior that occurs simply through associating some stimulus with another stimulus that naturally causes a reaction. The most famous classical conditioning experiment was performed by the behavioral psychologist Ivan Pavlov. Pavlov conducted experiments using dogs, meat powder (an **unconditioned stimulus** that naturally led to a salivation response), and a bell (a **conditioned stimulus** that did not lead to the response before it was paired with the powder).[30] The experiment revealed that the bell could eventually evoke the same behavior that the meat power naturally caused.

In the experiment, Pavlov began ringing the bell every time meat powder was provided to the dogs. Thus, the bell became associated with the meat powder. Eventually, Pavlov allowed the dogs to enter the experimental room and would ring the bell without providing the meat powder. As predicted, the bell proved enough to increase the amount of saliva the dogs produced. Originally, the dogs would salivate from being exposed to the unconditioned stimulus. The salivation was called an **unconditioned response**, which occurred naturally as a result of exposure to the unconditioned stimulus (the meat powder). The dogs eventually would respond in the same way to the exposure to the bell. This response became known as a **conditioned response**. Notice that the response became conditioned by the consistent pairing of the unconditioned and conditioned stimuli. Dogs do not allocate cognitive processing capacity in the way that we usually think that humans do. So, the dogs learned this response without trying to do so.

information processing perspective perspective that focuses on changes in thought and knowledge and how these precipitate behavioral changes

classical conditioning change in behavior that occurs simply through associating some stimulus with another stimulus that naturally causes some reaction; a type of unintentional learning

unconditioned stimulus stimulus with which a behavioral response is already associated

conditioned stimulus object or event that does not cause the desired response naturally but that can be conditioned to do so by pairing with an unconditioned stimulus

unconditioned response response that occurs naturally as a result of exposure to an unconditioned stimulus

conditioned response response that results from exposure to a conditioned stimulus that was originally associated with the unconditioned stimulus

For behaviorists, perception itself is an activity, not a mental process.

To be effective, the conditioned stimuli should be presented before the unconditioned stimuli, and the pairing of the two should be done consistently (and with repetition). The advertisement at the right illustrates a popular use of unintentional learning through classical conditioning—the use of sexual, or intimate, imagery.

Instrumental Conditioning

Much of what we know about instrumental (or operant) conditioning comes from the work of Skinner. With **instrumental conditioning**, behavior is conditioned through reinforcement. Reinforcers are stimuli that strengthen a desired response. Notice again that the focus is on behavior and behavioral change—not on mental processes that lead to learning. Specifically, with instrumental conditioning, the likelihood that a behavior will increase is influenced by the reinforcers (consequences) of the behavior. Note that the reinforcers are presented after the initial behavior has occurred.

As an example of instrumental conditioning, consider childhood development. When a parent is "potty training" a child, he or she is more concerned with getting the desired result than with teaching the child the benefits of using a toilet over a diaper. All parents know that it is very difficult to rationalize with young children. Therefore, attempting to get them to think about the various reasons to become trained is almost useless. So, the focus is on changing the behavior through reinforcement. When a child performs the desired behavior, he or she receives rewards in the form of hugs, kisses, and maybe even presents. These rewards reinforce the desired behavior.

Positive reinforcers come in many forms in the consumer environment, and often take the form of some type of reward. The effects can be seen by considering marketing efforts that encourage repeat purchase behavior. For example, many casinos have players' cards that accumulate points the more a customer plays. The casino keeps tracks of these points. As the points accumulate, various offers are provided to the consumer including free hotel rooms, meals, and other things that could otherwise be expensive for the consumer. In this case, the points are used to elicit a desired response—repeat purchase behavior.

RALPH LAUREN ROMANCE

Products become conditioned stimuli by consistent pairing with arousing images.

Discriminative Stimuli, Reinforcement, and Shaping. Discriminative stimuli are stimuli that are differentiated from other stimuli because they alone signal the presence of a reinforcer. These stimuli essentially signal that a type of reward will occur if a behavior is performed. Advertisements that feature special promotions represent marketing examples of discriminative stimuli. Here the ad informs consumers that they will receive some type of reward (for example, 10 percent off a purchase) if they perform the desirable behavior (for example, shop at a store). Notice that the stimulus serves as a signal that is presented before the behavior occurs and that the behavior must occur in order for the reinforcement to be delivered. Brand names can be discriminative stimuli because they signal potential customer satisfaction and value. For example, consumers realize that by using Federal Express, they can receive overnight delivery with outstanding quality. The reinforcer occurs after the behavior has been performed. Exhibit 3.7 presents this process. We again see the importance of exposure to the discriminative stimuli, further highlighting the relationship between perception and behavioral learning.

EXHIBIT 3.7
Discriminative Stimuli, Behavior, Reinforcer

DISCRIMINATIVE STIMULI → BEHAVIOR → REINFORCER

Shaping is a process through which the desired behavior is altered over time, in small increments. Here, the focus is on rewarding "small" behaviors that lead to the "big" behavior that is ultimately desired. For example, a motorcycle shop manager might offer free hot dogs and soft drinks to consumers on a special promotional day. When the consumers come in to the store and receive the food and drinks, the manager may offer them a coupon for free pizza simply for test-driving an ATV. Finally, the manager may offer the consumer a $200 rebate on the purchase of a new ATV. Notice that the behavior that is ultimately desired is the purchase of an ATV. The small rewards along the way help shape the desired behavior.

Not all reinforcement is positive. **Punishers** represent stimuli that decrease the likelihood that a behavior will occur again. Punishers are bad things! When children misbehave, they get punished. The hope is that the behavior will not occur again. In the same way, when consumers make poor decisions and purchase products that deliver less value than expected, they are punished. Chances are they won't buy those same products again! **Negative reinforcement**, on the other hand, refers to the *removal* of bad stimuli as a way of encouraging behavior.

Punishers and negative reinforcers are commonly confused. However, the concepts are not the same. A punisher is the presence of bad stimuli after an undesirable behavior has occurred, whereas a negative reinforcer represents the removal of undesirable events. Companies frequently use negative reinforcement techniques. For example, advertisements that focus on the bad outcomes associated with *not* using a company's products utilize this technique. The message is essentially "If only you would have tried us, this bad thing wouldn't have happened!"

Behaviors often cease when reinforcers are no longer present. This represents the concept of **extinction**. For example, consumers may become accustomed to receiving free donuts and coffee at a local service station every time they get their oil changed. If the station decides to stop offering the free food and drink, the consumers may eventually take their business elsewhere.

shaping process through which a desired behavior is altered over time, in small increments

punishers stimuli that decrease the likelihood that a behavior will persist

negative reinforcement removal of harmful stimuli as a way of encouraging behavior

extinction process through which behaviors cease because of lack of reinforcement

Loyalty rewards associate value with the desired behavior —such as using an AMEX card.

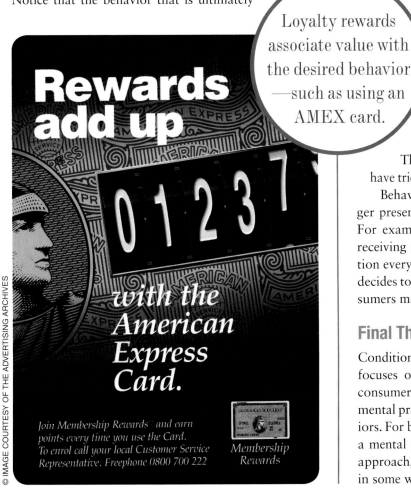

Rewards add up

0 1 2 3 7

with the American Express Card.

Join Membership Rewards™ and earn points every time you use the Card. To enrol call your local Customer Service Representative. Freephone 0800 700 222

Membership Rewards

Final Thought on Behavioral Conditioning

Conditioning represents a type of learning because it focuses on behavioral change that occurs through a consumer's interaction with the environment. Again, mental processes themselves are considered to be behaviors. For behaviorists, perception itself is an activity, not a mental process![31] Nevertheless, under the behavioral approach, consumers are exposed to stimuli and react in some way.

CASE

Chapter 3 Case

Golf Buggy has produced three-wheel golf carts for the U.K. market for over four decades. The basic design of the buggy, as they are referred to in the United Kingdom, has not changed. The buggy is characterized by a three-wheel design, with an open seat arrangement (like a convertible) and a steering arrangement that consists of a yoke rather than a steering wheel. Over recent years, they have faced increasing competition from Japanese and U.S. firms such as Club Car. These companies provide carts with more features and more power at a price slightly less than that offered by Golf Buggy. Golf Buggy traditionally used a sales force that directed their efforts toward golf clubs and tried to close the deal for an entire fleet of buggies for their course.

In response to the increased competition, Golf Buggy has designed a single-person golf cart that is low cost and has room for only one golfer and one golf bag. They have kept the basic three-wheel design so that it resembles somewhat a three-wheel scooter. In fact, Golf Buggy is even toying with the idea of a pedal model that would replace the conventional electric motor driven by a battery with a pedal, gears, and a chain. Given that batteries are so harmful to the environment, this product may appeal to more environmentally sensitive consumers. In addition, Golf Buggy is planning on a pull strategy that takes their products directly to individual consumers rather than directing marketing only toward golf clubs. This means advertising and sales training directed toward end consumers. The management team at Golf Buggy is looking at these moves in an effort to save the company. However, they know they must communicate the value of this product to consumers to have any chance of being successful. Will it work out?

Questions

1. Several advertising agencies are competing for the Golf Buggy account. Most are recommending communications that are consistent with an intentional method of learning. However, one agency is suggesting a behavioral or unintentional learning campaign. Should Golf Buggy give serious consideration to this agency based on its approach to consumer learning? Explain your choice.

2. How is a single-seat, three-wheel golf cart likely to be initially received in the marketplace? Use the steps in the consumer perception process to explain your opinion.

3. Would Golf Buggy have more success targeting a vehicle like this at non-golfers for use in large workplaces and perhaps even for consumers looking for an alternative to walking or driving when traveling short distances? Explain why.

Although marketers want to communicate value, many factors influence what a consumer comprehends in a given situation.

© CREATAS IMAGES/ JUPITERIMAGES

4

Comprehension, Memory, and Cognitive Learning

After studying this chapter, the student should be able to:

LO1 Understand the concept of comprehension and the factors that influence what gets comprehended.

LO2 Use the multiple store theory of memory to explain how knowledge, meaning, and value are inseparable.

LO3 Understand how consumers make associations with meaning as a key way to learn.

LO4 Use the concept of associative networks to map relevant consumer knowledge.

LO5 Apply the concept of a cognitive schema, including exemplars and prototypes, to understand how consumers react to new products.

Introduction

The previous chapter discussed the preliminary stages of perception and consumer learning. We defined learning as a change in behavior resulting from an interaction between a person and some stimulus. We also described the behaviorism approach to learning, an approach that focuses on behaviors rather than inner, mental processes. Cognitive learning focuses on *mental* processes occurring as consumers comprehend and elaborate upon information that they receive. The cognitive perspective views learning as an active, mental process wherein information is processed, associations are made, and knowledge is gained.

Cognitive learning takes place through information processing. Exhibit 4.1 breaks information processing down into its basic components. Note that we have already discussed several of the concepts presented in the exhibit, including exposure, attention, and comprehension. In the current chapter, we look more closely at comprehension and other issues related to cognitive learning, including elaboration and memory.

As we stated previously, because consumers are exposed to thousands of stimuli each day, they often practice selective perception. In fact, the chances can be slim that any one message will be attended to, comprehended, and elaborated upon in a way that will enable the consumer to accurately encode the message in memory. Accordingly, the chance that meaningful knowledge is gained in a way that will allow the consumer to actually use what has been learned is also slim. In a very real way, this is also why students often find studying to be difficult. One can only pay attention to, comprehend, and elaborate on so much information.

LO1
Comprehension: The Concept and Its Influencers

Comprehension refers to the interpretation or understanding that a consumer develops about some attended stimulus in order to assign meaning. This is a very important part of perception because the value a consumer obtains from consumption often depends on information. As an easy example, think of what happens when a consumer sees a "some assembly required" sticker. Of course, this means that the consumer will likely have to master a set of detailed instructions before consumption can begin. An easy-to-comprehend set of instructions would certainly contribute to the total value equation for the product. However, we all know how frustrating these instructions can be!

Other products contain warning labels that signal specific associated risks. Consider a typical cigarette package. A warning label will be effective only if consumers comprehend the intended message. Consumers, however, don't always comprehend messages correctly, as evidenced by consumers who interpret a cigarette warning label as contributing positively to the "rebellion" found in smoking. Consumers can also overestimate the dangers associated with smoking when they observe a typical package warning.[1] What's more, warning labels actually have only a small effect on consumer behavior![2] Thus, such warnings are often only moderately successful in curbing potentially dangerous consumer behaviors.

Ultimately, marketing messages can be effective only if consumers correctly comprehend the intended message, and getting consumers to comprehend the message correctly can be difficult. Here, we point out three important issues regarding comprehension:

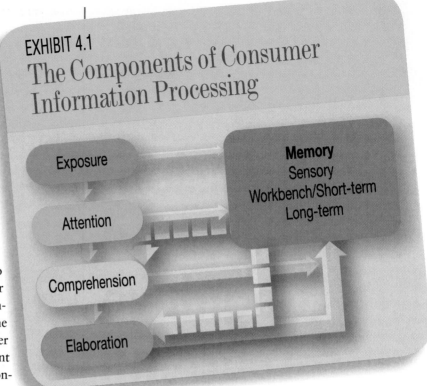

EXHIBIT 4.1
The Components of Consumer Information Processing

- Exposure
- Attention
- Comprehension
- Elaboration
- **Memory** Sensory Workbench/Short-term Long-term

- The process of comprehension is largely influenced by other internal factors within the consumer. Recall from a previous chapter that the factors that influence consumer behavior often interact with each other. Comprehension, consistent with this idea, is largely impacted by numerous components found in the CVF.

- Comprehension includes both *cognitive* and *affective* elements. Therefore, the process of comprehension involves both thoughts and feelings. As such, comprehension applies not only to consumer learning but to consumers' attitudes as well. For this reason, a number of the topics found in this chapter apply equally well to our chapter on attitude formation and change.

- Consumers don't always comprehend messages in the intended way, and to this extent, consumer comprehension is not always "correct." After all, perception leads to subjective reality, which may or may not equal objective reality! Quite simply, consumers sometimes just don't get it.

FACTORS AFFECTING CONSUMER COMPREHENSION

Meaning and value are inseparable, and consumers must comprehend marketing messages in order to learn the intended value of a product. Although marketers want to communicate value, many factors influence what a consumer comprehends in a given situation. Even though consumer researchers still have a great deal to learn about all the factors that influence comprehension, Exhibit 4.2 lists things we do know regarding these factors. Essentially, these factors can be divided into three categories:

- Characteristics of the message
- Characteristics of the message receiver
- Characteristics of the environment (information processing situation)

CHARACTERISTICS OF THE MESSAGE

Marketers obviously believe that they can affect consumer learning by carefully planning the execution of marketing messages. For instance, if you quickly flip through any popular magazine, you will see display advertisements with many different execution styles. Here are a few tools that can be used in an attempt to influence comprehension and control what consumers learn.

Physical Characteristics

The **physical characteristics** of a message refer to its attributes that are sensed directly. While these attributes can impact comprehension, you may note that some of these characteristics also impact the likelihood that attention will be devoted to stimuli. Here are just a few physical characteristics that can contribute to effective communication.

Meaning and value are inseparable, and consumers must comprehend marketing messages to learn the intended value of a product.

Intensity. Generally speaking, the larger the font, the larger the picture, or the more intense the sound, the more likely a consumer is to comprehend something from a message. For example, consumers can more easily read and interpret images when large print is used.

Color. Color affects the likelihood of gaining a consumer's attention, but it can also have an impact on comprehension. For example, colors mean different things in different cultures. Black is often seen as a somber color in western cultures, while white has these associations in some Eastern cultures. Accordingly, color can directly impact how an ad is comprehended.

Font. Consumers take meaning from both the actual text of a message and the visual presentation of the message. In fact, font style can influence comprehension. For example, the same brand or store name presented in a block font like courier may take on a different meaning if presented with a *script* font. Research suggests that some fonts, for example, portray a masculine image while others portray a feminine image. Consider the two examples below:

Nokona.com

Nokona.com

Most consumers would rate the first as more masculine than the second. But which is better? That probably depends on many factors, including the types of products

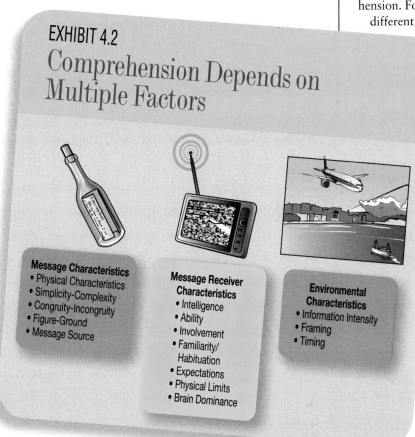

EXHIBIT 4.2
Comprehension Depends on Multiple Factors

Message Characteristics
- Physical Characteristics
- Simplicity-Complexity
- Congruity-Incongruity
- Figure-Ground
- Message Source

Message Receiver Characteristics
- Intelligence
- Ability
- Involvement
- Familiarity/ Habituation
- Expectations
- Physical Limits
- Brain Dominance

Environmental Characteristics
- Information Intensity
- Framing
- Timing

offered. Check out **www.nokona .com** and perhaps the answer to this question will become easier.

Numbers. In the 1980s, many discos around the world independently adopted the same name. They were called, in one way or another, 2001! In the 20th century, something with a year indicating the 21st century seemed progressive. Now, we would have to try a name like 3003 to create the same effect.

Many automobile companies use seemingly nonsensical combinations of letters and numbers when creating names for new car models. For example, makes and models include: Lexus GS, Acura TL 3.2, Mercedes CLS-550, Honda S2000, and Mazda RX-8. Compare these names with something like Volkswagen Rabbit or Chevrolet Impala. A car named after a rabbit would be expected to share characteristics of a rabbit, which has both good and bad characteristics. In contrast,

Keep Your Eyes on the Road!

Who pays attention to billboards? Consider all the competition for one's attention when going down the road. Typically, the radio, a companion, or a whole lot of billboards are competing for attention. Selective perception allows the consumer to deal with all of this and the billboards can easily lose out, thus lowering their effectiveness in conveying a message. Although advertisers employ a lot of creative approaches to try to get a consumer's attention with a billboard, research suggests that some simple rules can be employed to enhance billboard effectiveness. Two key factors involve (1) making the message clear and concise. Don't get cute – just convey a clear message and (2) locating the billboard near to the point of exchange (retail location). So, put the billboard close to the action and tell consumers how to get there, and billboards can be effective. Simple rules like this can help marketers communicate with billboards from Atlanta, Georgia to Tbilisi, Georgia (the country).

Sources: Taylor, C.R., G. Franke, and H.K. Bang (2006), "Use and Effectiveness of Billboards," Journal of Advertising, 35 (Winter), 21-34. Riza, A. A., E. Kaynak and S. Yalcin (2007), "Foreign Product Purchase Behavior in Transition Economies: An Empirical Analysis of Product Information Sources Among Georgian Consumers," Journal of Promotion Management, 13 (3), 321-337.

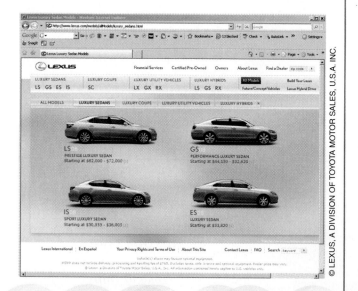

Auto makers often use combinations of letters and numbers when marketing their products.

combinations of numbers and letters are not tied to any one concrete meaning. This gives the company the advantage of being able to more easily shape the intended meaning of a brand. Additionally, names with letters and numbers used in combination tend to signify a "technologically based" meaning.

Simplicity–Complexity

Generally speaking, the simpler the message, the more likely a consumer is to develop meaningful comprehension, which, of course, relies on a consumer's ability to process information. For example, the U.S. Food and Drug Administration has performed considerable research to identify the simplest way to communicate important consumer information. Summary terms like *fat-free* and *low-fat* have replaced more complicated terms that were once linked to specific product attributes.[3] Thus, the Food and Drug Administration believes the new terminology represents easier ways to get consumers to comprehend the desired messages.

a practical standpoint, the decision to use highly consistent message content depends on the marketing goal. If the primary goal is to get consumers to simply remember information, some degree of incongruity is a good idea. If, however, the primary goal is to create a favorable attitude, then incongruity should be minimized.

The incongruity of a message with surrounding messages works in much the same way.[6] In fact, consumers will comprehend and remember more from an ad that is presented with incongruent material. So, if we return to the hair care example, the consumer will comprehend and remember more when presented with only one hair care advertisement in the three-ad sequence (see Exhibit 4.3).

> Simple phrases such as "light" often communicate more clearly than detailed information.

message congruity
extent to which a message is internally consistent and fits surrounding information

Message Congruity

Message congruity represents the extent to which a message is internally consistent and fits surrounding information. To illustrate, consider the question: "Does a consumer more effectively comprehend information when exposed to three ads about hair care products in a row, or when exposed to one hair care product ad preceded by a detergent ad and followed by an automobile ad?"

The conventional wisdom is that congruent content would lead to improved comprehension. However, this may not always be the case. For example, think about a typical television advertisement that contains background music. Music can be chosen to be either highly consistent or inconsistent with message content. Consider an advertisement for travel to China. Oriental music could be included in an effort to be consistent with the message content, whereas some type of western music could be used in an "inconsistent" way. In a situation such as this, consumers may actually comprehend more from the message with inconsistent background music.[4] The reason is that the incongruity motivates deeper processing than when everything in a message is highly congruent. The result is improved comprehension.

This doesn't mean that incongruent information is always better.[5] For example, an ad with inconsistent background music, such as an ad for China that includes western music, will generally be liked less than an ad with consistent music. Therefore, from

Figure and Ground

The focus of a marketing message can also affect comprehension. For example, any time someone takes a photograph, the photographer concentrates on capturing a focal image. Another way to look at this focal image, or the object that is intended to capture a person's

EXHIBIT 4.3
Congruent or Incongruent Message Sequences?

Congruent Messages

Consumer comprehends less about L'Oréal

Incongruent Messages

Consumer comprehends more about L'Oréal

figure object that is intended to capture a person's attention, the focal part of any message

ground background in a message

figure–ground distinction notion that each message can be separated into the focal point (figure) and the background (ground)

likeability extent to which a consumer likes the message source

expertise amount of knowledge that a source is perceived to have about a subject

trustworthiness how honest and unbiased the source is perceived to be

credibility extent to which a source is considered to be both an expert in a given area and trustworthy

counterarguments thoughts that contradict a message

support arguments thoughts that further support a message

EXHIBIT 4.4
The Figure and Ground Distinction

attention, is as the **figure** in the message. Everything else is supposed to be less important and simply represent the **ground** (or background) relative to the central message. The contrast between the two represents the psychological **figure–ground distinction**. In many ways, both the photographer's intent and the viewer's perception are relevant here.

One reason consumers do not always accurately comprehend the intended message is because the product that was intended to be the figure becomes the ground. Exhibit 4.4 illustrates how this occurs psychologically. As consumers assign different elements to figure and ground, respectively, ambigu-

ity in meaning occurs. In the exhibit, some consumers may have difficulty finding the word *TIE* in the image because the natural inclination is to treat the white as background and the black as figure. The second image demonstrates how consumers can comprehend a different meaning, either a chalice or two faces, depending on what part of the image becomes the focus.

Message Source

The source of a message also can influence comprehension. The source of the message could be a famous celebrity in an advertisement, a salesperson in a sales context, a family member giving "advice," or even a computer-animated avatar. A source's effectiveness in gaining comprehension is largely impacted by factors such as:[7]

1. Likeability
2. Expertise
3. Trustworthiness
4. Attractiveness[8]

Very simply, **likeability** refers to the extent to which a consumer likes the message source. A likeable source can change the interpretation of a stimulus. A fun example of likeability effects can be found with Mr. Clippy. Mr. Clippy is the familiar name for the paper clip avatar that pops up when Microsoft Word users need help. Many consumers dislike Mr. Clippy because they think he is impolite.[9] As a result, users often argue with advice he gives and become less likely to follow his guidance! This example illustrates how even with a fictitious source like a cartoon character, care needs to be given to make sure that consumers have a favorable impression. If not, the message may not be comprehended as intended.

Expertise refers to the amount of knowledge that a source is perceived to have about a subject, whereas **trustworthiness** refers to how honest and unbiased the source is perceived to be. Taken together, highly knowledgeable and trustworthy sources are seen as having **credibility**. Credibility is important because credible sources tend to lower the chances that consumers will develop **counterarguments** toward a message. Counterarguments are thoughts that contradict a message. **Support arguments** are thoughts that further support a message. Highly likeable sources also tend to reduce the number of counterarguments and increase the number of support arguments that occur as consumers comprehend messages. As we discuss in another chapter, attractive spokespeople also can affect how a message is comprehended. In general, attractive sources can be quite effective in delivering an intended message.

In summary, we can say that desirable characteristics positively affect how messages are comprehended. In fact, these characteristics are important even when a consumer isn't paying a lot of attention to an advertisement![10] We revisit source effects in the chapter on attitudes.

MESSAGE RECEIVER CHARACTERISTICS

Intelligence/Ability

As a general statement, intelligent and well-educated consumers are more likely to accurately comprehend a message than are less intelligent or less educated consumers. With this being said, we offer two caveats. First, a great deal of knowledge is specific to particular product categories. Therefore, a consumer who does not have a high overall IQ may be able to comprehend certain product information more readily than another consumer with a high IQ. Second, even a highly intelligent consumer would understand a simpler message better than a more complex message. Of course, as we have stated previously, marketers try to be very careful about clearly providing information pertaining to product warnings, usage instructions, or assembly directions.[11]

Involvement

Consumers are not equally involved with every message. As discussed in the perception chapter, highly involved consumers tend to pay more attention to messages. However, they also exert more effort in comprehending messages.[12] As a result, these consumers will also show better recall than consumers with lower levels of involvement and motivation.[13] Consider the consumer who views a website that is describing a new product. The highly involved consumer will click through more hyperlinks, exploring pages and comprehending more website information than will a less involved consumer.

Returning to the labeling/instructions issue, marketers face the challenge of designing messages that will be comprehended by consumers who are either highly involved or uninvolved. In fact, in 1990 the U.S. Congress passed the Nutrition Labeling and Education Act (NLEA), which had a goal of ensuring that consumers would understand product warnings and nutrition labels regardless of their level of involvement.

As a result of this act, marketers began to use simpler summary information on their labels. However, evidence suggests that even though this type of information is preferred, highly involved consumers still comprehend more from the labels than do those consumers with lower levels of involvement.[14]

© AP IMAGES/PRNEWSFOTO/STARDOLL

This website allows consumers access to many products with specific benefits. Consumers who are highly involved with their appearance will better comprehend the information than will other consumers.

Familiarity/Habituation

We discussed the concept of familiarity in the context of the mere exposure effect in a previous chapter. Familiarity is generally a good thing as consumers tend to like the familiar. However, in terms of comprehension, familiarity can *lower* a consumer's motivation to process a message. Thus, while some degree of familiarity may improve consumer attitude, high levels of familiarity may actually reduce comprehension.[15]

A closely related topic is consumer habituation. **Habituation** is the process by which continuous exposure to a stimulus affects the comprehension of and response to the stimulus. A psychological experiment demonstrates how strong habituation effects can be. In an experiment, subjects are asked to immerse their arms in extremely cold water (5°C) for 60 seconds. Obviously, this is an unpleasant task. Another group of subjects is asked to do the very same thing, except after the first immersion, they are asked to immediately immerse their arms into still very cold water that is only marginally warmer (10°C) for 30 additional seconds. At the end of the procedure both groups are asked to rate the task hedonically. For example, they are asked how much they enjoyed the experience of having their arms stuck in extremely cold water. Surprisingly, the group that immerses their arms for 90 seconds will generally rate the task more favorably than will the group that immerses their arms for only 60 seconds.

Habituation theory explains this result. The first 60 seconds of exposure to the extremely cold water habituated the subjects and created an **adaptation level**. As a result, when the second group was exposed to water that was still unpleasant, but slightly warmer than the first, a more favorable evaluation was obtained because the entire experience was framed by the relatively more valuable last 30 seconds.

To illustrate habituation in a consumer setting, consider that consumers in the United States, Canada, Australia, and throughout western Europe have long been habituated to fairly pleasant shopping experiences in which many goods and services are readily available. This hardly compares with many parts of the world, including third-world nations, where shopping as we know it hardly exists. For example, within the decade following the breakup of the Soviet Union, consumer researchers measured the hedonic and utilitarian shopping value Russian consumers received as they went about trying to obtain everyday goods and services.[16] The capitalist reforms had been slow to spread through-

The V's and G's

Habituation is a real factor in understanding the value consumers experience. One drawback to this is that as consumers use a product over and over again, they can become satiated, meaning that consumers experience a little less value with each consumption experience. You'll see marketers doing things to freshen up the experience. Due to the success of New Zealand's leading energy drink known as "V," consumers around the U.S. encountered a sports drink labeled "G" in 2009. What appeared at first to be a new product was really a reincarnation of America's favorite sports drink, Gatorade. The hope was to put new life into an old brand and create a "new" product to enhance value for consumers.

Sources: Redden, J.P. (2008), "Reducing Satiation: The Role of Categorization Level," *Journal of Consumer Research*, 34 (February), 624-634. NZ Marketing Magazine (2008), "Cornering the Market," 27 (4), 7.

© TERRI MILLER/E-VISUAL COMMUNICATIONS, INC.

out Russia and these consumers still faced shops with empty shelves and long lines to *dostats* things like boots or jackets. **Dostats** is a Russian word that can be roughly translated into English as acquiring things with great difficulty. Like the results of the water immersion experiment, the surprising result was that the Russian consumers reported similar amounts of shopping value compared to American shoppers. What is the explanation for this outcome? Even though shopping in Russia was certainly worse than shopping in America, shopping was still framed by their other life experiences. These life experiences provided a frame of reference in which shopping was *less* unpleasant than were many other activities.

The feature box above illustrates habituation further.

Expectations

Expectations are beliefs of what will happen in some situation. They play a very important role in many consumer behavior settings and can have a major impact on comprehension. We discuss expectations in more detail in our satisfaction chapter, but for now we note that what consumers expect to experience has an impact on their comprehension of the environment.

To illustrate, consider how packaging influences consumers' comprehension of products. Beverage marketers have realized for decades that packaging plays a major role in how beverages are perceived. In fact, studies indicate that consumers cannot even identify their "favorite" brand of beer if the package is removed.[17] Removing the label affects consumers' expectations, which in turn affects their comprehension. As another example, consider the marketing challenge that Coca-Cola faced just a few years ago with their new product, Coke Zero. Consumers hadn't developed accurate understandings of the product due largely to the fact that they didn't know what to expect.[18]

Physical Limits

A consumer's physical limitations can also influence comprehension. For example, we all have limits in our ability to hear, see, smell, taste, and think. Obviously, if someone can't hear, then they can't comprehend information found in an audio message. Also, consumers who are color blind will have difficulty comprehending information about color. For instance, if a caution or warning label is colored red as a way of signaling risk, a color blind consumer will not likely comprehend this aspect of the message.[19]

Brain Dominance

Brain dominance refers to the phenomena of *hemispheric lateralization*. Some people tend to be either right-brain or left-brain dominant. This, of course, does not mean that some consumers use *only* the left or right parts of their brains! Right-brain-dominant consumers tend to be visual processors, whereas left-brain-dominant consumers tend to deal better with verbal processing (words).

ENVIRONMENTAL CHARACTERISTICS

Information Intensity

Information intensity refers to the amount of information available for a consumer to process within a given environment. When consumers are overloaded, the overload not only affects their attention but also their comprehension and eventual reaction. For example, evidence suggests that the amount of information presented to consumers participating in online auctions

affects their bidding behavior, with highly intense information environments being associated with lower price sensitivity.[20]

Framing

Framing is a term that captures the idea that the same information can take on different meanings based on the way in which the information is presented. For example, think of what a driver comprehends when she sees that the gas gauge shows only a quarter of a tank of gas remaining. If she is driving through the suburbs of her hometown, she probably does not comprehend trouble. However, if she is driving through a sparsely populated desert, that same information may result in an entirely different comprehension and reaction.

Prospect theory hypothesizes that the way in which information is framed differentially affects risk assessments and any associated consumer decisions. For example, consumers are often presented with messages like "save 50 percent" or "you pay half price!" Or when buying beef, a consumer may see a label that says "95% lean" or "5% fat." Which one is better? Aren't they the same?

To illustrate prospect theory, consider what you have undoubtedly heard about risks associated with prolonged exposure to the sun. Consider the following two methods of presenting information about those risks:[21]

- Failing to use sunscreen leaves one vulnerable to skin cancer.

- Using sunscreen helps avoid skin cancer.

The first statement is negatively framed. Use this product or get skin cancer! The second statement is positively framed. Use this product and stay healthy! Importantly, negatively framed information generally has a greater impact on consumers.

Priming refers to the finding that the context or the environment frames thoughts and therefore both value and meaning. Importantly, negatively framed information often leads consumers to be more willing

information intensity amount of information available for a consumer to process within a given environment

framing process wherein the very same information can take on different meanings from situation to situation or based on the way that information is presented

prospect theory theory that suggests that a decision, or argument, can be framed in different ways and that the framing affects risk assessments consumers make

priming context or environment that frames thoughts and therefore both value and meaning to take risks. This is a key aspect of prospect theory. Exhibit 4.5 illustrates this aspect of framing.

When considering information in the exhibit, most consumers will chose option two in the first choice set. Notice that the frame is negative.[22] In the second choice set, where the frame is positive (priming gains), consumers will tend to opt for the certain gain. This happens even though the expected value ($E(v)$) for each choice is the same ($200). Thus, presenting a negative frame primes thoughts that lead to a consumer being more willing to take risks. In terms of prospect theory, we say that losses are weighted more heavily than gains. Losing $200 is certainly a loss! As such, consumers would be more willing to be risk takers in this example.

© AP PHOTO/EARL NEIKIRK

> Over time, Mountain Dew has taken on an entirely different meaning in consumers' memories.

© PRNEWSFOTO/PEPSI-COLA COMPANY

cess a message and *the point in time* at which the consumer receives the message. For example, consumers who have only a couple of seconds to process a message, such as when they are driving by a billboard advertisement, cannot possibly comprehend a message in as much depth as can a consumer who is not facing a timing issue.

The time of day can also affect the meaning and value of a product. For many consumers, coffee is a morning beverage. An advertisement for a brand of coffee can be comprehended quite differently based on the time of day in which it is aired. Many consumers may see a coffee advertisement in the morning as much more enticing than the same ad shown just before bedtime.

As you can see, several factors influence how a marketing message is comprehended. We now turn our focus to the other major concept in information processing and cognitive learning, memory.

EXHIBIT 4.5
An Illustration of Framing— What Would You Do?

Choose one of the two options below:
1. You lose $200.
2. You have a 20% chance of losing $1,000 and an 80 percent chance of losing nothing.

Choose one of the two options below:
1. You win $200.
2. You have a 20% chance of winning $1,000 and an 80 percent chance of winning nothing.

© ISTOCKPHOTO.COM/STEVE LUKER
© ISTOCKPHOTO.COM/JUSTIN HORROCKS

Although we generally think of negatively framed information as having a greater effect on comprehension than positively framed information, exceptions to this tendency exist.[23] In particular, when losses are viewed as temporary, a positively framed message may encourage consumers to try a product that has a certain degree of risk.

Timing

Timing can also affect comprehension. Here, timing refers to both the *amount of time* a consumer has to pro-

LO2 Multiple Store Theory of Memory and Storage of Knowledge

memory is the psychological process by which knowledge is recorded. As shown in Exhibit 4.1, all of the elements of the information processing model are in some way related to memory. You may remember from our perception chapter that we discussed the topics of implicit and explicit memory. Here, we discuss the major perspective of memory from the cognitive learning approach—the multiple store theory of memory.

MULTIPLE STORE THEORY OF MEMORY

The **multiple store theory of memory** views the memory process as utilizing three different storage areas within the human brain. The three areas are sensory memory, workbench (or short-term) memory, and long-term memory. Exhibit 4.6 illustrates this approach.

Sensory Memory

Sensory memory is the area in memory where the things that we encounter with any of the five human senses are stored. For example, when we hear something, sensory memory is responsible for storing the sounds. The consumer who is walking through a movie theater lobby encounters many sounds, smells, and sights. Sensory memory picks these things out and stores them even though the consumer has not yet allocated attention to any of these sensations. As such, this portion of memory is considered to be preattentive.

Sensory memory is truly remarkable. For one thing, sensory memory has unlimited capacity. As such, the sensory memory will store everything a person is exposed to, taking an exact record of what is encountered. Sensory memory also has different storage mechanisms, including iconic and echoic. **Iconic storage** is the storage of visual information. Things are stored in sensory memory as exact representations of the actual stimulus. **Echoic storage** is the storage of auditory information. Auditory information is also stored precisely in sensory memory. Thus, all sights, sounds, smells, tactile sensations, and tastes are recorded as exact replicas in the mind of the consumer.

If that is the case, then why can we recall only a fraction of what we encounter? Another remarkable aspect of sensory memory concerns duration. Sensory memory is very perishable and lasts only a very short time. In most cases, sensory memory begins to fade immediately after the sensation is recorded and lasts less than a second. Thus, the strength of sensory memory is capacity, but the weakness is duration.

Sensory memory can easily be illustrated. Take a quick look at an object and then close your eyes. What happens in the fractions of a second immediately after you shut your eyes? In most instances, your brain will hold the image immediately after you close your eyes—that is, you will be able to see the image mentally. However, very quickly things will start to fall out of the mental picture until eventually only the most central features can be pictured. If you are familiar with a strobe light, you may have noticed that when the light speeds up, images look continuous. This is because sensory memory is able to "hold" the image through the dark portion of the strobe, that is, until the next image is physically sensed.

Although sensory memory is important, its usefulness is limited because images are lost very quickly with this type of memory. Fortunately, sensory memory works in

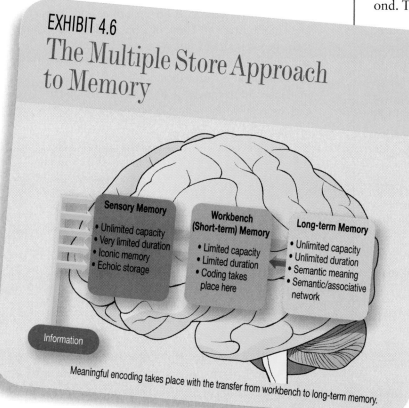

EXHIBIT 4.6
The Multiple Store Approach to Memory

Sensory Memory
- Unlimited capacity
- Very limited duration
- Iconic memory
- Echoic storage

Workbench (Short-term) Memory
- Limited capacity
- Limited duration
- Coding takes place here

Long-term Memory
- Unlimited capacity
- Unlimited duration
- Semantic meaning
- Semantic/associative network

Information

Meaningful encoding takes place with the transfer from workbench to long-term memory.

conjunction with other
memory functions allowing
a consumer to gain infor-
mation and knowledge.

Workbench Memory

Workbench memory is
the storage area in the
memory system where
information is stored and
encoded for placement in
long-term memory and,
eventually, retrieved for
future use. As we
will see, work-
bench memory works very closely with
long-term memory. **Encoding** is the process by which information is transferred
from workbench memory to long-
term memory for permanent storage.
Retrieval is the process by which information is transferred back into workbench memory for additional processing
when needed.

To illustrate workbench memory, imagine
a French consumer who is walking the aisles of an
Auchan hypermart (see **http://www.auchan.fr**). The
consumer places several produce items into the cart,
including some Camembert, Morbier, paté de canard,
and multiple household items including paper towels,
storage bags, bleach, and toilet tissue. How much do
you think all of this is going to cost the consumer? If he
doesn't physically write down each item's cost, can we
expect that he will be able to know what the total bill
will be? To some extent, his accuracy will depend on his
ability to hold prices in memory long enough to be able
to compute a total upon checkout.

Let's consider a single item. He picks up the Camembert, checks the price, and puts the item in the cart.
The price quickly enters his sensory memory and then
moves on to his workbench memory because he is trying to pay attention to the price. The relevancy of duration, capacity, and involvement quickly come into play.

- **Duration.** The term *short-term* is often used when
  describing workbench memory because this memory
  storage area, like sensory memory, has limited duration. The duration is not nearly as limited as sensory
  memory, but stimuli that enter short-term memory
  may stay there approximately 30 seconds or so
  without some intervention. Therefore, our consumer

Learning may not always be simple... but the key to meaning is tagging a stimulus in the brain's workbench!

can hardly be expected to remember the
prices for all items in his cart by the time the
checkout counter is reached.

- **Capacity.** Unlike sensory memory, workbench memory has limited capacity. Generally, the capacity limit
  for workbench memory is between three and seven
  units of information. Think of a physical workbench.
  If the bench is almost full, we cannot expect to put
  additional items on it. Some items must be removed
  first. Thus, our consumer cannot be expected to
  remember all the prices of all items in a shopping
  cart, especially if he is buying several products.

- **Involvement.** The capacity of workbench memory
  expands and contracts based on the level of a consumer's involvement. The more involved a consumer
  is with a message, the greater will be the capacity of
  his workbench memory. When involvement is very
  low, workbench memory capacity contracts to a
  minimum.

To test your own workbench memory, try to do the
following: Without looking back, name all the items
purchased by our French consumer. How many can you
remember? Don't feel bad if you can't remember them
all. In fact, most people would not be able to recall all
of the items. However, most consumers would be able
to recall at least two items. For instance, most would
recall that toilet tissue was one item. Unless a consumer
has some knowledge of French cheeses, the Camembert

and Morbier are not likely to be recalled. Prior knowledge helps consumers code and recall information. More is said about this issue later in this chapter.

LO3 Making Associations with Meaning as a Key Way to Learn

So, what kind of work goes on in workbench memory? Here, the task is to help a consumer recall things, both over a short period of time and over a long period of time. In other words, not only can the consumer recall the prices while in the store, but he or she can also recall the prices during the days and even weeks following the shopping trip.[24] When we use the term "remember something," we often are referring to the fact that some information can be recalled or made active in our minds intentionally. Four mental processes help consumers remember things:

1. **Repetition** is a process in which a thought is held in short-term memory by mentally "saying" the thought repeatedly.

2. **Dual Coding** is a process in which two different sensory "traces" are available to remember something. As we shall see, a *trace* is a mental path by which some thought becomes active.

3. **Meaningful Encoding** is a process that occurs when preexisting knowledge is used to assist in storing new information.

4. **Chunking** is a process of grouping stimuli by meaning so that multiple stimuli can become a single memory unit.

Note that meaningful encoding and chunking rely heavily on making associations between new information and meaning that is stored in long-term memory.

Repetition. Repetition is a commonly employed way of trying to remember something. Picture someone trying to remember the license plate number:

TT867-53-09

One way that this number could be remembered is by thinking it repeatedly. This process is also known as *rehearsal*. However, one major problem with this approach is **cognitive interference.**

Cognitive interference simply means that other things are vying for processing capacity when a consumer rehearses information. To illustrate, try to count backwards from 1,000 by 3. This seems like an easy task. But if you try to do this while someone is calling out random numbers at the same time, the task becomes much more difficult. All things equal, repetition is the weakest form of learning.

Dual Coding. Dual coding can be more effective than repetition. To illustrate dual-coding effects, consider Exhibit 4.7. This exhibit illustrates some all-time famous jingles. Putting words to music does help consumers remember information. Why is this? A consumer has two ways of retrieving information—both by the content of the message and by the sound of the music. Even though none of the jingles in Exhibit 4.7 are new, consumers can often remember them and fill in the blanks. Consumer research has demonstrated the effectiveness of dual coding in the form of music.[25] However, some say that jingles have lost favor recently in favor of recycled pop songs.[26]

Dual coding need not be in the form of music only. Sometimes a smell associated with a certain brand or store can aid recall. Pictures can also provide another

repetition simple mechanism in which a thought is kept alive in short-term memory by mentally repeating the thought

cognitive interference notion that everything else that the consumer is exposed to while trying to remember something is also vying for processing capacity and thus interfering with memory and comprehension

dual coding coding that occurs when two different sensory traces are available to remember something

EXHIBIT 4.7
All-Time Great Jingles

Brand Knowledge Quiz: How Many of these Blanks Can You Fill In?

- I'm loving it! _____
- It's the most original soft-drink ever in the whole,..wide,..world,... _____.
- And like a good neighbor, _____ is there!
- I am stuck on _____ brand, because _____'s stuck on me!
- MMM-Good, mmm-good, that's what _____ are, mmm-good!
- Give me a break, give me a break, break me off a piece of that _____ bar.
- For all you do, this _____'s for you!

Answers from first to last, respectively: McDonald's; Dr. Pepper; State Farm; Band-Aid/Band-Aid; Campbell's Soups; Kit-Kat; Bud

meaningful encoding coding that occurs when information from long-term memory is placed on the workbench and attached to the information on the workbench in a way that the information can be recalled and used later

chunking process of grouping stimuli by meaning so that multiple stimuli can become one memory unit

retrieval mechanism. For instance, consumers can use the image of an actual price on a sale sign to help remember the numbers representing the price.[27]

Meaningful Encoding

Meaningful encoding involves the association of active information in short-term memory with other information that is recalled from long-term memory. As such, new information is coded in meaningful ways. This is a third way in which information can be transferred from workbench to long-term memory.

To illustrate meaningful encoding, let's go back to the license plate example. First, note that consumers often find it difficult to associate anything meaningful with a number. However, a fan of 1980s pop rock would recognize the sequence of digits as the title of a famous hit by the rock artist Tommy Tutone. (In fact, the letter *T* followed by another letter *T* on the plate could signal this.) If the consumer were to retrieve memory of this song and attach this knowledge to the license plate number, the plate number would be much easier to remember. In a way, this example illustrates meaningful encoding because the music (also stored in memory) serves as a memory aid itself. For a consumer

> Chunking is an important mental activity because better chunking leads to improved recall.

who knows 1980s music, these numbers are *867- 5309*. (If you know the song, it's probably going to be stuck in your head now.)

Chunking. Chunking is the process of grouping stimuli by *meaning* so that multiple stimuli can become one memory unit. Remember that the capacity of workbench memory is rarely more than seven chunks of information. A **chunk** is a single memory unit. Here's a simple experiment that helps demonstrate what a chunk truly is. Show someone the following list of numbers for only a few seconds:

1 4 9 2 1 7 7 6 1 9 4 5

Does the humor used in this ad enhance comprehension?

After taking the list away, engage them in conversation for a couple of minutes. Then, ask the person to recall the list. You'll find that the task is difficult. Why is this? When the person treats each numeral as a distinct chunk of information, his or her memory capacity is exceeded. There are, after all, 12 numerals, or chunks, in the list.

Now, look at the list in this way:

1 4 9 2   1 7 7 6   1 9 4 5

If the person did well in American history class, the task should be considerably easier. That is, a history student should notice that these are all important dates in U.S. history. By grouping the numbers as shown, this is easy to see. The set of 12 numbers can now be stored and recalled as only three pieces of information instead of 12!

Marketers can also use humor to encourage chunking. Consider a coffee advertisement using the following lines spoken by two cartoon-type characters as a humor execution:[28] The first character says, "Other coffee tastes like mud"; then the other character says, "That's because they're ground every morning!" A tagline for the ad could be either "The Taste of Well-Balanced Coffee" or "The Taste of Exquisitely Ground Coffee." Here, the second tagline plays on the idea of ground coffee, which is included in the humor. Therefore, the second tagline would lead to better encoding and recall. Humor therefore helps to facilitate the process of encoding the message into a meaningful chunk.

Chunking is an important mental activity because better chunking leads to improved recall.[29] Marketers designing advertisements or websites, for example, should therefore be careful to group information together by meaning in order to assist consumers in encoding meaningful chunks of information.

Retrieval and Workbench Memory. As we have discussed, another task of workbench memory is with the retrieval of information from long-term memory. When a consumer retrieves information from long-term memory, it is processed once again in workbench memory. As a part of this process, long-term memory is scanned for relevant information. Through a process of **response generation**, consumers reconstruct memory traces into a formed recollection of the information they are trying to remember.

Marketers can help this process by ensuring that information that is placed in marketing messages is also placed on in-store promotions, and perhaps product packaging. One way of doing this is by using *integrated marketing communications* to ensure that a unified promotional message is sent across all consumer contacts.

Clearly, meaning and knowledge are the keys to effective coding and cognitive learning. To illustrate, consider the following list of words:

- Weep
- Sheep
- Deep
- Keep
- Peep

Suppose a subject is asked to look at a list like this and then the next day asked if the word *sleep* was on the list. Would there be many false recalls (indicating the word was on the list when it was not or vice versa)?

Now consider another list:

- Night
- Rest
- Awake
- Tired
- Dream

Would this list produce fewer false memories? The answer is yes. The key is that the second list enables more meaningful encoding and thus better memory.[30]

Long-Term Memory

A consumer's long-term memory also plays a very important role in learning. **Long-term memory** is a repository for all information that a person has encountered. This portion of memory has unlimited capacity and unlimited duration. Thus, barring some physical incapacity, long-term memory represents permanent information storage. Information that is stored in long-term memory is coded with **semantic coding**, which means the stimuli are converted to meaning that can be expressed verbally.

You may be wondering why consumers can't always recall information when needed if the storage is permanent. The problem is not usually found in storage but in retrieval. To illustrate, consider that even things that are processed at very low levels leave some memory trace. A **memory trace** is the mental path by which some thought becomes active. For example, the childhood Christmas memories of French consumers generally include a bouche de Noel (a Yule Log) more than any other food product. The memory traces that spread activation from Christmas to the bouche de Noel also spread to branded products associated with these products such as Hershey's cocoa and Domino powdered sugar.

Psychologically, a memory trace shows how cognitive activation spreads from one concept to another. This process is known as **spreading activation**. Marketers want their brand names to cause activation to spread to favorable, rather than unfavorable, thoughts. For example, consider the following brands:

- Tabasco
- KFC

Tabasco is most often associated with "hot." Generally, hot things are good. Hot music is good, hot fashions are good, and hot food is good. Therefore, consumers are willing to purchase Tabasco brand clothing (ties, shirts, etc.).

As another example, consider the effort that KFC undertook when the company changed its name from *Kentucky Fried Chicken* to *KFC*. A major reason for doing this was to change associations that consumers had with the idea of "fried" foods. Several years into this change, consumers can be expected to not think immediately of fried foods when they think of *KFC*. More recently, KFC has returned to signs with the

response generation reconstruction of memory traces into a formed recollection of information

long-term memory repository for all information that a person has encountered

semantic coding type of coding wherein stimuli are converted to meaning that can be expressed verbally

memory trace mental path by which some thought becomes active

spreading activation way cognitive activation spreads from one concept (or node) to another

© ISTOCKPHOTO.COM/CHRIS ELWELL

tag small piece of coded information that helps with the retrieval of knowledge

associative network network of mental pathways linking all knowledge within memory; sometimes referred to as a semantic network

declarative network cognitive components that represent facts

nodes concepts found in an associative network

paths representations of the association between nodes in an associative network

terms Kentucky Fried Chicken in many areas because they now realize that consumers actually associated wholesome, home-cooked food with the concept of fried chicken.

Mental Tagging. Let's look again at Exhibit 4.1. In psychological terms, a **tag** is a small piece of coded information that helps that particular piece of knowledge get retrieved. The tags function much like the bar-coded information on checked luggage. When everything works right, the information on the tag allows the luggage to be located. However, everything doesn't always go right, and as we all realize, luggage sometimes ends up in the wrong place. Similarly, if consumers do not tag information in a meaningful way, the encoding process results in errors.

To illustrate, most people have recalled some innocuous childhood memory later in life for what would seem to be no apparent reason. These types of memories illustrate how long-term memory is permanent and how events that were poorly tagged during encoding can emerge at practically any time. Things that consumers pay attention to but do not really comprehend or elaborate upon tend to get poorly tagged.

ASSOCIATIVE NETWORK GRAPHICS

Exhibit 4.8 illustrates the concept by showing a portion of a consumer's associative network that shows spreading activation from the Mercedes Benz brand. This illustrates the knowledge that can help identify a Mercedes Benz using nodes within a consumer's long-term memory. Alternatively, the network also shows where cognitive activation flows after the Mercedes concept becomes active.

DECLARATIVE KNOWLEDGE

Declarative knowledge is a term used in psychology to refer to cognitive components that represent facts. Declarative knowledge is represented in an associative network when two nodes are linked by a path. **Nodes** simply represent concepts in the network, while **paths** show the association between nodes in the network. Declarative knowledge can be compared with reality. Consumers may not always be correct about their declarative knowledge, but they do act upon the beliefs this knowledge represents. The following are examples of declarative knowledge shown in Exhibit 4.8:

A Mercedes is an automobile. A Mercedes is expensive. A Mercedes is luxurious. A Mercedes is silver. A Mercedes is a sedan. A sedan is an automobile. A Mercedes is German. Germans drink beer.

LO4 Associative Networks and Consumer Knowledge

knowledge in long-term memory is stored in an associative network. An **associative network**, sometimes referred to as a semantic network, is a network of mental pathways linking knowledge within memory. As an analogy, these networks are similar to family trees, as they represent known linkages between objects.

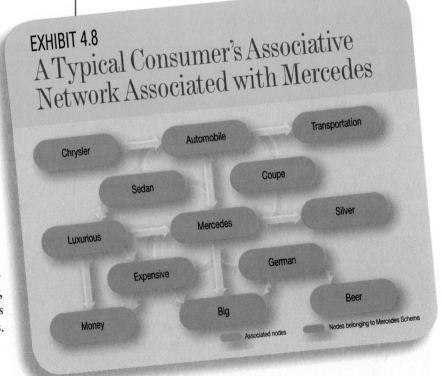

EXHIBIT 4.8
A Typical Consumer's Associative Network Associated with Mercedes

Notice from this slightly humorous example that all of these bits of knowledge can be compared with reality. Every time a consumer encounters a supportive instance of declarative knowledge, that knowledge becomes stronger. Consider: "A Mercedes is silver." All Mercedes are not silver. But when consumers are asked to respond with the first color that comes to mind when they think of Mercedes, they are most likely to say silver (with black coming in second). Every time a consumer sees a silver Mercedes, this belief becomes stronger, and so the association between Mercedes and silver becomes stronger. When the consumer sees a white Mercedes, the rule may diminish slightly in strength. In this sense, associative networks contain rules that become more likely to be used as they get stronger. Now consider: "Germans drink beer." If consumers hold this declarative knowledge, as they encounter more Germans, they will be more likely to expect to encounter Germans who are beer drinkers as opposed to Germans who enjoy sipping a Cabernet Sauvignon.

Amazingly, every concept within a consumer's associative network is linked to every other concept. Consider the following request:

List at least 10 *snack foods* in 60 seconds or less.

A typical consumer would produce a list that included things like potato chips, a power bar, a Twinkie, and a candy bar. Few would argue that these are indeed snack foods. All would be closely related to the snack concept and much further removed from other food categories—like dinner entrees. On the other hand, a glass of milk may also be a snack; however, the association between milk and snack food must first pass through several nodes. By that time, the association is weak. Selling milk as a snack, therefore, would be difficult. But, if milk can be packaged in a small container reminiscent of a snack food's plastic wrapper, the likelihood that consumers would view milk as a snack will increase, and the rule that milk can be a snack would subsequently increase in strength.

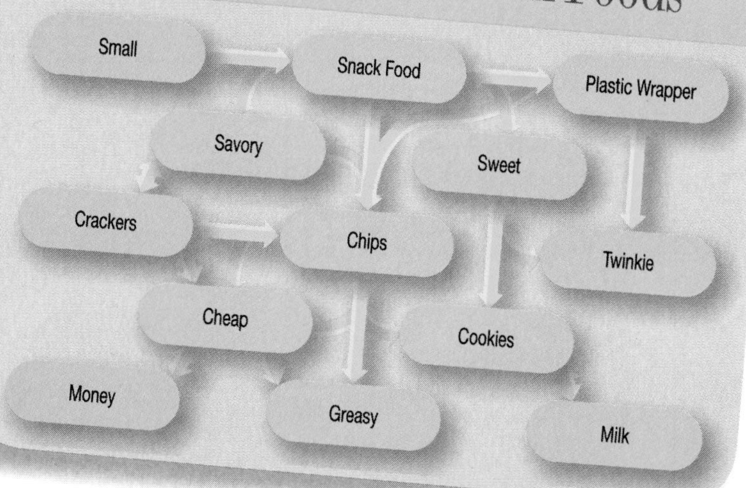

LO5 Cognitive Schemata and Reactions to New Products

a consumer's knowledge for a brand or for a product is contained in a schema. A **schema** is a type of associative network that works as a cognitive representation of a phenomenon that provides meaning to that entity. Exhibit 4.9 illustrates a product schema for snack food, whereas Exhibit 4.8 illustrates a brand schema for Mercedes Benz. Put another way, a brand schema is the small part of the total associative network responsible for defining a particular entity. Each time a consumer encounters something that could be a Mercedes Benz, the mind quickly compares all the characteristics observed to the schema to see if indeed the thought is correct. Several types of schemata (plural for schema) exist.

Exemplars

An **exemplar** is a concept within a schema that is the single best representative of some category. Exemplars can be different for different people. Following from our previous discussion, potato chips are often considered the exemplar for a snack food. Tiger Woods may be the category exemplar for a professional golfer. Disney World may be the exemplar for a vacation destination. All other instances of a category are compared to an exemplar. Thus, when a consumer encounters a carrot, the fit with chips as the exemplar of a snack food may not be high. But, if the retailer offers small bite-sized carrots enclosed in a

EXHIBIT 4.9
The Knowledge for Snack Foods

Small — Snack Food — Plastic Wrapper
Savory — Sweet
Crackers — Chips — Twinkie
Cheap — Cookies
Money — Greasy — Milk

small plastic bag, they may overlap enough with a bag of chips to fit into the snack food category. Exhibit 4.10 illustrates other possible category exemplars.

Prototypes

Some categories may not be represented by an exemplar. For instance, a car salesman category likely does not evoke a specific person by name who best represents that category. However, an image does appear in one's mind in association with the category. The image contains the characteristics most associated with a car salesperson in this example. Several characteristics may come to mind. This type of schema is known as a **prototype**. Whether represented by a prototype or an exemplar, new and unknown examples are compared to the standard by comparing features with those found in the schema.

REACTION TO NEW PRODUCTS/ BRANDS

When consumers encounter new products or brands, they react to them by comparing them to the existing schema. To illustrate, consider that Europeans are used to very small cars. Thus, when the smart car, a tiny two-seat coupe, was introduced, they were more likely to be able to accept it as an automobile than were American consumers. In the United States, the smart car shares much more in common with a golf cart! Therefore, American consumers will not fit the smart car in the auto category as easily. To the extent that a new product or brand can share the same nodes with an existing brand, consumers will more easily understand what the product does.

SCRIPT

A **script** is a schema representing an event. Consumers derive expectations for service encounters from these scripts. For instance, when a consumer dines in a nice Italian restaurant, the script probably contains things such as valet parking, being greeted by a mâitre d' in a nice suit, having to wait to be seated, and being seated

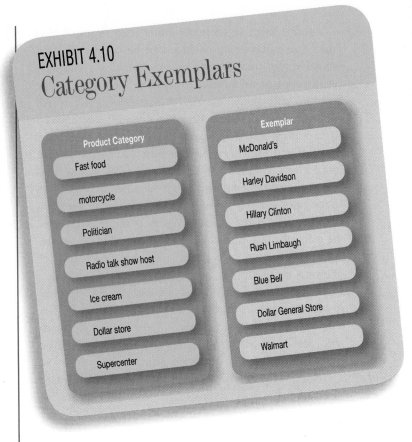

EXHIBIT 4.10
Category Exemplars

Product Category	Exemplar
Fast food	McDonald's
motorcycle	Harley Davidson
Politician	Hillary Clinton
Radio talk show host	Rush Limbaugh
Ice cream	Blue Bell
Dollar store	Dollar General Store
Supercenter	Walmart

at a table covered with a tablecloth. Because going to a nice Italian restaurant is generally a good experience, restaurant managers should try to not vary too much from expectations or risk confusing, and even frustrating, consumers.

Students can probably relate to the concept of a script every time an instructor hands back a graded test. For example, students have developed rules about how the tests are handed back. Many will believe that if their name is called out early, then the test result is generally good. If this script exists, the longer the student has to wait to get the test back, the more anxious he

Is it a car or a golf cart?

© DYNAMIC GRAPHICS/CREATAS IMAGES/JUPITERIMAGES

To Tell the Truth?

© SHERI GIBLIN/FOOD PIX/JUPITERIMAGES

Consumers will sometimes distort their memory of events. In other words, what someone says may not exactly match the episodic memory for an event. This is particularly so when consumers are trying to manage their own self-schema or the schema they believe other consumers hold for them. Similarly, when consumers go on job interviews, they may be tempted to exaggerate past events in their lives particularly when they involve achievement. If you are the interviewer, wouldn't you like to know if someone is lying? Well, when consumers are asked to discuss memories for past episodes in their lives, they can usually recall them quite quickly. One telltale sign of a liar is that he or she will take just a little longer to state the memory. However, people with the best social skills make the best liars in that they are able to lie more quickly than those without really good social skills. Maybe you'll pay a little closer attention the next time you are in a social setting and listening to others boast of their past glories.

Source: Argo, J., K. White, and D. W. Dahl (2006), "Social Comparison Theory and Deception in the Interpersonal Exchange of Consumer Information," *Journal of Consumer Research*, 33, 98–108; Walczyk, J. J., J. P. Schwartz, R. Clifton, B. Adams, M. Wei, and P. Zha (2005), "Lying Person-to-Person About Life Events: A Cognitive Framework for Lie Detection," *Personnel Psychology*, 58, 141–170.

---

episodic memory memory for past events in one's life

nostalgia yearning to relive past events, which can also be positively associated with purchase behavior

social schema cognitive representation that gives a specific type of person meaning

social stereotype another word for social schema

---

or she gets over the prospects of a poor grade.

EPISODIC MEMORY

Closely related to the concept of a script is **episodic memory**. Episodic memory refers to the memory for past events in one's life, and as such, they represent episodes from the past. A consumer may have fond memories of childhood holiday celebrations. Another consumer may remember graduating from college or getting a first job. These are all examples of episodes, which involve products and brands. Brands that get associated with positive events stored in episodic memory receive somewhat of a halo and tend to be preferred by consumers.[31] These events may also evoke **nostalgia**, a yearning to relive past events, which can also be positively associated with purchase behavior.

SOCIAL SCHEMATA

A **social schema** is the cognitive representation that gives a specific type of person meaning. Another word for social schema is **social stereotype**. The stereotype captures the role expectations that exist for a person of a specific type. For instance, consumers generally like it when service providers match existing stereotypes. Interestingly, even though consumers may not like politicians, they will likely vote for a typical candidate over an atypical candidate because at least the typical candidate matches the job description!

However, stereotypes, like all schemata, can also evoke emotion in the form of schema-based affect. Think about the way school kids react when they are called to the principal's office. Particularly, if the student finds a principal that really looks and acts like a principal, he or she is likely to be very apprehensive even if his or her conscience is clear. The fact is, the apprehension is an affect that is stored along with and becomes active along with the principal stereotype. Emotions in the form of schema-based affects can even interfere with information processing so that the student may not really remember a lot of the information he or she gets from the principal. Similarly, the emotions that a consumer experiences once a stereotype becomes active can interfere with information processing.

Consumers also realize that they belong to certain categories of person types. This phenomenon falls under the general heading of *social identity*. Most consumers will try to match the characteristics associated with the stereotype. For instance, male consumers often exhibit characteristics that protect their fit with the male stereotype. Male consumers' reactions to advertising containing relatively feminine characteristics are particularly less positive when viewed in the presence of another male consumer. This behavior may be the result of trying to protect their male identity.[32] Similarly, consumers sometimes seek out products that allow them to fit better into this category.

A social schema can be based on practically any characteristic that can describe a person, including occupation, age, sex, ethnicity, religion, and even product ownership. For example, what type of person drives a VW Beetle? Chances are most consumers' descriptions of a VW Beetle owner would overlap. Thus, social schemata are activated. Marketers can use this information in many ways. In fact, attempts to *demarket* a product can be implemented by stigmatizing consumption with a negative stereotype. Perhaps no better example exists than the stigmatization of smoking. A smoker, as opposed to a nonsmoker, is more likely to be attributed with the following characteristics: energetic, disgusting, offending, unkempt, and interesting.[33]

Additionally, a person described as a smoker is liked less than a similar person described as a nonsmoker, and interestingly, even smokers are more likely to describe a fellow smoker as disgusting and offensive. Thus, the stereotype seems pervasive. Obviously, a product associated with increasing the belief that a consumer is disgusting, unkempt, and offensive is more difficult to sell. Thus, to the extent that antismoking public policy messages have tried to stigmatize smokers, the messages have been effective.

ELABORATION

Elaboration refers to the extent to which a consumer continues processing a message even after an initial understanding is achieved in the comprehension stage.[34] With elaboration, more things from long-term memory are called up and attached to the new information. This means more and richer tags and a better chance of recall. In particular, **personal elaboration**, where the person imagines himself or herself somehow associating with a stimulus being processed, provides the deepest comprehension and greatest chance of accurate recall.

Notice that in Exhibit 4.1 the lines linking the information processing steps to memory get more pronounced from exposure through elaboration. The darker and more pronounced lines coming from comprehension and elaboration represent the strength with which incoming information is tagged. Remember, information is tagged so that it can be understood.

Consumers who reach the elaboration stage are most likely to meaningfully encode information so that intentional retrieval is possible later. In a marketing context, therefore, appeals that ask consumers to fill in aspects from their own lives are likely to lead to deeper comprehension and better recall.[35] Thus, when a consumer is asked, "Have you ever been in this situation?" or when a consumer is told, "Imagine yourself in a new Porsche Cayenne," these primes can trigger personal elaboration, resulting in better recall. Thus, personal elaboration is highly desirable when influence is expected to take place through cognitive reasoning.

© SOMOS/JUPITERIMAGES

"Young" consumers are expected to dress, look, and act as such—and their actions involve consumer behavior.

Chapter 4 Case

Antonio Parker works for one of the world's most prestigious brand names specializing in designer handbags. The company competes with other famous brands like Gucci. Antonio is responsible for production and is constantly facing pressures due to the increasingly high labor costs in Italy. Antonio is well aware that many fashion-oriented companies in Europe and in the United States have moved production to India, China, or some other place where labor is cheap. Even Italian companies making high-end designer suits have recently moved production to developing nations. They maintain that today, as opposed to the past, high-quality standards can be maintained and thus any material differences in the suits between one made in China and one made in Italy are not noticeable to the consumer.

So, although the company is proudly operated exclusively as an Italian company with 100% Italian production, Antonio is now considering opening a production facility in China. This would cut the costs involved in producing the designer bags by over 50%. Antonio is about to meet with the VP-Marketing. He anticipates a negative reaction because, in his opinion, marketing people rarely understand costs.

Questions

1. How important is the country of origin to consumers' comprehension of designer products like those sold by Antonio's company?

2. Play the role of the VP-Marketing. What would your reaction be? How could knowledge that the bag is produced in China potentially harm or enhance the brand?

3. Antonio suggests simply removing the stitching that says "Made in Italy" as a way of not misleading consumers. Would such a move address any ethical concerns that may exist once production is moved to China? Explain why.

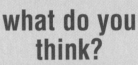

Marketing success

is determined by emotions because actions bring value to a consumer to the extent that desirable emotional states can be created.

5

Motivation and Emotion: Driving Consumer Behavior

After studying this chapter, the student should be able to:

LO1 Understand what initiates human behavior.

LO2 Classify basic consumer motivations.

LO3 Describe consumer emotions and demonstrate how they help shape value.

LO4 Apply different approaches to measuring consumer emotions.

LO5 Appreciate the fact that not all consumers express emotions in the same way.

LO6 Define the concept of schema-based affect.

LO1 What Drives Human Behavior?

how many times do people ask, "Why did I do that?" Sometimes the reason is simple. A consumer might ask, "Why did I eat that whole Big Mac?" The reason may be as simple as "I was hungry." Many consumers may also relate to another familiar question, "Why did I drink so much?" People usually ask this question the morning after a long night out. The reason here may not be as simple or obvious as "I was hungry." But ultimately, excessive drinking, like all acts, does indeed have an explanation.

motivations inner reasons or driving forces behind human actions as consumers are driven to address real needs

homeostasis state of equilibrium wherein the body naturally reacts in a way so as to maintain a constant, normal bloodstream

The basic consumption process (recall from Chapter 1) is a central component of the CVF and includes consumer needs as the first component. Consumer needs start the process because they kick-start or "motivate" subsequent thoughts, feelings, and behavior. Simply put, **motivations** are the inner reasons or driving forces behind human actions as consumers are driven to address real needs. As the CVF indicates, motivations do not completely determine behavior because other sources, including situational factors like the physical environment, influence behavior. However, motivations do much to provide the answer or intended reason for a consumer's actions.

HOMEOSTASIS

Human motivations are oriented toward two key groups of behavior. The first is behavior aimed at maintaining one in a current acceptable state. **Homeostasis** refers to the fact that the body naturally reacts in a way so as to maintain a constant, normal bloodstream. When one's blood sugar falls below an acceptable state, the physiological reaction is hunger. Hunger then motivates a consumer to have a Big Mac and restore the body to an acceptable state. Shivering motivates consumers to wear coats to keep their blood from becoming too cold. Thus, consumers act to maintain things the way they are.

SELF-IMPROVEMENT

The second group of behavior results from **self-improvement motivation**. These behaviors are aimed at changing one's current state to a level that is more ideal—not simply maintaining the current state of existence. Beyond some level, consumers exercise not to maintain themselves but to improve their health and well-being. When a consumer moves up from a Touchup handbag to a Prada handbag, she is not acting out a decision to maintain herself but to improve her status in life. Self-improvement leads us to acts normally involving an emotional payoff.

Basic motivations are relatively simple to understand. As with many psychological concepts, motives can be classified in several ways. We turn now toward two related classification schemes—one a general motivational classification and another aimed more specifically at consumer behavior.

LO2 A General Hierarchy of Motivation

Perhaps the most popular theory of human motivation in consumer and organizational behavior is **Maslow's hierarchy of needs**. This theory describes consumers as addressing a finite set of prioritized needs. The following list displays the set of needs starting with the most basic need.

- **Physiological.** Basic survival (food, drink, shelter, etc.)
- **Safety and security.** The need to be secure and protected
- **Belongingness and love.** The need to feel like a member of a family or community
- **Esteem.** The need to be recognized as a person of worth
  - **Self-actualization.** The need for personal fulfillment

According to Maslow's theory, consumers first seek value by satisfying the most basic needs. Thus, a starving consumer will risk safety to get something to eat. A consumer would find little value in things that might provide esteem or self-actualization when his or her survival is questioned. In contrast, when a successful businessperson retires, he or she may indeed find the most value in things that do not bring esteem, love, or safety but instead provide self-fulfillment. Several financial firms run advertisements showing retirees leaving high-paying careers to travel to far-off places or go off and work in a mission. This appeal typifies how consumer behavior can provide value by addressing the need for self-actualization.

For "Everything Else" there is Mastercard! And, the everything else can lead to self-actualization.

Further, consider how Maslow's hierarchy may operate differently around the world. In war-torn areas of the world, consumers may indeed risk their lives to buy basic necessities. Clearly, this type of shopping is providing only utilitarian value. In the United States, esteem may be found through performing well on the job and owning a large house. In Japan, however, space is so scarce that very few people own large homes. Therefore, esteem may manifest itself more in owning a nice car or in one's manner of dress.

Similarly, the things that provide self-actualization are likely to vary in different places around the world. Motivations can determine what type and amounts of value are sought by consumers. Generally, the most basic needs are addressed with utilitarian value, and as needs become more elaborate, hedonic value is sought to satiate the need state. Exhibit 5.1 illustrates the hierarchical aspect of needs and includes an example of the consumer behavior that goes with each. Notice too the tendency for the most basic needs to be addressed by utilitarian value, while more elaborate needs require hedonic value.

SIMPLER CLASSIFICATION OF CONSUMER MOTIVATIONS

The preceding discussion suggests that in the context of consumer behavior, motivations may be classified even more simply. Not surprisingly, the types of motivations match up with the types of needs. A simple but very useful way to understand consumer behavior is to classify motives based on whether a particular need can best be addressed by utilitarian or hedonic value.[1]

utilitarian motivation desire to acquire products that can be used to accomplish something

hedonic motivation desire to experience something emotionally gratifying

Utilitarian Motivation

Utilitarian motivation is a desire to acquire products that can be used to accomplish things. Utilitarian motivation bears much in common with the idea of maintaining behavior. When the consumer runs out of Kleenex® tissue, there will be a strong motivation to do something about this problem and acquire more Kleenex tissue. In the sense that utilitarian motivation helps a consumer maintain his or her state, these motivations work much like homeostasis.

Hedonic Motivation

Hedonic motivation involves a desire to experience something personally gratifying. These behaviors are usually emotionally satisfying. Interestingly, although sales via the Internet continue to grow, they account for less than 5% of all retailing. Perhaps part of the reason is that the process itself is not very rewarding. For people who really love to shop, the Internet may not provide the multisensory experience that a rich shopping environment can deliver. For these consumers, the Internet may be fine for acquiring things but disappointing as a rewarding shopping experience. Exhibit 5.2 illustrates some typical behaviors that are motivated by utilitarian or hedonic shopping motives.

CONSUMER INVOLVEMENT

Two American tourists are seated in a restaurant in Strasbourg, France. A waiter arrives at the table, provides them with English menus, and asks if anyone would like the special "entrée" du jour, fois gras d'oie avec marmalade. One customer responds by saying he isn't ready for his entrée while the other says, "Why yes that would be a terrific starter, and please serve it with crusty toast points, pickles and a bit of Cadillac." How are these consumers different? Well, many differences may exist, but one big difference is obviously the level

EXHIBIT 5.1
An Illustration of Consumer Motivations According to Maslow's Hierarchy

Self-actualization—Learning a foreign language for fun

Esteem—Describing one's life on MySpace.com

Belongingness and love—Home and family

Safety and security—Gated apartment

Physiological needs—Dumpster dining (finding food in garbage)

Hedonic Value

Utilitarian Value

consumer involvement degree of personal relevance a consumer finds in pursuing value from a given act of consumption

moderating variable variable that changes the nature of the relationship between two other variables

EXHIBIT 5.2
Utilitarian and Hedonic Motivations Lead to Consumer Behaviors

Utilitarian Motivations Lead to	Hedonic Motivations Lead to
Choosing the most convenient place to have lunch	Going out to a trendy, new restaurant for dinner
Buying a tank of gas for the car	Driving the car fast on a curvy road even when not rushed
Choosing to shop with retailers that are seen as useful and easy to use	Choosing to shop with retailers that are seen as fun and exciting
Using air freshener to cover up a strange smell in the apartment	Using air freshener because one really likes the smell
Going gift shopping out of a sense of obligation to give a gift	Giving a gift to enjoy the giving process and the joy the recipient experiences when opening the gift

of involvement each has in the food category.

Involvement is intimately linked to motivation because when one is highly involved with something, one is motivated to expend effort in consuming that thing.[2] **Consumer involvement** represents the degree of personal relevance a consumer finds in pursuing value from a given consumption act. When a consumer is involved in a product category, that category is very important to the consumer. Thus, when a consumer is highly involved, there is a greater chance that relatively high value can be achieved as long as things go as expected.

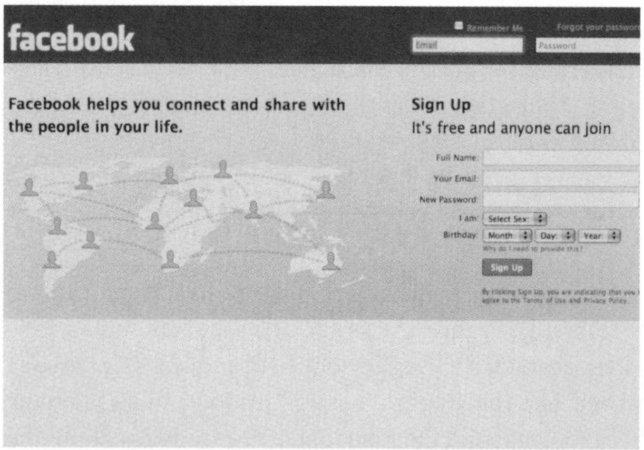
facebook
Facebook helps you connect and share with the people in your life.
Sign Up
It's free and anyone can join

© ORAMSTOCK/ALAMY

Do utilitarian or hedonic motivations drive consumers to share personal information freely via the Internet?

Consumer Involvement as a Moderator

Consumer researchers often consider involvement a key moderating variable. A **moderating variable** is one that changes the nature of a relationship between two other variables. For example, consider the relationship between the number of alternative brands of a product, perhaps running shoes, and the amount of time and effort a consumer spends choosing a pair of shoes. Logically, one might expect that the larger the selection, the greater the time needed to make a decision. However, would this be the case for all consumers? A highly involved consumer is likely to take more time because there are more attractive alternatives. He or she is willing (motivated) to spend time evaluating multiple pairs of shoes, trying them on, and comparing them on many attributes.

Value is closely tied to making the right choice. On the other hand, a consumer who lacks motivation to study shoes may be overwhelmed by all the brands and fall back to some simple choice decision like "pick the cutest." Additionally, some degree of involvement is needed to have an ability to effectively evaluate multiple brands. So, more brands will not affect the amount of time and effort expended by a consumer with low involvement. A consumer with high involvement, though, is likely to spend more time when there are more alternatives because the highly involved consumer is more likely to actually distinguish meaningful differences between brands.

Different Types of Involvement

Involvement can mean different things to different people. However, one way to bring different perspectives together is to realize that there are different types of involvement. In each case, high involvement still means high personal relevance and the fact that receiving value is highly important. Here are some key types of consumer involvement:

- **Product involvement** means that some product category has personal relevance. **Product enthusiasts** are consumers with very high involvement in some category. A relatively large segment of product enthusiasts can be found in the fashion market. These consumers find great value in learning about fashions, shopping for fashions, and wearing fashionable clothes. Thus, for every consumer some product categories are much more involving than others. Exhibit 5.3 contrasts products that are generally associated with low and high consumer product involvement.

EXHIBIT 5.3
Typical High and Low Product Involvement

High Product Involvement	Low Product Involvement
Dresses	
Televisions	Detergents
Champagne	Facial soap
Bras	Toothpaste
	Yogurt

- **Shopping involvement** represents the personal relevance of shopping activities. This relevance enhances personal shopping value. From a utilitarian value perspective, highly involved shoppers are more likely to process information about deals and are more likely to react to price reductions and limited offers that create better deals.[3]
- **Situational involvement** represents the temporary involvement associated with some imminent purchase situation. Situational involvement often comes about when consumers are shopping for something with relatively low involvement but a relatively high price. Things like household and kitchen appliances usually fit this category. For instance, few consumers are highly involved

with air conditioners. However, when a consumer is about to purchase an air conditioner, he or she may temporarily learn a lot about air conditioners to avoid paying too much or choosing an inappropriate unit.

- **Enduring involvement** can be contrasted with situational involvement.[4] Enduring involvement represents an ongoing interest in some product or activity. The consumer is always searching for opportunities to consume the product or participate in the activity. Enduring involvement is often associated with hedonic value because learning about, shopping for, or consuming a product for which a consumer has high enduring involvement is personally gratifying.
- **Emotional involvement** represents how emotional a consumer gets during some specific consumption activity. Emotional involvement is closely related to enduring involvement because the things that consumers care most about will eventually create high emotional involvement. Sports fans typify consumers

product involvement the personal relevance of a particular product category

product enthusiasts consumers with very high involvement in some product category

shopping involvement personal relevance of shopping activities

situational involvement temporary interest in some imminent purchase situation

enduring involvement ongoing interest in some product or opportunity

emotional involvement type of deep personal interest that evokes strongly felt feelings simply from the thoughts or behavior associated with some object or activity

Consumers with high enduring involvement sometimes even earn labels, such as *clothes horse*!

© FERNANDA CALFAT/ GETTY IMAGES

with high emotional involvement, and as we know, sports fans can be rowdy and do wild and crazy things.

LO3
Consuer Emotions and Value
EMOTION

What is *emotion*? Emotion is a difficult term to define. In fact, some refer to emotion as a "fuzzy" concept, believing that no exact definition exists. Rather, according to this view, the best that can be done is to list examples of emotion. Love, for example, is a primary example of an emotion, and all readers can relate to the experience of love. Yet, how is *love* defined?

> Both love and anger are controlling emotions in that they tend to shape one's behavior strongly.

Ask someone to put love into words and what generally happens is that people will provide examples or types of love such as romantic love, brotherly love, maternal love, or love for one's school. Although quite different, anger is another typical emotion sharing something in common with love. Both love and anger are controlling emotions in that they tend to shape one's behavior strongly.

While emotions are a bit "fuzzy," we can offer a simple definition. **Emotions** are psychobiological reactions to appraisals. Thus, when a consumer receives bad service in a restaurant, he or she appraises the situation and then reacts emotionally. When a consumer is contemplating vacation, she appraises different sites and thinks about the total vacation experience. She reacts differently to Las Vegas than Pigeon Forge, TN. Emotions are considered **psychobiological** because they involve psychological processing and physical responses.[5] Indeed, emotions create **visceral responses**, meaning that certain feeling states are tied to behavior

in a very direct way. Exhibit 5.4 lists some typical visceral responses to emotions.

Emotions are extremely important to consumer behavior and marketing because consumers react most immediately to their feelings.[6] Notice that the word *motivation* and the word *emotion* both contain "motion" as a root. The fact that emotions are hardwired to behavior has been explained as follows:

> *"[Emotions are] fuels for drives, for all motion, every performance, and any behavioral act."*[7]

Behaviors are closely tied to emotion, creating close links between emotions, consumer behavior, and value. Thus, to this extent, marketing success is determined by emotions because actions bring value to a consumer to the extent that desirable emotional states can be created.[8] One of the secrets to Starbucks's success is an environment that creates relaxing feelings, allowing the consumer an escape from his or her troubles for a few minutes while indulging in a good coffee and perhaps the company of a good friend.[9] These emotions end up contributing to the overall value of the Starbucks experience.

COGNITIVE APPRAISAL THEORY

What gives rise to consumer emotions? Psychologists have argued over all the different sources of emotions for decades, but **cognitive appraisal theory** represents an increasingly popular school of thought describing how specific types of thoughts can serve as a basis for specific emotions. When a consumer makes an appraisal, he or she is assessing some past, present, or future situation. Four types of cognitive appraisals are especially relevant for consumer behavior.[10]

1. **Anticipation appraisals.** Focuses on the future and can elicit emotions like hopefulness or anxiety

2. **Agency appraisals.** Reviews responsibility for events and can evoke gratefulness, frustration, or sadness

3. **Equity appraisal.** Considers how fair some event is and can evoke emotions like warmth or anger

4. **Outcomes appraisal.** Considers how something turned out relative to one's goals and can evoke emotions like joyfulness, satisfaction, sadness, or pride

Exhibit 5.4 illustrates each of these appraisal types. However, appraisals are often complicated enough to involve more than one type of appraisal. The consumer showing up at a party with out-of-place attire has

EXHIBIT 5.4
Visceral Responses to Emotions by Consumers

Type of Appraisal / Situation	Emotion	Behavioral Reaction
Anticipation appraisal—Consumer waits while doctor examines X-rays	Worry	Grim face with turned-down eyebrows and cheeks. Hands likely near face. Consumer would rather avoid situation.
Outcome appraisal—Consumer wins a contest	Joy	Genuine smile including turned-up cheeks and eyebrows and open hands. The consumer approaches the situation.
Equity appraisal—Consumer sees one customer receive faster and better service than he or she receives	Anger	Turned-down cheeks and eyebrows with clenched fists and hunched back. The consumer seeks to approach an agent of the company.
Agency appraisal—Consumer sees a waiter sneeze near a food preparation area	Disgust	Pinched-in facial expression and turned head. The body naturally withdraws (avoids) the situation.
Outcome appraisal—Consumer shows up at an important party inappropriately dressed	Embarrassment	Face blushes (turns red and feels hot), head cowers, and a strong desire to flee is experienced.

probably also made some type of agency appraisal addressing who was responsible for the misinformation. Understanding the basis for emotions is important because consumption situations might be better designed to avoid appraisals that produce avoidance reactions. Health services and facilities could be shaped to eliminate or minimize a consumer's anticipation following a diagnostic procedure by masking the procedure when possible or keeping the consumer occupied while test results are interpreted.

EMOTION TERMINOLOGY

Mood

Moods can be distinguished from the broader concept of emotion based on specificity and time. Consumer **mood** can be thought of as a transient (temporary and changing) and general feeling state often characterized with simple descriptors such as a "good mood," "bad mood," or even a "funky mood." Moods are generally considered less intense than many other emotional experiences; nevertheless, moods can influence consumer behavior. Consumers in good moods tend to make decisions faster and to outspend their bad-mood counterparts. In addition, consumer mood affects satisfaction, with a bad mood being particularly detrimental to consumer satisfaction.[11] In this sense, marketers do not have complete control of the satisfaction they deliver.

Employees' moods can also affect consumption outcomes as they interact with consumer mood. A salesperson in a bad mood can negatively affect a consumer's overall attitude and willingness to buy. Perhaps curiously, consumers who enter a situation in a bad mood react better to eservice providers who are also in a bad mood than they do to service providers in a good mood. Exhibit 5.5 provides an overview of results from a study investigating this phenomenon. Thus, consumers seem to be most receptive to an employee with a matching mood rather than to an employee who always has a positive mood.[12] However, this would not really lead to the suggestion that employees should try to match consumers' bad moods because later we will see how an employee's mood have the potential to also change a customer's mood.

Additionally, a consumer's mood can serve as a type of frame that can transfer into product value judgments. For example, when consumers are evaluating alternative vacation sites, they tend to rate sites more favorably when they evaluate them in a good mood as opposed to evaluating them when they are in a bad mood.[13] Consumers make **mood-congruent judgments** such as those in which the value of a target is influenced in a consistent way by one's mood. These effects are observed both when consumers are judging the value of products that they currently own and when they are considering purchasing.[14]

Affect

Affect is another term used to represent the feelings a consumer experiences when going through the consumption process. At times, affect is used as a general term encompassing both emotion and mood. However, in consumer behavior, **consumer affect** is more often used to represent the feelings a consumer has about a particular product or activity.[15] Thus, when consumers like Marlboro more than Winston, they are expressing their affect toward the Marlboro brand.

LO4 Measuring Emotion

marketing and consumer researchers place a great deal of emphasis on properly measuring consumer emotion because emotions play such a key role in shaping value. However, there is no consensus on the best way to measure consumer emotions. Two issues that regularly arise are whether consumers have introspection (can express verbally) to their emotions and how to best categorize these emotions if they can be communicated.

AUTONOMIC MEASURES

Perhaps the autonomic measures would offer the greatest validity in representing consumer emotions. **Autonomic measures** are those responses that are automatically recorded based on either automatic visceral reactions or neurological brain activity. These would include facial reactions, physiological responses such as sweating in a GSR (galvanic skin response) or lie detector test, heart rate, and brain imaging which can document activity in areas of the brain responsible for certain specific emotions.[16]

While these measurement approaches have the advantage of assessing emotional activity without requiring a volitional response from the consumer, they have the drawback of being intrusive because most require

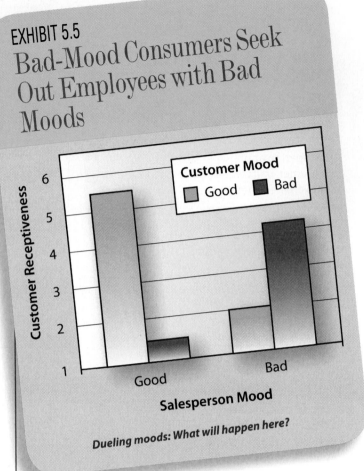

Dueling moods: What will happen here?

the consumer to be attached to some machine. Imagine a consumer wearing a net stocking cap attached to a computer by wires in a lab being told to watch some ads and to pretend he or she is in his or her own living room. This would be very difficult to do. So, the disadvantage of this approach is the obtrusiveness created by the measuring device. Interestingly however, research suggests that these autonomic responses generally correspond fairly well to introspective self-reports of emotional experience.[17]

SELF-REPORT MEASURES

Self-report measures are generally less obtrusive than biological measures because they don't involve physical contraptions. Self-report affect measures usually require consumers to recall their affect state from a recent experience or to state the affect they are feeling at a given point in time. These paper-and-pencil tests usually involve a questionnaire; they are not perfect but generally are valid enough to be useful to consumer and marketing researchers. However, many different options exist for applying self-report measures, and each option is usually based on a somewhat different perspective of emotion theory.

Charged Up!

Some actions require a charge to get things started. Consumer research shows how emotion causes behavior and thereby influences value (both utilitarian and hedonic). In particular, behaviors with an ethical angle often need a charge to get started.

What kinds of consumer behavior involve potential ethical angles? At a very simple level, some consumers may judge the actions of others based on whether or not they consider ethical factors in selecting brands. For instance, does a consumer consider the labor practices of competing companies before choosing a brand? Alternatively, green consumers may judge others' behaviors based on the way they behave and may even react emotionally when they see other consumers behaving in ways that are inconsistent with their beliefs such as using plastic bags at the supermarket. Interestingly, when consumers are judged by others they are viewed less favorably for not purchasing "ethical" products than they are viewed positively for purchasing ethical products. In the extreme, consumers practice unethical behaviors like shoplifting. Consumer emotions help explain why adolescents steal things from retailers. An emotional charge overrides thoughts and produces unethical behavior. So, a good lesson is to mind one's emotions!

Iwin, J.R. and Naylor, R.W. (2009), "Ethical Decisions and Response Mode Compatibility: Weighting of Ethical Attributes in Consideration Sets Formed by Excluding Versus Including Product Alternatives," Journal of Marketing Research, 46 (April), 234-246. Jiang, Y. and Wang, J.L. (2006), "The Impact of Affect on Service Quality and Satisfaction: The Moderation of Service Contexts," Journal of Services Marketing, 20 (4), 211-218. Babin, B.J., Griffin, M. and Boles, J.S. (2004), "Buyer Reactions to Ethical Beliefs in the Retail Environment," Journal of Business Research, 57 (October), 1155-1163.

PANAS

One of the most commonly applied ways to assess one's emotional state is by using the PANAS. PANAS stands for positive-affect-negative-affect scale and allows respondents to self-report the extent to which they feel one of 20 emotional adjectives. Exhibit 5.6 shows an example of the PANAS.

The PANAS is generally applied to capture the relative amount of positive and negative emotion experienced by a consumer at a given point in time. However, this raises several questions about the nature of emotion, including whether or not positive and negative emotions can coexist.

Positive and Negative Dimensions of Emotion

Look at the items making up the PANAS. Each can be identified as an example of a good or a bad feeling. Thus, one might wonder why "inspired" and "upset" would both need to be measured. If a consumer is inspired about a new product, it would seem that he or she certainly couldn't be upset at the same time. If feeling good excludes feeling bad, then wouldn't a researcher need only measure positive terms or negative terms to account for a consumer's feelings?

This might be an interesting academic question but the issue also has practical implications if consumers react differently to equal amounts of positive and negative emotions. Thus, considerable attention in psychology and marketing research has addressed this question and the evidence isn't crystal clear.[18] This answer can best be described as "sometimes." Consider the following situations:

One way a consumer in a positive mood protects her feelings is by not saying no to another "reward."

PAD self-report measure that asks respondents to rate feelings using semantic differential items. Acronym stands for pleasure–arousal–dominance

- A consumer rating the feelings experienced when a pop-up box shows up on an electronics retailer website.

- A consumer rating the feelings experienced when planning a wedding.

The first situation is quite simple. In situations like these, positive and negative emotions tend to be opposites. If people have bad feelings about the experience they are unlikely to have any good feelings. The second

situation is more complex and extends over a longer period of time. In situations such as these, bad and good feelings do not cancel each other out completely, and people can indeed experience some levels of both.

Thus, when consumer researchers are studying highly complex situations, a scale like that of the PANAS allows them to capture both positive and negative dimensions of emotional experience. The possibility exists that each dimension might explain somewhat unique experiences. For example, positive affect is highly related to spending but negative emotion is not. The more good feelings a consumer has, the more he or she buys. A consumer experiencing negative emotions may still complete the shopping task, but he or she may also be more likely to look for another place to shop next time.

PAD

PAD is an acronym that stands for pleasure–arousal–dominance. This scale asks consumers to rate their

> Marketing and consumer researchers place a great deal of emphasis on properly measuring consumer emotion.

EXHIBIT 5.6
A Short-Form PANAS Application

The scale below lists words that describe the feelings or emotions that you may have experienced while shopping at Hometown Bathshop today. Please use the items to record the way you felt while shopping by indicating the extent to which you felt each of the feelings described. The scale ranges from 1= very slightly or not at all to 5 = extremely.

	Very Slightly or Not at All	A Little	Moderately	Quite a Bit	Extremely
Upset	☐	☐	☐	☐	☐
Hostile	☐	☐	☐	☐	☐
Alert	☐	☐	☐	☐	☐
Ashamed	☐	☐	☐	☐	☐
Inspired	☐	☐	☐	☐	☐
Nervous	☐	☐	☐	☐	☐
Determined	☐	☐	☐	☐	☐
Attentive	☐	☐	☐	☐	☐
Afraid	☐	☐	☐	☐	☐
Active	☐	☐	☐	☐	☐

Source: Development and Validation of an Internationally Reliable Short-Form of the Positive and Negative Affect Schedule (PANAS), Edmund R. Thompson, *Journal of Cross-Cultural Psychology* 2007; 38; 227.

feelings using a number of semantic differential (bipolar opposites) items that capture emotions in these three dimensions. The theory behind PAD, unlike PANAS, is that pleasure—the evaluative dimension of emotion—is **bipolar**, meaning that if one feels joyful, he or she cannot also experience sadness.[19] Arousal, which is the degree to which one feels energized, excited, or interested, is also seen as bipolar in that a consumer is either aroused or bored. Likewise, dominance, the degree that one feels in control of a situation, is also bipolar. Thus, researchers have also combined the two approaches and applied adjectives taken from the PAD scale in a format similar to that shown in Exhibit 5.6 rather than a semantic differential.

The PAD approach has been applied widely in retail atmospherics, has been used to study behavior in all manner of environments, including museums and parks, and has also been applied to advertising contexts.[20] Because the scale captures arousal separately, the approach is advantageous when the degree of activation or excitement is of particular interest. For example, when consumers go to a movie, they may feel pleased but not excited. Similarly, the PAD approach allows a separate accounting for feelings of dominance, sometimes known as control. When consumers feel lower control, situational influences play a greater role in shaping their behavior.

LO5 Differences in Emotional Behavior

not all consumers react emotionally or show their emotions to the same extent or in the same way.[21] Two consumers may each receive the same poor service from a crowded retail store. One complains furiously to store management while the other simply walks away to find a more quiet shopping environment. Emotions, as discussed earlier, are deeply tied to personal motivations and traits. Thus, personality characteristics can affect the way consumers respond or demonstrate their emotions. For instance, neuroticism, an important personality trait, is positively related with the amount of negative affect a consumer reports in various service

settings.[22] However, other trait factors that directly reflect the emotional mannerisms of consumers have been studied.

> **bipolar** situation wherein if one feels joy he or she cannot also experience sadness

EMOTIONAL INVOLVEMENT

Motivation and involvement are closely related, as we discussed earlier in the chapter. The things that tap our deepest emotions have the ability to evoke the greatest value. This brings us to emotional involvement, meaning the type of deep personal interest that evokes strongly felt feelings simply from the thoughts or behavior associated with some object or activity. Thus, emotional involvement drives one to consume generally through relatively strong hedonic motivations. Often, emotional involvement can make a consumer appear irrational. Consider the amount of money and time a college alumnus and football fan will spend following his or her team. Some spend hundreds of thousands of dollars on motor homes used only on football weekends for tailgating. The consumer is deeply and emotionally involved with the team and in many ways becomes one with the team.

Other consumers may experience these deeply held feelings over certain fashion products, automobiles, music, or even wine. A consumer experiencing a fantastic dinner with a fantastic bottle of wine achieves a total customer experience, meaning achieving maximum value, through a combination of high emotional involvement and products that perform as expected or better than expected.[23]

Emotional involvement can be increased by providing something extra with products that are purchased. For instance, if someone buys

In situations like this, one consumer may become angry and another may become sad. This customer appears to be angry!

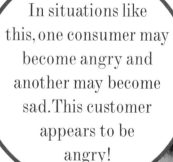

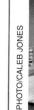

© AP PHOTO/CALEB JONES

a nice leather backpack, the company might consider adding a premium, which may include a phone holster, calculator, or gift certificate to a local pub. In this way, the consumer may develop an emotional attachment or become emotionally involved with the product and with the brand.[24]

Perhaps there is no better example of how different consumers react emotionally than the responses that different consumers have to motion pictures. Some consumers have difficulty getting through any "heart-touching" scene without tears coming to their eyes. Other consumers see the same scene and are simply bored and would rather be watching a classic slapstick movie like *Caddyshack* or *Dumb and Dumber*, which may also bring them to tears in an entirely different way. Similarly, consumers are expected to react differently to the emotions evoked through virtual reality experiences.[25]

Flow

All consumers can probably relate to the experience of enjoying a good book or a good movie so much that one loses awareness of time passing. When this occurs, a consumer has achieved a state of **flow**, meaning extremely high emotional involvement in which a consumer is engrossed in an activity.

A great deal of the work on flow deals with

> One question asked by many who study emotions is whether or not women are more emotional than men.

computer-related activities. For instance, consumers can become so involved in video games that they have little physical awareness of their surroundings. When a parent calls a child for dinner and the child seems to be ignoring him or her, the child may be so caught up in the video game that there really is no conscious awareness of being called. In the extreme, consumers can become addicted to video game consumption.[26]

The addiction is driven in part by a desire to achieve the state of flow and the resulting hedonic value that is produced.[27]

Highly involved shoppers are sometimes described as achieving a flow experience. When this occurs, the consumer is more likely to spend more time browsing, spend more money, be more likely to make repeat purchases and be more prone to impulse purchasing.[28] Online consumers can pursue a flow state while shopping; however, interruptions in Internet service, poor navigational clues, or slow page load times can all inhibit the flow experience and lower both utilitarian and hedonic shopping value.[29] If the consumer also achieves hedonic value, positive outcomes can result for both the consumer and the marketer when flow is achieved. However, the consumer must be able to maintain control of the situation to avoid compulsive or addictive behaviors.

EMOTIONAL EXPRESSIVENESS

Not all consumers express their emotions as obviously as do others. In this sense, **emotional expressiveness** can be thought of as the extent to which a consumer shows outward behavioral signs and otherwise reacts obviously to emotional experiences. The consumer with relatively high emotional expressiveness is likely to react in some way to outcomes that are not as expected. A bad poker player, for example, is unable to hide emotions from other players, and, as such, his/her reaction displays high emotional expressiveness.

Many who study emotions ask whether women are more emotional than men. Research on the matter does not provide a clear-cut answer.[30] For instance, psychologists interested in studying the human experience of and reaction to disgust have conducted experiments in which subjects are exposed to films depicting either an actual amputation or a man being swarmed by cockroaches.[31] Male and female subjects report the same average level of disgust while viewing the films. However, female respondents are more likely than males to react to the disgusting experience by leaving the room before the film is finished. Similar results have been found for other emotions beside disgust, both positive and negative.[32] Thus, when male and female consumers react with similar emotions, women are more likely to express these emotions.[33] Because of this, to the extent that a marketer can judge a consumer's emotional reaction, female consumers may prove more valuable in signaling poor or outstanding service than would male consumers.

EMOTIONAL INTELLIGENCE

Emotions can be useful in determining the most appropriate reaction to events. **Emotional intelligence** is a term used to capture one's awareness of the emotions experienced in a situation and the ability to control reactions to these emotions. This awareness includes awareness of the emotions experienced by the individual as well as an awareness and sympathy for the emotions experienced by others. Emotional intelligence (EI) is a multifaceted concept, and Exhibit 5.7 illustrates EI components.[34] High EI is characterized by high self-control.

In a marketing context, salespeople with high emotional intelligence are more effective in closing sales with consumers than are salespeople low in emotional intelligence.[35] Sales companies are increasingly realizing the benefits of employees with high EI. EI training is becoming commonplace as marketers attempt to get consumers to buy more and to be more satisfied with the things they do buy.[36]

LO6 Emotion, Meaning, and Schema-Based Affect

What is the relation between cognition and emotion? Intuitively, emotion and cognition seem so different that one can easily presume they are completely independent of each other. However, emotion and cognition are actually quite closely related, and this is seen clearly in the role that affect, mood, and emotion can play in signaling and developing meaning. This section focuses on the interplay between emotion and cognitive learning.

SEMANTIC WIRING

Cognitive concepts such as a "toaster" are closely linked with other concepts such as "breakfast" but remotely linked with other concepts like "hurricane." A consumer's ability to remember things about brands and products can be explained using theory developed around the principles of *semantic* networks. Recall that in a semantic network all concepts are connected or "wired" to all others.

Although the term *semantic* is more closely tied to cognitive thought processes, the active processing and storage of knowledge is significantly influenced by emotions in several ways. The general expression **"emotional effect on memory"** refers to relatively superior recall for information presented with mild affective content compared to similar information presented in an affectively neutral way.[37]

The implications for marketing are fairly direct. Marketing communications that present product information in a way that evokes mild levels of emotions will tend to be more effective in producing recall than communications that are affectively neutral.[38] Caution is needed in executing such a tactic because intense emotions are more complicated to deal with and can sometimes even distract consumers from the task of actually processing information. But clearly, emotion and cognition can become closely linked semantically in the mind of a consumer. Exhibit 5.8 illustrates this point.

EXHIBIT 5.7
Emotional Intelligence Consists of Multiple Elements

Self-control—ability to control one's emotions

Emotional empathy—ability to read and understand others' emotions

Emotional Intelligence

Upbeat—ability to maintain a generally upbeat and optimistic outlook

Productive—ability to turn emotions into value through better problem solving

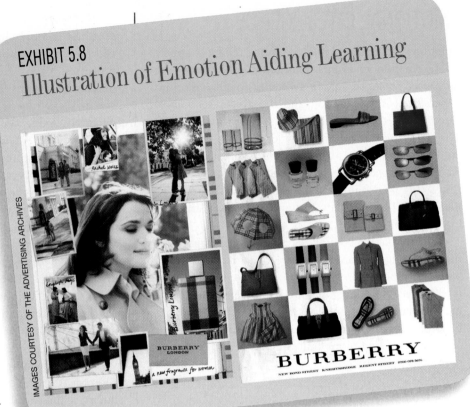

EXHIBIT 5.8
Illustration of Emotion Aiding Learning

IMAGES COURTESY OF THE ADVERTISING ARCHIVES

BURBERRY LONDON

a new fragrance for women

BURBERRY
NEW BOND STREET   KNIGHTSBRIDGE   REGENT STREET   0700 078 5676

MOOD-CONGRUENT RECALL

Many consumers can remember their first day of school, their first airplane trip, or their first visit to a theme park. In each case, products and brands are associated with the experience. Likewise, in each case, each event is associated with a fairly specific mood. For many consumers, the first day of school is filled with apprehension, the first airplane ride may be a blend of fear and excitement, and a visit to a theme park is associated with joyfulness.

Memories of previous, meaningful events in one's life are known as **autobiographical memories**. Consumers are more likely to recall autobiographical memories characterized by specific moods when the same mood occurs again in the future.[39] Simply put, moods tend to match memories.

Mood-congruent recall means that to the extent that a consumer's mood can be controlled, their memories and evaluations can be influenced. Music is one tool useful in inducing moods. Consumers in good moods tend to evaluate products relatively positively compared to consumers in bad moods and vice versa.[40]

NOSTALGIA

Nostalgia affects consumers in a manner similar to that of mood-congruent recall and autobiographical

memory. Nostalgia is discussed in more detail in another chapter. Generally, nostalgia is characterized by a yearning for the past motivated by the belief that previous times were somehow more pleasant. Nostalgia can motivate product purchases as consumers attempt to relive the pleasant feelings of the past. Music, toys, magazines, and movies are products that consumers report commonly buying in association with the feelings of nostalgia.[41] The large number of advertisements that include popular "oldies" songs illustrates attempts at evoking nostalgic feelings.

> Retro designs are increasingly popular and add value through the positive feelings created by nostalgia.

© ISTOCKPHOTO.COM/ZOOMSTUDIO

To Know It Really Is to Feel It!

O ne group of consumers who illustrate the close wiring between cognition and emotion are those who are fluent in multiple languages. Translation of ad copy from one language to another is certainly possible; however, the translation is not always 100% the same. This is particularly true for terms that are tied somehow to emotion. For example, in the United States, we may say we love our cars but such an expression would never be used in Japanese. Bilingual consumers report high but not exact overlap in the affect experienced when moving from one language to another. A Kia ad may be literally translated from Korean to English and retain all cognitive meaning, but the affect associated with the ad may be altered slightly. Thus, when consumers express terms in one language much but not all of the affective meaning is retained.

Additionally, nationalities themselves are embodied with schema-based affect among consumers. Thus, before exporting a product to another country, marketing managers may wish to know exactly what feelings may be present simply because of the knowledge that a product is manufactured in a particular company. Hyundai and Daewoo had to overcome relatively negative affect that was attached to South Korean cars. Interestingly, both brands' cars were rated highly by consumers who did not know the country of origin. Thus, culture and emotion are linked.

Sources: Han, S., S. Yoon, and P. T. Vargas (2005), "Think It's Good, but Feel It's Bad: Country-of-Origin Effect on Cognition, Affect and Behavior," *Advances in Consumer Research*, 33, 263–264; Luna, D., and L. A. Perrachio (1999), "What's in a Bilingual's Mind? How Bilingual Consumers Process Information," *Advances in Consumer Research*, 26, 306–311.

SCHEMA-BASED AFFECT

As we know from consumer information processing theory, knowledge of familiar things becomes organized in a cognitive unit of meaning known as a schema. A schema contains the knowledge of a brand, a product, or any concept. However, a schema is not a purely cognitive entity. Schemata are developed and reinforced through actual experience. So, we come to perceive what a "car salesperson" truly is based on our total experiences with that category. Experience involves more than cognition. When we encounter a car salesperson or hear stories that involve car salespeople, we also experience some type of affect or emotion. These emotions also become part of the meaning for a category in the form of **schema-based affect**.

Schema-based affect helps provide meaning and thus is another example of how affect and cognition are wired together. However, a consumer can actually experience the affect once a schema becomes active. For example, consumers who fear going to a dentist can actually experience true nervousness and apprehension simply by getting them to think about a visit to the dentist, which makes the dentist visit schema active.

Exhibit 5.9 displays a typical schema for a car salesperson including the schema-based affect.[42] The schema-based affect is shown in yellow. When managers realize that a category is associated with negative affect, as in this case, they may be wise either to change the characteristic attributes (in this case of the car salesperson) in an attempt to prevent the schema from becoming or remaining active or to activate an entirely different schema (i.e., professional salesperson). Further, negative schema-based emotions of this type can interfere with the consumer's ability to process information about the product—in this case an automobile. In recent years, many car dealerships have changed the appearance of their salespeople to avoid activating this schema.

> **schema-based affect**
> emotions that become stored as part of the meaning for a category (a schema)

emotional contagion
extent to which an emotional
display by one person influences the emotional state of a
bystander

Exhibit 5.10 displays examples of schema-based affect that
can influence consumers' reactions
to consumption experiences.

EMOTIONAL CONTAGION

Are emotions contagious? This
is the idea behind **emotional
contagion**, which represents the
extent to which an emotional
display by one person influ-
ences the emotional state of a bystander. Consumers
who perceive other consumers or employees surrounding them as either happy or sad may experience a corresponding change in actual happiness or sadness themselves. Emotional contagion means marketing managers
who have a mantra of "service with a smile" may have a

good reason to do so. When service providers maintain
an expression signaling positive affect (service with a
smile), consumers report higher incidences of positive
affect themselves.[43]

EXHIBIT 5.9
A Typical Car Salesperson Schema

Tie too short · Smiles · Flicks Butt Away · Bad Tie · "Cheesy" · Smokes · Overweight · Apprehensive · Pushy · Helpless · Male · Loud · Skeptical

EXHIBIT 5.10
Examples of Schema-Based Affect

Schema	Affect	Typical Consumer Reaction
Disney	Joyfulness, fun	Consumers have increased brand equity and lower price sensitivity for Disney products.
Individual countries (United Kingdom, France, United States, Japan, Israel, China)	Consumers may have slightly different affect associated with each country	Consumers are less favorable toward products manufactured in countries for which that consumer's schema evokes negative affect.
Telemarketing	Aggravation	Consumers often hang up quickly as a built-in avoidance response.
Baby	Tenderness, warmth	Products associated with babies are viewed more favorably.
Sports star	Excitement	Consumers may generalize excitement to products and services endorsed by the star.
Stereotypes	Each stereotype evokes slightly different affect	The affect associated with the stereotype can cause consumers to be more or less willing to approach and may alter information processing.

The Golden Shape Is as Good as Gold!

Schema-based affect can be evoked from practically any type of knowledge. For instance, even something as simple as a shape can be associated with specific affect. In fact, a fundamental principle of design that has survived for millennia is that people react favorably to rectangular shapes that have a ratio of width to height of about 1.6. The Parthenon, the famous fifth-century Greek temple, exhibits this dimension.

Thus, all things equal, consumers will prefer products designed with these dimensions. Similarly, consumers can react differently to package shapes depending on their knowledge. A uniquely shaped bottle, for instance, will evoke negative affect among highly involved consumers but positive affect among those who are not as involved. So, shapes matter in part because shapes evoke affect.

Sources: Bloch, P. H. (1995), "Seeking the Ideal Form: Product Design and Consumer Response," *Journal of Marketing,* 59 (July), 16–29; Bloch, Peter H., F. F. Brunel, and T. J. Arnold (2003), "Individual Differences in the Centrality of Visual Product Aesthetics: Concept and Measurement," *Journal of Consumer Research,* 29, 551–565; Rocchi, B., and S. Gianlucca (2006), "Consumers' Perception of Wine Packaging: A Case Study," *International Journal of Wine Marketing,* 18, 33–44.

© ISTOCKPHOTO.COM/CHRIS ZWAENEPOEL

A closely related topic is that of emotional labor. **Emotional labor** is performed by service workers who must overtly manage their own emotional displays as part of the requirements of the job. Thus, when airline flight attendants themselves feel angry, the requirements of their job ask them to hide their true feelings and express more positive emotions instead. While practically all service employees must perform emotional labor, including professional service providers such as physicians, the long-term impact on psychological well-being may not be positive unless the employees learn how to cope with the emotional conflict. One manner in which the employees may cope is to feed off the positive affect that comes back from customers in return for their emotional labor.[44]

Chapter 5 Case

Teens represent a sizable portion of the population (approximately 32 million), and they have tremendous buying power, as well as influence, over the buying power of their parents. Teens are worth approximately $150 billion annually as a market segment in the United States. This number is too large for marketers to ignore.

Today's young people, however, are generally unresponsive to traditional brand marketing messages. What they do respond to is something "cool." A *Frontline* film, *The Merchants of Cool*, shows how corporate marketing tries to catch cool in teen culture and how media giants try to become cool with media-savvy teens. In order for a marketer to find cool, they have to find a way into the young person's mind and learn how to "speak with teens' language" in the relationship existing between youth culture and the media.

How do teens decide what is cool? The *Merchants of Cool* shows how media contributes to the manufacture of the image of cool, even though their goal is to find out what is cool. Say a girl walks into her high school one day wearing a specific style of shoes. Where did she get the idea that those shoes were cool in the first place? Perhaps she saw them on the cool girl in her favorite reality TV show, or maybe she saw a cool celebrity wearing them in a magazine photo. It does seem that both the media and teens search for what is cool, and they tend to feed off one another in a circular fashion. For marketers, it comes down to finding the coolest of the cool—perhaps those that are, as of yet, the least emulated—and capitalizing on their coolness to reach teens.

To find the coolest of the cool, marketers need to reach teens using channels and settings through which they are likely to respond. In today's world, a marketer for MTV would not be likely to stop by a Wednesday night youth group meeting at a church to talk to teens about what is cool—this is not their demographic. Instead, they might set up a website that becomes a gathering place for teens with enticements such as chat rooms, blogs, games, photos, and contests; through this channel they could gather a vast amount of information from teens who are interacting among a group of their peers in a setting that encourages them to share their thoughts on what is cool.

Teens get excited when they try a new product and almost consider it a challenge. They look for new technology and new products and want to share their opinions on virtual environments. Tremor, a marketing service by the Procter & Gamble Company, is taking a different approach in that they promote their service with supporting teen word-of-mouth influences. Teens join the Tremor service for free not just to review products, listen to unreleased music, view movies, and help design a video game but also to acquire inside information related to product development.

A coolhunting firm is a marketing agency whose exclusive purpose is to research youth in areas of fashion, music, television, lifestyle, and culture. Understanding how to sell to teens requires knowing what teens think about. If companies can get in on a trend or subculture while it is still hidden, they can be the first to bring it to market. Information on what is cool can be used to create products that will reflect back exactly what the kids will want. So coolhunters—those who can track down the latest cool trends in teen life—can profit from this information.

Coolhunters are always seeking ways of seducing the attention of young people. They use pop culture to emphasize a new meaning in a cool trend and even create new trends in ever-changing youth cultures. At Trend Hunter, they want to "find out what's cool before it's cool." As the world of technology continues to evolve, marketers will continue to struggle with finding the product that entices teens into thinking it is cool. This service provides an opportunity that may give a company the boost it needs to sell their product and get into the teen market.[45]

Questions

1. How do teens create value through coolness of a product?

2. Teens respond to something cool, but cool keeps changing. So, if you're a marketer, how do you find cool?

3. Teens certainly appear to be a difficult demographic group to reach. What is different about this demographic group (teenagers) compared to other sectors of our society targeted by marketers?

LISTEN UP!

SHE DID

CB2 was designed for students just like you – busy people who want choices, flexibility, and multiple learning options.

CB2 delivers concise, focused information in a fresh and contemporary format. And… CB2 gives you a variety of online learning materials designed with you in mind.

At **4ltrpress.cengage.com/cb,** you'll find electronic resources such as **videos, audio downloads,** and **interactive quizzes** for each chapter.

These resources will help supplement your understanding of core concepts in a format that fits your busy lifestyle. Visit **4ltrpress.cengage.com/cb** to learn more about the multiple resources available to help you succeed!

what do you think?

My personality can easily be seen in the products that I buy.

1 2 3 4 5 6 7

strongly disagree   strongly agree

Although all consumers

ultimately seek value, some are more highly focused on value than are others.

6

Personality, Lifestyles, and the Self-Concept

Introduction

this chapter focuses on consumer personality, lifestyles, and self-concept. As such, the chapter deals with what are known as **individual difference variables**, which are descriptions of how individual consumers differ according to specific traits or patterns of behavior.[1] These concepts have several applications to both consumer research and marketing practice. Marketing managers are especially interested in identifying consumer characteristics that are associated with the likelihood of purchasing products. Concepts like personality, lifestyle, and self-concept help to describe these differences.

> **individual difference variables** descriptions of how individual consumers differ according to specific trait patterns of behavior
>
> **personality** totality of thoughts, emotions, intentions, and behaviors that a person exhibits consistently as he or she adapts to the environment

After studying this chapter, the student should be able to:

LO1 Define personality and know how various approaches to studying personality can be applied to consumer behavior.

LO2 Discuss major traits that have been examined in consumer research.

LO3 Understand why lifestyles and psychographics are important to the study of consumer behavior.

LO4 Comprehend the role of the self-concept in consumer behavior.

LO5 Understand the concept of self-congruency and how it applies to consumer behavior issues.

LO1 Personality and Consumer Behavior

personality has been studied for many years, and the term has been defined in a number of different ways. We define **personality** as the totality of thoughts, emotions, intentions, and behaviors that a person exhibits consistently as he or she adapts to his or her environment.[2] This definition highlights the *cognitive* (thoughts), *affective* (emotions), *motivational* (intentions), and *behavioral* (behaviors) aspects that are central to the study of personality. Personality is but one characteristic that helps explain why a particular behavior, like listening to the band Coldplay for example, provides great value to one consumer but none to another.

aggregation approach
approach to studying personality in which behavior is assessed at a number of points in time

psychoanalytic approach to personality approach to personality research, advocated by Sigmund Freud, that suggests personality results from a struggle between inner motives and societal pressures to follow rules and expectations

id the personality component in psychoanalytic theory that focuses on pleasure-seeking motives and immediate gratification

pleasure principle principle found in psychoanalytic theory that describes the factor that motivates pleasure-seeking behavior within the id

Personality exhibits a number of distinct qualities, including:

1. *Personality is unique to an individual.* Personality helps distinguish consumers from one another based on the relative degrees of characteristics each exhibits. Consumers differ in their personalities, although some characteristics, or traits, may be shared across individuals.

2. *Personality can be conceptualized as a combination of specific traits or characteristics.* Like all consumers, your overall personality is really a combination of many stable characteristics, or traits. In fact, for many psychologists, personality psychology deals exclusively with the study of human traits.[3]

3. *Personality traits are relatively stable and interact with situations to influence behavior.* Personality traits are expected to remain consistent across situations. However, consumer researchers do realize the importance of situational influences on behavior.[4] The combined influence of situations and traits has been shown to play a large role in influencing specific behaviors

(this is referred to as an *interaction* between the person and the situation).

4. *Specific behaviors can vary across time.* One major issue in personality research is that simply knowing that a consumer possesses a specific trait does not allow us to predict any one specific behavior. For example, simply knowing that a consumer is "materialistic" does not allow the researcher to predict the exact type of product the person may buy. For this reason, personality researchers often advocate an **aggregation approach** in which behaviors are measured over time rather than relying on a single measure of behavior at one point in time.

As we have mentioned, marketing managers are particularly interested in how consumers differ according to their personalities. Consistent patterns of thoughts, emotions, intentions, and behaviors can signal the need for individualized marketing campaigns, and today's marketers are becoming quite adept at individualizing messages. To understand how personalities differ across consumers, it is important to begin with a description of the various approaches to studying the concept. There are a number of ways to explore the human personality; however, here we focus on two popular approaches: the psychoanalytic approach and the trait approach. These approaches have received considerable consumer research attention.

Consistent patterns of thoughts, emotions, intentions, and behaviors can signal the need for individualized marketing campaigns.

PSYCHOANALYTIC APPROACH TO PERSONALITY

According to the famous psychologist Sigmund Freud, human behavior is influenced by an inner struggle between various systems within the personality system.[5] His approach, commonly referred to as the **psychoanalytic approach to personality**, is applicable to both motivation and personality inquiry. Freud's approach highlights the importance of unconscious mental processes in influencing behavior.

For Freud, the human personality consists of three important components: the id, the superego, and the ego. The **id** focuses on pleasure-seeking and immediate gratification. It operates on a **pleasure principle** that motivates a person to focus on maximizing pleasure and minimizing pain. One's id, therefore, focuses on hedonic value. Indeed, a key concept in the id is the *libido*. The libido represents a drive for sexual pleasure, although some researchers view it in slightly different ways. The **superego** works against the id by motivating behavior that matches societal norms and expectations. The superego can be conceptualized as being similar to a consumer's conscience. The ego focuses on resolving the conflicts between the *id* and the *superego*. The **ego** works largely in accordance with the **reality principle**. Under this principle, the ego seeks to satisfy the id within the constraints of society. As such, the ego attempts to balance the desires of the id with the constraints of, and expectations found in, the superego.

Psychoanalytic Approach and Motivation Research

In the early days of consumer research, researchers applied psychoanalytic tools to try to identify explanations for behavior. This was known as the **motivational research era**. Consumer researchers in this era utilized tools such as *depth interviews* and *focus groups* to improve their understanding of inner motives and needs.[6] Researchers applying depth interviews try to explore deep-seated motivations by asking consumers to describe an activity through a series of probing questions. As discussed in our motivation chapter, motivations are the reasons or driving forces behind actions.

Suppose a researcher is studying a consumer who strongly prefers hip hop music. The researcher might ask the following probing questions:

- "What does *hip hop* mean to you?"
- "How does *hip hop* make you feel?"

Does this ad appeal to some deeply held motivation?

- "Can you tell me more about what you are thinking about when you listen to *hip hop*?"
- "Why is *hip hop* important to you?"
- "What would you do if you could no longer buy and listen to *hip hop*?"

Although motivational research has been popular, in general, the motivational research era proved disappointing because it did not spawn any compelling, practical consumer behavior theories or guidelines for marketing actions. Nonetheless, Freud clearly influenced the study of personality and consumer behavior.[7] To this day, for instance, consumer researchers remain interested in discovering consumer motivations operating below the level of conscious awareness.

An example of the influence of deeply held motivations influencing behavior can be found when we consider the id. Although the use of sexual imagery in advertising is often criticized, overtly sexual advertisements are rather common. In fact, the old adage that "Sex sells!" may be directly tied to the Freudian approach. The use of phallic and ovarian symbols in advertising may be traced to a belief that such messages appeal to, and provide value for, the id.

TRAIT APPROACH TO PERSONALITY

While the psychoanalytic approach helped set the groundwork for much of consumer personality research, the **trait approach to personality** has received significant attention over the past few decades. A **trait** is defined as a distinguishable characteristic that describes one's tendency to act in a relatively consistent manner.

Not surprisingly, there are multiple approaches available for consumer researchers. Here, we discuss the

superego component in psychoanalytic theory that works against the id by motivating behavior that matches the expectations and norms of society

ego component in psychoanalytic theory that attempts to balance the struggle between the superego and the id

reality principle the principle in psychoanalytic theory under which the ego attempts to satisfy the id within societal constraints

motivational research era era in consumer research that focused heavily on psychoanalytic approaches

trait approach to personality approaches in personality research that focus on specific consumer traits as motivators of various consumer behaviors

trait distinguishable characteristic that describes one's tendency to act in a relatively consistent manner

nomothetic perspective variable-centered approach to personality that focuses on particular traits that exist across a number of people

idiographic perspective approach to personality that focuses on understanding the complexity of each individual consumer

single-trait approach approach in trait research wherein the focus is on one particular trait

multiple-trait approach approach in trait research wherein the focus remains on combinations of traits

value consciousness the extent to which consumers tend to maximize what they receive from a transaction as compared to what they give

differences between nomothetic and idiographic approaches, and between single- versus multi-trait approaches.

Nomothetic versus Idiographic Approaches

The nomothetic perspective and the idiographic perspective can be distinguished as follows.[8] The **nomothetic perspective** is a "variable-centered" approach that focuses on particular variables, or traits, that exist across a number of consumers. The goal of this perspective is to find common personality traits that can be studied across people.

An example helps to explain the nomothetic approach. Consider college sophomore Maria. One could say that Maria is "introverted." That is, she can be described as being shy, quiet, and bashful. Many consumers are introverted, and therefore, numerous other consumers can be described in this way. Here, the focus is on the introversion trait, and it is used to help describe the characteristics of a number consumers.

The **idiographic perspective** focuses on the total person and the uniqueness of his or her psychological makeup. Attention is not placed on individual traits or how they can be studied across multiple consumers. Rather, the focus is on understanding the complexity of each individual consumer.

The trait approach takes a nomothetic approach to personality. That is, the trait approach assumes that the human personality can be described as a combination of traits that can be studied across consumers. From this perspective, individuals can be described by using various trait descriptors.

Single-Trait and Multiple-Trait Approaches

We can further distinguish between single-trait and multi-trait approaches to consumer research. Under

a **single-trait approach,** the focus of the researcher is on one particular trait. Here, researchers can learn more about the trait and how it affects behavior. For example, a researcher may want to investigate the competitiveness trait and how it impacts the selection of athletic apparel. Perhaps highly competitive consumers will prefer one brand of athletic clothing over another.

With the **multiple-trait approach**, combinations of traits are examined and the total effect of the collection of traits is considered. Here, the researcher is interested in trait scores on numerous traits as potential predictors of consumer behavior. The prediction of individual behavior tends to be stronger with the multiple-trait approach when compared to the single-trait approach.[9] However, both the single- and multiple-trait approaches have been used extensively in consumer research.

LO2 Specific Traits Examined in Consumer Research

to say that there are many traits that can be studied would be a serious understatement! To illustrate, researchers Gordon Allport and Henry Odbert identified nearly 18,000 names for human characteristics found in Webster's Dictionary. And that was in 1936![10] Although numerous traits have received attention, we discuss only a handful of important traits found in consumer research including value consciousness, materialism, innovativeness, complaint proneness, and competitiveness.

Value Consciousness

As we have stated throughout this text, value is at the heart of consumer behavior. Although all consumers ultimately seek value, some consumers are more highly focused on value than are others. As such, value consciousness is often studied as a trait. **Value consciousness** represents the tendency for consumers to focus on maximizing what is received from a transaction as compared to what is given.

Research reveals that value consciousness is an important concept in consumer behavior. For example, value consciousness underlies tendencies to perform behaviors like redeeming coupons.[11] Value-conscious consumers can be expected to pay close attention to the resources that they devote to transactions and to the benefits that they receive. In today's turbulent economy, value consciousness is an important trait to study.

Materialism

Materialism refers to the extent to which material goods are important in a consumer's life. Most western cultures, including the U.S. culture, are generally thought of as being relatively materialistic. However, within each culture, the degree to which each individual is materialistic varies. Studying this trait has been very popular among consumer researchers, and numerous studies have examined the impact of materialism on various consumer behaviors.

Materialism is seen as consisting of three separate dimensions:[12]

- *Possessiveness.* A tendency to retain control and ownership over possessions
- *Nongenerosity.* An unwillingness to share with others
- *Envy.* Resentment that arises as a result of another's belongings and a desire to acquire similar possessions

Highly materialistic consumers tend to be possessive, nongenerous, and envious of other's possessions. Not surprisingly, these consumers view possessions as a means of achieving happiness and they tend to hold onto possessions as long as possible.[13]

Interestingly, consumers today commonly bring many of their favorite material possessions into the workplace. Personal possessions in the workplace can produce calm feelings and stabilize an employee's sense of self.[14] In this way, material possessions play an important part in self-expression. That is, material possessions help consumers express who they think they are, and even who they would like to become.[15] These issues are discussed later in the chapter.

Materialism tends to differ among generations, with lower materialism scores typically being found among older consumers.[16] Indeed, younger consumers have long been thought to be relatively materialistic. A change in the prevalence of materialism does appear to be occurring, however. Although the U.S. culture is widely viewed as being materialistic, research suggests that consumers are beginning to "downshift." Downshifting refers to a conscious decision to reduce one's material consumption. This may be a positive development considering that high levels of materialism can affect debt levels and personal relationships.[17] The recent economic downturn has contributed to a growth in consumer *frugality*, or the extent to which consumers

exhibit restraint when purchasing and using material goods.[18]

Innovativeness

Consumer **innovativeness** refers to the degree to which a consumer tends to be open to new ideas and buying new products, services, or experiences early in their introduction.[19] Innovative consumers are generally dynamic and curious, and they are often young, educated, and relatively affluent.[20] Obviously, consumer innovativeness is an important trait for marketers to consider when introducing new products.

Although researchers do not necessarily agree on the extent to which innovativeness is exhibited across product categories, a consumer with a strong degree of innovativeness may be expected to be innovative in a number of situations. For example, innovativeness has been shown to relate to a number of behaviors including new product adoption, novelty seeking, information seeking, and on-line shopping.[21]

Complaint Proneness

Complaint proneness refers to the extent to which consumers tend to voice complaints about unsatisfactory product purchases. Whereas some consumers may not complain after a bad experience, other consumers are quite ready to voice their frustrations to the company, other consumers, and/or outside parties.[22] Although the personal characteristics of complainers vary, research suggests that consumers who are highly complaint prone tend to be middle-aged, well-educated, upwardly mobile, and assertive.[23]

Although complaint proneness was identified several years ago, the trait remains important today.[24] Why do marketers care about complainers? Quite simply, marketers don't want to lose customers! In fact, the cost of acquiring new consumers far outweighs the costs associated with serving existing ones, and the negative word-of-mouth that complainers often spread can harm a firm's reputation.[25] Furthermore, with the Internet continuing to grow in popularity, marketers must realize that consumers now have more power than ever in spreading negative word-of-mouth.

materialism extent to which material goods have importance in a consumer's life

innovativeness degree to which an individual is open to new ideas and tends to be relatively early in adopting new products, services, or experiences

complaint proneness extent to which consumers tend to voice complaints about unsatisfactory product purchases

competitiveness enduring tendency to strive to be better than others

Competitiveness

The **competitiveness** trait may be defined as an enduring tendency to strive to be better than others. The predominance of competitiveness in consumer society is easy to see, and the use of competitive themes in marketing messages is widespread. Competition also comes in many forms on college campuses, as can be seen in the Ultimate Frisbee box.

A competitive person is generally easy to identify, and research reveals that the trait often emerges in the following ways:[26]

- When a consumer is directly competing with others (as when participating in a sport). The video gaming industry has seen significant growth over the past few years. Competitive gamers can now enjoy playing in national, and even international, video game tournaments. In fact, a recent Cyberathlete Professional League tournament in Dallas included a $150,000 cash prize![27] The sports network ESPN has even broadcast a reality-based series entitled *Madden Nation* to broadcast Madden NFL competitions. In the series, contestants battle for a $100,000 prize. Amateur gamers can also compete online while playing several popular video games. The growth of video "gaming" underscores one manifestation of consumer competitiveness in a technologically advanced environment.

- When a consumer enjoys winning vicariously through the efforts of others (as when we enjoy seeing "our team" win). Sports fans often bask in reflected glory (BIRG) when "their" team wins. This means that they will wear team apparel and display team merchandise when their team

Ultimate Frisbee

Although only a small percentage of high school athletes ever go on to play competitive sports in college, an up-and-coming sport promises fun and excitement for all. Ultimate Frisbee (named after Wham-O's trademarked toy) is rapidly becoming the sport of choice on many college campuses.

The sport, which originated in the 1960s, blends elements of football, soccer, and even basketball. Seven-member squads compete against each other on a field that is much like an American football field. Also like football, points are scored when a player catches the Frisbee in the opponent's "end zone."

One unique aspect of the sport is that the players themselves—not referees—make calls pertaining to the rules of play. Sportsmanship, therefore, is expected by all participants. Interestingly, the sport continues to grow without the use of referees, relying instead on sportsmanship qualities known as the "Spirit of the Game." Thanks to the fun and excitement of Ultimate Frisbee, the face of competition on college campuses is changing.

Sources: Based on online content retrieved at Ultimate Players Association **http://www.upa.org/ultimate**, March 9, 2009; also online content retrieved at **http://www.ultimatefrisbee.com/ultimate_frisbee_links.php** March 9, 2009; also "Ultimate Frisbee Tourney Whizzes into Town," *Herald-Sun, Durham, NC,* January 24, 2009; "Ultimate Frisbee Numbers on the Rise: Ultimate, a Sport Played with a Frisbee that Mixes Basketball, Soccer, and Football, is Exploding in Popularity," *Saint Paul Pioneer Press,* May 29, 2007; "Ultimate Frisbee Takes Off Among Region's Teens," *Pittsburgh Tribune-Review,* March 9, 2009.

is successful. By attempting to show an association between themselves and the team, consumers vicariously live through their team and proclaim things like "We're number one!" (As researchers point out, you hardly ever hear them say things like "They're number one!"[28]) BIRGing has been shown to be tied directly to consumer ego and self-esteem. Interestingly, fans also CORF. That is, they cut off reflected failure by hiding their association with losing teams. These fans would often be called "fair-weather" fans. Obviously, sports marketers love fan BIRGing behavior and hope to minimize fan CORFing.[29]

- When a consumer displays some superiority over others by openly displaying exclusive products (as when we flaunt a nice car in front of others). The term *conspicuous consumption* describes a tendency of the wealthy to flaunt their material possessions as a way of displaying their social class. Numerous product categories, ranging from automobiles to jewelry, help to signal a consumer's status and can be used to convey images of consumer "superiority." By buying and displaying the correct products, consumers often feel that they can send the "I'm better than you are!" message.

Other Traits Found in Consumer Research

It should be emphasized that the preceding traits represent only a small fraction of the many traits that have been investigated in consumer research. Exhibit 6.1 highlights other traits that are often studied. Again, we emphasize that there are many more!

EXHIBIT 6.1
Examples of Other Traits in Consumer Research

Frugality The tendency of a consumer to exhibit restraint when facing purchases and using resources.

Impulsiveness The tendency for consumers to make impulsive, unintended purchases.

Trait Anxiety A tendency to respond with anxiety when facing threatening events.

Bargaining Proneness The tendency for a consumer to engage in bargaining behaviors when making purchases.

Trait Vanity The tendency for consumers to take excessive pride in themselves, including their appearance and accomplishments.

The Five-Factor Model Approach

One of the most popular multiple-trait approaches found in both personality psychology and consumer research is the **five-factor model** (FFM) approach.[30] Numerous studies have examined the influence of the traits found in the FFM on a wide range of behaviors, including behaviors both inside and outside of the field of consumer research. The FFM proposes that five dominant traits are found in the human personality, including:

1. Extroversion
2. Agreeableness
3. Openness to Experience (also referred to as "creativity")
4. Stability (sometimes referred to in a clinical way as "neuroticism")
5. Conscientiousness

Extroverted consumers are outgoing and talkative with others. Agreeable consumers are kind-hearted to others and sympathetic. Creative consumers are imaginative and enjoy new ideas. Stable consumers tend to be able to control their emotions and avoid mood swings. Conscientious consumers are careful, orderly, and precise. These traits are presented in Exhibit 6.2.

> **five-factor model**
> multiple-trait perspective that proposes that the human personality consists of five traits: agreeableness, extroversion, openness to experience (or creativity), conscientiousness, and neuroticism (or stability)

As we have stated, the FFM approach is a multiple-trait approach, meaning that a consumer's personality is conceptualized as a *combination* of these traits and that each consumer will vary on the respective traits. For example, Corbin might possess relatively strong degrees of extroversion, agreeableness, and openness, but he may not be very stable or conscientious. By examining consumers across the five dimensions of the FFM, we gain an expanded view of how multiple traits influence specific consumer behaviors.

The FFM approach is indeed popular with consumer researchers, and the traits found in the FFM have been shown to have an impact on such consumer behaviors as complaining, bargaining, banking, compulsive shopping, mass media consumption, and commitment to buying environmentally friendly products.[31]

EXHIBIT 6.2
Five-Factor Model

Personality Trait	Description
Extroversion	Talkative, outgoing
Agreeableness	Kindhearted, sympathetic
Openness to Experience	Creative, open to new ideas, imaginative
Stability	Even-keeled, avoids mood swings
Conscientiousness	Precise, efficient, organized

Source: Based on McCrae, R. R., and P. T. Costa (2005), *Personality in Adulthood: A Five-Factor Theory Perspective*, 2nd ed., New York, Guilford.

hierarchical approaches to personality approaches to personality inquiry that assume that personality traits exist at varying levels of abstraction

Even though the FFM has proved useful for presenting an integrative approach to personality, the model is not universally accepted by all researchers. In fact, there have been some lively debates regarding its usefulness.

Hierarchical Approaches to Personality Traits

If you are beginning to think that there are so many different approaches to trait psychology theory that it is hard to keep them all straight, you are not alone! Organizing all of these traits is one of the goals of what are known as **hierarchical approaches to personality**.

Hierarchical approaches begin with the assumption that personality traits exist at varying levels of abstraction. That is, some traits are very specific (complaint propensity), and others are more broad (extroversion). Specific traits refer to tendencies to behave in very well-defined situations. For example, a complaint-prone consumer is much more likely to complain about a steak that is overcooked than is a consumer who is not complaint prone. Here, the situation is very specific. Broad traits refer to tendencies to behave across many different situations. For example, an extroverted consumer may be very outgoing when with friends, when in a restaurant, or when in a shopping mall.

As a general statement, specific traits tend to be better predictors of individual behaviors than do broad traits. For example, knowing that someone is complaint prone would give us a pretty good idea that she will complain if her order isn't just right, but simply knowing that she is extroverted might not. A number of researchers have argued for the existence of these hierarchies.[32]

Final Thoughts on the Trait Approach

The trait approach in consumer research is very popular today in large part due to its ability to objectively assign a personality trait score to an individual consumer. In this way, the approach has an advantage over the psychoanalytic approach in which personality dimensions are assigned based on the psychologist's subjective interpretation. We should emphasize, however, that the approach is not without criticism. Exhibit 6.3 reveals a number of criticisms that have been leveled against trait research. [33]

Personology

We discussed previously that personality and motivation are closely related topics. A relatively new approach to researching consumers that combines personality theory and motivation is the "personology" approach. This approach allows consumer researchers to better understand the uniqueness of the individual consumer by combining information on traits, goals, and even consumer life stories in order to gain a better understanding of the complexities of the human personality.[34]

As you can see, many ways to view the human personality exist, and several different approaches to exploring the influence of personality on consumer behavior have been used. Personality inquiry, while controversial and not without limitations, continues to be a fruitful avenue of research for consumer researchers.

BRAND PERSONALITY

Do brands have personalities? Does your favorite brand of soft drink have a personality? Does the personality of the drink match your personality? These questions may sound a bit strange at first, but upon closer reflection, consumers do describe

EXHIBIT 6.3
Criticisms of the Trait Approach

- Personality traits have not traditionally been shown to be strong predictors of consumer behavior relative to other explanatory variables.
- So many personality traits exist that researchers often select traits for study without any logical theoretical basis.
- Personality traits are sometimes hard to measure, and researchers often use measures with questionable validity.
- Personality inventories used to measure traits are often meant for use on specific populations, but they are frequently applied to practically any consumer group.
- Researchers often measure and use traits in ways not originally intended.
- Consumer traits generally do not predict specific brand selections.

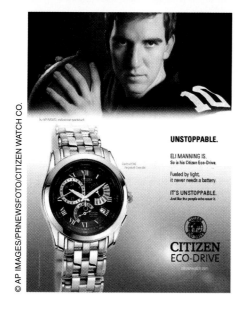

UNSTOPPABLE.

ELI MANNING IS.
So is his Citizen Eco-Drive.

Fueled by light,
it never needs a battery.

IT'S UNSTOPPABLE.
Just like the people who wear it.

CITIZEN
ECO-DRIVE

brands with human-like qualities. For example, how would you describe the personality of the Toyota Scion? What qualities are associated with Mountain Dew? How is Wrangler different from American Eagle?

Marketing managers and consumer researchers alike are very interested in the "personalities" of products. **Brand personality** refers to human characteristics that can be associated with a brand.[35] Brand personalities can be described across five dimensions including competence, excitement, ruggedness, sincerity, and sophistication. These dimensions are described in Exhibit 6.4.

Brand personalities represent opportunities for companies to differentiate their products. Accordingly, a brand's personality may be viewed as a part of its overall image.[36] A well-known Pepsi marketing campaign has attempted to position the brand as a "young and fun" brand. "Be Young! Have Fun!" is

the theme. Mountain Dew, a brand owned and marketed by PepsiCo, is an exciting, thrill-seeking brand. With cigarettes, Virginia Slims is often viewed as being feminine, while Marlboro is seen as being quite masculine.[37]

> **brand personality**
> collection of human characteristics that can be associated with a brand

Formation of Brand Personality

Many factors contribute to the development of a brand's personality.[38] A product's category can infer certain qualities. For example, if you hear the name *Sampson, Whitten, and Taylor* and find out that it is a law firm, you may develop an idea that the firm is serious, professional, and competent. If, however, you hear of a new brand of athletic wear called *Activesport*, you might expect the brand to be adventurous and outdoorsy. Other factors that contribute to the development of a brand's personality include packaging, price, sponsorships, symbols, and celebrity endorsers.

Personality and Brand Relationships

The brand personality concept is especially important when one considers that consumers, at least to some extent, have relationships with brands and that personality traits are important in the formation and maintenance of these relationships.[39] To illustrate, Coca-Cola's sincere and traditional personality enables the Coca-Cola Company to easily remind consumers that the brand has always been and will always be a part of their life. In fact, "Always Coca-Cola" is one of

EXHIBIT 6.4
Brand Personality Dimensions

Personality Trait	Description	Example
Competence	Responsible, reliable, dependable	Maytag—"Depend on Us"
Excitement	Daring, spirited	Mountain Dew—"Do the Dew!"
Ruggedness	Tough, strong	Ford Trucks—"Built Ford Tough"
Sincerity	Honest, genuine	Wrangler Jeans—"Genuine. Wrangler"
Sophistication	Glamorous, charming	Cartier jewelry—"Brilliance, Elegance, Exuberance"

Source: Based on Aaker, Jennifer (1997), "Dimensions of Brand Personality," *Journal of Marketing Research* (August), 347–356.

Coke's best-known advertising campaigns!

The concept of consumer–brand relationships has received considerable research attention, and several factors help indicate the level of relationship between a consumer and a brand. Consumer researcher Susan Fournier proposes that the overall quality of the relationship between consumer and brand can be described in terms of the following:[40]

- **Love and Passion.** A consumer may have such strong feelings about a brand that they actually describe it with the term *love*. A consumer may say, "I love my Dell Mini 10" or "I love Axe cologne."

- **Self-Connection.** Brands may help to express some central component of a consumer's identity. Research indicates that the correct match between a customer's personality and a perceived brand personality leads to higher overall satisfaction.[41]

- **Commitment.** In a strong consumer–brand relationship, consumers are very committed to their brands and feel very loyal to them. Harley-Davidson owners are well-known for their commitment to their bikes. In fact, the H.O.G. (Harley Owners' Group) is the largest factory-sponsored group in the world, with more than one million members![42]

- **Interdependence.** Consumer–brand relationships may be marked by interdependence between the product and the consumer. This can be described in terms of the frequency of use, the diversity of brand-related situations, and intense product usage. For example, consumers are often reminded that "Like a good neighbor, State Farm is there."

Demographics Today

The study of demographics is known as *demography*. Demographic variables include age, ethnicity, income, family size, and occupation.

- Age. Age is important not only because of its descriptive nature, but also because consumers who experience significant life events at approximately the same age are influenced greatly by the events. This is the "cohort effect." Groups such as "Tweens or Preteens" (born between 1998 - 2001), "Generation Y or Millennials" (born between 1981 – 1995), "Generation X" (born between 1966 – 1980), and "Baby Boomers" (born between 1946 – 1965) are identifiable segments. Baby boomers receive a lot of attention because of the group's size and spending power.

- Ethnicity. Diversity is growing in the United States. "Minority" groups (such as Hispanics, African Americans, and Asian Americans) are expected to grow considerably in the years to come. In fact, projections reveal that by 2050, the "minority" segment will exceed more than half of the total population![1]

- Income. Income is another important variable. "Engel's Law" states that as income increases, a smaller percentage of expenditures is devoted to food, and the percentage devoted to consumption rises slower than the rise in income.

These variables usually need to be combined with other variables, like psychographics. Failing to do so leads to the trap of assuming that all consumers of a certain description have the exact same tastes. An example is found in the concept of "psychological age." A person's actual age and his or her psychological age can be very different. As they say, "today's sixty is yesterday's forty." This is why researchers should always be cautious when relying on demographic information.

Sources: "An Older and More Diverse Nation By Midcentury", *U.S. Census Bureau News*, Washington, D.C., online content found at **http://www.census.gov/population/www/projections/index.html**, accessed March 20, 2009.

- **Intimacy.** Strong relationships between consumers and brands can be described as intimate. Deep-seated needs and desires of consumers can be tied directly to specific brands. For example, a need for intimacy and passion can be directly tied to a specific brand of perfume, like Obsession. A need for excitement or status can be related to a sporty automobile, like Porsche.

- **Brand Partner Quality.** In general, brands that are perceived to be of high quality contribute to the formation of consumer–brand relationships. In this sense, consumers develop feelings of trust regarding specific brands, and these feelings of trust foster consumer–brand relationships. Research reveals that brand personality traits also affect customer–brand relationship quality when service problems occur, with sincere brands suffering more than exciting brands when service breakdowns occur.[43]

LO3 Consumer Lifestyles and Psychographics

the term *lifestyle* is used commonly in everyday life. For example, we often speak of "healthy lifestyles," "unhealthy lifestyles," "alternative lifestyles," and even "dangerous lifestyles." The term has also been used in many ways in consumer research. Stated simply, consumer **lifestyles** refer to the ways consumers live and spend their time and money.

Personality and lifestyles are closely related topics. In fact, lifestyles have been referred to as context-specific personality traits.[44] This has implications for how the concepts are measured. That is, instead of asking a consumer if she is the "outdoor type," a lifestyle approach will ask the consumer about the amount of time she spends outdoors and what she does when she is outdoors. Importantly, lifestyles aren't completely determined by personality. Instead, they emerge from the influence of culture, group influence, and individual processes, including personality.[45] Not surprisingly, consumer lifestyles vary considerably across cultures.

Lifestyles have proved extremely valuable to marketers and others interested in predicting behavior. Purchase patterns are often influenced by consumer lifestyles, and numerous lifestyle categories can be identified. It shouldn't be surprising, therefore, that marketers often target consumers based on lifestyles. For example, Pepsi's Code Red has been aimed at active, young male consumers, while Dasani water appeals to the more health-conscious consumer. Because lifestyle can be directly tied to product purchase and consumption, consumer lifestyles are considered an important manifestation of social stratification.[46] In other words, they are very useful in identifying viable market segments.

Appealing to a consumer's lifestyle is so important that it's not uncommon to see advertisements focusing as much on lifestyle as on the actual product itself. One recent commercial for the Ford Freestyle shows a happy American family enjoying a nice weekend trip together, only to later reveal that the father is being dropped off alone at his apartment. This advertisement, addressing a serious change in family composition and lifestyle, signals the importance of letting customers know that a company understands their situations and lifestyles. Marketing messages like these become very personal when lifestyles are addressed.[47]

> Purchase patterns are often influenced by consumer lifestyles, and numerous lifestyle categories can be identified.

PSYCHOGRAPHICS

The term **psychographics** refers to the way consumer lifestyles are measured. Psychographic techniques use quantitative methods that can be used in developing lifestyle profiles. Notice that this is not the same thing as demographics. **Demographics** refers to observable, statistical aspects of populations including things such as age, gender, or income. Lifestyles, although also observable, refer to how consumers live.

Although psychographic research has been used to investigate lifestyles for many years, advances in technology have helped psychographics become even more popular with consumer researchers and marketing managers today. Psychographic analysis involves surveying consumers using **AIO statements**, which are used to gain an understanding of consumers' activities, interests, and opinions. These measurements can be narrowly defined (as relating to a specific product or product category) or broadly defined (as pertaining to general activities that the consumer enjoys).

Consumer segments very often contain consumers with similar lifestyles. As an example, one recent effort to identify segments in the European tourism industry resulted in the following lifestyle segment profiles:[48]

- **Home Loving.** Fundamentally focused on the family, this segment values product quality. These consumers enjoy cultural activities such as visiting art exhibits and monuments. The home-loving group takes the greatest number of long, family-oriented travel vacations.

- **Idealistic.** These responsible consumers believe that the road to success is based on bettering the world. They enjoy classical music and theater. Travel destinations for this group are primarily rural locations and country villages.

- **Autonomous.** These independent-thinking consumers strive to be upwardly mobile. They enjoy the nightlife and read few newspapers. This segment enjoys weekend travel.

- **Hedonistic.** The hedonistic segment values human relationships and work. They are interested in new product offerings and enjoy listening to music. These consumers enjoy visiting large cities.

- **Conservative.** Like the home-loving segment, this segment focuses largely on the family. These consumers tend to view success simply as doing a good job with their careers. This group dislikes nightlife and modern music and instead focuses on issues related to religion, law, and order. These consumers take few weekend trips, but they do enjoy visiting seaside destinations.

Another effort to segment the baby-boomer market (those consumers born between the years of 1945 and 1964) resulted in four distinct lifestyle groups: [49]

- **Upbeat Enjoyers.** These enthusiastic and upbeat consumers enjoy wearing the latest style in clothes and would enjoy one day living in condominiums.

- **Insecure.** These financially constrained boomers focus on satisfying their daily needs and products that make them appear younger (cosmetics, etc.).

- **Threatened Actives.** These successful active adults look for good times in the future. They would consider moving into safer neighborhoods after retirement.

- **Financial Positives.** These boomers have been successful in their careers and focus on the long term. They are quite savvy consumers who hope to enjoy retirement.

Other attempts to describe the psychographic profiles of various consumer groups have resulted in lifestyle segments being identified for Harley-Davidson owners (including "cocky misfits" and "classy capitalists"),[50] wine drinkers (including "conservatives," "experimenters," and "image oriented"),[51] and Porsche owners (including "top guns," "elitists," and "fantasists").[52] As you can see from the many examples here, there are several ways to segment consumers based on lifestyles.

Specificity of Lifestyle Segments

The lifestyle approaches that we have discussed here can be categorized in terms of specificity—either narrowly defined or more broadly defined. Generally, lifestyles are indeed quite specific. The magazine industry is particularly efficient at identifying consumer lifestyles and developing products around lifestyle segments. For example, consumers who skateboard can read magazines such as *Thrasher* while those who enjoy paintball can read *PB2Xtremes*. Exhibit 6.5 presents sample measures used for psychographic analysis for the leisure bowling segment.

VALS

When using lifestyle segmentation, a marketer can either identify his or her own segments or use established methods that are already available. One popular method in consumer research is the VALS™ approach.[53] Developed and marketed by SRI International, VALS is a very successful segmentation approach that has been adopted by several companies. **VALS** stands for "*Values and Lifestyles.*" The current approach, known as VALS2, classifies consumers into eight distinct segments that are based on resources available to the consumer (including financial, educational, and intellectual resources), as well as three primary motivations (ideals motivation, achievement motivation, and self-expression motivation).

VALS2 includes eight groups:

- **Innovators.** Innovators are successful, sophisticated people who have high self-esteem. They are motivated by achievement, ideals, and self-expression. Image is important to these consumers.

- **Thinkers.** Thinkers are ideal motivated. They are mature, reflective people who value order and knowledge. They have relatively high income and are conservative, practical consumers.

© COMSTOCK IMAGES/JUPITERIMAGES

EXHIBIT 6.5
Sample Psychographic Items for Segmenting the Bowling Market

TYPE OF ITEM	EXAMPLE	Strongly Disagree	Disagree	Neutral	Agree	Strongly Agree
Activity	I spend much of my free time bowling.	☐	☐	☐	☐	☐
Interest	I am very interested in the latest developments in bowling ball technology.	☐	☐	☐	☐	☐
Opinion	Bowling is truly "America's favorite sport."	☐	☐	☐	☐	☐

- **Achievers.** Achievers have an achievement motivation and are politically conservative. Their lives largely center around church, family, and career. Image is important to this group, and they prefer to purchase prestige products.

- **Experiencers.** Experiencers are self-expressive consumers who tend to be young, impulsive, and enthusiastic. These consumers value novelty and excitement.

- **Believers.** In some ways, believers are like thinkers. They are ideal motivated and conservative. They follow routines, and their lives largely center around home, family, and church. They do not have the amount of resources that thinkers have, however.

- **Strivers.** Strivers are achievement motivated, but they do not have the amount of resources that are available to achievers. For strivers, shopping is a way to demonstrate to others their ability to buy.

- **Makers.** Makers are like experiencers in that they are motivated by self-expression. They have fewer resources than do experiencers. They tend to express themselves through their activities such as raising children, fixing cars, and building houses.

- **Survivors.** Survivors are very low on resources and are constricted by this lack of resources. They tend to be elderly consumers who are concerned with health issues and who believe that the world is changing too quickly. They are not active in the marketplace, as their primary concerns center around safety, family, and security.

PRIZM

Another popular tool for lifestyle analysis is a geodemographic procedure known as PRIZM.[54] **Geodemo-** **graphic techniques** combine data on consumer expenditures and socioeconomic variables with geographic information in order to identify commonalities in consumption patterns of households in various regions. **PRIZM** is a popular lifestyle analysis technique that was developed by Claritas, Inc. (**http://www.claritas.com**). PRIZM, which stands for Potential Ratings Index by ZIP Market, is based on the premise that people with similar backgrounds and means tend to live close to one another and emulate each other's behaviors and lifestyles.

PRIZM combines demographic and behavioral information in a manner that enables marketers to better understand and target their customers. The technique uses 66 different segments as descriptors of individual households, which are ranked according to socioeconomic variables. Segments found using the PRIZM technique include "Movers and Shakers," "Money and

© CLARITAS, A NIELSEN COMPANY

You can explore PRIZM segments at the Claritas website. Check out your favorite U.S. ZIP Code!

Brains," "Red, White and Blues," and "Back Country Folks." There are other techniques that are available as well, including ESRI's GIS and Mapping Software (**http://www.esri.com**).

LO4 The Role of Self-Concept in Consumer Behavior

the self-concept is another important topic in consumer behavior. The term **self-concept** refers to the totality of thoughts and feelings that an individual has about him- or herself. Self-concept can also be thought of as the way a person defines or gives meaning to his or her own identity, as in a type of self-schema.

Consumers are motivated to act in accordance with their self-concepts. As such, consumers often use products as ways of revealing their self-concepts to others. According to a **symbolic interactionism** perspective, consumers agree on the shared meaning of products and symbols.[55] These symbols can become part of the self-concept if the consumer identifies with them strongly.

An important field of study that relates to the symbolic interactionism approach is semiotics. **Semiotics**

The Presentation of Self in Cyberspace

It will probably come as no surprise that the latest estimates reveal that 93% of American teenagers use the Internet and more than half of teenagers aged 12 – 17 use social networking sites such as MySpace and facebook. In addition, 55% of online teens have posted profiles about themselves on these websites.

Websites such as facebook.com and myspace.com allow users to post various aspects of their lives and present themselves in almost limitless ways. Although privacy concerns keep some posters from revealing too much about themselves, other posters seem to feel that almost any detail of their life is fair game. Some posters feel that most anything can be added to their profiles. This becomes a problem when too much information is given and stalkers view the postings and begin to stalk posters. Unfortunately, this is becoming more common. Also, employers are beginning to use these websites as a way to learn more about prospective employees. This brings a whole new perspective to the "ideal social self"! Although the Internet allows consumers to post all kinds of material about themselves, commonsense rules still apply.

Sources: Based on Duyn, Aline Van (2007), "Teenagers Love Social Networking Sites," *Financial Times* (January 8), 18; Smith, Diane (2007), "Kids Using Myspace Are Mostly Cautious," *Knight Ridder Tribune Business News* (January 9), 1; Rowland, Kara (2007), "Teens Using Network Sites Safely," *Knight Ridder Tribune Business News* (January 8), 1. *Pew Internet & American Life Project*, "*Teen Privacy and Online Social Networks*", April 18, 2007, online retrieval at: **http://pewinternet.org/pdfs/PIP_Teens_Privacy_SNS_Report_Final.pdf**, retrieved March 9, 2009.

refers to the study of symbols and their meanings. As we have stated, consumers use products as symbols to convey their self-concepts to others. In this sense, products are an essential part of self-expression.[56] The increased popularity of Internet blogging and websites like myspace.com and facebook.com allow consumers to have a new and exciting method of expressing their selves.[57]

Let's first explore various dimensions of the "self" before examining how a consumer's self-concept influences various behaviors. First, we note that a consumer will have a number of "concepts" about him- or herself that may emerge over time and surface in different social situations.[58] A few of the different "self-concepts" that may emerge include the actual self, the ideal self, the social self, the ideal social self, the possible self, and the extended self.[59]

The *actual self* refers to how a consumer currently perceives him- or herself (that is, who I am). The *ideal self* refers to how a consumer would like to perceive himself (that is, who I would like to be in the future). The *social self* refers to the beliefs that a consumer has about how he or she is seen by others. The social self is also called the "looking-glass" self because it denotes the image that a consumer has when he or she looks into the mirror and imagines how others see him or her. The *ideal social self* represents the image that a consumer would like others to have about him or her. The *possible self*, much like the ideal self, presents an image of what the consumer could become, whereas the *extended self* represents the various possessions that a consumer owns that helps him form perceptions about himself.

The relationship between consumer self-concept and product consumption is a two-way street. That is, consumers express their self-concepts by purchasing and displaying various products, while products help to define how the consumer sees himself or herself.[60] Note that the relationship between the self-concept and consumption is not limited to adult consumers only, as consumer–brand connections have been shown to form as early as childhood![61]

SELF-CONCEPT AND BODY PRESENTATION

The issue of self-concept in consumer behavior has several practical implications. For example, the cosmetics and weight-loss industries are well-known for offering products that purportedly help improve perceptions of one's self-image. The term **self-esteem** refers to the positivity of an individual's self-concept. The effect of advertising on consumers' self-esteem is an important topic in this area.

The fashion industry is constantly under fire for promoting overly thin models and body types. In fact, research confirms that consumers compare their bodies with those of models found in advertisements, and that these comparisons often have harmful effects. This is particularly the case for young females.[62]

In response to growing public concern regarding this issue, the Council of Fashion Designers of America (CFDA) recently released updated guidelines to encourage healthy eating habits and to discourage the use of overly thin models in advertisements. "The fashion business should be sensitive to the fact that we do have a responsibility in affecting young girls and their self-image," CFDA president Diane Von Furstenburg commented.[63] The problem is not solely for women, however, as evidence suggests that male consumers are also largely affected by unrealistic body imagery in advertising as well.[64] Although the industry has received much negative publicity, we do note that not all model effects are negative. In fact, consumers can sometimes feel better about themselves when they find similarities between their bodies and the bodies of models.[65]

Unilever Corp. recently addressed the issue of unrealistic body types with their Real Beauty campaign for the brand Dove. A basic motivation of the campaign is to provide more realistic views of beauty and to improve the self-esteem of both women and young girls.

self-esteem positivity of the self-concept that one holds

IMAGE COURTESY OF THE ADVERTISING ARCHIVES

curvy thighs, bigger bums, rounder stomachs. What better way to test our firming range?

Marketers like Unilever realize the importance of promoting realistic body images.

Cosmetic Surgery and Body Modification

Because of the many ways in which consumers compare themselves to others, it is easy to understand why many medical procedures that promise to improve a consumer's perception of his or her body are now being offered. According to the American Society for Aesthetic Plastic Surgery, nearly 11.7 million cosmetic procedures were performed in the U.S. in the year 2007 alone. Breast augmentation, lipoplasty, and eyelid surgery were common procedures for female patients, while liposuction and rhinopasty were popular among men. The majority of procedures were found among consumers aged 35–50.[66]

self-congruency theory
theory that proposes that much of consumer behavior can be explained by the congruence of a consumer's self-concept with the image of typical users of a focal product

Body Piercings and Tattooing

Body piercings and other forms of body decorations, such as tattooing, represent other methods of promoting one's self-concept. The growth of piercing among college-aged students is particularly noteworthy as it has been estimated that approximately 51% of undergraduate students have some form of piercing.[67] In fact, the growth in popularity of these behaviors suggests that new attitudes about the body and its role in self-presentation are emerging.[68]

While body piercings are popular forms of self-expression and are frequently used as innocent methods of self-expression, research also indicates that the use of piercings can sometimes be associated with increased levels of drug and alcohol use, unprotected sexual activity, trait anxiety, and depression.[69]

> For consumers, body piercing and tattooing have become more popular than ever.

LO5 Self-Congruency Theory and Consumer Behavior

reference group members share similar symbolic meanings. This is an important assumption of **self-congruency theory**. This theory proposes that much of consumer behavior can be explained by the congruence (match) between a consumer's self-concept and the image of typical users of a focal product.[70] For example, one study found that store loyalty is largely influenced by the degree of congruency between self-image and store image.[71] How would you describe shoppers of a popular store like PacSun? Hollister? American Eagle? Do you possess any of these characteristics?

SEGMENTATION AND SELF-CONGRUENCY

Marketers can use congruency theory by segmenting markets into groups of consumers who perceive high self-concept congruence with product-user image. Imagine a consumer who sees himself as being a stylish person. If he believes that people who drive Corvettes are stylish, then he will be motivated to drive a Corvette. In this way, brands become vehicles for self-expression.[72]

As discussed earlier, there are several types of self-concepts, and different products may relate to each concept. That is, one product may relate quite well to the actual self-concept, but not as strongly to the ideal self-concept. One study found that the purchase of privately consumable items (such as frozen dinners or suntan lotion) is heavily influenced by the actual self-concept while the purchase of publicly visible products (like clothing) is more strongly related to the ideal self-concept.[73]

A recent advertising campaign for Jaguar automobiles illustrates the importance of the ideal self-concept in consumer behavior. The ad presents a series of consumers simply looking into the camera and saying, "I will own a Jaguar." Here, the idea is that the consumers are moving closer to their ideal self-concept by being successful enough to own a Jaguar automobile. Rolex also has a long history of positioning its watches as the watch for the successful consumer who pursues excellence. Rolex is well-known for being the watch for people who have either "arrived" or who soon will be "arriving."

Final Thought on Personality, Lifestyles, and the Self-Concept

Personality, lifestyles, and the self-concept are all important topics in the study of consumer behavior. Consumers differ across each of these concepts, and these differences help signal the need for targeted marketing communications. As technological advancements continue to develop, it can be expected that marketing managers and consumer researchers alike will continue to be interested in these topics.

Chapter 6 Case

I t's Saturday morning in Manhattan Beach, California. The clock shows 6:00 A.M. when the phone rings. "Hello," Jon-Michael answers, knowing it's his buddy Ben.

The voice replies, "Dawn patrol! Wake up, Jonny! I just looked at it and it's going off . . . light offshore winds, two feet overhead, nice lines, outgoing tide. Insane! And it's only going to get better! Meet me in the water off Forty-second. Thirty minutes."

Jon-Michael replies, "Awesome! I'm hitting a cup of coffee and bagel, and I'll be there."

He kisses his wife's forehead and is out of bed in an instant. He and Ben are in the water, hitting amazing waves, before sunrise.

A bit later, at 10:00 A.M., the phone rings again. "Hello," Latonia answers, knowing it's her best friend Bebe. The voice replies, "Good morning, Latonia. Are you ready?" "Almost," Latonia replies. "Do you want to start at that cute café overlooking the water on Highland Avenue for breakfast?" "You mean Uncle Bob's Pancake Hut?" Bebe asks. "Yes!" Latonia answers. Bebe adds, "That sounds so good. Then I was thinking we could go to the mall. I heard Victoria's Secret is having a sale." "Great!" Latonia adds, "Let's do it!"

Jon-Michael and Latonia are a great couple, their values and principles are similar, and in many ways they can be segmented to the same categories. Here's how they can be described in marketing lingo:

Age: 25 to 30
Ethnicity: Caucasian
Socioeconomic: Upper-middle class
Education: Bachelor's or higher (both have Master's), well traveled
Income: $75,000 plus
Location: Prime beach community (Manhattan Beach) near large metropolitan city (Los Angeles)

Although they fit into these categories neatly, it's their personalities and lifestyles that create both challenges and opportunities for marketers. For example, consider these differences:

PRIORITY ACTIVITIES

Jon-Michael: surfing, fishing, diving, wakeboarding, snowboarding, hang gliding, going to concerts, traveling

Latonia: socializing, shopping, reading, relaxing on the beach

VIEW OF SHOPPING

Jon-Michael: Loathes shopping and shops only if it is absolutely necessary, that is, if the purchase serves a function. His purchases are deliberate. Shopping has to compete for his time.

Latonia: Loves shopping. It makes her feel good. She engages in shopping as an activity, and she's careful with her purchases. She makes time to shop!

PURCHASE MOTIVATORS

Both Jon-Michael and Latonia buy because the personality of the brand matches their personality. However, there are differences:

Jon-Michael: It's all about convenience and value. He does not like the name of the brand to show, and he buys more for what the product doesn't have—flash, apparent statements. Price is not as important as convenience.

Latonia: It's all about image. She prefers designer clothing. She likes the brand to be recognizable and for the message to be perceived almost immediately.

Questions

1. How can the use of a celebrity endorsement have a positive impact for Latonia and a negative impact for Jon-Michael?

2. To maximize value in the shopping experience, what attributes about shopping and the product should be emphasized if one were marketing to Latonia? What attributes about shopping and the product should be emphasized to Jon-Michael in order to maximize value?

3. How could researchers take a nomothetic approach to understanding the psychological makeup of these consumers?

4. How could self-congruency theory apply to this case?

5. What types of shopping value apply most readily to Jon-Michael and Latonia?

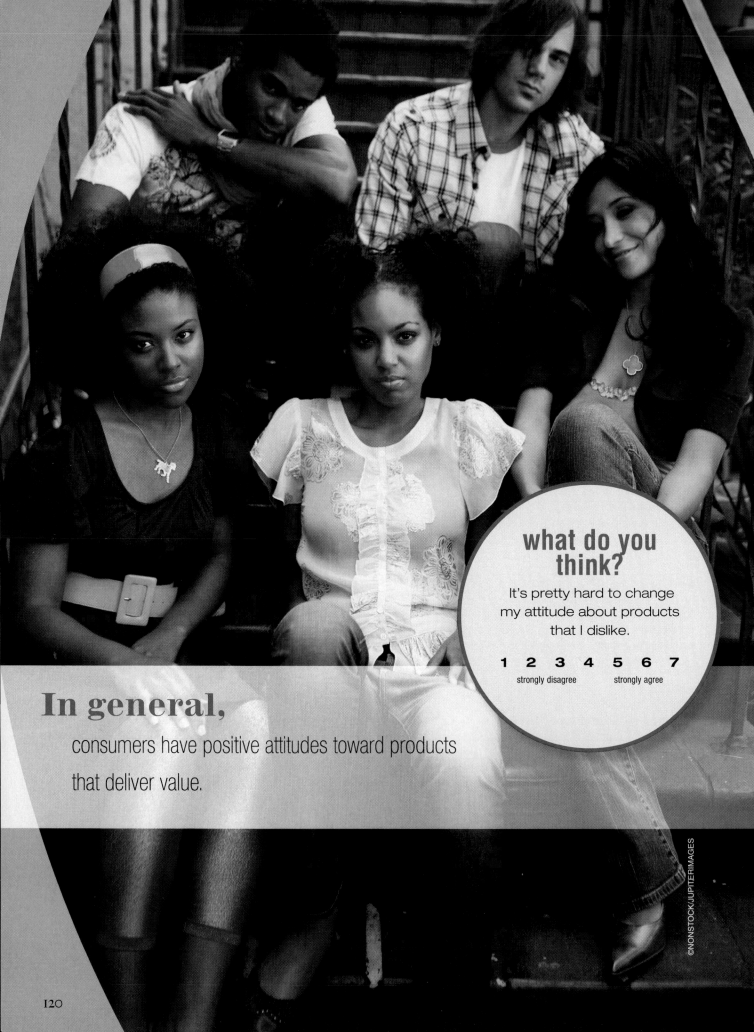

what do you think?

It's pretty hard to change my attitude about products that I dislike.

1 2 3 4 5 6 7

strongly disagree   strongly agree

In general,

consumers have positive attitudes toward products that deliver value.

7

Attitudes and Attitude Change

Introduction

rachel loves her new Honda Civic. She has owned Hondas in the past, and her new Civic is just what she has wanted. Although most of her friends don't seem to be very attached to their cars, Rachel loves hers and really likes the value that it provides. Although it may sound a bit extreme, she's even been known to write about her car on her Internet blog.

Getting consumers to feel this strongly about a product is something that marketers constantly try to achieve. When consumers have positive attitudes toward products, they often promote them to others. This is a win–

> **attitudes** relatively enduring overall evaluations of objects, products, services, issues, or people

win situation for both the customer and the company. Conversely, negative attitudes can have a profound impact as well. Some people become so upset with a company and its products that they boycott everything the company sells—and tell others that they should do the same.

Understanding the factors that influence consumer attitudes is very important for marketers. This may seem obvious, but the importance of consumer attitudes is found in nontraditional settings as well. For example, politicians want to know how voters *feel* about candidates. City managers want to know if citizens will *approve* of some new construction project. Musicians want to know if consumers will *like* their new album. In each of these examples, consumer attitudes are very important.

LO1 Attitudes and Attitude Components

he term *attitude* has been used in many ways. **Attitudes** are relatively enduring overall evaluations of objects, products, services, issues, or people.[1] Attitudes play a critical role in consumer behavior, and they

After studying this chapter, the student should be able to:

LO1 Define attitudes and describe attitude components.

LO2 Describe the functions of attitudes.

LO3 Understand how the hierarchy of effects concept applies to attitude theory.

LO4 Comprehend the major consumer attitude models.

LO5 Describe attitude change theories and their role in persuasion.

LO6 Understand how message and source effects influence persuasion.

ABC approach to attitudes approach that suggests that attitudes encompass one's **a**ffect, **b**ehavior, and **c**ognitions (or "beliefs") toward an object

functional theory of attitudes theory of attitudes that suggests that attitudes perform four basic functions

utilitarian function of attitudes function of attitudes in which consumers use attitudes as ways to maximize rewards and minimize punishment

knowledge function of attitudes function of attitudes whereby attitudes allow consumers to simplify decision-making processes

are especially important because they motivate people to behave in relatively consistent ways. It is therefore not surprising that the attitude concept is one of the most researched topics in the entire field of consumer research. In fact, attitude is one of the most popular concepts in all of the social sciences.

We note that attitudes and value are closely related. Recall from our opening example that Rachel is very pleased with the value that her Civic provides. In general, consumers have positive attitudes toward products that provide value. Likewise, when products deliver poor value, consumer attitudes are usually negative. In order to appreciate how attitudes influence consumer behavior, we need to distinguish between the various components of attitudes and the functions that attitudes perform.

COMPONENTS OF ATTITUDE

According to the **ABC approach to attitudes**, attitudes possess three important components: *a*ffect, *b*ehavior, and *c*ognitions (or beliefs). To understand these components, consider the following statements:

© AP IMAGES/PRNEWSFOTO/HONDA CIVIC TOUR

- "I really like my Honda Civic."
- "I always buy Honda products."
- "My Honda Civic gets good gas mileage."

These statements reflect the three components of a consumer's attitude found in the ABC approach. "I really like my Honda Civic" is a statement of affect because the feelings, or affection, a consumer has about a car is captured in liking. "I always buy Honda" refers to one's behavior regarding the Honda automobile. "My Honda Civic gets good gas mileage" is a cognitive statement that expresses the owner's belief about the car's gas mileage.

LO2 Functions of Attitudes

knowing that attitudes represent relatively enduring evaluations of products and that attitudes can be broken into three components is valuable. But what's the big deal about attitudes? What do they do for the consumer?

According to the **functional theory of attitudes**, attitudes perform four functions.[2] The four functions are the *utilitarian* function, the *knowledge* function, the *value-expressive* function, and the *ego-defensive* function. These functions are summarized in Exhibit 7.1.

Utilitarian Function

The **utilitarian function of attitudes** is based on the concept of reward and punishment. This means that consumers learn to use attitudes as ways to maximize rewards and minimize punishment. One way in which consumers maximize rewards through expressing attitudes is by gaining acceptance from others. Consumers often express their attitudes in order to develop and maintain relationships. A recent study of college sports fans presents an example. In the study, football fans revealed that one of the many reasons to wear their team's apparel is to help fans make and enjoy connections with new friends.[3] In other words, the outward behavior of wearing the apparel leads to the desired consequence of making friends and having fun.

Knowledge Function

The **knowledge function of attitudes** allows consumers to simplify decision-making processes. For instance, if

EXHIBIT 7.1
Functions of Consumer Attitudes

Attitude Function	Description	Example
Utilitarian	Attitudes are used as a method to obtain rewards and to minimize punishment.	Fraternity brothers express attitude to enjoy a sense of belonging to the group.
Knowledge	The knowledge function of attitudes allows consumers to simplify their decision-making processes.	Consumers may not like to listen to telemarketers and will therefore avoid calls from them.
Value-expressive	This function of attitudes enables consumers to express their core values, self-concept, and beliefs to others.	Consumers commonly attach bumper stickers to their cars to express their attitudes about products and social issues.
Ego-defensive	The ego-defensive function of attitudes works as a defense mechanism for consumers to avoid facts or to defend themselves from their own low self-concept.	Smokers use their positive feelings about smoking to filter out incoming information that suggests that the behavior is bad for their health.

value-expressive function of attitudes function of attitudes whereby attitudes allow consumers to express their core values, self-concept, and beliefs to others

ego-defensive function of attitudes function of attitudes whereby attitudes work as a defense mechanism for consumers

© AP IMAGES/PRNEWSFOTO/NEW ERA CAP COMPANY, INC.
© DAVE KAUP/REUTERS/LANDOV

the telephone rings during dinner and the caller I.D. says "unavailable," a consumer might think "I hate telemarketers!" and decide not to answer the phone. Or, a consumer might see a salesperson approaching him from a mall kiosk and realize that he doesn't like dealing with pushy salespeople, and decide to walk the other way. In each case, the decision-making process of the consumer is simplified. Attitudes therefore perform the important function of helping consumers avoid undesirable situations and approach more desirable situations.

Attitude components become stored in the associative network in consumers' long-term memory and become linked together to form rules that guide behavior. You may remember from our comprehension chapter that comprehension includes affective and cognitive elements. Here, one can easily see that attitudes are indeed related to both comprehension and knowledge.

Value-Expressive Function

The **value-expressive function of attitudes** is found in a number of consumer settings. This function enables a consumer to express his or her core values, self-concept, and beliefs to others. A good example of these expressions can be found in sports marketing. Most baseball fans know about the intense rivalry between the Boston Red Sox and the New York Yankees. A Red Sox fan is likely to express love for the team by wearing Red Sox clothing. A New York Yankee fan is likely to wear pinstripes and Yankee hats but never Red Sox gear. Wearing team apparel is a way to outwardly express love for a team or a product. Remember from our personality chapter that consumers also BIRG after their favorite team wins a big game.

Another setting where the value-expressive function can be seen at work is with products such as bumper stickers, posters, t-shirts, or even Internet blogs. Ultimately, the expression of attitudes becomes a mechanism by which consumers can make statements about closely held values.

Ego-Defensive Function

Finally, the **ego-defensive function of attitudes** works as a defense mechanism for consumers. There are a couple of ways in which this function works. First, the ego-defensive function enables a consumer to protect himself or herself

CHAPTER 7: ATTITUDES AND ATTITUDE CHANGE **123**

hierarchy of effects
attitude approach that suggests that affect, behavior, and cognitions form in a sequential order

from information that may be threatening. For example, people who like to smoke may discount any evidence that smoking is bad for their health. In this case, the attitude works as a defense mechanism that protects the individual from the reality that smoking isn't healthy.

Another example of the ego-defensive function is when a consumer develops positive attitudes toward products that enhance his or her self-image. Consider college freshman April. April likes to wear expensive brand name clothing because she is concerned about how people perceive her physical attractiveness. April's positive attitude toward expensive brands helps her to project a positive image.

LO3 Hierarchy of Effects

a s discussed earlier, the ABC approach to consumer attitudes suggests that there are three components to attitudes: affect, behavior, and cognition. Research indicates that these components may be formed in a sequential pattern. This attitude formation process is known as the **hierarchy of effects** approach.[4] According to this approach, affect, behavior, and cognitions form by following one of the four following hierarchies:

1. High-involvement (or standard learning) hierarchy
2. Low-involvement hierarchy
3. Experiential hierarchy
4. Behavioral influence hierarchy

These hierarchies are discussed in the next section and are presented in Exhibit 7.2.

HIGH-INVOLVEMENT HIERARCHY

The high-involvement, or standard learning, hierarchy of effects occurs when a consumer faces a high involvement decision. High-involvement decisions are important to a consumer and often contain significant risk. In this hierarchy, beliefs about products are formed first. The consumer carefully considers various product features and develops cognitions (beliefs) about each feature. Next, feelings, or evaluations, about the prod-

EXHIBIT 7.2
Hierarchy of Effects

Purchase Context	Hierarchy of Effects
High involvement	Belief–affect–behavior
Low involvement	Belief–behavior–affect
Experiential	Affect–behavior–belief
Behavioral Influence	Behavior–belief–affect

uct are formed. The consumer may begin to think the product is good and will suit his or her needs based on the beliefs that have been formed. Finally, after beliefs and feelings are formed, the consumer decides to act in some way toward the product. Here, a purchase decision is made. The consumer may decide to buy (or not buy) the product.

Imagine the process that Matt went through when he bought a new gaming system. Matt knew that it would be a significant purchase, and he was therefore careful about his selection. He first considered the various attributes of each system and began to develop favorable evaluations toward a few of the brands. Realizing that he felt best about the Xbox 360™, he decided that this would be the one to buy.

LOW-INVOLVEMENT HIERARCHY

This standard learning approach was once considered the best approach to take in order to understand consumer attitude formation. Marketers began to realize, however, that consumer purchases are often neither risky nor involving. In fact, many purchases are routine and boring.[5]

When low-involvement purchases are made, consumers often have some basic beliefs about products without necessarily having strong feelings toward them. Sam, a self-proclaimed computer geek, may not carefully consider the feelings that he has toward a brand of fabric softener. He may simply think, "Downy® is popular, so I'll buy it." Only after he buys and uses the product will he develop any type of feeling, or evaluation, of the softener. At first, he thinks "Downy is popular" (cognition) and he decides to buy it (behavior). Only later does he say "I like Downy" (affect). Chances are, however, that he would carefully consider computer features first, develop an overall like or dislike for each

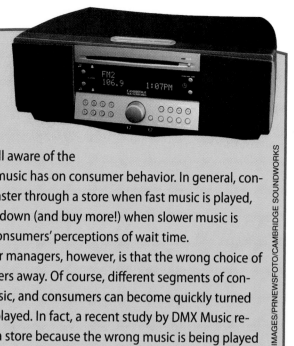

Change the Station, Please

Retail managers are well aware of the powerful effects that music has on consumer behavior. In general, consumers tend to walk faster through a store when fast music is played, and they tend to slow down (and buy more!) when slower music is played. Music can even impact consumers' perceptions of wait time.

What is equally important for managers, however, is that the wrong choice of music may actually drive customers away. Of course, different segments of consumers like different types of music, and consumers can become quickly turned off if the wrong kind of music is played. In fact, a recent study by DMX Music reveals that the tendency to leave a store because the wrong music is being played cuts across demographic segments. Quite simply, no one likes to be bombarded with bad music! As a major supplier for retail soundtracks, DMX understands that the right choice of background music can be a critical factor in retail success. Managers should pay close attention. Changing the station may significantly impact the bottom line!

Sources: Anonymous (2005), "Special Report: The Tills Are Alive," *In-Store* (October 7) 27; Ebenkamp, Becky (2004), "Songs in the Key of Flee," *Brandweek* (February 16) 17; Morrison, Michael, and Michael Beverland (2003), "In Search of the Right In-Store Music," *Business Horizons*, 46 (November–December), 77; Milliman, R.E. (1986), "Using Background Music to Affect the Behavior of Supermarket Shoppers," *Journal of Marketing*, 46, 86–91.

brand, and then buy one model or another. As such, it is easy to see that the purchase of a $1,200 computer system is much more involving for Sam than a $3.00 bottle of fabric softener.

EXPERIENTIAL HIERARCHY

Many purchases are based on feelings. That is, consumers purchase products or perform behaviors simply because it "feels good" or "feels right." For example, when a student decides to visit a new dance club, he makes the decision simply because it sounds like a fun thing to do.

Impulse purchases can be explained from the experiential perspective. These purchases are often motivated by feelings. Impulse purchasing means that a consumer buys a product spontaneously and with little concern for consequences. Dessert items are often purchased on impulse. When the waiter brings the tray by, the chocoholic feels strongly about one of the desserts and simply buys it on impulse. Here, she feels strongly and acts on those feelings. A great deal of research focuses on the experiential perspective as researchers explore the feelings and pleasures that accompany consumer purchases and behaviors.[6]

BEHAVIORAL INFLUENCE HIERARCHY

The behavioral influence hierarchy suggests that behavior occurs without either beliefs or affect being strongly formed beforehand. Strong environmental pressures lead to behaviors without belief or affect formation. An example of this may be found when a consumer eats at a restaurant playing soft, slow music. Restaurant managers know that one way to get people to relax and order more drinks is to play soft, soothing music. Consumers have been conditioned to slow down and relax when slow music is played. As such, behavior is influenced by environmental cues. This means that there are times when behaviors may be performed in the absence of strong beliefs or feelings.

LO4 Consumer Attitude Models

As you can see, understanding consumer attitudes is very important for understanding consumer behavior. This leads to the question of how to measure attitudes. As noted earlier, the study of attitudes has a long-established research tradition. It shouldn't be surprising, therefore, that several methods for measuring attitudes have been suggested. In this

attitude-toward-the-object model attitude model that considers three key elements including beliefs consumers have about salient attributes, the strength of the belief that an object possesses the attribute, and evaluation of the particular attribute

attribute feature of a product or object

section, some of the major approaches to measuring consumer attitudes are presented, beginning with a well-known approach advanced by Martin Fishbein and Icek Azjen, the attitude-toward-the-object model.[7]

ATTITUDE-TOWARD-THE-OBJECT MODEL

The **attitude-toward-the-object (ATO) model** (sometimes simply referred to as the *Fishbein model*) proposes that three key elements must be assessed to understand and predict a consumer's attitude. The first element consists of the *beliefs* a consumer has about salient **attributes**, *or* features, that the consumer thinks the product should possess. The second element is the *strength of the belief* that a certain brand does indeed have the feature. The third element is an *evaluation of the attribute* in question. These elements are combined to form the overall attitude toward the object (referred to as A_o, or attitude toward the object). This approach is known as a *multi-attribute* approach because consumers consider a number of attributes when forming attitudes in this way. The formula for predicting attitudes with this approach is

$$A_o = \sum_{I=1}^{N} (b_i)(e_i)$$

where A_o = attitude toward the object in question (or A_{brand}), b_i = strength of belief that the object possesses attribute i, e_i = evaluation of the attractiveness or goodness of attribute i, and N = number of attributes and beliefs.

The formula states that belief (*b*) and evaluative ratings (*e*) for product attributes are combined (multiplied) and the resulting product terms are added together to give a numerical expression of a consumer's attitude toward a product. This model can be used both for predicting a consumer's attitude and for understanding how salient attributes, beliefs, and evaluations influence attitude formation.

Using the ATO Approach

To understand this model, first consider how the various elements are measured. To begin, note that belief ratings can be measured on a 10-point scale such as:

How likely is it that the Sony television will give you a clear picture?

| 1 | 2 | 3 | 4 | 5 | 6 | 7 | 8 | 9 | 10 |

Extremely unlikely   *Extremely likely*

The evaluative *(e)* rating can then be measured on a -3 to $+3$ scale such as:

How bad/good is it that a television has a clear picture?

| -3 | -2 | -1 | 0 | $+1$ | $+2$ | $+3$ |

Very bad   *Very good*

The consumer would rate the Sony television and any other brand being considered, say Samsung, on every relevant attribute. They would also consider their evaluations of the attributes, and they would ultimately combine the information.

An example may help to clarify the use of this formula. Think of the situation that Brooke is facing with selecting a fitness center. How could we predict her attitude? This information is presented in Exhibit 7.3.

Brooke is thinking of joining one of the following fitness centers: Lifestyles Family Fitness, Curves for Women®, or Shapes®. She first considers the attributes that come to mind when she thinks of fitness centers. She considers the availability of circuit training, the variety of workout classes, the amenities (such as showers and lockers), the fees associated with joining, and

© ISTOCKPHOTO.COM/STEVE HARMON

EXHIBIT 7.3
Attitude-toward-the-Object Model Applied to Fitness Center Choice

Attribute	Lifestyles			Curves		Shapes	
	e	b	(b)(e)	b	(b)(e)	b	(b)(e)
Circuit training	−1	1	−1	10	−10	9	−9
Class variety	2	10	20	2	4	3	6
Amenities	1	9	9	5	5	5	5
Fees	−3	6	−18	4	−12	5	−15
Location	3	6	18	8	24	9	27
A_o			28		11		14

Note: "e" = evaluative ratings. These ratings are generally scaled from -3 to +3, with -3 being very negative and +3 being very positive. "b" = strength of belief that the object possesses the attribute in question. Beliefs are generally scaled from 1 to 10, with 1 meaning "highly unlikely" and 10 meaning "highly likely." "(b)(e)" is the product term that is derived by multiplying the evaluative ratings (e) by belief strength (b). A_o is the overall attitude toward the object. This is determined by adding the (b)(e) product terms for each object.

the physical proximity of the centers to her apartment. This example shows what Brooke's overall attitudes are toward each center and how belief and evaluations are combined to arrive at these attitudes.

After identifying the relevant attributes, Brooke thinks of how well each gym performs on the attributes, or how likely it is that the centers have these attributes. Brooke would be answering questions such as:

How likely is it that "CENTER X" offers a variety of classes?

1   2   3   4   5   6   7   8   9   10
Extremely unlikely   *Extremely likely*

Brooke rates each center across all relevant attributes. Brooke's belief (b) ratings for the centers are shown in Exhibit 7.3. From her belief ratings, we can see that Brooke thinks that Lifestyles Family Fitness performs better than other centers on the variety of classes (10).

Next, Brooke considers how she *feels* about the relevant attributes, or how good (or bad) the attributes are. A sample question would be:

How good/bad is it that a fitness center offers a variety of classes?

−3   −2   −1   0   +1   +2   +3
Very bad   *Very good*

Brooke isn't too focused on the variety of classes, but she does think variety is nice. She therefore gives this attribute an evaluative rating of 2.

It is important to emphasize that the evaluation ratings (e) do not vary across the brands under consideration while the belief ratings do.

Using this model, Brooke's attitude would be calculated by multiplying each belief rating (b) by the corresponding evaluation (e). For example, the belief rating of 10 (for Curves for Women, circuit training) would be multiplied by the evaluation of −1 for circuit training to arrive at −10. Similarly, the belief rating of 9 for Lifestyles, amenities, would be multiplied by the evaluation of 1 to arrive at 9. This is performed for all belief ratings and evaluations. Finally, the product terms are added together to arrive at a predicted attitude score. From Exhibit 7.3, we see that Brooke's most positive attitude is toward Lifestyles (A_o = 28), followed by Shapes (A_o = 14), and finally Curves (A_o = 11).

What was it that led to the higher attitude toward Lifestyles versus the other two centers? An examination of Exhibit 7.3 reveals that Lifestyles was rated much higher than the other two centers on the variety of classes attribute. Note also that Curves and Shapes were both rated highly on circuit training. Brooke evaluated that attribute rather poorly (e = −1).

An examination of the table also reveals that Lifestyles received the highest attitude rating even though it scored highest on the attribute that Brooke rated most poorly, high fees. It can be said that the higher ratings on other attributes (such as variety of classes) compensated for the belief that Lifestyles has higher fees than the other centers. Accordingly, the ATO approach is known as a **compensatory model**. With compensatory models, attitudes are formed holistically across a number of attributes with poor ratings on one attribute being compensated for by higher ratings on another attribute.

Implications of the ATO Approach

Information obtained from this model has important marketing implications. First, we note that attitude research is most often performed on entire market segments rather than on individuals. For example, marketing researchers would generally want to understand how an entire segment of consumers feels about the various fitness center options. Information would then be gathered from a sample of several women in the segment. An important marketing issue would be developing an understanding of what women think about each of the relevant product attributes. What do members of our target segment think about the amenities that are offered in health clubs? What do they think about circuit training? What do they think about variety in class offerings?

> Consumers think about relevant features of products, how much they value the features, and how each product rates on the features.

An equally important issue for managers would be an understanding of the extent to which women believe that their specific centers offer the relevant attributes. Does our target segment know that we offer variety in our classes? Do they think that we have high fees? If managers were to find out that the target segment does not know that there is plenty of variety offered in the club, this would be something that they should emphasize in advertising campaigns. This would particularly be the case if the attribute was highly valued by the consumers. Therefore, both belief (*b*) and evaluative (*e*) ratings have important implications.

As a general statement, it would be easier for managers to convince the target segment that they do offer a lot of variety (in other words, to change a belief rating) than it would be to attempt to convince the segment that variety is a bad thing (or to change an evaluation). Accordingly, marketers need to perform extensive research up front to gain clear understandings of attributes that are highly valued and then develop their products and services around these features.

A couple of questions commonly arise regarding this approach. "Do consumers really form attitudes in this way?" Most consumer researchers would respond "Yes." It is easy to think of a person considering the purchase of a new cell phone. Chances are that they will first think of the features that are relevant. Next, they will rate each brand on how well it performs on those features. They will also consider how they feel about each of the features. Finally, they will combine their beliefs with the evaluations and make a decision. Granted, *they may not sit down and follow this exact formula*, but consumers think about relevant features of products, how much they value the features, and how each product rates on the features.

The next question that is commonly asked is: "Do consumer researchers really do this?" Again, the answer is "Yes." Researchers are very interested in how consumer attitudes are formed and the approach presented here can easily be performed through consumer surveys. This information can have a significant impact on marketing strategy. As the fitness center example reveals, this type of research can affect both product development and promotional strategy. For example, a manager could decide that he should improve features that are desired by the targeted segment. Or, he could focus on improving customer awareness that the center does have features that the targeted consumers want. Of course, he could also do both of these things.

Overall, the attitude toward the object model has value from both an academic and practical viewpoint. We do note, however, that one difficulty with the model is that the weights that are associated with the various attributes do not necessarily remain constant over time and the list of relevant attributes may indeed change. For this reason, managers should ensure that they attempt to stay current on these issues.

Do Attitudes Always Predict Behavior?

Marketing managers and researchers alike realize that just because a consumer has a positive attitude towards a product, this doesn't mean that he or she will always purchase the product. In fact, there would be little need for sales promotion if this were the case. **Attitude–behavior consistency** refers to the extent to which a strong relationship exists between attitudes and actual behavior. A number of situations may keep a consumer from selecting a product to which a positive attitude is held.[8] In general, attitudes are stronger predictors of behavior when the decision to be made is classified as high involvement, when situational factors do not impede the product selection (for example, the product is out of stock or the consumer doesn't have enough money), and when attitudes toward the product are very strong. Because attitudes don't always predict behavior, other approaches, including the behavioral intentions model, have been developed to improve upon the ATO approach.

BEHAVIORAL INTENTIONS MODEL

The **behavioral intentions model**, sometimes referred to as the *theory of reasoned action*, has been offered as an improvement over the attitude-toward-the-object model. This model differs from the attitude-toward-the-object model in a number of important ways.[9] First, rather than focusing explicitly on attitudes, the model focuses on intentions to act in some way. Second, the model adds a component that assesses the consumer's perceptions of what other people think they should do. This is referred to as the *subjective norm*. Finally, the model explicitly focuses on the consumer's attitude toward the behavior of buying rather than the attitude toward the object.

The formula for the behavioral intentions model is as follows:[10]

$$B \quad BI = w_1 (A_{behavior}) + w_2 (SN)$$

where B = behavior, BI = behavioral intention, $A_{behavior}$ = attitude toward performing the behavior (or, A_{act}), SN = subjective norm, and w_1, w_2 = empirical weights.

This model states that a consumer's behavior is influenced by the intention to perform that behavior (BI), and that this intention is determined by the attitude toward performing the behavior ($A_{behavior}$) and *subjective norms (SN)*.

From our fitness center example, the $A_{behavior}$ component includes the belief that the behavior will lead to a consequence (for example, "I'll lose a lot of weight if I go there") and an evaluation of the consequence (for example, "Losing weight is a good thing."). The SN component includes a consumer's belief that a reference group thinks that he or she should (or should not) perform the behavior (for example, Brooke's friends think she should choose Lifestyles) and the extent to which the consumer wants to comply with the suggestions of others (for example, does Brooke want to do what her friends say?).

The aspects of the behavioral intentions model are presented in Exhibit 7.4.

The behavioral intentions model was indeed introduced as an improvement to the ATO model. Again, two major differences are found in the attitude toward the behavior and subjective norm components. For marketers, a clear understanding of the perceived consequences of product selection is crucial. Researchers must determine the consequences that are highly valued

attitude–behavior consistency extent to which a strong relationship exists between attitudes and actual behavior

behavioral intentions model model, developed to improve upon the ATO model, that focuses on behavioral intentions, subjective norms, and attitude toward a particular behavior

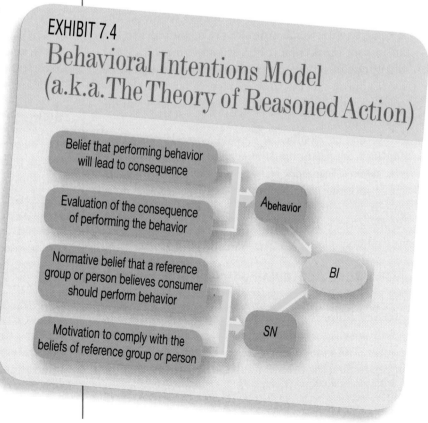

EXHIBIT 7.4

Behavioral Intentions Model (a.k.a. The Theory of Reasoned Action)

- Belief that performing behavior will lead to consequence
- Evaluation of the consequence of performing the behavior

  → $A_{behavior}$

- Normative belief that a reference group or person believes consumer should perform behavior
- Motivation to comply with the beliefs of reference group or person

  → SN

  → BI

theory of planned action attitudinal measurement approach that expands upon the behavioral intentions model by including a perceived control component

attitude tracking effort of a marketer or researcher to track changes in consumer attitudes over time

by their targeted consumer segments. Consumers don't always select products for the most predictable reason. Losing weight isn't the only reason people join a fitness center. Consumers may join simply to meet people and make friends.

Marketing managers should also pay close attention to the subjective norm component of the model. Word-of-mouth communications are becoming critical for marketers. What do referent others think that the consumer should do? To what extent are they motivated to comply with the input of these people? The answers to these questions would be quite valuable.

Factors That Weaken Attitude–Behavior Relationship

Although consumer attitude models are very popular in consumer research, researchers note that a number of factors can detract from the accuracy of this approach. For example, as the length of time between attitude measurement and overt behavior grows, the predictive ability of attitudinal models weakens. The specificity with which attitudes are measured also has an impact on accuracy. For example, measuring the intentions of buying a new Sony television would be more appropriate for Sony managers than would measuring one's intentions to buy a new "television" in the next month.

Strong environmental pressures can also keep consumers from performing intended behaviors. For example, when consumers feel rushed, decisions are often made in haste. Finally, attitude–behavior models tend to not perform very well in impulse-buying situations. As discussed earlier, these behaviors are quite common in a number of consumer contexts.

Alternative Approaches to Attitude

One small variation of this theory is the **theory of planned action**, which expands upon the behavioral intentions model by including a *perceived control* component. This component assesses the difficulty involved in performing the behavior and the extent to which the consumer perceives that he or she is in control of the

product selection.[11] Products can be difficult to purchase, especially if they are in short supply.

Expanding the Attitude Object

The definition of attitudes presented earlier states that attitudes are relatively enduring evaluations of objects, products, services, issues, or people. For this reason, consumer researchers often study attitudes toward several different entities, not just brands or products.

One area that has received considerable consumer research attention is *attitude toward the advertisement*. Research has shown that there is generally a positive relationship between a consumer's attitude towards an advertisement and his or her attitude towards a particular product.[12] We note, however, that several factors have been shown to affect this relationship including the overall liking of the television program in which the ad is embedded, the vividness of the imagery in the ad, the ad context, and the mood of the consumer.[13]

A growing area of research interest has also focused on attitude toward the company. What consumers know or believe about a company (sometimes referred to as *corporate associations*) can influence the attitude they have toward its products.[14] The study of consumer beliefs toward companies is therefore gaining considerable attention from consumer researchers. Of particular importance for many consumers is the question of how responsible companies are with their business practices. In general, consumers who feel positively about a company's business practices are likely to react more favorably toward the brands that the company markets.[15]

Attitude Tracking

Assessing one's attitude toward a specific product, brand, purchase act, advertisement, or company at only one specific point in time can also limit the accuracy of attitudinal models. Researchers therefore track how attitudes change over time. Because attitudes toward a brand can be influenced by several things, including attitude toward advertisements and companies, it is especially important to study changes in consumer attitudes. **Attitude tracking** refers to the extent to which a company actively monitors its customers' attitudes over time. What is important to understand is that even though attitudes are relatively enduring evaluations of objects, products, services, issues, or people, these attitudes should be monitored over time to gauge changes that may occur.

Who's Setting the Table?

I t used to be common to see a family dinner table crowded with food—and families. In today's fast-paced environment, however, this behavior is becoming much less common. MTV Networks recently embarked on an initiative that was aimed at reversing this trend by selecting its TV Land and Nick at Night networks for a campaign entitled "Family Table: Share More Than Meals."

The campaign, which utilizes airtime on the networks to promote the benefits of families sharing time together, represents an explicit attempt to improve attitudes toward the simple family practice of sharing time together. MTV Networks donated $11 million in airtime and more than 20 public service announcements (PSAs) to encourage this behavior. Thanks to these efforts, perhaps the dinner table can again become what it once was—a place for family connections, conversation, and togetherness.

Sources: Lipp, Danielle (2006), "Initiative Helps Families Connect," *PRWeek* (October 23), 27; Bergantini-Grillo, Jean (2005), "Family Meals are Hip Again," *Broadcasting & Cable* (November 21), 18; Anonymous (2005), "Nick, TV Land Back Family Dinner Day," *Executive Quote and Information Service* (August 29).

© GO PHOTO/STOCKFOOD CREATIVE/GETTY IMAGES

LO5 Attitude Change Theories and Persuasion

a n important issue in the study of consumer behavior is how attitudes are changed. Marketers frequently want to change consumer attitudes about their products, and they focus their efforts on developing persuasive messages. Advertising obviously plays a major role in this effort. The term **persuasion** refers to specific attempts to change attitudes. Usually, the hope is that by changing beliefs or feelings, marketers can also change behavior.

There are many different persuasive techniques, and the following discussion presents the theoretical mechanisms through which persuasion may occur. These include the ATO approach, the behavioral influence approach, the schema-based affect approach, the elaboration likelihood model, the balance theory approach, and the social judgment theory approach.

ATTITUDE-TOWARD-THE-OBJECT APPROACH

According to the ATO model, both beliefs about product attributes and evaluations of those attributes play important roles in attitude formation. By focusing on these components, the ATO approach presents marketers with a number of alternatives for changing consumer attitudes. To change attitudes according to this approach, marketers can attempt to change beliefs, create new beliefs about product features, or change evaluations of product attributes.

Changing Beliefs

As discussed in our fitness center example, marketers may attempt to change consumers' beliefs. Again consider our example. If consumers do not believe that Shapes offers a variety of classes, then the center could increase the actual number of classes offered and promote this change to its consumers. Or, let's assume that the center actually does offer a number of classes and consumers simply don't realize that they do. In this case, the center would need to advertise its variety of classes to its targeted consumers. With each effort, the focus is on improving the belief rating for an attribute that is evaluated positively (here, variety of classes).

Another approach would be to focus on decreasing the strength of belief regarding a negatively evaluated attribute. For example, since price is evaluated quite negatively (-3), the center might decide to promote the overall value that comes from club membership or the relatively low price of the center as compared to the competition. Here, the focus is on decreasing the belief rating of a negatively evaluated attribute. As we have discussed throughout this text, communicating value is an important marketing task.

Adding Beliefs about New Attributes

Another strategy for changing attitudes under the ATO approach is adding a salient attribute to the product or service. Like the changing beliefs approach, this may require a physical change to the product itself. For example, a fitness center might add a supervised "play room" for children so that parents can use the facilities without having to make arrangements for their kids. Here, a new attribute that is likely to be evaluated positively by consumers is added. When a valued attribute that was not previously considered is added, the overall attitude toward the fitness center may be improved, and the fitness center may become the preferred option for targeted consumers.

At other times, the new beliefs may not be exactly tied to a "new" attribute. Rather, they may simply emphasize something that consumers had previously not considered. To illustrate, consider what has happened with the marketing of red wine. In the 1980s, Robert Mondavi Winery added labeling to its wines that referred to the health-related benefits that

> À votre santé! The belief that wine is healthy can lead people to like it even more.

© STEFANO OPPO/PHOTONICA/GETTY IMAGES

Changing Evaluations

As noted earlier, marketers may also attempt to change the evaluation of an attribute. Here, the marketer would try to convince consumers that an attribute is not as positive (or negative) as they may think. For example, a fitness center may attempt to convince consumers that location is not always a positive thing. They may advertise to their customers that any gym can be "around the corner" but a good gym is worth the drive. Or, the center may attempt to change evaluations of circuit training by emphasizing that circuit training leads to quicker weight loss and muscle development.

Changing evaluations of an attribute is more difficult than changing the strength of a belief regarding that attribute. Quite simply, consumers know what they like, and they make selections accordingly.

> Another strategy commonly applied by marketers is directly changing behaviors without first attempting to change either beliefs or feelings.

come from drinking wine. Initially, the FDA reacted and stopped this practice based on the notion that the label was misleading and detrimental to consumers. However, after years of research, the health-giving properties of wine cannot be argued. Red wine is beneficial in reducing risks associated with both heart disease and cancer, and this information has now been widely promoted. Thus, although the health-related benefits of red wine are nothing new, only in the last few years has the belief become prominently known and accepted. By adding a new belief, wine marketers have increased the market share of wine relative to beer and spirits.

BEHAVIORAL INFLUENCE APPROACH

Another strategy commonly applied by marketers is directly changing behaviors without first attempting to change either beliefs or feelings. According to the behavioral influence hierarchy, behavior change can precede belief and attitude change. Changing a retail store's design or atmospherics can have a direct influence on behavior. In fact, an entire industry called scent marketing (that is, using scents to influence behavior) is emerging.

You may remember from our discussion on conditioning in an earlier chapter that behavioral conditioning can be very effective. Consumers respond to marketing stimuli in certain ways, and behaviors frequently result independently of either beliefs or affect occurring prior to the behaviors.

© AP IMAGES/PRNEWSFOTO/VIZIO, INC.

Digital TV Transition

Few developments in television broadcasting have been as notable as the transition to digital programming that occurred officially on June 12, 2009. The transition to digital programming promised better picture quality and sound for consumers, as well as more channels. The conversion also cleared the airwaves for alternative uses for analog broadcasting.

Getting millions of consumers to change their viewing habits was a major undertaking for the U.S. government. Consumers were forced to either upgrade their televisions to digital models or purchase a digital converter box for their older, analog sets. The government provided coupons to assist consumers with the costs involved with the purchase of the converter boxes (although the program did originally run out of coupons), but consumers were still forced to change their behaviors by buying the boxes or new TV sets. There were no attempts to change beliefs or feelings about the switch, rather, consumers were simply informed that they *had* to make the switch. Of course, most consumers complied with the directives and bought the converter boxes or newer sets.

The DTV transition is an example of how behaviors can be changed directly without either belief or affect change occurring beforehand. In this situation, consumers simply had little choice but to comply. Fortunately, most consumers were prepared for the switch. For these consumers, the transition was relatively easy and the switch was largely considered a success.

Sources: Frenzel, Louis E. (2009), "The DTV Transition: Will it Happen? What Can We Expect?" *Electronic Design*, 57 (3), pg. 20 – 21; *Anonymous* (2009), "DTV: So Far, So Good," *Broadcasting & Cable*, 139 (8), pg. 26; *Anonymous* (2009), "I Want My DTV," *Wall Street Journal*, February 17, pg. A14.; *Anonymous* (2008), "Are You Set for All-Digital TV?" *Consumer Reports*, March, 73 (3), pg. 32; Wildstrom, Stephen H. (2008), "Digital TV: Rough on Rabbit Ears," *Business Week*, August 25, Issue 4097, pg. 93.

CHANGING SCHEMA-BASED AFFECT

We introduced the notion of schema-based affect in a previous chapter. From an attitude perspective, schema-based affect refers to the idea that schemas contain affective and emotional meanings. If the affect found in a schema can be changed, then the attitude toward a brand or product will change as well.

To illustrate, consider what happened when Domino's Pizza first entered Japan. Initially, the company had to deal with a commonly held belief that tomatoes were unhealthy and that delivery food was not clean. Rather than trying to change these beliefs directly, Domino's

created funny delivery carts and advertisements that attempted to attach positive feelings to the product schema and to their brand. Thus, the positive attitude was shaped by this feeling found within the schema. This attitude-change technique can be effective if performed properly.

THE ELABORATION LIKELIHOOD MODEL

Another popular approach for conceptualizing attitude change is found in the **elaboration likelihood model.**[16] The elaboration likelihood model (or ELM for short) illustrates how attitudes are changed based on differing levels of consumer involvement. Numerous research studies have examined the usefulness of the ELM in explaining the attitude change process. This model is shown in Exhibit 7.5.

According to the ELM, a consumer begins to process a message as soon as it is received. Depending on the level of involvement and a consumer's ability and motivation to process a message, the persuasion process then follows one of two routes: a *central route* or a *peripheral route*.[17]

The Central Route

If the consumer finds that the incoming message is particularly relevant to his or her situation (and thus highly involved), then he or she will likely expend considerable

> **elaboration likelihood model** attitudinal change model that shows attitudes are changed based on differing levels of consumer involvement through either central or peripheral processing

central route to persuasion path to persuasion found in ELM where the consumer has high involvement, motivation, and/or ability to process a message

counterarguments arguments that contradict a message

support arguments arguments that support a message

central cues information presented in a message about the product itself, its attributes, or the consequences of its use

peripheral route to persuasion path to persuasion found in ELM where the consumer has low involvement, motivation, and/or ability to process a message

peripheral cues nonproduct-related information presented in a message

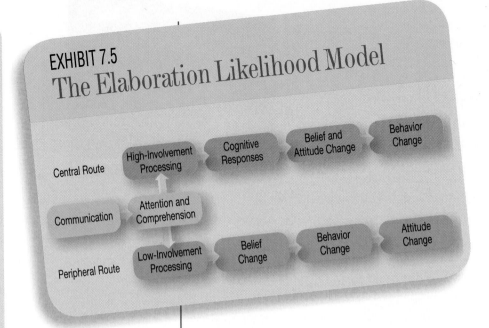

EXHIBIT 7.5
The Elaboration Likelihood Model

effort in comprehending the message. In this case, high-involvement processing occurs, and the **central route to persuasion** is activated. Here, the consumer develops a number of thoughts (or cognitive responses) regarding the incoming message that may either support or contradict the information. Contradicting thoughts are known as **counterarguments**. Thoughts that support the main argument presented are known as **support arguments**.

In the central route, the consumer relies on **central cues**. Central cues refer specifically to information found in the message that pertains directly to the product, its attributes, its advantages, or the consequences of its use.

To illustrate this process, imagine an experienced photographer who sees an advertisement for Sony cameras. Because he knows a lot about cameras and is highly interested in them, he will likely think carefully about the message he sees and the arguments that are presented for why Sony cameras are the best cameras on the market. The arguments presented in the ad are critical. The photographer will consider the arguments presented and compare them to his current beliefs. He may even form counterarguments against the ad. For example, he may think "Canons are better." Or, he may think, "Sony cameras really are better than Canons after all." (It is important to note that responses can be either negative or positive.)

If the consumer's beliefs are changed as a result of message exposure, attitude and behavior change will follow. Because the consumer is highly involved, and because he has taken the effort to carefully attend to the message, it is likely that the attitude change will be relatively enduring. This is an important aspect of the central route to persuasion: *Attitude change tends to be relatively enduring when it occurs in the central route.*

The Peripheral Route

If a consumer is not involved with a message or lacks either the motivation or ability to process information, the **peripheral route to persuasion** will be followed. In this route, the consumer is unlikely to develop cognitive responses to the message (either supporting arguments or counterarguments), and he is more likely to pay attention to things like the attractiveness of the person delivering the message, the number of arguments presented, the expertise of the spokesperson, and the imagery or music presented along with the message. These elements of the message (that is, nonproduct-related information) are referred to as **peripheral cues**.

If the consumer is influenced more by peripheral cues than central cues, any resulting belief or attitude change will likely be only temporary. That is, because the consumer is not highly engaged in the process, it is unlikely that attitude change will be enduring.

A popular ad campaign for Corona beer illustrates peripheral processing. The campaign includes a series of advertisements that show a man and woman relaxing on a beach. In the ads, there is no ad copy at all other than the tag-line "Corona—Miles from Ordinary." Although there is little ad copy, the ads are full of

The use of beautiful scenery represents peripheral cues.

peripheral cues—from the soothing sound of the waves hitting the sand to the beautiful imagery of the ocean. These cues play a major role in persuasion even if the consumer isn't presented with a list of reasons of why they should buy Corona or why Corona is the best beer available on the market.

Low-Involvement Processing in the Consumer Environment

It is important to note that the vast majority of advertisements to which consumers are exposed are processed with low-involvement processing. Consumers are simply not motivated to carefully attend to the thousands of ads that they are exposed to each day! Therefore, advertisers tend to rely heavily on the use of peripheral cues—attractive models, enticing imagery, upbeat music—when developing advertisements.

BALANCE THEORY

Another way to conceptualize attitude change processes is through balance theory. The **balance theory** approach was introduced by social psychologist Fritz Heider.[18] The basic premise of balance theory is that consumers are motivated to maintain perceived consistency in the relations found in mental systems. Accordingly, this approach is based on the **consistency principle**. This principle states that human beings prefer consistency among their beliefs, attitudes, and behaviors.

Balance theory focuses on the associations, or relations, that are perceived between a person (or observer), another person, and an attitudinal object. The relations between these elements may be perceived as being either positive or negative. An example is shown in Exhibit 7.6.

Note that the system (composed of observer, person, and object) is referred to as a *triad* because it consists of a set of three elements. The relations between the elements are referred to either as sentiment relations or unit relations. *Sentiment relations* are the relations between the observer (consumer) and the other elements in the system. In Exhibit 7.6, the observer–person relation and the observer–object relation are referred to as

balance theory theory that states that consumers are motivated to maintain perceived consistency in the relations found in a system

consistency principle principle that states that human beings prefer consistency among their beliefs, attitudes, and behaviors

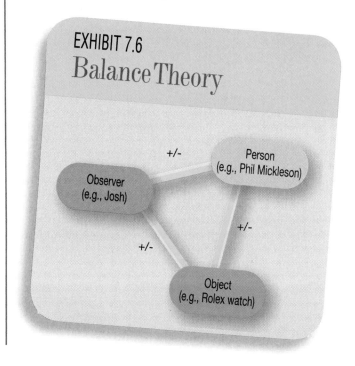

EXHIBIT 7.6
Balance Theory

sentiment relations. The object–person relation is referred to as a *unit relation*. Unit relations are based on the idea that two elements are in some way connected to one another.

Again, the basic premise of balance theory is that consumers are motivated to maintain perceived consistency in the relations found in the triad. Importantly, the perceived relations between the cognitive elements in the balance theory system may be changed when inconsistency occurs.

To illustrate, look carefully at Exhibit 7.6. Assume that Josh really likes his favorite golfer, Phil Mickleson. That is, there is a positive (+) sentiment connection between Josh and Phil Mickleson. If Josh sees that Phil is endorsing an expensive watch like Rolex (an attitudinal object), he would perceive a positive unit relation (+) between Phil and the watch. That is, Josh assumes that Phil endorses the brand because he really likes it. How would Josh feel about Rolex? Well, in order to maintain balance in this triad, he would

Balance theory applies to celebrity endorsements.

© ROSS KINNAIRD/GETTY IMAGES

develop positive feelings toward the watch, resulting in a positive sentiment connection between himself and the brand.

This example illustrates a key premise of balance theory: *Consistency in the triad is maintained when the multiplication of the signs in the sentiment and unit relations result in a positive value.* When the resulting value is negative, consumers are motivated to change the signs (feelings) associated with one of the relations.

Suppose Josh doesn't like Phil Mickleson. That is, suppose there is a negative (–) sentiment relation between Josh and the star. Because he perceives a positive unit relation between Phil and the brand, he will be motivated to form a negative sentiment relation between himself and the brand (note that $[-] \times [+] \times [-] = +$). According to the theory, weak perceived relations are generally changed, while stronger relations remain unchanged. Here, Josh would be turned off by the advertisement and would develop a negative sentiment relation between himself and the brand. We note that while balance theory is often used to explain endorser effectiveness, the theory has also been applied in several other contexts including product placements in television shows,[19] goal-oriented behavior,[20] and consumer–brand relationships.[21]

It should also be noted that marketers who rely on this approach should be careful to monitor any changes that occur in how a target market perceives an endorser. As we have seen, public attitudes toward celebrities can change nearly overnight. In this case, the sentiment connection between the endorser and the consumer can become negative, leading the brand being advertised to trouble!

SOCIAL JUDGMENT THEORY

Social judgment theory is yet another theory for explaining attitude change.[22] This theory proposes that consumers compare incoming information to their existing attitudes about a particular object or issue. The initial attitude acts as a frame of reference, or standard, against which the incoming message is compared. Around these initial reference points are *latitudes of acceptance* and *latitudes of rejection*. For a message to fall within the latitude of acceptance, the information presented must be perceived as being close to the original attitude position. A message that is perceived as being far away from, or opposed to, the original attitude position will fall within the latitude of rejection. These aspects of the theory are presented in Exhibit 7.7.

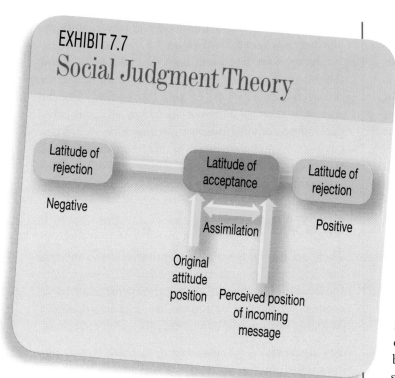

EXHIBIT 7.7
Social Judgment Theory

According to the theory, when an incoming message falls within the latitude of acceptance, *assimilation* occurs. This means that the message is viewed as being congruent with the initial attitudinal position, and the message is received favorably. In fact, the message may be viewed as being even more congruent with the initial attitudinal position than it really is. As a result, the consumer is likely to agree with the content of a message falling within the latitude of acceptance, and the attitude would change in the direction of the message.

If the message is perceived as falling in the latitude of rejection, an opposite effect occurs. In fact, the message will be viewed as being even more opposed to the original attitude than it really is, and the message will be rejected. In this way, a *contrast effect* is said to occur.

The implication for marketers is that messages should be constructed so that they fall within the latitude of acceptance of the targeted consumer. An important finding in this line of research is that when the original attitude is held with much conviction (either positive or negative), the latitude of acceptance is quite small and the latitude of rejection is large. On the contrary, when the original attitude is weak (either positive or negative), the latitude of acceptance is large and the latitude of rejection is small. This finding helps to explain why it is difficult to change a person's attitude when his or her attitude is very strong.

LO6 Message and Source Effects and Persuasion

an important part of understanding persuasion is comprehending the many ways in which communication occurs. Marketing messages come to consumers in a variety of ways. As we have discussed, consumers are exposed to literally thousands of messages every day. Many of these messages come directly from marketers. Other messages come from other consumers. In both cases, the message being sent and the source delivering the message influence persuasiveness. For this reason, it is important to consider the roles of message effects and source effects in persuasion.

Message effects is a term that is used to describe how the appeal of a message and its construction affect persuasion. **Source effects** refer to the characteristics of the person or character delivering a message that influence persuasion. To understand how message and source effects work, we must begin by introducing a simple communication model. A basic communication model is shown in Exhibit 7.8.

> **message effects** how the appeal of a message and its construction affects persuasiveness
>
> **source effects** characteristics of a source that impact the persuasiveness of a message

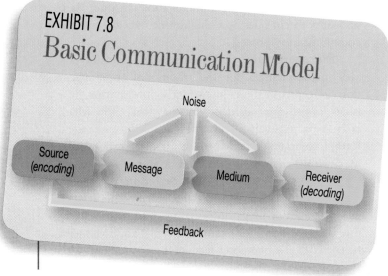

EXHIBIT 7.8
Basic Communication Model

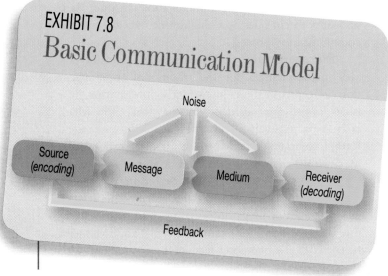

According to this model, a source encodes a message and delivers the message through some medium. The medium could be personal (for example, when one consumer talks to another, or when a salesperson speaks with a customer) or impersonal (for example, when a company places an ad on television, radio, or on a web page). The receiver (consumer) decodes the message and responds to it in some way. Feedback consists of the responses that the receiver sends back to the source. For example, a consumer might voice an objection to a sales pitch or decide to call a 1-800 number to receive additional product information.

The *noise* concept is very important to this model. Noise represents all the stimuli in the environment that disrupt the communication process. In today's environment, noise comes in many different forms. For example, the popularity of online pop-up blockers is evidence of the number of distractions that are found on the Web. From a traditional advertising perspective, the basic communication model is referred to as a "one-to-many" approach because it illustrates how a marketer may attempt to communicate with numerous consumers.[23]

INTERACTIVE COMMUNICATIONS

The one-to-many communications model works well when examining personal communications or traditional advertising media (television or radio). However, interactive communications (including the Internet, cell phones, text messaging, e-commerce, and personal data assistants) have radically changed the communication paradigm. In fact, current estimates reveal that 22% of the world's population is using the Internet (more than 1.5 billion consumers).[24] Due to the rapid adoption of the Internet as a major communications medium, it is necessary to consider how the Internet has affected the communication process.

The interactivity that the Internet provides creates major changes for the traditional communication conceptualization. Importantly, information flow is no longer considered a "one-way street" in which consumers passively receive messages from marketers. Rather, communication is seen as an interactive process that enables a flow of information among consumers and/or firms in what might be referred to as a many-to-many approach.[25] Senders can place content (such as web pages or blogs) into the medium or communicate directly (with, for example, e-mails and IMs) with receivers in the computer-mediated environment. This

changes the communication model. A newer conceptualization is presented in Exhibit 7.9.

As we have discussed, both the message itself and the person delivering the message have an impact on the overall effectiveness of an advertisement. For this reason, marketers must consider both elements when developing communication strategies. This section discusses a number of findings regarding message and source effects. As you may remember, some of these topics were first introduced in our comprehension chapter.

MESSAGE APPEAL

There are several ways to conceptualize how a message may impact the persuasiveness of an advertisement. Here, we focus on the appeal (or general content) of an advertisement. A number of appeals are used by advertisers including sex appeals, humor appeals, and fear appeals.

Sex Appeals. A popular saying in marketing is that "sex sells!" and using sexual imagery in advertisements certainly is popular in many parts of the world. In fact, European media usually contain stronger and more explicit sexual appeals than do American media. As we discussed in our personality chapter, the rationale for this approach is found within the psychoanalytic approach, which assumes that behavior is influenced by deep-seated desires for pleasure.

Interestingly, consumers often find sexually appealing ads to be persuasive, even when they consider them to be exploitative or offensive![26] However, consumers' reactions to the strategy depend on a number of factors. Moderate levels of nudity appear to be most preferred,

EXHIBIT 7.9
Communication in a Computer-Mediated Environment

Source: Adapted from: Hoffman, Donna L., and Thomas P. Novak (1996), "Marketing in Hypermedia Computer-Mediated Environments: Conceptual Foundations," *Journal of Marketing*, 60 (3), 50–68.

as highly explicit content tends to direct attention away from the product.

Gender plays a role in advertising effectiveness regarding nudity. For example, one study found that women react negatively to the use of female nudity in advertising but that men respond favorably toward the practice.[27] Conversely, a later study revealed men react negatively toward the use of male nudity in ads and that women responded favorably. The type of product being advertised also plays an important role. That is, the use of nudity is most effective for products that have some level of intimate appeal.[28]

Finally, research also reveals that including a romantic theme (rather than focusing on the explicit pleasure of sex) may have positive benefits for marketers. This is good news for fragrance marketers, who often focus their ads on romantic situations and settings.[29]

Humor Appeals. Marketers also frequently use humorous ads. In today's age of tremendous adver-

VISA GOLD. He who has the gold makes the rules.

Humorous ads can attract attention and create a positive mood.

tising clutter, ads that are humorous can be effective. In general, humorous ads can attract attention, create a positive mood, and enhance the credibility of a source.[30] However, research suggests that the use of humor should relate to the product being advertised.[31]

The overall effectiveness of a humorous ad depends, in part, on the characteristics of both the individual consumer and the advertisement. For example, research indicates that humor is more effective when a consumer's need for cognition is high rather than low[32] and when a consumer has a high need for humor.[33] Furthermore, the initial attitude that a consumer has regarding the product plays an important role as humorous ads appear to be most effective when the consumer's attitudes are initially positive rather than negative.[34]

The amount of humor to place in an advertisement is another issue. High levels of humor can cause consumers to fail to pay attention to the product being advertised, and high levels can also limit information processing.[35] Obviously, marketers don't want to spend millions of dollars on ad campaigns simply for entertainment purposes.

Fear Appeals. In addition to using sexual and humor appeals, advertisers also frequently attempt to evoke some level of fear in their target audiences as a means of changing attitudes and behaviors. These ads often rely on the relationship between a threat (an undesirable consequence of behavior) and fear (an emotional response).[36] The product being advertised is often promoted as a type of "hero" that will remove the threat.

For example, an insurance company might try to evoke fear in consumers by suggesting that their loved ones may fall into financial hardship if the consumer doesn't carry enough life insurance. Public service announcements may attempt to evoke fear in consumers by highlighting the tragic consequences of unsafe sexual practices (for example, HIV). Security monitoring services may use fear appeals to draw attention to the frightening consequences of home invasions.

Numerous research studies have addressed the effectiveness of fear appeals in marketing. As a general statement, research suggests that the use of fear appeals can be effective. However, the level of fear that results is very important. Overly high levels of fear may lead consumers to focus on the threat so much that they lose focus on the proposed solution.[37] Also, different consumers are likely to react in different ways to the exact same fear appeal, complicating the issue further.[38] As a result, it is very difficult to predict how an individual consumer will react to any fear appeal. The context in

primacy effect effect that occurs when the information placed early in a message has the most impact

recency effect effect that occurs when the information placed late in a message has the most impact

which fear appeals are placed can also influence their effectiveness. For example, attitudes toward a fear-inducing ad have been found to be less positive when the ad is embedded in a sad television program than when the ad is placed in a happy (comedic) program.[39]

As an overall statement, fear appeals appear to be effective when they (1) introduce the severity of a threat, (2) present the probability of occurrence, (3) explain the effectiveness of a coping strategy, and (4) show how easy it is to implement the desired response.[40]

Although the use of fear appeals is popular among advertisers, it is important to note that there is an ethical question regarding their use. Critics often argue that the use of fear appeals in advertising is essentially a means of unfair manipulation.[41]

MESSAGE CONSTRUCTION

The way that the message is constructed also impacts its persuasiveness. Advertisers must consider a number of issues when constructing a message. Here, we present a number of questions that marketers must answer.

- *Should an ad present a conclusion or should the consumer be allowed to reach his own conclusion?*

Advertisements that allow consumers to arrive at their own conclusions

tend to be more persuasive when the audience has a high level of involvement with the product. Conversely, when the audience is not engaged with the message, it is generally better to draw the conclusion for consumers.[42]

- *Should comparative ads that directly compare one brand against another be developed?*

Advertisers generally have three alternatives when developing an ad. First, they can promote their brands without mentioning competing brands. Second, the can promote their brands and compare them generically to "the competition." Third, they can actively compare their products against specific competitors by explicitly naming the competing brands in the advertisement.

Directly comparing one brand against specific competitors can be effective—especially when the brand being promoted is not already the market leader.[43] Promoting a brand as being "superior to all competition" can also be very persuasive when a firm hopes to court users away from all competing brands.[44]

- *Where should important information be placed?*

When material presented early in a message is most influential, a **primacy effect** is said to occur. When material presented later in the message has the most impact, a **recency effect** is said to occur.[45]

Research suggests that primacy effects are likely to occur when the audience is highly engaged (highly involved) and when verbal (versus pictorial) content is present.[46] If marketers are attempting to reach a highly involved audience, important information should be placed earlier in the message. Marketers can also attempt to gain the consumer's attention as early as possible and encourage careful processing of information by using statements such as "an important message" or "listen carefully." For audiences with lower levels of involvement, important information can be placed later in the message.

- *Should the message be straightforward and simple or complex?*

In general, complex ads take more effort on the part of the consumer and require deep information processing. Overly complex messages can cause frustration within consumers and lead to unfavorable reactions. As presented earlier in the section on the ELM, the number of arguments presented in an ad is considered a peripheral cue. Highly involved consumers are more motivated to attend to a larger number of arguments than are less motivated consumers.

Advertisers must consider both message and source effects.

As you can see, a marketer must consider numerous message-related issues.

SOURCE EFFECTS

Another important issue in the study of persuasion is how the source of a message (a spokesperson or model, for example) influences consumers' attitudes. Source effects include issues such as credibility, attractiveness, likeability, and meaningfulness.

Source Credibility. Source credibility plays an important role in advertising effectiveness. In general, credible sources tend to be more persuasive than less credible sources. This effect tends to be highest when consumers lack the ability or motivation to expend effort attending to the details of an ad (low involvement).[47] However, credible sources also influence highly involved consumers, especially if their credentials are clearly communicated early in a message.[48]

As we discussed in our comprehension chapter, credibility consists of two elements: expertise and trustworthiness. *Expertise* refers to the amount of knowledge that a spokesperson is perceived to have about the product or issue in question. You may remember from our presentation on the ELM that source expertise represents a peripheral cue in advertising. Expertise can be an important quality for a spokesperson to possess. In fact, a major review of source effects has revealed that source expertise has the biggest influence of all source effects on consumer responses to advertisements.[49]

Trustworthiness refers to a perception of the extent to which a spokesperson is presenting a message that he or she truly believes, with no reason to present false information. Interestingly, expertise and trustworthiness can independently influence persuasion. That is, trustworthy sources can be persuasive even if they're not experts, and expert sources can be persuasive even if they're perceived as being untrustworthy.[50]

Finally, we note that source credibility, although generally conceptualized as pertaining to a spokesperson or model, also applies to the sponsoring company. In fact, research reveals that the credibility of both the spokesperson and the company influences the effectiveness of an advertisement, with the credibility of the spokesperson having a stronger influence than the credibility of the company.[51]

Source Attractiveness. Source attractiveness is another quality that has received a great deal of attention. Attractive models are often thought to possess desirable qualities and personalities. They also tend to be more persuasive than unattractive spokespeople.[52] However, the type of product plays an important role in the process. Much like the research regarding the use of sex appeals, research into attractiveness reveals that attractive models are more effective when promoting products that have an intimate appeal, whereas unattractive models are more effective when promoting products that have no intimate appeal.[53] This is particularly the case when consumers have the ability and motivation to process the message being presented.[54]

matchup hypothesis
hypothesis that states that a source feature is most effective when it is matched with relevant products

Source Likeability. Source likeability also affects a spokesperson's effectiveness. Likeable sources tend to be persuasive. Of course, individuals differ in terms of what celebrities they like and dislike, and marketers are very interested in finding the best possible spokesperson for a given market segment. The advertising industry relies heavily on a Q-score rating provided by Marketing Evaluations, Inc., as an indication of the overall appeal of celebrities.[55]

Source Meaningfulness. Celebrities have images and cultural meanings that resonate with consumers. For example, a famous athlete like LeBron James embodies the image of hard work and success. Pairing LeBron with athletic apparel or footwear simply makes sense. You should recall that research on the use of sexual imagery and source attractiveness suggests that these characteristics should be matched with the type of product being advertised. This is true for source meaningfulness as well. That is, the dominant characteristics of a source should match the characteristics of the product. This is a key concept that is found in the **matchup hypothesis**, which states that a source feature is most effective when it is matched with relevant products.[56] As such, we should expect LeBron James to be an effective spokesperson for footwear and less effective when promoting a product that has no athletic qualities at all.

As you can see, marketers face a number of decisions when constructing campaigns that are aimed at changing consumer attitudes.

Chapter 7 Case

The explosion of the market for coffee beverages can be seen in the responses to the mere mention of the name Starbucks. Recent trends in the United States among consumers regarding beverages have notably included both coffee drinks and energy drinks. How do beverage companies that are not typically in the market of coffee beverages compete? Specialty coffee drinks are a $10 billion a year industry in the United States and are expected to continue growing at a rate of approximately 7%. Therefore, targeting those in the group that are the heaviest consumers of specialty coffee drinks would be logical.

Coca-Cola has been a part of American culture for over a century. The product's image is graven deeply in American hearts regardless of consumer segmentation. Using brand recognition, Coca-Cola introduced Coca-Cola BläK in an attempt to gain a share of the coffee market.

From the beginning in April of 2006, Coca-Cola BläK has been available at supermarkets and convenience retail stores nationwide, in both individual bottles and four-packs. They target adult consumers. According to Coca-Cola North America, "There is no other beverage available today quite like Coca-Cola BläK. Imagine the refreshing taste of an ice-cold Coca-Cola that finishes with a rich essence of coffee. Only Coca-Cola can deliver that distinct combination of flavors." Coca-Cola BläK has the texture of coffee and a cappuccino style that will compete against Pepsi Max Cino.

By focusing on the innovative idea of combining coffee with the classic beverage, the company tries to appeal to the wider range of the market as a new category of soft drink. According to Brian Tracy, a business editor at MSNBC, the target market is the Starbucks and Red Bull consumers.

Advertising messages with sophisticated and stylish graphics were employed to attract adult consumers. Marketing supports for the new brand began with a teaser television ad, which aired during the live Red Carpet preshow broadcast of the 78th Annual Academy Awards® on ABC. The 15-second commercial titled "POParazzi" presented Coca-Cola BläK as a glamorous star appearing before throngs of media, complete with flashing camera lights. Beginning the following April in cities across the United States, additional support for the brand consisted of a fully integrated program featuring both traditional and nontraditional media, including television, print, and outdoor advertising, in-store displays, and targeted sampling programs designed to engage consumers and pique their interest in Coca-Cola BläK.

It is apparent that the product is advertised as a premium blend—something that is high-class but that can be purchased by anyone. If Coca-Cola gets high-class personalities to promote the product, it will be successful. In America, people don't mind spending a few extra dollars to have what they believe is a quality product. If high-power celebrities endorse Coca-Cola BläK, people's attitudes can be positive toward the image of this unknown product.

Coca-Cola Classic doesn't have that many advertisements anymore because everyone knows what Classic tastes like and it has been a valued drink for several decades. However, Coke needs to make sure they start their new product off on the right foot with immense advertising efforts, showing in an ad how much BläK helps the average person to stay awake and keeps him or her focused on the task at hand. Again, it all falls back on the belief that this product tastes good and that people don't mind spending the extra cents on a beverage that actually will help them through the day.

The biggest challenge Coca-Cola BläK is going to face is that coffee and cola together might not sound very appealing to many consumers. Many people may prefer either the coffeehouse flavor or the flavor of original Coca-Cola alone, but not necessarily together. For example, cola/coffee drink mixes are not a new concept. In the mid-1990s, Pepsi Kona, Java Cola, and Café Cola were introduced, but they did not gain the attention of consumers and disappeared from the market. While incorporating the Coca-Cola brand name, Coca-Cola BläK needs different positioning between the soft drink and coffee markets. As Coca-Cola instilled a fresh image to consumers in the past, Coca-Cola BläK might need a new concept of drink in this new area.[57]

Questions

1. If you are in charge of the marketing strategy for Coca-Cola BläK in America, who should be your target consumers be? Why?

2. What kinds of advertising messages would appeal to the target consumer to cause an attitude change toward Coca-Cola BläK?

3. Compared to ordinary Coca-Cola, Coca-Cola BläK is expensive ($1.99). How should Coca-Cola BläK be positioned?pass 2 page 143 replace this "Listen Up" ad with the new Review Card ad

REVIEW

HE DID

CB2 puts a multitude of study aids at your fingertips. After reading the chapters, check out these resources for further help:

- **Chapter in Review cards**, found in the back of your book, include all learning outcomes, definitions, and visual summaries for each chapter.

- **Online printable flash cards** give you three additional ways to check your comprehension of key concepts.

Other great ways to help you study include **interactive games, podcasts, audio downloads, and online tutorial quizzes with feedback**.

You can find it all at **4ltrpress.cengage.com/cb**.

what do you think?

Men should always pay for their date's dinner.

1 2 3 4 5 6 7
strongly disagree   strongly agree

Without culture,

consumers would have little guidance as to the appropriate actions in many consumer situations.

8

Consumer Culture

After studying this chapter, the student should be able to:

LO1 Understand how culture provides the true meaning of objects and activities.

LO2 Use the key dimensions of core societal values to understand the concept of cultural distance.

LO3 Define acculturation and enculturation.

LO4 List fundamental elements of verbal and nonverbal communication.

LO5 Discuss current emerging consumer markets and scan for opportunities.

LO1 Culture and Meaning Are Inseparable

grandé doppio latté, please! What language is this? A consumer can use this expression in over two dozen countries and get exactly what he or she wants with no translation. The popularity of Starbucks, clearly a company with American roots, has led to a universal language describing coffee consumption.

Americans do not really have a deep history as gourmet coffee lovers. In fact, prior to the last few years, the typical American coffee was cheap, weak, and, outside of Seattle and New Orleans, nondescript at best. In America, coffee is and remains the first choice for a morning beverage. In much of Europe, coffee is consumed not only in the morning but in the afternoon and evening as well. In much of Asia, coffee consumption is relatively rare as tea is viewed as the beverage of choice in the morning and throughout the day.

With all these different coffee-drinking habits and orientations, how could a single coffee company succeed with the same basic formula in so many different places around the world? In fact, the feature "The World *Is* Their Cup" describes how Starbucks defied the odds in expanding in new and different cultures like China. In the United States, a $2 cup of coffee may seem relatively high compared to traditional convenience store prices, but $2 is within reach of nearly all Americans and is hardly viewed as a luxury product. However, consider how a $2 price tag might compare in countries like Poland, Mexico, or China. For Starbucks to succeed, they have to offer an experience that adds value to the lives of consumers who come from many different backgrounds and many different orientations toward beverage consumption. Thus, Starbucks's success depends on being accepted by culture and somehow creating a meaning that conveys value in the coffee shop experience.

WHAT IS CULTURE?

Consumers make very simple decisions involving things like coffee drinking and very important and meaningful decisions involving things like religious affiliations. In all cases, what a person consumes helps determine how accepted one is by other consumers in society. Likewise, the consumption act itself generally has no absolute meaning, only meaning relative to the environment in which the act takes place. Culture, therefore, embodies meaning.

Consumer culture can be thought of as commonly held societal beliefs that define what is socially gratifying. Culture shapes value by framing everyday life in terms of these commonly held beliefs. The fact that the average price for a cup of coffee in the United States has risen indicates that in America, the beliefs that people have about the coffee-drinking experience have certainly changed and define a more valuable experience than in decades past. Culture ultimately determines what consumption behaviors are acceptable.

Although American adults enjoy coffee, some consumers believe that providing coffee to a child is unacceptable. In other areas, however, this behavior is seen as normal. Culture shapes the value of most beverages as it does with other products. Exhibit 8.1 lists some consumption behaviors that vary in meaning, value, and acceptability from culture to culture.

Culture is Hierarchical

Culture is a universal phenomenon. It is everywhere and ultimately explains the habits and idiosyncrasies

The World *Is* Their Cup!

Starbucks has over 10,000 stores in practically every corner of the world. Starbucks has even been successful in places like Paris where "experts" told them the concept was too American and inconsistent with the Parisian idea of a coffeehouse. However, can Starbucks succeed in a place where consumers associate coffee with the sensation of a Saharan desert?

This is the challenge that faces Starbucks. China is a tea-drinking country and one where a $4 grandé latté is truly a luxury. The average income in this area is under $4,000 per year. Starbucks's strategy in China is to capitalize on the stores as a gathering place. So, the stores are generally bigger with larger sitting areas than in a typical U.S. Starbucks. The ambiance is clearly Starbucks. Additionally, an emphasis on sweeter products, more food items, and fresh-brewed tea is the recipe they will follow. Starbucks hopes to deliver a high-hedonic-value experience and one that will lead to success for most of its more than 400 stores across China.

Sources: Adamy, J. (2006), "Eyeing a Billion Tea Drinkers, Starbucks Pours it on in China," *Wall Street Journal* (11/29), A1; Chao, L. (2006), "Starbucks Raises Stake in Beijing, Tianjin Stores, *Wall Street Journal* Online (11/25), **http:online.wsj.com/article/SB116167895560901902.cb.html,** accessed October 25, 2006; Adamy, J. (2007), "Starbucks Chairman Says Trouble May be Brewing," *Wall Street Journal* (2/24), A4.

of all groups of consumers. In fact, each consumer belongs to many cultural groups. For instance, a college student attending a state university in Texas is likely part of American culture, Texas culture, perhaps some ethnically defined culture such as Hispanic culture, university culture, and possibly Greek culture should he or she belong to a fraternity or sorority. In this way, culture is hierarchical. A consumer can belong to one large national culture and then to one of many smaller cultural groups existing within that culture. Exhibit 8.2 illustrates a cultural hierarchy.

The fact that this particular consumer is Texan also typifies culture. Texas has a unique and identifiable culture, and this point is illustrated by the fact that consumers have generally consistent associations with the "Texan" social schema. A student who wears

EXHIBIT 8.1
Culture, Meaning, and Value

Behavior	Meaning in United States	Alternate Meaning
Consumer age 14–18 consuming beer or wine in a restaurant	Unacceptable or even illegal in most areas.	Wine is part of a nice family meal in other areas, including much of western Europe.
People gathering to eat barbecue pork ribs	This menu is part of a pleasant social event.	Pork is not an acceptable food item among Hebrews and Muslims.
Supervisors and employees socializing together	Supervisors and coworkers can be friendly with each other.	Employees and supervisors should keep their distance away from work. An employee who acts too casually with a "senior" could incur a sanction.
Kissing	Purely a family or romantic activity.	In many nations, kissing is common when making a new acquaintance or greeting a friend.

ful soccer experience and reinforcing his or her identity as a soccer hooligan. Anthropologists have studied this cultural phenomenon by immersing themselves with the hooligan group. Some hooligans are professional people who find involvement in soccer to be a way to escape other realities, and, thus, they find hedonic value in hooligan activities.

Culture, Meaning, and Value

The focus of this chapter is on culture. This focus acknowledges that the marketplace today truly is global. Modern technology has greatly reduced the geographic barriers that prevented consumers from doing business with marketers in other parts of the world. Without culture, consumers would have little guidance as to the appropriate actions in many common consumer situations. Thus, culture performs important functions for consumers. These functions shape the value of consumer activities and include:

boots, jeans, and a Stetson to school in Massachusetts may stand out in the crowd, but this manner of dress helps a Texan fit in. This particular consumer likely also identifies with a specific age-based or generational culture and makes consumer choices that either reinforce this social identity or send the signal that he or she does not wish to be part of this group. Think about how these decisions explain simple things like music preferences.

The term **subculture** is sometimes used to refer to a culture existing at a lower level than overall culture. Thus, Exhibit 8.2 illustrates how culture can be broken down into multiple subcultures. Generational culture can be referred to as a subculture of regional culture, which is a subculture of ethnic culture and so forth.

Group membership changes the value of things. American consumers, for instance, generally find watching soccer dull and thus a low-value activity. In contrast, consumers all around Europe and in other parts of the world find soccer to be the number one spectator sport. Cultural groups even arise within sports fans, and an extreme soccer fan may even become a *soccer hooligan* who participates in extreme and sometimes violent behaviors as a way of creating a personally meaning-

1. **Giving meaning to objects.** Consider how much culture defines the meaning of food, religious objects, and everyday items like furniture. For instance, in Japan, refrigerators are tiny by most western standards.

EXHIBIT 8.2
Culture Is Hierarchical

National Culture

Ethnic Culture

Regional Culture

Generational Culture

University Culture

2. Giving meaning to activities. Consider, for example, the role of things as simple as recreational activities and even washing (hygiene). A daily shower is not a universally accepted norm.

3. Facilitating communication. The shared meaning of things facilitates communication. When strangers meet, culture indicates whether a handshake, hug, or kiss is most appropriate. Things as simple as making eye contact can take on dramatically different meanings from one culture to another.

CULTURAL NORMS

Culture, meaning, and value are very closely intertwined. For this reason, culture determines things that are socially rewarding (valuable) or socially unrewarding (not valuable). A consumer who acts inconsistently with cultural expectations risks being socially ostracized. The term **cultural norm** refers to a rule that specifies the appropriate behavior in a given situation within a specific culture. Most, but not all, cultural norms are unwritten and simply understood by members of a cultural group.

In Korea, for example, a consumer is not expected to pour a drink for himself or herself when out in a bar or restaurant with friends or family. The cultural norm is that one pours a drink for friends and family. Thus, by pouring drinks for others and waiting for someone else to pour a drink for him or her, the consumer has performed a socially rewarding (valuable) act consistent with the norms of that society.

CULTURAL SANCTIONS

So, what happens to a consumer who performs an act inconsistent with cultural norms? Unfortunately, the consumer is likely to experience a cultural sanction. A **cultural sanction** refers to the penalties associated with performing a nongratifying or culturally inconsistent behavior. Cultural sanctions often are relatively innocuous. For instance, if one were to pour her own drink in

Korea, she is likely to only get a curious look or to suffer some innocent teasing from members of the group. In other instances however, a culturally inconsistent act may mean being shunned or suffering banishment from a group.

Many societies still have strong cultural norms about marrying outside of one's social class, religion, or ethnic group. Violation of this norm can result in isolation from family or worse. Physically or socially harming a family member for fraternizing beyond one's cultural group represents a fairly strong cultural sanction.

Popular Culture

Popular culture captures cultural trends and also shapes norms and sanctions within society. A few decades ago, a male American college student might routinely wear platform shoes, silk shirts, sideburns, and maybe even an Afro hairstyle. For a student in the 1970s, all of these consumer behaviors would be consistent with popular culture. A student who showed up at class in this fashion today would certainly stand out from his or her classmates and might face at the least one or two curious glances. Pop icons such as the Jonas Brothers or Taylor Swift help determine acceptable style for many groups of admirers who desire to fit in with today's popular culture.

Sex Roles

Sex roles refer to the societal expectations for men and women among members of a cultural group. Sex roles are ubiquitous in society, and inconsistency with them can be a source of sanctions. The difference between societal expectations of men and women vary less in western cultures than they do in eastern cultures where sex-based divisions in roles remain more obvious.[1] Recent comparisons of brand personality tend to show greater androgyny, meaning neither clearly male nor female, among U.S. perceptions of brands relative to Korean brands.[2]

That said, even in western cultures, certain responsibilities such as child care and household cleaning still remain unevenly spread among cultures. In Italy, a relatively feminine culture by western standards, women spend a great deal of time keeping their houses clean. Even an Italian woman who works outside of the home is likely to wash the floors of her home at least twice a week. Women who do not work outside the home likely

© MIKE KEMP/RUBBERBALL/JUPITERIMAGES

wash the floors nearly every day. In addition, they tend to use stronger cleaners than their U.S. counterparts. Clearly, all of this cleaning provides utilitarian value through the result of a clean house, but Italian women also take inner gratification from the activities because they help fulfill their specific societal sex role.[3] In western culture, men traditionally picked up the tab during a date, but as cultures become more androgynous, this tradition may be falling by the wayside.

Marketers need to be aware of the relative sex roles within societies. Men and women may share purchasing responsibilities differently from culture to culture. In the United States, the woman in the family remains the primary purchasing agent for most things. Men are generally allowed to make purchase decisions alone for things such as lawn care equipment and beer. The woman even purchases the majority of clothing for the male of the house. However, in Italy men place great pride in their business attire and are more likely to want control of these purchase decisions. Marketers therefore need to do research to help identify these roles or else run the risk of targeting the wrong family member with marketing communications.

LO2 Using Core Societal Values

WHERE DOES CULTURE COME FROM?

Culture is commonly used to explain and predict consumer behavior.[4] Estimates suggest that out of all academic explanations of consumer behavior, more than 10% of all explanations include culture as a key factor.[5] Cultural beliefs define what religion is acceptable, what types of art and recreation are preferred, what manners are considered polite, the roles for different types of individuals including expectations for men and women in a society, and much more. Distinguishing the unique effects of culture over these more specific things is extremely difficult since as part of culture, these things tend to function together. But, as a whole, there is little doubt that culture causes differences in the value consumers perceive from different products and experiences.[6]

How do people in one nation end up with a culture distinct from that of people in another? In other words, what causes culture? The answer to this question involves two important components.

First, ecological factors cause differences in culture because they change the relative value of objects. **Ecological factors** are the physical characteristics that describe the physical environment and habitat of a particular place. Thus, for example, consumers from groups that have traditionally lived in desert areas place a great value on water relative to consumers from areas filled with freshwater lakes. As a result, consumers from this area may have different habits when it comes to hygiene, including the frequency and duration of baths or showers. This can affect sales of beauty products, soaps, and toilet water and also things like hotel room and building design.

While tradition can be thought of as influencing culture, one can safely say that, in the long run, culture also defines tradition.

Second, over time, tradition develops among groups of peoples, and these traditions carry forward to structure society. **Tradition** in this sense refers to the customs and accepted ways of structuring society. Traditions include things like the family and political structures of a society. In the United States, Australia, Canada, and much of Europe, families traditionally consist of two generations (parents and children) living in a household, where a husband and wife share decision making. In other cultures, India for instance, more than two generations (grandparents, parents, and children) may share a household, and the key decision maker is the oldest male living in the house. Thus, consumer advertising may need to be completely redesigned based on the traditional family decision-making style associated with a culture. While tradition can be thought of as influencing culture, one can safely say that, in the long run, culture also defines tradition.

Exhibit 8.3 illustrates how tradition and ecology come together to influence culture, with each culture being described by different amounts of core societal values (discussed later in this chapter), and these

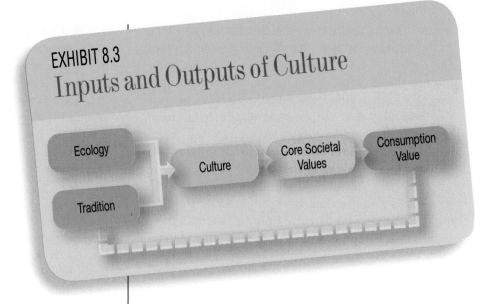

EXHIBIT 8.3
Inputs and Outputs of Culture

values driving differences in consumer behaviors and the value derived from them. Over time, traditions become embedded in culture and become relatively stable. However, while stable, they do slowly change as illustrated by the changes in places where people could traditionally smoke without fear of sanctions. In this sense, not only are the choices and behaviors of consumers influenced by culture, but, in the long run, subtle changes in these choices and behaviors also influence culture.

© FOODPIX/JUPITERIMAGES

Religious traditions shape consumption experiences.

DIMENSIONS OF CULTURAL VALUES

Although conflicting views exist on what exactly are the best dimensions to describe differences in cultural values, the most widely applied dimensions are those developed by Geert Hofstede.[7] This theory of value-based differences in cultures is based on five key dimensions with each dimension representing a core societal value. **Core societal values (CSV)**, or **cultural values**, represent a commonly agreed-upon consensus about the most preferable ways of living within a society. Even though not all members of a culture may share precisely the same values to the same degree, a specific cultural group will tend to have common worldviews along these dimensions. Exhibit 8.3 illustrates how core societal values serve as the mechanism by which culture affects value. The values can be classified using multiple dimensions. In some cases, the dimensions overlap with each other or are related to one another.

Individualism

The first CSV dimension contrasts cultures based on relative amounts of individualism.[8] **Individualism** as a CSV means the extent to which people are expected to take care of themselves and their immediate family. Highly individualistic societies place high value on self-reliance, individual initiative, and personal achievement. In contrast, nations with low individualism are seen as high in **collectivism**, which refers to the extent to which an individual's life is intertwined with a large cohesive group. Highly collectivistic societies tend to live in extended fami-

A typical advertisement appealing to individualism as a CSV.

lies, take their identity from the groups to which they belong, and be very loyal to these groups.

Clearly, this dimension has important implications for the way consumers make decisions and the way that value is extracted from consumption (see the CVF in Chapter 2 for an illustration). In the United States, the value of various products often is communicated by illustrating the extent to which personal freedom can be achieved through consumption. American consumers often see important purchases as an extension of themselves. Advertisements for cigarettes, jeans, ATVs, and even laptop computers commonly use adjectives such as *rugged*, *tough*, and *dependable*.[9] In contrast, an advertisement for a collective culture may rely more on adjectives such as *honest* or *friendly*.

Generally, western societies tend to be more individualistic, whereas eastern nations tend to be more collectivistic. This generality is just that—a generality! There are exceptions to this rule. Later, we'll discuss specific scores on all dimensions across many countries.

Masculinity

The **masculinity** CSV dimension captures distinctions existing in societies based on mannerisms typically associated with male traits such as valuing assertiveness and control over traditional feminine traits such as caring, conciliation, and community. **Femininity** is seen as the opposite of masculinity, but in this case, the term does not refer to a political or social movement or even to the prominence that women have within a society. In fact, women's traits tend to vary less from nation to nation than do those of men, so this dimension is most clearly obvious within a masculine culture. In other words, in a culture with low masculinity, men also tend to share some female traits.[10]

Advertisements for laptop computers in a highly masculine nation such as Japan may emphasize the computer's ability to help one get ahead. So a newer, faster computer with more features can help one assert himself in the workplace or at school. In contrast, in a more feminine country such as Mexico, an advertisement for the same laptop computer might emphasize the benefit of being able to stay in touch with family and friends through e-mail and web-based communication.

Power Distance

Power distance is the extent to which authority and privilege are divided among different groups within society and the extent to which these facts of life are accepted by the people within the society. Social class distinctions become a very real issue among consumers in high-power-distance nations. However, the distinctions go beyond just social class and affect relationships between supervisory and subordinate employees and even between students and teachers.

Low-power-distance nations tend to be more egalitarian. First names are commonly used even among people of different social classes and even between employees and supervisors. In high-power-distance nations, those with less status must show deference to those with greater status; therefore, the lower-status

masculinity sex role distinction within a group that values assertiveness and control; CSV opposite of femininity

femininity sex role distinction within a group that emphasizes the prioritization of relational variables such as caring, conciliation, and community; CSV opposite of masculinity

power distance extent to which authority and privileges are divided among different groups within society and the extent to which these facts of life are accepted by the people within the society person would not likely call a person of higher status by first name.

In many Asian nations, where power distance is relatively high compared to that in the United States, the terms *senior* and *junior* are often used to capture status distinctions. A student might be junior to a faculty supervisor or even to another student who preceded him or her through a program of study. When one is unclear about whether or not he or she is junior or senior to another, he or she might well ask the other consumer, "How old are you?" Age would be a tiebreaker with older people having more status than younger people. Senior and junior status can affect simple things such as seating arrangements and whether or not one carries his or her own briefcase. Juniors may need to be careful in what they buy and do so as not to seem superior in any substantive way to a senior. A consumer violating a custom and acting more "senior" than appropriate may well face cultural sanctions for the behavior.

> Uncertainty avoidance has important implications for consumer behavior because marketing success and improved quality of life often depend on obtaining value from something innovative and, therefore, somewhat unfamiliar.

In high-power-distance nations, certain consumer behaviors are designated exclusively to individuals by class or status. For example, in high-power-distance nations, golf is seen as an activity only for those with very high status. Additionally, authority appeals in marketing are more effective when power distance is high.[11]

Uncertainty Avoidance

Uncertainty avoidance is just what the term implies. A culture high in uncertainty avoidance is uncomfortable with things that are ambiguous or unknown. Consumers high in uncertainty avoidance prefer the known, avoid taking risks, and like life to be structured and routine. Uncertainty avoidance has important implications for consumer behavior because marketing success and improved quality of life often depend on obtaining value from something innovative and, therefore, somewhat unfamiliar. The task becomes making the unfamiliar seem familiar in appealing to consumers high in uncertainty avoidance.

Nations that are high in uncertainty avoidance will be slower to adopt product innovations. Additionally, nations that are relatively high in uncertainty avoidance, such as France, will react differently to basic CB generalizations. For instance, one such generalization is that scarcity affects the perceived value of products. A scarce product is worth more, and consumers are more likely to purchase a product perceived to be scarce. However, the extent to which scarcity drives actual purchase intentions is more pronounced among cultures high in uncertainty avoidance.[12] In other words, consumers in high-uncertainty-avoidance cultures are quicker to buy something because of perceived scarcity.

Basic consumer principles such as the price–quality relationship are also affected by differing CSV. For instance, the price–quality relationship is not as strong among cultures with high uncertainty avoidance. These consumers are more skeptical and likely to discern individual features of products separately. Such is the case with Chinese consumers, who are more likely to perceive a price–risk relationship than a price–quality relationship. In other words, higher price means higher risk in conditions of uncertainty.[13]

Consumers from high-uncertainty-avoidance cultures also demand greater amounts of product information and explanation. Bosch automotive industries, based in Germany, designs different packages for products sold in Europe and products sold in the United States. For example, a packet containing replacement windshield wipers might be sold in a simple cellophane package in the United States. The same product might require a box through much of Europe, not because the products differ in size but because the box allows more room to write product information about the wipers and how to install them than does a plastic wrapper. As a result, the European customers find more value and experience greater job satisfaction on these projects.

Long-Term Orientation

The final CSV dimension is long-term orientation. **Long-term orientation** reflects values consistent with Confucian philosophy and a prioritization of future rewards over short-term benefits. As such, high long-term orientation means that a consumer values thriftiness and perseverance as well as the maintenance of long-term relationships.[14] Relationships need time to develop and are intended to last for a lifetime. As a result, negotiations between suppliers and buyers are more likely to consider long-term effects to both parties in high-long-term-orientation cultures such as Japan.[15] At the other end of the spectrum, a short-term orientation is associated more with immediate payoffs and face saving.[16]

Guanxi (pronounced gawn-zeye) is the Chinese term for a way of doing business in which parties must first invest time and resources in getting to know one another and becoming comfortable with one another before consummating any important deal. Guanxi is a common mode of operation among cultures with high long-term orientation—as with many nations in the Far East.[17] Western consumers depend on credit cards for everyday purchases and even in many cases as instant financing for luxury items. Thus, American consumers often have multiple credit cards, each from a different bank or credit company. As the Chinese economy develops, the principles of guanxi and long-term orientation present barriers for credit card companies.[18] The Chinese consumers are loath to take a card from a company they do not know or fully understand. Also, the idea of financing consumer products remains *foreign*.

THE CSV SCOREBOARD

A CSV scoreboard can be put together using historical CSV dimension scores found in many resources including the Hofstede website **www.geert-hofstede.com**. How does your country stack up on the CSV scoreboard? The CSV scores for a given country can be essential information for marketers wishing to appeal to consumers in another country. The more similar the CSV scores, the more likely consumers find value in the same or similar products and experiences.

BRIC

Exhibit 8.4 shows a CSV scoreboard for a few select nations. Brazil, Russia, India, and China represent widely accepted emerging economies. The acronym **BRIC** refers to the collective economies of these nations. These nations are key targets for foreign investment, and the ripple effect is that consumers in these nations are becoming wealthier and better targets for all manner of goods and services. Doing business in these nations is

guanxi (pronounced gawn-zeye) Chinese term for a way of doing business in which parties must first invest time and resources in getting to know one another and becoming comfortable with one another before consummating any important deal

BRIC acronym that refers to the collective economies of Brazil, Russia, India, and China

EXHIBIT 8.4
CSV Scoreboard for the United States, Australia, United Kingdom, Brazil, Russia, India, and China

	Power Distance	Individualism	Masculinity	Uncertainty Avoidance	Long-Term Orientation
United States	40	91	62	46	29
Australia	36	90	61	51	31
United Kingdom	35	89	66	35	25
Brazil	69	38	49	76	65
Russia	93	39	36	95	55a
India	77	48	56	40	61
China *	80	20	66	30	118

a LTO score for Russia is not available. This value represents the average LTO score for these countries. Averages: PDI, 59; IDV, 44; MAS, 51; UAI, 66; LTO, 45.

hardly the same, though, as their CSV scores show. Thus, in this truly global marketplace, serving consumers in emerging markets can be an important route to business success. Some are now considering where the next emerging nations will be.[19]

© VARIO IMAGES GMBH & CO.KG/ALAMY

CSV Leaders

Among all nations with CSV scores, Austria has the lowest power-distance scores, and Malaysia has the highest. The United States has relatively low power distance with only 15 nations reporting lower scores. For individualism, Guatemala reports the lowest score, and the United States has the highest. Sweden reports the lowest masculinity score, and Japan the highest with the exception of the Slovak nations. The United States is neither clearly masculine nor clearly feminine. Singapore reports the lowest uncertainty avoidance score and Greece the highest. The United States is relatively low on uncertainty avoidance with only 12 nations reporting a lower score. Long-term orientation scores are available for only a few nations. But, among those with scores, Pakistan has the lowest (meaning that it is the most short-term oriented), and China has the highest.

CULTURAL DISTANCE

More and more businesses are considering reaching out to markets outside of their own country. Certainly, the Internet has helped reduce the market separations caused by geographic distance. However, consider businesses like Carrefour, Subway, Accor Hotels, and Zaras. Each already operates many stores in many countries. How should a company decide where it should expand internationally? In other words, where will it be successful?

Two approaches to this important question can be taken. First, perhaps the most intuitive response is to look to neighboring countries with which the home country shares a border. Certainly, many U.S. businesses exist in Canada and vice versa. This approach is based on geographic distance. Countries are attractive because they are nearby and can be easily reached both in terms of marketing communications and physical distribution.

The second approach looks more at how similar a target nation's consumers are to the home consumers.

> How should a company decide where it should expand internationally?

This approach is based more on **cultural distance**, which represents how disparate one nation is from another in terms of their CSVs. Thus, with this approach, consumers can be compared by using scores available in a CSV scoreboard. For example, Exhibit 8.5 shows the difference scores for all nations depicted in the CSV scoreboard compared to those of the U.S.A. These are obtained simply by subtracting the score for each nation on each dimension from the corresponding score for U.S. consumers.

Notice the small scores on each dimension for the differences between Australia, the United Kingdom, and the United States compared to the other nations. The total cultural difference between nations can be summarized with a simple formula. One might consider simply adding up the difference scores; however, the negative and positive scores could cancel each other out, making two nations that are really quite different appear similar. Thus, one way to correct this problem is by using the squared differences much as would be the case in computing statistical variation. For example, the following formula is used to compute the total cultural distances from the United States for each nation shown in Exhibit 8.5:

$$CD = \sqrt{\sum_{i=1}^{5} (TCSV_i - BCSV_i)^2}$$

where CD = cultural distance, TCSV = target country value score on dimension i, and BCSV = baseline country value score on dimension i.

Thus, for example, the CD for Australia from the United States is

$$CD = \sqrt{\begin{array}{c}(36 - 40)^2 + (90 - 91)^2 + (61 - 62)^2 + \\ (51 - 46)^2 + (31 - 29)^2\end{array}} = \sqrt{47} = 6.9$$

Among all comparisons, few would show so little difference as this. Compare these with the CD scores for the

BRIC countries. The CD score can be easily computed for all nations for which CSV scores are available.

So, countries with relatively low CD scores are more similar and thus, they tend to value the same types of consumption experiences. In fact, the term **CANZUS** is sometimes used to refer to the close similarity in values between Canada, Australia, New Zealand, and the United States.[20] Additionally, the U could also represent the United Kingdom because the nations are nearly identical from a CD perspective. Not surprisingly, common consumer products, retailers, and restaurant chains that are successful in one of these countries tend to be successful in the others as well.

International expansion decisions should consider CD as well as geography.

LO3 How Is Culture Learned?

Culture is a learned process. Consumers learn culture through one of two socialization processes discussed in this section. **Socialization** involves learning through observation and the active processing of information about lived, everyday experience. The process takes place in a sequence something like this:

Social interaction ↦ modeling ↦ reinforcement

As consumers interact they begin to model (meaning enact) behaviors learned or seen. Reinforcement occurs through the process of rewarding reactions or sanctions. Additionally, learning results in CSVs that are relatively enduring. Societal values are not easily changed, and the clash between peoples with differing CSVs has been around since the beginning of time.

CANZUS acronym that refers to the close similarity in values between Canada, Australia, New Zealand, and the United States

socialization learning through observation of and the active processing of information about lived, everyday experience

enculturation way a person learns his or her native culture

ENCULTURATION

The most basic way by which consumers learn a culture is through an enculturation process. **Enculturation** represents the way a person learns his or her native culture. In other words, enculturation represents the way in which a consumer learns and develops shared understandings of things with his or her family.[21]

Why do some consumers like wasabi or hot peppers? The answer is enculturation. Consumers are not born liking very pungent food. But, early in life, children observe the diets of their parents and relatives and come to mimic those behaviors. When they do, they receive

EXHIBIT 8.5
CSV Difference Scores Relative to American Consumers

	Power Distance	Individualism	Masculinity	Uncertainty Avoidance	Long-Term Orientation	Total Distance Score
Australia	−4	−1	−1	5	2	6.9
United Kingdom	−5	−2	4	−11	−4	13.5
Brazil	29	−53	−13	30	36	77.6
Russia	53	−52	−26	49	26	96.3
India	37	−43	−6	−6	32	65.7
China	40	−71	4	−6	89	121.8

overt social rewards, thereby reinforcing their dietary choice. In Kyrgyzstan, children grow up drinking fermented mare's milk. Although *Kumis*, the Kyrg name for fermented mare's milk, has what can kindly be called a "peculiar" flavor by most standards, the fact that one grows up drinking this creates the acquired taste that makes it palatable or even tasty. The entire idea of habituation, discussed in an earlier chapter, provides a mechanism that helps make this type of enculturation possible.

ACCULTURATION

Acculturation is the process by which consumers come to learn a culture other than their natural, native culture—that is, the culture to which one may adapt when exposed to a new set of CSVs. Acculturation is a learning process. Therefore, when a consumer becomes acculturated, chances are that old beliefs have been replaced by new beliefs. Therefore, children generally become acculturated more quickly than adults.[22] Retail managers at Sainsbury's supermarket in the U.K. are aiming more lines of food products specifically at children. As a marketing tool, this may attract more shoppers, but as an image tool, Sainsbury is positioned as providing more healthy alternatives for children.[22a]

However, not all consumers who are introduced into a new culture acculturate. Several factors can inhibit acculturation. For example, strong **ethnic identification**, the degree to which consumers feel a sense of belonging to the culture of their ethnic origins, can make consumers feel close-minded about adopting products from a different culture. When ethnic identification is strong, consumers in a new land may even avoid learning the language of a new land. For instance,

pockets of Chinese immigrants in Canada with strong ethnic identification choose to live the majority of their lives interacting with only other Chinese immigrants, purchasing Chinese products nearly exclusively, and paying attention to only Chinese language media.[23]

Consumer ethnocentrism is a belief among consumers that their ethnic group is superior to others and that the products that come from their native land are superior to other products. Consumers who are highly ethnocentric believe that it is only right to support workers in their native country by buying products from that country. Ethnocentrism is highly related to the concept of uncertainty avoidance. When ethnocentrism is very high, consumers who are in a foreign land may create their own communities within a larger enclave and display little interaction with the outside "world." Many Turkish neighborhoods exist in Germany, for instance, and many of these Turks have little contact with people outside their own neighborhoods.

Exhibit 8.6 illustrates factors that either inhibit or encourage consumer acculturation. Simply put, male consumers who have high ethnic identification, high ethnocentrism, and are relatively old are the worst targets for adopting products of a different or new culture. Interestingly, from an international marketing perspective, CSV profiles characterized by high uncertainty avoidance and strong masculinity are likely not good targets for imported goods relative to other countries. The inhibitions that consumers have about "foreign" products distract from the value the products offer because their very meaning is inconsistent with the consumer's current belief structure.

©ISTOCKPHOTO.COM/BOLESLAW KUBICA

QUARTET OF INSTITUTIONS

So, consumers *get* culture through either enculturation or acculturation. Each of these is a learning process. Consumers learn primarily through the influence of cultural institutions. Previously, consumer behavior theory suggested that a triad of institutions accounted for much of the cultural learning process. However, more recently a fourth institution has been recognized. Thus,

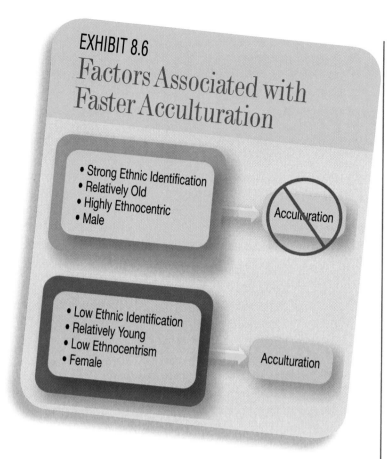

EXHIBIT 8.6
Factors Associated with Faster Acculturation

- Strong Ethnic Identification
- Relatively Old
- Highly Ethnocentric
- Male

→ ⊘ Acculturation

- Low Ethnic Identification
- Relatively Young
- Low Ethnocentrism
- Female

→ Acculturation

we now recognize a **quartet of institutions** that are responsible for communicating the CSV through both formal and informal processes from one generation to another. The four institutions comprising the quartet are (see Exhibit 8.7):

1. **Family**
2. **School**
3. **Church**
4. **Media**

Family, school, and church have long been recognized as primary agents for acculturation and enculturation. Each of these is recognized as a vehicle for teaching values to children; therefore, they are agents of enculturation. Consumers become socialized by the behaviors that are affiliated with specific institutions.

More recently the impact of media on culture has been recognized. For instance, many nations actively limit the amount of American media that is allowed in a country in the belief that this will protect their culture from becoming overly Americanized or westernized. An influx of nonnative media can indeed influence the rate of acculturation.[24] In addition, children who watch more television have a more distorted view of reality and generally presume that the typical family owns more luxury items and is better off materialistically than families in that particular culture really are. Children who watch more television become more acculturated to consumer society and are more materialistic than children who view less television.[25] Therefore, many families try to actively limit the amount of television viewed by their children.[26]

> **quartet of institutions** four groups responsible for communicating the CSV through both formal and informal processes from one generation to another: family, school, church, and media

World Teen Culture?

Consumer media involve more than just television. Radio, print publications, music, and web-based communication all can play a role in shaping culture and, therefore, the things that consumers value.[27] The Internet facilitates communication among consumers around the world, contributing to what some believe is a more universally similar **world teen culture**. Evidence of similar tastes among teenaged consumers around the world is obvious if one takes a look at teen purchase and consumption patterns. Many of these tastes are influenced by the western media's depiction of celebrities. Thus, fashion and entertainment companies in particular may find segmenting based on age as useful as geography.

EXHIBIT 8.7
The Quartet of Institutions

Church

What should I do today? What do I value?

Family

School

Media

world teen culture
speculation that teenagers around the world are more similar to each other than to people from other generations in the same culture

modeling process of imitating others' behavior; a form of observational learning

Brands listed in Exhibit 8.8 have particular appeal to teens in practically all corners of the world. Coca-Cola and McDonald's, for example, are brand names that are listed among teens' favorite brands throughout much of the world.[28] Coca-Cola hopes to build brand reputation even further among teens by taking advantage of virtual media. Through **secondlife.com**, Coke has launched a major presence that includes opportunities for consumers to build a virtual vending machine which grants wishes to loyal Coke drinkers.[29] Thus, Coke is attempting to use the latest media to create virtual experiences that help build loyalty among the teen market segment.

Although teens around the world may find value in many of the same types of music and clothing, research suggests that the cultural values of their home nation remain relatively distinct from nation to nation, particularly among personal products.[30] American teen consumers, for instance, still rate freedom as the most important CSV. In contrast, teens from Arab countries list faith as the most important CSV.[31] These differences translate into different consumption habits. For example, even though McDonald's is popular among teens practically everywhere, preferences for fast-food brands still differ between Asians and Americans.[32]

Culture and Policy-Related Consumer Communication

Differences in CSVs may have public policy implications as well. A study of teen consumers in countries such as Italy, Austria, Slovenia, Uzbekistan, Russia, and the United States, among others, found that antismoking ads were not equally effective. The results suggest that antismoking ads targeted toward countries high in individualism should emphasize the ill effects of smoking to one's self. In contrast, in countries with high collectivism, anti-

Young consumers from different cultures around the world appear to have similar tastes in apparel.

smoking ads that emphasize the negative effects of smoking on other consumers are more effective.[33]

Studies measuring CSV among consumers still show distinctions consistent with the profiles discussed earlier. Thus, beyond the teen years particularly, differences in tastes, political views, and preferences are expected to remain somewhat distinct from culture to culture.

Modeling

Modeling is an important way in which consumers are socialized into a specific culture either through acculturation or enculturation. A famous cliché says that imitation is the sincerest form of flattery. Well, **modeling** is precisely a process of imitating others' behavior. Modeling is a form of observational learning.[34] Young children, for instance, will tend to model their parents' behavior.

As children become older, they may choose to model the behavior of older peers more than they model that

EXHIBIT 8.8
Similarities and Differences among Teen Consumers

Favorite Brands	Similar Activities	Less Similar Choices
Coca-Cola	Listening to Music	Religious Ideas/Activities
McDonald's	Using Mobile Phone	Cosmetic Brands
Nike	Surfing the Internet	Political Ideas
Disney	Video Games	Equality of Sexes
Cadbury	Smoking	
Nokia		

What Consumers Do Know Can Hurt Them?

T he Chinese government certainly believes that electronic media can affect the core societal values of consumers. Chinese officials are actively engaged in censoring the Internet sites available to the typical Chinese consumer. This censorship has caused problems for companies like Google, Microsoft, and Yahoo, all of which have been scrutinized by U.S. officials for participating in China's censorship efforts. Google actually places a disclaimer along with its searches that notifies the Chinese consumer that content has been censored. This simple act may actually cost Google advertising share in China. Baidu, a search engine originating in China, has seen its ad share increase relative to that of Google as Google receives more attention for acting rebellious toward the censorship activities. Baidu also participates in the censorship but does so without resistance. Thus, Chinese consumers appear relatively comfortable with the idea of censorship relative to western consumers. The acceptance of censorship may be a clear demonstration of the high uncertainty avoidance present in Chinese culture.

Sources: Einhorn, B. (2006), "Testing China's Web Tolerance," *Business Week Online* (1/23), 10; Zhao, M. (2006), "Don't Hand Me That Gu Ge," *Forbes Asia*, 2 (9/4), 39.

shaping socialization process by which consumers' behaviors slowly adapt to a culture through a series of rewards and sanctions

verbal communication transfer of information through either the literal spoken or written word

of normative influences.[36] Not all cultures reward complaining in the same way.[37] In collectivistic cultures, complaining can be a sign of disrespect and may be looked at as inappropriate for minor inconveniences. American consumers who complain about their hotel room being slightly too warm are not likely to risk sanction. However, in a more collectivistic culture, complaining about a room that is slightly warm can be looked down upon. Therefore, the extra added value that comes from group acceptance is greater among cultures where collectivism is stronger than individualism.

of their parents. Adolescent children's attitudes toward smoking as well as their actual smoking behavior are largely influenced by the activities of peer referents.[35] In other words, adolescents will tend to model the behavior of those they aspire to become.

Shaping

Shaping is a socialization process by which consumers' behaviors slowly adapt to a culture through a series of rewards and sanctions. Reference group influence will be discussed in more detail in the next chapter. At this point, however, think about how one might modify his or her behavior to win acceptance from a group. A child might decide to wear different clothes to school as a way of trying to fit in. The way that other students react to the new attire can serve to shape the student's future behavior.

The CSV profile of a culture can influence the effectiveness of cultural shaping. For instance, more individualistic cultures are less susceptible to these types

LO4 Fundamental Elements of Communication

VERBAL COMMUNICATION

Obviously, language can sometimes be a problem. Anyone who has ever needed directions to some location in a place where he or she doesn't know the language can appreciate this. However, sometimes, even when the correct language is used, communication can still be awkward or difficult. The term Chinglish is used to refer to the awkward use of English traditionally common in China.[38]

In this section, **verbal communication** refers to the transfer of information through either the literal spoken or written word. Consumers will have difficulty finding value in things they cannot understand. Marketers have long wrestled with the problem of translating advertisements, research instruments, product labels, and promotional materials into foreign languages for foreign markets. This problem is only made more prevalent in today's truly international marketplace.

Verbal communication can even be difficult within a single language. Almost every language is spoken slightly differently from place to place—or with several unique **dialects**. English in the United States isn't exactly the same as English in England, which is not the same as English in Australia, which is not the same as English in Ireland or other places where English is spoken. Thus, translation alone is insufficient to guarantee effective communication. Exhibit 8.9 provides some examples of difficulties in communicating even simple ideas through the spoken or written word. And, we are not even considering the complications added by slang!

Translation Equivalence

Bilingual speakers realize that often, more than one way exists to potentially express the meaning of one language in another. In some cases, words that exist in one language have no precise equivalent in another. In other instances, even when the same word may exist, people in other cultures do not use the word the same way. Thus, interpretation errors and blunders are understandable unless great care is taken.

Translational equivalence exists when two phrases share the same precise meaning in two different cultures. Translation–back translation is a way to try to produce translational equivalence. With this process, one bilingual speaker takes the original phrase and translates it from the original language into the new language. Then, a second, independent bilingual speaker translates the phrase from the new language back into the original language. Assuming the retranslated phrase matches the first, translational equivalence exists. If not, either the phrase needs to be dropped or more work possibly involving even other speakers fluent in both languages is needed to determine if a common meaning can be found by changing the words in one or both languages.

EXHIBIT 8.9
Example Problems with Verbal Communication

Communication	Situation	Intended Communication	Problem
"Yo vi la Papa!"	Spanish-language slogan on t-shirts prior to Pope's visit to Mexico	"I saw the Pope!"	"La Papa" is "the potato." El (or al) Papa is the Pope. So, the t-shirts said "I saw the potato."
"Boy, am I stuffed!"	English-language restaurant slogan spoken by middle-aged man.	"Boy, am I full!" (meaning had a lot to eat)	Slogan works fine in the United States; however, in Australia, "stuffed" means pregnant. So, slogan depicts middle-aged, slightly overweight man saying "Boy, am I pregnant!"
"Strawberry Crap Dessert"	English placed on pre-prepared, refrigerated pancakes by Japanese firm intending product for Chinese market.	"Strawberry crêpe"	English can convey a quality image to products in much of Asia even if most consumers can't read the words. Here, the phonics are probably just a little off.
"Bite the waxed tadpole"	Chinese label for Coca-Cola	"Coca-Cola"	Coke tried to find the best phonetic way to produce something sounding like "Coca-Cola." In some Chinese dialects, but not all, strange interpretations like this resulted.
"Mist-stick for your hair!"	Clairol's name for a new hair care product introduced in Germany	A "mist stick"	Mist-stick, when pronounced, is the German word for "diarrhea."

CAUTIOU SUIPPERY

© JON BOWER CHINA/ALAMY

What Do You Get When You Cross Chinese and English? Lost??

The 2008 Olympic Games were held in Beijing, China. With the Olympics, thousands upon thousands of visitors flocked to China. Chinese officials launched a campaign in 2002 to clean up something they felt was embarrassing and something that others felt was charming. What were they cleaning up? The Chinglish, which is the awkward English translations of simple phrases, which exists throughout China. Imagine encountering signs with the following messages:

- Execution in progress!
- The slippery are very crafty.
- Dongda Hospital for Anus and Intestine Disease Beijing
- Show mercy to the Slender Grass.
- Be careful not to let skies fall.

China is not alone in slip-ups like these, and the international traveler can be both bewildered and amused. Retailers and service providers operating internationally need to take care that their translations are accurate and send the right message. Obviously, the Chinese government understands that even your non-native words can shape a consumer's image of a country or brand.

Okay, here is the intended meaning of the lines above, respectively: Caution—Work in progress, Wet floor, Proctology hospital, Keep off the grass, and Hold on to your skis so they don't fall (from a chair lift)!

Sources: Xinhua (2007), "Ahead of Olympics, Beijing Says Goodbye to 'Chinglish'," Yahoo Sports India, **http://in.sports.yahoo.com/070929/43/6lcge.html**, accessed 2/20/2008. Fong, Mei (2007), "Tired of Laughter, Beijing Gets Rid of Bad Translations," *Wall Street Journal*, February 5, A1.

rated a young woman who was 5 feet 2 inches tall for height, she might be rated quite tall. However, if a Norwegian rated the same person, she would be rated as quite short.

Metric equivalence refers to the state in which consumers are shown to use numbers to represent quantities the same way across cultures. Metric equivalence is necessary to draw basic comparisons about consumers from different countries concerning important consumer relationships. Comparing average scores for consumer attitudes from one culture to the next requires another form of equivalence known as scalar equivalence. The procedures for performing tests of metric equivalence are beyond the scope of this text, but students of consumer behavior and international marketing should be aware of these approaches because comparing quantities across cultures can be tricky.[39]

NONVERBAL COMMUNICATION

Metric Equivalence

Once a common meaning is established, things could still go wrong when consumer researchers compare consumer reactions from one country with those from another. Researchers who apply typical survey techniques such as Likert scales or semantic differentials may wish to compare scores from one culture with those from another. This is valid only if the two culture–language combinations use numbers in a somewhat similar fashion. For example, if a Chinese consumer

A conductor at a train station in Germany is approached by an American tourist who wants to know how many stops it will be until he reaches his destination. The train is noisy and filled with people so the conductor holds up his pointer finger in response. When the train stops, the tourist quickly exits. However, he'll soon realize he is not in the right location. Why? In Germany, one would be indicated by holding up the thumb.

Nonverbal communication refers to information passed through some nonverbal act—in other words, communication not involving the literal spoken or written word. This example illustrates intentional nonverbal communication; however, much communication through this means is unintentional or automatic. Many nonverbal communication cues are culturally laden so that the meaning depends on culture.

Exhibit 8.10 depicts several aspects of nonverbal communication and the way they come together to create effective communication. High-context cultures emphasize communication through nonverbal elements. In contrast, low-context cultures, such as Germany, emphasize the spoken word and what you say is truly what you mean. The elements of nonverbal communication are touched on briefly in the following sections.

Time

In America, the expression "time is money" is often used. Americans typically place a high value on time and timeliness. The high value placed on timeliness may be due to the importance of individualism and achievement as core values. When an American consumer plans a formal dinner meeting for 7:30 P.M., he or she expects everyone to be present at 7:30 P.M.

Consumers from some other cultures do not value timeliness in the same way. For example, in Spain, where individualism is much lower than the United States, a formal dinner scheduled for 9:00 P.M. will certainly not begin at 9:00 P.M. The exact starting time is uncertain, but chances are dinner will not be served until some time much later than 9:00 P.M.

Asian cultures also show much more patience consistent with high long-term orientation. Thus, while CANZUS and many western European salespeople will want to close a sale on the first meeting, such an approach with Asian buyers will not come across well. Asian exchange partners need time to get to know one another and are not anxious to either close a sale or be closed until guanxi is established.

Mannerisms/Body Language

Body language refers to the nonverbal communication cues signaled by somatic (uncontrollable biological) responses. Consumers may use certain mannerisms when discussing issues with other consumers or salespeople. These cues can be more telling than the words that are spoken. The mannerisms that reveal meaning include the following characteristics:

- Facial expressions
- Posture
- Arm/leg position
- Skin conditions
- Voice

Most consumers sometimes have to pretend to be happy. This requires a fake smile. While most people can easily make their mouths produce a grin, true happiness would also be indicated by smiling eyebrows, slightly dilated pupils, and a tilted head (back). Similarly, the posture of a truly happy person generally indicates a willingness to approach the object of the emotion. Salespeople can be trained to detect if a consumer is truly experiencing pleasant emotion or if they are only pretending by close observation of facial expressions and posture.

Service providers may be successful in trying to guess which consumers will complain out of anger long before any negative words are voiced.[40] Thus, if anger is detected, intervention may actually turn the experience into something positive through proactive measures to remedy the situation causing the anger.

In addition, in today's virtual marketplace, nonverbal communication extends to virtual employees. Marketers are currently studying the mannerisms of avatars to investigate the way their messages are interpreted. In

EXHIBIT 8.10

Nonverbal Communication Affects the Message Comprehended

Avatars communicate both verbally and nonverbally. The avatar's body language can establish the image of a commercial site.

other words, how do you make an avatar seem agreeable, or disagreeable, or welcoming, or even trustful? Currently, the effects of avatars alone are small; however, the combination of verbal communication along with an avatar may contribute to higher trust and to increased hedonic value from the shopping experience.[41] So, an interesting question for web retailers is how to get an avatar to communicate a message that will be understood by all consumers.

Space

In places like the United States and Australia, there is a lot of space! Relative to many parts of the world, like Japan or western Europe, the United States and Australia are relatively sparsely populated. Thus, space varies in importance. The typical consumer in Seoul lives in a large high-rise condominium in a small flat identical to that of many neighbors living in the same building. For many Americans or Australians, the fact that so many people would be packed into a tight space may make them uncomfortable. For citizens of Seoul, being very close to other people is a fact of life.

The value that consumers place on space affects communication styles, too. Generally, CANZUS consumers, for instance, do not like to be too close to each other. When having a conversation, they remain at "arm's length." However, Italian, Armenian, or many Arabian consumers are comfortable communicating when they are so close to each other that they

are physically touching. The CANZUS consumer engaged in a conversation with an Armenian, for instance, will likely automatically try to obtain some space in the conversation by leaning backward at the waist as if an escape were possible! The differing approaches to space have implications for sales approaches, the way other consumers are depicted in advertising, and the design of retail environments.

> **etiquette** customary mannerisms consumers use in common social situations

Etiquette/Manners

When Americans greet each other, the typical response, particularly if a man is involved, is a handshake. Different handshakes may communicate different impressions. However, Asian consumers would expect a bow as a greeting and show of respect, while many Europeans may plant a kiss or two on the cheek. Greeting a business client with a kiss on the cheek would be a definite no-no in the United States; however, in France, a couple of kisses to the cheek could be an appropriate greeting.

Different cultures have different etiquettes for handling various social situations. **Etiquette** represents the customary mannerisms consumers use in common social situations. Dining etiquette varies considerably from one culture to another. In the United States, a consumer cuts food with the right hand, places the knife down, then places a fork in the right hand to place food into his or her mouth. In Europe, however, good manners dictate that the knife stays in the right hand and the fork in the other. One cuts with the right hand and uses the left to efficiently scoop food into one's mouth. In any event, violating etiquette can lead to a cultural sanction.

Service providers need to be sensitive to the various differences in etiquette. For example, although no formal airline passenger etiquette exists, there is an informal code, and passengers who break these unwritten rules can actually decrease the satisfaction of other passengers. This situation is exaggerated by airlines carrying multinational groups of passengers. These passengers have different rules about space, privacy, dress, and hygiene. Passengers with body odor or who dress inappropriately (for example, men in tank tops are generally considered inappropriate for such close company in western cultures) can ruin the experience for other consumers. When consumers are unaware or lack concern for the proper etiquette in a given situation, consumers and the service provider may pay the price.[42]

Relationships

How do consumers respond to attempts by marketers to build a personal relationship? Earlier, we discussed the Asian principle of guanxi and the different ways that a relationship may develop under this principle as opposed to conventional western principles. However, differing CSVs have other implications for consumer–brand or consumer–service provider relationships.

For example, with high collectivism, the idea of a relationship is no longer personal. Consumers from collectivist nations define relationships in terms of the ties between a brand or service provider and a family or relevant group of consumers. Therefore, marketing appeals aimed at building personal relationships should emphasize the collective preference of this group rather than the individual.[43]

Deutschland Donald

Even the communication of the words, actions and symbolic meaning of cartoon characters changes with culture. Americans clearly have an affinity for Donald Duck—the ill-tempered Disney duck. But that affinity is surpassed by that of German consumers. Germans purchase over 250,000 copies of Donald Duck comic books each week. Why? In Germany, Donald Duck in translation has a philosophical meaning over and above his free-spirited mannerisms. His popularity exceeds that of his less complex American counterpart.

Source: Note: Bernofsky, S. (2009), "Why Donald Duck is the Jerry Lewis of Germany," *Wall Street Journal*, May 25, **http://air.wsj.com**, accessed May 25, 2009.

© WONDERFUL WORLD OF DISNEY, THE, DONALD DUCK, 1997/EVERETT COLLECTION

Just over 1 billion consumers live in India. Today, the largest group of consumers is between 12 and 20 years old.

Agreement

How is agreement indicated and what does it mean? An Asian consumer who responds to a sales appeal with "yes" is not indicating agreement. Instead, this "yes" is more a way of indicating that he or she understands what is being said. Further, many Asian cultures will avoid strong affirmative or negative responses and instead use expressions like "that is possible" or "that may be difficult" to indicate agreement or lack of agreement.

Additionally, the extent to which a contract is seen as binding varies from place to place. Traditionally, South Koreans have not been accustomed to signing contracts. The fact that one would be asked to sign such an agreement was seen as a bit of an insult. Thus, western firms may have to adjust their practices to indicate formal agreements when doing business in these cultures.

Symbols

The chapter began by emphasizing the link between culture and meaning. Because different cultures have different value profiles, objects and activities take on different symbolic or semiotic meaning. Perhaps nowhere is this more obvious than in the arena of religious objects. A large wooden cross is a device used to execute people in some cultures, but to Christians, a cross is an important symbol signifying everlasting life.

The symbolic meaning of objects also affects gift giving from culture to culture. In some western cultures, particularly among French cultures including Quebec and south Louisiana, a knife is seen as an inappropriate gift because of the risk that a knife symbolizes cutting a relationship. In China, clocks and watches are inappropriate as gift items because they symbolize the finite nature of life—time is running out. Also in Japan, the term *omiyage* refers to the custom of bringing gifts to friends from foreign trips. In particular, an omiyage gift of a famous brand can help symbolize freedom for the typical female office worker.[44] Marketers need to take care against unintentionally promoting offensive items based on cultural symbolism.

LO5 Emerging Cultures

marketing efforts are largely directed at consumers from developed nations. However, less-developed nations can offer attractive markets and many may represent emerging economies. Even low-income consumers in third-world nations can represent attractive markets to serve, particularly if low-priced, basic products can be offered. Market segments in developing nations offer tremendous opportunities, but communicating and delivering value in these segments means that the nuances of culture must be known and understood.

Exhibit 8.11 displays the most attractive national consumer markets. Countries like the United States, United Kingdom, and Germany have long been recognized as important consumer markets; however, many nations on this list are emerging in the sense that they would not have been considered leading consumer markets a decade or two ago. Sociopolitical changes have allowed these markets to emerge.

BRIC MARKETS

As discussed previously, the acronym BRIC stands for Brazil, Russia, India, and China. These four nations are often singled out as having economies that are growing very rapidly. In each market, large middle classes are emerging as consumers who formerly would have had little opportunity for a good job have benefited from corporate capital investment. As a result, consumers in these nations have rising standards of living and they have become attractive markets for many goods and services.

Exhibit 8.12 tracks the **purchasing power parity (PPP)** of the 10 most attractive consumer markets. The PPP gives an idea of the total size of the consumer market in each country in terms of total buying power. By 2020, China is expected to match or exceed the total purchasing power of the United States.

CHINDIA

The term **Chindia** refers to the combined market and business potential of China and India. The

consumer demographics of India today compare favorably to those of the United States in 1970. Just over one billion consumers live in India. Today, the largest group of consumers is between 12 and 20 years old. This cohort group is similar to

purchasing power parity (PPP) total size of the consumer market in each country in terms of total buying power

Chindia combined market and business potential of China and India

EXHIBIT 8.11
Attractive Consumer Markets for Foreign Direct Investment (FDI)[45]

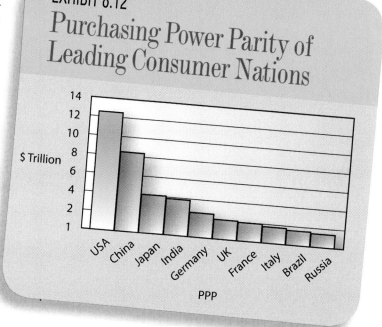

EXHIBIT 8.12
Purchasing Power Parity of Leading Consumer Nations

the baby-boomer generation in the United States, which was responsible for tremendous economic growth domestically and abroad.

Over 185 million households call India home. Today, 135 million of those households are considered aspiring consumers with equivalent household incomes under $2,500 per year. However, by 2010, expectations are that the Indian middle class will total just over 100 million households—doubling its size in less than a decade. As Indian incomes rise, the market potential of India expands as well.[46]

Some idea of the market potential can be seen in the mobile phone market. More than one-half billion consumers currently own a mobile phone in China.[47] Soon, that number is expected to *exceed* one billion. The key for marketers is to provide a functional product to consumers who are unaccustomed to elaborately designed products and who, to a large extent, are unable to read or write very well.

GLOCALIZATION

How should a company from another country appeal to these emerging but foreign consumer markets? Certainly, these countries offer a significantly different CSV profile than those in the United States. The term *glocalization* represents one alternative that allows flexibility in responding to the unique value profiles of consumers. **Glocalization** represents the idea that the marketing strategy may be global but the implementation of that strategy at the marketing tactics level should be local.

Reef Brazil beachwear (**www.reef.com**) executes a global branding strategy that appeals to the youth market by portraying a cool, carefree image.[47a] This corporate strategy may be set by executives in Brazil. However, rather than dictating how this plan would be implemented, Reef could practice glocalization by letting managers and consultants in the foreign markets decide how this strategy should be carried out in their own particular markets.[48] By doing so, local consumers can comprehend the global theme and share the same meaning for the brand.

What's Next?

During the days of the cold war, consumer markets like those in Russia and China were hardly seen as attractive to marketers in North America and Europe. However, times have changed. The advancement of free market economies has led to increased standards of living in many corners of the globe.

However, the fact is that half the world's consumer population remains illiterate and struggles to maintain anything more than a meager way of life. As the emerging economies advance today, so will the cost of doing business in those countries. Companies will search for cheaper places to do business and through this process, new emerging economies will develop. Much of Africa, for example, remains without the type of industrial or technological development necessary to create good jobs and the incomes that lead to a higher standard of living. Africa has a total population of nearly 800 million people. Even though parts of South Africa and northern Africa are developed, much of the rest remains destitute. Perhaps this area too will be a new emerging market for later in this century.

Like other places though, the cultural barriers presented there are more than trivial. The cultural barriers go beyond dealing with consumers, but they also are engrained in the sociopolitical environment. Therefore, changes in the government institutions will probably be needed before many companies will feel comfortable doing business there.[49]

Chapter 8 Case

Al Pratt steps through the sliding doors of the grocery store and picks up a red basket. With his shopping list in one hand and the basket nestled firmly in the crook of his arm, he makes his way into the produce section. There, he is confronted with all the colorful bins of fruits and vegetables available for him to purchase. He checks his list to see what he needs. Potatoes top the list. He sees that five-pound bags of potatoes are on sale for $2.99, which seems like a really good deal to him; however, he chooses to purchase only two potatoes at almost a dollar apiece instead. Al is a single man who lives by himself and knows that he can't possibly eat all of a bag of potatoes without wasting most of them.

As Al's situation demonstrates, we need to be careful as marketers in assuming that all citizens of a particular culture fit the norms and assumptions of that culture. In America, marriage and couplehood are accepted as the cultural norm; however, the singles market is a rapidly growing segment of the marketplace (DePaulo, 2007). As of the 2005 American Community Survey provided by the U.S. Census Bureau, over 30 million men and women in the United States are currently living by themselves. Many of these include individuals who have chosen to put off marriage while they work on careers or educational pursuits, and many of them are people who are of retirement age and beyond who find themselves living alone for a variety of reasons including both widowhood and divorce. As the single segment grows in the coming decades, marketers may need to be more conscious of their more mundane needs as well as their dating and mating needs.

For many of life's simple and seemingly mundane tasks, Al is intimately aware of his single status. For instance, when he goes to the grocery store, he feels put off upon seeing deals for bulk items or "buy one get one free" promotions in which, because he does not want to waste food or money, he cannot participate. Also, since most cookbooks are written with multiple servings in mind, Al may be forced to adjust the ingredient portions prior to the shopping excursion or, as is often the case, simply skip certain meals suggested by cookbooks or online recipes because he cannot adjust the ingredient portions accordingly. Additionally, Al refrains from purchasing certain items like celery because he knows that most of it will go to waste.

In a culture that prizes marriage, Al feels punished for being single. As he states, "A lot of times, especially with coupons, I don't want to buy two just to save this much money. I just want to buy one. Why am I punished just because I need one? Well, a family could use two . . . or buy four. I don't want four. It's almost like . . . the only way you can take advantage of it, especially if it's perishable, is if you're in a family." Additionally, Al does not like having to go all over the store in order to purchase the "single" items he needs, and he is not a fan of the carrying alternatives open to him. A grocery cart is too big for the shopping he does and makes him feel inadequate in comparison to others he sees in the store, but the basket that grocery stores provide is not always big enough for his needs and becomes very heavy as he shops.

In many ways, this inability to take advantage of certain discount prices or to break bulk items into smaller quantities adds to Al's feelings of alienation as he moves quietly through the grocery store, waiting patiently for the couples who are shopping together to move out of his way or eying the grocery carts full of meat and other items that are obviously intended for a family. And Al is not necessarily alone in these feelings of alienation and punishment in the grocery store. Others like him, both male and female, are expressing their dissatisfaction with grocery stores and other retail establishments for not catering to their nonfamilial needs. As a group, little attention has been paid to single people who live alone and how such a living arrangement affects the various decisions such individuals make.[50]

Questions

1. According to the text, consumer culture is defined as the commonly held societal beliefs that define what is socially gratifying. How does this case defy commonly held societal beliefs in American consumer culture? What CSV dimensions are most involved?

2. Imagine yourself as the store manager of the grocery store where Al is shopping. How might you address his needs and the needs of the growing numbers of singles without compromising the needs of the families that also shop at your store?

3. What problems directly related to socialization and culture do you see within this case?

4. What other emerging markets can you think of that may need to be addressed by grocery stores? How might they best address these markets?

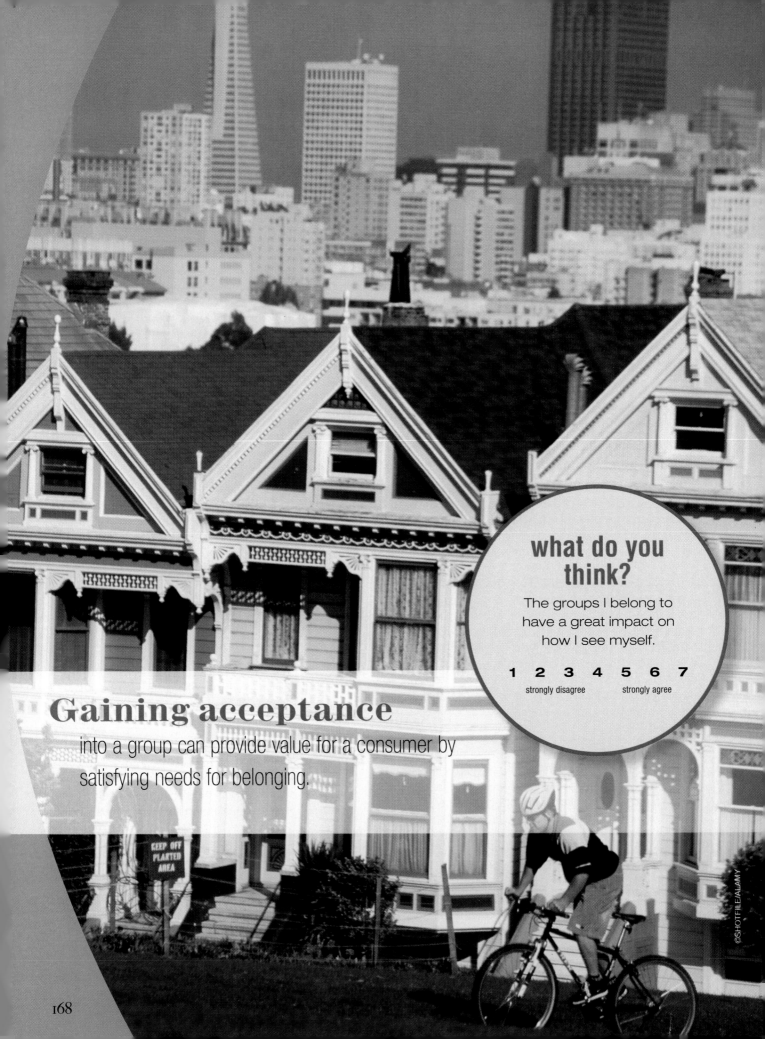

Gaining acceptance

into a group can provide value for a consumer by satisfying needs for belonging.

what do you think?

The groups I belong to have a great impact on how I see myself.

1 2 3 4 5 6 7

strongly disagree   strongly agree

9

Group Influence

Introduction

The motivation to belong is an important part of human life. Consumers are social creatures who desire contact and affiliation with others. As a result, consumers often belong to (or aspire to belong to) a number of formal or informal groups. These groups can exert significant influence over consumer behavior. In this chapter, we discuss a number of issues relating to the concept of group influence and how these concepts apply to value. We begin by discussing the various types of reference groups that influence consumer behavior.

> **reference group** individuals who have significant relevance for a consumer and who have an impact on the consumer's evaluations, aspirations, and behavior

After studying this chapter, the student should be able to:

LO1 Understand the different types of reference groups that influence consumers and how reference groups influence value perceptions.

LO2 Describe the various types of social power that reference groups exert on members.

LO3 Comprehend the difference between informational, utilitarian, and value-expressive reference group influence.

LO4 Understand the importance of word-of-mouth communications in consumer behavior.

LO5 Comprehend the role of household influence in consumer behavior.

LO1 Reference Groups

A **reference group** is a group of individuals who has significant relevance for a consumer and who has an impact on the consumer's evaluations, aspirations, and behavior.[1] This influence affects the ways that consumers seek and receive value from consumption. Even the decision to get a tattoo can mean one thing to a particular consumer because of the way it reflects his or her membership within a group. The same tattoo might mean little to another consumer. However, within the tattoo-wearing consumer's primary reference group, the tattoo can help be the key to gaining acceptance and can express belongingness explicitly.

If you stop and think of all the ways in which reference groups influence you daily, you'd probably be really surprised. This is because reference groups typically exert great influence on their members. In order to explore how groups influence their members' behaviors, we must begin by defining exactly what we mean by "group influence."

GROUP INFLUENCE

Group influence refers to the ways in which group members influence the attitudes, opinions, and behaviors of others within the group. As we have noted, groups are an important part of social life, and group processes profoundly affect consumer behavior. Gaining acceptance into a group can provide value for a consumer by satisfying his or her needs for belonging. Consider the following aspects of group life:

- Group members share common goals and interests.
- Group members communicate with, and influence, one another.
- Group members share a set of expectations, rules, and roles.
- Group members view themselves as members of a common social unit.[2]

These qualities of group membership are important. Sorority sisters share a common set of expectations that ultimately influences members' decisions about things such as activities, attire, and social involvement. A student marketing club organizes fundraisers for an end-of-the-year field trip, with all members sharing a common goal. An "over-fifty" student organization meets regularly to discuss the difficulties associated with being a nontraditional student.

Group influence does not just affect buying behavior. Consumer attitudes, opinions, and value perceptions also are heavily influenced by reference groups, even if a specific purchase does not directly result. Many groups influence consumer behavior, but not all groups have the same influence.

Primary/Secondary Groups

A **primary group** is a group that includes members who have frequent, direct contact with one another. Primary reference groups generally have the most influence on their members, and *social ties* for these groups are very strong. A social tie is a measure of the strength of connection between group members. An example of a primary reference group is the family unit. Family members generally have much influence on one another, and many times it directly affects behavior in the marketplace. For example, studies reveal that parental influence on children's shopping and saving behavior can be quite strong.[3] Parents who openly discuss financial matters, such as developing savings accounts, can greatly influence these behaviors.

In a **secondary group**, interaction within the group is much less frequent than in a primary group. Professional organizations and social clubs are examples of secondary groups. Usually, the influence of these groups on members is not as strong as the influence of primary groups on their members. Furthermore, social ties are not as strong in secondary groups as they are in primary groups.

One special type of secondary group is a **brand community**. Brand communities are groups of consumers who develop relationships based on shared interests or product usage.[4] A popular example of a brand community is Harley-Davidson's H.O.G. (*Harley Owners' Group*). Fans of Harley-Davidson meet regularly at events that marketers refer to as *brandfests*.

In general, connections that are found in brand communities lead to positive outcomes for consumers and companies. Consumers learn more about the products they enjoy, and they develop bonds with other users. Companies reap the rewards of positive consumer attitudes. The brand devotion that community members share helps members strongly identify with each other.[5]

Sorority sisters often have a great deal of influence on each other.

© ISTOCKPHOTO.COM/MINH TANG

Formal/Informal Groups

A **formal group** is a group in which a consumer formally becomes a member. For example, a consumer becomes a formal member of a church congregation. Formal groups generally have a set of stated rules, accepted values, and codes of conduct that members are expected to adhere to.

An **informal group** is a group that has no membership or application requirements, and codes of conduct may be nonexistent. Examples of informal groups include groups that meet regularly to exercise, have coffee, or go to sporting events. Although informal group influence may not be as strong as formal group influence, these groups can have an impact on consumer behavior.

Aspirational/Dissociative Groups

An **aspirational group** is a group in which a consumer desires to become a member. Aspirational group membership often appeals to the consumer's *ideal* self. The ideal self is an important part of the consumer's self-concept, and consumers often visualize themselves as belonging to certain groups. For example, a business student may desire to become a member of a professional business association once he earns his degree. Consumers frequently emulate the members of aspirational groups and perform behaviors that they believe will lead to formal acceptance into the group. Getting the first job would be the first step for joining a business organization.

A **dissociative group** is a group to which a consumer does not want to belong. For example, a Republican might want to avoid being perceived as belonging to a Democratic group (and vice-versa). Recent college graduates may want to disassociate themselves with groups from their past as they take the next step into adulthood.

CONFORMITY

An important topic in the study of reference group influence is conformity. **Conformity** occurs when an individual yields to the attitudes and behaviors of other consumers. Conformity is very similar to the concept of persuasion. The key difference between persuasion and conformity is that with conformity, the other party does not necessarily defend its position. That is, a group may give no reason for why it expects its group members to act or think a certain way. Persuasion, on the other hand, relies on one party defending its position to another party in an explicit attempt to change attitude or behavior.[6]

Peer Pressure

Peer pressure and conformity are also closely related topics. **Peer pressure** is the pressure an individual feels to behave in accordance with group expectations. Peer pressure can greatly influence behavior. In fact, peer pressure is often the strongest type of influence a consumer experiences in daily life.

Consumers of all ages feel peer pressure. In fact, very young children often desire to wear the types of clothing and brands that will allow them to feel accepted. One study found that children as young as 10 years of age prefer to wear brand-name footwear (e.g., Nike) so that they will fit in with their peers.[7]

> Within the Parrot-Head community, all things Buffet have enhanced value.

formal group group in which a consumer formally becomes a member

informal group group that has no membership or application requirements and that may have no codes of conduct

aspirational group group in which a consumer desires to become a member

dissociative group group to which a consumer does not want to belong

conformity result of group influence in which an individual yields to the attitudes and behaviors of others

peer pressure extent to which group members feel pressure to behave in accordance with group expectations

© REUTERS/CORBIS

Negative Peer Pressure

Peer pressure to wear a certain brand of clothing is not necessarily a bad thing. Unfortunately, negative consumer behaviors are often heavily influenced by peer pressure. Consumers are often pressured by others to engage in unethical, perhaps illegal, behaviors.

Peer pressure is frequently cited as being particularly persuasive for young consumers. One topic that receives much media attention is peer pressure related to illegal alcohol consumption and underage smoking. Binge drinking among underage consumers is a serious societal problem that can have disastrous, and sometimes fatal, effects. Peer pressure often plays a large role in this behavior. Although this form of peer pressure is negative, marketers can harness the power of peer pressure in positive ways. For example, advertisements that encourage young consumers to abstain from negative behaviors (like underage drinking) can be effective when peer group members deliver the message.[8]

© ISTOCKPHOTO.COM/MICHELLE_D

> Friends are especially influencial during the teen years.

> Peer pressure can greatly influence behavior. In fact, it is among the strongest types of influence a consumer experiences in daily life.

Adolescents are particularly susceptible to peer pressure and are often compelled to rebel against their families in favor of behaviors that win acceptance of their peers. Teens commonly go against family expectations and parental rules. At this stage in social development, friends begin to take on additional importance and exert greater influence in teens' lives. This can be considered a natural part of a child's development; nevertheless, negative influences including conflict within the family can result.

Peer pressure is not confined only to the consumer behavior of children and teens. Adults also feel peer pressure, and sometimes the pressure can be directed toward negative behaviors. In fact, one study of adult consumers revealed that respondents reported a greater likelihood to buy an illicit product (counterfeit or stolen merchandise) if their friends did the same.[9] As with influence on children, this form of peer pressure is negative and can affect consumers, marketers, and society as a whole.

LO2 Social Power

another important topic in the study of reference groups and group influence is social power. **Social power** refers to the ability of an individual or a group to alter the actions of others.[10] Consumers often believe that others hold a great deal of power over their own behavior. As a result, social power can greatly influence the types of products that consumers buy, the attitudes that consumers hold, and the activities in which they participate.

TYPES OF SOCIAL POWER

Social power can be classified into five categories.[11] These categories include *referent power*, *legitimate power*, *expert power*, *reward power*, and *coercive power*. These forms of power can be exerted both by referent groups and by other individuals. These power bases are presented in Exhibit 9.1 and then discussed in more detail.

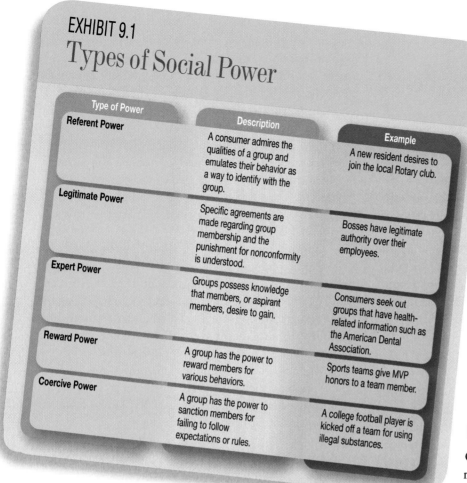

EXHIBIT 9.1
Types of Social Power

Type of Power	Description	Example
Referent Power	A consumer admires the qualities of a group and emulates their behavior as a way to identify with the group.	A new resident desires to join the local Rotary club.
Legitimate Power	Specific agreements are made regarding group membership and the punishment for nonconformity is understood.	Bosses have legitimate authority over their employees.
Expert Power	Groups possess knowledge that members, or aspirant members, desire to gain.	Consumers seek out groups that have health-related information such as the American Dental Association.
Reward Power	A group has the power to reward members for various behaviors.	Sports teams give MVP honors to a team member.
Coercive Power	A group has the power to sanction members for failing to follow expectations or rules.	A college football player is kicked off a team for using illegal substances.

Referent Power

Consumers often imitate the behaviors and attitudes of groups as a means of identifying with the group. For example, a new resident of a city might desire to join the local Rotary club, or perhaps a country club. In these cases, it is likely that the behaviors of other group members will be imitated. Belonging to such groups often allows consumers to feel as though they are fitting in.

Legitimate Power

In many situations, social arrangements dictate that differing levels of power are dependent upon one's position in a group. Legitimate power is used to describe this type of power, and it is associated with *authority*. For example, bosses have legitimate power and authority over their employees. A boss has the authority to fire his or her employees. Notice that employees are usually very limited in any power that they can exert over a boss.

Expert Power

An important motivation in consumer behavior is the motivation to understand the environment. Expert power refers to the ability of a group or individual to influence a consumer due to the group's or individual's knowledge of, or experience with, a specific subject matter. For example, consumers often find advice on health issues by consulting groups such as the American Heart Association or American Diabetes Association. Medical patients also often consult various online discussion groups for information. By consulting these groups for advice and direction relating to specific medical issues, consumers can alter their behaviors based on the perceived expertise of the source of information.

Reward Power

Groups frequently have the power to reward members for compliance with expectations. For example, at season's end, sports teams often distribute "most valuable player" awards based on performance. The desirability of the rewards is very important. If the reward isn't valued by the group members, then the motivation to perform the desired behavior is not overly strong.

Coercive Power

Groups may also exert coercive power over their members. When consumers fail to give in to group expectations or rules, disapproval can be harsh and may even result in loss of membership. For example, college athletes can be kicked off sports teams for using illegal substances like steroids. As mentioned earlier, groups may sanction members based on their legitimate power to do so, or they may revoke the membership of members who do not comply with group rules.

How does social power originate? Social power actually depends upon a member's agreement to, or acceptance of, the fact that the power bases do indeed exist. That is, members must (a) *be aware that the power base exists* and (b) *desire to maintain or establish membership into the group* in order for the power base to be effective.

LO3
Reference Group Influence

the study of reference groups requires an understanding of group influence processes. Reference group influence generally falls into one of three categories: *informational influence*, *utilitarian influence*, and *value-expressive influence*. These categories of influence are discussed next.[12]

INFORMATIONAL INFLUENCE

The **informational influence** of groups refers to the ways in which consumers use the behaviors and attitudes of reference groups as information for making their own decisions. Reference groups often provide members with product- or issue-related information, and consumers often consider group-related information when purchasing products or services. Consumers desire to make informed decisions, and reference groups are often perceived as being effective sources of information.[13] Groups can be very influential in this way. Informational influence can be a result of explicit searching behavior. For example, when a consumer is seeking a doctor, friends may influence the choice by saying "this doctor is very good."

Informational influence is also present even when the consumer is *not* explicitly searching for product-related information, but rather when he or she is observing others' behaviors. For example, a consumer may simply see another person drinking a new soft drink and decide to try one.[14]

Informational influence helps to explain why word-of-mouth communication is so persuasive. Consumers share all kinds of information about products, services, and experiences, and this information can have a significant impact on consumer behavior. Internet discussion groups, in particular, have rapidly become important sources of information for group members.

The informational influence of a group is particularly strong if the group is seen as being credible. Credibility is often associated with expertise. Professional groups are often perceived as being very credible, and for this reason, they can exert significant informational influence even if a consumer is not a member of the group. For example, a consumer may be persuaded by a message that proclaims that "four of five dentists recommend brand X." This same information obtained from the American Dental Association can affect a dentist's decisions as well, as informational influence is directly related to expert power.

UTILITARIAN INFLUENCE

The **utilitarian influence** occurs when consumers conform to group expectations to receive a reward or avoid punishment (this is sometimes referred to as "normative" influence). Compliance with group expectations often leads to valued rewards.

As discussed earlier, young consumers often think they need to buy the correct brand of shoes or clothing to fit in. By wearing apparel approved by the reference group, a child feels accepted (the reward). If the wrong clothing is selected, the child may feel shunned by the group (a punishment). When the group is perceived as being able to give rewards and punishment based on compliance, then this influence is quite strong. Importantly, rewards can be either social (the feeling of fitting in) or economic (the attainment of direct monetary value).

Gaining membership in groups often provides direct rewards for music fans.

© NEWSCOM/PRNEWSFOTO

Reference material provided in this website may provide informational influence on dentists.

We've Got Connections

Fan clubs are very important entities for rock bands.

The formation of a fan club allows bands to identify a solid core of consumers who are devoted to their music. However, fan club membership can be quite valuable for members as well. Fan clubs have long offered their members memorabilia and concert updates, but real economic incentives are now the norm.

One economic benefit of fan club membership is the availability of choice seats at concerts. It is referred to as the *10% club rule*. The arrangement requires that 10% of seats for concerts be reserved for fan club members. By joining a club, members are able to forgo the frustration that is often felt by buying tickets through large ticket brokers.

This fan club benefit is well known, and artists ranging from Kelly Clarkson to Dave Matthews Band offer these incentives. No longer is it a matter of standing in line or trying to get through a jammed phone service. By joining these clubs, fans can truly say that they've "got connections."

Sources: Waddell, Ray (2007), "The Ticks Hit the Fans," *Billboard*, 119 (13), 11; Fitch, Asa (2007), "The Last-Second Save—and Other Ticket Strategies," *Money*, 36 (2), 23; Garrity, Brian (2002), "Online Fan Clubs Emerge as Potential Profit Centers," *Billboard*, 114 (31), 1–2.

> **value-expressive influence** ways in which a consumer internalizes a group's values or the extent to which a consumer joins groups in order to express his or her own closely held values and beliefs

Consumers may also use group membership as a way to project their own self-image. Importantly, the self-image of the individual is influenced by the group, and group membership helps the individual project his or her desired image. For example, a consumer may choose to join Mothers Against Drunk Driving because she feels strongly about the drunk driving issue. Once she has joined, she can project the values of the group as well.

VALUE AND REFERENCE GROUPS

External influences have a direct impact on the value of many activities. Reference groups and value are related in various ways.

From a utilitarian value perspective, joining a campus organization (for example, Students in Free Enterprise) can be quite a valuable experience. The benefits associated with membership (networking, work experience, accomplishment) may be greater than the work that is put into the organization (work performed to complete a project, hours devoted to planning and meetings). In this way, utilitarian value is derived from belonging to the group, and group membership becomes a means to a valued end state.

Group membership also involves hedonic value perceptions. Value can be derived from simply enjoying group meetings and activities. Here, value is an end in and of itself. Attending functions such as sorority functions and dances can be quite enjoyable beyond any utilitarian benefits that come from membership.

Utilitarian influence of groups is not limited to any age group or demographic profile. Adult consumers often perceive a great deal of utilitarian influence from reference groups. Driving the right car, living in the right neighborhood, and belonging to the right clubs can make adults feel accepted. Here, we can see that utilitarian influence is related to reward power.

VALUE-EXPRESSIVE INFLUENCE

Consumers often desire to seek membership into groups that hold values that are similar to their own. They also choose to adopt the values that are held by the desirable group. The **value-expressive influence** of groups refers to the ways in which consumers internalize a group's values or the extent to which consumers join groups to express their own closely held values and beliefs. This influence is related to referent power.

Simply enjoying the fun is enough! Motivations and emotions are closely related topics. The motivation to belong to, or be affiliated with, a group can bring happiness and joy. Many students join sororities and fraternities not for long-term benefits but for short-term fun!

Reference group influences affect value perceptions in other ways. Because consumers learn about products and services from referent others, the information that is obtained from groups directly affects consumer expectations about product benefits such as quality and convenience. If you hear from your friends that a product is good, you'll probably believe it! These expectations, in turn, affect value perceptions and satisfaction.

Expectations, satisfaction, and value are all closely related concepts. Belonging to a group can also lead to economic benefits such as those described in the fan club example.

REFERENCE GROUP INFLUENCE ON PRODUCT SELECTION

A number of things affect how much influence reference groups have on product selection. First, the situation in which the product is consumed must be considered. "Public" products are easily seen by others (for example, a watch). "Private" products are not (for example, an electric blanket). Second, the extent to which the product is considered to be a necessity or a luxury affects the level of reference group influence.[15] We really do need some products (for example, a refrigerator). Others aren't so necessary (for example, a hot tub). Third, reference group influence differs depending on whether a type of product or a particular brand is being selected. Obviously, a watch is a product. Rolex is a very expensive brand of watch. These elements are presented in Exhibit 9.2.

For necessities, reference group influence is weak for product selection (boxes #1 and #2). Reference groups rarely influence the decision to wear blue jeans. With public necessities, however, the influence of reference groups on brand selection is also strong (for example, "You should get some Apple Bottom jeans!" box #1). For luxuries, reference group influence is strong for product selection (boxes #2 and #4). However, group influence on brand selection is only strong for public luxuries (box #2). Reference group members could influence the choice of product (for example, "Don't you have a set of golf clubs?") and the brand used (for example, Callaway). A careful look at the exhibit reveals that group influence on brand selection is strong for all publicly viewed products!

INDIVIDUAL DIFFERENCES IN SUSCEPTIBILITY TO GROUP INFLUENCE

Although group influence plays an important role in influencing consumer behavior, not all consumers conform to group expectations equally. Individual difference variables play an important role in the extent to which consumers conform to the expectations of others. They also influence how one behaves in the presence of others. Three important variables are susceptibility to interpersonal influence, attention to social comparison information, and separateness-connectedness.

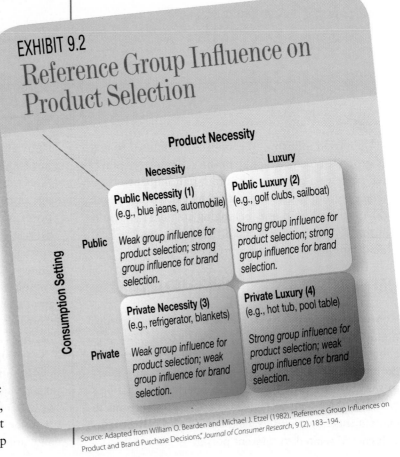

EXHIBIT 9.2
Reference Group Influence on Product Selection

Product Necessity

	Necessity	**Luxury**
Public	**Public Necessity (1)** (e.g., blue jeans, automobile) — Weak group influence for product selection; strong group influence for brand selection.	**Public Luxury (2)** (e.g., golf clubs, sailboat) — Strong group influence for product selection; strong group influence for brand selection.
Private	**Private Necessity (3)** (e.g., refrigerator, blankets) — Weak group influence for product selection; weak group influence for brand selection.	**Private Luxury (4)** (e.g., hot tub, pool table) — Strong group influence for product selection; weak group influence for brand selection.

Consumption Setting

Source: Adapted from William O. Bearden and Michael J. Etzel (1982), "Reference Group Influences on Product and Brand Purchase Decisions," *Journal of Consumer Research*, 9 (2), 183–194.

Susceptibility to Interpersonal Influence

One individual difference variable, **susceptibility to interpersonal influence,** assesses the individual's need to enhance his or her image in terms of others by acquiring and using products, conforming to the expectations of others, and learning about products by observing others.[16] Exhibit 9.3 shows sample items of how this trait is measured. Notice that this trait includes both a normative dimension (what others think I should do) and an informative dimension (my tendency to gather information from others).

Studies reveal that consumers who are particularly susceptible to interpersonal influence are more likely to value conspicuous items (that is, highly valued items like luxury automobiles or jewelry).[17] From the value equation (value = what you get − what you give), the benefits of quality and image would be weighted heavily in their perception of value.

Seeking approval of others through product ownership is very important to these consumers. Consumers who score highly on the susceptibility to interpersonal influence scale are also more likely to desire avoiding negative impressions in public settings.[18] For example, wearing "uncool" clothes in a shopping mall would be much more distressing to a consumer who is highly susceptible to interpersonal influence than to other consumers.

Attention to Social Comparison Information

Another individual difference variable that affects consumer behavior related to group influence is **attention to social comparison information (ATSCI).** Consumers who score highly on this measure are concerned about how other people react to their behavior.[19] This trait is closely related to susceptibility to interpersonal influence.

The ATSCI trait often emerges when a consumer is shopping, as consumers with a strong degree of the trait tend to modify their purchasing behaviors when they are shopping with others. For example, a consumer who has a strong degree of ATSCI might buy an imported beer when he is shopping with others. He would buy a less expensive domestic beer when he is shopping alone. Paying attention to what others think is likely to lead consumers to conform to others' expectations, and studies have shown that consumers with a strong degree of ATSCI are more likely to conform to the expectations of others.[20]

Separateness—Connectedness

Consumers differ in their feelings of "connectedness" to other consumers. A consumer with a **separated self-schema** perceives himself or herself as distinct and separate from others, while a consumer with a **connected self-schema** sees himself

susceptibility to interpersonal influence individual difference variable that assesses a consumer's need to enhance his or her image with others by acquiring and using products, conforming to the expectations of others, and learning about products by observing others

attention to social comparison information (ATSCI) individual difference variable that assesses the extent to which a consumer is concerned about how other people react to his or her behavior

separated self-schema self-conceptualization of the extent to which a consumer perceives himself or herself as distinct and separate from others

connected self-schema self-conceptualization of the extent to which a consumer perceives himself or herself as being an integral part of a group

EXHIBIT 9.3
Susceptibility to Interpersonal Influence

Normative Influence (a focus on what others think I should do)

1. I rarely purchase the latest fashion styles until I am sure my friends approve of them.
2. It is important that others like the products and brands I buy.
3. When buying products, I generally purchase those brands that I think others will approve of.

Informational Influence (a focus on obtaining information from a group)

4. To make sure I buy the right product or brand, I often observe what others are buying and using.
5. If I have little experience with a product, I often ask my friends about the product.
6. I often consult with other people to help choose the best alternative available from a product class.

Adapted from Bearden, William O., Richard G. Netemeyer, and Jesse E. Teel (1989), "Measurement of Consumer Susceptibility to Interpersonal Influence," *Journal of Consumer Research, 15 (4), 473–481.*

or herself as an integral part of a group.[21] Marketers are well aware of the differences in how people view their relationships with groups, and marketing messages are often based on "connected" or "separated" themes. One study found that consumers who feel connected respond more favorably to advertisements that promote group belonging and cohesion.[22]

Culture plays an important role in how separated or connected consumers feel. For example, consumers in eastern cultures tend to feel more connected to others, while consumers in western cultures tend to feel more separate and distinct. Advertising themes in collectivist cultures (a culture that focuses heavily on the interdependence of citizens) therefore often promote connected themes, while advertisements in the United States tend to emphasize separate themes.[23]

> WOM is very influential because, in general, consumers tend to believe other consumers more than they believe advertisements.

Social Influence and Embarrassment

The impact of groups on consumers cannot be overstated. In fact, the mere presence of others in a specific situation can make one feel uncomfortable.[24] This is especially the case when consumers are consuming or buying personal products. Consumers can feel very uneasy, or even embarrassed, by the presence of others when purchasing these items.

One study revealed that college students were particularly embarrassed with the purchase of condoms when other consumers were present.[25] This influence was affected, however, by the amount of experience the students had with buying condoms. Consumers who were familiar with the act of buying the product did not feel significantly higher levels of embarrassment if others were present during the purchase. Many consumers are uncomfortable working out in a gym for fear of how they appear to others!

Consumers with connected self-schemas respond favorably to advertisements promoting togetherness.

LO4 Word-of-Mouth

another important concept in the study of interpersonal influence is word-of-mouth behavior. **Word-of-mouth (WOM)** is information about products, services, and experiences that is transmitted from consumer to consumer. WOM includes all kinds of information that can be spread about various consumer behaviors.

Two types of WOM influences can be distinguished: *organic* and *amplified*. The distinction between the concepts is highlighted by the Word of Mouth Marketing Association (or, WOMMA). According to WOMMA, organic WOM occurs naturally when consumers truly enjoy a product or service and they want to share their experiences with others. Amplified WOM occurs when marketers attempt to launch or accelerate WOM in existing customer circles, or when they develop entirely new forums for WOM (such as discussion boards on web pages).[26]

Consumers are heavily influenced by WOM, and its power is impressive. Consumers tell each other about products, services, and experiences all day long. If a movie is really good, moviegoers tell others. It's no wonder that word-of-mouth influences the vast majority of consumer product sales! WOM is influential because, in general, consumers tend to believe other consumers more than they believe advertisements and explicit marketing messages from companies.

POSITIVE AND NEGATIVE WOM

The more satisfied consumers are with a company or product, the more likely they are to spread positive WOM. If consumers believe strongly in a company and its products, they are more likely to talk to others about it.[27] Terms such as *brand advocate* or *brand ambassador* are beginning to emerge in marketing to describe consumers who believe strongly in a brand and tell others about it.

Consumers are also more likely to spread WOM when a product is particularly relevant to their own self-concept and when they are highly involved with the product category.[28] For example, a motorcycle enthusiast is more likely to spread WOM about motorcycle products than a consumer who doesn't even like motorcycles.

Marketers realize that negative WOM can be extremely damaging. The reason why negative WOM is so damaging to a company is that this form of WOM is especially influential. In general, negative word-of-mouth is more influential than is positive word-of-mouth.[29] Hearing that the food at a restaurant is terrible is much more influential than hearing that it is good! Consumers also tend to tell more people about unsatisfactory experiences than pleasing ones.

Value and Word-of-Mouth

As noted earlier, group influence processes are closely related to consumer perceptions of value. Similarly, WOM is affected in large part by the perceived value that consumers receive from products and services. One recent study, performed in a South Korean service setting, found that both utilitarian and hedonic value positively influence WOM intentions.[30] Customers who believed the restaurant allowed them to efficiently address their hunger received utilitarian value, and those who enjoyed the experience beyond addressing hunger received hedonic value. When this value was perceived as being particularly high, consumers were motivated

to encourage their families and friends to go that restaurant as well. The more value that consumers receive, the more likely they are to tell others about their experiences with products and services!

online social network
a computer-mediated portal that allows consumers to post information about themselves, their hobbies, their interests, and products that they enjoy

Word-of-Mouth in the Digital Age

The rapid adoption and acceptance of the Internet has had a major impact on WOM. Of course, the Internet allows consumers to connect with others in ways that have never before been possible, and information contained in chat rooms, discussion boards, and blogs can strongly influence consumer behavior.[31] It shouldn't be surprising that the vast majority of Internet users have participated in online groups. One estimate revealed that as many as 84% of all Internet users have participated in online discussion groups.[32]

Companies often encourage their customers to discuss products and services online. In fact, it is common to see corporate websites that include discussion board links. In this way, companies assist in the development and maintenance of brand communities. Sprint Telecommunications recently utilized a "Spring Ambassador Program" by identifying influential bloggers and giving them free cell phones as compensation for writing positive comments online about the phones.[33]

While companies actively encourage online WOM chat by giving away free products or services, one growing trend is to hire posters to talk about products and services.

As we discussed earlier, negative WOM is very influential. Because it is so influential, marketers are interested in learning what customers are saying about their company's performance. This is especially true in the online community because not all information spread online is positive. In fact, it is becoming quite common to see what can be called *anti-brand communities*, or communities in which members spread negative information about companies and products to other users.[34]

Online Social Networking

Online social networking also has an impact on consumer behavior. In sociology, a social network is viewed as a set of individuals who share information and experiences. An **online social network** is similar.

However, with an online social network, social influence occurs over the Internet. Therefore, an *online social network* can be defined as a computer-mediated portal that allows consumers to post information about themselves, their hobbies, their interests, and the products they enjoy.

Today, many popular networks are available including sites such as **facebook.com** and **myspace.com**. Networking is obviously very popular, and the information that is shared via networking is highly valued. In fact, many consumers turn to online networks for advice on personal issues. One recent study found that 60 million Americans have sought input into major life decisions, including health, personal, and financial decisions, from online networks![35]

The popularity of sites such as facebook and myspace is undeniable. Millions of consumers frequent these sites multiple times per day, sharing information and maintaining contact with friends who may only be known in the digital world. Social networking sites are particularly popular among teenagers. In fact, nearly 65% of online teens have profiles on social networking sites as compared with only 35% of online adults aged 18 and over.[36] The popularity of these sites (and related sites) makes them tremendous vehicles for spreading WOM.

Many of today's companies that cater to specific segments have ventured into the online world. The popular website **momjunction.com** illustrates how online social networking is used by moms.

BUZZ MARKETING

One evolving form of marketing that utilizes word-of-mouth processes is termed **buzz marketing.** Buzz marketing includes marketing efforts that focus on generating excitement (buzz) that is spread from consumer to consumer. Successful buzz marketing can be a powerful tool for marketers, as information about products and services can spread quickly. Buzz marketing is one form of what is called **guerrilla marketing,** or the marketing of a product using unconventional means.

Although marketers have attempted to get consumers talking about their products for years, generating a buzz around products and services is currently becoming very popular. And, in today's age of mass media fragmentation and advertising clutter, these techniques can be very effective. Ford Motor Company utilized this technique when it gave a handful of consumers new Ford Focus automobiles to drive around and be seen in. By having consumers see the new automobile in use and receive WOM from others, Ford was able to take advantage of the power of buzz marketing.[37]

One buzz marketing tactic that relates directly to WOM is termed viral marketing. **Viral marketing** uses online technologies to facilitate WOM by having consumers spread marketing messages through their online conversations. For example, **hotmail.com** includes messages aimed at promoting their service that are included at the bottom of e-mail messages. Other forms of viral marketing include encouraging consumers to simply refer others to various websites and discussion boards.

Although buzz marketing is facilitated through online message boards and networking sites such as **myspace.com**, buzz marketing is not limited to online WOM content. The term *buzz marketing* is used much more broadly than that with tools such as the Internet and other public communication vehicles helping to spread the buzz.

STEALTH MARKETING

Another form of marketing that uses WOM that is more controversial is stealth marketing. **Stealth marketing** is a guerrilla marketing tactic that is similar to buzz

© AP IMAGE/PRNEWSFOTO/MOMJUNCTION

Websites like **momjunction.com** *have grown in popularity.*

Flat screen plasma TV | Yahoo! Search

the new
YAHOO! search
Faster. Easier. Bingo.
yahoo.com

OPINION LEADERS

Buzz marketing techniques are especially effective when opinion leaders are used. **Opinion leaders** are consumers who have great influence on the behavior of others relating to product adoption and purchase. Opinion leaders are knowledgeable about specific products or services and have a high level of involvement with those products. Characteristics of opinion leaders depend largely on the type of product under consideration, but in general, opinion leaders are socially active and self-confident.

The recent launch of a perfume exemplifies the use of opinion leaders. BCB-Girl, a perfume marketed by BCBG fashion, was introduced when the company sent bottles of the fragrance to teen trendsetters, along with 100 samples that each was expected to share with friends. The tactic was a success, as the perfume became the best-selling product in the selected cities the week of its full product launch.[40] By including opinion leaders in the marketing campaign for BCBGirl, BCBG fashion was able to harness the power of WOM processes.

> Opinion leaders have a great deal of influence on other consumers.

marketing, but a key difference between the terms is the degree to which consumers realize that they are being targeted by a marketing message. With stealth marketing, consumers are completely unaware that they are being marketed to (hence, the term *stealth*). As an example of stealth marketing, imagine a camera marketer that has employees pose as tourists. These "tourists" then ask others to take their pictures with a new camera. Of course, the picture takers don't realize that the tourists are employed by the company and that they are being targeted by a marketing message.[38]

The use of stealth marketing techniques, though growing, is considered questionable by many marketing professional organizations, and WOMMA is opposed to the stealth tactics. In fact, WOMMA has developed several categories of what it considers "unethical" marketing practices, including the following types of marketing techniques:[39]

- **Stealth marketing.** Deceiving consumers about the involvement of marketers in a communication
- **Shilling.** Compensating consumers to talk about, or promote, products without disclosing that they are working for the company
- **Infiltrating.** Using fake identities in online discussions to promote a product

Market Mavens and Surrogate Consumers

Opinion leaders are not the only influential consumers that have been identified. Market mavens and surrogate consumers also exert much influence on others. A **market maven** is a consumer who spreads information about all types of products and services that are available in the marketplace. The key difference between an opinion leader and a market maven is that the market maven's influence is not category specific. That is, market mavens spread information about numerous products and services.

Consumers can also be heavily influenced by what are termed surrogate consumers. A **surrogate consumer** is a consumer who is hired by another to provide input into a purchase decision. Interior decorators, travel consultants, and stock brokers can all be considered

diffusion process way in which new products are adopted and spread throughout a marketplace

surrogate consumers. Surrogate consumers can be very influential, and marketers should carefully consider the level of influence of these individuals.[41] Because of their extensive product expertise, surrogate consumers can often help others derive the maximum amount of value out of their transactions by maximizing the benefits associated with product purchase.

DIFFUSION PROCESSES

One area of interest in the study of group processes is the diffusion process. The **diffusion process** refers to the way in which new products are adopted and spread throughout a marketplace. Researchers have learned that different groups of consumers tend to adopt new products at different rates. One group may adopt a new product (for example, a hybrid automobile) very early in the product's life cycle, while another group may be very slow to adopt the product if it adopts the product at all. A product life cycle is a description of the life of a product from the time it is introduced to the time it dies off.

In all, five categories of consumers have been identified. They include innovators, early adopters, early majority, late majority, and laggards. These groups are presented in Exhibit 9.4.[42]

What makes group influence relevant to the diffusion process is that each group learns about new products not only from seeing marketing messages but also from talking with other consumers and observing their

© ERIC CARR/ALAMY

Maybe Talk Isn't Cheap

Marketers are excited about the many opportunities that are available in cyberspace. One of the fastest-growing opportunities can be found with blogging. Many popular sites exist, including **blogger.com**. These sites allow consumers to voice their opinions on a number of different topics. Blogging has even become a part of the marketing mix for many companies!

A number of websites that allow companies to hire bloggers to write blogs about their products have been introduced. Sites such as **payperpost.com**, **sponsoredreviews.com**, and **reviewme.com** are growing in popularity. Although the requirements for each site vary, the basic idea is that bloggers are given the opportunity to blog about products or companies for pay. Advertisers tell bloggers what products or services they want included in the blog, and the blogger agrees to write about it. The arrangement can be a win–win situation for both the blogger and advertiser. Of course, this practice may be considered to be unethical by some. Nevertheless, this form of Internet promotion is rapidly becoming an important component of buzz marketing, and given the popularity of the Internet blog, it is likely that this practice will continue to grow in popularity.

Sources: Johnson, Carolyn Y. (2007), "Blogging for Dollars," *Knight Ridder Tribune Business News* (April 16), 1; Fernando, Angelo (2007), "Transparency Under Attack," *Communication World*, 24 (2), 9–11; Schwartz, Matthew (2007), "Can Paid Blog Reviews Pay Off?," *B to B*, 92 (2), 1–3; Frazier, Mya (2006), "Want to Build Up Blog Buzz? Starting Writing Checks for $8," *Advertising Age*, 77 (44): 3–4; Armstrong, Stephen (2006), "Bloggers for Hire," *New Statesman*, 135 (4807), 26–27.

behavior. Group influence processes therefore apply to these categories.

Innovators and early majority consumers tend to be influential when discussing products and services with members of other groups. As such, they tend to be opinion leaders for specific product categories. Innovators are often risk takers and financially well-off. Early majority consumers are generally young and well-educated. Members of other groups, including early and late majority consumers, and laggards, tend to be more cautious about buying new products and wait significantly longer to buy the latest innovations. These consumers also tend to be somewhat older with lower levels of education and spending power.

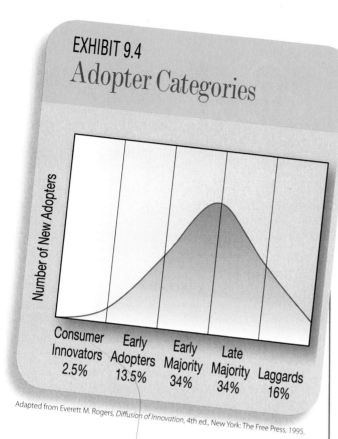

EXHIBIT 9.4
Adopter Categories

Number of New Adopters

Consumer Innovators 2.5%
Early Adopters 13.5%
Early Majority 34%
Late Majority 34%
Laggards 16%

Adapted from Everett M. Rogers, *Diffusion of Innovation*, 4th ed., New York: The Free Press, 1995.

LO5 Household Decision Making

as we discussed previously, the family unit is an important primary reference group for consumers. Family members typically have a great deal of influence over one another's attitudes, thoughts, and behaviors. Consider the many ways that the family has an impact on consumer behavior. **Household decision making** is the process through which household units choose between alternative courses of action. To begin with, we first discuss the various conceptualizations of the term *household*.

TRADITIONAL FAMILY STRUCTURE

The ways in which society views the family unit have changed dramatically in recent decades. Traditionally, the **family household** has been viewed as at least two people who are related by blood or marriage and who occupy a housing unit. In fact, this is how the U.S. Census Bureau defines a family unit. Other traditional family definitions include the *nuclear* family and the *extended* family.

The **nuclear family** consists of a mother, a father, and a set of siblings. The **extended family** consists of three or more generations of family members, including grandparents, parents, children, and grandchildren. In individualistic cultures like that in the United States, emphasis is placed on the nuclear family. However, in collectivist cultures, more focus is placed on the extended family, and it is not uncommon to see households that are comprised of extended family members living together.

Emerging Trends in Family Structure

As mentioned previously, the traditional views of the family have changed over time. Today, many nontraditional household arrangements exist throughout the United States. Societal trends toward people of opposite sex sharing living quarters (termed POSSLQ or cohabitation) and homosexual households have altered the way in which family households are conceptualized. In fact, 33% of households accounted for in the latest census information are defined as nonfamily households (that is, consumers sharing the same living quarters who are not related by blood or marriage).[43] Realize that even if a household is categorized as a nonfamily household, members still exert significant influence on one another.

Divorce rates tend to be quite high in the United States. Nearly 50% of all marriages in the United States eventually end in divorce. Divorces have dramatically altered the composition of the American family, and they have led to *blended families.* Blended families consist of previously married spouses and children from the previous marriages. Although the divorce rate in the United States is high, the latest estimates reveal that the rates are at their lowest point in over 30 years, at 3.6 divorces per 1,000 people. The highest rate recorded was in 1981, when the rate was 5.8 per 1,000 people.[44] Even with a divorce rate of 50%, less than half of all Americans who get married get divorced. This may seem paradoxical, but the explanation simply lies in the fact that those who do get one divorce become highly likely to get a second divorce or perhaps more.

Many people simply decide to never marry, even when children are present. In fact, it has been reported that more American women are now living without a

household decision making process by which decisions are made in household units

family household at least two people who are related by blood or marriage who occupy a housing unit

nuclear family a mother, a father, and a set of siblings

extended family three or more generations of family members

household life cycle (HLC) segmentation technique that acknowledges that changes in family composition and income alter household demand for products and services

husband than with one.[45] As a result of this trend and the high divorce rate, single-parent households have increased dramatically. Approximately 26% of U.S. children lived with only one parent in the year 2007.[46] Of course, not all women have children either by choice or inability. In fact, it is estimated that 20% of women aged 40-44 in 2006 (latest data available) had never had children. This number is twice the percentage of women in the same age group without children in 1976.[47] Another growing trend is that single men are adopting children at a rate higher than ever before.[48]

Finally, we note that the meaning of the term *nonfamily* is open to debate and interpretation. One topic of current debate is same-sex marriages. Same-sex marriages are becoming increasingly common, and the debate over the legality of same-sex marriages continues. Marketers increasingly target same-sex couples in many of their advertisements.

Even though each of these trends offers opportunities for marketers, one clear fact remains based on the census data of households in the United States. Despite widespread attention to nontraditional households, census data reveal that the largest portion of American consumers still live in something resembling a traditional household consisting of a married couple who either have yet to have children, have children living under the same roof, or have already raised children who no longer live at home. Also, the data reveal that the majority of American children reside in a traditional household, as is shown in Exhibit 9.5.

The prevalence of products such as SUVs and minivans as well as family-oriented movies such as *Shrek* and the *Harry Potter* franchise and the profitability of retailers such as Sam's Club owe at least a portion of their success to the large numbers of traditional family units.

Household Life Cycle

An important concept in the study of the family unit is the **household life cycle (HLC)**. The HLC represents a segmentation technique that acknowledges that changes in family composition and income alter household demand for products and services.

The traditional HLC segments families into a num-

> Family members greatly influence one another.

ber of groups based on the number of adults present and the age of the head of household. Based on this conceptualization, a number of segments are present including consumers who never marry (Bachelor 1, 2, and 3); two-adult, childless households (Young Couple, Childless Couple, and Older Couple); two adults with children (Full Nest 1, 2, and 3 and Delayed Full Nest); and one adult with children (Single Parent 1, 2, and 3). This conceptualization is presented in Exhibit 9.6.

The categorization of the household is important for consumer researchers.[49] Product expenditures vary greatly by stage in the HLC, and at each stage, consumers often try to obtain the most value that they can from their purchases. For example, Full Nest 1 consumers often face costly expenses related to raising young children, including the cost of baby clothes, furniture, and day care. These young consumers often have to search for new living accommodations in the form of larger apartments, or a starter home, when children are born. Single parents face the same challenges as two-adult families, but they must face these challenges alone. A great strain is therefore placed on the income of single parents. Older, childless couples have more disposable income to spend on their own needs. They are much more likely to enjoy luxuries such as vacation homes, financial investments, and upscale automobiles. Couples older than 64 often enjoy their retirement years, or choose to remain employed beyond retirement age.

The categories and assumptions in the HLC are representative of general patterns of spending behavior. That is, not every consumer will fall neatly into one specific category. Rather, the categories help to explain the living situations and expenditures of many consumers. Obviously, each consumer faces his or her own situation.

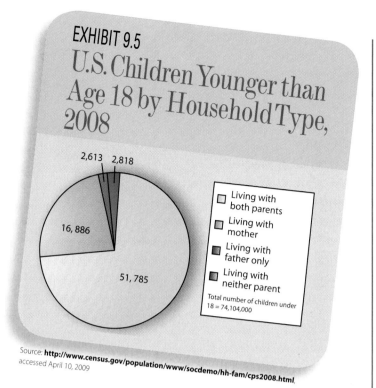

EXHIBIT 9.5

U.S. Children Younger than Age 18 by Household Type, 2008

2,613   2,818

16,886

51,785

Living with both parents

Living with mother

Living with father only

Living with neither parent

Total number of children under 18 = 74,104,000

Source: **http://www.census.gov/population/www/socdemo/hh-fam/cps2008.html**, accessed April 10, 2009

Middle-Aged Consumers: Boomerang Kids and the Sandwich Generation

Two evolving issues that are currently of interest to consumer researchers are boomerang kids and the sandwich generation. **Boomerang kids** are young adults, aged 18 to 34, who graduate from college and move back home with their parents. Quite often, the motivation is to reduce debt that has accumulated in the college years. Some have suggested the term *adultolesence* to describe this stage. The trend is growing, and it is estimated that nearly 65% of college graduates move back home with their parents today, compared to 53% who moved back with their parents in 2002.[50] As college tuition and student loan debts continue to rise, this number may be expected to increase in the future. This trend challenges the traditional HLC, and it greatly impacts how middle-aged consumers spend their money. In fact, it has been estimated that boomerang kids cost their parents $5,000 per year in disposable income.[51] The long-term implications of this trend are yet to be seen.

Financial and emotional strains on middle-aged consumers also come from belonging to the sandwich generation. The **sandwich generation** consists of those consumers who must take care of both their own children and their aging parents. An estimated 20 million consumers in the United States are members of the sandwich generation.[52] This number is also expected to increase dramatically over the next decade as millions of baby-boomers enter into their retirement years. Taking care of both children and parents obviously affects the behavior of these consumers as income is devoted

boomerang kids young adults, between the ages of 18 and 34, who move back home with their parents after they graduate from college

sandwich generation consumers who must take care of both their own children and their aging parents

EXHIBIT 9.6

Traditional Household Life Cycle Categories

	Under 35 Years	35 – 64 Years	Older than 64 Years
One-adult household	Bachelor 1	Bachelor 2	Bachelor 3
Two-adult household	Young Couple	Childless Couple	Older Couple
Two adults + children	Full Nest 1 (children < 6 years old) Full Nest 2 (children > 6 years old)	Delayed Full Nest (children < 6 years old) Full Nest 3 (children > 6 years old)	
One adult + children	Single Parent 1 (children < 6 years old) Single Parent 2 (children > 6 years old)	Single Parent 3	

Adapted from Mary C. Gilly and Ben M. Enis (1982), "Recycling the Family Lifecycle: A Proposal for Redefinition," in *Advances in Consumer Research*, Vol. 9, Andrew A. Mitchell, ed., Ann Arbor, MI: Association for Consumer Research, 271–276.

sex role orientation (SRO) family's set of beliefs regarding the ways in which household decisions are reached

to the needs of others. In fact, the average cost of caring for others aged 50-plus is nearly $6,000 per year. For consumers who must care for others long distance, the cost is nearly $9,000 per year.[53]

Household Purchase Roles

Each member of a household plays a specific role in product purchase. Five important roles in the household purchase process can be identified:

- *Influencer.* The person in the household who recognizes a need and provides information about a potential purchase to others

- *Gatekeeper.* The person who controls information flow into the household (for example, a mother who blocks unwanted e-mail solicitations from her child's e-mail account)

- *User.* The actual user of the product under consideration

- *Decision maker.* The person who makes the final decision regarding product purchase or nonpurchase

- *Purchaser.* The person who actually buys the product under consideration

Each role is important in product consideration and selection. The final purchase of the product is largely influenced by beliefs regarding the role of each person in the household.

Sex Roles and Household Decision Making

Like many of the concepts pertaining to household composition, societal views on sex roles and family decision making have evolved over time. Traditionally, men were viewed as having the primary responsibility

The Child's Role in CB

It is widely known that the child consumer of today is very different from the child consumer of yesteryear. Today's child is much more consumer savvy and has much more power in the marketplace. Children influence as much as $600 billion per year in consumer spending, and have more disposable income of their own than ever before. The influence of children on household spending ranges across spending categories from groceries to vacation destinations to automobile purchases.

Not everyone agrees that the commercialization of children is a positive development. For many, children should be off-limits to advertisers, or at least they should be targeted less frequently. Marketers often believe that parents should play a more active role in limiting commercial exposure while parents argue that marketers should cut back on advertisements aimed at kids. Still others believe strongly in the consumer socialization concept and that consumer education should begin early in life.

What is interesting about children today is that they are active not only as influencers, but also as gatekeepers of marketing information. Because they spend more time online than ever before, children are more likely to find marketplace information and relay the information on to the actual decision maker or purchaser: their parents! Therefore the power of children in the marketplace is not only increasing from a monetary standpoint, but the roles that children play in household purchasing are evolving as well.

Sources: Schor, Juliet (2008), "Understanding the Child Consumer," *Journal of the American Academy of Child and Adolescent Psychiatry*, 47 (5), 486 -490; Anonymous (2006), "Business: Trillion Dollar Kids; Marketing to Children," *The Economist*, 381 (8506), 74; Tapscott, Don (2008), "Net Gen Transforms Marketing," *BusinessWeek (online)*, November 17, 2008, **http://www.businessweek.com/technology/content/nov2008/tc20081114_882532.htm**, accessed April 10, 2009.

© DAVID DAVIS/SHUTTERSTOCK/IMAGES LLC

of providing for the family, while women were expected to meet everyday family needs and take care of the home.[54] However, changes in the education of women and the acceleration in the number of double-income families have challenged these conceptualizations.

An important concept in sex roles and family decision making is **sex role orientation (SRO)**. A family's SRO influences the ways in which household decisions are reached. Families that have a traditional SRO believe that it is the responsibility of the male head of household to make large purchase decisions, while families with a "modern" SRO believe in a more democratic approach.[55] Given the evolving nature of the typical household in the United States, it is not surprising that SROs are changing. In particular, the role of women in household decision making is more prevalent than in previous years. Indeed, studies have revealed that women are playing a bigger role in decision making in all household decision areas.[56]

Kid Power

The role of children in household decision making is also evolving. Although children were once thought to have relatively little impact on purchasing decisions outside of what toy to buy, marketers are realizing that children are playing a much larger role in influencing household purchases than ever before. One recent study revealed that 36% of parents with children between the ages of 6 and 11 reported that their children significantly influence their purchasing decisions.[57]

The power of the children's market has grown substantially over the past few decades. Today, children between the ages of 8 and 12 spend $30 billion per year of their own money and influence another $600 billion per year in total household spending.[58] Furthermore, the teen segment frequently sees its disposable income grow at a rate that is unlike that found in any other segment. For example, the typical American 12-year-old has $1,500 per year to spend. However, this number leaps to $4,500 per year by the time the child reaches age 17.[59] Much of this income is earned income, even if it is a weekly allowance provided by parents. Obviously, older children earn much of their income from jobs outside of the home.

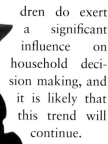

An important issue in the development of the child consumer is known as consumer socialization. **Consumer socialization** is defined as the process through which young consumers develop attitudes and learn skills that help them function in the marketplace.[60] Sometimes these skills are learned at a surprisingly young age, and children have largely begun to seek products that were once considered to be "too old" for their age segment. This has led to the development of a well-known marketing catchphrase, K.G.O.Y. (Kids Growing Older, Younger).

Although many consider the issue of kid power and marketing to children controversial, it is clear that children do exert a significant influence on household decision making, and it is likely that this trend will continue.

consumer socialization the process through which young consumers develop attitudes and learn skills that help them function in the marketplace

Chapter 9 Case

I n 1993, Apple introduced the first personal digital assistant (PDA), the Newton, to the market. The Newton included handwriting recognition software, a backlight, and a stylus that was used to input most commands. It also supported modems, ethernet and wireless network cards, and flash memory. However, due to Apple's rush to beat competitors to the market, engineers did not have adequate time to test the Newton, and bugs were later found in its software. In addition, many consumers thought the Newton had too many features and was not user-friendly. This perception, combined with the Newton's size, which was larger than the PalmPilot and other PDAs introduced later, made it unpopular with most consumers. Sales of the Newton were sluggish so it was dropped from Apple's product line in early 1998, shortly after Steve Jobs became CEO of Apple.

During its brief time with Apple, though, a brand community consisting of about 200,000 highly loyal Newton users coalesced. Many members of this community thought that the discontinuation of the Newton was directly due to Steve Jobs becoming Apple's CEO, while others believed that the product had not been given a fair chance and was simply too far ahead of its time. Thus, in a surprising result, the Newton brand community did not disappear with the removal of the Newton from the market; rather, the community flourished. The members of the brand community became even more committed to the Newton and served as devout advocates of the Newton. Online community forums dedicated to the Newton were filled with accounts of Newton users convincing others of the product's worth, stories about how Microsoft and its users were bullying the Newton, and rumors about the Newton being reintroduced. Almost mythical descriptions of the Newton's performance, such as its compatibility with other products or recovery after seemingly "fatal" accidents, were also quite normal.

Mystical and spiritual themes were widespread among members' comments about the Newton. Marketing researchers have even noted that many members of this brand community almost treated it as a religion. Many members of the community treated competing products like a false religion, comparing users of other PDAs and Microsoft products to cattle who were simply going with the flow and unaware of the real value of the Newton. When members of the community felt that the community was threatened, their resolve to stay with the community and be all the more dedicated to it was reinforced.[61]

Questions

1. Why did a brand community develop around the Newton?

2. Why did the Newton brand community thrive after Apple abandoned the Newton?

3. Could the Newton brand community have existed without the Internet? Why or why not?

what do you think?

I never let anything get in the way of preparing for my consumer behavior class.

1 2 3 4 5 6 7

strongly disagree   strongly agree

The social environment,

referring to the other customers and employees in a service or shopping environment, cannot be ignored when explaining how "place" affects consumer behavior.

10

Consumers in Situations

After studying this chapter, the student should be able to:

LO1 Understand how value varies with situations.

LO2 Know the different ways that time affects consumer behavior.

LO3 Analyze shopping as a consumer activity using the different categories of shopping activities.

LO4 Distinguish the concepts of unplanned, impulse, and compulsive consumer behavior.

LO5 Use the concept of atmospherics to create consumer value.

LO6 Understand what is meant by antecedent conditions.

LO1 Value in Situations?

for most American tourists, a trip to London is not complete without spending some time at Harrods of Knightsbridge. Harrods's six stories of upscale retailing presents consumers with some of the most fabulously merchandised products to be found anywhere. Harrods spares no expense in creating a unique experience. For instance, most department stores have background music of some type, but Harrods entertains shoppers with a full-fledged orchestra on busy days. Certainly, the excitement created by live music helps frame purchase situations, and who could possibly leave Harrods without some souvenir that helps capture the experience in an enduring way?

While these American tourists are on their way to London, their plane may well pass a plane full of British travelers on their way to America's heartland. British travelers can take off from London and fly for a one-day shopping spree at none other than the Mall of America in Minneapolis. They leave behind Harrods and other British merchandisers such as Marks and Spencer; climb aboard one of several airliners offering nonstop flights from London to Minneapolis; and spend their time, albeit limited, shopping in a different place. Certainly, after flying all the way to Minnesota, will any of these shoppers come back empty-handed? It's unlikely!

What makes these experiences different from "regular" shopping? Some of the factors involved in explaining these outcomes include:

- Exchange rates
- Time of year
- Time available for shopping
- Credit policies/financing
- Who is accompanying the shopper
- The purpose of the trip—fun or work?
- Airline baggage regulations

Each of these factors and others can affect the value one experiences in exchange.

SITUATIONS AND VALUE

This chapter focuses on precisely how the value a consumer obtains from a purchase or consumption act varies based on the context in which the act takes place. These contextual effects, meaning effects

> Situational influences are neither enduring characteristics of a particular consumer nor the product or brand involved.

independent of enduring consumer, brand, or product characteristics, are known as **situational influences**. As can be seen in the CVF framework, situational influences can directly affect both consumer decision making and the eventual value experienced. Situational influences are neither enduring characteristics of a particular consumer nor the product or brand involved. Indeed, situational influences are ephemeral, meaning they are temporary conditions in a real sense. Contexts can affect communication, shopping, brand preference, purchase, actual consumption, and the evaluation of that consumption.

Situational influences are typified by the movie theater experience. If the movie is a matinee, the consumer expects to pay a lower price than he or she would pay in the evening. Even though the movie hasn't changed, the number of people available to go to the movie has changed from the evening hours. Therefore, the lower demand entices the theater to offer lower prices. In contrast, in the evening far fewer people are working and thus are more likely to be able to fill a theater seat.

The same consumer goes to the concession stand and pays $10 for a Coke and some popcorn. For some, Coke and popcorn with a movie is a highly ritualized tradition, and the entire experience is diminished without this treat. The fact that the theater doesn't permit

© CHUCK SAVAGE/CORBIS

> Popcorn becomes more valuable when the consumers are at the movies.

outside food and drink also enhances the value of the products sold at the concession stand because competition is practically eliminated. Situational influences change the desirability of consuming things and therefore change the value of these things.

Situational influences can be classified into one of three categories. These categories represent different influences due to:

- Time
- Place
- Conditions

Exhibit 10.1 provides a snapshot of examples of these influences and the way they operate. The following sections discuss each of these groups of influence in more detail with an emphasis on how value changes with each.

EXHIBIT 10.1
Situational Influence Categories

1. Time can influence consumers by changing the way information is processed. A consumer shopping for a computer near the store's closing time may not deliberate and consider as much information as usual. This may shift decision making to limited problem solving when the consumer would otherwise use extended problem solving and ultimately affect brand choice.

2. Place can frame any purchase, consumption, or information processing situation. Think about how the theme of a restaurant as captured by the atmosphere of the place will shape the types of foods consumed there and the value they provide. Sushi is the best in an environment with an Asian genre.

3. Conditions also can influence consumption. Beverage choices are different when a consumer is cold than when a consumer is hot. Also, social settings affect choice. Consumers in crowded restaurants and bars are more likely to choose name brand beverages than when the social condition does not involve crowds.

LO2 Time and Consumer Behavior

time can be thought of as a consumer's most valuable resource. Time is truly scarce. In some ways, time is a consumer's only real resource because it can be converted into economic resources. Time is necessary for consumption to occur. In addition, time-related factors can affect a consumer's thoughts, feelings, and behavior, all of which come together to create differing perceptions of value. Time can affect consumption in any of these forms:

- Time pressure
- Time of year
- Time of day

The term **temporal factors** is sometimes used to refer to situational characteristics related to time. Thus, each of the time forms listed here represents a different temporal factor.

TIME PRESSURE

A consumer sits down with five coworkers for lunch. The waiter comes by and asks, "Are you ready to order?" All the others at the table are ready. The consumer experiences a sense of urgency and hastily settles for a hamburger. Would the consumer have made a different choice if he or she had not felt compelled to rush to a decision rather than make the others wait?

This situation exemplifies an intense time pressure. **Time pressure** is represented by an urgency to act based on some real or self-imposed deadline. In this situation, the consumer imposes a deadline of ordering at the same time as the others at the table. Therefore, he or she is rushed to make a decision without the due deliberation that would likely take place otherwise.

Time pressure affects consumers in several ways. First, when time is scarce, consumers process less information because time is a critical resource necessary for problem solving. Consumers who experience time pressure, for instance, are able to recall less information about product choices than are consumers in the same situation who are not under the situational influence of time pressure.[1] Additionally, consumers experiencing time pressure are more likely to rely on simple choice heuristics than are those in less tense situations.[2] Consumers who might otherwise consider many attributes in reaching a decision may simply rely on a price-quality heuristic under time pressure.[3]

Time pressure shapes the value consumers perceive in products by influencing their quality and price perceptions.[4] Because consumers rely more on price-quality heuristics than they do beliefs about financial sacrifice, brands that are positioned as relatively high quality may benefit in situations characterized by high time pressure. Consumers may simply choose the well-known and potentially higher-priced brand because they don't have time to weigh off different attributes against the price. Conversely, other consumers may simply choose the lowest price alternative and risk being disappointed by a brand that does not deliver the expected benefits.

TIME OF YEAR

Seasonality refers to regularly occurring conditions that vary with the time of year. The fact is, consumers'

temporal factors situational characteristics related to time

time pressure urgency to act based on some real or self-imposed deadline

seasonality regularly occurring conditions that vary with the time of year value perceptions also vary with the time of the year. A cup of hot chocolate is simply not worth as much to a consumer on a hot, sunny summer afternoon as it is on a cold, cloudy winter day.

Even though this tendency may seem as obvious as consumers purchasing more coats and sweaters during the winter, seasonality has other effects that are perhaps not so obvious.[5] Consumers tend to shop earlier in the day during winter months, and, overall, they tend to spend more during the summer months.[6] Almost all products are susceptible to some type of seasonal influence. Fashion may lead the way with traditional spring, summer, fall, and winter fashions. However, many food items vary in demand with the season. Champagne is consumed predominantly during the holidays. The challenge for those who sell seasonal products like champagne is to position the product more as an everyday option.

TIME OF DAY/CIRCADIAN CYCLES

What beverage do most consumers around the world wake up to? Traditionally, Danes, Italians, and the French have been almost exclusively coffee drinkers. Consumers in the United Kingdom and in many parts of Asia wake to tea in the morning. During the 1990s, American consumers turned away from coffee toward soft drinks, particularly among young consumers. Today, however, coffee sales are on the rise, and college-aged Americans have returned to drinking coffee in the morning. Coffee sales are also increasing in the United Kingdom as coffee shops, including Starbucks, can be found in all major cities.

The increase in coffee consumption in the United States has come largely at the expense of carbonated soft drinks. Tea sales are also increasing in the United States, and although tea has largely been an afternoon and evening beverage in the past, Americans now are turning to tea, even iced tea, as a beverage to wake up to.[7]

Whether it's beverage consumption, attire, or choice of entertainment, the time of day affects the value of products and activities. Some of this influence is due to scheduled events during the day such as one's working hours. But, part is also biological. In fact, our bodies have a rhythm that varies with the time of day. This rhythm is known as the **circadian cycle**. One aspect of the circadian cycle deals with our sleeping and waking times. Consumers would prefer to sleep between the hours of midnight and 6 A.M. and from about 1 to 3 P.M. Consumers who tend to shop during the "odd hours" will do so with less energy and efficiency. However, they can also do so with less interference from other consumers.

Our circadian cycle is responsible for productivity in many activities. However, ill effects follow from circadian cycles as traffic fatalities due to drowsy driving also vary with natural circadian cycles.[8] A host of products exist to try to aid consumers through the low-

Let the Madness Begin

Most college sports fans are aware of the madness that occurs in March—the month when the NCAA Men's Basketball Tournament begins. The tournament ends in April with the all-important championship game. Sixty-four teams compete across four, sixteen-team "regional" tournaments with the goal of eventually being crowned champions.

The tournament has become a marketer's dream. Although fans watch games on-and-off throughout the season, millions of consumers become glued to television sets during the tournament. In fact, overall work productivity decreases during the tournament because many workers spend work time watching games on Internet broadcasts or simply talking about games around the water cooler! Software packages even have "boss buttons" that allow the user to switch quickly away from a game on the computer screen to a spreadsheet to make it look like they are actually working and not watching. Estimates suggest that millions of dollars of productivity are lost each year due to the tournament. Of course, college basketball delivers value for millions of fans throughout the season. But from March until April, value perceptions greatly increase due to that annual sports phenomenon known as "madness."

Energy drinks like those offered by Monster provide an alternative to coffee as a pick-me-up beverage. The drinks particularly appeal to younger demographics looking for something to get them over the daily down times that go with the circadian cycle.

energy periods of the day, but perhaps the best fix is a quick nap!

ADVERTIMING

Are you having trouble sleeping? Try Rozeram! A popular ad campaign for a Japanese pharmaceutical product uses Abraham Lincoln, a beaver, and other assorted characters to convince the consumer that this product will indeed solve sleeping related problems—primarily, the lack of sleep.

What is the best time to communicate to consumers who have difficulty sleeping? Rozeram runs television ads mainly from about midnight through the early morning hours. At this time, the assumption is that consumers will be most sensitive to problems with sleeping. Maybe they're having trouble going to sleep and are up late or they are drowsy in the morning because of an inability to sleep well through the night.

Companies sometimes buy advertising with a schedule that runs the advertisement primarily at times when customers will be most receptive to the message. This practice is known as **advertiming**. Advertising also can be based on seasonal patterns or even on day-to-day changes in the weather.[9] Swimming pool marketers realize that consumers are more receptive to their ads in the spring or summer, as do marketers of products such as jet skis and power boats.

LO3 Place Shapes Shopping Activities

INTRODUCTION

The economy depends on consumers buying things. Consumers depend on purchases to receive value. Buying is the end result of the shopping process. Thus, marketers understand that shopping holds the key to value creation that stimulates economies and ultimately raises standards of living.

Many of the activities involved in the CVF and consumer behavior theory in general take place in the shopping process. What exactly is shopping? Perhaps the following questions can help put shopping in perspective:

- Do consumers have to buy to shop?
- Is a store necessary for shopping?
- What motivates consumer shopping?

Marketers naturally hope that consumers will purchase things while shopping. But not every shopping act culminates in a purchase. Sometimes a consumer goes shopping only to find out that the desired product is out of stock. Rather than buying a less desirable product, the consumer may simply pass or put off product acquisition indefinitely.

More and more, a physical store isn't necessary for shopping to take place. Consumers shop using their computers, their PDAs, vending machines, or more traditional "nonstore" alternatives like catalogs. Sometimes, consumers facing an important decision like a new home or an upcoming vacation are so involved in the buying process that they can't stop thinking about their choices. In this case, they may be shopping simply from the things they hold in memory.

WHAT IS SHOPPING?

Shopping can be defined as the set of value-producing consumer activities that directly increase the likelihood that something will be purchased. Thus, when a consumer surfs the Internet looking for a song for her iPod, she is shopping. When a consumer visits a car dealer after hours to peruse the options on new cars, he is shopping.

acquisitional shopping
activities oriented toward a specific, intended purchase or purchases

epistemic shopping
activities oriented toward acquiring knowledge about products

experiential shopping
recreationally oriented activities designed to provide interest, excitement, relaxation, fun, or some other desired feeling

impulsive shopping
spontaneous activities characterized by a diminished regard for consequences, spontaneity, and a desire for immediate self-fulfillment

Shopping enhances purchase behavior. What happens when the situation involves shopping with a friend?

When a consumer visits the mall as a regular weekend activity, she is shopping. Earlier, marketing was discussed as business activities that enhance the likelihood of purchase. In this sense, shopping can be looked at as the inverse of marketing. Both marketing and shopping make purchase more likely, but one involves activities of marketing people and the other involves activities of shoppers.

> Both marketing and shopping make purchase more likely, but one involves activities of marketing people and the other involves activities of shoppers.

SHOPPING ACTIVITIES

Shopping activities take place in specific places, over time, and under specific conditions or contexts. Shopping thus occurs in situations that are not easily controlled by a consumer and often not by the marketer either. The consumer may be either alone or in a crowded place, rushed or relaxed, in a good mood or a bad mood. In other words, shoppers are subjected to many situational influences that affect decision making and value. Whether the shoppers are American,

European, or Asian, situational variables are at least as important in explaining eventual buying behavior as are personal characteristics or product beliefs.[10] Even the online shopping experience is largely shaped by situational variables.[11] Practically all shopping activities are influenced by contextual sources.

Shopping activities can be divided into four different types. Any given shopping experience is characterized by at least one of these types, but sometimes the shopper can combine more than one type into a single shopping trip. The four types of shopping activities are

1. **Acquisitional shopping.** Activities oriented toward a specific, intended purchase or purchases

2. **Epistemic shopping.** Activities oriented toward acquiring knowledge about products

3. **Experiential shopping.** Recreationally oriented activities designed to provide interest, excitement, relaxation, fun, or some other desired feeling

4. **Impulsive shopping.** Spontaneous activities characterized by a diminished regard for consequences, heightened emotional involvement, and a desire for immediate self-fulfillment

Acquisitional Shopping

A consumer who runs out to the store on her lunch hour to buy a gift for a coworker's baby shower is strongly oriented toward getting a gift. Thus, shopping is more like a task, and this particular activity depends on high utilitarian value as an outcome.

Epistemic Shopping

Epistemic activities include finding information on some purchase that is imminent. Alternatively, epistemic activities include shopping simply to increase an ever-growing body of knowledge about some product category of interest. In this sense, epistemic activities can be associated with either situational involvement or enduring involvement, respectively.

Experiential Shopping

Experiential activities include things done just for the experience. Many consumers go shopping on the weekends just to do something. In other words, experiential shopping can be motivated by boredom. On the other hand, consumers who are on vacation often take in the local shopping venues. In this way, they experience something new and possibly unique. **Outshopping** is a term used to refer to consumers who are shopping in a city or town they must travel to rather than in their own hometown. Outshopping is often motivated simply by the desire for the experience. The outshopping consumer sees this as a value opportunity and is more likely to make purchases in this less familiar and perhaps more intriguing place.

Impulsive Shopping

Impulsive behaviors represent a unique group of shopping activities. These will be discussed in more detail later. However, impulsive activities also illustrate how a single shopping trip can result in more than one type of activity. A shopper may simply go to a big box store to acquire a gift. However, while there, they may get into the environment of the store and experience strong emotions. These may also encourage the consumer to act impulsively.

Exhibit 10.2 provides examples of each type of activity and ties the activities to the types of value they are more associated with.

SHOPPING VALUE

All shopping activities are aimed at one key result—value. Consistent with the view of value from a previous chapter, **personal shopping value**, or **PSV**, is the overall subjective worth of a shopping activity considering all associated costs and benefits. Like value overall, PSV can be usefully divided into two types. **Utilitarian shopping value** represents the worth obtained because some shopping task or job is completed successfully. **Hedonic shopping value** represents the worth of an activity because the time spent doing the activity itself is personally gratifying.[12]

outshopping shopping in a city or town to which consumers must travel rather than in their own hometowns

personal shopping value (PSV) overall subjective worth of a shopping activity considering all associated costs and benefits

utilitarian shopping value worth obtained because some shopping task or job is completed successfully

hedonic shopping value worth of an activity because the time spent doing the activity itself is personally gratifying

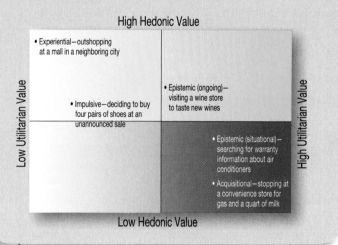

EXHIBIT 10.2
Shopping Activities and Shopping Value

High Hedonic Value

Low Utilitarian Value — High Utilitarian Value

- Experiential—outshopping at a mall in a neighboring city
- Epistemic (ongoing)—visiting a wine store to taste new wines
- Impulsive—deciding to buy four pairs of shoes at an unannounced sale
- Epistemic (situational)—searching for warranty information about air conditioners
- Acquisitional—stopping at a convenience store for gas and a quart of milk

Low Hedonic Value

COURTESY OF SPA HAMPTON

Day spas have become increasingly popular. After indulging in spa treatments, consumers may impulsively purchase products to bring home.

Value and Shopping Activities

Thus, the activities shown in Exhibit 10.2 all provide value, but they provide value in different ways to different consumers. The old term *window shopping* illustrates this point. Some consumers window shop to find information so that an upcoming shopping trip might be more successful. In this way, window shopping is a means to the end of a more successful future shopping task. Consumers may also window shop simply as a way of passing time in a gratifying way. Thus, window shopping can provide utilitarian and/or hedonic shopping value, respectively.

Situational influences may affect the type of shopping value desired by consumers. Time pressure, for example, may lead consumers to be more concerned with simple product acquisition than they might otherwise be. On the other hand, consumers who are in a bad mood may choose to change it by going shopping. The pleasant emotions can be personally gratifying and can potentially improve a shopper's mood.[13] Thus, hedonic shopping value becomes important. Both value dimensions are related to both customer share and customer loyalty. However, research suggests that hedonic shopping value may be more strongly related to loyalty than is utilitarian shopping value.[14]

Retail Personality

Retailers specializing in things like a wide selection of goods, low prices, guarantees, and knowledgeable employees can provide high proportions of utilitarian shopping value. This type of positioning emphasizes the **functional quality** of a retail store by facilitating the task of shopping. In contrast, retailers specializing in a unique environment, an impressive décor, friendly employees, and pleasant emotions can provide relatively high hedonic shopping value. This type of positioning

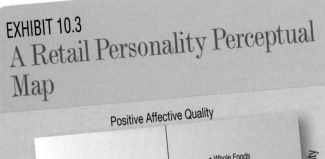

EXHIBIT 10.3
A Retail Personality Perceptual Map

emphasizes the **affective quality** of a retail store. The affective quality can be managed to create an emotionally rewarding environment capable of producing high hedonic shopping value. Together, the functional and affective qualities come together to shape retail personality. More specifically, **retail personality** is the way a retail store is defined in the mind of a shopper based on the combination of functional and affective qualities.[15]

From a strategic perspective, these two retail personality dimensions are extremely useful as perceptual map dimensions (see Exhibit 10.3). Once again, a perceptual map of this type reveals which retail choices consumers view as most similar. As consumers' choices become more similar, they are more likely to compete with each other.

LO4 Impulsive Shopping and Consumption

mpulsive shopping activities take place every day. Some retailers and service providers survive largely as a result of consumers' compulsive activities. For instance, many behaviors associated with indulgence can be driven by impulsive motivations.

So, just what is an impulsive consumption act? As the definition implies, **impulsive consumption** is largely characterized by three components:

1. Impulsive acts are usually spontaneous and involve at least short-term feelings of liberation.

2. Impulsive acts are usually associated with a diminished regard for any costs or consequences (negative aspects) associated with the act.

3. Impulsive acts are usually motivated by a need for immediate self-fulfillment and are thus usually highly involving emotionally and associated with hedonic shopping value.

Activities characterized by these features are likely to be impulsive. For example, a consumer might have a bad morning at work and decide to cancel a business lunch to take a break shopping for self-gifts or "happies" via the Internet. This activity is likely characterized as impulsive and can be a way to suppress negative emotions and evoke more positive feelings.[16] The behavior can be broken down to demonstrate the impulsiveness involved as follows:

1. The act involves willingly deviating from previous plans and thus shows spontaneity and no doubt feelings of liberation from the negative events of the day.

2. The act shows diminished regard for consequences either for missing the business lunch or for any expense incurred.

3. The act fulfills the need to maintain a positive outlook on the self and thus provides hedonic value.

Internet shopping, although often viewed as utilitarian in nature, can provide hedonic value in this way.[17]

IMPULSIVE VERSUS UNPLANNED CONSUMER BEHAVIOR

Impulsive purchasing is not synonymous with unplanned purchasing behavior. **Unplanned shopping,** buying, and consuming share some, but not all, characteristics of truly impulsive consumer behavior. Exhibit 10.4 illustrates the relationship between impulsive and unplanned consumer activity. The right side of the exhibit shows that unplanned consumer acts are characterized by

1. Situational memory

2. Utilitarian orientation

3. Spontaneity

Situational memory characterizes unplanned acts because something in the environment, such as a point-of-purchase display, usually triggers the knowledge in memory that something is needed. A consumer may enter the grocery store without Doublemint gum on her grocery list. However, the candy counter at the checkout provides a convenient reminder that her office inventory of her favorite breath freshener is depleted.

Simply put, unplanned purchases are usually driven by utilitarian motivations. This consumer who purchases Doublemint gum is probably not very emotionally moved by the gum purchase. However, the purchase allows her to fulfill a need to replenish her supply of the product.

Unplanned acts are spontaneous, and to some extent, they share this characteristic with impulsivity. They are, by definition, unplanned and therefore done without any significant deliberation or prior decision making. The gum buyer certainly had not put a lot of thought into the decision to buy Doublemint as she planned the shopping trip.

> **unplanned shopping**
> shopping activity that shares some, but not all, characteristics of truly impulsive consumer behavior; being characterized by situational memory, a utilitarian orientation, and feelings of spontaneity

EXHIBIT 10.4
Impulsive versus Unplanned Shopping Behavior

Impulsive Behavior
- Diminished Regard for Consequences
- Impulse Shopping/Behavior
- Emotional-Hedonic
- Spontaneous

Unplanned Behavior
- Situational Memory
- Unplanned Shopping/Behavior
- Utilitarian

DISTINGUISHING IMPULSIVE AND UNPLANNED CONSUMER BEHAVIOR

The line between impulsive and unplanned purchases is not always clear because some unplanned acts are impulsive and many impulsive acts are unplanned. Las Vegas tourism for years has used a tagline that says:

What Happens in Vegas, Stays in Vegas

While some trips to Vegas may be completely spontaneous, most involve some degree of planning. But the tagline emphasizes the impulsive nature of consumer behavior in Las Vegas. Certainly, the campaign illustrates the high hedonic value that can be obtained and encourages consumers not to worry so much about the consequences. So perhaps an impulsive consumption act, like going to Vegas, can even be planned. Simple

© IMAGE COURTESY OF THE ADVERTISING ARCHIVES

A spontaneous gum purchase may be unplanned, but is it impulsive?

unplanned purchases may lack the impulsive characteristics captured so well by this campaign.

Simple unplanned purchases usually lack any real emotional involvement or significant amounts of self-gratification. Additionally, unplanned purchases often involve only minimal negative consequences and thus fail to really qualify as having negative consequences. A pack of gum is not likely to cause severe financial problems for very many consumers.

SUSCEPTIBILITY TO SITUATIONAL EFFECTS

Are all consumers susceptible to unplanned and impulsive behavior? The answer is "yes," but not all consumers are equally susceptible. Individual difference characteristics can play a role. For example, **impulsivity** is a personality trait that represents how sensitive a consumer is to immediate rewards. A consumer shopping for a gift for a friend may see shoes on sale at half off and be compelled to purchase these and obtain the *reward*.[18] Naturally, consumers with high impulsivity are more prone to impulsive acts.[19]

Consumers with attention deficit disorder, for example, typically have high degrees of impulsivity, which makes them more prone to impulsive acts. One consequence is that such consumers are even less likely than others to follow step-by-step instructions for assembling or using a product.[20] Thus, they may fail to get the full value from the product because the assembly is incomplete or wrong.

Situational characteristics also influence impulse shopping.[21] For example, a consumer shopping for a purple dress for a special occasion may encounter a different black dress on the 40% off rack. The low-price cue may encourage an impulse purchase in this case. Atmospheric characteristics such as the colors, music, free samples, merchandising, and salespeople also can encourage purchase. Online retailers can facilitate the actual buying process by making the transaction a simple one-step process.[22] Exhibit 10.5 summarizes things that retailers can do to encourage unplanned and impulse purchasing.

CONSUMER SELF-REGULATION

Another key personality trait that affects a consumer's tendency to do things that are unplanned or impulsive is self-regulatory capacity. **Consumer self-regulation**, in this sense, refers to a tendency for consumers to inhibit outside, or situational, influences from interfering with

EXHIBIT 10.5
Retail Approaches at Encouraging Impulse Purchases

TOOL	EXAMPLE
1. Merchandise complementary products together	Placing beer near the charcoal triggers memory so that the consumer remembers how well beer goes with barbecue.
2. Encourage "add-on" purchases	Asking consumers to buy socks after they have agreed to buy shoes seems like a small request, and turning the request down risks creating negative feelings. Add-on purchases also serve as a trigger in memory.
3. Create an emotionally charged atmosphere	Positive emotions, in particular excitement, are associated with larger purchases. Giving free samples can be one way of making consumer feel good.
4. Make things easy to buy	Consumers have less time to think about the purchase and perhaps decide the product is not worth the price. A consumer who allows his credit card number to be automatically used by a website will be more prone to unplanned and impulse purchases.
5. Provide a discount	Buy one watch get a second for half price. The consequences become even easier to diminish.

shopping intentions. Consumers with a high capacity to self-regulate their behavior are sometimes referred to as **action-oriented**, whereas consumers with a low capacity to self-regulate are referred to as **state-oriented**.[23] Action-oriented consumers are affected less by emotions generated by a retail atmosphere than are state-oriented consumers. Recall the three dimensions of atmospheric emotions discussed in an earlier chapter: pleasure, arousal, and dominance. State-oriented shoppers who are emotionally aroused are far more likely to make additional purchases beyond what was planned than are action-oriented shoppers. Likewise, state-oriented shoppers' spending behavior is strongly affected by feelings of dominance in the environment. Further, feelings of dominance among state-oriented shoppers increase hedonic shopping value and decrease utilitarian shopping value. In contrast, action-oriented shoppers' purchasing and shopping value perceptions are unaffected by dominance.

New electronics can be a tempting element in a shopping environment. Self-regulation is related to a consumer's desire, and intention, to purchase such new products. A state-oriented consumer who enters an upbeat electronics store is more likely to buy a new product than an action-oriented consumer would be under the same circumstances.[24] Retailers with a high proportion of state-oriented consumers in their target market are more likely to thrive on consumers' impulse purchases.

Exhibit 10.6 lists some questions that can distinguish consumers based on self-regulatory capacity. The exhibit shows a statement and then demonstrates the way a consumer would respond to the situation. Consumers with a high ability to self-regulate their behavior, in other words the action-oriented consumers, generally form rules that they stick by to limit the amount to which situational influences determine their behavior. For example, if they know they will be tempted to overspend during a shopping trip, they may decide not to take their credit cards with them while shopping. In this way, they can resist the overspending that sometimes accompanies unplanned and impulse purchases.[25]

Although Exhibit 10.5 lists some things retailers can do to encourage unplanned or impulse purchases, one might ask, are such actions ethical? Or, do such actions simply encourage consumers to buy things wastefully? This certainly can be the case, but unplanned purchases are often simply things consumers would indeed intend to buy if they had remembered them before they started shopping. Impulse purchases can also be a relatively harmless way that consumers control their emotions and improve their outlook on life. Impulse purchases

STATEMENT	ACTION-ORIENTED CONSUMERS' TYPICAL RESPONSE	STATE-ORIENTED CONSUMERS' TYPICAL RESPONSE
If I had to work at home…	I would get started right away	I would often have problems getting started
When I have important things to buy…	I make a shopping plan and stick to it	I don't know how to get started
When I have an important assignment to finish in an afternoon…	I can easily concentrate on the assignment	It often happens that things will distract me
When it is absolutely necessary to do some unpleasant task…	I finish it as soon as possible	It takes a while before I can start on it

do provide value as long as the consequences of the purchases are relatively harmless. In this way, impulse shopping can be therapeutic and emotionally uplifting. This isn't always the case though.

IMPULSIVE VERSUS COMPULSIVE BEHAVIOR

Impulsive and compulsive consumer behavior shares many of the same characteristics. Compulsive behavior can be emotionally involving and certainly entails the possibility of negative consequences. Compulsive consumer behavior can be distinguished from impulsive consumer behavior. The three distinguishing characteristics are:

- Compulsive consumer behavior is harmful.

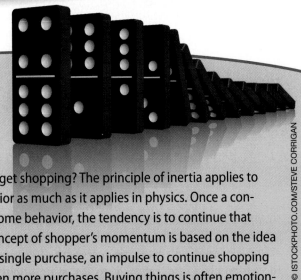

© ISTOCKPHOTO.COM/STEVE CORRIGAN

Domino Shopping

Does shopping beget shopping? The principle of inertia applies to consumer behavior as much as it applies in physics. Once a consumer initiates some behavior, the tendency is to continue that behavior. The concept of shopper's momentum is based on the idea that once a shopper makes a single purchase, an impulse to continue shopping develops, which results in even more purchases. Buying things is often emotionally rewarding. So, if one purchase creates good feelings, and perhaps hedonic shopping value, then two purchases must be even better—right?

Shoppers' momentum may also exist for nonpurchase. Inaction inertia is a term used to refer to the fact that once a consumer passes on buying a brand that he or she is used to buying, not buying that brand becomes easier. This becomes particularly apparent when a consumer misses an opportunity to buy an often-used brand on sale. That consumer is actually less likely to buy that brand again the next time the need becomes apparent. So, not buying can grow on a consumer just as buying can!

Sources: Dhar, R., J. Huber and U. Khan (2007), "The Shopping Momentum Effect," *Journal of Marketing Research*, 44 (August), 370–378; Zeelenberg, M., and Puttun, Van Marijke (2005), "The Dark Side of Discounts: An Inaction Inertia Perspective on the Post-Promotional Dip," *Psychology & Marketing*, 22 (September), 611–622.

- Compulsive consumer behavior seems to be uncontrollable.
- Compulsive consumer behavior is driven by chronic depression.

Compulsive consumer behavior is defined and discussed in more detail in a later chapter.

LO5 Places Have Atmospheres

all consumer behavior takes place in some physical space. This statement isn't really profound. Sometimes marketing managers easily forget that the physical environment can play a significant role in shaping buying behavior and the value a consumer receives from shopping or service. Perhaps nowhere is the true impact of place more obvious than in retail and service environments.

RETAIL AND SERVICE ATMOSPHERICS

In consumer behavior, **atmospherics** refers to the emotional nature of an environment or, more precisely, to the feelings created by the total aura of physical attributes that comprise the physical environment. A total list of things that make up the atmosphere would be difficult to compile; however, they can be summarized by two dimensions.[26] Exhibit 10.7 provides a summary of the dimensions and what they can create.

The term **servicescape** is sometimes used to refer to the physical environment in which consumer services are performed.[27] Each servicescape has its own unique environment. Others have used terms like *e-scape* to refer to a virtual shopping environment as portrayed by a website

or *festivalscape* to refer to the array of environmental characteristics a consumer encounters when attending a festival.[28] Thus, Mardi Gras in New Orleans creates an atmosphere where consumers feel uninhibited and sometimes perform extreme behaviors including acts of public nudity, which they probably would not even consider doing in another atmosphere. While consumers sometimes do things they may regret later, this feeling is a defining part of the Mardi Gras experience. No matter the "scape," atmosphere works through the same sequence:

Environment → Thoughts → Feelings → Behavior → Value

Functional Quality

As mentioned earlier, the functional quality of an environment describes the meaning created by the total result of attributes that facilitate and make efficient the function performed there. In a shopping environment,

> **atmospherics** emotional nature of an environment or the feelings created by the total aura of physical attributes that comprise a physical environment

> **servicescape** physical environment in which consumer services are performed

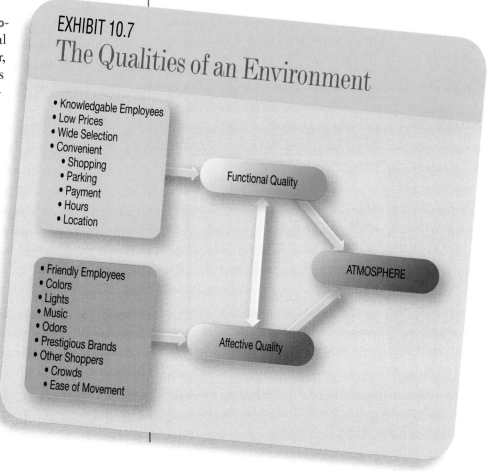

EXHIBIT 10.7
The Qualities of an Environment

- Knowledgable Employees
- Low Prices
- Wide Selection
- Convenient
  - Shopping
  - Parking
  - Payment
  - Hours
  - Location

- Friendly Employees
- Colors
- Lights
- Music
- Odors
- Prestigious Brands
- Other Shoppers
  - Crowds
  - Ease of Movement

Functional Quality

Affective Quality

ATMOSPHERE

this includes convenience in all forms: the price levels, the number and helpfulness of employees, and the breadth and depth of merchandise, along with other characteristics that facilitate the shopping task. In a service environment, the amount and expertise of service employees, the convenience of the environment, and the capability of the support staff, among other things, all contribute to the functional quality of the service environment.[29] These are often thought of as core aspects of service as some are essential for the benefits to be realized by consumers.

Affective Quality

The affective quality represents the emotional meaning of an environment, which results from the sum effect of all ambient attributes that affect the way one feels in that place. A friendly service employee can make the environment more pleasant, cool colors can be relaxing, upbeat music can be exciting, and a crowded environment that restricts movement can be distressing. Although many managers focus more on core aspects, these more relational aspects also influence value and satisfaction.

Restaurants, for example, often go out of business despite having excellent food and a good location. A primary reason for their lack of competitiveness is a lack of attention to the environment. As a result, the restaurant lacks style or creates a distressing or boring affective quality. All consumers are susceptible to the effects of affective quality; however, female consumers appear much more demanding based on how they react to a place with a negative affective quality.[30]

So, does a retail environment with a distinctly high functional quality necessarily have an uninteresting or poor affective quality? Quite the contrary! If anything, the two dimensions are positively related. An environment with a favorable functional quality tends to be associated with some degree of positive affect. Adolescent girls, for example, find an environment with high levels of functional qualities like accessibility and safety features to also be more pleasing places to shop.[31] Thus, retailers should keep this in mind and realize that even things that are built to create shopper safety can affect both the functional and affective meaning of a particular retailer.

ATMOSPHERE ELEMENTS

The way an atmosphere makes a consumer feel is really determined by the consumer's perception of all the elements in a given environment working together. Therefore, naming all the elements that eventually affect the retail or service atmosphere is impossible. However, a more distinct atmosphere creates a feeling that can ultimately result in a core competitive advantage based on the unique feeling. Two factors help merchandisers and retail designers create just such an atmosphere:[32]

- **Fit** refers to how appropriate the elements of an environment are for a given environment.

- **Congruity** refers to how consistent the elements of an environment are with each other.

Buffalo Wild Wings is a popular restaurant that operates outlets in nearly all fifty states in the U.S. The concept of the restaurant is to offer their patrons a fun, exciting atmosphere while delivering high-quality food and drink products. The atmosphere is largely based on a sports bar model, with numerous flat screen televisions placed throughout the restaurants with various sports games being shown. The fit and congruity of the atmospheric elements work perfectly, giving patrons a fun and exciting place where they can bring their entire families to enjoy good times and great food. The company has even won numerous "best sports bar" awards. While other restaurants can attempt to offer similar food products, none can duplicate the Buffalo Wild Wings atmosphere.

© LAMBERT'S CAFE

Lambert's Café has a unique environment and personality for a restaurant. The key feature of Lambert's is the "throwed roll," and even their URL takes on this label. Lambert's certainly has a strong situational influence.

Although an atmosphere is created by a combination of elements, researchers often study elements in isolation or in combination with only one or two other attributes. In the following sections, a few of the more prominent environmental elements are singled out as being particularly effective in changing or shaping an environment's atmosphere.

Odors

Believe it or not, in Manchester, U.K., the industrial revolution museum includes a tribute to sewerage systems with a sewer museum. What should a sewer museum smell like? Well, the folks at the museum in Manchester have a sewer that smells like a sewer, and the sewer museum certainly wouldn't be the same with the scent of roses piped in. The fact is, odors are prominent environmental elements that affect both a consumer's cognitive processing and affective reaction.

Olfactory is a term that refers to humans' physical and psychological processing of smells. When shoppers process ambient citrus odors, they tend to feel higher levels of pleasant emotions while shopping and to be more receptive to product information. Citrus odors produce positive responses in practically all consumers. Even more positive reactions can be obtained by matching odors with a target market. For example, women respond more favorably to floral scents while men respond more favorably to food scents like pumpkin pie. No kidding! Perhaps the way to a man's heart, or wallet, really is through his stomach.

Retailers like the Knot Shop, a chain of specialty stores for men's fashion accessories, spend considerable amounts of time and money managing the scents in their shops. In the Knot Shop, a masculine odor reminiscent of leather and tobacco is given off to help frame the shopping environment as masculine. The smell fits and helps create the store image! Retailers can also trigger greater arousal by introducing a moderately incongruent odor into an environment. In an experimental study, wine store consumers paid more attention to label information when an incongruent and slightly less pleasant odor was present and became less risk averse and more willing to try different wines when more pleasing and consistent odors were present.[33] Odors also seem to have a greater effect when other more intrusive elements like crowding are not too strong.[34]

Music

Fast music means fast dancing. Slow music means slow dancing. Even though consumers don't always dance through the aisles of stores, this image is fairly accurate in describing the way background music affects consumers. Both foreground and background music affect consumers, but they do so in different ways. **Foreground music** is music that becomes the focal point of attention and can have strong effects on a consumer's willingness to approach or avoid an environment. Consumers who dislike rap or country music will likely have a difficult time hanging around a place with loud rap or country music.

From a consumer behavior standpoint, **background music,** which is music played below the audible threshold that would make it the center of attention, is perhaps more interesting than foreground music. Service providers and retailers generally provide some type of background music for customers. Muzak is one of several companies whose business is providing the appropriate background music for a particular service or retail setting. Several effects are attributable to background music:

- The speed of the background music determines the speed at which consumers shop. Slower music means slower shopping. Faster music means faster shopping.
- The tempo of music affects the patience of consumers. Faster music makes consumers less patient.
- The presence of background music enhances service quality perceptions relative to an environment with no background music.
- Pop music used in the background contributes to discount store perceptions.
- Incongruent music lowers consumers' quality perceptions.

These factors are important for retail managers interested in managing quality and value perceptions.

> **olfactory** refers to humans' physical and psychological processing of smells
>
> **foreground music** music that becomes the focal point of attention and can have strong effects on a consumer's willingness to approach or avoid an environment
>
> **background music** music played below the audible threshold that would make it the center of attention

However, background music can also affect the bottom line. In restaurants, for instance, consumers who dine with slow background music are more patient and in less of a hurry to leave. As a result, they linger longer and tend to buy more beverages than consumers dining with faster background music. Thus, gross margins can actually be increased by slowing down the background music particularly in light of the higher margins realized on drink sales relative to food sales.[35]

Color

Color is another tool that marketing managers can use to alter consumer reactions. Some colors are more liked than other colors, but liking isn't really the key to understanding consumer reactions to color. Blue is perhaps the most universally liked color. Blue presents few cultural taboos. Red, white, and black, however, all present cultural barriers associated with bad omens and death in some cultures. Red is a risky color in Japan, as is white in China and black in western cultures. Color, like other environmental elements, helps frame the shopping experience. Therefore, choosing the right color depends on how consumers react in terms of both their thoughts and their feelings.

Color, for example, affects both quality and price perceptions. Consumers who perceive a product in a predominantly blue background tend to think the product is of higher quality, and they are willing to pay more for that product.[36] In contrast, warm colors like red and orange tend to promote expectations of poor quality and low price. Exhibit 10.8 illustrates the way these effects can play out in a retail environment. Color changes behavior by framing the way one thinks about a product and also by changing the way one feels. Thus, the perceived value of an object can vary with color.

Exhibit 10.8 clearly illustrates how color can frame consumer information processing. The same product at the identical price, in this case $100, will be viewed as priced more fairly with a blue background than with an orange or red background. Consumers also express more positive feelings when presented with blue background. Not surprisingly, consumers are also more willing to buy a product presented in a blue background than a red or orange background.

Is This Going to Take Long?

© KEVIN MAZUR/WIREIMAGE/GETTY IMAGES

Music impacts consumers in many ways. As we have discussed, the tempo of music can determine the speed at which consumers shop, dine, and even browse. Tempo also affects perceptions about waiting. It even impacts how consumers feel about waiting! Fast-tempo music is generally disliked for short waits and slow tempo music is disliked for long waits. So maybe some Vivaldi would be good if the wait is short, but Green Day would be better if it's going to be a while!

Sources: Oakes, Steve (2003), "Musical Tempo and Waiting Perceptions," *Psychology & Marketing*, 29 (8), 685 – 713; Areni, Charles (2003), "Exploring Managers' Implicit Theories of Atmospheric Music: Comparing Academic Analysis to Industry Insight," *Journal of Services Marketing*, 17 (2/3), 161 – 184; Kellaris J.J. and R.J. Kent (1992), "The Influence of Music on Consumers' Temporal Perceptions: Does Time Fly When You're Having Fun?", *Journal of Consumer Psychology*, 1, 365 – 376.

EXHIBIT 10.8
The Way Color Works

$100

- High Quality
- Worth $100
- Believe Price Is Fair
- Feel Pleased
- More Willing to Buy

$100

- Low Quality/Discount
- Not Worth $100
- Believe Price not as Fair
- Feel More Distressed
- Less Willing to Buy

Background colors can affect consumer price and quality perceptions.

So, is blue always a good color? Like many aspects of consumer behavior, the story isn't quite that simple. Blue has drawbacks. For instance, blue is a cool color. Thus, blue does not attract attention as effectively as a warm color like red or orange does. Also, like other situational effects due to the environment, color does not work alone. Lighting can have dramatic effects on the environment and even reverse color's effect. For example, the effects above hold for bright lights. Change a store's lighting to soft lights and consumers' opinions regarding the product change considerably. For instance, soft lights and an orange background can eliminate the advantage for blue in that the price fairness perceptions, quality perceptions, affect, and purchase intentions are now equal to or slightly better than the combination of blue and soft lights.[37] Victoria's Secret for many years merchandised stores with predominantly warm colors; however, their soft lighting eliminated any bad effects that might be present with bright lights.

Like other elements too, a marketer must be aware of the image. If the brand is closely associated with a color, then that association may be more important than the effects discussed here. So, if you are in a bad mood, change the color of your space, and things may improve!

Social Settings

An old saying about Bishop Berkeley's forest goes:

If a tree falls in the forest and nobody is there to hear it, does it make any noise?

Well, if a consumer goes to the Magnificent Mile in Chicago and there are no other people, is there really an atmosphere? People are a huge part of the environment, and if the people are removed, the atmosphere of that environment also is removed. Thus, the **social environment**, referring to the other customers and employees in a service or shopping environment, cannot be ignored when explaining how atmosphere affects consumer behavior.

Crowding refers generally to the density of people and objects within a given space. A space can be crowded without any people. However, *shopper density*, meaning the number of consumers in a given exchange environment, can still exert relatively strong influences on consumer behavior. Crowding actually exerts a **nonlinear effect** on consumers, meaning that a plot of the effect by the amount of crowding does not make a straight line.

Exhibit 10.9 illustrates the way crowding works, particularly with respect to shopper density. Generally, consumers are not particularly attracted to an environment with no other consumers. The lack of consumers can be

> **social environment** the other customers and employees in a service or shopping environment

> **crowding** density of people and objects within a given space

> **nonlinear effect** a plot of the effect by the amount of crowding, which does not make a straight line

> *The sheer volume of shoppers in downtown Chicago adds to the excitement of this atmosphere.*

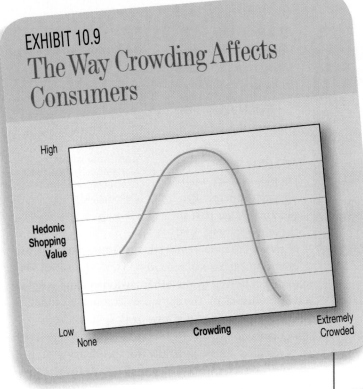

EXHIBIT 10.9
The Way Crowding Affects Consumers

Hedonic Shopping Value

High

Low

None — Crowding — Extremely Crowded

perceived as a sign of poor quality or in other cases, an absence of other consumers can simply be awkward. For example, a consumer who enters a restaurant alone, particularly with no other diners, may well feel quite uncomfortable. In contrast, a mild degree of crowding produces the most positive outcomes in terms of shopping affect, purchase behavior, consumer satisfaction, and shopping value.[38] Thus, the upside down U shape generally shows the way crowding affects positive consumer outcomes to varying extents. For instance, crowding affects utilitarian shopping value less strongly than hedonic shopping value in part because of the negative affect caused by crowding.

Hypermart chains like Carrefour, Auchan, or even Walmart can unintentionally diminish the hedonic shopping value consumers experience by placing large displays on the sales floor that compound the negative affect occurring during busy shopping times. In contrast, savvy retailers can actually increase sales by decreasing the amount of merchandise on the sales floor and creating a less crowded shopping environment.

Both the number and type of salespeople can also affect shoppers. For example, the presence of more salespeople in a shopping environment can actually increase shopper purchase intentions. This effect occurs in full-service and discount store environments.[39] However, the type of salespeople can also influence shoppers' purchasing and value perceptions. In particular, salespeople and service providers should have an appropriate appearance for the type of product sold.[40] A cosmetic salesperson should look the part or else run the risk of creating an awkward shopping experience. The salespeople should simply fit the part. At Disney theme parks, employees are referred to as "cast members" in part because their appearance is tightly controlled to fit the particular environment in which they work.

The other shoppers can also influence buying. Shopping buddies, meaning shopping companions, generally are associated with greater amounts of buying compared to shopping alone. The shopping buddy can help reinforce positive feelings about products and thus encourage purchase. A simple statement like "those jeans look great on you" can tilt the scale toward purchase. Reference group influence is more salient when the referents are actually with the shopper. Thus, teens' behavior at the mall is particularly affected by the presence of a peer group.[41]

Virtual Shopping Situations

Shopping via the Internet is just about as commonplace as catalog shopping. Many effects seen in real "bricks and mortar" shopping environments are also seen in the virtual shopping world. For example, the effects of color and sounds can work in much the same way. A website with a blue background can enhance quality perceptions just as the background in a real store might. Additionally, images placed in the background of a website can produce active thoughts, particularly when consumer expertise or knowledge is low. A web-based furniture retailer using pictures of clouds in the web background, for instance, can produce thoughts of soft and comfortable furniture. Similarly, images related to money can produce thoughts related to discounts.[42]

More and more, virtual retail sites include avatars or images of real people playing the social role of a helpful salesclerk. Does a virtual salesperson have any effect on shoppers? The answer is "Yes!"[43] People tend to respond favorably to a website that contains social images. The advantages to these sites are seen in increased purchase likelihood and utilitarian shopping value as the virtual people are helpful, but the additional social context particularly improves hedonic shopping value.

LO6 Antecedent Conditions

t he term **antecedent conditions** refers to situational characteristics that a consumer brings to a particular information processing, purchase, or consumption environment. Events occurring prior to this particular point in time have created a situation. Antecedent conditions include things like economic resources, mood, and other emotional perceptions such as fear. They can shape the value in a situation by framing the events that take place. The following sections elaborate.

ECONOMIC RESOURCES

Buying Power

The economic resources a consumer brings to a particular purchase setting refer to the consumer's buying power. Buying power can be in the form of cash on hand, credit card spending limits, or money available by draft or debit card. Most places in the United States today accept credit cards for payment (Visa, MasterCard, Discover, American Express); however, a few businesses still insist on cash payment. Businesses not accepting "card payment" are much more common in other countries. Thus, the amount of money a consumer has on hand can determine where he or she will shop or dine. For consumers short on cash, McDonald's may be a better option than Outback.

However, other issues arise. What if consumers are near their credit limits? This can also change their shopping behavior. Companies may put together special financing packages to deal with consumers whose credit is good enough to receive a major credit card even though they maintain high debt levels. Many consumers live paycheck to paycheck. If so, buying may increase around the day that consumers are paid. Then, they may actually have more cash on hand, but even if they do not, the awareness that they are financially better off because of payday may stimulate increased spending. Check advance services take advantage of payday timing by offering to prepay consumers in return for a portion of the total paycheck. Thus, these consumer services offer utilitarian value to consumers by providing a way for them to receive their pay before the company they work for actually issues a check. The ethical implications of check advance services are discussed in a later chapter.

Consumer Budgeting

In the 1990s, consumer debt ballooned to unprecedented levels. Much of this was in the form of credit card debt. The fact is, if credit card companies can charge a high interest rate (such as 18% percent or more), then they can afford to take a few credit risks and still maintain a profitable business. Thus, credit became easy to get. As a result, the general rule is that consumers can avoid delaying gratification and have things today. However, when consumers find themselves having difficulty making payments, their spending habits must change or they run the risk of losing their credit and worse.

During 2007 and 2008, a mortgage crisis in the United States rippled through financial markets around the world. Many consumers had taken variable rate mortgages that offered very low rates in the first few years of the loan. However, as interest rates rose, these very same consumers sometimes found themselves in a position where their home mortgage was taking 50% or more of their total income. As these rates rose, the consumers found themselves shopping less and buying less because their buying power was reduced. Eventually, many consumers who faced foreclosure because of the rising rates learned the hard way about the risks of a variable rate loan.

Most consumers do not perform a formal budgeting process; however, those consumers who do budget end up with different spending habits than those who do not. Generally, budgeting is associated with frugality.

Many consumers who do not prepare a formal budget do perform mental budgeting. **Mental budgeting** is simply a memory accounting for recent spending. One result is that a consumer who has recently splurged on spending in one category will tend to make up for the exuberance through underconsumption in another category.[44] In other words, they buy less than they typically would. Thus, a consumer who splurges on the weekend in Vegas and doesn't hit it big on the gaming floor may spend less on food for dinner or restaurants for a few days. Thus, the fact that the consumer has splurged recently in one area creates an antecedent condition that affects spending in another.

MOOD

Mood was defined earlier as a transient affective state. While shopping and consuming can alter a consumer's

antecedent conditions situational characteristics that a consumer brings to information processing

mental budgeting memory accounting for recent spending

mood, each consumer brings his or her current mood to the particular consumption situation. Consumers in particularly bad moods may have a tendency to binge consume. For example, a consumer in a foul mood may down an entire pint of Ben and Jerry's ice cream. If the mood is particularly disagreeable, perhaps a quart is more likely to do the trick. The temporary value of the ice cream is enhanced because it provides not just hedonic value (tastes great) but is also therapeutic in that it at least temporarily restores a more favorable affective state. In this way, things like ice cream can provide some utilitarian value, too.

Mood can also affect shopping. The mood that consumers bring to the shopping environment can exaggerate the actual experience. A consumer in a good mood may find even greater hedonic shopping value in a pleasant shopping experience than he or she may otherwise find.[45] Mood can also affect spending and consumer satisfaction. Shoppers who go shopping in a bad mood are particularly liable to buy less and experience lower consumer satisfaction than consumers in good moods. One reason is that consumers in bad moods buy no more than what they absolutely have to buy to complete their shopping.[46]

SECURITY AND FEARFULNESS

Consumers today live with ever-present reminders of vandalism, crime and even terrorism. Large parking lots such as commonly found at Walmart stores or conventional shopping centers attract criminals who prey on seemingly defenseless consumers. Stories of abductions, muggings, assaults, car jackings, and other heinous criminal acts taking place understandably create fear among some shoppers, particularly those who view themselves as vulnerable.[47] Shopping malls, markets, airports, and other places where large numbers of consumers gather are consistently mentioned as potential terrorist targets providing another reason for consumers to feel less secure.

Fearfulness can affect consumers in multiple ways. A consumer who goes shopping in a fearful mood will not go about his or her shopping in the same way. A fearful consumer will tend to buy less and enjoy the experience less. Alternatively, a consumer may cope with fear of shopping by turning to nonstore outlets such as the Internet as a seemingly safer way of doing business. But, even here, consumers sometimes fear providing private information often needed to complete a transaction. Thus, retailers who pay attention to making their parking and shopping environments more secure can help eliminate the feelings of fear some shoppers may have otherwise. Exhibit 10.10 lists some ways fearfulness may be reduced among consumers.

EXHIBIT 10.10
Enhancing Value by Making Consumers Feel More Safe

- Increase number and visibility of security personnel
- Increase number and prominence of security cameras in parking lots
- Have brightly lit parking lots
- Add carry-out service for consumers—particularly for those shopping alone
- Maintain an uncrowded, open entrance
- Clearly mark all exits
- Prevent loitering
- Discourage gangs from visiting the center

Chapter 10 Case

Watch Replica is a retailer that, true to its name, specializes in selling famous name brand watch replicas. It offers replicas of famous Swiss brands including Rolex, Omega, Tag Heuer, and even Patek Philippe, perhaps the most prestigious name brand among watches. Watch Replica makes no bones about what it sells and is not ashamed to offer replicas. Watch Replica tries hard to stand out from the image of shady street vendors who offer replicas that often truly are junk. In contrast, Watch Replica offers high-quality watches that it believes will stand the test of time. It backs every watch it sells with an iron-clad warranty that allows consumers to return a watch for any reason for three months, and it backs the watch against defects for a full year. Watch Replica watches contain genuine Swiss movements that are obtained from the same firm that supplies movements to genuine Swiss watch companies like Cartier. "These are not Chinese-made dime-store watches." The prices are also not dime-store prices. A Patek Philippe Calatrava replica is priced at nearly £400, about the same price as a Rolex Day and Date replica. The real things can retail for over $10,000.

Watch Replica does business currently out of the United Kingdom, but it is considering the future. Most of its business is conducted via its website (**http://watchreplica.com**). One possibility for its future is opening retail stores in the United States and France. Two strategies are offered for opening these stores. One is to locate in tourist areas. Thus, Watch Replica is considering retail locations in better outlet shopping centers and malls near Orlando, Las Vegas, and New Orleans, and in New York City. In France, it is considering retail locations in Paris near the Champs Elysées, in Normandy, and along the French Riviera. An alternative is to locate in major train stations and airports in the United States and France including New York's Grand Central Station, Atlanta's Hartsfield Airport, and Paris's Charles de Gaulle Airport.

Questions

1. Which of the two location strategies is more likely to be successful?

2. Are there consumer situations that might affect the value of the Watch Replica brand?

3. Given the four different types of shopping discussed in the chapter, which do you think is most likely to attract a consumer into a Watch Replica store? Explain.

4. How might time, place, and social conditions influence a consumer's behavior toward Watch Replica?

5. Would you be more comfortable shopping at the Watch Replica website or in a genuine Watch Replica store?

what do you think?

Most of the time I am a rational decision maker.

1 2 3 4 5 6 7

strongly disagree   strongly agree

Both utilitarian

and hedonic value are associated with consumer decision making.

11

Decision Making I: Need Recognition and Search

After studying this chapter, the student should be able to:

LO1 Understand the activities involved in the consumer decision-making process.

LO2 Describe the three major decision-making research perspectives.

LO3 Explain the three major types of decision-making approaches.

LO4 Understand the importance of the consideration set in the decision-making process.

LO5 Understand the factors that influence the amount of search performed by consumers.

LO1 Consumer Decision Making

Consumers encounter problem situations each and every day. Most of the time there are so many situations that it's hard to recall them all. You can run out of milk, be low on gasoline, search for a new apartment, take your car to the shop, and look for an outfit for a job interview all in the same day. In each of these situations, needs are recognized. When needs occur, decision making must take place. What kind of milk should I buy? Where should I get gasoline? Should I shop at Kohl's or Macy's?

Some situations require big decisions. For example, when a student recognizes a need for a new laptop computer, a big decision usually follows. In other situations, the decisions are relatively small. For example, when you run out of milk, the decision of which brand, or even where to shop, usually doesn't take much time or effort.

You may recall the basic consumer behavior consumption process that was presented in our opening chapter. This process is shown again in Exhibit 11.1. The process revolves around value-seeking activities that consumers perform as they go about satisfying needs. The consumer first realizes she has a particular need. She then moves through a series of steps that will help her find a desirable way to fill the need. Exchange then takes place, and she ultimately derives value from the process. As with other consumer behavior concepts, we see that value is at the heart of the process.

The decision-making process has been added to the exhibit. As you can see, decision-making processes generally include five activities: (1) need recognition, (2) search for information, (3) evaluation of alternatives, (4) choice, and (5) postchoice evaluation. In the current chapter, we focus on the first two stages of the process: need recognition and information search. The following chapter discusses evaluation of alternatives and choice.

To better visualize this process, consider Exhibit 11.2. Here, Mike is faced with a need for a new laptop

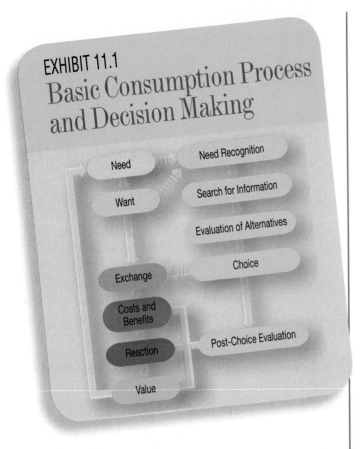

EXHIBIT 11.1
Basic Consumption Process and Decision Making

- Need
- Want
- Exchange
- Costs and Benefits
- Reaction
- Value

- Need Recognition
- Search for Information
- Evaluation of Alternatives
- Choice
- Post-Choice Evaluation

as he leaves for college. To learn about his options, he begins to read reports about laptops and he asks friends what type of laptop they think he should buy. After considering all of the information that he has gathered, Mike evaluates the alternatives that are realistically available. From there, he makes a choice and an exchange occurs. Finally, Mike thinks of all the costs and benefits associated with each brand and he considers the overall value that he has received from his purchase.

Note that the activities found in the decision-making process are not referred to as steps. The reason is that consumers do not always proceed through the activities in sequential fashion, nor do they always complete the process. Because consumers face numerous decision-making situations daily, they often decide to simply defer a decision until a later time. Consumers can also uncover additional problems or unmet needs as they search for information—moving them from information search to need recognition.

DECISION MAKING AND CHOICE

Decision-making processes lead to consumer choice. The term choice is important. *Choice* does not neces-

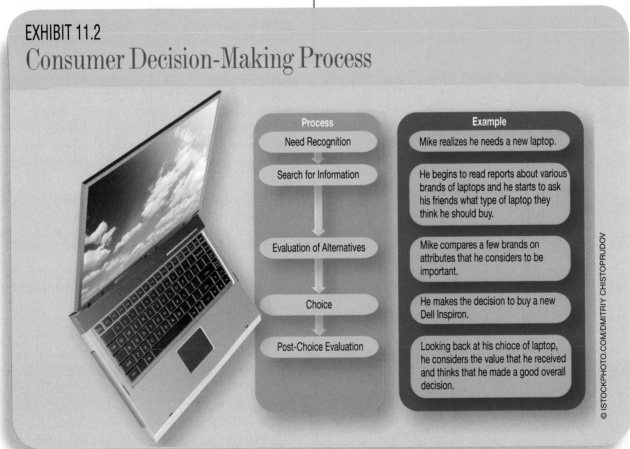

EXHIBIT 11.2
Consumer Decision-Making Process

Process	Example
Need Recognition	Mike realizes he needs a new laptop.
Search for Information	He begins to read reports about various brands of laptops and he starts to ask his friends what type of laptop they think he should buy.
Evaluation of Alternatives	Mike compares a few brands on attributes that he considers to be important.
Choice	He makes the decision to buy a new Dell Inspiron.
Post-Choice Evaluation	Looking back at his chioce of laptop, he considers the value that he received and thinks that he made a good overall decision.

Decision Making 101

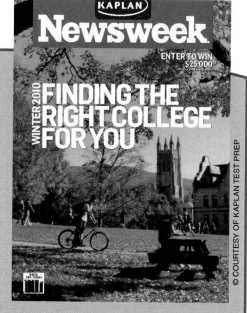

Newsweek KAPLAN

WINTER 2010 **FINDING THE RIGHT COLLEGE FOR YOU**

ENTER TO WIN $25,000

© COURTESY OF KAPLAN TEST PREP

For most consumers, selecting a college is one of the biggest decisions that they face. The educational landscape has become quite competitive, and students now regularly receive information and brochures from prospective colleges while they are in their early high school years, if not sooner.

Experts in the area of college choice suggest that students pay close attention to finding the college that fits best with their personal needs and goals. Big-name colleges aren't always the best solution for students, even though the familiar names may be attractive. In fact, many times, the so-called best schools do not offer the best fit for a student. For this reason, students are encouraged to carefully search for relevant information by visiting websites, talking with guidance counselors, taking campus tours, and seeking out independent research sources. The information provided can go a long way toward helping them reach the final college decision. Although students may spend only a handful of years on a college campus, this choice can have a profound impact on the rest of their lives.

Sources: Coleman, Christina (2007), "The 'Best' School Might Not Be Best for You," *Chronicle of Higher Education*, 52 (44), 66; Conboy, Katie (2007), "Big-Name Schools Aren't Always Best," *Christian Science Monitor*, 99 (69), 9; Knight, Mimi Greenwood (2006), "The Beginner's Guide to the College Search," *Ignite Your Faith*, 65 (3), 44–46.

sarily mean identifying what brand of product to buy. In fact, one of the very first choices that consumers need to make when facing a decision is whether any purchase will be made at all![1] Consumers commonly either delay the purchase of a product or forgo purchases altogether.

Decision-making processes also frequently do not involve finding a tangible product. Rather, consumers make choices about behaviors not relating directly to a purchase. For example, a consumer may be trying to decide if she should volunteer at a community theater. Here, the decision involves whether time should be exchanged in return for greater involvement with the theatre. Thus, consumer decision making does not always focus on the purchase of a tangible product, but it does always involve choices linked to value.

Decision Making and Value

Both utilitarian value and hedonic value are associated with consumer decision making. As we have discussed previously, the car-buying experience involves both value types. First, a car is in itself a means to an end. That is, owning a car enables the consumer to transport himself or herself from place to place. As such, an automobile delivers utilitarian value. Second, much of the car-buying (and car-owning) experience is based on hedonic value. The image associated with a particular model of car and the feelings that go with sporty handling are hedonic benefits. Many other consumption activities also provide both hedonic value and utilitarian value. For example, a $400 Coach purse may provide the same utilitarian value as an $8 purse from Target. However, the hedonic value of each would differ based on the feelings involved with consumption.

Value perceptions also influence the activities found in the decision-making process itself. For example, consumers generally continue searching for information about products only to the point where the perceived benefits that come from searching exceed the perceived costs associated with the process.

Decision Making and Motivation

As discussed in our motivation chapter, motivations are the inner reasons or driving forces behind human actions as consumers are driven to address needs. It isn't surprising, therefore, that decision making and motivation are closely related concepts.[2] For example, a student may notice that the ink in his printer is low and perceive a need to fix the problem (a utilitarian motivation). Or, the same student may be bored on a Saturday afternoon and decide to play paintball (a hedonic motivation). The relationship between decision making and motivation is well-known and almost all consumer decisions revolve around goal-pursuit.[3]

> The decision-making process can be very emotional depending on the type of product being considered or the need that has arisen.

Decision Making and Emotion

Consumer decision making is also closely related to emotion. The decision-making process can be very emotional depending on the type of product being considered or the need that has arisen. Because the decision-making process can be draining, consumers frequently have feelings of frustration, irritation, or even anger as they attempt to satisfy needs. This is especially true when consumers must make difficult decisions, cannot find acceptable solutions to problems, or must make tradeoffs by giving up one alternative for another.[4] As a college student, you may soon face the difficult task of deciding which job offer to take. Perhaps there will be a job offer many miles away, or one that is closer to your family. Decisions like these can be quite emotional.

LO2 Decision-Making Perspectives

Consumer researchers view the decision-making process from three perspectives: the rational decision-making perspective, the experiential decision-making perspective, and the behavioral

influence decision-making perspective.[5] These perspectives are similar to the attitude hierarchies that we discussed in our attitude chapter.

It is important to remember two important aspects of these perspectives. First, each perspective serves as a theoretical framework from which decision making can be viewed. That is, the perspectives pertain to how consumer researchers view the decision-making process, and they are not consumer decision-making strategies. Second, most consumer decisions can be analyzed from a combination of these perspectives. The perspectives are presented in Exhibit 11.3.

RATIONAL DECISION-MAKING PERSPECTIVE

The early study of consumer decision making centered upon what is referred to as the rational decision-making perspective. This perspective is considered by many to be the traditional approach to studying decision making. The **rational decision-making perspective** assumes that consumers diligently gather information about purchases, carefully compare various brands of products on salient attributes, and make informed decisions regarding what brand to buy. This approach centers on the assumption that human beings are rational creatures who carefully consider their decisions and that they can identify the expected value associated with a purchase. The act of selecting either cable or satellite television often follows a rational process.

EXHIBIT 11.3
Perspectives on Consumer Decision Making

Perspective	Description	Example
Rational perspective	Consumers are rational and they carefully arrive at decisions.	Zach carefully considers a number of options when buying a new car.
Experiential perspective	Decision making is often influenced by the feelings associated with consumption.	Marcie decides to go to a day spa for the pleasure and relaxation it provides.
Behavioral influence perspective	Decisions are responses to environmental influences.	The relaxing environment at the restaurant leads Jackie to stay and buy another drink.

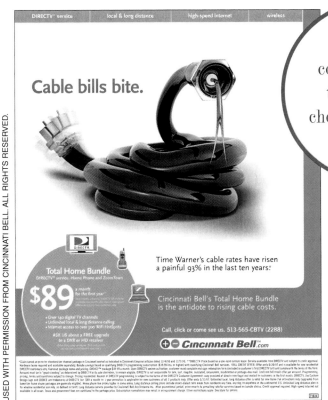

Cable bills bite.

Time Warner's cable rates have risen a painful 93% in the last ten years.*

Total Home Bundle
DIRECTV® service, Home Phone and ZoomTown

$89 a month for the first year*

- Over 140 digital TV channels
- Unlimited local & long distance calling
- Internet access to over 300 WiFi Hotspots

ASK US about a FREE upgrade to a DVR or HD receiver

Cincinnati Bell's Total Home Bundle is the antidote to rising cable costs.

Call, click or come see us. 513-565-CBTV (2288)

⊕⊙ *Cincinnati Bell*.com

> Consumers consider many things when choosing cable or satellite TV.

Consumers will often compare service, features, and prices carefully when making these purchases. The rational perspective fits very well with the concept of utilitarian value.

Even though the rational perspective makes sense, we cannot assume that consumers follow this process in all situations. In fact, consumers often make purchases and satisfy needs with very little cognitive effort or rationality. We simply don't want to think extensively about every single product choice that we make. Nor could we!

The assumption that consumers are "rational" is also debatable. Of course, what is rational to some may be irrational to others. Paying over $1,000 for a single season ticket to a sporting event could hardly be considered rational to some, but sports fans do it every single year! Although researchers focused on the rational perspective for several years, the experiential and behavioral influence perspectives have recently gained significant attention.

EXPERIENTIAL DECISION-MAKING PERSPECTIVE

The **experiential decision-making perspective** assumes that consumers often make purchases and reach decisions based on the affect, or feeling, attached to the product or behavior under consideration. Recall from the discussion in our attitude chapter that consumers sometimes follow

a "feel-do-think" hierarchy. That is, behaviors are based largely on the sheer enjoyment involved with consumption rather than on extensive cognitive effort.

Experiential decision processes often focus on hedonic value. For example, a consumer may decide to spend time at a day spa as the result of an experiential decision-making process. Here, decisions are based on feeling—not on a drawn-out decision-making process. That is, the value comes from the experience, not from an end result.

BEHAVIORAL INFLUENCE DECISION-MAKING PERSPECTIVE

The **behavioral influence decision-making perspective** assumes that many decisions are actually learned responses to environmental influences. For example, soft music and dim lighting can have a strong influence on consumer behavior in a restaurant. These influences generally lead consumers to slow down, stay in the restaurant for a longer time, and buy more drinks and dessert. Here, behavior is influenced by environmental forces rather than by cognitive decision making.

The behavioral influence perspective also helps to explain how consumers react to the store layout, store design, and POP (point-of-purchase) displays. Traffic flows in a grocery store greatly influence grocery shopping behavior. In fact, consumers often buy products that are placed on display simply because they are on display! Retailers use the "brand-lift index" to measure the incremental sales that occur when a product is on display. Lift indices can be impressive. In fact, a recent study indicated that POP displays in convenience stores can increase product sales by nearly 10%. This is a sizable amount. Considering that incremental sales opportunities for POP materials in grocery stores can be in the billions of dollars, retailers should pay close attention to the behavioral influence perspective![6]

LO3 Decision-Making Approaches

Consumers reach decisions in a number of different ways. The decision-making approach that is used depends heavily on the amount of involvement a consumer has with a product category or purchase and the amount of purchase risk involved with the decision. Note that involvement can be associated with either the product, the purchase situation, or both. In general, as involvement and risk increase, consumers are motivated to move more carefully through the decision-making process.

You may remember from an earlier chapter that consumer involvement represents the degree of personal relevance that a consumer finds in pursuing value from a given act. **Perceived risk** refers to the perception of the negative consequences that are likely to result from a course of action and the uncertainty of which course of action is best to take. Consumers face several types of risk, including[7]:

- **Financial risk.** Risk associated with the cost of the product
- **Social risk.** Risk associated with how other consumers will view the purchase
- **Performance risk.** Risk associated with the likelihood of a product performing as expected
- **Physical risk.** Risk associated with the safety of the product and the likelihood that physical harm will result from its consumption
- **Time risk.** Risk associated with the time required to search for the product and the time necessary for the product to be serviced or maintained

Risk varies across consumers and situations. For example, signing a year-long apartment lease is a financially risky process for most consumers. For the very

perceived risk perception of the negative consequences that are likely to result from a course of action and the uncertainty of which course of action is best to take

extended decision making assumes consumers move diligently through various problem-solving activities in search of the best information that will help them reach a decision

wealthy, this may not be the case at all. Likewise, buying a new dress shirt is usually not perceived as being risky, unless one is making the purchase to wear on a first date!

Decision-making approaches can be classified into three categories: extended decision making, limited decision making, and habitual (or "routine") decision making. Remember, these are approaches that consumers use, and they differ from the researcher perspectives discussed previously. Exhibit 11.4 presents these categories in the form of a continuum based on involvement and risk.

EXTENDED DECISION MAKING

When consumers engage in **extended decision making**, they tend to search diligently for information that will help them reach a satisfactory decision. This information can come from both internal sources (for example, previous experiences) and external sources (for example, websites such as **shopping.com**). Consumers carefully assimilate the information they have gathered and evaluate each alternative based on its potential to satisfy their need. This process is generally rather lengthy. Extended decision making occurs when involvement is high and when there is a significant amount of purchase risk involved with the decision. Expensive products such as houses, automobiles, and televisions are usually purchased only after an extended decision-making process has occurred.

LIMITED DECISION MAKING

With limited decision making, consumers search very little for information and often reach decisions based on prior beliefs about products and their attributes. There is little comparison between brands. Given the

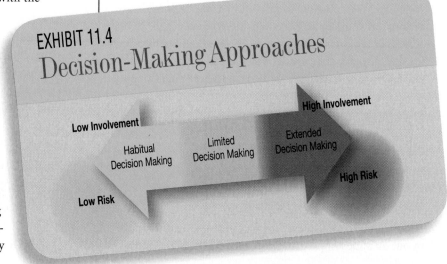

EXHIBIT 11.4
Decision-Making Approaches

High Involvement

Low Involvement

Habitual Decision Making

Limited Decision Making

Extended Decision Making

High Risk

Low Risk

time constraints that consumers often feel, this type of decision making occurs with great frequency.

Limited decision making usually occurs when there are relatively low amounts of purchase risk and product involvement. For example, a consumer may need to buy a new a roll of adhesive tape, and there may be very few attributes that are considered in the process. Perhaps the consumer will want to find a roll that is designed to be "invisible." Any brand that offers this feature would likely be selected.

HABITUAL DECISION MAKING

With **habitual decision making** (sometimes referred to as "routine" decision making), consumers generally do not seek information at all when a problem is recognized. Choice is often based on habit. Here, consumers generally have a specific brand in mind that will solve the problem, and they believe that the consumption of the product will deliver value. For example, most consumers have a favorite type of soft drink that they habitually buy when they are thirsty.

Two topics are of special importance concerning habitual decision making: *brand loyalty* and *brand inertia*. **Brand loyalty** may be defined as a deeply held commitment to rebuy a product or service regardless of situational influences that could lead to switching behavior.[8] For a consumer to truly be brand loyal, he or she must have a bond with the product and believe that the consumption activity delivers value. Companies often attempt to reward loyalty with rewards programs as found in frequent flier miles, hotel reward points, and credit card cash-back deals. However, in order for these tactics to be successful, consumers must ultimately value both the product and the incentives offered.[9] This leads to a key difference between loyalty and what is referred to as brand inertia. **Brand inertia** is present when a consumer simply buys a product repeatedly without any real attachment. Loyalty, on the other hand, includes an attitudinal component that reflects a true affection for the product.[10] Strictly speaking, a consumer is not loyal simply because he or she habitually buys the same product.

Brand loyalty affects consumption value in a number of ways. First, loyalty enables consumers to reduce searching time drastically by insisting on the brand to which they are loyal. This leads to a benefit of convenience. Second, loyalty creates value for a consumer through the benefits associated with brand image. Ford trucks are well-known for their ruggedness and durability, and the Ford image is one benefit of owning the product. Finally, loyalty enables consumers to enjoy the benefits that come from long-term relationships with companies. For example, a consumer might enjoy special incentives that are offered to long-time Ford purchasers.

Brand loyalty also has an impact on the value of the brand to the firm. As branding expert David Aaker asserts, consumer brand loyalty influences the value of a product to a firm because (a) it costs much less to

Hotel reward points can be a successful method of rewarding loyalty if consumers value both the product and the incentives offered.

retain current customers than to attract new ones, and (b) highly loyal customers generate predictable revenue streams.[11] As can be seen, brand loyalty has benefits for both the consumer and the marketer.

Final Thought on Decision-Making Approaches

Consumers go through decision-making processes, but these processes do not guarantee maximum value from a consumption experience. Consumers often make mistakes or settle for alternatives that they are really unsure about. In reality, many consumer purchases are made with very little prepurchase decision effort.[12] Most purchases made on a daily basis are low-involvement purchases that do not entail significant risk. Also, con-

sumers are not always motivated to make the "best" decision. In fact, in many situations, consumers engage in what is called satisficing. **Satisficing** is the practice of using decision-making shortcuts to arrive at satisfactory, rather than optimal, decisions.[13] When a consumer says to herself "this is good enough," satisficing has occurred. Time pressures, search fatigue, and budgetary constraints often lead consumers to engage in satisficing.

LO4 Need Recognition, Internal Search, and the Consideration Set

a s we have discussed, the recognition of a need leads the consumer to begin searching for information. Several important issues are relevant here.

NEED RECOGNITION

The decision-making process begins with the recognition of a need. Simply put, a need is recognized when a consumer perceives a difference between an actual state and a desired state. A consumer's **actual state** is his or her perceived current state, while the **desired state** is the perceived state for which the consumer strives. A consumer recognizes a need when there is a gap between these two. Note that either the actual state or the desired state can change, leading to a perceptual imbalance between the two. When the actual state begins to drop, for example when a consumer runs out of deodorant, a need is recognized. Obviously, needs like this are recognized many times each day. Importantly, however, marketers also focus on what

Isn't Variety a Good Thing?

I t is easy to think that a little bit of variety is a good thing. A common problem for consumers today is that in many situations there are simply *too many alternatives* from which to choose. A simple walk down any grocery store aisle will confirm that the average consumer is bombarded with hundreds—if not thousands—of product varieties every day. Whereas previous generations often faced the problem of not having enough products to choose from, today there are often too many!

When should a shopper stop looking for information? Frequently, the answer comes when one finds an acceptable, rather than optimal, solution. This is what satisficing is all about. Shoppers often simply focus on finding the first alternative that meets their minimum requirements. So, instead of finding the best paper towel available, they'll simply look for the one that delivers an acceptable level of value and move on. The decision-making process becomes much easier for consumers who "satisfice."

Sources: Douglas, Kate, and Dan Jones (2007), "How to Make Better Choices," *New Scientist*, 194 (2602), 35-43; Pelusi, Nando (2007), "When to Choose is to Lose," *Psychology Today*, 40 (5), 69 – 70; Moyer, Don (2007), "Satisficing," *Harvard Business Review*, (April), 144; Wright, Peter (1975), "Consumer Choice Strategies: Simplifying Vs. Optimizing," *Journal of Marketing Research*, 12 (February), 60 – 67.

© RAGNAROCK/SHUTTERSTOCK IMAGES LLC

Desired states changed dramatically with the introduction of the iPhone.

they term *opportunity recognition*. Here, a consumer's actual state doesn't change, but his or her desired state changes in some significant way.

To illustrate how a desired state can be changed, consider how happy consumers once were with their cell phones—that is, before the iPhone was released. After the iPhone was introduced, the desired state for many consumers changed dramatically. Phones became much more than just phones!

Desired states can be affected by many factors, including reference group information, consumer novelty seeking, and cognitive thought processes.[14] As we discussed in our group influence chapter, reference groups are important sources of information for consumers and the information that is gathered from others directly affects what consumers think they should do and what types of products they think they should buy. Desired states are also influenced by novelty. Many times consumers desire to try a new product simply because of boredom or because of a motivation to engage in variety-seeking. Finally, consumers have the ability to cognitively plan their actions by anticipating future needs. For example, college graduates realize after graduation that they face the need for all types of insurance they may not have considered before, including life, health, and homeowner's insurance.

Not all needs are satisfied quickly nor does the recognition of a need always trigger the other activities found in the decision-making process. Value is again important here. If the end goal is not highly valued, consumers may simply put off a decision. For example, a consumer may realize that the leather on the seat of her bicycle has ripped, but this does not necessarily mean that she will begin to search for information on where to buy a new seat. She may simply realize that there is a problem that eventually needs to be fixed. In fact, she may have to be reminded of this need several times before she does anything about it. Or, she may decide to do nothing at all about it. For instance, she may simply sell her bike and buy a new one. From this example, we are again reminded of why we don't refer to the activities found in decision making as steps. That is, the sequential ordering of the activities is not concrete.

We should once again clarify the distinction between a want and a need. Both of these terms have been discussed in a previous chapter. As you many remember, a want is the way in which a consumer goes about addressing a need. It's quite common for marketers to be criticized for attempting to turn wants into needs. For example, a consumer may want to fulfill a need for transporting personal items by buying an expensive purse like Prada, even though a much less expensive purse would suffice.

Luxury brands like Prada appeal to customers' desired states.

SEARCH BEHAVIOR

When consumers perceive a difference between an actual state (an empty gas tank) and a desired state (a full tank), the decision-making process is triggered.[15] **Consumer search behavior** refers to the behaviors that consumers engage in as they seek information that can be used to satisfy needs. Consumers seek all types of information about potential solutions to needs, including: (1) the number of alternatives available, (2) the price of various alternatives, (3) the relevant attributes that should be considered and their importance, and (4) the performance of each alternative on the attributes.[16] Consumer search behaviors can be categorized in a number of ways, including ongoing search, prepurchase search, internal search, and external search.

Ongoing and Prepurchase Search

A consumer performs an **ongoing search** when she seeks information simply because she is interested in a particular topic (such as a product or an organization). Here, the search effort is not necessarily focused on an upcoming purchase or decision, rather the effort is focused on simply staying up to date on a topic of interest. Consumers who perform ongoing searches are usually highly involved with the product category and seek information simply for enjoyment. They also tend to spend more in the relevant product category than do consumers who do not regularly search for information.[17]

Prepurchase search activities are focused on locating information that will enable the consumer to reach a decision for a specific problem. These searches are purchase-specific. Prepurchase search can also be exhibited in browsing behavior. When consumers browse, they are simply gathering information that can be used in decisions that involve a longer time frame. Note that browsing and ongoing searches are similar. The difference between ongoing searches and browsing behavior is that an ongoing search is performed when consumers have an enduring interest or involvement with the product, not simply when information is being gathered for a specific purchase.

The concept of information search has changed dramatically in recent years due to the mass adoption of the Internet as well as the proliferation of mobile information technologies like cell phones and personal data assistants. In today's environment, finding information generally isn't a problem. The problem is that there is simply too much information out there![18] Information overload is therefore a more important topic than ever before. **Information overload** refers to the situation in which consumers are presented with so much information that they cannot assimilate it all.

THE CONSIDERATION SET

Internal search includes the retrieval of knowledge about products, services, and experiences that is stored in memory. This type of knowledge is related directly to consumers' experiences with products and services. When confronted with a need, consumers begin to scan their memories for available solutions to the problem that can aid in decision making. As such, consumers most often perform internal searches before any other type of search begins.

Marketers find it valuable to understand the **consideration set** of their customers in order to learn

© COURTESY OF ACTION VILLAGE, INC.

Paintball enthusiasts can browse popular sites to learn about products.

about the total number of brands, or alternatives, that are considered in consumer decision making.[19] The conceptualization of a consideration set is presented in Exhibit 11.5.

The total collection of all possible solutions to a recognized need (for example, the total number of brands of deodorant available on the market) is referred to as the **universal set** of alternatives. Although the universal set may be quite large, consumers generally do not realize how many solutions are potentially available when a need arises. In fact, decision making is limited by what is referred to as the awareness set. The **awareness set** includes, quite simply, the set of brands or alternatives of which a consumer is aware. Alternatives that have been previously selected are included in this set,[20] and the size of the awareness set increases as external search proceeds.

Within the awareness set, three categories of alternatives are found. The first is the consideration set (or the "evoked set"). The consideration set includes the brands, or alternatives, that are considered acceptable for further consideration in decision making. There are also alternatives in the awareness set that are deemed to be unacceptable for further consideration. These alternatives comprise the **inept set**. The **inert set** includes those alternatives to which consumers are indifferent, or for which strong feelings are not held.

Exhibit 11.5 demonstrates how the size of both the awareness set and consideration set is smaller than the universal set. This is because, for most decisions, these sets are much smaller than the universal set. Research confirms that consumers generally consider only a small fraction of the actual number of problem solutions that are available.[21] Note that although the consideration set is held internally in a consumer's memory, alternatives that are found in external search can be added to the set as the decision-making process continues. Of course, good marketers ensure that their brands are placed in consumers' consideration sets.

universal set total collection of all possible solutions to a consumer problem

awareness set set of alternatives of which a consumer is aware

inept set alternatives in the awareness set that are deemed to be unacceptable for further consideration

inert set alternatives in the awareness set about which consumers are indifferent or do not hold strong feelings

external search gathering of information from sources external to the consumer such as friends, family, salespeople, advertising, independent research reports, and the Internet

LO5 External Search

frequently, consumers do not have stored in their memories enough information that will lead to adequate problem solving. For this reason, external search efforts are often necessary. **External search** includes the gathering of information from sources external to the consumer, including friends, family, salespeople, advertising, independent research reports (such as *Consumer Reports*), or the Internet. In selecting the best information source, consumers consider factors such as

- The ease of obtaining information from the source
- The objectivity of the source
- The trustworthiness of the source
- The speed with which the information can be obtained

In general, consumers find that information from family and friends is dependable but that information from commercial sources (like advertising or salespeople) is less credible for input into decision making.[22]

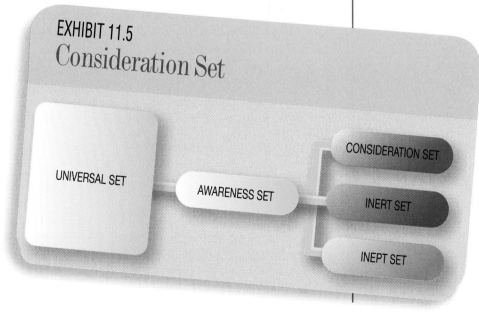

EXHIBIT 11.5
Consideration Set

UNIVERSAL SET

AWARENESS SET

CONSIDERATION SET

INERT SET

INEPT SET

THE ROLE OF PRICE AND QUALITY IN THE SEARCH PROCESS

The term *evaluative criteria* is used to refer to the attributes of a product that consumers consider when reviewing possible solutions to a problem. Many things can become evaluative criteria. However, two evaluative criteria are used across almost all consumer decisions: price and quality. Consumers tend to seek out information about these concepts early in the search process, and they play important roles in external search.

Price represents an important type of information that consumers generally seek. But what is a price? A price is really a piece of information. More specifically, price is information signaling how much potential value may be derived from consuming something. In this sense, price is like the physical concept of potential energy.

> Price and quality perceptions are related as consumers generally assume that higher prices mean higher quality.

Generally, we think of a high price as being a bad thing. In other words, a higher price means greater sacrifice to obtain some product. This view of price is referred to as the negative role of price. From this view, needless to say, a lower price is more desirable. Some consumers are very sensitive to the negative role of price. They tend to be very bargain conscious and do things like collect and redeem coupons.

However, a positive role of price also exists. In this sense, price signals how desirable a product is and how much prestige may be associated with owning the product. Some consumers are more sensitive to the positive role of price and tend to desire things with high prices as a way of signaling prestige and desirability to others.[23] You may remember from an earlier discussion that a backward sloping demand curve is not necessarily rare.

Consider a consumer shopping for a new outfit to wear "out on the town." She may find a cute outfit at Target, but this outfit may not offer enough value given that it will be worn in a socially sensitive situation. Therefore, she may opt for a higher-priced outfit that may be somewhat similar. The higher price will signal more prestige. Thus, she may feel more comfortable shopping at Banana Republic or some other more prestigious fashion retailer.

Consumers also commonly search for information about a product's quality. Consumers nearly always consider quality as an important evaluative criterion. Although quality can mean many things to many people, from a consumer perspective, **quality** represents the perceived overall goodness or badness of some product. In other words, consumers generally use the word *quality* as a synonym for relative goodness. A high-quality hotel room is a good hotel room and a low-quality hotel room is a bad hotel room.

Quality perceptions take place both before and after purchase. However, consumers do not always seek high quality because many times, consumers do not need the "best" product available. Although Fairfield Inns may not offer as high quality of an experience as does a Hyatt Regency hotel, it does adequately address the need for a place to sleep on a cross-country drive.

Consumers almost always use price and quality when making decisions. Indeed, price and quality perceptions are related as consumers generally assume that higher prices mean higher quality. This issue is discussed in more detail in our next chapter.

EXTERNAL SEARCH AND THE INTERNET

As we mentioned earlier, the Internet has become a powerful search tool for consumers, and it has simplified the search process for many product categories. Due to the popularity of various search engines like

Google, consumers can find solutions to all sorts of problems online. Of course, this has simplified search processes to a large extent. In today's fast-paced information-rich environment, tremendous amounts of information are at our fingertips, and the Internet has quickly become an extremely popular consumer search tool.[24]

The Internet improves consumer search activities in several ways. First, the Internet can lower the costs associated with search and can also make the process more productive.[25] Second, the search process itself can be enjoyable and deliver hedonic value to the consumer.[26] Third, consumers have the ability to control information flow much more efficiently than if they are viewing product information on a television commercial or hearing about a product from radio ads. In general, the ability to control information flow increases the value of information and increases the consumers' ability to remember information that is gathered.[27]

Studies have indicated that Internet search behavior depends heavily on website construction. For example, one recent study found that consumers spend more time searching in three-dimensional, interactive web environments than in two-dimensional web spaces. However, the study also revealed that the number of brands examined was actually higher for two-dimensional web pages than for three-dimensional sites.[28] Of course, website design is very important! We can expect consumers to use the Internet even more as technology continues to improve and computer availability becomes more widespread.

AMOUNT OF SEARCH

The amount of search that a consumer performs related to decision making can be measured in a number of ways including the number of stores visited, the number of Internet sites visited, the number of personal sources (friends, family, salespeople) used, the number of alternatives considered, and the number of advertisements studied.

Many factors influence information search effort, including previous experience with a product, involvement, perceived risk, value of search effort, time availability, attitudes toward shopping, personal factors, and situational influencers.[29]

© VARIO IMAGES GMBH & CO. KG/ALAMY

After searching internally, consumers turn to external sources like the Internet.

Product Experience. Prior product experience with a product has been shown to influence how much a consumer searches. A number of researchers have examined this issue, sometimes with conflicting results. As a general statement, evidence shows that moderately experienced consumers search for purchase-related information more than do either experienced or inexperienced consumers. This finding is shown in Exhibit 11.6.[30]

One explanation for the finding that moderately experienced consumers search more than other consumers is that individuals with little experience are unable to make fine distinctions between product differences and will likely see product alternatives as being similar. As such, they find little value in extensive information search. Highly experienced consumers can make fine distinctions between products and may know so much about products that they do not need to search at all. Moderately experienced consumers, on the other hand, perceive some differences among brands and are more likely to value information about these distinctions.[31]

Involvement. As noted earlier, purchase involvement is positively associated with search activities, especially for ongoing searches. Because involvement represents a level of arousal and interest in a product, search tends to increase when a consumer possesses a high level of purchase involvement.[32]

Perceived Risk. As perceived risk increases, search effort increases.[33] As discussed earlier in the chapter, a number of risks can be associated with the consumption act including financial, social, performance, physical, and time risks. Consumers are usually motivated to reduce these risks as much as possible and will therefore expend considerable time and effort in searching for information.

Value of Search Effort. Value can be obtained from the search process itself. When the benefits received from searching exceed the associated costs, consumers derive value. When searching costs are greater than the benefits of the search process, consumers no longer value the activity and search stops.[34] Costs associated with search can be either monetary (for example, the cost of driving around town looking for a new bedroom dresser) or nonmonetary (for example, psychological or physical exhaustion or stress).

Time Availability. All other things being equal, more time to spend on search usually results in increased search activity.[35] Because time is valued so highly by most consumers, search will decrease dramatically when time constraints are present.

Attitude toward Shopping. Consumers who value shopping and who possess positive attitudes toward shopping generally spend more time searching for product information.[36]

Personal Factors. Search tends to increase as a consumer's level of education and income increases. Search also tends to decrease as consumers become older.[37]

Situational Influencers. Situational factors also influence the amount of search that takes place. Perceived urgency, financial pressure, and mood can all impact search behavior. The purchase occasion can also affect the search. Consumers sometimes have such an urgent need for a product that they will select the first option they come across. As an example of a purchase occasion, when a product is being purchased as a gift, the amount of search will depend on the nature of the relationship between the giver and the receiver and on the amount of time before the occasion.

External Search Often Minimized

While many factors influence the amount of search that takes place, consumers tend to search surprisingly little for most products.[38] This is true for both high- and

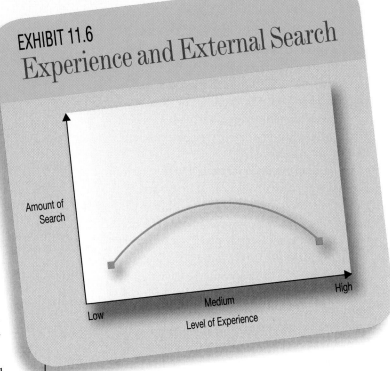

EXHIBIT 11.6
Experience and External Search

Amount of Search (vertical axis)

Level of Experience (horizontal axis): Low — Medium — High

low-involvement products. Consumers may already have a stored rule in memory for low-involvement products and may engage in extensive ongoing search activities and have acceptable alternative solutions in mind for high-involvement categories.[39]

SEARCH REGRET

As we have discussed, emotions and decision making are closely related topics. The search process can lead directly to emotional responses for consumers as well. The term **search regret** refers to the negative emotions that come from failed search processes. Many times, consumers are simply not able to find an acceptable solution to their problems. As a result, the decision-making process stops. In these situations, consumers may feel as if the entire search process was a waste of time, and they will start to feel search regret. Feelings of search regret are directly related to the overall amount of search effort, the emotions felt during the search process, and the use of unfamiliar search techniques.[40]

Many issues relate to the topics of need recognition and search. Our next chapter discusses evaluation of alternatives and choice.

Get In, Get Out!

One thing that retailers love is for their customers to stay in their stores as long as possible. Longer visits usually lead to increased sales! However, in today's hectic environment, it is increasingly difficult to get consumers to spend hardly any time at all in a store. Due to extremely busy schedules, many consumers simply enter a store, quickly find what they are looking for, and leave. There is usually very little time for browsing or for searching for product information.

Consumers with young children face especially difficult tasks as they attend to their kids while they shop. Retailers attempt to ease the burden of these consumers in various ways such as by adding playgrounds, family facilities, and comfortable seating areas to make the shopping experience as easy and relaxing as possible. Although these additions are certainly welcomed, the clock continues to tick, and parents try to the find the quickest solutions to their problems. No wonder Internet shopping continues to grow in popularity!

Sources: Dickenson, Helen (2006), "We're a Nation of Impatient Shoppers," *Marketing* (July 12), 13; Chater, Amanda (2006), "Soccer Mom's Goal Is One-Stop Shopping," *Drug Store News*, 28 (8), 129; Weber, Lauren (2005), "Malls Try to Win Back Young Families," *Knight Ridder Tribune Business News* (July 24), 1.

Chapter 11 Case

What do consumers think about bottled water? Many of them say "I never saw the need." Even though consumers in the United States enjoy a vast quantity of clean, public source drinking water (a true privilege considering that many countries have a dire shortage of good-quality water), Americans consumed more than 8 billion gallons of bottled water in 2006 alone.[41] The increasing trend toward bottled water consumption simply baffles many marketing experts and critics worldwide. How can it be that a society that has good-quality public water systems consumes so much bottled water? Also, given the strain that all of those plastic bottles put on the environment, why do consumers tend to look the other way?

It is generally well known that older consumers have a hard time understanding the trend. For them, buying bottled water is expensive and nonsensical. On a per-ounce basis, bottled water is extremely expensive especially compared to tap water. Although this is true, many consumers wholeheartedly trust that bottled water is simply better for them because it offers true health-related benefits.

Because consumers today are generally more health-conscious than ever before, bottled water is certainly attractive. Bottled water seemingly fills an important consumer need for better health, and younger consumers have grown up with the belief that bottled water is simply better at delivering health-related benefits. Convenience is another important issue. Bottled water packaged in plastic containers is simply easier to carry around during the day. Convenience is not as important as health, however, and for the first time in 20 years, sales volume for soda declined in 2005[42] while sales of bottled water surged. Of course, other beverages like teas, juices, and isotonics (sports drinks) have also enjoyed category growth due largely to the new focus on health. But how much better is bottled water than tap water, really? This is a question that is currently garnering a lot of public attention.

Bottled water consumption clearly puts a strain on the environment. It has been estimated that nearly 80% of empty bottles end up in landfills or incinerators.[43] When 8 billion gallons have been consumed, that's a lot of empties going straight to the landfill! Also, oil is required to produce the plastic bottles, resulting in a double whammy for the environment. As a result of these issues, among others, local governments are beginning to take action against bottled water marketers. For example, the city of Chicago has recently begun a citywide tax on bottled water that is expected to bring in as much as $10.5 million in tax revenue annually.[44]

Although the pressures from outside groups can be considerable, consumer perceptions of health benefits are still key. As long as consumers perceive that bottled water sufficiently fulfills a true need and delivers good value, the product is likely to continue to grow in popularity. Although other consumers consider such purchases as wasteful and foolish, bottled water enthusiasts strongly disagree.

Questions and Activities

1. How does the need recognition portion of the consumer decision-making process apply to this case? What need is being addressed?

2. What brands of bottled water are you familiar with? Do these brands easily come to mind when you think of bottled water? Explain this issue from the perspective of the consideration set. How would you describe your consideration set for bottled water?

3. The next time you are in the classroom, take note of how many students are drinking bottled water as compared to soda. Does this surprise you? Ask a friend why he or she chooses bottled water over soda. Can you relate? Do you agree with his or her reasoning?

4. Go to a website that markets bottled water. Does it explain the health benefits of the product? If so, what does it claim? Why do you believe or disbelieve the information that you have found? Do you believe that the water is significantly better for you than is tap water? Explain.

SPEAK UP!

SHE DID

CB2 was built on a simple principle: to create a new teaching and learning solution that reflects the way today's faculty teach and the way you learn.

Through conversations, focus groups, surveys, and interviews, we collected data that drove the creation of the current version of CB2 that you are using today. But it doesn't stop there – in order to make CB2 an even better learning experience, we'd like you to SPEAK UP and tell us how CB2 worked for you.

What did you like about it? What would you change? Are there additional ideas you have that would help us build a better product for next semester's students?

At **4ltrpress.cengage.com/cb** you'll find all of the resources you need to succeed – **videos, audio downloads, flash cards, interactive quizzes** and more!

Speak Up! Go to **4ltrpress.cengage.com/cb.**

what do you think?

Getting a hair style for under $10 is a very good thing.

1 2 3 4 5 6 7

strongly disagree   strongly agree

The value that

consumers believe they will receive from a product directly impacts their evaluation of that product.

12

Decision Making II: Alternative Evaluation and Choice

After studying this chapter, the student should be able to:

LO1 Understand the difference between evaluative criteria and determinant criteria.

LO2 Comprehend how value affects the evaluation of alternatives.

LO3 Explain the importance of product categorization in the evaluation of alternatives process.

LO4 Distinguish between compensatory and noncompensatory rules that guide consumer choice.

Introduction

Selecting a new apartment is obviously a big decision. There are many issues to consider. Which location is best? How much rent will I have to pay? Is this apartment complex safe? Are utilities included in the rent? What kind of lease do I have to sign? Making a final decision can be draining. Thankfully, not every decision we face is this difficult.

As you will remember from our first decision-making chapter, the decision-making process includes need recognition, search for information, alternative evaluation, choice, and postchoice evaluation. The decision-making model is shown once again in Exhibit 12.1. In the current chapter, we focus on evaluation of alternatives and choice.

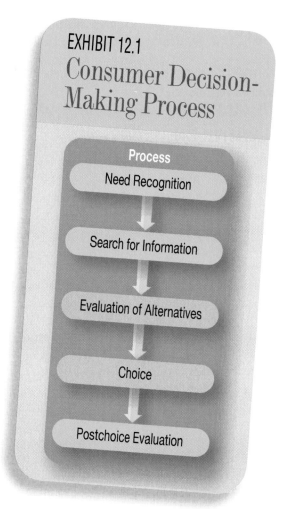

EXHIBIT 12.1
Consumer Decision-Making Process

Process

Need Recognition

↓

Search for Information

↓

Evaluation of Alternatives

↓

Choice

↓

Postchoice Evaluation

LO1 Evaluations of Alternatives: Criteria

a very important part of decision making is evaluating alternative solutions to problems. As we have discussed throughout this text, consumers are bombarded daily by a blistering array of product varieties, brands, and experiences from which to choose. For example, consumers can select from hundreds of varieties of breakfast cereals, snack foods, and athletic shoes. Musical choices are no different. A quick look at a popular music website like iTunes reveals thousands of songs to download! Trying to make sense out of all the alternatives can be very difficult. Fortunately, consumer researchers have learned much about how consumers evaluate alternatives. The first issue to address is how consumers select criteria that can be used in differentiating one alternative from another.

evaluative criteria attributes that consumers consider when reviewing alternative solutions to a problem

feature performance characteristic of an object

benefit perceived favorable results derived from a particular feature

determinant criteria criteria that are most carefully considered and directly related to the actual choice that is made

EVALUATIVE CRITERIA

After a need is recognized and a search process has taken place, consumers begin to examine the criteria that will be used for making a choice. **Evaluative criteria** are the attributes, features, or potential benefits that consumers consider when reviewing possible solutions to a problem. A **feature** is a performance characteristic of an object. Remember from our attitude chapter that features are often referred to as attributes. A **benefit** is a perceived favorable result that is derived from the presence of a particular feature.[1] A snooze button on an alarm clock is a feature. A benefit of the button is that it provides a kinder way to wake up. These concepts are illustrated in Exhibit 12.2.

Benefits play an important role in the value equation. A consumer doesn't buy an alarm clock because of a snooze button. Rather, the snooze button allows the benefit of a few extra minutes of sleep before facing the day. You may remember that benefits represent "what you get" in the value equation.

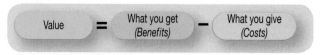

| Value | = | What you get (Benefits) | − | What you give (Costs) |

DETERMINANT CRITERIA

Not all evaluative criteria are equally important. **Determinant criteria** (sometimes called determinant attributes) are the evaluative criteria that are related to the actual choice that is made.[2] Consumers don't always reveal, or may not even know, the criteria that truly are determinant. This is true even when several attributes are considered to be important. For example, airline safety is definitely an important feature of an airline, and consumers would quickly voice this opinion. But, because consumers do not perceive a difference in safety among major airlines, safety does not actually determine the airline that is eventually selected. For this reason, statistical tools are often needed to establish determinance.

Which criteria are determinant can depend largely on the situation in which a product is consumed. For example, a consumer might consider gas mileage as a determinant criterion when buying a car for himself. However, the safety of a car would likely be a determinant factor if he is buying a car for his daughter.

Marketers frequently position products on the determinant criteria that their customers use when making a final selection. With the introduction of video capabilities to MP3 players, many consumers now use this feature as a determinant criterion

> Most people would prefer not to own one of these. But features that make waking easier add utilitarian value.

© ISTOCKPHOTO.COM/ZORAN DJEKIC

EXHIBIT 12.2
Product, Feature, and Benefit

Product	Feature	Benefit
Alarm clock	Snooze button	A kinder way to wake up
HDTV	1080p reception capability	A bright, clear picture
Laptop computer	Wireless Internet card	Freedom to connect to the Internet

when choosing a player. The Apple MacBook Air is designed as the flattest laptop computer on the market. The sleekness of the design can be a determinant criterion for consumers who are evaluating laptops.

LO2 Value and Alternative Evaluation

t o understand how alternatives are evaluated and how final choices are made, we must again highlight the key role that value plays in decision making. The value that consumers believe they will receive

The ultra-sleek design of the MacBook Air makes thinness a determinant criterion for consumers.

from a product has a direct impact on their evaluation of that product. In fact, the word *evaluate* literally means to set a value or worth to an object. Remember that benefits are at the heart of the value equation, and value is a function of both benefits and costs.

HEDONIC AND UTILITARIAN VALUE

As we have discussed several times in this text, hedonic and utilitarian value are both very important for consumers. The criteria that consumers use when evaluating a product can also often be classified as either hedonic or utilitarian.[3] Hedonic criteria include emotional, symbolic, and subjective attributes or benefits that are associated with an alternative. For example, the prestige that one associates with owning a Mercedes Benz is a hedonic criterion. These criteria are largely experiential. Utilitarian criteria pertain to functional or economic aspects associated with an alternative. For example, the gas mileage of a Mercedes Benz is a utilitarian criterion.

Marketers often promote both utilitarian and hedonic potential of a product. For example, the advertisements presented in Exhibit 12.3 promote utilitarian and hedonic automobile attributes. Consumers often use both categories of criteria when evaluating alternatives and making a final choice.

Rationality, Effort, and Variety

As discussed previously, consumers are not always rational when they are evaluating and choosing from possible solutions to a problem. What's more, consumers often have limited ability to process all the information that's available in the environment. The term **bounded rationality** describes the idea that perfectly rational decisions are not always feasible due to constraints found in information processing.

Even when consumers have the ability to consider all possible solutions to a problem, they do not always

affect-based evaluation evaluative process wherein consumers evaluate products based on the overall feeling that is evoked by the alternative

attribute-based evaluation evaluative process wherein alternatives are evaluated across a set of attributes that are considered relevant to the purchase situation

do so. Quite simply, sometimes the task just isn't worth it. In fact, consumers often minimize the effort that they put into alternative evaluation and choice. As we discussed in our need recognition and information search chapter, consumers often settle for a solution that is simply good enough to solve a problem. Realistically, there are just too many choices out there. In fact, even though variety is a good thing, studies indicate that too much variety actually contributes to feelings of discontent and unhappiness![4]

AFFECT-BASED AND ATTRIBUTE-BASED EVALUATIONS

We can distinguish between two major types of evaluation processes: affect-based and attribute-based. With **affect-based evaluation**, consumers evaluate products based on the overall feeling that is evoked by the alternative.[5] When consumers say something like, "I'm not even sure why I bought this sweater, I just liked it," an affect-based process is reflected. Emotions play a big role in affect-based evaluation, as do mood states.[6]

> In general, positive mood states lead to positive evaluations while negative mood states lead to negative evaluations.

In general, positive mood states lead to positive evaluations while negative mood states lead to negative evaluations. Mood is also influential when limited information is found about an alternative.[7] For example, when you are in a good mood, you may evaluate a product positively even if there is not a lot of information given about the product.

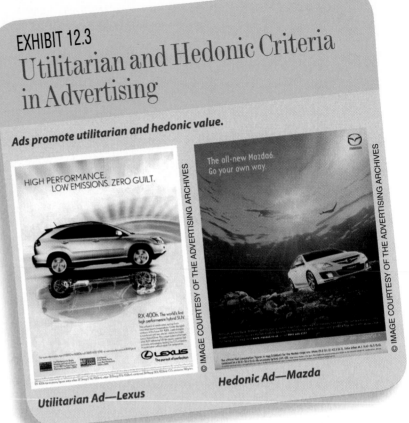

EXHIBIT 12.3
Utilitarian and Hedonic Criteria in Advertising

Ads promote utilitarian and hedonic value.

HIGH PERFORMANCE. LOW EMISSIONS. ZERO GUILT.

The all-new Mazda6. Go your own way.

Utilitarian Ad—Lexus

Hedonic Ad—Mazda

Strong feelings also motivate consumers to seek variety as a means of escaping boredom. Beverage marketers like Coca-Cola and Pepsi-Cola frequently update their offerings in order to combat consumer boredom.

With **attribute-based evaluation**, alternatives are evaluated across a set of attributes that are considered relevant to the purchase situation. As we have noted, the rational decision-making process assumes that consumers carefully integrate information about product attributes and make careful comparisons between products. This process illustrates attribute-based evaluation.

LO3 Product Categorization and Criteria Selection

One of the first things that a consumer does when she receives information from the environment is attempt to make sense of the information by placing it in the context of a familiar category. Existing schemas, as discussed in our comprehension chapter, allow consumers to provide meaning to objects. Within

Something New

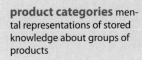

Major soft drink companies like PepsiCo and Coca-Cola Company are well known for their extremely popular product lines. The companies also excel at understanding consumer wants and responding to these wants with quality products. Today, it's much more than just being "cola kings."

It seems that what consumers really want today is variety. A casual walk down the grocery store aisle reveals that the product lines of these marketing giants have grown very large over the years. It's all about variety and excitement from the consumer's perspective. Consumers like seeing something new, and new products can lead to excitement.

Consumers have sought variety in their beverages for years, and today the focus is really on healthier alternatives. In water alone, Coca-Cola offers Dasani, Dasani Flavors, Glaceau fruitwater, and others. Not to be outdone, Pepsi offers Aquafina, Aquafina Alive!, Aquafina Sparkling, and Aquafina FlavorSplash. This doesn't even cover their sports drinks, teas, juices, iced coffees, frappuccinos, or vitamin-fortified soft drinks. By staying on top of consumer trends and offering variety, marketing success continues for the cola kings!

Sources: Garcia, Tonya (2007), "Coke Keeps Plus Debut Simple," *PRweek*, 10 (19), 5; Foote, Andrea (2006), "A Taste for the Good Life," *Beverage World*, 125 (1763), 44–45; Bachmann, Tom (2004), "The State of Our Industry," *Beverage Industry*, 93 (6), 8.

these schemas, both product categories and brand categories are found.

Product categories are mental representations of stored knowledge about groups of products. When considering a new product, consumers rely on the knowledge that they have regarding the relevant product category. Knowledge about the existing category is then transferred to the novel item. For example, when consumers view a slide phone for the first time, they start to compare it with existing cell phone categories and draw from their knowledge of phones. Even if a product is very different from products that are currently available, consumers still draw on existing category knowledge to guide their expectations and attitudes toward the new product.[8] The successful launch of the iPhone is a good example of this.

CATEGORY LEVELS

Consumers possess different levels of product categories. The number of levels and details within each level is influenced by familiarity and expertise with products.[9] Consumers know the differences between snacks, breakfast, and dinner. Further distinctions can be made within any of these categories. For example, within the "snack" category, distinctions can be made between salty snacks, sweet snacks, fruits, and vegetables. Even finer distinctions can be made at yet a third level. Salty snacks may be broken down into crackers, chips, snack mix, and so on. Therefore, distinctions at basic levels are generally made across product categories (for example, snacks, breakfast foods, dinner foods). Distinctions at subsequent levels increase in specificity, ultimately to the brand and attribute level.[10] Expertise and familiarity play important roles in this process.

Superordinate and Subordinate Categories

The different levels of product categories can be referred to as being either superordinate or subordinate.[11] *Superordinate categories* are abstract in nature and represent the highest level of categorization. A superordinate category would be video game. *Subordinate categories* are more detailed. Here, the consumer examines the knowledge that he has stored about various options. For example, a consumer would proceed through superordinate and subordinate categories like video game, console, and Playstation 3. This concept is shown in Exhibit 12.4.

Evaluations are generally more relevant and meaningful at subordinate levels.[12] That is, specific differences can be easily noticed like "the price of the Xbox is higher than the price of the Wii." Recall from our memory chapter that exemplars are first thought of within any category. New alternatives will be compared to exemplars first and then to other brands that are found in the brand category. For example, when someone sees an advertisement for a new video game, she will quickly move through the video game and console categories and arrive at Playstation 3. Playstation 3 will then be used as the first benchmark. Other brand comparisons will then occur.

Perceptual and Underlying Attributes

When evaluating products, consumers also distinguish between perceptual and underlying attributes. **Perceptual attributes** are visually apparent and easily recognizable. Size, shape, color, and price are perceptual attributes. These attributes are sometimes referred to as search qualities because they can easily be evaluated prior to actual purchase.

Underlying attributes are not readily apparent and can only be learned through experience with the product. These attributes are sometimes referred to as experience qualities because they are often perceived only during consumption. An example of an underlying attribute is product quality. The distinction between the two types is important because consumers most often infer the existence of underlying attributes through perceptual attributes. As we discussed in our search chapter, the price of a product often tells the consumer something about its quality. In this way, price is used as a signal of quality. A **signal** is a characteristic that allows a consumer to diagnose something distinctive about an

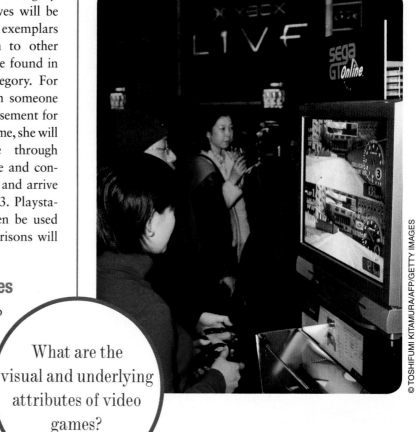

© TOSHIFUMI KITAMURA/AFP/GETTY IMAGES

What are the visual and underlying attributes of video games?

EXHIBIT 12.4
Superordinate and Subordinate Categorization

Superordinate — Video Game

Subordinate — Portable, Console, Arcade

Console: XBOX 360, Playstation 3, Nintendo Wii, New Console Game

Features	XBOX 360	Playstation 3	Nintendo Wii	New Console Game
Price:	Moderate	High	Low	?
Graphics:	Excellent	Excellent	Moderate	?
Resolution:	1080i	1080p	480p	?
Console Size:	Medium	Big	Very Small	?

© ISTOCKPHOTO.COM/PAWEL TALAJKOWSKI

"Real" Estate Downsize

It's well known that the housing market played a major role in the worldwide economic tailspin of the last few years. Lenders lent money to risky borrowers and the subprime mortgage business boomed. Housing prices escalated to unrealistic levels and adjustable rate mortgage payments eventually began to climb. The market finally burst as many consumers began to default on their mortgages. Obviously, severe economic ramifications resulted.

One of the direct results of the housing market collapse is that many consumers today are intentionally "downsizing" their home purchases. Granted, mortgages are harder to come by than in recent years, but for those home buyers who can qualify for mortgages, many are deciding to buy well below their means. This has actually put an increased demand on smaller, rather than larger homes. Whereas a very large home with all the bells and whistles has long been considered a status symbol, many consumers are readjusting their ways of thinking.

Sources: Gopal, Prashant (2009), "Even Once-Strong Housing Markets Stumble," *Business Week (online)*, January 28, 2009; Gardner, Dave (2008), "The Incredible Shrinking House," *Northeast Pennsylvania Business Journal*, 23 (10). 77; Farrell, Christopher (2998), "Choosing Where to Grow Old," *Business Week*, July 14, 2008 (4092), 44; Gandel, Stephen (2008), "Real Estate's Next Evolution," *Money*, June, 37 (6), 98; Evans, Kelly (2007), "Size of New Homes Starts Shrinking as Builders Battle Housing Slump," *Wall Street Journal*, September 12, 2007, A1.

alternative. When a retailer offers a price-matching guarantee, meaning that they will match any competitor's advertised price, they give off a signal that consumers will enjoy low prices when they shop at this particular store.

Signals such as brand name, price, appearance, and retailer reputation often infer information about product quality. This is particularly so in the following situations:

- When the consumer is trying to reduce risk
- When purchase involvement is low
- When the consumer lacks product expertise[13]

Interestingly, young and inexperienced consumers rely more heavily on perceptual attributes than do older consumers.[14]

CRITERIA SELECTION

What Determines the Type of Evaluative Criteria That Consumers Use?

A number of factors influence the type of criteria that consumers use when evaluating alternatives. Situational influences, product knowledge, social influences, expert opinions, online sources, and marketing communications all influence the type of criteria that are used.

1. **Situational Influences.** As discussed earlier in this chapter, the type of criteria that are considered depends heavily on situational influences. If a product is being purchased as a gift, the buyer may pay close attention to hedonic attributes such as the image of the product and its reputation. For example, when buying perfume for a loved one, brand name and imagery can be very important. These criteria would therefore be weighted heavily in the evaluation process. Perhaps a consumer buying perfume for personal consumption may rely more heavily on other criteria such as price and convenience.

2. **Product Knowledge.** As a consumer's level of knowledge increases, he or she is able to focus on criteria that are most important in making a selection and to discount irrelevant information.[15] As such, an expert would be expected to be able to quickly discern what information is important and what is not.

3. **Expert Opinions.** Because brand experts have well-developed knowledge banks for products, they can be used to help others determine what types of information to pay attention to when evaluating products. For example, a computer science professor would be able to guide students in selecting the most important criteria to consider when buying a new computer. Market mavens are also trusted sources who can guide consumers in focusing on various product attributes.

4. **Social Influences.** Friends, family members, and reference groups also have an impact on the type of criteria that are used for decision making. This is especially true for socially visible products like automobiles or clothing.[16] Friends and families are considered to be trustworthy sources of information, and guidance that they give into what type of attributes to consider is usually closely followed.

5. **Online Sources.** Numerous websites can assist consumers with information on product attributes

and brand differences. **Consumerreports.com** explains what types of criteria to consider when buying products. Popular retail sites like **bestbuy .com** also explain what attributes consumers should consider.

6. **Marketing Communications.** Marketing communications also assist consumers in deciding what features to consider when buying a particular product. Marketers generally promote the attributes that their products excel on and attempt to convince consumers that these are the most important. For example, Papa John's Pizza is well known for advertising "Better Ingredients, Better Pizza." While the company claims that their pizza contains better ingredients than that of their competitors, they also attempt to convince consumers that ingredients are important criteria to consider when buying pizza.

Marketing communications influence the choice of evaluative criteria.

© MICHAEL NEWMAN/PHOTOEDIT

Are Consumers Accurate in Their Assessment of Evaluative Criteria?

The accuracy of a consumer's evaluation depends heavily on the quality of judgments that they make. **Judgments** are mental assessments of the presence of attributes and the benefits associated with those attributes. Consumer judgments are affected by the amount of knowledge or experience a consumer has with a particular object. During the evaluation process, consumers make judgments about the following:

-   **Presence of features.** Does this MP3 player play videos?

-   **Feature levels.** How many videos can be stored?

-   **Benefits associated with features.** I'd be able to watch a movie on a long trip.

-   **Value associated with the benefit.** That would be nice.

-   **How objects differ from each other.** The other one doesn't have this.

There are several issues that affect consumer judgments. We review a few of these issues here.

1. **Just Noticeable Difference.** The ability of a consumer to make accurate judgments when evaluating alternatives is influenced by his or her ability to perceive differences in levels of stimuli between two options. As was discussed in our perception chapter, the just noticeable difference (JND) represents how much stronger one stimulus must be compared to another if someone is to notice that the two are not the same. For example, when judging sound quality, a consumer may not be able to discern the difference between speakers that have a frequency range between 47 Hz and 20 kHz and those that have a range between 50 Hz and 20 kHz. If consumers cannot tell the difference, then their judgments about the products may not be accurate.

Sometimes, the same manufacturer offers different brands or models that are very similar to each other. The term *branded variants* is used to describe the practice of offering essentially identical products with different model numbers or names.[17] Even if differences are perceived, the differences might not be very meaningful. As we discussed earlier, the JND concept is also important.

The impact of the JND on consumer judgments applies to how consumers react to counterfeit products. Some counterfeits are so much like the original that consumers simply can't perceive the difference between them. This is, of course, a bad situation for marketers of the original. The

Get Real feature on page 240 discusses the issue of counterfeit products.

2. **Attribution Correlation.** Consumers often make judgments about features based on their perceived relationship with other features. For example, earlier we stated that price is often used as a signal for quality. Here, consumers rely on **attribute correlation** to describe the perceived relationship between attributes of products.[18] Recall from our consumer search chapter that price and quality are often assumed to be positively correlated. That is, when a product has a high price, consumers often assume it will be high quality.

Attributes can also be negatively correlated. For example, if a consumer's wait time at a bank is long, he or she might think that the bank offers poor service. Here, the consumer assumes that as wait time goes up, service quality goes down (hence, a negative correlation). This can be a faulty assumption because a long wait time may simply mean that consumers get individualized attention and really good service. Some things are worth waiting for!

3. **Quality Perceptions.** Marketers have long realized that consumer perception is critical to marketing success. As we have discussed, perceptions are not always in line with reality. One issue that pertains to consumer judgments is the difference between objective quality and perceived quality. *Objective quality* refers to the actual quality of a product that can be assessed through industry specification or expert rating. For example, a cell phone provider may advertise that its service has been proven to have the fewest dropped calls in the industry. *Perceived quality* is based on consumer perceptions. Even if the cell phone has objectively been shown to have the best coverage in the industry, consumers may still perceive poor quality if the coverage in their immediate area is not good.

Companies spend a great deal of time and money on improving the objective quality of their products. These efforts are limited, however, by consumer perceptions of quality. In fact, a recent study revealed that improvements in objective quality may take as many as six years to be fully recognized by consumers![19] You may remember from our discussion in the comprehension chapter that consumers act on declarative knowledge even if the knowledge

is incorrect. So if a company invests in improving the quality of its products, consumers may still act on the assumption that the product's quality is not good.

attribute correlation
perceived relationship between product features

4. **Brand Name Associations.** Brand names also have an impact on consumer judgments. Much like price, brand names can be used as signals of quality. In fact, studies have found that brand names are even stronger signals of quality than is price.[20] For example, Energizer batteries are assumed to last a long time and Gillette razors are believed to be the best a man can get.

Unusual product names also influence consumer judgments. One technique that marketers have used for several years is coming up with unexpected, even humorous, names for products. This is especially true in the snack food industry. Hot sauce brands are known for their funny names. Names like Arizona Gunslinger and Java Hot Sauce are quite common. Research indicates that unexpected names can lead to increased product preference and choice.[21]

How Many Criteria Are Necessary to Evaluate Alternatives Effectively?

As we have discussed, too many alternatives can be draining for consumers. However, research suggests that consumers can handle a surprisingly high number of comparisons before overload sets in. One study revealed that consumers can evaluate as many as ten product alternatives and fifteen attributes before overload occurs.[22] Even though consumers can handle this much information, they rarely like to do so. And they generally do not

> What can a brand name tell you about a product?

© MARK YAMAMOTO/ORANGE COUNTY REGISTER/NEWSCOM

conjoint analysis
technique used to develop an understanding of the attributes that guide consumer preferences by having consumers compare product preferences across varying levels of evaluative criteria and expected utility

consider this many alternatives. In fact, consumers are often able to make good choices when considering only a single attribute.[23]

What If Information Is Missing?

Consumers may have a good understanding of the types of attributes that they would like to use for alternative evaluation, but sometimes attribute information is not available. This actually happens quite frequently in the marketplace. For example, consider the information given in Exhibit 12.5. Here, information is given for two televisions that a consumer collects from print advertisements. Assume that both televisions cost roughly the same amount, say $1,000. As you can see, the information for television A lacks the details for picture quality while the information given for television B lacks the details regarding the product's warranty. Consumer satisfaction ratings are available for both products.

Get Real!

A serious problem for many marketers today is the proliferation of counterfeit products. In fact, counterfeit products often cost industries millions of dollars in lost sales. Everyone loses with counterfeits—that is, if the perpetrator is caught. Companies lose sales, consumers get ripped off, and the criminals go to jail.

At the heart of the issue with counterfeit products is whether consumers can tell the difference between a fake and the original. The just noticeable difference applies here. Many times consumers can't discern the subtle differences between the original and the clone.

One signal that consumers can use is where the product is sold. You shouldn't expect to see high-class products like Rolex watches or Louis Vuitton handbags available on the street corner at knockoff prices. Surprisingly, these counterfeits can sometimes find their way into popular retail outlets, meaning that consumers must beware. As usual, if it seems too good to be true, it probably is.

Sources: Ward, Stephanie Francois (2007), "Knockoffs Landing on Retail Shelves," *ABA Journal*, 93 (February), 10–11; Anonymous (2006), "Counterfeit Crackdown," *MicroScope* (May 22), 3; Jackson, Lee Anna (2004), "Duped by Designer Doubles," *Black Enterprise*, 35 (2), 188.

> Consumers are often able to make good choices when considering only a single attribute.

To help solve this dilemma, consumers tend to weigh the criteria that are common to both alternatives quite heavily in the evaluation. They also tend to discount information that is missing for the option that performs better on the common criteria. For example,

satisfaction ratings are given for both sets in this exhibit. Consumers would likely discount the missing warranty information for television B because this alternative performs better on the common criterion of consumer satisfaction ratings.[24]

How Do Marketers Determine Which Criteria Consumers Use?

Marketers can use several techniques to determine the criteria that consumers use when judging products. They can directly ask consumers through surveys. They can also gather information from warranty registrations that ask consumers to indicate the specific criteria that were used in arriving at a purchase decision.

Marketers also use techniques such as perceptual mapping and conjoint analysis to assess choice criteria. Perceptual mapping was discussed in a previous chapter. **Conjoint analysis** is used to understand the attributes that guide preferences by having

EXHIBIT 12.5
Missing Information

Features	Television A	Television B
Consumer satisfaction ratings	Good	Excellent
Warranty	2 years parts & labor	Not given
Picture quality	Not given	Good

Source: Kivetz, Ran, and Itamar Simonson (2000), "The Effects of Incomplete Information on Consumer Choice," *Journal of Marketing Research*, 37 (4), 427–448.

consumers compare products across levels of evaluative criteria and the expected utility associated with the alternatives.[25]

LO4 Consumer Choice: Decision Rules

Once consumers have evaluated alternative solutions to a problem, they begin to make a choice. "Choice" does not mean that a particular alternative will be chosen. Rather, consumers may simply choose to delay a choice until a future date or to forgo a selection indefinitely.

There are two major types of rules that consumers use when selecting products: compensatory rules and noncompensatory rules. **Compensatory rules** allow consumers to select products that may perform poorly on one attribute by compensating for the poor performance by good performance on another attribute. A consumer using a compensatory rule might say something like "It's OK that this car isn't very stylish; it gets good gas mileage. I'll buy it."

Noncompensatory models do not allow for this process to take place. Rather, when **noncompensatory rules** are used, strict guidelines are set prior to selection, and any option that does not meet the specifications is eliminated from consideration. For example, a consumer might say "I'll only choose a car that gets good gas mileage. I am not budging on that."

COMPENSATORY MODELS

The attitude-toward-the-object model (Fishbein model) that was presented in our attitude chapter represents a compensatory approach. The formula $[A_o = \sum(b_i)(e_i)]$ allows for poor scores on one attribute to be compensated for by good scores on another. Our example from that chapter is again shown in Exhibit 12.6. This example revealed that Lifestyles fitness center was selected even though it scored highest on the attribute that Brooke rated most poorly, high fees. The high ratings on other attributes compensated for Brooke's belief that Lifestyles has high fees.

NONCOMPENSATORY MODELS

Consumer researchers have identified four major categories of noncompensatory rules.[26] They include the conjunctive rule, the disjunctive rule, the lexicographic rule, and the elimination-by-aspects (EBA) rule.

1. Following the **conjunctive rule**, the consumer sets a minimum mental cutoff point for various features and rejects any product that fails to meet or exceed this cutoff point across all features.

2. Following the **disjunctive rule**, the consumer sets a minimum mental cutoff for various features. This is similar to the conjunctive rule. However, with the disjunctive rule, the cutoff point is usually high. The product that meets or exceeds this cutoff on any feature is selected.

3. Following the **lexicographic rule**, the consumer selects the product that he or she believes performs best on the most important feature.

compensatory rule decision-making rule that allows consumers to select products that may perform poorly on one criterion by compensating for the poor performance on one attribute by good performance on another

noncompensatory rule decision-making rule in which strict guidelines are set prior to selection and any option that does not meet the guidelines is eliminated from consideration

conjunctive rule noncompensatory decision rule where the option selected must surpass a minimum cutoff across all relevant attributes

disjunctive rule noncompensatory decision rule where the option selected surpasses a relatively high cutoff point on any attribute

lexicographic rule noncompensatory decision rule where the option selected is thought to perform best on the most important attribute

EXHIBIT 12.6
A Compensatory Approach

Attribute	e	LIFESTYLE b	LIFESTYLE (b)(e)	CURVES b	CURVES (b)(e)	SHAPES b	SHAPES (b)(e)
Circuit training	−1	1	−1	10	−10	9	−9
Class variety	2	10	20	2	4	3	6
Amenities	1	9	9	5	5	5	5
Fees	−3	6	−18	4	−12	5	−15
Location	3	6	18	8	24	9	27
A_o			28		11		14

Note: "e" = evaluative ratings. These ratings are generally scaled from −3 to +3, with −3 being very negative and +3 being very positive. "b" = strength of belief that the object possesses the attribute in question. Beliefs are generally scaled from 1 to 10, with 1 meaning "highly unlikely" and 10 meaning "highly likely". "(b)(e)" is the product term that is derived by multiplying the evaluative ratings (e) by belief strength (b). A_o is the overall attitude toward the object. This is determined by adding the (b)(e) product terms for each object.

4. Following the **elimination-by-aspects rule (EBA)**, the consumer sets minimum cutoff points for the attributes. Beginning with the most important feature, he or she then eliminates options that don't meet or surpass the cutoff point on this important feature. The consumer then moves on to the next most important feature and repeats the process and does this until only one option remains and a choice is made.

To illustrate these rules, consider the information that is presented in Exhibit 12.7. Here, the consumer is evaluating different makes and models of cars.

The process involved with each decision rule would be as follows:

1. **Conjunctive Rule.** Assume that all features must meet or surpass a mental cutoff of 5 in order for the car to be selected. Looking across the various features for the cars, we see that only the Ford Focus has performance ratings at or above 5 on all features. Using this rule, the Ford Focus would therefore be selected. Its performance ratings are, respectively: 7, 6, 8, 8, 6, 5. Notice that at least one of the performance ratings for the attributes of the other cars falls below the cutoff of 5.

2. **Disjunctive Rule.** Assume that the consumer wants a car that excels at any of the features. Here, he would set a high cutoff of, say, 10. The only car

EXHIBIT 12.7
Noncompensatory Decision Approaches

Attribute	Importance	Chevy Aveo Belief Ratings	Ford Focus Belief Ratings	Honda Fit Belief Ratings	Hyundai Accent Belief Ratings
Gas mileage	10	5	7	9	8
Low price	9	8	6	7	10
Styling	8	9	8	4	4
Warranty	5	4	8	9	8
Service	6	5	6	7	3
Handling	7	6	5	3	3

Note: Belief ratings are performance judgments scaled from 1 = very poor to 9 = very good. Importance ratings are scaled so that 10 = most important, 9 = next most important, and so on.
Source: Wright, Peter (1975), "Consumer Choice Strategies: Simplifying Vs. Optimizing," *Journal of Marketing Research*, 12 (1), 60–67.

Choosing a car is a highly involving decision and probably involves both compensatory and noncompensatory rules.

that offers a performance rating of 10 on any attribute is the Hyundai Accent. The "low price" criterion is particularly strong for this car, and the consumer rates this feature as a 10. Using the disjunctive rule, the Hyundai Accent would be selected. He is considering performance ratings, and not the importance of the attributes.

3. **Lexicographic Rule.** Here, the product that is thought to perform best on the most important attribute is selected. In this example, the Honda Fit would be selected because it scores highest (9) on the most important attribute, gas mileage.

4. **EBA Rule.** Assuming a minimum cutoff point of 5 once again, the consumer begins with the most important attribute, gas mileage. Any product that does not meet or surpass the cutoff of 5 on this attribute would be eliminated. All options meet or surpass 5 on the gas mileage attribute and no products are eliminated. Next, the consumer looks at the next most important attribute, low price. Again, all options meet the 5 criterion and no options are eliminated.

On the next most important attribute, styling, two options are eliminated because they don't reach the 5 cutoff—the Honda Fit and the Hyundai Accent. The consumer continues on with the next most important attribute, handling. Both the Aveo and the Focus surpass the 5 cutoff on this attribute. The same is true for the next most important attribute, service. Finally, on the final attribute, warranty, the Aveo is eliminated from consideration because it does not reach the cutoff and the Ford Focus is ultimately selected. Notice that the conjunctive and EBA rules

can result in the same decision. This will occur if the same cutoff points are used for both rules.

USE OF DECISION RULES

Noncompensatory rules are often used in low-involvement situations because these rules allow consumers to simplify their thought processes. However, these rules are also used in high-involvement purchase situations. The decision of what car to buy is certainly a high-involvement decision for most people.

Consumers can combine decision rules in order to arrive at a final solution. For example, a consumer might begin with a conjunctive rule to narrow down the choices and then use a compensatory approach to finalize the decision.

You may be wondering what type of rule consumers use most often. Studies have revealed that the lexicographic rule is very common. This is because consumers usually know what features are most important, and they simply select the product that offers the best performance on that feature.

You may also wonder how often consumers use these rules. Actually, the rules are used quite frequently. We should emphasize, however, that the processes are indeed mental. That is, the comparisons are almost always made mentally, without the strict use of a mathematical formula. Nevertheless, by considering issues such as cutoff points, researchers are able to gain a better understanding of the processes behind consumer choice.

RETAIL OUTLET SELECTION

Up to this point, we have emphasized the processes that consumers use when selecting from alternative solutions to a problem. Consumers must also choose where they will buy the product. Sometimes, consumers will decide *where* they will buy before they determine *what* they will buy. One consumer says to another: "I'm going to the store; what do we need?" The other replies, "Where are you going?" Here, the decision of what product to buy hinges on where you are shopping.

As we have noted earlier in this text, consumers have gradually become less brand loyal and more store loyal. This underscores the importance of store choice in consumer behavior research. Several factors influence the choice of retail outlet including objective and subjective criteria such as product variety, store image, location, service, and product quality.[27] Of course, consumers may also decide to make their purchases on the Internet. The Internet has quickly become the channel of choice for many consumers. The actual decision of which website to use is based on several factors including the availability of product variety and information, customer service, security, and navigational ease.[28] Of course, many large retailers have both physical presence (a bricks-and-mortar store) and an online presence (website).

As you can tell, evaluating alternatives and making final purchase decisions are part of an involved process. Our next chapter will consider the processes that occur after a choice has been made.

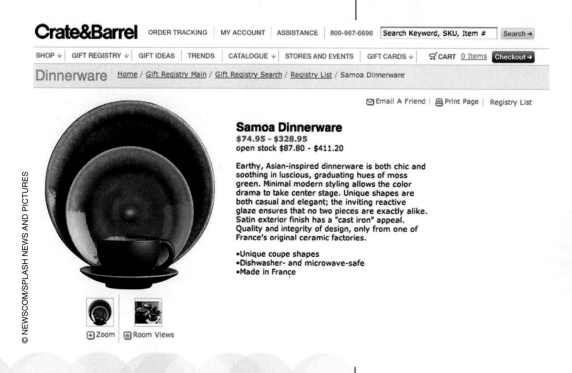

Online retailers have to thoroughly describe the evaluative criteria that consumers may use.

Chapter 12 Case

Not too long ago, it seemed relatively simple for consumers to select a camera. The Polaroid One-Step camera was very popular and it worked on a simple idea: "point and click." For those consumers who haven't kept up with advances in technology, however, selecting a camera is suddenly a big deal. In fact, it can be downright perplexing.

Now, there are many product attributes that are totally new to consumers including megapixels, digital zoom / optical zoom, single-lens reflex features, and all sorts of storage media. Whereas consumers once knew that they could get 24 exposures on a roll of film, the storage capacity of today's media depends on things like megapixels. Many brands are also available, including Canon, Casio, Kodak, Sony, Panasonic, Fujifilm, and Nikon. Of course, consumers can make inferences of quality based on what they know about the company or brand. Also, the price ranges vary dramatically. For example, lower-end cameras can retail for as little as $79, while higher-end cameras can go for thousands of dollars.

At the most basic level, the central question is how the camera will be used. However, making sense of all of these differences and evaluating different models is still not easy. This is especially the case when consumers are presented with information like that shown in the chart below.

Popular websites like **myproductadvisor.com** make the process a bit easier. By simply answering a number of questions about the way in which the camera will be used, what features are important, and what price range is desirable, the consumer can get a number of recommendations about both brands and features. Guiding consumers through an otherwise complex process of brand selection is quite valuable. However, the final decision of which brand to buy still remains with the consumer.

Sites like **myproductadvisor.com** are gaining in popularity. Obviously, visiting websites for product recommendations has both advantages and disadvantages. A major advantage is that all kinds of information can be gathered in almost limitless fashion at any time of the day or night. The disadvantage is that consumers don't always know which sites to trust, and they are usually limited in the amount of conversation that can take place with service representatives. Nonetheless, these sites are popular and very helpful in the alternative evaluation process.

Major retail sites such as **bestbuy.com**, **circuitcity.com**, and even **walmart.com** also allow consumers to view product information and make comparisons with relative ease. Of course, here the hope is that the consumer will make the actual purchase on the website. Making the evaluation process as easy as possible can greatly help the retailer gain more sales. Nevertheless, consumers still often like to shop around.

Whether using a recommendation site like **myproductadvisor.com** or a major retail site like **bestbuy.com**, consumers can gather a great deal of information and evaluate alternatives all from the comfort of their own keyboards. Given that there are literally hundreds of models and features available, most consumers value this convenience highly.[29]

Questions and Activities

1. What types of decision-making rules can be used for selecting a digital camera? How would they apply to this case?

2. How can consumers deal with the problem of missing information for one, or several, of the alternatives?

3. What role does the brand name of a camera play in the selection process?

4. Compare two popular websites such as **bestbuy.com** and **myproductadvisor.com** on how they present alternatives and explain differences among cameras. How helpful do you find these sites to be?

	Price	Resolution	Speed	Aperture	Digital Zoom	Optical Zoom
Camera A	$1,300	10.2 mpxi	3 fr/sec	F/3.5–5.6	1X	7.5X
Camera B	$1,100	10.1 mpxi	3 fr/sec	F/4.0–5.6	1X	5X
Camera C	$970	8.2 mpxi	5 fr/sec	F/3.5–5.6	1X	3X

what do you think?

When I'm treated unfairly by a business, dissatisfaction describes my feelings well.

1 2 3 4 5 6 7

strongly disagree   strongly agree

Marketers can be

extremely successful by focusing on value. In fact, Walmart's success is more about value than satisfaction.

13

Consumption to Satisfaction

LO1 Consumption, Value, and Satisfaction

Consumption is at the heart of all consumer behavior. Obviously, a consumer *consumes*! In fact, it can be argued that all human activity focuses on some form of consumption. Even when we work, we consume things so that we can earn money to consume more![1] In the **consumption process**, consumers use the product, service, or experience that has been selected. Ultimately, consumers consume products in order to receive value.

> **consumption process** process in which consumers use the product, service, or experience that has been selected
>
> **durable goods** goods that are usually consumed over a long period of time
>
> **nondurable goods** goods that are usually consumed quickly

After studying this chapter, the student should be able to:

LO1 Gain an appreciation of the link from consumption to value to satisfaction.

LO2 Discuss the relative importance of satisfaction and value in consumer behavior.

LO3 Know that emotions other than satisfaction can affect postconsumption behavior.

LO4 Use expectancy disconfirmation, equity, and attribution theory approaches to explain consumers' postconsumption reactions.

LO5 Understand problems with commonly applied satisfaction measures.

LO6 Describe some ways that consumers dispose of products.

CONSUMPTION LEADS TO VALUE

The important role of consumption becomes apparent when one considers that without consumption, there is no value. Accordingly, consumer value is directly derived from product consumption.[2] Earlier, consumption was defined as the process that converts time and goods, services, or ideas into value. Consumption experiences potentially produce utilitarian and/or hedonic value.

The basic consumption process that is at the heart of the CVF is shown again in Exhibit 13.1.

CONSUMPTION AND PRODUCT CLASSIFICATION

Many issues go along with the consumption of goods, services, and experiences. Important differences exist for the consumption of durable and nondurable goods. **Durable goods** are goods that are consumed over long periods of time. A dishwasher is a durable good. **Nondurable goods** are consumed quickly. Soft drinks are nondurable goods.

For nondurable goods especially, marketers try to increase consumption frequency as much as possible. **Consumption frequency** refers to the number of times a product or service is consumed in a given time period. Credit card companies have made it easier and easier for consumers to use their cards on routine shopping trips. Visa and MasterCard were once thought of as inappropriate for routine purchases like groceries. Today, however, consumers often use these for all manner of everyday purchases.

Marketers also attempt to increase the amount of product that is consumed. For example, soft drink marketers gradually increased the average size of soft drinks over time. Many students may be surprised to find out that the traditional Coke bottle was much smaller than today—weighing in at a mere $6\frac{1}{2}$ ounces. Pepsi's selling point was a 10-ounce bottle at the same price. Today consumers often consume 20-ounce or even 1-liter bottles a number of times per day! The soft drink industry has slowly worked to increase the average consumption of cola.

Services and experiences are often classified as being "nondurable" by default. However, some services are more clearly consumed over extended time periods. For example, insurance is consumed daily even though consumers may pay premiums on only a few occasions throughout the year. Experiences are complete when consumption stops. However, marketers of these products encourage repeat consumption of their products by

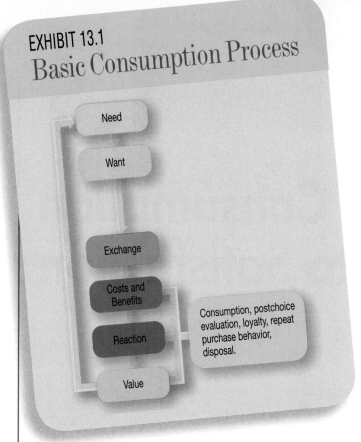

EXHIBIT 13.1
Basic Consumption Process

Need

Want

Exchange

Costs and Benefits

Reaction

Consumption, postchoice evaluation, loyalty, repeat purchase behavior, disposal.

Value

offering season tickets, club memberships, and special invitations to events. By encouraging increased consumption, these marketers are able to foster customer relationships.

SITUATIONS AND CONSUMER REACTIONS

As discussed previously, consumption situations and settings have a significant impact on the consumer experience. The temporal factors, antecedent conditions, and physical environment are particularly influential on the consumption experience. How and what we consume is largely dependent upon the environment that we're in.

For example, when football fans enjoy the tailgating experience, they are likely to consume a number of products that supply added value to the occasion. Beer, burgers, and brats are the standard fare at typical tailgates. For many consumers, the consumption of these products becomes part of the tailgating ritual. Here, the social context directly influences the overall consumption experience.

The environment plays a large role in influencing consumption and consumer satisfaction. When golfers play a crowded golf course, the pace of play is determined more by others. Although proper etiquette is

Insurance is consumed daily even though consumers may pay premiums on only a few occasions throughout the year.

Tailgate 101

Social settings play a large role in consumption. Just ask tailgaters. Estimates indicate that over 50 million consumers tailgate at football stadiums each year, and the number is increasing quickly. Although tailgates were once simple affairs, these pregame rituals have become quite extravagant in recent years.

College campuses appear to be the setting of choice, although professional sports stadiums come in a close second. Tailgates often include a variety of drinks and food, from simple hamburgers and brats to catered dinners and seafood! The setting is what it's all about. Combined with friends, family, and fans, it's a fun event for everyone involved. And tailgaters are attractive to marketers because many of them earn over $75,000 per year.

For many consumers, it is difficult to separate the party from the food. The game can almost be an afterthought. The experience is what it's all about. Clearly, there is an enormous hedonic aspect to tailgating. After all, it's all about friends, food, and football.

Sources: Flynn, Kimberly, Eric Lenkowitz, and Elizabeth Ward (2007), "Tailgating 101," *Men's Fitness*, 23 (7), 128–129; Valdez, Andrea (2007), "Tailgating," *Texas Monthly*, **http://www.texasmonthly.com/preview/2007-09-01/themanual.com**, accessed 3/13/08; Megerian, Christopher (2007), "The Prize in the Parking Lot," *Business Week*, 11 (4048), 11; Major, Meg (2007), "Fresh Gains Yardage," *Progressive Grocer*, 86 (11), 60–63.

---

meaning transference process through which cultural meaning is transferred to a product and onto the consumer

Meaning transference begins with culture. Value is affected largely by the meaning of goods, services, and experiences. Important cultural ideals or values are transferred onto products by marketing efforts like advertising and by word-of-mouth that occurs between consumers. If a freedom theme can be attached to a product—for example, a motorcycle—then a consumer not only consumes the motorcycle itself, but also the meaning attached to the bike. Ultimately, the meaning of the product becomes an important part of the consumption experience.[3] The transfer of meaning in the consumption process is illustrated in Exhibit 13.2.

---

to allow faster players to pass slower golfers on the course, the interference with one's usual pace of play distracts from the enjoyment of the experience. Some courses have employees who will even require a group that is playing too slowly to skip a hole. Environmental factors like this influence how much value consumers receive and how satisfied they are with the experience.

CONSUMPTION, MEANING, AND TRANSFERENCE

Consumers' lives are very much intertwined with consumption. Value depends on a process called **meaning transference**. From a utilitarian standpoint, the meaning of consumption is straightforward. Consumers buy shoe polish to polish their shoes. That's easy. What is not as straightforward is the hedonic component of consumption. Here, inner meanings, including cultural meaning, must be considered.

EXHIBIT 13.2
Transfer of Meaning in Consumption

- Culturally defined meaning
- Product, service, experience
- Consumer

Source: McCracken, Grant (1986), "Culture and Consumption: A Theoretical Account of the Structure and Movement of the Cultural Meaning of Consumer Goods," *Journal of Consumer Research*, 13 (1), 71–84.

CONSUMPTION AND EMOTION

Consumers choose products, services, and experiences that they believe will deliver value and satisfy their wants and needs. This implies that anticipated outcomes are considered as a product is selected. Consumers usually hope that the products will be "good" and that their needs will be satisfied.[4] The hopes and desires that consumers have affect the emotions that they feel during consumption. Consumers experience a variety of emotions during the consumption experience, including feelings of pleasure, arousal, joy, disgust, fear, and sadness.[5] The emotional side of consumption is very important because consumers frequently base decisions on emotions rather than on any rational, carefully thought-out criteria. Fantasies, fun, and feelings all are associated with consumption, and these elements of consumption are closely tied to perceived value.[6] That is, consumers receive value not only from the utilitarian aspects of an exchange but also through the hedonic components of consumption.

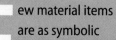

For Better or For Worse

Few material items are as symbolic as the diamond wedding ring. The diamond is a well-known symbol of love and commitment, and diamond rings bring about feelings of love, fulfillment, and excitement for the bride-to-be.

Consumer researchers carefully observed diamond ring sales during the recent economic downturn. What they found was that although the demand for diamonds did fall, the symbolism of the diamond ring ensured that wedding rings would still sell. Of course, people continue to marry whether the economy is good or bad. Many consumers simply turned away from high-end diamonds to less-pricey alternatives.

The demand for diamond rings highlights the importance of product symbolism and the strong impact that emotions have on consumption even during economic hard times. Economic conditions can sour, but diamonds still hold their symbolic meaning. When it comes to marriage, diamonds are still a girl's best friend!

Sources: Barbee, Jeffrey (2009), "Diamonds Are Forever?", GlobalPost, May 13, 2009, online content found at **www.globalpost.com/dispatch/aftrica/090512/diamonds-are-forever.htm**. Mortished, Carl (2009), "Now Cheaper, Are Diamonds Still a Girl's Best Friend", *The Times*, April 11, 2009, p. 49; Greene, Jay (2008), "Blue Nile: A Guy's Best Friend," *Business Week*, June 09, 2008, pg. 39.

> Fantasies, fun, and feelings all are associated with consumption, and these elements of consumption are closely tied to perceived value.

Consumption, value, and satisfaction are closely related concepts. Not surprisingly, consumers tend to be more satisfied with exchanges they find valuable, as value is at the heart of marketing transactions. Value perceptions, therefore, directly influence consumer satisfaction.[7] The relationship between consumption, value, and satisfaction is shown in Exhibit 13.3. However, the link between value and satisfaction is nowhere near perfect, as will be seen later.

EXHIBIT 13.3
Consumption, Value, and Satisfaction

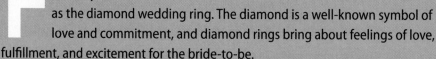

Consumption | Value | Satisfaction

LO2 Value and Satisfaction

Satisfaction is a key variable, and certainly companies should strive to satisfy customers. However, is satisfaction *the* key outcome variable for marketers and consumers? Consider Exhibit 13.4. It plots scores from the ACSI, which is the American Consumer Satisfaction Index. This index plots satisfaction scores for many major companies. This particular chart plots satisfaction for retail companies operating in the United States.

Notice that Kohl's has the highest customer satisfaction ratings over the last four years according to the ACSI. Notice also that Kohl's, JCPenney, Target, and Dillard's all have higher satisfaction ratings than Walmart. However, which retailer is most successful? Has any retailer enjoyed more success than Walmart in recent years? But, as the ACSI shows, Walmart is hardly a leader in satisfaction. In fact, Walmart's satisfaction ratings are the lowest of all listed retailers according to the ACSI. What can explain this? The answer lies in value. Even if Walmart does not provide high customer satisfaction, it does provide leadership in value, particularly the perception that high utilitarian value can be achieved by shopping at Walmart. Thus, Walmart should continue to strive to prioritize value over satisfaction.[8]

The importance of value in the consumption experience cannot be overstated. In fact, value creation is the reason for a firm's very existence.[10] Exhibit 13.3 shows how value comes from the consumption process, and

Scores By Industry
Apparel

	Base-line	95	96	97	98	99	00	01	02	03	04	05	06	07	08*	Previous Year % Change	First Year % Change
Jones Apparel Group, Inc.	NM	NM	NM	NM	NM	NM	NM	79	78	78	77	82	79	81	84	3.7	6.3
VF Corporation	83	80	80	81	79	78	82	84	82	84	79	82	82	84	83	-1.2	0.0
Apparel	82	81	78	77	79	79	79	79	80	80	79	81	80	82	80	-2.4	-2.4
Hanesbrands, Inc.	83	81	75	81	77	78	78	76	78	80	79	79	82	82	80	-2.4	-3.6
All Others	79	80	78	77	79	79	79	79	80	80	79	81	80	82	79	-3.7	0.0
Liz Claiborne, Inc.	84	81	81	77	78	76	79	79	80	78	79	78	81	79	79	0.0	-6.0
Levi Strauss & Co.	84	83	80	81	75	76	79	80	78	80	80	79	79	80	78	-2.5	-7.1
Fruit of the Loom	83	80	78	77	80	80	79	NM	NM	NM	NM	NM	NM	NM	NM	N/A	N/A

*At the end of 2004, ACSI adopted the North American Industry Classification System (NAICS) to replace the Standard Industrial Classification (SIC) for the organization of ACSI measured sectors and industries. The NAICS classification moves the limited-service restaurant industry from the Retail sector, measured in fourth quarter, to the Accommodation & Food Services sector, measured in first quarter. Therefore, the Q4 2004 measurement of the limited-service restaurant industry was delayed until Q1 2005 and the industry will continue to be measured in the first quarter thereafter.

The ACSI for famous apparel brands. Do you agree?

Is satisfaction the key outcome variable for marketers and consumers?

that value, in turn, influences customer satisfaction.[11] As stated in a previous chapter and suggested by the ACSI scores, value is at the heart of consumer behavior, and value can therefore be thought of as the key outcome variable in the consumption experience.[12]

EXHIBIT 13.4
The ACSI Scores for U.S. Retailers[9]

ACSI Scores

- Kohl's Corporation
- J.C. Penney Corporation, Inc.
- Target Corporation
- Dillard's, Inc.
- Macy's, Inc.
- Army and Air Force Exchange Service (AAFES)
- Walmart Stores, Inc.

Customer satisfaction has received much attention from consumer researchers and marketing managers. However, satisfaction is often defined differently by different people and often is confused with numerous closely related concepts, including quality and cognitive dissonance. However, satisfaction is distinct from these concepts. If marketers ever face the decision of providing value or satisfaction, value should be prioritized because, as illustrated by the ACSI, firms can do well even when they do not enjoy the highest industry satisfaction scores, but the firm that does not provide value cannot do well.

Consumer emotions play an important role in influencing behavior.

© PHOTOS.COM/JUPITERIMAGES

© RADIUS IMAGES/JUPITERIMAGES

WHAT IS CONSUMER SATISFACTION?

Consumer satisfaction is a mild, positive emotional state resulting from a favorable appraisal of a consumption outcome. Several points distinguish consumer satisfaction from other important consumer behavior concepts:

- Consumer satisfaction is a postconsumption phenomenon because it is a reaction to an outcome.

- Like other emotions, satisfaction results from a cognitive appraisal. Some refer to this appraisal as the satisfaction judgment.

- Satisfaction is a relatively mild emotion that does not create strong behavioral reactions.

Other key consumer variables like expectations, quality, or attitude are generally more relevant preconsumption or even prepurchase in explaining consumer behavior.[13] Nevertheless, managers consider consumer satisfaction to be important because consumer's word-of-mouth, repeat purchase, and ultimately, consumer loyalty correlate with consumer satisfaction scores. These relationships are discussed in detail in the next chapter.

WHAT IS CONSUMER DISSATISFACTION?

Recall from the material on consumer information processing (CIP) that consumers react quite differently when responding to losses than when responding to gains. Additionally, some debate exists over whether or not low satisfaction necessarily means a consumer has high dissatisfaction. For reasons like these, consumer behavior theory distinguishes consumer dissatisfaction from consumer satisfaction. Therefore, consumer dissatisfaction can be defined as a mild, negative affective reaction resulting from an unfavorable appraisal of a consumption outcome.[14] Even though conceptually dissatisfaction is an opposite concept to satisfaction, the fact that consumers react differently to negative contexts means that dissatisfaction will explain behaviors that satisfaction cannot.

LO3 Other Postconsumption Reactions

although *satisfaction* is often used as a colloquialism for everything that happens after a consumer buys something, many other things, including other emotions, may also occur postconsumption. This view can cause other important postconsumption reactions to be overlooked. Among these are specific emotions, including delight, disgust, surprise, exhilaration, and even anger.[15] These particular emotions are often much more strongly linked to behavior because although they are also emotional reactions to appraisals, they are often much stronger.

An angry consumer exhibits much more noticeable and persistent behavior than does a consumer with low satisfaction. The angry consumer likely complains and sometimes shouts and, in extreme cases, begins boycott initiatives against a company that is the target of anger. A consumer with low satisfaction would not likely exhibit any visible signs of irritation. The particular emotion experienced by consumers will do much to determine the behavioral reaction as we will see in the following chapter when we discuss complaining in more detail.

LO4 Theories of Postconsumption Reactions

EXPECTANCY/DISCONFIRMATION

The most commonly accepted theory of consumer satisfaction is the **expectancy/disconfirmation theory**. The basic disconfirmation model proposes that consumers enter into a consumption experience with predetermined cognitive expectations of a product's performance. These expectations are used as a type of benchmark against which actual performance perceptions are judged.

Disconfirmation becomes central in explaining consumer satisfaction. When performance perceptions are more positive than what was expected, **positive disconfirmation** occurs. Positive disconfirmation leads to consumer satisfaction. When performance perceptions do not meet expectations, meaning performance is less than expected, **negative disconfirmation** occurs. Negative disconfirmation leads to dissatisfaction. Finally, if performance perceptions exactly match what was expected, confirmation (sometimes simply referred to as neutral disconfirmation) is said to occur.

The expectancy disconfirmation approach is shown in Exhibit 13.5. Taken together, disconfirmation represents the cognitive appraisal that produces postconsumption emotions like consumer satisfaction. Using different terminology, disconfirmation is the satisfaction judgment. The blue boxes represent cognitive postconsumption reactions, whereas the green box represents an affective or emotional postconsumption reaction. The relationships between the concepts are explained in the section that follows.

Expectations

Expectations may be thought of as preconsumption beliefs of what will occur during an exchange and/or consumption of a product. Consumer expectations have two components: (1) The probability that something will occur and (2) an evaluation of that potential occurrence.[16] Exhibit 13.5 reveals that expectations also can have a direct impact on satisfaction (by the dotted line), independent of their role in the disconfirmation process.[17] This can occur when the consumer has very little involvement. In these cases, little effort is put into either expectation or performance appraisal, and satisfaction formation is largely impacted by consumer expectations alone. In other words, with low involvement, high expectations will be associated directly with increased satisfaction, and low expectations will be associated directly with increased dissatisfaction.

The same sort of effect can be found with very high involvement. In these cases, balance theory kicks in and consumers may adjust their reactions automatically as a way of protecting themselves from the realization that they may have made a poor choice. When consumers go on Spring Break they may anticipate the

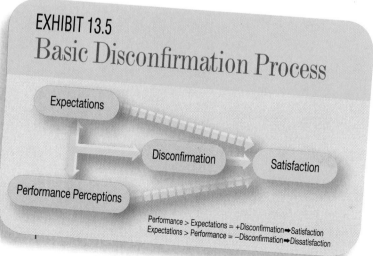

EXHIBIT 13.5
Basic Disconfirmation Process

Expectations → Disconfirmation → Satisfaction

Performance Perceptions

Performance > Expectations = +Disconfirmation→Satisfaction
Expectations > Performance = −Disconfirmation→Dissatisfaction

event so highly that they block out some of the bad things that happen so that their satisfaction reaction adjusts to their preconsumption expectations. Thus, under conditions of very low or very high involvement, expectations can influence satisfaction directly.

Types of Expectations

Consumers bring different types of expectations into a consumption situation.

- **Predictive Expectations.** Expectations that form about what a consumer thinks will actually occur during an experience.
- **Normative Expectations.** Expectations of what a consumer thinks should happen given past experiences with a product or service.
- **Ideal Expectations.** Expectations about what a consumer really wants to happen during an experience if everything were ideal.
- **Equitable Expectations.** Expectations that a consumer forms regarding what he or she thinks should happen given the level of work that he or she has put into the experience.

Source of Expectations

How do consumers form expectations? In other words, what are the sources of information that allow consumers to form expectations? In reality, consumers form expectations based on a number of different sources.[18] Word-of-mouth communication from other consumers is an important source of information. When a close friend tells you that a new television show is good, you'll probably expect it to be good. A consumer's experience also influences expectations. If you've gone to a dentist who was caring and respectful of your feelings, then you would expect

the same kind of treatment during the next visit. Explicit promises such as advertisements and promotions create consumer expectations as well. If a company promises that it will deliver a package within two days, you expect that the package will indeed be delivered! Personal factors also influence expectations. Some people simply expect more out of products and services than do others. Perhaps you know people who expect restaurant meals to be perfect or flights to arrive on time in any conditions. Here, personal factors influence the expectations that they have about the service.

Expectation Confidence and Performance Perceptions

The disconfirmation approach seems to be relatively straightforward; however, the processes behind the approach can be complex. This is especially true given the roles of performance perceptions, expectation confidence, and the "confirmatory bias."

Performance Perceptions

Recall that perception plays a very important role in consumer behavior. "Perception *is* reality!" Marketers are well aware of this. Perception directly influences how a consumer interacts with the world.

Perception is also very important for the consumption and postconsumption processes. As is the case with expectations, performance perceptions can also directly influence consumer satisfaction formation independent of the disconfirmation process (dotted line in Exhibit 13.5). This is particularly the case when expectations are low. For example, if a consumer buys a brand of product that he or she knows will be bad, expectations are likely to be low. Even if these low expectations are met by performance perceptions, the consumer is likely to be dissatisfied. Also, if a consumer has no previous experience or expectation regarding a product (for example, a new product), then perceptions can directly influence satisfaction.[19]

Marketers may think twice about setting expectations too firmly among consumers. Domino's Pizza once emphasized the 30-minute delivery guarantee for their pizzas. Consumers then began to expect this performance so strongly that they became very dissatisfied when the expectation was not met, so much so that the drivers became hazards on the road in an effort to meet the

Consumers have many types of expectations.

30-minute deadline. In the end, Domino's had to back off the guarantee to avoid legal liability for accidents incurred by drivers who could easily be accused of driving recklessly in an effort to meet the 30-minute promise.

Confidence in Expectations and the Confirmatory Bias

Another issue that is important in satisfaction theory is the degree to which consumers are confident in their expectations. For example, if a complete stranger tells a consumer that a movie is good, the consumer may not be very confident in his or her expectations. However, if a family member tells the consumer that a movie is good, then the consumer might feel much more confident in expecting the movie to be good. Research has indicated that when expectations are held with a strong degree of confidence, both disconfirmation and performance perceptions affect satisfaction. However, when expectations are not held with a strong degree of confidence, perceived performance more strongly influences satisfaction.[20]

Not only do expectations play a key role in satisfaction formation, they also can affect how consumers see things. That is, expectations can affect performance perceptions.[21] Imagine a student who goes into a class thinking, "This class is going to be really bad!" There is a tendency for an expectation like this to actually alter his or her perception of the class experience. If the student thinks it's going to be bad, he or she may very well look for evidence to support this expectation! The term to explain this phenomenon is **confirmatory bias**. The confirmatory bias works in conjunction with self-perception theory. **Self-perception theory** states that consumers are motivated to act in accordance with their attitudes and behaviors. Here, consumers are motivated to perceive their environment through the lens of their expectations. The confirmatory influence of expectations on perceptions is especially strong when consumers are quite confident in what to expect.[22]

Expectations and Service Quality

Service quality can be thought of as the overall goodness or badness of a service provided. Service quality is often discussed as the difference between consumer expectations of different service aspects and the actual service that is delivered. When a gap exists, for example, when a dental hygienist is not as empathetic as a consumer expected, then quality perceptions are diminished. In fact, the **SERVQUAL** scale, a commonly applied approach for measuring service quality, takes this approach. From this perspective, service quality is really a disconfirmation approach.[23] Perhaps it goes without saying, but service quality then becomes a key driver of consumer satisfaction or dissatisfaction.

Desires and Satisfaction

Although expectations play a major role in satisfaction formation, consumer desires are also very important. **Desires** are the level of a particular benefit that will lead to a valued end state. Studies have shown that desires directly impact satisfaction, beyond the influence of disconfirmation alone.[26] What consumers truly desire, rather than expect, from a product, service, or experience is therefore very important.

Emotions, Meaning, and Satisfaction

As discussed earlier, emotions and meaning play important roles in consumption. These elements are also an important part of satisfaction formation. Positive emotions that consumers feel while shopping can influence

confirmatory bias tendency for expectations to guide performance perceptions

self-perception theory theory that states that consumers are motivated to act in accordance with their attitudes and behaviors

service quality overall goodness or badness of a service experience, which is often measured by SERVQUAL

SERVQUAL way of measuring service quality that captures consumers' disconfirmation of service expectations

desires level of a particular benefit that will lead to a valued end state

J.D. Power and Associates measures customer satisfaction with numerous products and services based on feedback from consumers who have owned or used the products or service—here, ratings for small business banking are shown.

equity theory theory that proposes that people compare their own level of inputs and outcomes to those of another party in an exchange

overall product satisfaction.[27] This is true of the consumption of products, services, and experiences. If a consumer is in a bad mood when he or she goes to a restaurant, overall satisfaction with the experience will likely be affected in a mood-congruent direction. Furthermore, the meaning behind the meal contributes to satisfaction as well. For example, perhaps that meal is one with a loved one, or a business meal that will be used to seal an important business agreement. Here, the overall satisfaction with the meal would be affected by the meaning of the consumption experience, independently of prior expectations or perceptions. An interpretive study of river-rafting consumers revealed that the emotions that consumers felt while consuming the experience were strongly related to the value they experienced during the trip.[28]

How are the emotions of river-rafting consumers related to the value they experience during the trip?

EQUITY THEORY AND CONSUMER SATISFACTION

Perceptions of fairness can also have an impact on consumer satisfaction. **Equity theory** proposes that consumers cognitively compare their own level of inputs and outcomes to those of another party in an exchange.[29] Equitable exchanges occur when these ratios are equal. In equation form:

$$outcomes_A/inputs_A \approx outcomes_B/inputs_B$$

The equation states that as long as comparisons of outcomes to inputs for consumer A are approximately the same as the same ratio for another party (for example, a company or another consumer), then satisfaction will be positively affected. So, an inequitable exchange can occur when a consumer believes that he or she has been taken advantage of by a company or when another customer has been treated more favorably.

When a consumer sets out to buy a computer, she will put quite a bit of effort into finding just the right one. She will take time to visit a store such as Best Buy, talk with friends about what brand to buy, visit websites such as **Dell.com**, and try to figure out the best way to finance the computer. All of these efforts are considered inputs into the transaction. What will the consumer get when she buys the computer? Of course, she will get a computer, but she will also get a warranty, service contract, and maybe even in-home installation. These things represent her outcomes.

The computer salesperson should put time into understanding the consumer's desires and the way she will use the computer and then try to match these with a good arrangement of product features. Perhaps the salesperson will show effort by listening and physically searching store inventory for the most appropriate product. These are inputs for the salesperson. Salesperson outcomes include a salary and any commission tied directly to the sale. When consumers put a lot into an important purchase, they don't like to be shortchanged by an apathetic employee. That wouldn't be fair, and the output-to-input ratios would reflect this. Fairness perceptions affect satisfaction in addition to any influence of disconfirmation.[30]

Inequitable Treatment

Perhaps more often, equity perceptions involve inequitable treatment of customers. A single customer enters a restaurant for lunch and puts in an order. A few minutes later, a couple enters and sits beside the first customer at the next table. They place their order. After ten minutes, the couple receives their food and the original customer is still waiting. To the original customer, this may seem unfair and be a source of dissatisfaction. Thus, service providers need to be keenly aware of how customers are treated in public to maintain perceptions that all customers are treated in much the same way—or at least treated in a fair way.

The idea of "no charge" could increase a consumer's perceptions of equity by creating the perception of getting something for nothing.

Inequitable Consumers

Some consumers will try to take advantage of situations. Even though treatment is inequitable, if the inequity is in the consumers' favor, these particular customers may be very satisfied. For example, some consumers may take a minor mishap and complain so fiercely that managers feel compelled to offer something overly generous as a way of calming the consumer down. Other consumers may realize that a cashier has made a significant error and given them significantly too much change and not correct the mistake. These consumers may be satisfied because the equity balance favors them. However, their actions can sometimes disadvantage other consumers.

ATTRIBUTION THEORY AND CONSUMER SATISFACTION

Another approach to satisfaction can be found in attribution theory. **Attribution theory** focuses on explaining why a certain event has occurred. When consumers select and consume products, they are motivated to make attributions as to why good or bad things happen. Humans are innately curious. There are three key ele-

ments to the attribution theory approach: *locus*, *control*, and *stability*.[31]

- **Locus.** Judgments of who is responsible for an event. Consumers can assign the locus to themselves or to an external entity like a service provider. A self-ascribed event occurs when a consumer blames himself or herself for a bad event. For example, a consumer might say to himself, "I took way too long between oil changes, it's no wonder that my engine blew up!" Self-ascribed causes are referred to as internal attributions. If an event is attributed to a product or company, an external attribution is made. For example, a consumer might say, "I changed my oil regularly! It's not my fault that the engine blew up! Chrysler is still turning out junk!" This type of attribution of blame toward a marketing entity increases consumer dissatisfaction.

- **Control.** The extent to which an outcome was controllable or not. Here, consumers ask themselves, "Should this company have been able to control this event?" Two consumers are stranded

> **attribution theory**
> theory that proposes that consumers look for the cause of particular consumption experiences when arriving at satisfaction judgments

When service breakdowns occur, consumers make all kinds of attributions.

cognitive dissonance
an uncomfortable feeling that occurs when a consumer has lingering doubts about a decision that has occurred

in the Frankfurt, Germany, airport overnight because their destination airport, Dallas Fort Worth, is iced over. One consumer is irate (beyond dissatisfaction) with the airline because he believes the airline should have equipment to clear the ice off the runway—even in the southern part of the country. Another consumer who is booked on the same flight is not happy about the situation but does not blame the airline because she understands that weather events are uncontrollable. Therefore, the situation does not significantly affect her satisfaction process.

- **Stability.** The likelihood that an event will occur again in the future. Here, consumers ask themselves, "If I buy this product again, is another bad outcome likely to happen?" Let's briefly return to the Frankfurt airport example. If a customer has recently been stranded because of weather problems in Dallas on occasions other than the recent ice storm, he naturally comes to believe that this is a stable situation and his satisfaction with the airline will be diminished. On the other hand, if the other consumer has never before been stranded due to problems at the Dallas airport, her satisfaction with the airline is not likely to be affected by the current situation.

> Dissonance has also been responsible for more than a few cold feet in the days before a wedding day.

COGNITIVE DISSONANCE

Consumers also can experience what is known as cognitive dissonance following a purchase or a big decision. As was discussed with the balance theory approach, consumers prefer consistency among their beliefs. When faced with the knowledge that a bad decision may have been made, consumers experience dissonance (literally meaning "lack of agreement") between the thought that they are a good decision maker and that they made a bad decision. **Cognitive dissonance** refers to lingering doubts about a decision that has already been made.[32] Dissonance is sometimes known as buyer's regret. For example, a consumer may reach a decision to buy one house and then experience

discomfort due to doubt that creeps in when the consumer realizes there were many other attractive houses available in addition to the one purchased.

Cognitive dissonance does not occur for all decisions. For high ticket items like automobiles or homes though, dissonance is a real possibility if not a probability. Dissonance has also been responsible for more than a few cold feet in the days before a wedding day. These are situations that naturally lend themselves to the experience of dissonance. A consumer is more likely to experience true dissonance following a purchase when the following conditions exist:

1. The consumer is aware that there are many attractive alternatives that may offer comparable value relative to the product/brand purchased.

2. The decision is difficult to reverse.

3. The decision is important and involves risk.

4. The consumer has low self-confidence.

The dissonance among consumers' beliefs following a consumption experience can be very discomforting and be a source of negative postconsumption emotions. Consumers may therefore be motivated to lessen this discomfort. Furthermore, effective marketing can target consumers after purchase to take steps to reinforce their customers' decisions to select a brand. Many universities automatically send graduates university-sponsored magazines in order to maintain relationships and to reinforce the idea that choosing the school was indeed a good idea.

To lessen feelings of discomfort following purchase, consumers may engage in any, or all, of the activities listed in Exhibit 13.6.

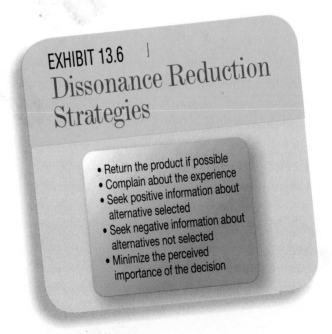

EXHIBIT 13.6
Dissonance Reduction Strategies

- Return the product if possible
- Complain about the experience
- Seek positive information about alternative selected
- Seek negative information about alternatives not selected
- Minimize the perceived importance of the decision

Cognitive Dissonance and Satisfaction

Satisfaction and cognitive dissonance are closely related topics. The major difference between the two concepts is that satisfaction is generally felt *after* a consumption experience but dissonance may be experienced even *before* consumption begins. For example, after a decision has been made, a consumer might immediately think, "I should have bought the other one!" Note that this reaction is often based on the uncertainty of events that might occur.[33]

LO5 Consumer Satisfaction / Dissatisfaction Measurement Issues

there are many ways that marketers can measure consumer satisfaction. Three popular ways are through direct measures, difference scores, and disconfirmation.

- **Direct, Global Measure.** Simply asks consumers to assess their satisfaction on a scale such as:

  How do you rate your overall satisfaction with your television?

  completely dissatisfied — dissatisfied — satisfied — completely satisfied
  ☐ ☐ ☐ ☐

- **Attribute-Specific.** Assesses a consumer's satisfaction with various components, or attributes, of a product, service, or experience, such as:

  How satisfied are you with the following attribute of your television?

  Picture Quality

  completely dissatisfied   completely satisfied
  1   2   3   4   5

- **Disconfirmation.** Compares the difference between expectations and performance perceptions. This measure can be taken in a direct, subjective fashion, such as:[24]

  Compared to my expectations, this television performs . . .

  much worse than I expected   much better than I expected
  1   2   3   4   5

IMPROVING SATISFACTION MEASURES

Satisfaction is one of the most commonly measured concepts in consumer behavior but is also one of the most difficult to measure accurately. For example, the typical four-choice satisfaction approach as is shown in the direct global measure example actually proves quite problematic in practice. The problems can be severe and limit the ability to use satisfaction ratings to explain or predict other outcomes including whether or not the consumer will return.

Consider that marketers measure satisfaction among existing customers most frequently. These customers have already decided to patronize a business. So, a web pop-up for **Amazon.com** may ask a consumer to rate satisfaction with a simple measure of this type. This consumer should already be favorable because he or she has decided to purposefully visit **Amazon.com** and shop using this site. Thus, he or she already feels favorable toward **Amazon.com**. Therefore, we would expect even without knowing what happened during the visit that the customer would report some degree of satisfaction. In fact, typical consumer responses to this type of measure show that the vast majority of consumers, 80% or more, choose "satisfied" or "completely satisfied." Statistically speaking, these data are **left skewed**, in this instance meaning that the bulk of consumers have indicated that they are satisfied or completely satisfied with the product or service.

Does this reflect reality, or is the scale simply inadequate in truly differentiating consumers experiencing different levels of satisfaction? The truth is that both possibilities are likely true to some extent. From a measurement perspective, giving consumers more choices to respond to may increase the amount of variance displayed in the satisfaction measure and thereby increase its usefulness in trying to use satisfaction to predict and explain other behaviors. An alternative would be to have consumers score their satisfaction on a 0 (no satisfaction) to 100 (complete satisfaction) point scale. The results will still typically show an average satisfaction score above 50 points; however, the statistical properties are much improved, making for a more useful measure. Even better, a researcher might have a respondent rate his or her satisfaction with multiple scale items.

left skewed distribution of responses consistent with most respondents choosing responses such that the distribution is not evenly spread among responses but clustered toward the positive end of the scale

consumer refuse any packaging that is no longer necessary for consumption to take place or, in some cases, the actual good that is no longer providing value to the consumer

Exhibit 13.7 displays an improved way of measuring consumer satisfaction using multiple scale items. The scale mitigates problems with skewness and/or bias by providing scales with more response points and by using different response formats for each response item. The scale also focuses only on satisfaction. Although a marketer may choose to measure only satisfaction, this scale suggests that dissatisfaction should be measured with its own scale. A dissatisfaction scale can be formed by substituting the word *dissatisfaction* for satisfaction in each of the four items. Even if a total of eight items are used (four satisfaction and four dissatisfaction items), a consumer can typically respond to these items in less than one minute. The question of whether or not dissatisfaction is more than just low satisfaction can be sorted out statistically. That topic is left for another course.

LO6 Disposing of Refuse

DISPOSAL DECISIONS

A final step in consumption is disposal of any consumer refuse. **Consumer refuse** is any packaging that is no longer necessary for consumption to take place or, in some cases, the actual good that is no longer providing value to the consumer. Many consumers have old computers that they no longer use but have not yet disposed of because of various concerns including security issues. At first, this may seem like a straightforward pro-

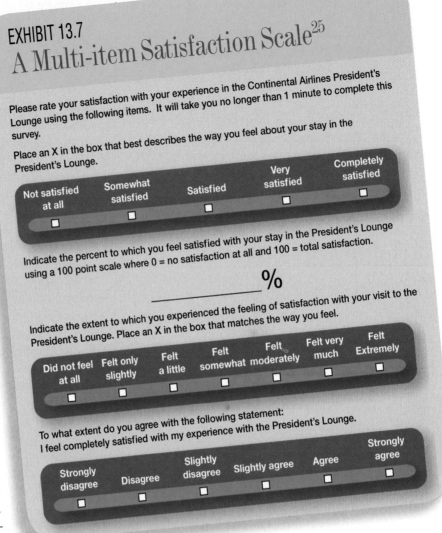

EXHIBIT 13.7
A Multi-item Satisfaction Scale[25]

Please rate your satisfaction with your experience in the Continental Airlines President's Lounge using the following items. It will take you no longer than 1 minute to complete this survey.

Place an X in the box that best describes the way you feel about your stay in the President's Lounge.

| Not satisfied at all | Somewhat satisfied | Satisfied | Very satisfied | Completely satisfied |

Indicate the percent to which you feel satisfied with your stay in the President's Lounge using a 100 point scale where 0 = no satisfaction at all and 100 = total satisfaction.

_____ %

Indicate the extent to which you experienced the feeling of satisfaction with your visit to the President's Lounge. Place an X in the box that matches the way you feel.

| Did not feel at all | Felt only slightly | Felt a little | Felt somewhat | Felt moderately | Felt very much | Felt Extremely |

To what extent do you agree with the following statement:
I feel completely satisfied with my experience with the President's Lounge.

| Strongly disagree | Disagree | Slightly disagree | Slightly agree | Agree | Strongly agree |

cess wherein the consumer simply throws away their trash. However, a number of disposal alternatives are available. These include trashing, recycling, converting to another use, trading, donating, or reselling.[34]

- **Trashing.** One alternative that a consumer has is to simply throw away waste material including unused products, packaging, and by-products. Of course, there are environmental concerns with this alternative. According to the Environmental Protection Agency (EPA), approximately 254 million tons of municipal garbage is generated each year, or an average of 4.6 pounds of garbage per person, per day![35] Many marketers have turned to so-called green marketing initiatives, which aim to use packaging materials that cut down on the environmental impact of waste.

- **Recycling.** Another alternative for consumers is to recycle used products or packaging. Recycling cuts down on

Buy, Sell, and Trade the Online Way

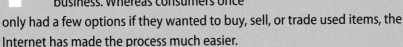

From **eBay.com** to **Craigslist.com** to **Kijiji.com**, online buying, selling, and trading has become a huge business. Whereas consumers once only had a few options if they wanted to buy, sell, or trade used items, the Internet has made the process much easier.

Of course, the Internet phenomenon eBay has long been the benchmark in the online trading world. The Internet giant that is well-known for allowing consumers to auction off their belongings in an online marketplace has been wildly successful for several years. Rival **Craigslist.com**, which focuses on online classified advertising, has also experienced rapid growth, and the site currently accounts for over 90% of online classified listing traffic. Not to be outdone, eBay's **Kijiji.com**, which also focuses on online classified advertising, is becoming a major player in the growing industry.

Thanks to sites such as these, consumers can now auction their products, place classified ads online, or simply browse local pages for good deals. The ease and availability of these sites are rapidly changing how consumers buy and sell goods and, ultimately, how consumers interact with one another.

Sources: Fowler, Geoffrey A. (2009), "Auctions Fade in eBay's Bid for Growth," *Wall Street Journal (online)*, May 26, 2009, pg. A1, accessed June 15, 2009; MacMilliam, Douglas (2009), "Craigslist Fuels Online Classified-Ad Surge," *BusinessWeek (online)*, New York: May 25, 2009, accessed June 15, 2009; Dell, Kristina (2008), "eBay Bids for Revitalization," *Time (online)*, 172 (25), December 22, 2008, pg. G1, accessed June 15, 2009.

garbage while providing raw materials for other new products. Consumers can then buy new products made of recycled materials.

- **Converting.** Consumers can convert products, or product packaging, into new products in a number of creative ways. For example, consumers often use old t-shirts and socks as car-wash rags. Of course, consumers know many uses for old products!

- **Trading.** Another alternative for consumers is to trade in old products for new products. The automotive industry has encouraged this practice for years. Consumers can often get thousands of dollars off of a new automobile purchase by trading in an old model. Even a car that doesn't run has some value in the form of spare parts.

- **Donating.** Consumers also have the ability to donate used products to various causes. Eyeglasses, clothing, and (surprisingly) automobiles are often donated in order to help other consumers who may not be able to afford new products.

- **Reselling.** One of the most popular methods for permanently disposing of used products is to simply sell them. Garage sales and swap meets are popular means of disposing of products in this way. Of course, online methods such as eBay and Craigslist are also quite popular with consumers.

DISPOSAL, EMOTIONS, AND PRODUCT SYMBOLISM

Consumers often develop emotional bonds with their possessions. As discussed in an earlier chapter, possessions can help express a consumer's self-concept. The decision to part with belongings can therefore be very emotional, especially for older consumers who place much symbolic value on many products.[36] Strong feelings of attachment may be placed on many goods, especially those goods that are considered to be family heirlooms. Selling, giving away, or donating these goods can lead consumers to feel as if they have lost a part of themselves. In other situations, consumers can be quite ready to dispose of products that bring back bad memories, or that lead the consumers to have uneasy feelings about themselves or their past.[37]

Some consumers are very reluctant to part ways with their possessions. The term *packrat* is used to describe a person who keeps possessions that fulfill no utilitarian or hedonic need and who have a difficult time disposing of products. Packrats are likely to visit garage sales, swap meets, and flea markets to purchase products that serve no immediate need.[38] Even though the term *packrat* is often used loosely, the packrat behavior can be associated with various psychological conditions including obsessive–compulsive disorder.

Chapter 13 Case

According to eBay's report of its 2006 financial results, it had approximately $6 billion in revenue in 2006, up nearly 33% from 2005. The total value of all successful auctions was a record $52 billion. eBay has grown faster than any other company in history, including Microsoft, Dell, and Walmart. Some 72 million active users bought and sold merchandise on eBay in 2005, and this number increased to 82 million in 2006, an increase of nearly 14% in one year. If eBay was a brick-and-mortar retailer, rather than the world's largest on-line marketplace, it would be larger than Best Buy and Lowe's.

Consumers are increasingly discovering the value of utilizing eBay to obtain items more inexpensively, more conveniently, and so on. As the economy continues to be in a state of flux and consumers are uncertain about such things as gas prices and the future of interest rates, they will likely continue to turn to eBay as an alternative means of obtaining the items they seek. Consumers purchase anything from clothing to automobiles on eBay. In fact, they are shopping for more than 100 million items that are available for sale on eBay every day. With such numbers in an e-tailing environment, customer satisfaction is a major concern for eBay. Finding ways to both assess customer satisfaction and deal with customer dissatisfaction is an ongoing problem for the company.

One tool eBay has established is a rating system. The rating system operates by each party of a transaction (buyer and seller) rating each other. Most eBay participants rate soon after the transaction is completed. For example, a buyer will normally rate the seller as soon as the purchased item is received and a cursory examination is accomplished to ensure the item is as described in the eBay auction. The seller, then, upon receiving the feedback from the buyer, knows the item arrived at its destination and considers the transaction to be complete, so he or she then rates the buyer. The parts of the consumption process that are evaluated in these ratings are whether the buyer pays for the item soon after winning the auction, whether the seller ships the item in a timely manner and adequately protects the item in the shipping process, and whether the product is as represented, usually after only a quick and not in-depth examination.

This rating, or "feedback," system is really just a tool for buyers and sellers to help them determine whether or not to trust the other participant before engaging in a transaction. eBay has the opportunity to use the information generated by this feedback system; however, it is common knowledge among eBay users that the feedback is grossly inflated. In order to avoid negative ratings from others, both buyers and sellers often give only positive feedback, even though the transaction did not go well.

Many consumers like to shop for a product. Shopping may include visiting several stores, trying out the product, trying on clothing, and socializing with shopping partners. The consumption situation and experience are important determinants of consumer satisfaction, and many of these shopping consumers are seeking the specific situation and experiences that shopping can bring. When consumers shop on eBay, however, the shopping experience is totally different. The possibility of trying on clothing, for example, is completely nonexistent. Rarely do eBay shoppers socialize with shopping partners while finding and bidding on eBay items. Because of these factors, eBay focuses on making this online shopping experience as positive as possible.

Despite these efforts, eBay's ACSI is only a B−, and it decreased in the last year. Look at the table for details. In fact, according to the ACSI, customer satisfaction was the same in 2006 for eBay as it was in 2000. Part of the reason for less-than-satisfactory customer satisfaction may be due to the fact that consumers cannot see and inspect the product before purchasing it. Most sellers provide pictures of the products they are selling, but the quality of these pictures varies, and the possibility of consumer prepurchase actions, such as trying on shoes and clothing, just cannot be provided. Thus, consumers face a greater risk getting something different than expected.

Company Name	ACSI SCORES BY YEAR						
	2000	2001	2002	2003	2004	2005	2006
Amazon.com	84	84	88	88	84	87	87
eBay Inc.	*80*	*82*	*82*	*84*	*80*	*81*	*80*
E*TRADE	66	66	69	71	70	71	74
Expedia, Inc.	NA	NA	80	78	76	79	78
Google Inc.	NA	NA	80	82	82	82	81
uBid.com	67	69	70	73	73	73	74
Yahoo! Inc.	74	73	76	78	78	80	76

Questions

1. Does eBay assess the entire consumption process of its consumers? Why or why not? Suggest different methods for assessing consumer satisfaction that may be useful in eBay's case.

2. How does the consumption situation differ between eBay consumers and consumers at brick-and-mortar retailers?

3. How much did the ACSI score for eBay change from 2005 to 2006, by percentage? What is the significance of these scores and changes, as compared to other large Internet companies represented in the table?

4. Use the website for the ACSI scores (**www.theacsi.org**), to find out how the scores for eBay compare with brick-and-mortar retailers, such as Kohl's, J.C. Penney, Target, Dillard's, Macy's, Nordstrom, and Walmart. Explain your findings.

5. According to the expectancy/disconfirmation theory, what could be one of the problems eBay faces in attempting to increase its consumer satisfaction?

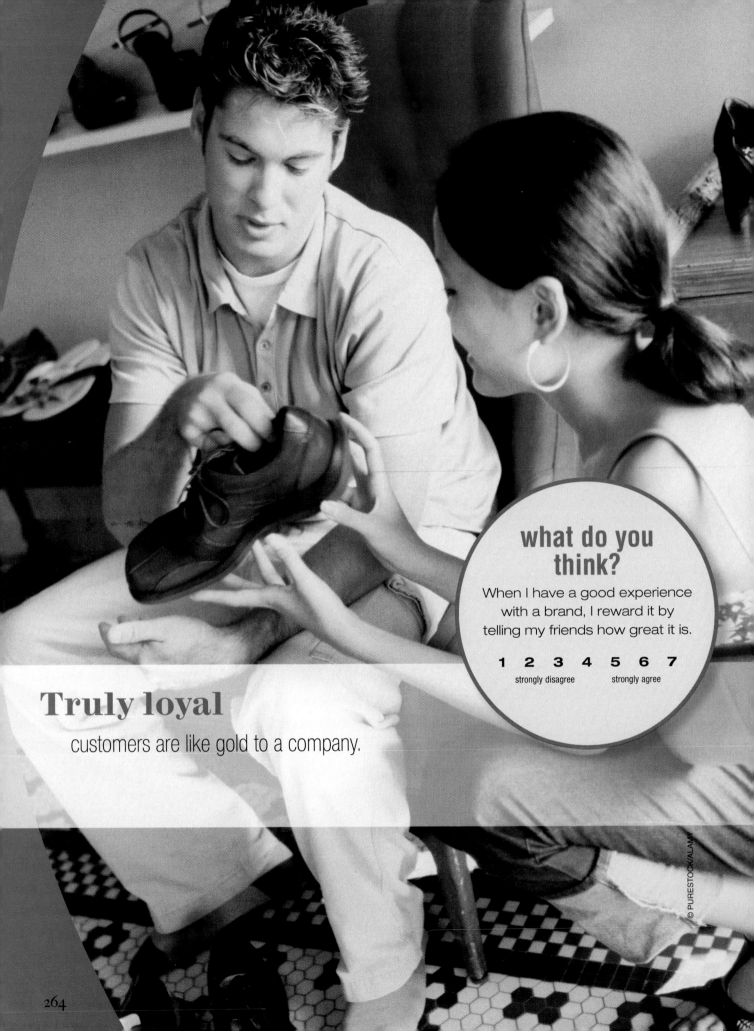

what do you think?

When I have a good experience with a brand, I reward it by telling my friends how great it is.

1 2 3 4 5 6 7

strongly disagree   strongly agree

Truly loyal

customers are like gold to a company.

14

Consumer Relationships

LO1 Outcomes of Consumption

t he previous chapter focused significantly on customer satisfaction/dissatisfaction. Many companies have satisfaction guarantees: *100% Satisfaction or Your Money Back!*

Assuming that marketers' motivations for such guarantees are well intentioned, are companies really interested in satisfaction? If consumers could not return to do business again, the pursuit of satisfaction would be relegated to a purely altruistic exercise. Many firms might lose interest in serving customers well if this were the case. However, firms are interested in what happens after a consumer is satisfied or dissatisfied because they would like customers to return to do business again. Thus, this chapter picks up where the previous chapter left off. Here, the focus is squarely on postconsumption reactions—the things that happen after a consumer has received most consumption benefits.

Exhibit 14.1 expands the disconfirmation framework traditionally used to explain consumer satisfaction. This particular chart divides up the different concepts into three groups. The green color variables represent things that are predominantly cognitive. These include the actual disconfirmation formation process that results from comparing actual performance with expected performance. Additionally, consumer's attribution and equity cognitions are also included among cognitions.

Postconsumption cognitions lead to an affective reaction that most conventionally is represented by consumer satisfaction/dissatisfaction (CS/D). This particular model recognizes that the evaluation process could lead to any number of varying affective outcomes, many of which have stronger behavioral reactions than CS/D. The affective variables are shown in blue in the exhibit.

Finally, the exhibit shows behavioral outcomes of the postconsumption process in red boxes. Indeed, this is why marketers are interested in pursuing satisfaction. The behaviors that complete this process do much to determine the success or failure of competitive enterprises. Never has this been more true than in today's relationship marketing era. While the negative behaviors like complaining perhaps receive more attention as reactions to consumption, positive outcomes, including positive word-of-mouth behavior and ultimately the development of a strong relationship, are essential elements to success.

We begin this chapter by looking at some common behaviors that follow consumption. Exhibit 14.1 lists the behaviors; and although all but the last, loyalty, may seem negative, if properly managed the firm can turn these negative behaviors into positive value experiences. When this is done, customers are more likely to become loyal, and loyalty is the positive outcome relationship-oriented firms seek.

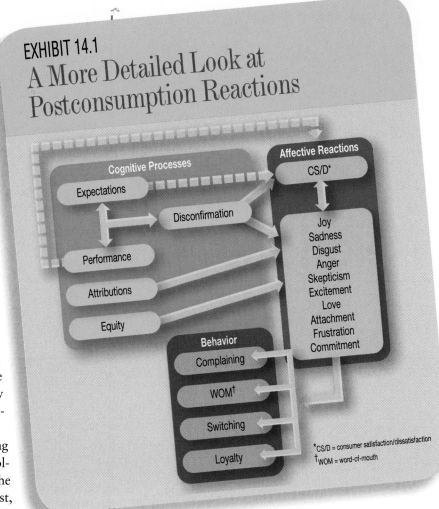

EXHIBIT 14.1
A More Detailed Look at Postconsumption Reactions

*CS/D = consumer satisfaction/dissatisfaction
†WOM = word-of-mouth

LO2 Complaining and Spreading WOM
COMPLAINING BEHAVIOR

Complaining behavior occurs when a consumer actively seeks out someone to share an opinion with regarding a negative consumption event. The person may be a service provider, a supervisor, or someone designated by a company to take complaints. Think about this question:

How long should a consumer have to wait for service before complaining?

The answer to this may depend on several factors, including the type of service involved. A 30-minute wait may be unacceptable and evoke negative disconfirmation, a negative affective consequence, and an active complaint if a consumer is waiting to be served for lunch. However, a consumer waiting to see a doctor for 30 minutes may not experience the same reaction because the expectation is that one will wait for 30 minutes or more. Even if one waits longer than expected to see a doctor, the consumer still may not complain for other reasons.

Complainers

Generally, we think of dissatisfied customers as complainers. Not all customers reporting dissatisfaction complain. In fact, far less than half of customers experiencing some dissatisfaction complain to management. Only 17% of healthcare consumers complain upon experiencing some problem with the service or care they are receiving, and a recent survey among restaurant consumers suggests that no more than 5% of consumers with a problem complain.[1] What makes a *complainer* different? Consumers who do complain react with different emotions than do those who do not complain. In contrast to consumers who are merely dissatisfied, consumers who experience anger in response to an evaluation of the consumption experience are very likely to complain.[2]

A potentially worse outcome for a business occurs when a consumer has a negative experience, realizes this, and then reacts more with disgust than anger. Compared to the angry customer, a disgusted or hopeless consumer is not likely to complain.[3] Consumers' behavioral reactions can be understood by considering whether the emotions they experience evoke approach or avoidance reactions. Negative approach emotions like anger are most likely to precede complaining behavior.

The consumer who reacts with disgust is very unlikely to complain. Disgust evokes an avoidance response, and as a result, a disgusted consumer avoids a potential confrontation and simply goes away. When the disgusted consumer simply goes away, the information that caused the problem in the first place also goes away. Complainers, although sometimes unpleasant to deal with, are valuable sources of feedback about potential problems in service quality, product performance, or system malfunction.

When a consumer complains, the marketer has a chance to rectify the negative situation. A consumer that sulks away takes the valuable information with him or her. A truly consumer-oriented company should encourage customers to complain when things go wrong. If "100% satisfaction" is not just a slogan, the company must encourage its customers to act like whistle blowers when something goes wrong. In this sense, an angry customer is not the worst possible outcome for a business!

> Actively listening to the complaints of annoyed customers can lead to greatly improved service.

The company must encourage its customers to act like whistle blowers when something goes wrong ... an angry customer is not the worst possible outcome for a business.

The Result of Complaining

Exhibit 14.2 provides a summary of what happens when consumers do or do not complain. The fact of the matter is that for consumers as well as marketers, complaining pays off. When consumers complain, more often than not, some corrective action is taken that culminates with the consumer feeling satisfied when he or she reevaluates the situation. A consumer who complains

EXHIBIT 14.2
The Complainer versus the Noncomplainer and Negative Word-of-Mouth

© PHOTODISC RF/GETTY IMAGES/NEWSCOM

- More likely to become a satisfied customer
- More likely to return
- Tells others when company responds poorly
- Valuable source of information

© MARCIO EUGENIO/ SHUTTERSTOCK

- Unlikely to return
- May well tell others about experience
- Can become a satisfied customer if firm can take preemptive action despite the lack of a complaint

about a noisy hotel room gets moved to another room, perhaps a suite! In such a case, the customer is likely to believe that he or she was treated fairly after complaining, and these thoughts evoke a more positive outcome. This positive outcome can represent a win–win situation.

Earlier, we mentioned that only about 5% of restaurant customers with a service problem actually complained to management. However, among those who complained, 95% were likely to remain customers of the restaurant when their complaint was handled quickly and responsively. The following list gives service providers advice for handling consumer complaints effectively:[4]

1. Thank the guest for providing the information.

2. Ask questions to clarify the issue.

3. Apologize sincerely.

4. Show empathy for the customer's situation.

5. Explain the corrective action that will take place.

6. Act quickly.

7. Follow up with the customer after the corrective action.

The Result of Not Complaining

So, what happens when the consumer does not complain? Let's return to the noisy hotel room. A customer may simply put up with the inconvenience and end up leaving miserable after a poor night's sleep. Is this the end of the story? Not really! The consumer may well remember this incident and be less likely to do business

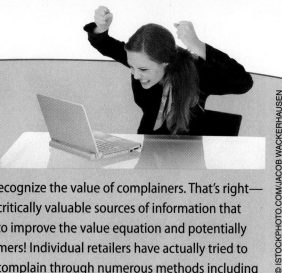

Complaining Made Easy!

Marketers should recognize the value of complainers. That's right—complainers are critically valuable sources of information that allow marketers to improve the value equation and potentially benefit all consumers! Individual retailers have actually tried to make it easier for consumers to complain through numerous methods including a lenient return policy. Although this policy may increase costs to retailers, the benefit is increased intelligence and the opportunity to turn a negative value experience for consumers into a positive value experience. Today it's easier than ever for consumers to complain publicly. Check out websites like these:

- **www.complaints.com**
- **http://esupport.fcc.gov/complaints.htm**
- **http://www.bbb.org/**

These websites allow consumers to lodge formal complaints, make their complaints public, and get advice on the proper steps to follow should the consumer need to take further official action. Even customers who have a strong relationship with a company will complain, and particularly when a customer believes the firm could've responded to the situation better, complaining can even become retaliation. So, it's best to deal with complaints sooner rather than later.

Sources: Huppertz, J.W. (2007), "Firms' Complaint Handling Policies and Consumer Complaint Voicing," *Journal of Consumer Marketing*, 24 (July), 428-437. Gregoire, Y. and R. Fisher (2006), "The Effects of Relationship Quality on Customer Retaliation," *Marketing Letters*, 17 (1), 31-46.

with this hotel again. He or she may also tell others about the episode. Interestingly, though, when marketers can take action to address a negative situation before a consumer complains, a very positive outcome can result. So, imagine that a bell clerk reports the noise in one of the halls of the hotel to management. Management then takes action by calling the adjacent rooms to suggest that they move to a better room. These customers are likely to be very appreciative and become more likely to return again.[5]

WORD-OF-MOUTH

Just because a consumer doesn't complain to the offending company doesn't mean he or she just keeps the episode inside. **Negative word-of-mouth** (negative

WOM) takes place when consumers pass on negative information about a company from one to another. As can be seen from Exhibit 14.2, both the complainer and the noncomplainer may well participate in this kind of potentially destructive behavior. Some estimates suggest that a consumer who fails to achieve a valuable consumption experience is likely to tell his or her story to more than ten other consumers.[6] Recall that as a source of information, WOM is powerful because of relatively high source credibility. The fact that most consumers who participate in WOM do so to multiple consumers makes the matter all the more important.

This website provides consumers with a place to publicly complain to potentially large numbers of other consumers.

WOM is not always negative. In fact, **positive WOM** occurs when consumers spread information from one to another about positive consumption experiences with companies. Conventionally, negative WOM is seen as more common than positive WOM. However, in the television industry, consumers appear more likely to spread the word about shows they find valuable rather than those they do not.[7] Whether positive or negative, WOM exerts very strong influences on other consumers. As we will see later, a consumer spreading positive WOM is likely to be an asset to a business.

Negative Public Publicity

When negative WOM spreads to a relatively large scale, it can result in **negative public publicity**. Negative public publicity could even involve media coverage. Thus, most large companies have employees whose job it is to try to quell or respond to negative public publicity. A Delta Air Lines customer had a camera stolen from a checked bag. After personally investigating the situation, he was able to track down the culprit, a Delta baggage handler. Eventually, the story was reported in the media, at which point a Delta Air Lines official contacted the customer and refunded him the price of the original flight.[8] In this case, the negative publicity paid off for the customer.

Today, consumers can easily make their complaints public using the World Wide Web. Numerous websites that facilitate just this sort of behavior exist. One such site is **www.consumeraffairs.com**. The site featured a story on "unintended acceleration" of late model (2000–2007) Jeep Grand Cherokee SUVs. According to the consumers voicing the complaints, the vehicles would suddenly and without prompting accelerate after the car was put into gear. A formal complaint was filed with the NHTSA (National Highway and Traffic Safety Authority). Thus far, the NHTSA has not found a defect with the vehicle, but the matter is far from closed.[9] Interestingly, in the 1980s Audi's U.S. market share was virtually wiped out within a short period after the news show *60 Minutes* ran a segment claiming that Audis were susceptible to sudden acceleration syndrome. In reality, *60 Minutes* producers had rigged an Audi sedan to appear to be driving in circles with no driver in the car as a way of trying to convince viewers that Audis were indeed dangerous.[10] After over a decade of study, Audi was actually cleared of this charge with the cases being attributed to driver error—hitting the accelerator when meaning to press the brake. Whether the sudden acceleration syndrome claims about the Jeep Grand Cherokee also are attributable to driver error or not is yet to be seen, but the PR team at Jeep may face a crisis should this story hit the mainstream media.

How should a firm handle negative public publicity? Here are some alternative courses of action:

1. Do nothing; the news will eventually go away.

2. Deny responsibility for any negative event.

3. Take responsibility for any negative events and be visible in the public eye.

4. Release information allowing the public to draw its own conclusion.

What is the best approach?

Doing Nothing or Denying Responsibility

Doing nothing is neither the best nor the worst option. Taking action seems to be a responsible thing to do, but the action can backfire. Even when the basis for the negative publicity is simply rumor, denying any responsibility can be a very bad idea.

Common sense should suggest that McDonald's would never substitute worms for ground beef simply on the basis of cost alone (worms would have to be more expensive than ground beef). Enough consumers believed this rumor at one point in time that McDonald's market share suffered. McDonald's reacted with a 100% beef ad campaign; and even Ray Croc, the founder of McDonald's, did interviews suggesting the idea had no basis in common sense or reality.[11] In essence, this was a denial response. Claiming the burgers were 100% beef was much the same as saying they are 0% worm! Denying a ridiculous claim only gives it credibility and results in negative effects for the brand.[12]

At Snopes.com, you can find information about all the well-known and latest urban legends. Many involve famous brands like Disney and McDonald's.

Taking Responsibility

One might easily see that attribution theory plays a role in dealing with negative publicity. If consumers blame the company for the event surrounding the negative publicity, then the potential repercussions appear serious. However, public action to deal with any consequences of a negative event can mollify any negative effects.

One of the most famous negative publicity cases of all time involves Tylenol pain medicine. In the fall of 1982, over half a dozen consumer deaths in the Chicago area were attributed to cyanide traces in Tylenol capsules. Tylenol executives considered their options, including plausible deniability, and decided to take action by immediately having all Tylenol removed from shelves all around the country immediately. In addition, they agreed to take steps to make sure they discovered what had happened and to make sure it could not happen again. The dramatic action helped convince consumers that Tylenol truly cared about the welfare of customers and wanted to make sure this never happened again. Even though they were quite certain they had no culpability in what appears to be senseless murder, they acted in a way that led to a huge short-term loss. However, this action saved Tylenol's reputation. In fact, many younger consumers may wonder how we came to have tamper-proof packaging for over-the-counter medications and now practically all food products. While today government mandates require such packaging in many instances, the beginning of tamper-proof packaging goes back to Tylenol's response to this potentially damaging negative publicity associated with these murders.

Releasing Information

Sometimes, a company may be able to release some counter-PR to media that allows consumers to make up their own minds about the potential source of any negative PR. If this is done properly, the company does not publicly deny any allegation about the event and instead insists that actions are being taken to get to the bottom of the event.

In the mid-1990s, a consumer made the news by claiming that he was simply drinking a Pepsi when a hypodermic needle began to flow out of the can and stuck his lip. Within two days of this story going public, dozens of consumers from all around the country made the same claim. Pepsi, rather than denying any responsibility, opened the doors of canning operations around North America. Film crews were allowed to come in and videotape cans streaming down an assembly line at high speed. Pepsi released information about the number of canning plants that exist and how they are spread around the country. This action worked to prevent any negative fallout for Pepsi. The media coverage allowed consumers to draw their own conclusions. Obviously, if a needle would get into some Pepsi cans, the chances that this would happen at multiple canning plants all around the country seemed unlikely. Thus, how could this be happening all over? Also, watching the canning operations made clear the fact that nobody could possibly slip a needle into a can at the speeds the assembly line operates. This entire incident was over in just a couple of weeks. All of the alleged needle victims confessed to making up the stories with the hope of getting some part of any settlement that Pepsi might be forced to pay. Thus, this appears to be a textbook way to deal with negative publicity for an implausible event.

Participating in Negative WOM

One of the factors that helps determine negative word-of-mouth returns to the issue of equity. Consumers who believe they have not been treated with fairness or justice become particularly likely to tell others and, in some cases, report the incident to the media.[13]

Consumers can be angry when they believe they have been wronged in this way, and these actions are a small way of trying to get revenge. Consumers who spread negative WOM without complaining to the company itself are particularly likely not to ever do business with that company again.[14] This tendency provides all the more reason for companies to make consumers feel comfortable about complaining and to try to create the impression of genuine concern for the consumer's situation.

Implications of Negative WOM

One reason consumers share negative WOM is as a way of preventing other consumers from falling victim to a company. Thus, negative WOM can hurt sales. However, this is not the only potential negative effect. Negative WOM also can damage the image of the firm. When a consumer hears the negative WOM from a credible source, that information is very likely to become strongly attached to the schema for that brand. Thus, not only is the consumer's attitude toward the brand lowered but the consumer will also find the firm's advertising harder to believe.[15]

In extreme cases, the negative WOM attached to one company can have effects that spill over to an entire industry. For instance, news attributing accidents at one amusement park to a lack of maintenance will certainly damage the image of that particular amusement park. However, a consumer hearing this news may end up not feeling very comfortable about any amusement park deemed similar to the one being accused. Thus, firms must be wary of negative WOM not just for their own brand, but for the industry as well.[16]

Negative WOM does not affect all consumers in the same way. Consumers who have very strong, positive feelings about a brand may have a difficult time accepting negative WOM. Once again, this can be due to balance theory as consumers try to maintain their existing belief systems. If the relationship with the brand is strong, accepting negative information also diminishes the consumer's self-concept. Thus, a consumer who holds strong convictions about a brand is less likely to be affected by negative WOM or negative publicity. Brands whose images are strongly linked to positive emotions such that the emotions help provide meaning can also insulate themselves from negative WOM to some degree.[17]

LO3 Switching Behavior

e xhibit 14.1 suggests that a consumer evaluates a consumption experience, reacts emotionally, and then, perhaps, practices switching behavior. **Switching** in a consumer behavior context refers to the times when a consumer chooses a competing choice, rather than the previously purchased choice, on the next purchase occasion. If a consumer visited Dunkin' Donuts for breakfast last Tuesday, and chooses Krispy Kreme on Saturday, the next time she goes out for breakfast, the consumer has practiced switching behavior. This could be due to any number of reasons, but perhaps the last experience at Dunkin' Donuts was less than satisfying.

All things considered, consumers prefer the status quo. Change brings about, well . . . change, and this can mean costs that diminish the value of an experience. If the consumer has been a regular Dunkin' Donuts customer, she now has to learn the new assortment of doughnuts available at Krispy Kreme, may lose the

All things considered, consumers prefer the status quo. Change brings about, well ... change, and this can mean costs that diminish the value of an experience.

benefits of any accumulated loyalty card from Dunkin' Donuts, and cannot refill her Dunkin' Donuts insulated coffee mug.

Thus, the consumer will incur some **switching costs**, or the costs associated with changing from one choice (brand/retailer/service provider) to another. Switching costs are one reason why a consumer may be dissatisfied with a service provider but will continue to do business with them. Switching costs can be divided into three categories:[18]

1. Procedural
2. Financial
3. Relational

PROCEDURAL SWITCHING COSTS

Procedural switching costs involve lost time and effort. Although Apple computers have a stellar reputation for being easy to use, most computer users stick with PC models. Why? Even if an Apple is easy to use, a consumer familiar with a PC-based Windows operating platform would have to forgo this knowledge to learn how to use an Apple. Thus, the effort that went into learning the PC system is lost and replaced by effort that would be needed to learn how to use an Apple. Most consumers would not want to invest the time and effort needed to learn a new system that would, in their minds, produce similar benefits. Thus, when consumers master a technologically complex product, they become very resistant to switching.[19]

Procedural switching costs are a reality in today's technological marketplace. Nintendo Wii games do not play on Playstation 3, and the games that play on it do not play on XBox 360. Thus, one reason why a consumer may not try a competing video game platform is due to the large costs associated with acquiring new games and the sunk costs associated with games that cannot be used on the new platform. The infamous so-called loyalty cards that reward consumers with a discount or product promotion after a targeted purchase level is reached can also create procedural switching costs.

© ISTOCKPHOTO.COM/MURAT BAYSAN

How do procedural switching costs influence loyalty to computer brands?

FINANCIAL SWITCHING COSTS

Financial switching costs consist of the total economic resources that must be spent or invested as a consumer learns how to obtain value from a new product choice. A consumer in Rivel, France, plans a summer vacation to the Mexican Riviera. A few weeks later, the consumer hears friends discussing their upcoming vacation in Florida and suffers cognitive dissonance. Even though the vacation to Florida now seems better, he has already purchased airfare for his family and the airlines would impose a €50 penalty on each ticket. This financial cost of switching does much to influence the final decision to go to Mexico.

RELATIONAL SWITCHING COSTS

The **relational switching cost** refers to the emotional and psychological consequences of changing from one brand/retailer/service provider to another. Imagine a consumer who has used the same hairstylist for five years. When she goes to college, however, she finds another hair salon that is more

© NEWSCOM

convenient. She is greeted by a stylist named Karla just after entering the salon. Although Karla seems nice, the consumer is very uneasy during the entire salon visit. In fact, she even feels a bit guilty for letting Karla do her hair. This uneasiness is an example of a typical relational switching cost.

UNDERSTANDING SWITCHING COSTS

Exhibit 14.3 demonstrates conventional consumer behavior theory that explains switching costs. Consumers become dissatisfied for any number of reasons, and these reasons and dissatisfaction together determine how likely a consumer is to return on the next purchase occasion.[20] Equity judgments, in particular perceptions of unfair treatment, are particularly prone to lead consumers to switch. Perceptions of unfair prices may make consumers temporarily angry, but they also create lasting memories. When coastal building centers raise plywood prices immediately before a hurricane's landfall, they may

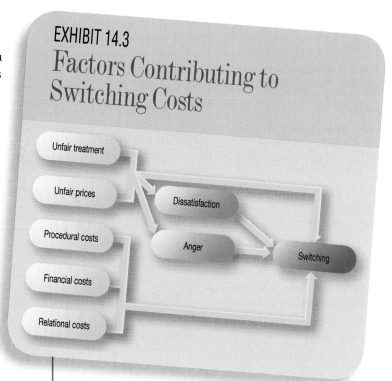

EXHIBIT 14.3
Factors Contributing to Switching Costs

- Unfair treatment
- Unfair prices
- Procedural costs
- Financial costs
- Relational costs

Dissatisfaction → Anger → Switching

Home Depot may build up relational switching costs with the choice to not take advantage of hurricanes by raising prices on essential items like plywood.

enjoy a short-term profit, but consumers will probably remember this and switch to a different retailer the next time they need a building center.[21] Retailers like Home Depot make a point of advertising policies that they maintain prices during weather crises like hurricanes.

Furthermore, even though all types of functional costs can prevent switching, evidence suggests that relational barriers may be the most resistant to influence. Retailers who build up procedural switching costs, particularly through the use of loyalty cards and other similar programs, may gain temporary repeat purchase behavior, but they fail to establish the connection with the customer that wins them true loyalty.[22] Additionally, the inability of web-based retailers to build in anything other than procedural loyalty may be responsible for the low levels of loyalty observed for pure play (Internet only) retailers.[23]

SATISFACTION AND SWITCHING

The intermingling of consumer satisfaction/dissatisfaction and switching costs has received considerable attention. In fact, in addition to the measurement difficulties associated with CS/D, switching costs are another important reason why CS/D results often fail to predict future purchasing behavior. Exhibit 14.4 summarizes how vulnerable a company is to consumer defections based on the interaction between switching costs, competitive intensity, and consumer satisfaction.

As can be seen in Exhibit 14.4, dissatisfaction does not always mean that the consumer is going to switch.

competitive intensity
number of firms competing
for business within a specific
category

customer share portion
of resources allocated to one
brand from among the set of
competing brands

share of wallet customer
share

EXHIBIT 14.4
Vulnerability to Defections Based on CS/D

CUSTOMERS	HIGH COMPETITIVE INTENSITY		LOW COMPETITIVE INTENSITY	
	SWITCHING COSTS		SWITCHING COSTS	
	Low	High	Low	High
Satisfied	Vulnerable	Low vulnerability	Low vulnerability	No vulnerability
Dissatisfied	Highly vulnerable	Vulnerable	Vulnerable	Low vulnerability

Before reaching a conclusion on vulnerability to losing a customer, one also has to take into account at least two other factors. For instance, the amount of competition and the competitive intensity also play a role in determining who switches. **Competitive intensity** refers to the number of firms competing for business within a specific category. At one time, consumers in the United States had only one choice for telephone service—Ma Bell. So, competitive intensity was low. Today, consumers have many choices for phone service. Even though Bell Telephone as it was known no longer exists, consumers can choose AT&T, Sprint, Alltel, or an Internet provider like Skype.com.

When competitive intensity is high and switching costs are low, a company is vulnerable to consumers who will switch providers even when customers are satisfied. The consumer has many companies vying for the business and changing presents little barrier. Today, a consumer has many choices for getting the car's oil changed, and the switching costs are virtually negligible. So, even if a consumer is satisfied with the corner Jiffy Lube, he or she may try 5-Minute Oil Change the next time if the location is slightly more convenient. In contrast, under conditions of high competitive intensity and low switching costs, dissatisfied consumers are almost certain to switch.

In contrast, Exhibit 14.4 suggests that even when consumers are dissatisfied, consumers may not switch. Consider the case when competitive intensity is low, meaning there are few alternatives for the consumer and switching costs are high. In this case, even dissatisfied consumers may return time and time again. In many small- to medium-size markets in the United States, Walmart Supercenters dominate the mass merchandising landscape. Many conventional grocery stores were unable to compete in these markets; as a result, the Walmart Supercenter becomes practically the only choice for buying groceries on any large scale. Thus, although consumers may experience dissatisfaction, the fact that there are few places to turn to and the costs of switching might involve a long drive to the next larger city in the area makes Walmart only slightly vulnerable to defections due to low consumer satisfaction.

LO4 Consumer Loyalty
CUSTOMER SHARE

Marketing managers have come to accept the fact that getting business from a customer who has already done business with the company before is easier and less expensive than getting a new customer. This basic belief motivates much of relationship marketing. The rubrics that determine marketing success then switch from pure sales and margin toward indicators that take into account marketing efficiencies. One important concept is **customer share**, which is the portion of resources allocated to one brand from among the set of competing brands. Here, *brand* is used loosely to capture any type of consumer alternative including a retailer, service provider, or actual product brand. The term **share of wallet** is sometimes used to refer to customer share. Exhibit 14.5 shows how the concept works.[24]

Exhibit 14.5 shows the choices made by two consumers who make daily coffee shop visits. Customer A chose Starbucks (S) eight out of ten times and spent $60 out of the $80 she spent at Starbucks. Customer B chose Starbucks only three times consumer inertia situation in which a consumer tends to continue a pattern of behavior until some stronger force motivates him or her to change

Breaking Up Is Hard to Do!

Breaking up a relationship nearly always causes some pain. But, as painful as breaking up is for individual consumers, breaking up can be devastating for an entire company when a business switches service providers. At times, businesses may even try to build in switching costs to their products as a way of making it more difficult for competitors to compete successfully for business. Think about all the computer systems necessary to manage a large organization. SAP is a provider of software for businesses, including Customer Relationship Management (CRM) software programs and even more generalized systems known as enterprise suites. Many firms that implement CRM programs are dissatisfied with their decision. However, even though they are dissatisfied, they often stick with the software systems because changing would mean significant procedural and financial switching costs as well as facing the trauma that goes along with sunk costs incurred from implementing the system. As a result, these employees, who are consumers of the software, must cope with the consequences. Thus, breaking up the relationship, in this case between a firm and a software systems provider, really is hard to do. In much the same way, many consumers who are less than satisfied with things like digital entertainment and communication services also hang in there and try to reconcile because of the financial costs involved with breaking a service contract and the procedural costs involved in learning a new system.

Sources: Porter, M. E. (2008), "The Five Competitive Forces that Shape Strategy," *Harvard Business Review*, 86 (January), 78–93; Whitten, D., and K. W. Green, Jr. (2005), "The Effect of Switching Costs on Intent to Switch: An Application in IS Service Provision Markets," *International Journal of Mobile Communication*, 3 (4), 1.

tenet of relationship marketing is that a company's marketing is much more efficient when most of the business comes from repeat customers. In this sense, customer A is a more valuable consumer to Starbucks than is customer B.

Customer share represents a behavioral component that is indicative of customer loyalty. When customers don't switch, they repeat their purchase behavior over again. At times, they repeat the behavior over and over and over again. The question of whether or not a consumer is truly loyal can be addressed only by examining why a consumer is repeating behavior. This brings us to the concept of consumer inertia.

Consumer Inertia

In physics, inertia refers to the fact that a mass that is in motion (at rest) will stay in motion (at rest) unless the mass is acted upon by a greater force. The concept of consumer inertia presents an analogy. **Consumer inertia** means that a consumer will tend to continue a pattern

out of the ten visits to a coffee shop and spent $20 out of the $70 total with Starbucks. Thus, Starbucks gets considerably greater customer share from A than from B. The

EXHIBIT 14.5
Customer Share Information for Two Coffee Shop Customers

	Date of Visit										Total Spent
	7-1	7-2	7-3	7-4	7-5	7-6	7-7	7-8	7-9	7-10	
Customer A Choice	S	S	CC	S	S	CC	S	S	S	S	
$$ Spent	5	10	10	5	15	10	5	5	10	5	$80
Customer B Choice	S	CC	M	M	S	M	CC	S	CC	M	
$$ Spent	5	15	5	5	5	5	10	10	5	5	$70

S = Starbucks
CC = CC's
M = McDonald's

© AP IMAGES/PRNEWSFOTO/HILL'S PET NUTRITION INC.

loyalty card/program
device that keeps track of the amount of purchasing a consumer has had with a given marketer once some level is reached

customer commitment
sense of attachment, dedication, and identification

of behavior until some stronger force motivates him or her to change. In fact, resistance to change is one of the biggest reasons why new products fail in the marketplace.[25] Also, change often means consumers must give something up. For example, why hasn't satellite radio been a bigger hit? Although consumers gain access to a much wider array of programming with satellite radio, they also give up the long-held benefit of free music via over-the-air radio. Remember that losses loom larger than gains and thus the potential loss motivates consumers even more to continue with what they already have.

> Loyalty card programs are meant to reward loyal customers, not those looking for big discounts.

Loyalty Programs

Many marketers have experimented with loyalty cards or programs as a way of increasing customer share. Loyalty cards also allow marketers to learn more about customer groups' demographics and shopping patterns. A **loyalty card/program** is a device that keeps track of the amount of purchasing a consumer has had with a given marketer (as well as a list of actual items purchased by the consumer) and once some level is reached, a reward is offered usually in terms of future purchase incentives. Loyalty programs differ somewhat based on the firms offering them. Today, European firms typically offer the standard reward in terms of a future purchase incentive, but in the United States, loyalty programs

more often work by offering on-the-spot discounts on selected items. One result is a two-tiered pricing system where there is one price for customers who comply with the card program, and a higher price for those who do not use the card on those selected items.

However, the results are mixed with respect to the effectiveness of loyalty cards. In fact, they can sometimes even backfire by appealing too strongly to consumers who are bargain shoppers. Consumers with a strong economic orientation display lower customer share with all competitors instead choosing to shop in the place with the current best offer.[26]

While these programs are referred to as "loyalty" programs, the question occurs as to exactly what constitutes loyalty. Customer share reflects a behavioral component of loyalty by reflecting repeated behavior. Consumer A in Exhibit 14.5 repeats similar behavior over again and thus, appears to be loyal to Starbucks, but is she really? This is the focus of the next section.

CUSTOMER COMMITMENT

Consumer A does appear at least partially loyal to Starbucks. However, loyalty cannot be answered by behavior alone. True consumer loyalty consists of both a pattern of repeated behavior as evidenced by high customer share and a strong feeling of attachment, dedication, and sense of identification with a brand. This sense of attachment, dedication, and identification is known as **customer commitment**. Exhibit 14.6 depicts the components of loyalty. Customer share is behavioral, and commitment is an affective component of loyalty.

Customers who feel true commitment are true assets to the company. They are willing to sacrifice to continue doing business with the brand and serve as a source of promotion by spreading positive WOM. If we look at a consumer with a pattern of consistent

COURTESY OF CASPIAN CONSUMER PRIVACY—WWW.NOCARDS.ORG

This screen shot shows a website (www.nocards.org) that encourages consumer efforts and boycotts of those companies who do use loyalty cards or in this case, RFID tags which can track patterns of repeated behavior to understand consumer purchase behavior.

EXHIBIT 14.6
True Loyalty Requires Customer Commitment

behavior like customer A in Exhibit 14.5, the question becomes whether the behavior is simply inertia or motivated by true commitment. Perhaps this particular customer simply happens to live next door to a Starbucks and thus getting coffee there is simply the easiest thing to continue to do. If a CC's Coffee Shop were to take over the current Starbucks location, the customer would simply buy her coffee there. However, if customer A were truly committed, she would seek out another Starbucks location even if the one next to her place were to close or be rented out to a different coffee competitor. This distinguishes inertia from a truly loyal customer. Even if Starbucks is not the most convenient or least expensive alternative, the truly loyal consumer will still seek out Starbucks!

Truly loyal customers are like gold to the company. The CLV (Customer Lifetime Value equation from Chapter 2) concept demonstrates why. The certainty of a lengthy stream of revenues is much less for a customer acting only on inertia. In addition, the customer acting on inertia alone is likely not contributing on the equity side of the equation as is the truly committed customer. A firm that concentrates on repeated behavior alone, perhaps by always being convenient, can do well but remains more vulnerable to competitors. The reason for the vulnerability is that tangible assets like convenience are easily duplicated; but the intangible assets, like the feel associated with a choice or place, like the feelings consumers have for visiting Starbucks or drinking a Coke, are very hard to duplicate.

ANTILOYALTY

Loyalty is almost always discussed from a positive perspective. However, at times consumers can become anti-

loyal. **Antiloyal consumers** are those who will do everything possible to avoid doing business with a particular marketer. These consumers generally are driven by a severe dislike of this particular company and the negative emotions that go along with the aversion. Antiloyalty is often motivated by a bad experience between a consumer and the marketer in which the marketer could not redress the problem.

> **antiloyal consumers** consumers who will do everything possible to avoid doing business with a particular marketer

Loyalty cannot be answered by behavior alone.

Frustration is driven by such things as attributes a marketer builds in to a product to create procedural switching costs. These attributes include parts that are incompatible with widely available replacements or a mobile phone contract that locks a consumer into a specific service set for a lengthy period of time. Consumers may wonder if their mobile phone number is transferable. In fact, many consumers may be frustrated with their mobile phone carrier but feel locked in particularly if the phone number is not transferable.[27]

Antiloyal customers are often consumers who have switched and treat the former marketing partner as a jilted partner. They obviously have no net positive lifetime value for the target firm. Moreover, these antiloyal consumers who are former customers become perhaps the most frequent source for negative word-of-mouth.[28] Thus, antiloyal consumers can be a major force to reckon with.

VALUE AND SWITCHING

Exhibit 14.7 reproduces the center portion of the CVF. The exhibit clearly shows that value plays a role in the postconsumption process. During an exchange, the consumer goes through the consumption process, and the result produces some amount and type of value. The value, in turn, shapes what happens next. Thus, the CVF makes up for a shortcoming of the disconfirmation theory approach (as displayed in Exhibit 14.1) by explicitly accounting for value.

For a host of reasons, consumers may end up maintaining a relationship even if they experience dissatisfaction. However, consumers do not maintain relationships

relationship quality degree of connectedness between a consumer and a retailer

in which they find no value. Even if consumers do not enjoy shopping at Walmart, they tend to repeat the behavior because of high utilitarian value. Also, even though a consumer may be able to bank at a more convenient location, he might continue doing business with his original bank because he enjoys the personal relationships he has developed with bank personnel. Thus, both utilitarian and hedonic value can be a key in preventing consumers from switching to a competitor and creating true loyalty among consumers.

Is one type of value more important than the other in preventing switching behavior? The answer to this question depends on the nature of the goods or services being consumed. For functional types of services, such as banking, utilitarian value is more strongly related to customer share (and therefore preventing switching) than is hedonic value.[29] However, for more experiential types of services, such as mall shopping, hedonic value is more strongly related to customer share.[30]

Value also is linked to the affective side of loyalty, customer commitment. Again, both value dimensions relate positively to commitment. But hedonic value plays a larger role in creating this important outcome. In

particular, customers who have switched service providers are more likely to become loyal customers when they experience increased hedonic value compared to the previous service provider.[31] Exhibit 14.8 suggests ways that value plays a role in shaping loyalty and preventing switching behavior for different types of businesses.

EXHIBIT 14.8
Value Types and Loyalty

Functional	
• Banking	Utilitarian value brings them back a bit more than hedonic value
• Pharmacies	
• Fast-food (adults)	
• Internet services	

Experiential	
• Mall shopping	Hedonic value brings them back a bit more than utilitarian value
• Spa/salon services	
• Fine dining	
• Resort hotels	

LO5 Value, Relationships, and Consumers

RELATIONSHIPS AND THE MARKETING FIRM

Marketers have come to realize that the exchange between a business and a consumer comprise a relationship. Two factors help make this clear:

1. Customers have a lifetime value to the firm.

2. True loyalty involves both a continuing series of interactions and feelings of attachment between the customer and the firm.

In return, many firms that truly adopt a relationship marketing approach with customers enjoy improved performance.[32] This is particularly the case as the relationship between customer and seller becomes very personal and involves trust.

Taken together, CS/D, complaining behavior, switching, customer share, and commitment all indicate relationship quality. Generally, **relationship quality**

EXHIBIT 14.7
Value and Relationship Outcomes

Consumption Process
- Needs
- Wants
- Exchange
- Costs and Benefits
- Reactions

Value
- Utilitarian
- Hedonic

Relationship Quality
- CS/D
- Switching Behavior
- Customer Share
- Customer Commitment

Takes Three to Tango!

Consumers and salespeople have many different types of relationships. Marketing firms often realize that salespeople often hold the key to building effective relationships with customers. In fact, salespeople are often seen as the key to successfully implementing a relationship marketing strategy. When customers like the salespeople they deal with, they often turn to this person first when they need assistance from the company. Even though the salesperson's first job may be to sell, a relationship-marketing-oriented firm will encourage its salespeople to spend the time necessary to see that the customer's problem is satisfactorily addressed. In this way, the salesperson returns the loyalty shown by the customer, and as a result, the customer is also loyal to the company. The same sort of three-way relationship can exist with service providers where the customer becomes loyal to a particular service provider who shows loyalty to the customer, and as a result, the bond is built between the customer and the firm.

Sources: Palmatier, R. W., L. K. Scheer, M. B. Houston, K. R. Evans, and S. Gopalakrishna (2007), "Use of Relationship Marketing Programs in Building Customer-Salesperson and Customer-Firm Relationships: Differential Influences on Financial Outcomes," *Journal of Services Marketing*, 24 (September), 210–223. Macintosh, G. (2007), "Customer Orientation, Relationship Quality, and Relational Benefits to the Firm," *Journal of Services Marketing*, 21 (3), 150–157.

For the marketer, the regular consumer does not have to be resold and thus much of the selling effort required to convert a new customer is not necessary.

In fact, when relationship quality is very strong, the marketer and the customer act as partners. When something bad happens to the marketer, the customer is affected.[33] When something bad happens to the customer, the marketer is affected. Customers and sellers often act very closely as partners in business-to-business contexts. However, relationship quality can be very important in business-to-consumer contexts, too. When a parent sends a child off to college, chances are that a strong relationship exists or will soon exist between the family and the college. The family will don school colors on game day and become a prime target for fund-raising campaigns. The strong relationship quality means that the family and the university share many common goals.

Exhibit 14.9 displays some of the characteristics of a marketing relationship that is very healthy. Consider this

represents the degree of connectedness between a consumer and a retailer. When relationship quality is high, the prospects for a continued series of mutually valuable exchanges exist. Relationship quality can be thought of as capturing the health of the relationship so that, in all likelihood, it will continue. When consumers are truly loyal, and this loyalty is returned by the marketer, relationship quality is high.

> Universities hope a high-value experience leads graduates to continue a life-long relationship with the school.

VALUE AND RELATIONSHIP QUALITY

A healthy relationship between a consumer and a marketer enhances value both for the consumer and the marketer. For the consumer, decision making becomes simpler, enhancing utilitarian value, and relational exchanges often involve pleasant relational and experiential elements, enhancing hedonic value.

EXHIBIT 14.9
The Characteristics of Relationship Quality

- **Competence** Consumer views company and service providers as knowledgeable and capable
- **Communication** Consumer and firm understand each other and "speak the same language"
- **Trust** Buyer and seller can depend on each other
- **Equity** Both buyer and seller see equity in exchange and are able to equitably resolve conflicts
- **Personalization** Buyer treats the customer as an individual with unique desires and requirements
- **Customer oriented** Strong relationships are more likely to develop when a firm practices a marketing orientation, and this filters down to service providers and salespeople

example. A consumer uses the same travel agent for practically all travel. When the consumer calls the agent, the agent does not have to ask the customer for preferences or personal information, not even a credit card number, because she has all the information about the customer. She knows the customer is a Delta SkyMiles member so she tries to always book on Delta when possible. She knows the customer doesn't like close connections (under an hour), so she tries to always allow at least an hour and a half between connecting flights. Whenever the customer flies, the agent monitors the flight status. If there is a delay, she phones the customer to exchange information and begins rebooking any connecting flights, hotel reservations, or car rentals in case the delay is so lengthy that plans must be changed. In this case, we can see that many of the characteristics displayed in Exhibit 14.9 are illustrated.[34] This agent is customer oriented, has a personal relationship with the customer, communicates well, and is competent; the relationship is characterized by trust. Chances are that this customer will be loyal for quite some time.

Chapter 14 Case

Avant Healthcare is an international medical staffing firm based in Orlando, Florida. It brings healthcare professionals (HCPs) from all over the world into healthcare facilities throughout the United States. The international medical staffing industry serves a much-needed niche by filling staffing voids in the medical field. Bringing qualified HCPs to the United States is a complicated process. From the time an HCP is recruited, it takes between 16 and 24 months to bring that person into the United States and have him or her fully documented and ready to work. As soon as an agency starts the process of bringing in a HCP, there are great costs involved. For HCPs, there is a great commitment of time, mostly as a result of the many documents they must submit and the difficult exams they must prepare for. Furthermore, most agencies have the HCPs sign a contract with significant financial penalties for those HCPs who switch agencies or drop out of the process.

CUSTOMERS

One of the main customers of international medical staffing firms is the HCPs. Even though the HCPs are employed by the medical staffing firm, they are still seen as one of the main customers because they are the revenue generators for the firms. Moreover, with the shortage of healthcare professionals throughout the United States, these HCPs have the option of working with many different agencies.

Within the industry, there is a large problem with HCP commitment and loyalty. This difficulty is largely due to the fact that the HCPs do not communicate with the agency. Often the HCPs do not voice their problems or displeasure with the medical firms they are working for. Instead, they complain to friends and colleagues about their dissatisfaction. They also spread their displeasure through other means such as anonymous web blogs like the ones listed below from the popular nurse networking site **www.allnurses.com**: "I would definitely stay away from *Agency X*.* I have seen too many horror stories, especially from nurses from the UK about them. They didn't deliver on what they promise and that is a major 'no-no' in my book." and *"Agency X"* are a bunch of nurse-cheating crooks. Stay away from them!"

Feedback from blogs like this and negative word-of-mouth hurt the medical staffing companies because they lose future HCPs that would become customers. They also affect the firms because, even with the aforementioned high switching costs, it is not uncommon for HCPs to switch agencies. In some cases, international medical companies are seeing 30% or more of their HCPs leaving assignments before their contracts are complete. Most of these firms do little but accept this dropout and negativity as part of their operating model. They view the complainers as thorns in their sides that will eventually go away. Occasionally, these firms have countered these negative sentiments with marketing campaigns in trade journals and shows that portray their HCPs as completely enjoying their experience. In some other cases, the international medical staffing firms have attempted to appease the HCPs by giving them raises and better benefits. However, in most cases, this was not the root of the problem and only served as a temporary fix.

AVANT'S CUSTOMER LOYALTY

Compared with other companies within the industry, Avant's HCPs are loyal. There are four main ways that they have accomplished this. First, they establish very open and clear communication about the immigration process and what the HCPs should expect on every step of the way. Second, Avant employs a diverse support staff that is effective at communicating and relating to the foreign HCPs. Third, Avant asks regularly for feedback from their HCPs on how Avant can improve the process. Fourth, Avant works with the HCPs to quickly identify and resolve any concerns they might have. The net effect of all these efforts has been an extremely high level of satisfaction and loyalty by Avant's HCPs. Avant has been able to leverage this brand loyalty to attracting many HCPs through referrals. This loyalty has also greatly reduced the dropout or switching of HCPs from Avant to other agencies.

Questions

1. How can Avant Healthcare further leverage its brand loyalty from its HCPs to helping its business?

2. What is the importance of Avant proactively asking its HCPs about possible concerns? How does this help Avant build brand loyalty?

3. How do the international medical staffing firms that view customer complaints as nothing more than a pain in their side contribute to customer disconfirmation formation by their HCPs?

4. What kinds of long-term implications can the negative word-of-mouth have on international medical staffing firms?

*"Agency X" has been substituted for the real name of the firm in the all nurses blog.

what do you think?

Binge drinking is a serious problem for college students today.

1 2 3 4 5 6 7

strongly disagree   strongly agree

In order for exchanges

to occur in an orderly fashion, the expectations of the consumer, the marketer, and even other consumers must coincide with one another.

15

Consumer Misbehavior

Introduction

m ost of the behaviors that we have discussed so far in this text are generally considered acceptable or normal by societal standards. A number of important consumer-related topics, however, fall outside of what would be considered acceptable. Here's a question to consider: Would you steal sunglasses from Hot Topic if you knew that you wouldn't get caught? Why or why not? Or, would you buy a new outfit with the sole intention of wearing it once and then taking it back the next day for a refund?

In this chapter, we focus on what is referred to as consumer misbehavior. The term *misbehavior* is used cautiously because opinions regarding what is acceptable or normal depend on our ethical beliefs and ideologies. Of course, these beliefs differ across consumers and across cultures.

> **consumer misbehavior**
> behavior that violates gen- erally accepted norms of conduct

Many behaviors can be considered misbehaviors. For example, consumers shoplift products from stores, download music illegally, drink and drive, and engage in fraudulent activities. By performing these behaviors, consumers violate accepted norms and break established laws. They also hurt other people. Understanding the motivations behind all these behaviors can be difficult.

LO1 Conceptualization of Consumer Misbehavior

i n its most basic form, **consumer misbehavior** may be viewed as a subset of a more general topic, *human deviance*. The deviance topic has a long history of research attention in the field of sociology. Because of this, many of the

After studying this chapter, the student should be able to:

LO1 Understand the consumer misbehavior phenomenon and how it affects the exchange process.

LO2 Describe the role of value in consumer misbehavior.

LO3 Comprehend how consumers' moral beliefs and evaluations influence the choice to engage in consumer misbehavior.

LO4 Distinguish between consumer misbehavior and consumer problem behavior.

LO5 Understand specific consumer misbehaviors and problem behaviors.

concepts that pertain to the study of consumer misbehavior are similar to topics studied in sociology and human deviance research.

Consumer misbehavior can be referred to in several ways. We define consumer misbehavior as behavior that violates generally accepted norms of conduct.[1] Behavior that violates norms also disrupts the flow of consumption activities. For example, a consumer screaming loudly and cursing at a waiter because his order is wrong will likely make other consumers feel uncomfortable. This action disrupts others' meals and may even ruin the entire evening. Chances are that the waiter who endures the scolding will perform poorly during the rest of the evening after the tongue-lashing. In this way, all customers are affected by a single consumer's actions.

Researchers sometimes call misbehavior the "dark side" of consumer behavior, and there are certainly many ways to describe it. Words such as *aberrant*, *illicit*, *negative*, *dysfunctional*, and *deviant* have been used to describe misbehavior. Some behaviors are clearly illegal, while others are simply immoral. Obviously, there's a difference. For example, shoplifting is illegal and almost always considered immoral. Speeding, however, is illegal but may not be considered immoral. Not returning excess change that is mistakenly given at a store is immoral but not illegal.[2] The "Can I Get My Money Back?" feature details one specific form of consumer misbehavior that many will consider immoral, **retail borrowing**.

CONSUMER MISBEHAVIOR AND EXCHANGE

As described earlier, consumer misbehavior can profoundly affect the exchange process. In fact, in order for exchanges to occur in an orderly fashion, the expectations of the consumer, the marketer, and even other consumers must coincide with one another.[3] For example, when we attend a movie theater, we can expect to wait in line in to purchase concessions. We hope that our wait won't be long, and management does all that it can to ensure that the wait isn't long. Management expects us to act orderly, keep our place in line, and wait our turn. Other consumers expect the same from us. When we see consumers becoming abusive, cutting in line, or making other people uncomfortable, the exchange process is disrupted. Like a bad customer at a restaurant, a bad customer at a movie theater can ruin everything!

Of course, abusive consumers aren't the only ones to disrupt the exchange process. Consumers who shoplift disrupt the exchange process and increase costs for all consumers. In much the same way, consumers who make fraudulent insurance claims also increase costs for other consumers. Computer users who send spam or spread computer viruses slow down electronic commerce and lower overall business productivity. Belligerent sports fans turn otherwise joyous occasions into embarrassing and annoying events for everybody. Drunk drivers kill people! All sorts of consumer misbehaviors affect the exchange process.

© ISTOCKPHOTO.COM/JAMES STEIDL

LO2 The Focus of Misbehavior: Value

as we have discussed throughout this text, a central component for understanding consumer behavior is value. It shouldn't be surprising then that the focal motivation for consumer misbehavior is also value.[4] However, *how* consumers attempt to obtain value is an important issue in consumer misbehavior research.

Rowdy sports fans think that the best way to obtain value from their admission into a sporting event is to be obnoxious. Identity thieves believe that the best way to obtain value is to not pay for anything and steal from others! In each instance, consumers seek to maximize the benefits they receive from an action while minimizing, or eliminating, associated costs. Unfortunately, other consumers suffer while misbehaving consumers break societal norms and laws. In this way, consumer misbehavior is, quite simply, selfish.

Can I Get My Money Back?

A trend is occurring in the retail sector. Consumers are returning products like crazy. This seems fairly normal. After all, retailers have offered returned-merchandise policies for years. Hold on to your receipt, and you're good to go!

What's different about this trend is that the behavior is premeditated. That is, consumers *plan* to return merchandise after using it even when there is nothing wrong with it! It's been called retail borrowing or deshopping, and it's happening more and more. The behaviors range from women "borrowing" dresses to wear to special occasions to shoppers "borrowing" camcorders to record personal events. Most retailers are aware of the problem. They should be aware because fraudulent returns cost the retail sector over $3.5 billion annually!

Retail managers are currently implementing costly methods to combat this growing problem. Efforts include collecting detailed information about customers to help identify patterns of fraud, installing new software programs that allow clerks to detail the histories of each transaction, and simply getting rid of cash refunds in favor of store credit. In the end, retail borrowing obviously hurts retailers, but it also hurts all consumers in the form of increased prices and more stringent return policies.

Sources: Landy, Heather (2006), "Retailers Bracing for Returns," *Knight Ridder Tribune News* (December),1; Giovis, Jaclyn (2006), "Smart Shoppers Will Need Their Receipts to Bring Merchandise Back to Many Stores," *Knight Ridder Tribune News* (December 18), 1; Schmidt, Ruth A., Fiona Sturrock, Philippa Ward, and Gaynor Lea-Greenwood (1999), "Deshopping: The Art of Illicit Consumption," *International Journal of Retail & Distribution Management*, 27, 290–301; Wirtz, Jochen, and Doreen Kum (2004), "Consumer Cheating on Service Guarantees," *Journal of the Academy of Marketing Science*, (Spring), 159–175.

© TERRI MILLER/E-VISUAL COMMUNICATIONS, INC.

moral beliefs beliefs about the perceived ethicality or morality of behaviors

moral equity beliefs regarding an act's fairness or justness

part, by a type of *ethical* decision making.[5] In this section, we discuss how moral beliefs and evaluations influence the decision to perform these behaviors.

MORAL BELIEFS

Moral beliefs, or beliefs about the perceived ethicality or morality of behaviors, play important roles in ethical decision making.[6] The effect of moral beliefs on ethical decision making and consumer misbehavior is shown in Exhibit 15.1.

Notice that a consumer's moral beliefs are comprised of three components: moral equity, contractualism, and relativism.[7]

- **Moral equity** represents beliefs regarding an act's fairness or justness. Do I consider this action to be fair? Is it fair for me to shoplift this item?

LO3 Consumer Ethics and Misbehavior

a s we discussed in our decision-making chapters, consumer actions result from some form of decision making. In fact, all aspects of consumer behavior are guided, at least in

EXHIBIT 15.1
Moral Beliefs, Ethical Decision Making, and Behavior

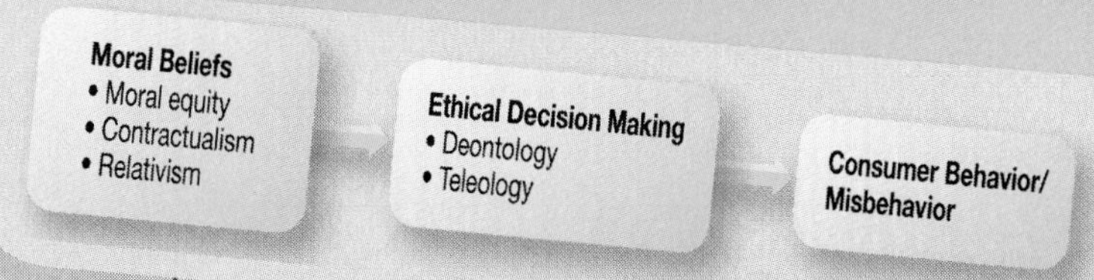

Moral Beliefs
- Moral equity
- Contractualism
- Relativism

Ethical Decision Making
- Deontology
- Teleology

Consumer Behavior/ Misbehavior

contractualism beliefs about the violation of written (or unwritten) laws

relativism beliefs about the social acceptability of an act

deontological evaluations evaluations regarding the inherent rightness or wrongness of specific actions

teleological evaluations consumers' assessment of the goodness or badness of the consequences of actions

anomie state that occurs when there is a disconnect between cultural goals and norms and the capacities of members of society to act within societal norms in an effort to achieve those goals

- **Contractualism** refers to beliefs about the violation of written (or unwritten) laws. Does this action break a law? Does it break an unwritten promise of how I should act? Is shoplifting illegal?

- **Relativism** represents beliefs about the social acceptability of an act. Is this action culturally acceptable? Is shoplifting acceptable in this culture? Does it matter if it is acceptable in this culture? Is it acceptable to me?

BEHAVIORAL EVALUATION

Consumers bring their moral beliefs into all decision-making settings. Once a consumer enters into a situation that calls for an ethical decision (*"should I steal this CD or not?"*), he or she considers the various alternative courses of action. Here, two sets of ethical evaluations occur: deontological evaluations and teleological evaluations.[8]

Deontological evaluations focus on specific *actions*. Is this action "right"? As such, deontology focuses on *how* people accomplish their goals. In fact, how people accomplish goals (that is, how they act) is actually given more consideration than what they actually accomplish. The deontological perspective is, in large part, attributed to the work of German philosopher Immanuel Kant. Kant's *Categorical Imperative* suggests that one should act in a way that would be considered a universal law for all people facing the same situation.

Teleological evaluations focus on the *consequences* of the behaviors and the individual's assessment of those consequences. How much "good" will result from this decision? Four major issues are considered with teleological evaluations:

- The perceived consequences of the actions for various stakeholders

- The probability that the consequence will occur

> There are many motivations for consumer misbehavior.

- The desirability of the consequences for the stakeholders

- The importance of the stakeholder groups to the consumer[9]

Both deontological and teleological evaluations come into play when consumers face an ethical decision.

MOTIVATIONS OF MISBEHAVIOR

Moral beliefs and behavioral evaluations indeed play important roles in consumer misbehavior. However, the question remains: Why do consumers misbehave? Many motives for consumer misbehavior have been suggested. Researchers Ronald Fullerton and Girish Punj offer the following motivations of consumer misbehavior:[10]

- **Unfulfilled Aspirations.** Many consumers have unfulfilled aspirations that influence their misbehavior. An important concept here is **anomie**. To understand the concept of anomie, consider first the goals that are generally accepted in a given culture. For example, it's pretty easy to say that the U.S. culture places a great deal of emphasis on attaining material possessions and "getting ahead." However, it could be argued that not all members of the U.S. society have the necessary tools, skills, and resources to be able to get ahead and enjoy the things that society deems important. As a result, some consumers may turn to deviant actions in order to achieve what society teaches them they should enjoy. It's when societal goals are seemingly out of reach given the means to achieve them that deviance often occurs.[11]

From this perspective, consumers misbehave because they do not believe that they can get what they want in any other way. For example, shoplifters decide that stealing is the only way to acquire the products they desire. ID thieves may think that the best way to acquire products that they can't get otherwise is by defrauding others. Obviously, anomie does not mean that all people who feel deprived will resort to illegal acts. If this were the case, crime would indeed be rampant. Nonetheless, from a sociological perspective, anomie does help to explain these behaviors.

- **Thrill-seeking.** For some consumers, the simple thrill of the action leads consumers to misbehave. Breaking the speed limit and driving very fast can be exciting for some consumers. As we've seen in this text, thrill-seeking can be a motivation for many consumer behaviors, and misbehavior is no different.

- **Lack of Moral Constraints.** Some consumers simply don't have a set of moral beliefs that are in agreement with society's expectations. These consumers see no problem with their misbehaviors. For example, consumers who hurt others by scaring them with aggressive driving may believe that the other drivers "deserve it!"

- **Differential Association.** Sociologists use the theory of differential association to explain why groups of people replace one set of acceptable norms with another set that others view as unacceptable. By acting in opposition to the prevailing acceptable standards, group members are able to forge their own identities and strengthen their sense of group cohesion.[12] Here, consumers view deviant behavior as a way to belong to a specific group. For example, gang members often accept behaviors and ideals that other members of society would find unacceptable.

- **Pathological Socialization.** Consumers may view misbehavior as a way of getting revenge against big companies. The sheer size of major companies can produce feelings of resentment, and consumers can view misbehavior as a method of "getting back" at big business. For example, stealing from very large corporations may seem less severe than stealing from a locally owned hardware store, and consumers can believe that big companies deserve it.

- **Provocative Situational Factors.** Factors like retail crowding, flight delays, excessive heat, or noise can all contribute to consumer misbehavior. Clearly, situational factors play important roles in guiding behavior. For example, a well-mannered, quiet person may lose his or her cool after having to wait in line for 20 minutes at a local drive-through restaurant.

- **Opportunism.** Misbehavior can also be the outcome of a deliberate, rational decision-making process that weighs the risks and rewards of the behavior. Consumers may simply believe that the rewards associated with a behavior (for example, stealing cable television) outweigh the risks involved (that is, getting caught). Opportunism focuses specifically on self-interest above all other considerations. In this way, consumers seek the first opportunity to misbehave when they think that they can get away with it.

> **consumer problem behavior** consumer behavior that is deemed to be unacceptable but that is seemingly beyond the control of the consumer

LO4 Distinguish Consumer Misbehavior and Problem Behavior

Consumer misbehavior and what we refer to as consumer "problem behavior" can be distinguished in important ways. The misbehavior term is used to describe behavior deliberately harmful to another party in an exchange process. **Consumer problem behavior**, on the other hand, refers to behaviors that are seemingly outside of a consumer's control. For example, some people compulsively shop. Some people are addicted to drugs and/or cigarettes. Some consumers have alcohol problems. In cases like these, consumers may express a desire to stop the behaviors but simply find quitting to be too difficult.

Although the line between consumer misbehavior and problem behaviors can be somewhat blurred, we distinguish between the two areas by considering the issue of self-control. Exhibit 15.2 presents examples of consumer misbehaviors and problem behaviors. Some behaviors can be considered either consumer misbehaviors or problem behaviors. Drug addiction is listed as a problem behavior, but when someone drives under the influence of drugs, the individual risks injuring or killing someone else.

EXHIBIT 15.2
Consumer Misbehavior and Problem Behavior

CONSUMER MISBEHAVIOR	CONSUMER PROBLEM BEHAVIOR
• Shoplifting • Computer-mediated behaviors: illicit sharing of software and music, computer attacks, cyberbullying • Fraud • Abusive consumer behavior • Dysfunctional sports behaviors • Illegitimate complaining • Product misuse: aggressive driving, drunk driving, cell phone use	• Compulsive buying • Compulsive shopping • Eating disorders • Binge drinking • Problem gambling • Drug abuse

LO5 Specific Consumer Misbehaviors and Problem Behaviors

as you can see, there are many different types of consumer misbehaviors and problem behaviors. Many of the behaviors that are listed in Exhibit 15.2 are discussed frequently in the popular press and various news outlets. In fact, you may have heard stories in the news media about the devastating effects of binge drinking or problem gambling. You may even know someone who struggles with these behaviors. Although there are many different type of behaviors that we could discuss, we limit our discussion to a number of behaviors that tend to gather significant consumer research attention.

CONSUMER MISBEHAVIOR

As we have stated, consumer misbehavior represents behaviors that are deliberately harmful to other parties in an exchange process. Here, we discuss shoplifting, computer-mediated behaviors, fraud, abusive behavior, dysfunctional sports behavior, illegitimate complaining, and product misuse.

Shoplifting

Did you know that consumers steal more than $35 million of products from retailers every day? That's over $13 billion per year! In fact, more than 10 million people have been caught shoplifting in the last 5 years.[13] That's a lot of people! How could these figures be so high? Consumers' motivations for shoplifting are similar to motivations for other forms of misbehavior, and include the following:[14]

- **The temptation is so strong.** Consumers sometimes shoplift largely because the temptation is so strong. Retailers present merchandise in a way that is so enticing that a consumer is willing to steal the product to obtain the value that is offered. This also typifies underage consumers who steal cigarettes and alcohol that they cannot legally buy.

- **Consumers believe retailers can absorb the loss.** Much like the motivation for misbehaving in other contexts, consumers who shoplift often think that businesses deserve what they get and can absorb losses. In other words, many consumers have an antibusiness sentiment that influences shoplifting behaviors.

- **Consumers perceive the likelihood of getting caught is low.** Consumers often believe only a small portion of offenders actually get caught. When stores are crowded and busy, consumers often think there's no way they'll be noticed, and shoplifting becomes easy.

- **Consumers desire to gain acceptance into a group.** Consumers, particularly adolescents, often steal in order to show off. The strong reference group influence to fit in with others who see shoplifting as funny or cool can motivate the behavior.

- **Shoplifting is exciting and risky.** Some people steal for the excitement associated with the activity. Again, adolescents are particularly susceptible to this type of influence.

Emotions and Shoplifting. Emotions and feelings play a large role in shoplifting. Fear of being caught plays an important role in predicting shoplifting intentions, especially among young consumers. Interestingly, the shoplifting intentions of adolescent consumers appear to be more heavily influenced by emotions than by moral beliefs. The opposite occurs in older consumers. Research also suggests that consumers who shoplift are sometimes motivated by repressed feelings of stress and anger.[15]

Age and Shoplifting. Interestingly, shoplifting behavior appears to peak during the adolescent years. This may be because adolescents are yet to fully mature and often find themselves in the stressful transition from childhood to adulthood. As such, adolescents often "act out" in ways that are self-harming. Adolescents also tend to consider shoplifting as being more ethical than do adult shoppers.[16]

Computer-Mediated Behaviors: Illegal Sharing of Software and Music

Due to improvements in computer technologies, consumers often have the ability to illicitly download electronic material from a number of sources. Major problems here include the pirating of computer software, video games, and music.

The software industry loses billions of dollars annually due to illegal copying. In fact, the Business Software Alliance estimates that $53 billion was lost globally due to the illegal theft and use of software products in 2008.[17] The music industry has also been hit hard by these actions. The U.S. Digital Millennium Copyright Act deems the sharing of copyrighted music as illegal. The most well-known case of illicit music downloading came to the public eye when Napster lost a court case that accused the company of violating applicable copyright protection laws. In recent years, numerous other legal download services have become available including **itunes.com**, **zune.com**, and **rhapsody.com**. However, consumers continue to share music in illicit and illegal ways.

Research reveals that how consumers view illegal downloading depends on the motivation for the behavior. That is, if the motivation is primarily based on utilitarian value (that is, for personal gain), then the act is viewed as less morally ethical and socially acceptable than if the behavior occurs based on hedonic value (that is, for "fun").[18]

Computer-Mediated Behaviors: Attacks

Computers present other opportunities for misbehavior. Did you know that consumers in the United States send more spam than do consumers in any other nation? Losses from clogging up computers and slowing Internet connectivity result in losses of up to $17 billion annually in business productivity![19] Computer viruses are another major problem. Today there are literally thousands of computer viruses being circulated from computer to computer. The effects of viruses range from being mildly annoying to devastating.

An emerging form of computer misbehavior is known as cyberbullying. Cyberbullying, the attack of innocent people on the Internet, is an especially big problem among young consumers. Currently, the behaviors most often affect young girls, as research indicates that girls tend to be targeted by, and instigate, cyberattacks more often than boys do.[20] Regardless of gender, cyberbullying is a serious issue and can have very harmful effects on victims. In fact, it has been estimated that as many as 1 in 3 teenagers have been victims of cyberbullying.[21] Unfortunately, many of these children never report the incidents.

Consumer Fraud

A number of behaviors may be classified as consumer fraud. For instance, consumers fraudulently obtain credit cards, open

> Consumer fraud is growing due in large part to the popularity of the Internet.

© ISTOCKPHOTO.COM/ED HIDDEN

culture jamming
attempts to disrupt advertisements and marketing campaigns by altering the messages in some meaningful way

bank accounts, and turn in bogus insurance claims. Although it is difficult to estimate exactly how much consumer fraud ends up costing consumers, the Coalition Against Insurance Fraud estimates that insurance fraud alone costs Americans at least $80 billion per year.[22]

Identity theft is another major public concern. The Federal Trade Commission estimates that as many as 9 million consumers have their identities stolen each year, and this number appears to be growing.[23] Lawmakers are combating the problem, and laws such as the Identity Theft and Assumption Deterrence Act of 1998 and the Identity Theft Penalty Enhancement Act of 2004 have been passed in efforts to curb the crime. The increased reliance on computer technology for transactions has contributed to the spread of identity theft. It is no wonder that information privacy and security concerns are becoming hot topics for consumers.

Abusive Consumer Behavior

Have you ever seen a consumer who was so abusive and hostile toward a company representative that the consumer simply couldn't be calmed down? Some consumers become so incredibly upset when they don't get their way that they become obnoxious and belligerent. Problem customers or just downright rude customers can be found in just about any setting.

Although there really isn't just one definition of exactly what is meant by abusive consumer behavior, we can say that consumers who are aggressive or rude can be abusive.[24] One early study in the area of problem customers suggested that four categories of customers can

Too Much Is Too Much

Some consumer behavior texts have suggested that overconsumption in and of itself is indeed misbehavior. When is too much simply too much?

The advertising world sends all kinds of messages wrapped around promises to make consumers younger-looking, sexier, more popular, better-loved, and more successful. As a result consumers often buy many more products and services than are really necessary! What's more, the value that the advertising world attempts to place on possessions, money, physical appearance, and success actually leads to overconsumption, which can lead to unhappiness, anxiety, financial problems, or even mental disorders.

Some consumers have actually fought back on the temptation to overconsume by voluntarily simplifying their lives. This was particularly noted by consumer researchers during the economic turndown of 2008 – 2009. Many consumers adjusted their perspectives to move their focus away from overconsumption to "voluntary simplicity." Attitudes towards buying, credit, and saving all changed markedly during this time period.

Even though attitudes towards overconsumption appear to have changed slightly, the issue remains important. The impact of overconsumption on personal finance, pollution, and personal happiness continues to be noted. Sometimes enough is simply enough!

Sources: Ives, Nat (2009), "Marketers Fear Frugality May Just Be Here to Stay," Advertising Age, June 1, 2009, 80 (21), pg 1-2; Evans, Kelly (2009), "The Outlook: Frugality Forged in Today's Recession Has Potential to Outlast it," Wall Street Journal, April 6, 2009, pg. A2; James, Oliver (2008), "It's More than Enough to Make You Sick," Marketing, January 23, 2008, pg. 26 -28.

© ISTOCKPHOTO.COM/NIKOLA HRISTOVSKI

be identified: *verbally or physically abusive customers, uncooperative customers, drunken customers,* and *customers who break company policy.*[25] Needless to say, employees don't like to deal with customers who act this way.

Little is known about the specific effects of abusive consumer behavior. However, abusive behaviors can have negative effects on employee self-esteem and morale, as well as on other consumers.[26]

Another controversial consumer behavior today is found with culture jamming. **Culture jamming** refers to attempts to disrupt advertisements and marketing campaigns by altering the messages in some meaningful way. For example, billboards can be defaced or altered in a way that delivers messages that conflict with those originally intended. Cigarette

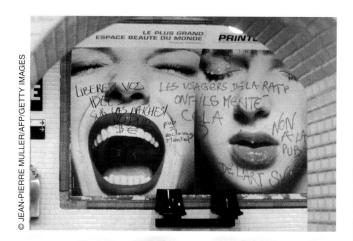

Culture jamming such as this is pervasive in urban areas throughout North America and Europe.

billboards are frequently targeted by groups of consumers who are strongly opposed to smoking. Websites that attempt to disrupt marketing efforts are sometimes started. For example, sites like **amexsux.com** and **unitedparcelsmashers.com** have popped up in the online world. Of course, calling culture jamming an "abusive" behavior depends on your personal perspective! Nevertheless, the actions clearly are uncooperative with marketing efforts. Proponents of culture jamming, however, firmly believe that their behaviors are good for society because they present opposing viewpoints to commercial messages.

Dysfunctional Sports Behaviors

Abusive behavior has also found its way into the consumption of sporting events. Over the past decade, what may be referred to as "dysfunctional" fan behavior has grown steadily. **Dysfunctional fan behavior** refers to abnormal or impaired functioning relating to sporting event consumption.[27] Simply stated, dysfunctional fan behavior is bad fan behavior!

Although terms like *fanatics* or *devoted fans* are often reserved for fans who have very strong attachments to their teams, the term *dysfunctional* implies something much, much darker. Dysfunctional fans are often verbally abusive to others, are loud and obnoxious at sporting events, and can sometimes be violent to others at sporting events. Fans like these disrupt what would otherwise be enjoyable sporting events.

Unfortunately, dysfunctional fan behavior is all too common at sporting events. These behaviors also take place immediately after games are over. For example, several college towns have suffered through the effects

of riots that have occurred after big losses (or wins) of the home team. Unfortunately, riots like these can quickly escalate into very violent behavior, even resulting in the deaths of innocent bystanders. Some think that this behavior is simply a result of an increasingly violent society.[28]

dysfunctional fan behavior abnormal functioning relating to sporting event consumption

Can dysfunctional sports fans be identified easily? One study revealed that these fans differ from other fans in a few ways. First, they tend to consume more alcohol during sporting events than do other fans. They also are much more vocal during games, verbally blasting players, officials, and other fans. As for demographics, research reveals that dysfunctional fans are often young males with relatively low incomes, who are single, and who have lower levels of education than do other fans.[29] Of course, these aren't the only fans who behave like this! One alarming trend is for parents to become unruly and aggressive during their children's games.

Dysfunctional fans who take things too far can even be arrested during sporting events. Needless to say, this can have long-term legal implications.

Illegitimate Complaining

Consumers also complain about products and services even when there really isn't a problem. As with other consumer misbehaviors, little is currently known about the motivations of illegitimate consumer complaining. However, one study did find that illegitimate complaining behavior is motivated by the following needs:

- Desire for monetary gain (that is, to receive free goods without experiencing a failure as when a customer deshops)
- Desire to evade personal responsibility for product misuse
- Desire to enhance the consumer's ego
- Desire to look good to others
- Desire to harm a service provider or company[30]

Product Misuse

Consumers also often use products in ways that were not intended by the marketer. In fact, a major issue with consumer-product packaging and safety warnings is ensuring that consumers understand the ways in which products should be used. Even when warnings and instructions are provided, however, consumers still use safe products in unsafe ways. Consumers can become injured, or even killed, as a result of misusing products. These injuries can be very costly to the economy. In fact, statistics from the Consumer Product Safety Commission reveal that deaths and injuries resulting from product consumption cost the United States over $800 billion annually.[31]

As with other consumer misbehaviors, many examples of product misuse can be discussed. Consumers sometimes simply ignore safety guidelines. For example, consumers commonly climb ladders beyond the rung that is deemed safe by ladder manufacturers. Some consumers also use products in ways that are completely at odds with their intended purpose. For example, some consumers sniff glue or household cleaners to get a "high."

Why do consumers use safe products in unsafe ways? A number of explanations have been offered. Consumers may simply not pay attention to what they are doing, may feel as though they always get away with the risky behavior, may have a tendency to be error prone, or may focus more on the thrill of misuse rather than the actual risk of the behavior.[32] As with other consumer misbehaviors, we see that the "thrill" of the act is a strong motivating factor.

We could discuss a number of different consumer behaviors related to product misuse; however, we will discuss three major issues regarding the misuse of a highly visible product: the automobile.

Aggressive Driving. Aggressive driving may range from mild displays of anger to seriously violent acts while driving. Although aggressive driving is often thought of as an act by a solitary consumer, aggressive driving problems often involve multiple drivers. In fact, a recent study revealed that approximately half of all people who are subjected to aggressive

© MUSKOPF PHOTOGRAPHY, LLC/ALAMY

Consumer Misbehavior: Sexting

One growing form of consumer misbehavior is the practice known as "sexting." It's the practice of taking nude photos of oneself and sending them to another person via cell phone. The practice seems to occur most frequently among teen-aged consumers and it is becoming increasingly common.

According to multiple media reports, many teens seem to feel like sexting isn't harmful. Parents and school administrators don't feel the same way. Parents are concerned that the images can be passed from person to person, and eventually onto the Internet. Sexting also raises moral, ethical and legal issues for teens and their parents.

One major concern with sexting is that it can lead to child pornography charges. If a minor is charged with possession or distribution of child pornography, he or she may have to register as a sex offender. There are many legal issues that surround sexting, and it's often unclear exactly who should be charged in these cases.

Should the person taking the photo be charged or the person receiving the photo? What about people to whom the images are forwarded? While legal authorities wrestle with questions such as these, it is clear that the cell phone was never meant to be used for sending or receiving pornography, making sexting another case of consumer misbehavior.

Sources: Searcy, Dionne (2009), "Currents: A Lawyer, Some Teens and a Fight Over Sexting" *Wall Street Journal* April 21, 2009, Pg. A17; Kingston, Anne (2009), "The Sexting Scare," Maclean's, March 16, 2009, Pg. 52; Koch, Wendy (2009), "Teens Caught 'Sexting' Face Porn Charges," USA Today (online edition), March 11, 2009, online content retrieved at: **http://www.usatoday.com/tech/wireless/2009-03-11-sexting_N.htm**, accessed June 18, 2009.

driving behaviors respond aggressively themselves![33] Clearly, when one consumer responds aggressively to the actions of another, the problem becomes much, much worse.

Age, gender, and education have all been shown to be associated with the occurrence of aggressive driving behaviors. In general, younger, less-educated males are more likely to engage in aggressive driving behavior.[34] Situational factors, such as intense traffic congestion, driver stress, and high temperatures play major roles in aggressive driving. Personal factors, such as personality, also influence the behavior. In particular, traits like instability and competitiveness have been found to be associated with the behavior.[35] Road rage, an extreme manifestation of aggressive driving, continues to be an important consumer behavior and public policy issue.

MADD works hard to prevent drunk driving.

use, a growing area of public concern involves the use of cell phones while driving. Like drinking and driving, neither behavior in isolation is considered to be a problem. However, the use of the two products at the same time is generating significant public attention and scrutiny. Studies reveal that the use of cell phones is the single biggest distraction for today's driver.[42] Among teens, the problem is especially serious as nearly 50% of teens recently surveyed report using cell phones while driving[43] and over 40% report texting while driving![43a]

The problem is not confined to the United States. In fact, currently 40 countries worldwide either restrict or ban the use of cell phones while driving. Numerous pieces of legislation aimed at banning the use of cell phones while driving have been introduced in the United States, and several states have actually passed laws regarding the practice.[44] Given the increased popularity of cell phone technologies, this issue is likely to remain under intense public scrutiny.

CONSUMER PROBLEM BEHAVIOR

There are other behaviors that can be considered consumer problem areas that do not necessarily break any specific laws or generally accepted societal norms. For example, some consumers simply shop too much. Some consumers rack up too much credit card debt. Some consumers harm their own bodies in desperate attempts to look thin. In many cases, these behaviors are caused by psychological problems.

Drunk Driving. The latest statistics reveal that nearly 13,000 people died from alcohol-related traffic accidents in the year 2007 alone. What's more, nearly three out of every ten Americans will be involved in an alcohol-related crash at some point in their lives.[36] Sadly, approximately one out of every six fatalities among children aged 14 and younger are due to alcohol-related accidents.[37] Furthermore, nearly 64% of all drivers aged 15–20 who were involved in fatal accidents had blood alcohol levels above .08.[38] Of course, this group is under the legal drinking age!

Drunk driving is a serious societal problem that may be classified as consumer misbehavior. Neither drinking nor driving is an illegal behavior. However, mixing the two is illegal, and the problem appears to be growing. In fact, one recent study revealed that the number of people reporting that they had driven a motor vehicle while under the influence of alcohol jumped 57% between 2000 and 2005.[39]

Not surprisingly, drunk driving (also referred to as alcohol-impaired driving or *AID*) is often related to binge drinking. In fact, over 80% of respondents who reported AID also reported engaging in binge drinking behaviors.[40] Once again, we see that several consumer misbehaviors are related to one another.

Cell Phone Use in Cars. Over 230 million U.S. consumers now have mobile phone service.[41] Given the popularity of cell phone

Texting while driving is extremely dangerous.

compulsive consumption repetitive, excessive, and purposeful consumer behaviors that are performed as a response to tension, anxiety, or obtrusive thoughts

addictive consumption physiological dependency on the consumption of a consumer product

compulsive buying chronic, repetitive purchasing that is a response to negative events or feelings

In the sections that follow, we discuss several of these behaviors. We begin with an issue that has received considerable attention, compulsive consumption.

Compulsive Consumption

Compulsive consumption is a serious consumer behavior issue. **Compulsive consumption** refers to repetitive, excessive, and purposeful consumer behaviors that are performed as a response to tension, anxiety, or obtrusive thoughts.[45] The term *compulsive consumption* is often used broadly and consists of a number of specific behaviors related to the purchase and use of consumer products and services.[46]

Although this ad is humorous, compulsive consumption is no laughing matter.

Compulsive consumption should not be confused with *addictive consumption*, although the terms are often used interchangeably. **Addictive consumption** refers to a physiological dependency on the consumption of a product. The word *dependency* is very important, and in the strictest sense, addictions are characterized by the physical inability to discontinue a behavior. A person who is addicted to a product physically needs that product. Compulsivity is more psychologically oriented, but to a consumer, compulsions can be equally controlling.

Some problem areas, such as the newly recognized *Internet addiction*, are often described in both ways. In other words, consumers may seemingly have the inability to stop the behavior (as when a consumer surfs online for hours on end), and they also tend to release stress by engaging in the behavior (as when a consumer plays games online as a way to escape). Of course, the degree to which a consumer becomes physically dependent on the Internet is highly questionable. However, we can see from this example that the two terms can be used rather loosely.

Whether classified as real addiction or compulsion, several consumer behaviors become problematic. Compulsive consumption often takes two forms: *compulsive buying* and *compulsive shopping*.

Compulsive Buying. **Compulsive buying** may be defined as chronic, repetitive *purchasing* behaviors that are in response to negative events or feelings.[47] Compulsive buying can have very harmful results including the accumulation of high levels of debt, domestic problems, and feelings of frustration. At a time when personal debt is at an all-time high in the United States, the issue of compulsive consumption is very important.

Several factors are related to compulsive buying. Influencers of this form of buying include feelings of low self-esteem and self-adequacy, obsessive–compulsive tendencies, fantasy-seeking motivations, and materialism.[48] Among adolescent consumers, compulsive buying may also be a response to a disruption in family structure, such as parental divorce.[49] The same negative feelings that influence compulsive buying can also result from the behavior itself. That is, a consumer who buys compulsively as a reaction to negative feelings often experiences even more negative feelings after going on buying binges.[50] As you can see, compulsive buying can be described as a vicious circle!

Compulsive Shopping. Compulsive shopping is another manifestation of compulsive consumption that

© IMAGE COURTESY OF THE ADVERTISING ARCHIVES

is closely related to compulsive buying. To buy, you must shop! **Compulsive shopping** refers to repetitive *shopping* behaviors. The word *oniomania* is sometimes used to describe this behavior. Compulsive shoppers frequently shop four to seven days per week, think about shopping for nine or more hours per week, and spend two or more hours shopping during each trip.[51] While compulsive buying and shopping are closely related, a key difference between the concepts is that compulsive buying behavior is focused on purchasing, whereas compulsive shopping is focused on shopping, browsing, and the mental highs associated with "the hunt."[52]

Early research on this issue revealed that compulsive shopping was predominately a problem for women.[53] However, recent evidence suggests that both women and men engage in compulsive shopping. In fact, a recent study confirmed that equal proportions of men and women are compulsive shoppers, with 6% of women and 5.5% of men being classified as compulsive.[54]

Eating Disorders

Binge eating refers to the consumption of large amounts of food while feeling a general loss of control over intake. Binge eating may result in medical complications, including high cholesterol, high blood pressure, and heart disease. Exhibit 15.3 presents a description of the binge eating disorder.

As mentioned previously, compulsive tendencies are often related to one another, and binge eating has been shown to be associated with compulsive buying. This is particularly the case for obese consumers. In fact, obese consumers who engage in binge eating are likely to have

EXHIBIT 15.3
Binge Eating Disorder

Binge eating disorder consists of:
- Frequent eating episodes that include large quantities of food in short time periods.
- A felt loss of control over eating behavior.
- Feelings of shame, guilt, and/or disgust about the amount of food consumed.
- The consumption of food when one is not hungry.
- The consumption of food in secret.

Source: Based on National Eating Disorders Association, **www.nationaleatingdisorders.org**.

other psychiatric disorders that require treatment.[55] Unfortunately, many consumers who have problems with binge eating often fail to seek medical treatment. Binge eating is also often associated with *bulimia*, a disorder that includes binge eating episodes followed by self-induced vomiting or purging. Another eating-related problem area for many consumers is *anorexia*, or the starving of one's body in the pursuit of "thinness."

Binge drinking can have serious consequences. In fact, it has been linked to suicide attempts, unsafe sexual practices, legal problems, academic disruptions, and even death.

Binge Drinking

Binge drinking is a very serious problem in society today. This behavior is defined as the consumption of five or more drinks in a single drinking session for men and four or more drinks for women.[56] It is particularly prevalent among college students. In fact estimates reveal that binge drinking rates among full-time college students are over 40%, compared to only 17% for students not enrolled full time.[57] The behavior is not confined to students in the United States, however, as another study revealed that students in the United Kingdom often binge drink for the sole purpose of getting drunk. Indeed, the results indicated that respondents view "getting drunk" as a key feature of college life.[58] Binge drinking can have serious consequences. In fact, it has been linked to suicide attempts, unsafe sexual practices, legal problems, academic disruptions, and even death.[59]

Personal values, such as values for self-actualization and for social affiliation, appear to be related to attitudes toward alcohol consumption. College students who have higher self-actualization values generally have lower attitudes toward drinking, whereas students who value affiliation tend to have more positive attitudes toward the behavior.[60]

Importantly, binge drinking problems are not confined only to the college population. Rather, binge drinking cuts across demographic groups. One particularly alarming trend is the occurrence of binge drinking among underage consumers. In fact, nearly half of the alcohol consumed on four-year college campuses is consumed by underage consumers.[61]

Problem Gambling

Problem gambling (also referred to as pathological gambling) is another serious consumer behavior issue. This behavior may be described as an obsession with gambling and the loss of control over gambling behavior and its consequences.[62] Problem gambling emerges in a number of ways. Consumers who are problem gamblers frequently gamble longer than planned, borrow money to finance their gambling, and feel major depression due to their gambling behaviors. Although casino and online gambling receive much research attention, lottery-ticket and scratch-ticket purchases can also be considered problem gambling behaviors.[63]

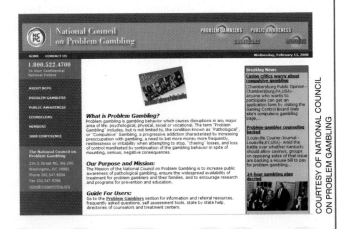

The National Council on Problem Gambling is a valuable resource for problem gamblers.

Estimates reveal that as many as three million consumers meet the criteria of pathological gambling behavior.[64] Although problem gambling is often thought of as being primarily an issue for middle-aged consumers, this is not the case. In fact, approximately 8% of college students gamble problematically.[65] What's more, a recent study revealed that nearly 70% of seniors older than 65 had gambled at least once in the previous year and nearly 11% were considered at "at risk" for problem gambling.[66]

As is the case with many compulsive behaviors, problem gambling is associated with other consumer compulsions. For example, research indicates that problem gambling is often associated with compulsive buying and compulsive drug abuse.[67]

Drug Abuse

Another problem area for many consumers is the consumption of drugs. Both illegal and legal drugs (such as over-the-counter medications and prescription drugs) can become problematic for consumers. In fact, a recent study by the Partnership for a Drug Free America revealed that nearly one in five teenagers report using prescription drugs to get high, and nearly one in ten report abusing cough medicine to get high. Even more troubling is the finding that nearly 40% of teenagers sampled believe that abusing prescription drugs is "safer" than abusing illegal drugs such as marijuana or cocaine.[68]

The abuse of illegal drugs (including marijuana, cocaine, hallucinogens, and heroin) has been a major problem for years. The problem is particularly serious for young consumers. In fact, a 2008 study revealed that over 14% of eighth graders in the U.S. reported using illicit drugs in the previous year. Given that these data rely on self-report measures, the number may actually be higher than this![69]

Final Thought on Consumer Problem Areas

We've discussed only a handful of behaviors that may be considered consumer problem areas, and there are many other behaviors that may be discussed. Indeed, space prohibits a complete discussion of these issues. Nevertheless, the topics discussed in this chapter are quite popular in today's consumer culture.

Chapter 15 Case

I n 2005, over 100,000 U.S. consumers were alarmed to learn that their personal information might have fallen into the wrong hands. ChoicePoint, a suburban Atlanta-based company, reported that these individuals' identities were at risk of being used for fraudulent purposes. This incident was one of many reported cases of identity theft, a criminal offense.

ChoicePoint is part of a growing industry of data brokers, or companies that specialize in collecting and selling background information on adult consumers. ChoicePoint offers names, Social Security numbers, birth dates, employment information, and credit histories to customers, which include governmental agencies and private companies. ChoicePoint's business clients use consumer data for marketing purposes. To perform this crime, a group of individuals set up over fifty different accounts under fictitious company names and fraudulently purchased consumer background information.

Over 750 victims reported that their personal information had been used to buy jewelry and consumer electronics products. Many victims were unaware that this information had been collected at all. Some expressed outrage toward the data brokerage industry and demanded that their personal information be protected from criminals and businesses alike. The Federal Trade Commission (FTC) charged ChoicePoint with failing to maintain reasonable standards for screening prospective clients and filed a civil suit against the company. As a consequence, ChoicePoint was ordered to pay $10 million in civil penalties and $5 million redress to consumers to settle the FTC's charges. Some victims are experiencing the aftermath effects

of identity theft and continued to have difficulty with harassing creditors. One victim reported still owing close to $140,000 in fraudulent debt one month after the crime was reported, despite following Justice Department protocol for resolving his credit problems.

As the text indicates, as many as 9 million consumers fall victim to identity theft each year. According to the FTC, there are various forms of identity theft. Traditionally, identity theft has been limited to obtaining personal information through false solicitation (preapproved credit applications) or "shoulder surfing," in which criminals observe others as they provide information in public places. Others will "dumpster dive," searching discarded papers for personal information. Recently, the rise of Internet transactions has opened another realm in which criminals can obtain personal information for fraudulent use through false e-mail solicitations, or "phishing." There are many more methods in which criminals steal the identities of others, as evidenced by the ChoicePoint case. The FTC emphasizes that identity theft can happen to anyone, and the consequences can be devastating.[70]

Questions

1. What measures can consumers take in order to prevent becoming victims of identity theft?

2. Even though selling consumer data is a legal business practice, many people question the data brokering practice. Is it ethical to sell consumer data for profit?

3. Will Internet identity theft stop consumers from carrying out transactions online?

Being socially

responsible is one way in which businesses can attempt to do well by doing the right things.

what do you think?

Consumers are generally more ethical than the typical businessperson.

1 2 3 4 5 6 7
strongly disagree   strongly agree

16

Marketing Ethics, Misbehavior, and Value

After studying this chapter, the student should be able to:

LO1 Discuss marketing ethics and how marketing ethics guide the development of marketing programs.

LO2 Describe the consumerism movement and how the movement has affected marketing practice.

LO3 Comprehend the role of corporate social responsibility in the field of marketing.

LO4 Understand the various forms of regulation that affect marketing practice.

LO5 Comprehend the major areas of criticism to which marketers are subjected.

LO6 Understand how products liability issues can provide both positive and negative results for consumers.

Introduction

a fair marketplace depends on each party in an exchange acting fairly and with due respect for each other. Thus, consumers, marketing entities, and government officials who regulate business activity must all act with integrity. Whenever anyone acts unethically, inefficiencies result and chances are that somebody will suffer. As such, consumer misbehavior is not the only misbehavior that deserves attention.

Media reports all too often describe company actions that are at best questionable, at times immoral, and at worst illegal. News headlines frequently highlight stories of accounting scandals, manipulative marketing practices, and deceptive advertising. Unscrupulous actions of companies directly impact the marketplace because they upset the value equation associated with a given exchange. When a company misrepresents a product, consumers are led to expect more than is actually delivered. Unfair exchanges result. A fair value exchange exists when marketers and consumers act with good faith, complete disclosure, and trust. When trust is violated, value perceptions are harmed.

> **ethics** standards or moral codes of conduct to which a person, group, or organization adheres

LO1 Marketing Ethics and Marketing Strategy

t he issue of marketer misbehavior is not easy to discuss because not everyone will agree on what behaviors really should be considered "misbehaviors." As discussed in our consumer misbehavior chapter, discussions of misbehavior center on the concept of ethics. The term **ethics** has been used in many ways, and ethical issues permeate our everyday lives. The term refers to standards or moral codes of conduct to which a person, group, or organization adheres. **Marketing ethics** consist of societal and professional standards of right and fair practices that are expected of marketing managers as they develop and implement marketing strategies.[1] More simply, ethics determines how much tolerance one has for actions that take advantage of others.

Many organizations have explicitly stated rules and codes of conduct for their employees. Most professional organizations do as well. Exhibit 16.1 presents the Code of Conduct for the American Marketing Association (that is, the AMA).

As we have discussed previously, misbehavior can be viewed as a subset of the *deviance* topic. Accordingly, for a marketer to misbehave, he or she must be aware that an action will be considered unethical and act with deviance to cover the true intent of the action. According to this perspective, the marketing organization or employee that misbehaves must know that the actions are considered inappropriate and carry through with them anyway. Sometimes, firms and employees do not intend to misbehave. Rather, simple mistakes are made in marketing execution. As in a court of law, proving intent is not an easy thing to do, and, of course, agreement on many of these issues will likely never happen.

Complete agreement on exactly what is meant by an action being either "right" or "wrong" is not likely to be found. Obviously, these labels are dependent upon personal perspectives, morals, ideals, and culture. What is more certain, however, is that certain actions break laws and that some actions violate consumer trust.

LO2 Consumerism

the **marketing concept** proposes that all the functions of the organization should work together in satisfying its customers' wants and needs. This is important for any business. When businesses begin taking advantage of consum-

ers, consumers lose, businesses lose, and society as a whole eventually loses. In fact, it can be said that the ethical treatment of consumers is a cornerstone of a fair marketplace.[2]

As a simple example, consider what happens when a business knowingly deceives consumers. Perhaps a water filtration salesperson knowingly contaminates a water clarity test by adding certain minerals to a water sample. Consumers may become alarmed at the poor quality of their water and decide to buy a filtration system. If they later find that the test was tainted, they may complain to the company or even the Better Business Bureau. Obviously, the value of the transaction to the consumer is severely harmed. If word gets around that the marketer is acting unethically, the company may even go out of business. Employees will be lost, storefronts will suddenly become vacant, and consumers will be left with unnecessary products.

This example makes clear how one simple act of a salesperson can have detrimental effects on the salesperson's customers, town, and even self!

Much of the pressure that has been placed on marketers comes directly from consumer groups. **Consumerism** is used to describe the activities of various groups to protect basic consumer rights. Many years ago, the voice of the consumer simply didn't garner much attention. In the early days of mass production, much of the focus was on production efficiencies and "cost per unit," with little attention to consumer concerns. This changed gradually throughout the 20th century, however. The voice of the consumer grew steadily, and consumer movements were greatly helped by the adoption of the Consumer Bill of Rights.

> The Consumer Bill of Rights dramatically changed how businesses viewed the consumer.

© BETTMANN/CORBIS

EXHIBIT 16.1
American Marketing Association Code of Ethics

Preamble The American Marketing Association commits itself to promoting the highest standard of professional ethical norms and values for its members. Norms are established standards of conduct that are expected and maintained by society and/or professional organizations. Values represent the collective conception of what people find desirable, important and morally proper. Values serve as the criteria for evaluating the actions of others. Marketing practitioners must recognize that they not only serve their enterprises but also act as stewards of society in creating, facilitating and executing the efficient and effective transactions that are part of the greater economy. In this role, marketers should embrace the highest ethical *norms* of practicing professionals and the ethical *values* implied by their responsibility toward stakeholders (e.g., customers, employees, investors, channel members, regulators and the host community).

General Norms:

1. Marketers must do no harm. This means doing work for which they are appropriately trained or experienced so that they can actively add value to their organizations and customers. It also means adhering to all applicable laws and regulations and embodying high ethical standards in the choices they make.

2. Marketers must foster trust in the marketing system. This means that products are appropriate for their intended and promoted uses. It requires that marketing communications about goods and services are not intentionally deceptive or misleading. It suggests building relationships that provide for the equitable adjustment and/or redress of customer grievances. It implies striving for good faith and fair dealing so as to contribute toward the efficacy of the exchange process.

3. Marketers must embrace, communicate and practice the fundamental ethical values that will improve consumer confidence in the integrity of the marketing exchange system. These basic *values* are intentionally aspirational and include honesty, responsibility, fairness, respect, openness and citizenship.

Ethical Values

Honesty—to be truthful and forthright in our dealings with customers and stakeholders. We will tell the truth in all situations and at all times. We will offer products of value that do what we claim in our communications. We will stand behind our products if they fail to deliver their claimed benefits. We will honor our explicit and implicit commitments and promises.

Responsibility—to accept the consequences of our marketing decisions and strategies. We will make strenuous efforts to serve the needs of our customers. We will avoid using coercion with all stakeholders. We will acknowledge the social obligations to stakeholders that come with increased marketing and economic power. We will recognize our special commitments to economically vulnerable segments of the market such as children, the elderly and others who may be substantially disadvantaged.

Fairness—to try to balance justly the needs of the buyer with the interests of the seller. We will represent our products in a clear way in selling, advertising and other forms of communication; this includes the avoidance of false, misleading and deceptive promotion. We will reject manipulations and sales tactics that harm customer trust. We will not engage in price fixing, predatory pricing, price gouging or "bait-and-switch" tactics. We will not knowingly participate in material conflicts of interest.

Respect—to acknowledge the basic human dignity of all stakeholders. We will value individual differences even as we avoid stereotyping customers or depicting demographic groups (e.g., gender, race, sexual orientation) in a negative or dehumanizing way in our promotions. We will listen to the needs of our customers and make all reasonable efforts to monitor and improve their satisfaction on an ongoing basis. We will make a special effort to understand suppliers, intermediaries and distributors from other cultures. We will appropriately acknowledge the contributions of others, such as consultants, employees and coworkers, to our marketing endeavors.

Openness—to create transparency in our marketing operations. We will strive to communicate clearly with all our constituencies. We will accept constructive criticism from our customers and other stakeholders. We will explain significant product or service risks, component substitutions or other foreseeable eventualities that could affect customers or their perception of the purchase decision. We will fully disclose list prices and terms of financing as well as available price deals and adjustments.

Citizenship—to fulfill the economic, legal, philanthropic and societal responsibilities that serve stakeholders in a strategic manner. We will strive to protect the natural environment in the execution of marketing campaigns. We will give back to the community through volunteerism and charitable donations. We will work to contribute to the overall betterment of marketing and its reputation. We will encourage supply chain members to ensure that trade is fair for all participants, including producers in developing countries.

Implementation Finally, we recognize that every industry sector and marketing subdiscipline (e.g., marketing research, e-commerce, direct selling, direct marketing, advertising) has its own specific ethical issues that require policies and commentary. An array of such codes can be accessed through links on the AMA website. We encourage all such groups to develop and/or refine their industry and discipline-specific codes of ethics to supplement these general norms and values.

The **Consumer Bill of Rights** was introduced in 1962, and included:

1. The right to safety
2. The right to be informed
3. The right to redress and to be heard
4. The right to choice

The Consumer Bill of Rights stands today as a foundation of the consumerism movement. Of course, these rights were introduced years ago and prior to the advent of the Internet. Internet security has become a huge topic and unsuspecting consumers often fall victim to phishing and cybersquatting scams. By falling victim to such scams, the consumers' rights to safety, information, and choice are violated. These issues are discussed in the Cyber-What? feature.

THE MARKETING CONCEPT AND THE CONSUMER

The marketing concept developed greatly in the 1960s. It was early in this time period that famed author Theodore Levitt published an article in the *Harvard Business Review* entitled "Marketing Myopia." Among other things, Levitt's work brought about a new perspective that argued that businesses should define themselves in terms of the consumer needs that they satisfy rather than in terms of the products that they make. Levitt argued that a firm's long-term health depends on its ability to exist as a consumer-satisfying entity rather than a goods-producing entity. Levitt's work was important for the large-scale adoption of the marketing

Cyber-What?

The practice of cybersquatting, by which deceptive individuals attempt to purchase and control websites that mimic popular commercial sites, has become a very serious issue in Internet marketing. In fact, it has been estimated that cybersquatting costs brand-name marketers over $1 billion per year.

Although cybersquatting is illegal under the Anti-Cybersquatting Consumer Protection Act of 1999, the problem continues. The practice actually started in the 1990s when entrepreneurs would attempt to buy the rights to a popular name such as "michaeljordan.com" and then sell the name to the appropriate owner, often for very large sums of money. These attempts have continued, and in 2006 alone the majority of cybersquatting complaints came from companies who were approached by individuals trying to sell website domain names.

Cybersquatting can also harm consumers because they often don't realize that they are visiting a suspicious website. A big problem exists when consumers mistype popular website addresses and find themselves on a cybersquatting site. Many times, the website looks practically identical to the intended site. So pay close attention to the websites you visit. You may find yourself in the cybersquatting world.

Sources: Schnitzler, Peter (2007), "We Have Your Website," *Indianapolis Business Journal*, 28 (18) (July 9), 17; Torbenson, Eric (2007), "Cashing In on Human Error: Your Fingers Have Fumbled, and Now You're Looking at the Wrong Web Site," *Knight Ridder Tribune Business News* (May 24), 1; Cowlett, Mary (2007), "Protecting Companies from Cybersquatters," *PR Week* (April 20), 21.

concept. As we discussed in an earlier chapter, a key assertion of this concept is that the long-term survival of the firm depends on its ability to focus on customer needs as a means of achieving organizational success.

While many companies today adhere to the marketing concept, numerous questions arise regarding actual marketing practice. For example, companies often come under criticism for marketing products that some consider harmful. In particular, the fast-food, cereal, tobacco, and alcohol industries are often under fire from various groups. Even though freedom of choice is a central tenet of the U.S. economic system, these products are among the many that society often considers harmful.

The Marketing Mix and the Consumer

Marketers should use the tools found in the marketing mix carefully as they target consumers. Decision makers have been under increased public pressure to use their tools ethically. When consumers question the way in which they are treated, they are likely to spread negative information through word-of-mouth.

All areas of the marketing mix can be brought into question by consumer groups. One of the most visible elements of the marketing mix is pricing, and for this reason pricing policies are often questioned. When consumers believe that a firm's prices are unfair, they are likely to leave the firm and spread negative information about it.[3] Consumers also complain that marketing efforts lead to overall higher prices. Marketers counter by explaining that marketing expenditures allow for increased economies of scale that contribute to lower overall production costs. As with other issues in this chapter, pricing issues are certainly debatable. Exhibit 16.2 presents the four P's of marketing as well as their ethical and unethical uses.

The product portion of the marketing mix also commonly comes under fire. One of the major concerns is the extent to which products are actually harmful to either the consumer or society in the long run. That is, many products can lead to short-term customer satisfaction, but they can also lead to long-term problems for both the consumer and society. Consider the following categories of products that were originally introduced by Philip Kotler:[4]

- **Deficient products** are products that have little to no potential to create value of any type (for example, faulty appliances).

- **Salutary products** are products that are good for both consumers and society in the long run (for example, air bags). These products offer high utilitarian value, but do not provide hedonic value.

- **Pleasing products** are products that provide hedonic value to consumers but may be harmful in the long run (for example, cigarettes).

- **Desirable products** are products that deliver high utilitarian and hedonic value and that benefit both consumers and society in the long run (for example, pleasant-tasting weight-loss products).

deficient products products that have little or no potential to create value of any type

salutary products products that are good for both consumers and society in the long run and that provide high utilitarian value, but no hedonic value

pleasing products products that provide hedonic value for consumers but may be harmful in the long run

desirable products products that deliver high utilitarian and hedonic value and that benefit both consumers and society in the long run

Marketers would clearly want to avoid offering *deficient* products. The difficult issue comes with the marketing of *pleasing* products. Many consumers know that the products they enjoy are indeed harmful, but they buy them anyway! Needless to say, the tobacco industry has been under criticism for years for marketing products that many think are unsafe. Again, individual responsibility and freedom are important factors in consumer decisions to use these products. Most of the time, these companies deliver both customer satisfaction and value.

The promotion and place elements of the marketing mix are also often questioned. Many times consumers believe that products are promoted in a way that is simply "too good to be true." We discuss this issue later in the chapter. Consumers also question distribution tactics used by marketers. For example, they

EXHIBIT 16.2
The Marketing Mix and Business Ethics

TOOL	COMMON USE	UNETHICAL USE
Product	The development of a good, service, or experience that will satisfy consumers' needs.	Failure to disclose that product won't function properly without necessary component parts.
Place	The distribution of a marketing offer through various channels of delivery.	Limiting product availability in certain markets as a means of raising prices.
Price	The marketer's statement of value received from an offering that may be monetary or non-monetary.	Stating that a regular price is really a "sales" price. This practice is prohibited by law.
Promotion	Communicating an offering's value through techniques such as advertising, sales promotion, and word-of-mouth.	Promoting one item as being on sale and then informing the customer that the product is out of stock and that a more expensive item should be bought. This practice, known as "bait and switch," is illegal.

often complain about tickets to major events being made available in only a few very select channels. As a result, consumers often feel like they are being treated unfairly. In 2009, Bruce Springsteen fans were enraged when they tried to buy tickets to his New Jersey concerts through ticketmaster.com. After logging on at the appropriate time, fans were given a website error message and re-directed to the Ticketmaster-owned site "ticketsnow.com." The problem was that the ticket prices were much higher than face value on ticketsnow.com. Springsteen strongly condemned the practice and Ticketmaster later apologized.[4a]

© MIKE MARSLAND/WIREIMAGE/GETTY IMAGES

> Restricting tickets to popular events can ultimately harm consumers.

Consumer Vulnerability and Product Harmfulness

Two important issues to consider when discussing marketing ethics are product harmfulness and consumer vulnerability.[5] A classification of product harmfulness/consumer vulnerability applied to marketing decision making is presented in Exhibit 16.3. Public criticism of marketing strategies tends to be most intense when a marketer targets vulnerable consumer groups with harmful products, as is the case when a marketer targets high-alcohol-content beverages to segments that have a large proportion of alcohol problems.

Of course, what constitutes a "harmful" product is up to the interpretation of the individual, as is the definition of a "vulnerable" consumer. For example, many would argue that fast food is harmful only if it is consumed in large quantities over time. Others may argue that the quantity consumed is not relevant as long as the consumer exercises regularly. Many would agree that children and undereducated or elderly consumers could be considered vulnerable. Others may not agree with this categorization. As with other ethical issues, it is difficult to come to complete agreement on these issues.

One issue that is currently a hot topic is the growth in obesity among U.S. consumers. Both media attention and public pressure have led fast-food marketers to rethink their menu offerings.

Employee Behavior

Individual employees play an important part in the execution of marketing programs. Of course, consumers hope that a firm's employees are acting in good faith, but this is obviously not always the case. When a used car salesperson sets the odometer back on automobiles, the salesperson knows that the act is unethical and illegal. This is straightforward, and all salespeople should know this. However, not all situations are this straightforward.

To illustrate, consider a different salesperson facing the temptation to use bribery as a means of obtaining a sale. In some cultures, this practice is commonplace and acceptable; however, the practice is prohibited in the United States. But what if

EXHIBIT 16.3
Product Harmfulness and Consumer Vulnerability

Product Harmfulness

	Less Harmful	More Harmful
Less Vulnerable	Low-fat fast-food item promoted to above-average income segment consumers	High-interest-rate credit cards marketed to above-average income segment consumers
More Vulnerable	Low-nicotine cigarette promoted to undereducated consumers	High-alcohol-content drink marketed to consumer groups known to have disproportionate levels of alcohol problems

Consumer Vulnerability

Source: Adapted from Smith, N. Craig, and Elizabeth Cooper-Martin (1997), "Ethics and Target Marketing: The Role of Product Harm and Consumer Vulnerability," *Journal of Marketing*, 61 (3), 1–20.

the salesperson is dealing with a customer who is living in the United States but is from a country where bribes are commonplace? One would hope that the salesperson acts in accordance with expectations of his own home country, but you can see how difficulties can emerge.

Individual behavior is guided not only by a sense of what members of society would believe is ethical or unethical in a particular situation but also by the individual's morals. **Morals** are personal standards and beliefs that are used to guide individual action. Certainly, morals and ethics go hand in hand, and each individual must answer to his or her own belief system.

As we discussed in our consumer misbehavior chapter, ethical and moral beliefs affect all types of behaviors. In fact, professors are even under pressure to ensure that they act ethically in the classroom. Several actions, such as using unfair grading techniques, manipulating teaching evaluations, or showing favoritism to students, are all considered to be unethical.[6]

Actions such as these lower the value that students receive from their education!

morals personal standards and beliefs used to guide individual action

corporate social responsibility organization's activities and status related to its societal obligations

LO3
Corporate Social Responsibility

an important topic in business today is corporate social responsibility, and a popular catch-phrase for socially responsible businesses is "doing well by doing good." That is, a company will perform well if it does good things. Being socially responsible is one way in which businesses can attempt to do well by doing the right things. **Corporate social responsibility** may be defined as an organization's activities and status related to its societal obligations.[7] Due to increased pressure from consumer and media groups, companies are finding that they must be socially responsible with their activities.

There are many ways in which companies can be responsible. Activities such as making donations to causes, supporting minority programs, ensuring responsible manufacturing processes and environmental protectionism, acting quickly when product defects are detected, focusing on employee safety, and encouraging employees to volunteer for local causes are some of the many ways in which companies can exhibit their social responsibility.[8] The popular ice cream giant, Ben & Jerry's, is well-known for its cause-related and philanthropic marketing efforts.

Basically, the actions described here fall into one of three categories:

Peanut Butter Safety

A major outbreak of sallmonella poisoning struck unsuspecting peanut butter consumers in late 2008 and early 2009. The outbreak highlighted just how complex the American food distribution system is and how poor managerial decisions can result in devastating effects. By mid-2009, approximately 700 people were sickened by the outbreak, with at least 46 states being affected.

The source of the outbreak was a manufacturing facility in Georgia operated by the Peanut Butter Corporation of America, which shipped bulk peanut butter and peanut paste to institutional customers. Peanut butter and paste is found in numerous products ranging from cookies to ice cream to pet treats.

Reports quickly surfaced that the company knowingly shipped tainted products even after tests revealed that salmonella was present in the peanut butter. A criminal investigation was launched by the federal government in January 2009, and the company later filed for bankruptcy protection in February 2009. The problems with the salmonella poisoning highlight the importance of ensuring that consumer safety, confidence, and trust is maintained for all marketing organizations.

Sources: Hill, Catey (2009), "Officials Want Criminal Probe of Peanut Butter Corporation for Shipping Salmonella-Tainted Peanut Butter, *New York Daily News* (online), online content retrieved at: **http://www.nydailynews.com/money/2009/01/28/2009-01-28_officials_want_criminal_probe_of_peanut_-4.html**, accessed June 19, 2009; Investigation update April 29, 2009, Center for Disease Control, online content retrieved at **http://www.cdc.gov/salmonella/typhimurium/update.html**, accessed June 19, 2009. Anonymous (2009), "Peanut Butter Recall," *New York Times* (online), online content retrieved at: **http://topics.nytimes.com/top/reference/timestopics/subjects/f/food_safety_peanut_butter_recall_2009/index.html**, accessed June 19, 2009. Hartman, Brian and Kate Barett (2009), "Timeline of the Salmonella Outbreak, ABC News (online), online content retrieved at : **http://i.abcnews.com/Health/Story?id=6837291&page=1**, retrieved June 22, 2009.

© ISTOCKPHOTO.COM/LUCAS CORNWELL

ethical duties expectations placed on a firm to act within ethical boundaries

altruistic duties expectations placed upon a firm to give back to communities through philanthropic activities

strategic initiatives process of strategically engaging in socially responsible activities in order to increase the value of the firm

societal marketing concept marketing concept that states that marketers should consider not only the wants and needs of consumers but also the needs of society

- **Ethical duties** include acting within expected ethical boundaries.

- **Altruistic duties** include giving back to communities through philanthropic activities.

- **Strategic initiatives** include strategically engaging in socially responsible activities in order to increase the value of the firm.[9]

Socially responsible marketing creates positive outcomes. For example, socially responsible marketing is associated with more favorable consumer evaluations, increased customer satisfaction, and the likelihood of more sales. This is particularly the case when an individual consumer identifies with the company and the causes to which it contributes.[10]

THE SOCIETAL MARKETING CONCEPT

The **societal marketing concept** emerged out of recognition of the effects that a marketing system has on society as a whole. This concept considers not only the wants and needs of individual consumers but also the needs of society.[11]

Society is comprised of all kinds of stakeholders for a firm, and the effects of marketing actions on these stakeholder groups should be considered in all marketing decisions. For example, a firm may develop and market a profitable product to a targeted group of consumers, but if the campaign achieves profitability at the expense of the general good, then the effort should not be undertaken. Again, *all* the stakeholders of the firm should be considered when marketing programs are initiated. This assertion is found in Exhibit 16.4, which presents prescriptions for improved marketing ethics.

There are many ways in which companies can be socially responsible.

EXHIBIT 16.4
Prescriptions for Improved Marketing Ethics

Prescriptions for Improved Marketing Ethics

- Marketers must put people first and consider the effects of their actions on all stakeholders.

- Actions must be based on standards that go beyond laws and regulations.

- Marketers must be held responsible for the means they use to achieve their desired ends. Focusing on profit motivations is not enough.

- Marketing organizations should focus on training employees in ethical decision making.

- Marketing organizations should embrace and disseminate a core set of ethical principles.

- Decision makers must adopt a stakeholder orientation that leads to an appreciation of how marketing decisions affect all relevant parties.

- Marketing organizations should specify ethical decision-making protocols.

Source: Laczniak, Gene R., and Patrick E. Murphy (2006), "Normative Perspectives for Ethical and Socially Responsible Marketing," *Journal of Macromarketing*, 26 (2), 154–177.

LO4 Regulation of Marketing Activities

many federal, state, and local laws were established in order to protect consumers from many forms of marketer misbehavior. Federal regulatory bodies such as the Federal Trade Commission (FTC) and the Food and Drug Administration (FDA) monitor exchanges that take place between consumers and marketing organizations. Other groups, such as the Better Business Bureau (BBB) and the American Association of Advertising Agencies (AAAA), also play important roles in monitoring marketing activities. Although these groups attempt to bring fairness to the marketplace, it is ultimately up to managers to ensure that the actions of their firms fall within generally accepted business guidelines.

Exhibit 16.5 presents legislation that has been enacted in an effort to regulate commerce and ensure free trade. Many of these acts are aimed at maintaining or improving the general welfare of consumers in a free marketplace. They also protect the value that consumers receive from exchanges by prohibiting acts such as deceptive advertising and the selling of defective or unreasonably dangerous products.

LO5 Public Criticism of Marketing

there are many areas in marketing that come under public scrutiny. Before we discuss some of these areas, however, we should again emphasize the difference between simple marketing mistakes and truly unethical behavior. Unethical marketers intend to do harm in some way, act negligently, and/or manipulate consumers. Much of our attention has focused on these issues. However, marketers can simply make innocent mistakes. For example, a company may not discover a product defect until the product has already been released for public consumption. Product recalls are all too common, and recalls are found in many industries. Marketers can, however, intentionally release harmful products to their target markets. This, of course, would be considered unethical. At issue is the *intent* and *knowledge* of the firm. Consumer perceptions of incidents such as these are also important, as bad events can mean disaster for the firm in terms of lost business, customer boycotts, and bad publicity.

We could discuss any number of different issues regarding public criticism of marketing; however, we focus on only a handful of issues here.

EXHIBIT 16.5
Major Acts Affecting Commerce and Consumer Safety

Sherman Antitrust Act (1890)	Prohibits restraint of free trade
Federal Food and Drug Act (1906)	Prohibits misleading practices associated with food and drug marketing
Clayton Act (1914)	Restricts price discrimination, exclusive dealing, and tying contracts
Wheeler Lea Act (1938)	Provides FTC with jurisdiction over misleading or false advertising
Fair Packaging and Labeling Act (1966)	Marketers must present proper packaging and content information about products
Child Protection Act (1966)	Prohibits the marketing of dangerous toys
Truth In Lending Act (1968)	Lenders required to disclose complete costs associated with loans
Consumer Product Safety Act (1972)	Created Consumer Product Safety Commission
Children's Online Privacy Protection Act (1998)	Establishes rules governing online marketing practices aimed at children
Anticybersquatting Consumer Protection Act (1999)	Prohibits the act of cybersquatting
Consumer Telephone Records Act (2006)	Prohibits the sale of consumer cell phone records
Consumer Product Safety Improvement Act of 2008	Establishes product safety standards and other requirements for children's products
Credit Card Accountability, Responsibility, and Disclosure Act (2009)	Amends Truth in Lending Act to establish fair and transparent practices relating to consumer credit
Helping Families Save Their Homes Act (2009)	Prevents mortgage foreclosures and enhances mortgage availability

DECEPTIVE ADVERTISING

Deceptive advertising (sometimes called false or misleading advertising) is a very important issue for marketers. Deceptive advertising is covered under the Wheeler Lea Act (1938). This act amended the Federal Trade Commission Act by including false advertising issues. The Federal Trade Commission exists to protect consumers from acts of fraud, deception, and unfair business practices, and the Wheeler Lea Amendment plays an important role in regulating advertising practices, as highlighted in Exhibit 16.5. This act gives the FTC power to issue cease-and-desist orders and to issue fines against firms that are found guilty of deceptive advertising.

According to the FTC, **deceptive advertising** is advertising that (a) contains or omits information that is important in influencing a consumer's buying behavior and (b) is likely to mislead consumers who are acting "reasonably."[12] Of course, the extent to which advertisers *intentionally* misrepresent their products is an important issue in deceptive advertising allegations.

Although regulatory mechanisms are in place to protect consumers from deceptive advertising, most businesses prefer forms of self-regulation over governmental regulation. In fact, self-regulatory bodies, such as the National Advertising Review Council (NARC), work to ensure that advertising practices are truthful. The NARC provides guidelines and sets standards for truth and accuracy for national advertisers.[13] National organizations such as the American Association of Advertising Agencies and the American Advertising Federation also monitor the advertising practices of their members.

Although the FTC defines what deceptive advertising is, actual deception can be sometimes difficult to prove in practice. In fact, an important distinction in practice is the difference between deceptive advertising and *puffery*. The term **puffery** describes the practice of making exaggerated claims about a product and its superiority. Puffery differs from deceptive advertising in that there is no overt attempt to deceive a targeted consumer.

A popular tactic is for a firm to advertise a product as being the "best" available. Advertisements commonly proclaim things like "the best steak in town!" These claims are generally considered to be puffery. In general, the more detailed the claim, the more it must

Stating that a product is "best" is an example of puffery.

be supported by empirical evidence. For example, if a steakhouse claims that "consumers prefer our steak two-to-one over the competition!" then this claim would need to be supported. The industry refers to this as *substantiation* for a claim, and it is vital in cases of alleged deceptive advertising. In general, objective claims must be substantiated. In fact, the American Advertising Federation openly promotes the idea that advertising claims must be, among other things, truthful and substantiated.[14] The line between puffery and deception can indeed be blurry.

MARKETING TO CHILDREN

Children typify a "vulnerable" group because many believe that children lack the knowledge to behave as responsible consumers. Two important issues arise with marketing to children. First is the issue of whether children can understand that some marketing messages may not offer a literal interpretation of the real world. For example, many toys are shown in unrealistic settings. An action figure may be shown in a man-made waterfall that the child simply doesn't have. Second, the sheer quantity of marketing messages to which children are exposed can be called into question. In fact, it has been estimated that the average American child sees more than 40,000 television commercials per year—or an average of over 100 commercials per day.[15] The Children's Television Act of 1990 was put into effect to limit the amount of advertising to which children are exposed. The act limits the amount of commercial airtime during children's programming to 10.5 minutes per hour on weekends and 12 minutes on weekdays.

Marketing to children is a controversial issue.

The Children's Advertising Review Unit (CARU) of the Better Business Bureau is an important self-regulatory body that examines marketing activities that are aimed at children. Among other things, the CARU insists that advertisers take into account the limited knowledge and comprehension that children have regarding marketing issues. Furthermore, the CARU maintains that advertisers should play close attention to the educational role that advertising plays in a child's development and that advertising should stress positive behaviors.[16]

Another important issue with marketing to children is found in Internet marketing. The **Children's Online Privacy Protection Act** went into effect in 2000. This act applies specifically to the online collection of personal information from children who are younger than 13 years of age. It specifies what marketers must include in privacy policies, when and how to seek consent from parents, and the responsibilities that marketers have to protect children's privacy and safety online.[17] In general, the act places strict restrictions on the collection and dissemination of information that is collected from children online.

Some argue that children today are growing up in a society that is far too commercialized and that the messages children receive harm their psychological development and lead them to focus too heavily on material goods. Others believe that advertising and marketing messages simply add to a socialization process in which children learn marketplace skills that will enable them to function properly as consumers. Of course, agreement on this issue is very difficult to reach!

> **Children's Online Privacy Protection Act** act that was established to protect children's privacy in online environments

POLLUTION

Marketing systems exist in order to provide value through consumption. The process of marketing a product, however, often leads to pollution. As a result, marketers are often criticized for harming the environment. Of course, consumption also leads to waste and pollution.[18] Most would agree, therefore, that both marketers and consumers play important roles in environmental protection.

The issue of environmental protection continues to grow in importance, and several popular culture movies and events highlight consumer pressure on businesses and government to move toward increased environmental protectionism. In fact, the "Live Earth" concert held on July 7, 2007, was formed to bring attention to global warming and how businesses and consumers should react to climate problems. Although Live Earth 2008 was cancelled due to violence in India, the organization continues to work towards solving important environmental issues and concerns.

Like other criticisms of marketing, environmental issues are indeed complicated. In fact, many "experts" disagree about the

> Live Earth represented a major effort to highlight environmental issues.

causes and reality of issues like global warming. What is clear, however, is that consumer groups are quite vocal with their efforts to put pressure on businesses to protect the environment. Regulating bodies such as the Environmental Protection Agency play key roles in the reduction of pollution problems.[19]

PLANNED OBSOLESCENCE

Marketers are also criticized for intentionally phasing out products before their usefulness truly wears out. For example, video game manufacturers are often criticized for releasing new and seemingly "improved" gaming consoles even when older models haven't been on the market for very long.

The practice of managing and intentionally setting discontinue dates for products is known as **planned obsolescence**. Critics charge that it is both wasteful and greedy for marketers to engage in planned obsolescence. Marketers counter by arguing that by continually offering improved products, consumers are able to enjoy increased standards of living. A very visual example of obsolescence is the transition from analog to digital television signals. Although there are many issues involved with this transition, millions of consumers are affected by the switch.

TRUE VERSUS ARTIFICIAL NEEDS

Marketers are often criticized for imposing what might be called "artificial" needs on consumers. At issue here is the difference between a want and a need. You may recall that a want represents the way in which a con-

Exaggerated Claims

The line between puffery and deceptive advertising can be blurry. Marketers are often criticized by groups that allege that unfair statements are made about products, even when the intent of marketers is innocuous.

Two recent cases highlight the scrutiny under which cereal marketers operate. General Mills came under fire from the FDA for stating that Cheerios is clinically proven to reduce cholesterol by 4 percent in 6 weeks and that it helps reduce the risk of heart disease. The FDA determined that the claims could qualify Cheerios as being a drug. Although Cheerios does contain whole grains which are known to lower cholesterol, the problem was with how the information was presented in packaging and in advertisements. As such, it wasn't the product that was being questioned, rather, it was the message itself.

In another case, Kellogg's settled allegations from the FTC that it falsely advertised that Frosted Mini-Wheats would raise children's attentiveness. Although studies did show that the cereal impacts attentiveness, the FTC alleged that the statements used constituted false advertising.

Both companies worked with regulators to settle the cases. Obviously, health claims are monitored closely, and marketers must be careful to ensure that claims are made appropriately. Scientific claims often draw the attention of regulating bodies.

Sources: Larkin, Catherine and Duane Stanford (2009), "Cheerios Cereal Isn't So Wholesome as Package Claims," Bloomberg. Com, May 12, 2009, online content retrieved at: **http://www.bloomberg.com/apps/news?pid=20601202&sid=ajfZZtGplemc**, accessed June 19th, 2009; La Jeunesse, William (2009), "FDA Takes Cheerios to Task for Boastful Labels," Fox News (online), June 19, 2009, online content retrieved at: **www.foxnews.com/politics/2009/06/19/fda-takes-cheerios-task-boastful-labels/**, accessed June 19, 2009; Anonymous (2009), "FDA to General Mills: Cholesterol Claims Render Cheerios a Drug," NutritionBusinessJournal.com, online content retrieved at: **http://nutritionbusinessjournal.com/healthy-foods/news/0512-FDA-General-Mills-cholesterol-claims-cheerios-drug-nutrition-business-journal/**, accessed June 19, 2009.

sumer goes about addressing a need. Also, remember that consumers have many different needs, ranging from utilitarian needs to hedonic needs. A consumer might have a need for food and sustenance, but have the want to fulfill that need with an expensive steak dinner.

Marketers often come under fire for leading consumers into confusing wants with needs. The old adage "keeping up with the Joneses" comes into play here. For example, do consumers really need a 50-inch plasma HDTV? Also, do consumers really need whiter teeth? A recent barrage of advertisements suggests that they do. Of course, some may believe that whiter teeth falls into the want category rather than the need category. Do consumers really need $150 sneakers when $30 sneakers would work just as well? As with other issues discussed here, the line can become blurred quite easily.

As mentioned earlier, another common complaint of consumers is that advertisers unfairly create unrealistic expectations in their advertisements. For example, a consumer might argue that an advertiser is sending the message that by wearing a certain type of cologne, he will automatically become much more attractive to romantic partners. Sometimes these expectations can be set too high. Health-related items also promote quite lofty expectations. Advertisers include disclaimers such as "results vary" or "results are not typical" in their advertisements, but consumers rarely notice them. This is often the case with popular weight-loss medications.

CASH ADVANCE LOANS

Cash advance loans, also referred to as payday loans, have become another hot topic for consumer groups. These loans represent one of the fastest-growing sectors of the consumer finance industry. With a cash advance loan, a borrower usually writes a check for the specific amount that he or she wants to borrow plus a fee. The lender gives the borrower the amount that she wished to borrow and holds the check until the borrower's payday at which point the lender cashes the check and keeps the fee as payment.

Problems arise when the fees associated with the service amount to an extremely high interest rate. Truth-in-lending laws require lenders to disclose the real cost of the loan; however, many times consumers simply don't consider these costs. Of course, the consumer has the freedom to choose whether to accept the loan or not. Like many of the activities discussed in this chapter, cash advance loans cannot be considered to be unethical in an absolute sense. Indeed, reputable

The Community Financial Services Association of America promotes responsible regulation of the cash advance industry.

associations such as the Community Financial Services Association of America (CFSA) are dedicated to promoting the responsible use and regulation of these loans. It should also be pointed out that many consumers benefit from the immediacy of the financial service. Critics charge, however, that consumers of these services are most often vulnerable. We do note that CFSA members adhere to a mandated set of industry best practices.

> **sales orientation** practice of using sales techniques that are aimed at satisfying the salesperson's own needs and motives for short-term sales success
>
> **customer orientation** practice of using sales techniques that focus on customer needs
>
> **ingratiation** tactics that are used to become more attractive and likable to another person or party

Several studies have shown that having a customer orientation leads to favorable results for salespeople.

MANIPULATIVE SALES TACTICS

Several personal selling tactics are often called into question. High-pressure and manipulative sales pitches are often the cause of consumer dissatisfaction. For example, a realtor might tell a client that several other people have looked at a particular house when they actually haven't. Or a salesperson might tell a customer that a product is in short supply when it really isn't.

Salespeople who adhere to a **sales orientation** are often guilty of these types of high-pressure tactics. To have a sales orientation means that the salesperson is more focused on the immediate sale and short-term results than on long-term customer satisfaction and relationship development. A more appropriate way to approach a sale is to adhere to what is referred to as a customer orientation. When using a **customer orientation**, the salesperson focuses on customer needs. Several studies have shown that having a customer orientation leads to favorable results for salespeople.

There are other tactics that are often used by salespeople that can be called into question. **Ingratiation** tactics are used subtly by salespeople in order to

foot–in–the–door technique ingratiation technique used in personal selling in which a salesperson begins with a small request and slowly leads up to one major request

door-in-the-face technique ingratiation technique used in personal selling in which a salesperson begins with a major request and then follows with a series of smaller requests

even-a-penny-will-help technique ingratiation technique in which a marketing message is sent that suggests that even the smallest donation, such as a penny or a dollar, will help a cause

"I'm working for you!" technique technique used by salespeople to create the perception that they are working as hard as possible to close a sale when they really are not doing so

equity theory theory of satisfaction in which a consumer compares the ratio of his or her own outcomes and inputs to the same ratio for another party in a transaction

Consumers are often unaware of manipulative tactics.

© THINKSTOCK/GETTY IMAGES

warm up to a prospective customer, motivate some type of response, and potentially get a sale. In general, ingratiation techniques are often viewed as being manipulative. There are several, well-known techniques that salespeople use.[20] These include the foot-in-the-door technique, the door-in-the-face technique, the even-a-penny-will-help technique, and the "I'm working for you!" technique.

• A salesperson using the **foot-in-the-door technique** focuses on simply getting a "foot in the door." When consumers realize that they have opened themselves up to a sales pitch (or literally, opened their door to a salesperson!), they are more likely to listen to the pitch, and they are also more likely to buy a product. Typically, the salesperson first makes a small request such as "May I have a few minutes of your time?" It is followed by a larger request such as "May I show you how this works?" and then by the largest request, "May I have your order?" The foot-in-the-door technique is based on *self-perception theory*, which proposes that consumers use perceptions of their own actions when forming attitudes. That is, the consumer realizes that he has "let the salesperson in" and has given in to a small request; therefore, he must be the type of person who would give in to larger requests and ultimately buy the product being sold!

• With the **door-in-the-face technique**, a salesperson begins by making a very large request of a customer. For example, the salesperson might begin with "Can

I get you to buy this car today?" Realizing that very few, if any, customers would say "Yes!" the salesperson prepares for the dreaded "No!" Showing that her feelings are clearly hurt, the salesperson follows with a guilt-ridden statement like "Well, can I show you its features?" Many consumers would feel bad about initially responding negatively to the first request and would allow the salesperson to explain the car's features. This tactic relies on the *reciprocity norm*, which states that individuals are motivated to give back to those who have given them something. By feeling that he just rejected a salesperson, the customer may think that he at least owes the salesperson the courtesy of listening to her pitch. Here, guilt just might work!

• Using the **even-a-penny-will-help technique**, cause-related marketers suggest to potential donors that even the smallest donation will go a long way toward reaching the desired end goal, such as ending child abuse, feeding the hungry, or sheltering the homeless. The idea is to make the donor feel ashamed to give such a small amount. If the donors do feel shame, they are more likely to give more than is requested. Instead of giving the penny, they may give a dollar. Instead of giving the requested dollar, they may give ten! Studies reveal that this technique can be effective.[21] However, the tactic is implicitly following a guilt-ridden marketing message.

• Using the **"I'm working for you!" technique**, salespeople attempt to lead customers into believing that they are working as hard as possible to give them the best deal when in reality they are simply following a script or a routine. This method is common with automobile sales. A salesperson walks away from his office during a sales negotiation to "go check with the manager" when he is really going to get coffee or simply stepping outside for fresh air. The salesperson returns and says something like "I'm really working for you!" or "I am trying so hard to get you the best deal."

This technique relies on **equity theory**, which was discussed in an earlier chapter. Equity theory states that consumers become satisfied when they believe that the ratio of their outcomes to inputs approximates the ratio of the other party. Here, the consumer would think that the salesperson is working hard, thereby raising the denominator in the comparison equation and leading to higher levels of satisfaction, and potentially purchase likelihood. Of course, salespeople often do consult with sales managers and work as hard as possible to give their customers the best deal. Nevertheless, this tactic is one of the oldest in the books!

The ingratiation techniques discussed here may be considered unethical to the extent that consumers do not realize that they targeted with the tactics. At issue is the degree to which manipulation is occurring. When consumers are not aware that they are being subjected to these techniques, ethical questions arise. Of course, these techniques may also be used innocently.

STEALTH MARKETING

One area of marketing that is currently receiving increased attention is the use of stealth marketing. Stealth marketing (sometimes referred to as covert marketing) was discussed earlier, but we again highlight its use here because it is commonly called into question on moral grounds. Is it ethical for businesses to market products to consumers when the consumers do not realize that they are being targeted by marketing messages?

As you may remember from our earlier discussion, with **stealth marketing**, consumers are completely unaware that they are being marketed to (hence, the term *stealth*). Again, WOMMA (Word of Mouth Marketing Association) is opposed to such tactics and considers their use to be unethical.[22]

LO6 Products Liability

big business is often criticized for marketing unsafe products. The Consumer Product Safety Commission (CPSC) is the main body that monitors product safety. The right to be safe is a basic consumer right listed in the Consumer Bill of Rights. As stated previously,

deaths, injuries, and/or property damage from consumer products in the United States cost the nation more than $800 billion annually.[23]

Another organization with which consumers are familiar is the Insurance Institute for Highway Safety. This organization is an independent, nonprofit body that focuses on deaths, injuries, and property damage from automobile accidents on the nation's highways. The institute regularly tests the safety of automobiles and releases its findings for public review.

Product safety is governed in different ways around the world. American consumers are largely protected by rules and regulations resulting from tort law. In other words, when a consumer is harmed by a product, he or she has the right to sue the party believed to be responsible for causing the injury. The issue of **products liability**, which is the extent to which businesses are held responsible for product-related injuries, is determined through this process. At one extreme, the consumer could live by the "buyer beware" principle and face responsibility for all injuries. At the other, firms could be responsible for any consumer injury. In the latter case, the marketplace would be so restricted that few if any firms could actually afford to operate successfully.

The primary legal doctrine governing products liability in the United States today is strict liability. With **strict liability**, consumers can win a legal action against a firm if they can demonstrate in court that an injury occurred and that the product associated with the injury was faulty in some way. This doctrine has become more prominent in recent years than the former guiding doctrine of negligence. With **negligence**, an injured consumer

Product safety is a very important issue.

stealth marketing marketing technique in which consumers do not realize that they are being targeted for a particular product promotion

products liability extent to which businesses are held responsible for product-related injuries

strict liability legal action against a firm whereby a consumer demonstrates in court that an injury occurred and that the product associated with the injury was faulty in some way

negligence situation whereby an injured consumer attempts to show that a firm could foresee a potential injury might occur and then decided not to act on that knowledge

punitive damages damages that are sought to punish a company for behavior associated with an injury

compensatory damages damages that are intended to cover costs incurred by a consumer due to an injury

would have to show that the firm could foresee a potential injury that might occur and then decided not to act on that knowledge. As might be obvious, the doctrine of strict liability means that firms face increased exposure to costs associated with product injury lawsuits.

A famous consumer legal action involved McDonald's and a customer who ordered a cup of coffee. The incident occurred in the United States and involved a woman spilling coffee onto her legs. She obtained legal counsel and attempted to sue McDonald's for millions of dollars. Under negligence, the plaintiff would have to prove that McDonald's knew such an injury could occur and did nothing to prevent such a mishap. However, under strict liability, the consumer needed to demonstrate that an injury occurred (a burn) and that the product was faulty. In this case, an action under strict liability was pursued on the basis that the consumer was burned and the coffee, being hot, was faulty. The woman ended up winning the lawsuit. A similar action led to Wendy's discontinuing the sale of hot chocolate because if "being hot" made the chocolate faulty, there was little need in offering the product for sale! As a result of these events, fast-food companies began to place warning labels on their products.

The costs of products liability are extremely high in many industries. Physicians in the United States face enormous costs due to the amount of liability insurance they must carry. Some claim that the single greatest cost element to an automobile is the cost of liability exposure. Companies have little choice but to pass the financial costs on to customers. So, when a consumer purchases a ladder, a significant portion of the price covers liability-related issues. However, a potentially greater cost comes from stifled innovation as firms fear introducing products that are truly novel because they could be considered faulty in some way. Companies like Cessna, Piper, and Beechcraft produce piston engine aircraft using the same basic technology that existed in 1950. More innovative aircraft are produced in the "kit plane" industry where the consumer has the responsibility of manufacturing the airplane himself or herself. In this way, the firm avoids significant liability

© BILL FRITSCH/BRAND X PICTURES/JUPITERIMAGES

Finding the balance between consumer protection and market freedom is difficult.

exposure.

Generally, firms face higher liability costs in the United States than in most other countries. One reason is because liability lawsuits that actually reach a courtroom often involve jury trials. In Europe, for example, most liability actions would be overseen by a magistrate rather than a jury. For a host of reasons, juries tend to be more sympathetic to a consumer who is claiming a product injury and are much more likely to award substantial punitive damages as well as compensatory damages. **Punitive damages** are intended to punish a company for behavior associated with an injury and **compensatory damages** are intended to cover costs incurred by a consumer due to an injury.

The issue of products liability is a good way to illustrate the importance of public policy to consumer behavior. Certainly, the answers are never clear because the issue can be terribly complicated and emotional. But, while tilting the balance of bearing the burden of product injuries toward firms may seem reasonable based on a belief that big business has deep pockets, such tilting actually restricts market freedom by driving businesses out of certain industries and restricting the choices of consumers. Thus, if pharmaceutical firms face costs that are too high and regulations that are too stringent, they simply may stop producing potentially life-saving medications because of product risk. The key to effective public policy is finding the proper balance, which offers consumers reasonable protection but still provides a high degree of freedom in the marketplace. This, of course, is no easy task.

Chapter 16 Case

Kelly sits down at a brand new computer and logs on to the Internet. Sipping a heavily sugared cup of coffee, he downloads the latest generation of file-sharing software, installs it on his hard drive, and activates it. After thinking for a moment about whether or not he should, Kelly enters the name of his favorite Rolling Stones song into the search grid; almost immediately, thousands of copies of the song are available for him to download for free. He selects one, and within a few short seconds he is listening to Mick Jagger sing "You Can't Always Get What You Want." Cracking his knuckles, and singing along with the line "but if you try sometimes . . . you might find . . . you get what you need" (Jagger and Richards 1969), Kelly spends the rest of his evening seeking out songs to download and listen to at will. Toward morning, he searches everywhere to find Led Zeppelin's "Kashmir" but to no avail—eventually, a buddy tells him Zeppelin isn't available for download. Kelly is frustrated and thinks, "That isn't fair! There should be a law!!"

The path to this particular example of consumer misbehavior began with a seemingly innocuous little bit of consumer ingenuity. In January of 1999, Shawn Fanning, a 19-year-old college dropout with a passion for tinkering with computer code and listening to music, had little idea that he was about to begin a revolution. Constantly frustrated in his search for easily and quickly downloadable MP3 music files, he sought to create a search engine that would allow people to look for copies of music files on the Internet and, once found, copy those files onto their own hard drives. The search engine that he created, Napster, was released onto the Internet for free download and quickly became one of the most recognized brand names on the planet (Menn 2003).

Napster allows music pirates unlimited access to a seemingly unlimited supply of music. The reaction, to this point, by the music industry, led by the Recording Industry Association of America (RIAA), is to find legislative or litigious means of reining in the growing threat of music piracy. To this point, the RIAA has filed over 26,000 lawsuits in federal court (Freed 2007). The industry has also attempted a "grassroots approach to both educate the public on the legal aspects of file-sharing copyrighted music and publicize the damage that it is doing to the industry" (Wade 2004, p. 12). Such a reaction is understandable considering the apparent cost music piracy has had on the industry in recent years.

The RIAA claims that much of the recent loss of revenues, nearly 25% between 1999 and 2003, is attributable to illegal downloading (Mamudi 2003). That figure amounts to an estimated $300 million in revenues per year (Langenderfer and Cook 2001) and represents a decline of 31% percent in units shipped since 2000 (Wade 2004). As a result, the industry, along with the RIAA, has maintained a staunch position against piracy, utilizing all the tools in its arsenal to fight what has amounted to a war of attrition. Despite legal wranglings and various interpretations of U.S. and international copyright law, neither side has given ground. However, if predictions hold true and the next generation of file-sharing software succeeds in providing anonymity based upon the encryption of files and of users that not even ISPs will be able to decode (Taylor 2003, p. 42), then it may amount to a war that the industry will lose.

However, what the RIAA and others have failed to take into account is the notion that individual consumers don't think that this music piracy is even wrong or unethical. One individual who has gone to trial for sharing copyrighted music even claims that file-sharing is not illegal, citing as evidence of this a case study she wrote during her MBA program (Freed 2007). Others engage in the behavior without a second thought for the legality or the consequences. Despite the introduction of legitimate pay services like iTunes, Rhapsody, and the new Napster, consumers simply go forward with their search for free music, comforted by the thought that *everyone else is doing it* or *so many people are doing it, how can I possibly be caught?* or something similar.

Kelly is also not convinced that the RIAA acts ethically. In fact, he's heard of companies placing rootfiles and spyware on computers via CDs. Any company that does that can't be trusted, he thinks. Also, he believes that the problem with sagging industry sales is not file-sharing, but simply that the industry is delivering poor quality. He can't stand all those flashy dancers in music videos and the perfect-looking people. He thinks they're selling fluff—not music. They try to hook consumers with a flashy video and one good song, and then expect them to pay for an entire album that just isn't good. That's the real reason why sales are dipping.

If this continues, what then can the record industry and the RIAA really do? How will they address the next generation of downloaders who are kept safe behind encryptions and firewalls and other items designed to protect this particular consumer misbehavior? How can consumers respond to actions that they think are unethical on the part of the RIAA companies?[24]

Questions

1. How do file-sharing and music piracy disrupt the exchange process? How have they enhanced the exchange process?

2. Do government restrictions on file-sharing activity interfere with the consumer bill of rights?

3. The case provides an example of the three components of moral beliefs. Describe each of those examples and explain why each fits with those components.

4. What is your opinion? Do perceived unethical actions by a company or industry justify unethical actions in return? Do you believe that the music industry deserves some protection from illicit file-sharing?

Chapter 1

1. See Walters, C. Glenn, and Gordon W. Paul (1970), *Consumer Behavior: An Integrated Approach*, 3rd Edition. Irwin, Homewood, IL; Howard, John L., and Jagdish Sheth (1969), *The Theory of Buyer Behavior*, Wiley, New York.
2. See http://dictionary.laborlawtalk.com/ **Economics** for different perspectives on economics; accessed January 8, 2007.
3. Pan, Suwen, Cheng Fang, and Jaime Malaga (2006), "Alcoholic Beverage Consumption in China: a Censored Demand System Approach," *Applied Economics Letters*, 13 (12/15), 975–979.
4. Christie, Jennifer, Dan Fisher, John C. Kozup, Scott Smith, Scott Burton, and Elizabeth H. Creyer (2001), "The Effects of Bar-Sponsored Alcohol Beverage Promotions Across Binge and Nonbinge Drinkers," *Journal of Public Policy & Marketing*, 20 (Fall), 240–253.
5. Tyler, Leona E. (1981), "More Stately Mansions—Psychology Extends its Boundaries," *Annual Review of Psychology*, 32, 1–20.
6. Yoon, Carolyn, Gilles Laurent, Helen H. Fung, Richard Gonzales, Angela H. Gutchess, Trey Hedden, Raphaelle Lambert-Pandraud, Mara Mather, Denise C. Park, Ellen Peters, and Ian Skurnik (2005), "Cognition, Persuasion and Decision Making in Older Consumers," *Marketing Letters*, 16 (3), 429–441.
7. Darroch, Jenny, Morgan P. Miles, Andrew Jardine, and Ernest F. Cooke (2004), "The 2004 AMA Definition of *Marketing* and Its Relationship to a Market Orientation: An Extension of Cooke, Rayburn, & Abercrombie (1992)," *Journal of Marketing Theory & Practice*, 12 (Fall), 29–38.
8. Mittelstaedt, Robert A. (1990), "Economics, Psychology, and the Literature of the Subdiscipline of Consumer Behavior," *Journal of the Academy of Marketing Science*, 18 (4), 303–311.
9. Zinkhan, George M., Martin S. Roth, and Mary Jane Saxton (1992), "Knowledge Development and Scientific Status in Consumer-Behavior Research: A Social Exchange Perspective," *Journal of Consumer Research*, 19 (September), 282–291.
10. Ibid.
11. Henry, G. T., and Theodore Poister (1994), "Citizen Ratings of Public and Private Service Quality: A Comparative Perspective," *Public Administration Review*, 54, 11a; Winkler, C. (2003), "When Yanking the Mainframe Isn't an Option," *Computerworld*, 37, 35–36.
12. Weiss, E.M. (2002), "DMV Waits Irk Customers; Holiday, New Closings Aggravate End-of-Month Crunch," *Washington Post*, (December 1, 2002), p. C03. Kinney, M.Y. (2009), "Speeding Welcome Behind the Counter at License Bureaus," *Philadelphia Inquirer*, (May 17), p. B01.
13. Narver, J. C., and S. F. Slater (1990), "The Effect of a Market Orientation on Business Profitability," *Journal of Marketing*, 54 (October), 20–35. Narver, J. C., S. Slater, and B. Tietje (1998), "Creating a Market Orientation," *Journal of Market Focused Management*, 2 (3), 241–55.
14. Voss , G. B., and Z. G. Voss (2000), "Strategic Orientation and Firm Performance in an Artistic Environment," *Journal of Marketing*, 64, 67–83. Auh, Seigyoung, and B. Menguc (2006), "Diversity at the Executive Suite: A Resource-Based Approach to the Customer Orientation–Organizational Performance Relationship," *Journal of Business Research*, 59, 564–572.
15. Skogland, I., and J. A. Siguaw (2004), "Are Your Satisfied Customers Loyal?" *Cornell Hotel and Restaurant Administration Quarterly*, 45, 221–234. Berger, P. D., N. Eechambadi, G. Morris, D. R. Lehmann, R. Rizley, and R. Venkatesan (2006), "From Customer Lifetime Value to Shareholder Value: Theory, Empirical Evidence and Issues for Future Research," *Journal of Services Research*, 9, 156–167.
16. Neslin, S. A., D. Grewal, R. Leghorn, V. Shankar, M. L. Teerling, J. S. Thomas, and P. C. Verhoef (2006), "Challenges and Opportunities in Multichannel Customer Management," *Journal of Services Research*, 9, 95–112.
17. Hunt, S. D. (1997), "Competing Through Relationships; Grounding Relationship Marketing in Resource Advantage Theory," *Journal of Marketing Management* 13 (5), 431–445.
18. All dates taken from company websites. Samsung was originally founded in 1938 but as a Korean food exporter. In 1969, Samsung Electronics was created.
19. Christenson, C. M., S. Cook, and T. Hall (2005), "Marketing Malpractice: The Cause and the Cure," *Harvard Business Review*, 83, 74–83.
19a. Tryhorn, C., (2009), "Mobile Phone Use Passes a Milestone," The Guardian, (March 06), p. 9.
20. Gumbel, P., and T. Demos (2007), "The Bomb in Your Wallet," *Fortune*, 156, 9–10.
21. *Market Europe* (2006), "UK Consumers Carry a Heavy Load of Debt," 17 (October), 3.
22. Pinto, M. B., P. M. Mansfield, and D. H. Parente (2004), "Relationship of Credit Attitude and Debt to Self-Esteem, and Locus of Control in College-Age Consumers," *Psychological Reports*, 94, 1405–1418.
23. Zikmund, W. G., and B. J. Babin (2007), *Exploring Marketing Research*, Thomson South-Western, Mason, OH.
24. Bode, Mathias (2006), "Now That's What I Call Music! An Interpretive Approach to Music in Advertising," *Advances in Consumer Research*, 33, 580–585.
25. Tadajewski, M. (2006), "Remembering Motivation Research: Toward an Alternative Genealogy of Interpretive Consumer Research," *Marketing Theory*, 6, 429–466.
26. Moe, W., and P. Fader (2001), "Measuring Hedonic Portfolio Products: A Joint Segmentation Analysis of Music Compact Disc Sales," *Journal of Marketing Research*, 38, 376–385.
27. Chiou, J. S., C. Y. Huang, and H. H. Lee (2005), "The Antecedents of Music Piracy Attitudes and Intentions," *Journal of Business Ethics*, 57, 161–174.
28. Zikmund and Babin (2007), p. 131.
28a. http://www.starbucks.com.aboutus/ Company_Factsheet.pdf
29. http://academic.emporia.edu/ smithwil/00spmg456/eja/pieschl. html#Sears.
30. *Payment News* (2005), "US Internet Sales up 24 Percent," (May 22), http:// www.paymentsnews.com/2005/05/ us_internet_ret.html; accessed January 24, 2007.
31. eMarketer, April 2003, www.eMarketer .com; April 2003.
32. U.S. Census Bureau International Data Base, April 2004, www.census.gov/ipc/ www/idbnew.html.
33. Axelrad, Marge (2007), "Explaining 'Value' Regardless of the Price," Vision, 21 (9/24), 5.

Chapter 2

1. Seattle Post-Intelligencer News Services (2003), "Rock Still the Most Popular Music Genre," SeattlePI.com (May 13), http://seattlepi.nwsource.com/ pop/122353_tf217.html, accessed February 26, 2006.
2. Grégoire, Yany, and Robert Fisher (2006), "The Effects of Relationship Quality on Customer Retaliation," *Marketing Letters*, 17 (1), 31–46; Kressmann, Frank, M. Joseph Sirgy, Andreas Herrmann, Frank Huber, Stephanie Huber, and Dong-Jin Lee (2006), "Direct and Indirect Effects

of Self-image Congruence on Brand Loyalty," *Journal of Business Research,* 59 (September), 955–964.

3. Popp, Jamie (2005), "Libations, Libations," *Restaurants and Institutions,* 115 (8/15), 43–50.

4. Treacy, Michael, and Fred Wiersema (1993), "Customer Intimacy and Other Value Disciplines," *Harvard Business Review,* 71 (Jan./Feb.), 84–93.

5. Babin, B. J., W. R. Darden, and M. Griffin (1994), "Work and/or Fun: Measuring Hedonic and Utilitarian Shopping Value," *Journal of Consumer Research,* 20 (March), 644–656.

6. Seeking Alpha (2007), "Coke, Pepsi Losing Market Share," (March 9), **http://seekingalpha.com/article/29100-coke-pepsi-losing-market-share,** accessed May 24, 2009.

7. Halliday, Jean (2005), "Total Value Promise a Total Mess for GM Sales," *Advertising Age,* 76, 3.

8. Adner, R. (2006), "Match Your Innovation Strategy to Your Innovation Ecosystem," *Harvard Business Review,* 84 (April), 98–108.

9. Dickson, P. R., and J. L. Ginter (1987), "Market Segmentation, Product Differentiation and Marketing Strategy," *Journal of Marketing,* 51, 1–10.

10. Orth, U. R., M. McDaniel, T. Shellhamer, and K. Lopetcharat (2004), "Promoting Brand Benefits: The Role of Consumer Psychographics and Lifestyle," *Journal of Consumer Marketing,* 21, 97–108.

11. Rust, R., and N. Donthu (1994), "Positioning a Radio Station," *Journal of Applied Business Research,* 10, 21–27.

12. Sunil, G., D. Hanssens, B. Hardie, W. Kahn, V. Kumar, L. Nathaniel, and N.R. Sriram (2006), "Modeling Customer Lifetime Value," *Journal of Service Research,* 9 (November), 139–155.

13. Kumar, V., D. Shah, and R. Venkatesan (2006), "Managing Retailer Profitability—One Customer at a Time!" *Journal of Retailing,* 82, 277–294.

14. Ibid.

15. CVS/pharmacy website http://www.cvs.com.

16. Gale Group, Copyright 2002. Business & Company Resource Center, see www.galegroup.com.

17. Drug Store News (2002), "Edging out the Competition," (3/25).

18. Business Wire (2001), "CVS Corporation August Sales Increase 10.9%," CVS Press Release, (9/5).

Chapter 3

1. See Levinsky, D. L., and T. Youm (2004), "The More Food Young Adults Are Served, the More they Overeat," *Journal of Nutrition,* 134, 2546–2549; Rolls, B. J., L. S. Roe, and J. S. Meengs (2006), "Reductions in Portion Size and Energy Density of Foods Are Additive and Lead to Sustained Decreases in Energy Intake," *American Journal of Clinical Nutrition,* 83, 11–17.

2. Raghunathan, Rajagopal, and Julie R. Irwin (2001), "Walking the Hedonic Product Treadmill: Default Contrast and Mood-Based Assimilation in Judgments of Predicted Happiness with a Target Product," *Journal of Consumer Research,* 28, 355–368.

3. Meyers-Levy, Joan, and Alice M. Tybout (1989), "Schema Congruity as a Basis for Product Evaluation," *Journal of Consumer Research,* 16 (1): 39–54.

4. Sylvie, M., L. Dubé, and J. C. Chebat (2007), "The Role of Pleasant Music in Servicescapes: A Test of the Dual Model of Environmental Perception," *Journal of Retailing,* 83, 115–130.

5. Kim, J., A. M. Flore, and H. H. Lee (2006), "Influences of Online Store Perception, Shopping Enjoyment, and Shopping Involvement on Consumer Patronage Behavior Towards an Online Retailer," *Journal of Retailing and Consumer Services,* 14, 95–107.

6. See Merkile, P. M. (2000), "Subliminal Perception," *Encyclopedia of Psychology,* 7, 497–499.

7. Gable, M., H. Wilkens, L. Harris, and R. Feinbert (1987), "An Evaluation of Subliminally Embedded Sexual Stimuli in Graphics," *Journal of Advertising,* 16, 26–31.

8. Broyles, S. J. (2006), "Misplaced Paranoia over Subliminal Advertising: What's the Big Uproar?" Journal of Consumer Marketing, 23, 312–313.

9. Broyles, S. J. (2006), "Subliminal Advertising and the Perceptual Popularity of Playing to People's Paranoia," *Journal of Consumer Affairs,* 40, 392–406.

10. See Lantos, G. (1996), "Ice Cube Sex: The Truth about Subliminal Advertising: Book Review," *Journal of Consumer Marketing,* 13, 62–64.

11. See Key, W. B. (1974), *Subliminal Seduction: Ad Media's Manipulation of a Not so Innocent America,* Signet, New York; Packard, V. (1957), *The Hidden Persuaders,* D. McKay Co., New York.

12. Cook, W. A. (1993), "Looking Behind Ice Cubes," *Journal of Advertising Research,* 33 (Mar/Apr), 7–8.

13. *Advertising Age* (2000).

14. Vroomen, J., and M. Keetels (2006), "The Spatial Constraint in Intersensory Pairing: No Role in Temporal Ventriloquism," *Journal of Experimental Psychology,* 32, 1063–1071.

15. Miller, Richard L. (1962), "Dr. Weber and the Consumer," *Journal of Marketing,* 57–67.

16. Kalyanam, K., and T. S. Shively (1998), "Estimating Irregular Pricing Effects: A Stochastic Spline Regression Approach," *Journal of Marketing Research,* 35, 16–29.

17. Miller, op. cit.

18. Janiszewski, Chris (1993), "Preattentive Mere Exposure Effects," *Journal of Consumer Research,* 20 (3): 376–392.

19. Smith, Gene F. (1982), "Further Evidence of the Mediating Effect of Learning in the "Mere Exposure"

Phenomenon," *Journal of General Psychology,* 197: 175–178; Stang, D. J. (1975), "Effects of "Mere Exposure" on Learning and Affect," *Journal of Personality and Social Psychology,* 31: 7–12.

20. Gustav, K., and Z. Dienes (2005), "Implicit Learning of Nonlocal Musical Rules: Implicitly Learning More than Chunks," *Journal of Experimental Psychology/Learning, Memory & Cognition,* 31 (Nov.), 1417–1432; Chakraborty, G., V. Lala, and D. Warran (2003), "What Do Customers Consider Important in B2B Websites?" *Journal of Advertising Research,* (March), 50.

21. Janiszewski, op. cit.

22. Leavitt, C., A. Greenwald, and C. Obermiller (1981), "What Is Low Involvement In?" *Advances in Consumer Research,* 8, 15–19.

23. Yang, M., D. Roskos-Ewoldson, L. Dinu, and L. M. Arpan (2006), "The Effectiveness of 'In-Game' Advertising," *Journal of Advertising,* 35 (Winter), 143–152.

24. Auty, S., and C. Lewis (2004), "Exploring Children's Choice: The Reminder Effect of Product Placement," *Psychology & Marketing,* 21 (9), 697–713.

25. Ang, S. H., S. M. Leong, and W. Yeo (1999), "When Silence Is Golden: Effects of Silence on Consumer Ad Reponses," *Advances in Consumer Research,* 26, 295–299.

26. David, B., D. W. Wooten (2006), "From Labeling Possessions to Possessing Labels: Ridicule and Socialization among Adolescents," *Journal of Consumer Research,* 33, 188–198.

27. Skinner, B. F. (1989), "The Origins of Cognitive Thought," *American Psychologist,* 44 (1): 13–18.

28. Ibid.

29. Malone, John C., Jr., and Natalie M. Cruchon (2001), "Radical Behaviorism and the Rest of Psychology: A Review/Precis of Skinner's About Behaviorism," *Behavior and Philosophy,* 29, 31–57.

30. **http://www.simplypsychology.pwp.blueyonder.co.uk/behaviourism.html,** accessed February 4, 2007.

31. Malone and Cruchon, op. cit.

Chapter 4

1. Viscusi, K. (1990), "The Impact of Safety Warnings on Perception and Memory," *Journal of Political Economy,* 98, 253–269; Lepkowska-White, E., and A. Parsons (2001), "Comprehension of Warnings and Resulting Attitudes," *Journal of Consumer Affairs,* 35, 278–294.

2. Argo, J. J., and K. J. Main (2004), "Meta-Analysis of the Effectiveness of Warning Labels," *Journal of Public Policy and Marketing,* 23 (Fall), 193–208.

3. Madhubalan, V., and M. Hastak (2002), "The Role of Summary Information in Facilitating Consumers' Comprehension of Nutrition Infor-

mation," *Journal of Public Policy & Marketing*, 21, 305–318.

4. Shen, Y. C., and T. C. Chen (2006), "When East Meets West: The Effect of Cultural Tone Congruity in Ad Music and Message on Consumer Ad Memory and Attitude," *International Journal of Advertising*, 25, 51–70.

5. See Kellaris, J. J., A. D. Cox, and D. Cox (1993), "The Effects of Background Music on Ad Processing: A Contingency Explanation," *Journal of Marketing*, 57, 114–125.

6. Burke, R.R., and T. K. Srull (1988), "Competitive Interference and Consumer Memory for Advertisements," *Journal of Consumer Research*, 15 (June), 55–68.

7. Dholokia, R. R., and B. Sternthal (1997), "Highly Credible Sources Persuasive Facilitator or Persuasive Liabilities?" *Journal of Consumer Research*, 3, 223–232.

8. Singh, J., and R. Jayanti (2004), "The Collective-Relational Paradox in Consumer Trust Judgments: Framework and Propositions," *Advances in Consumer Research*, 31, 343–357.

9. Whitworth, Brian (2005), "Behaviour & Information Technology," 24, 353–363.

10. Kang, Yoon-Sung and Paul M. Herr (2006), "Beauty and the Beholder: Toward an Integrative Model of Communication Source Effects," *Journal of Consumer Research*, 33 (1): 123–130.

11. Taylor, V. A., and A. B. Bower (2004), "Improving Product Instruction Compliance: If You Tell Me Why, I Might Comply," *Psychology & Marketing*, 21, 229–245.

12. Celsi, Richard L., and Jerry C. Olson (1988), "The Role of Involvement in Attention and Comprehension Processes," *Journal of Consumer Research*, 15 (2): 210–224.

13. Menon, S., and D. Soman (2004), "Managing the Power of Curiosity for Effective Web Advertising Strategies," *Journal of Advertising*, 31, 1–14.

14. Moorman, Christine (1996), "A Quasi Experiment to Access the Consumer and Informational Determinants of Nutrition Information Processing Activities: The Case of the Nutrition Labeling and Education Act," *Journal of Public Policy and Marketing*, 15, 28–44.

15. See Nordhielm, C. L. (2002), "The Influence of Levels of Processing on Advertising Repetition Effects," *Journal of Consumer Research*, 29 (December), 371–382.

16. Griffin, M., B. J. Babin, and D. Modianos (2000), "Shopping Values of Russian Consumers: The Impact of Habituation in a Developing Economy," *Journal of Retailing*, 76, 33–52.

17. Allison, Ralph I., and Kenneth P. Uhl (1964), "Influence of Beer Brand Identification on Taste Perception," *Journal of Marketing Research*, August (1): 36–39.

18. Terhune, Chad (2005), "Coke Zero Looks for Positive Spin," *Wall Street Journal*, August 12, B2.

19. Kaufman-Scarborough, C. (2000), "Seeing through the Eyes of the Color-Deficient Shopper: Consumer Issues for Public Policy," *Journal of Consumer Policy*, 23, 461–492.

20. Bapna, Ravi, P. Goes, A. Gupta, and G. Karuga (2002), "Optimal Design of the Online Auction Channel: Empirical and Computational Insights," *Decision Sciences*, 33, 557–577.

21. Cox, A. D., D. Cox, and G. Zimet (2006), "Understanding Consumer Responses to Product Risk Information," *Journal of Marketing*, 70 (January), 79–91.

22. Tversky, A., and D. Kahneman (1981), "The Framing of Decisions and the Psychology of Choice," *Science*, 211, 453–458.

23. Cox, Cox and Zimet, op. cit.; Roggeveen, A. L., D. Grewal, and J. Gotlieb (2006), "Does the Frame of a Comparative Ad Moderate the Effectiveness of Extrinsic Information Cues?" *Journal of Consumer Research*, 33, 115–122.

24. Vanhuele, M., and X. Drèze (2002), "Measuring the Price Knowledge Consumers Bring to the Store," *Journal of Marketing*, 66, 72–85.

25. Stewart, D. and *Journal of Business Research*.

26. Dawson, B. (2005), "Jingles' Best Days May Be Behind Them," *Minneapolis Star Tribune*, April 13, http://www .ocregister.com/ocr/sections/life/ lf_trends/article_478162.php, accessed April 4, 2007.

27. Vanhuele, M., G. Laurent, and X. Drèze (2006), "Consumers Immediate Memory for Prices," *Journal of Consumer Research*, 33, 153–172.

28. Cline, T. W., and J. J. Kellaris (2007), "The Influence of Humor Strength and Humor-Message Relatedness and Ad Memorability," *Journal of Advertising*, 36, 55–67.

29. Fiser, J., and R. Aslin (2005), "Encoding Multi-Element Scenes: Statistical Learning of Visual Feature Hierarchies," *Journal of Experimental Psychology: General*, 134, 521–537; see also Hansen, D. E. (2003), "Using the Voeke Method to Improve Student Learning in Principles of Marketing Classes," *Journal of Marketing Education*, 25, 108–117. For an example of research involving chunking, see

30. Chan, J. C. K., K. B. McDermott, J. M. Watson, and D. A. Gallo (2005), "The Importance of Material-Processing Interactions in Inducing False Memories," *Memory & Cognition*, 33, 389–395.

31. Lee, A. Y., and B. Sternthal (1999), "The Effects of Positive Mood on Memory," *Journal of Consumer Research*, 26, 115–127.

32. Fisher, R. J., and L. Dubé (2005), "Gender Differences in Responses to Emotional Advertising: A Social Desirability Perspective," *Journal of Consumer Research*, 31, 850–858.

33. Moore, R.S. (2005), "The Sociological Impact of Attitudes Toward Smoking: Secondary Effects of the Demarketing of Smoking," *Journal of Social Psychology*, 145, 703–718.

34. Celsi and Olson, op. cit.

35. Saegert, J. (1979), "A Demonstration of Levels of Processing Theory in Memory for Advertisements," *Advances in Consumer Research*, 6, 82–84.

Chapter 5

1. Childers, T. L., C. L. Carr, J. Peck, and S. Carson (2001), "Hedonic and Utilitarian Motivations for Online Retail Shopping Behavior," *Journal of Retailing*, 77 (Winter), 511–535.

2. Laurent, G., and J. N. Kapferer (1985), "Measuring Consumer Involvement Profiles," *Journal of Marketing Research*, 22 (February), 41–53.

3. Howard, D. J., and R. A. Kerin (2006), "Broadening the Scope of Reference Price Advertising Research: A Field Study of Shopping Involvement," *Journal of Marketing*, 70 (October), 185–204.

4. Day, E., M. R. Stafford, and A. Camacho (1995), "Opportunities for Involvement Research: A Scale Development Approach," *Journal of Advertising*, 24, 69–75; Houston, Michael J., and Michael L. Rothschild (1978), "Conceptual and Methodological Perspectives on Involvement," in *Research Frontiers in Marketing: Dialogues and Directions*, Subhash C. Jain, ed., Chicago: *American Marketing Association*, 184–187.

5. Plutchik, R. (2003), *Emotions and Life: Perspectives from Psychology, Biology and Evolution*, Washington DC: American Psychological Association.

6. O'Shaughnessy, J., and N. J. O'Shaughnessy (2003). *The Marketing Power of Emotions*. Oxford: Oxford University Press; Slama, M. E. (2003). "Book Review: Emotions and Life: Perspectives from Psychology, Biology and Evolution," *Psychology & Marketing*, 22 (January), 97–101.

7. Fonberg, E. (1986), "Amygdala: Emotions, Motivation, and Depressive States," in *Emotion: Theory, Research, and Experience*, R. Plutchik et al., eds., New York: Kluwer Press, 302.

8. Babin, B. J., W. R. Darden, and L. A. Babin (1998), "Negative Emotions in Marketing Research: Affect of Artifact?" *Journal of Business Research*, 42, 271–285. Russell, J. A., and J. Snodgrass (1987), "Emotion and the Environment," in *Environment and Psychology*, D. Stokols and I. Altman, eds., New York: John Wiley and Sons, 245–280.

9. Price, P. (2007), "Unleash Emotions for Business Growth," *Advertising Age*, 78 (November), 20.

10. Watson, L., and M. Spencer (2007), "Causes and Consequences of Emotions on Consumer Behaviour: A Review and Integrative Cognitive Appraisal Theory,"

European Journal of Marketing, 41, 487–511; Stephens, N., and K. Gwinner (1998), "Why Don't Some People Complain: A Cognitive-Emotive Process Model of Consumer Behavior," *Journal of the Academy of Marketing Science*, 26, 172–189.

11. Babin, B. J., and W. R. Darden (1996), "Good and Bad Shopping Vibes: Spending and Patronage Satisfaction," *Journal of Business Research*, 35, 201–206.

12. Pucinelli, N. M. (2006), "Putting Your Best Foot Forward: The Impact of Customer Mood on Salesperson Evaluation," *Journal of Consumer Psychology*, 16, 156–162.

13. Raghunathan, R., and J. R. Irwin (2001), "Walking the Hedonic Product Treadmill: Default Contrast and Mood-Based Assimilation in Judgments of Predicted Happiness with a Target Product," *Journal of Consumer Research*, 28 (December), 355–368.

14. Detwiler-Bedell, B., J. Detwiler-Bedell, and P. Salovey (2006), "Mood-Congruent Perceptions of Success Depend on Self-Other Framing," *Cognition & Emotion*, 20, 196–216; Forgas, J. P., and J. Ciarrochi (2001), "On Being Happy and Possessive: The Interactive Effects of Mood and Personality on Consumer Judgments," *Psychology & Marketing*, 18 (March), 239–260; Meloy, Margaret G. (2000), "Mood-Driven Distortion of Product Information," *Journal of Consumer Research*, 27 (December), 345–359.

15. Raghubir, P. (2006), "An Information Processing View of the Subjective Value of Money and Prices," *Journal of Business Research*, 59, 1053–1062.

16. See Karolein, P., and S. Dewitte (2006), "How to Capture the Heart? Twenty Years of Emotion Measurement in Advertising," *Journal of Advertising*, 46, 18–37.

17. For an overview, see Drake, R. A., and L. R. Myers (2006), "Visual Attention, Emotion, and Action Tendency: Feeling Active or Passive," *Cognition and Emotion*, 20, 608–622.

18. Babin et al. (1998); Bagozzi, R. P. (1993), "An Examination of the Psychometric Properties of Measures of Negative Affect in the PANAS-X Scales," *Journal of Personality & Social Psychology*, 65 (October), 836–891; Watson, D., L. A. Clark, and A. Tellegen (1998), "Development and Validation of Brief Measures of Positive and Negative Affect," *Journal of Personality and Social Psychology*, 47, 1063–1070; Crawford, J. R., and J. D. Henry (2004), "The Positive and Negative Affect Schedule (PANAS): Construct Validity, Measurement Properties and Normative Data in a Large Clinical Sample," *British Journal of Clinical Psychology*, 43, 245–265.

19. Russell, J. A., and G. Pratt (1979), "Affect Space Is Bipolar," *Journal of Personality and Social Psychology*, 37, 1161–1178; Babin et al. (1998).

20. Havlena, W. J., and M. B. Holbrook (1986), "The Varieties of Consumption Experience: Comparing Two Typologies of Emotion in Consumer Behavior," *Journal of Consumer Research*, 13, 97–112. Kottasz, R. (2006), "Understanding the Influences of Atmospheric Cues on the Emotional Responses and Behaviours of Museum Visitors," *Journal of Nonprofit & Public Sector Marketing*, 16, 95–121.

21. White, C., and Y. Yi-Ting (2005), "Satisfaction Emotions and Consumer Behavioral Intentions," *Journal of Services Marketing*, 19, 411–420; Chebat, J. C., and W. Sluszrczyk (2005), "How Emotions Mediate the Effects of Perceived Justice on Loyalty in Service Recovery Situations: An Empirical Study," *Journal of Business Research*, 56, 664–673.

22. Mooradian, T. A., and J. M. Oliver (1997), "I Can't Get No Satisfaction: The Impact of Personality and Emotion on Postpurchase Processes," *Psychology & Marketing*, 14, 379–393.

23. Mascarenhas, O., R. Kesavan, and M. Bernacchi (2006), "Lasting Customer Loyalty: A Total Customer Experience Approach," *Journal of Consumer Marketing*, 23, 397–405.

24. Hiam, A. (2000), "Match Premiums to Marketing Strategies," *Marketing News*, 34 (20), 12.

25. Riva, Giuseppe, F. Mantovani, C. S. Capideville, A. Preziosa, F. Morganti, D. Villani, A. Gaggioli, C. Botella, and M. Alcañiz (2007), "Affective Interactions Using Virtual Reality: The Link between Presence and Emotions," *CyberPsychology & Behavior*, 10, 45–56.

26. Chou, T. J., and C. C. Ting (2003), "The Role of *Flow* Experience in Cyber-Game Addiction," *CyberPsychology & Behavior*, 6, 663–675.

27. Sénécal, Sylvain, J. E. Gharbi, and J. Nantel (2002), "The Influence of Flow on Utilitarian and Hedonic Shopping Values," *Advances in Consumer Research*, 29, 483–484.

28. Smith, Donnavieve N., and K. Sivakumar (2004), "Flow and Internet Shopping Behavior," *Journal of Business Research*, 57, 1199–1208.

29. Dailey, L. (2004), "Navigational Web Atmospherics: Explaining the Influence of Restrictive Navigation Cues," *Journal of Business Research*, 57, 795–803.

30. Babin, B. J., M. Griffin, and J. Boles (1997), "Keeping Your Customers: An Exploratory Investigation of Patronage Loyalty," presented at The American Marketing Association's Summer Educators' Conference, Chicago, IL, August 11, 1997.

31. Gottman J. M., and R. W. Leveson (1992), "Emotional Suppression: Physiology, Self-Report, and Expressive Behavior," *Journal of Personality and Social Psychology*, 64 (April), 970–986.

32. Gross, J. J., and O. P. John (1997), "Revealing Feelings: Facets of Emotional Expressivity in Self-Reports, Peer Ratings, and Behavior," *Journal of Personality and Social Psychology*, 72 (February), 435–448.

33. Particularly when the emotions are consistent with the sex-role expectations of the female social schema. Social schemata are discussed in a later chapter.

34. Various authors have defined EI with different numbers of emotions and using different terms to capture dimensions. These are a composite of common dimensions. For a review, see Frye, C. M., R. Bennett, and S. Caldwell (2006), "Team Emotional Intelligence and Team Interpersonal Process Effectiveness," *Mid-American Journal of Business*, 21, 49–56.

35. Rozell, E. J., C. E. Pettijohn, and R. S. Parker (2006), "Emotional Intelligence and Dispositional Affectivity as Predictors of Performance in Salespeople," *Journal of Marketing Theory and Practice*, 14, 113–124.

36. Chang, J. (2003), "Born to Sell?" *Sales & Marketing Management*, 155, 34–39.

37. Ferré, P. (2003), "Effects of Level of Processing on Memory for Affectively Valenced Words," *Cognition and Emotion*, 17, 859–880, quotation taken from p. 859.

38. Baird, Thomas R., R. G. Wahlers, and C. K. Cooper (2007), "Non-Recognition of Print Advertising: Emotion Arousal and Gender Effects," *Journal of Marketing Communications*, 13, 39–57.

39. Miranda, R., and J. F. Kihlstrom (2005), "Mood Congruence in Childhood and Recent Autobiographical Memory," *Cognition and Emotion*, 19, 981–998.

40. Forgas, J. P., and J. Ciarrochi (2001), "On Being Happy and Possessive: The Interactive Effects on Mood and Personality on Consumer Judgments," *Psychology & Marketing*, 239–260.

41. Sierra, J. J., and S. McQuitty (2007), "Attitudes and Emotions as Determinants of Nostalgic Purchases: An Application of Social Identity Theory," *Journal of Marketing Theory and Practice*, 15, 99–112.

42. Schema adapted from Babin, B. J., J. S. Boles, and W. R. Darden (1995), "Salesperson Stereotypes, Consumer Emotions, and Their Impact on Information Processing," *Journal of the Academy of Marketing Science*, 23, 94–105.

43. Gountas, S., M. T. Ewing, and J. I. Gountas (2007), "Testing Airline Passengers' Responses to Flight Attendants' Expressive Displays: The Effects of Positive Affect," *Journal of Business Research*, 60, 81–83; Tsai, W. C., and Y. M. Huang (2002), "Mechanisms Linking Employee Affective Delivery and Customer Behavioral Intentions," *Journal of Applied Psychology*, 87, 1001–1008; Hennig-Thurau, T., M. Groth, P. Michael, and D. D. Gremier (2006), "Are All Smiles Created Equal? How Emotional Contagion

and Emotional Labor Affect Service Relationships," *Journal of Marketing*, 70, 58–73.

44. Hennig-Thurau et al. (2006); Morris, J., and D. Feldman (1997), "The Dimensions, Antecedents and Consequences of Emotional Labour," *Academy of Management Journal*, 21, 989–1010.

45. http://www.tremor.com, accccessed December 15, 2007; http://www.pbs.org/wobh/pages/frontline/shows/cool/, accessed December 11, 2007; "The Merchant of Cool: Cool Hunters Seek Us Out for Our Opinions and Then Sell Them Right Back to Us," http://findarticles.com/p/articles/mi_m0GER/is_2002_Summer/ai_89646387, accessed December 13, 2007; http://en.wikipedia.org/wiki/Coolhunting, accessed December 11, 2007; Trend Hunter, http://www.trendhunter.com/about-trend-hunter, accessed December 11, 2007; "Teen Market Profile" 2004, Mediamark Research Inc. for Magazine Publisher of America, www.magazine.org/content/files/teenprofile04.pdf, accessed December 12, 2007; Marketing to the Young, http://www.desjardins.com/en/particuliers/clienteles/parents/conseils/marketing_et_jeunes.jsp., accessed December 12, 2007.

Chapter 6

1. For a discussion of individual difference variables in consumer research and marketing practice, see Mowen, John C. (2000), *The 3M Model of Motivation and Personality: Theory and Empirical Applications to Consumer Behavior*, Boston, Kluwer Academic Publishers.

2. This definition is based on a number of different works found in the personality psychology literature including Allport, G. W. (1961), *Pattern and Growth in Personality*, New York, Holt, Rinehart, and Winston; Pervin, L. A., and O. P. John (1977), *Personality Theory and Research*, New York, John Wiley & Sons; Brody, Nathan, and Howard Ehrlichman (1998), *Personality Psychology: The Science of Individuality*, Upper Saddle River, NJ, Prentice Hall; Mowen (2000).

3. Angleitner, Alois (1991), "Personality Psychology: Trends and Developments," *European Journal of Personality*, 5, 185–197.

4. A discussion of the debate regarding personality and behavioral consistency across situations may be found in Mischel, W., and P. K. Peake (1983), "Some Facets of Consistency: Replies to Epstein, Funder, and Bem," *Psychological Review*, 89, 394–402; Epstein, S. (1983), "The Stability of Confusion: A Reply to Mischel and Peake," Psychological Review, 90, 179–194; Buss, David (1989), "Personality as Traits," *American Psychologist*, 44, 1378–1388.

5. For a discussion of psychoanalytical theory and applications to marketing, see Kassarjian, Harold H. (1971), "Personality and Consumer Behavior: A Review," *Journal of Marketing Research*, 8 (November), 409–418. Also see Kassarjian, Harold H., and Mary Jane Sheffet (1991), "Personality and Consumer Behavior: An Update," in *Perspectives in Consumer Behavior*, 4th ed., Harold H. Kassarjian and Thomas S. Robertson, eds., Upper Saddle River NJ, Prentice Hall, 1991: 81–303. For a general description of the psychoanalytical approach in psychology, see Brody and Ehrlichman (1998).

6. Interesting examples of the early use of these motivational techniques can be found in Gustafson, Philip (1958), "You Can Gauge Customers' Wants," *Nation's Business*, 49 (April), 76–84.

7. Kassarjian, Harold H. (1971), "Personality and Consumer Behavior: A Review," *Journal of Marketing Research*, 8 (November), 409–418.

8. Brody and Ehrlichman (1998).

9. Buss, David (1989), "Personality as Traits," *American Psychologist*, 44, 1378–1388.

10. Allport, G. W., and H. S. Odbert (1936), "Trait Names," *Psychological Monographs*, 47 (211), 1–37.

11. Lichtenstein, Donald R., Richard G. Netemeyer, and Scot Burton (1990), "Distinguishing Coupon Proneness from Value Consciousness: An Acquisition-Transaction Utility Theory Perspective," *Journal of Marketing*, 54 (3), 54–67.

12. Belk, Russell W. (1985), "Materialism: Trait Aspects of Living in the Material World," *Journal of Consumer Research*, (December), 12 (3), 265–280.

13. Richins, Marsha L. (1994), "Special Possessions and the Expression of Material Values," *Journal of Consumer Research*, (December), 21 (3), 522–533; Belk (1985).

14. Tian, Kelly, and Russell W. Belk (2005), "Extended Self and Possessions in the Workplace," *Journal of Consumer Research*, (September), 32 (2), 297–310.

15. Wallendorf, Melanie, and Eric J. Arnould (1988), "My Favorite Things: A Cross-Cultural Inquiry into Object Attachment, Possessiveness, and Social Linkage," *Journal of Consumer Research*, (March), 14 (4), 531–547.

16. Belk (1985).

17. Graham, Judy F. (1999), "Materialism and Consumer Behavior: Toward a Clearer Understanding," *Journal of Social Behavior & Personality* (June), 14 (2), 241–259; Loftus, Mary (2004), "Till Debt Do Us Part," *Psychology Today*, (November/December), 37 (6), 42–50.

18. Lastovicka, John L., Lance A. Bettencourt, Renee Shaw Hughner, and Ronald J. Kuntze (1999), "Lifestyle of the Tight and Frugal: Theory and Measurement," *Journal of Consumer Research*, (June), 26 (1), 85–98.

19. This definition is based on the works of Midgley, David F., and Grahame R. Dowling (1978), "Innovativeness: The Concept and Its Measurement," *Journal of Consumer Research*, 229–242; Rogers, Everett M., and Floyd F. Shoemaker (1971), *Communication of Innovations*, New York, The Free Press.

20. Hartman, Jonathan B., Kenneth C. Gerht, and Kittichai Watchravesringkan (2004), "Re-Examination of the Concept of Innovativeness in the Context of the Adolescent Segment: Development of a Measurement Scale," *Journal of Targeting, Measurement and Analysis for Marketing*, 12, 353–366; Wood, Stacy L., and Joffre Swait (2002), "Psychological Indicators of Innovation Adoption: Cross-Classification Based on Need for Cognition and Need for Change," *Journal of Consumer Psychology*, 12, 1–13; Goldsmith, Ronald E., and Charles E. Hofacker (1991), "Measuring Consumer Innovativeness," *Journal of the Academy of Marketing Science*, 19, 209–221; Venkatraman, Meera A. (1991), "The Impact of Innovativeness and Innovation Type on Product Adoption," *Journal of Retailing*, 67, 51–67.

21. Hirunyawipada, Tanawat, and Audhesh K. Paswan (2006), "Consumer Innovativeness and Perceived Risk: Implications for High Technology Product Adoption," *Journal of Consumer Marketing*, 23/24, 182–198; Hirschman, Elizabeth C. (1980), "Innovativeness, Novelty Seeking, and Consumer Creativity," *Journal of Consumer Research*, 7, 283–295; Manning, Kenneth C., William O. Bearden, and Thomas J. Madden (1995), "Consumer Innovativeness and the Adoption Process," *Journal of Consumer Psychology*, 4, 329–345; Citrin, A. V., D. E. Sprott, S. N. Silverman, and D. E. Stem (2000), "Adoption of Internet Shopping: The Role of Consumer Innovativeness," *Industrial Management & Data Systems*, 100, 294–300.

22. Harris, Eric G., and John C. Mowen (2001), "The Influence of Cardinal-, Central-, and Surface-Level Personality Traits on Consumers' Bargaining and Complaint Intentions," *Psychology & Marketing* (November), 18 (11), 1155–1185.

23. Moyer, Mel S. (1984), "Characteristics of Consumer Complaints: Implications for Marketing and Public Policy," *Journal of Public Policy & Marketing*, 3, 67–85; Richins, Marsha L. (1983), "An Analysis of Consumer Interaction Styles in the Marketplace," *Journal of Consumer Research*, 10, 73–82.

24. Juhl, Hans J., John Thogersen, and Carsten S. Poulsen (2006), "Is the Propensity to Complain Increasing Over Time?," *Journal of Consumer Satisfaction, Dissatisfaction, and Complaining Behavior*, 19, 118–127.

25. Kiger, Patrick J. (2002), "Why Customer Satisfaction Begins with HR," *Workforce*, (May), 26–28.

26. Mowen, John C., (2004), "Exploring the Trait of Competitiveness and Its Consumer Behavior Consequences," *Journal of Consumer Psychology*, 14, 52–63.

27. Moore, Dave (2007), "Gaming League Reaches 17–24-year-old Crowd," *Dallas Business Journal*, (January 7), 5.

28. Cialdini, Robert B., Richard J. Borden, Avril Thorne, Marcus R. Walker, Stephen Freeman, and Lloyd R. Sloan (1976), "Basking in Reflected Glory: Three (Football) Field Studies," *Journal of Personality and Social Psychology,* 34 (3), 366–375.

29. Pons, Frank, and Mehdi Mourali (2006), "Consumer Orientation Toward Sporting Events," *Journal of Service Research,* (February), 8 (3), 276–287.

30. A number of researchers have contributed to the development of the Five-Factor Model. For example, see Costa, P. T., and R. R. McCrae (1985), *The NEO Personality Inventory Manual*, Odessa, FL, Psychological Assessment Resources; Goldberg, L. R. (1992), "The Development of Matters for the Big-Five Factor Structure," *Psychological Assessment*, 4, 26–42; Wiggins, J. S. (1996), *The Five-Factor Model of Personality*, New York, Guilford Press.

31. Harris, Eric G., and John C. Mowen (2001), "The Influence of Cardinal, Central-, and Surface-Level Personality Traits on Consumers' Bargaining and Complaining Behaviors," *Psychology & Marketing,* (November), 18 (11), 1150–1185; Harris, Eric G., and David E. Fleming (2005), "Assessing the Human Element in Service Personality Formation: Personality Congruency and the Five Factor Model," *Journal of Services Marketing*, 19 (4), 187–198; Mowen, John C., and Nancy Spears (1999), "Understanding Compulsive Buying among College Students," *Journal of Consumer Psychology,* 8 (4), 407–430; Finn, Seth (1997), "Origins of Media Exposure: Linking Personality Traits to TV, Radio, Print, and Film Use," *Communication Research,* (October), 24 (5), 507–530; Fraj, Elena, and Eva Martinez (2006), "Influence of Personality on Ecological Consumer Behaviour," *Journal of Consumer Behaviour*, 5, 167–181.

32. Notable works in this area include Eysenck, H. J. (1947), *Dimensions of Personality*, London, Routledge & Kegan Paul; Allport, G. W. (1961), *Pattern and Growth in Personality*, New York, Holt, Rinehart, and Winston; Paunonen, S. V. (1998), "Hierarchical Organization of Personality and Prediction of Behavior," *Journal of Personality and Social Psychology*, 74, 538–556; Mowen (2000).

33. This section is based on a number of sources that have discussed problems with the trait approach in consumer behavior including Kassarjian, Harold H. (1971), "Personality and Consumer Behavior: A Review," *Journal of Marketing Research*, 8 (November), 409–418; Kassarjian and Sheffet (1991); Lastovicka, John L., and Eric A. Joachimsthaler (1988), "Improving the Detection of Personality-Behavior Relationships," *Journal of Consumer Research*, (March): 583–587, 14 (4); Mowen (2000).

34. Baumgartner, Hans (2002), "Toward a Personology of the Consumer," *Journal of Consumer Research*, (September), 29 (2), 286–292; also McAdams, Dan P. (1996), "Personality, Modernity, and the Storied Self: A Contemporary Framework for Studying Persons," Psychological Inquiry, 7 (4), 295–321.

35. Aaker, Jennifer (1997), "Dimensions of Brand Personality," *Journal of Marketing Research* (August), 34 (3), 347–356.

36. Gwinner, K. P., and J. Eaton (1999), "Building Brand Image Through Event Sponsorship: The Role of Image Transfer, *Journal of Advertising*, 38, 47–57.

37. Aaker, David A. (1996), *Building Strong Brands*, New York, Free Press.

38. This section based on Aaker (1996).

39. Fournier, Susan (1998), "Consumers and Their Brands: Developing Relationship Theory in Consumer Research," *Journal of Consumer Research*, (March), 343–373; Aaker, Jennifer, Susan Fournier, and S. Adam Brasel (2004), "When Good Brands Do Bad," *Journal of Consumer Research*, (June), 1–16.

40. Fournier (1998).

41. Harris, Eric G., and David E. Fleming (2005), "Assessing the Human Element in Services Personality Formation: Personality Congruency and The Five-Factor Model," *Journal of Services Marketing,* 19, 187–198.

42. This information from: www.harleydavidson.com, accessed February 25, 2008.

43. Aaker, Fournier, and Brasel (2004).

44. Darden, W. R., and D. Ashton (1974), "Psychographics Profiles of Patronage Preference Groups," *Journal of Retailing*, 50 (Winter), 99–112.

45. Lazer, W. (1963), "Lifestyle Concepts and Marketing," in S. Greyer (ed.), *Towards Scientific Marketing*, Chicago, American Marketing Association.

46. Lawson, Rob, and Sarah Todd (2002), "Consumer Lifestyles: A Social Stratification Perspective," *Marketing Theory*, 2, 295–307.

47. Geist, Laura Clark (2006), "Ford Commercials Focus on People, Not Product," *Automotive News* (September 18), 30.

48. Gonzalez, Ana M., and Laurentino Bello (2002), "The Construct 'Lifestyle' in Market Segmentation: The Behaviour of Tourist Consumers," *European Journal of Marketing*, 36, 51–85.

49. Morgan, Carol M., and Doran J. Levy (2002), "The Boomer Attitude," *American Demographics* (October), 24 (9), 42–45.

50. Benezra, Karen (1998), "The Fragging of the American Mind," *Brandweek*, (June), S12–S19.

51. Johnson, Trent, and Johan Bruwer (2003), "An Empirical Confirmation of Win-Related Lifestyle Segments in the Australian Wine Market," *International Journal of Wine Marketing*, 15, 5–33.

52. Taylor, A. (1995), "Porsche Slices Up its Buyers," *Fortune* (January 16), 24.

53. This section based on information obtained on the SRI International website, **www.sri-bi.com**, accessed February 23, 2008.

54. This information based on materials found at **www.claritas.com**, accessed February 23, 2008.

55. Ridgeway, Cecilia L., and Henry A. Walker (1995), "Status Structures," in *Sociological Perspectives on Social Psychology,* Karen S. Cook, Gary A. Fine, and James S. House, eds., Boston, Allyn and Bacon, 281–310.

56. Mead, George H. (1934), *Mind, Self and Society,* Chicago, University of Chicago Press; Mick, David Glen (1986), "Consumer Research and Semiotics: Exploring the Morphology of Signs, Symbols, and Significance," *Journal of Consumer Research,* (September), 13 (2), 196–213; Holbrook, Morris B. (2001), "The Millennial Consumer in the Texts of Our Times: Exhibitionism," *Journal of Macromarketing*, 21, 81–95; Chaudhuri, Himadri Roy, and Sitanath Majumdar (2006), "Of Diamonds and Desires: Understanding Conspicuous Consumption from a Contemporary Marketing Perspective," *Academy of Marketing Science Review*, (2006), 1.

57. See also Schau, Hope Jensen, and Mary Gilly (2003), "We Are What We Post? Self-Presentation in Personal Web Space," 30 (3), *Journal of Consumer Research* (December), 385–404; Trammell, Kaye D., and Ana Keshelashvili (2005), "Examining the New Influencers: A Self-Presentation Study of A-List Blogs," *Journalism and Mass Communication Quarterly* (Winter), 82 (4), 968–983.

58. Aaker, Jennifer (1999), "The Malleable Self: The Role of Self-Expression in Persuasion," *Journal of Marketing Research* (February), 36 (1), 45–57.

59. These concepts based on Sirgy, M. Joseph (1982), "Self-Concept in Consumer Behavior: A Critical Review," *Journal of Consumer Research* (December), 9 (3), 287–300; Belk, Russell (1988), "Possessions and the Extended Self," *Journal of Consumer Research* (September), 15 (2), 139–168.

60. Ahuvia, Aaron C. (2005), "Beyond the Extended Self: Loved Objects and Consumers' Identity Narratives," *Journal of Consumer Research* (June), 32 (1), 171–184; Escalas, Jennifer, and James R. Bettman (2005), "Self-Construal, Reference Groups, and Brand Meaning," *Journal of Consumer Research* (December), 32 (3), 378–389.

61. Chaplin, Lon Nguyen, and Debrah Roedder John (2005), "The Development of Self-Brand Connections in

Children and Adolescents," *Journal of Consumer Research* (June), 32 (1), 119–130.

62. Smeesters, Dirk, and Naomi Mandel (2006), "Positive and Negative Media Image Effects on the Self," *Journal of Consumer Research* (March), 32 (4), 576–582; Richins, Marsha (1991), "Social Comparison and the Idealized Images of Advertising," *Journal of Consumer Research* (June), 18 (1), 71–83; Grogan, Sarah (1999), *Understanding Body Dissatisfaction in Men, Women, and Children*, London, Routledge.

63. Tan, Cheryl Lu-Lien (2007), "Fashion Group Sets Guides to Rein in Ultra-Thin Models," *Wall Street Journal* (January 8), B4.

64. Keim, Brandon (2006), "Media Messes with Mens' Minds Too," *Psychology Today* (September/October), 39 (5), 26.

65. Hafner, Michael (2004), "How Dissimilar Others May Still Resemble the Self: Assimilation and Contrast after Social Comparison," *Journal of Consumer Psychology*, 14, 187–196.

66. This information from American Society for Aesthetic Plastic Surgery website: **www.surgery.org/press/news-release.php?iid-465**, accessed February 23, 2008.

67. Mayers, L.B. and S.H. Chiffriller (2008), "Body Art Among Undergraduate University Students: Then and Now", *Journal of Adolescent Health*, 42 (2): pgs. 201–203.

68. Brumberg, Joan Jacobs (2006), "Are We Facing an Epidemic of Self-Injury?" *Chronicle of Higher Education*, 53, B6–B8.

69. Braithwaite, R., A. Robillard, T. Woodring, T. Stephens, and K. J. Arriola (2001), "Tattooing and Body Piercing Among Adolescent Detainees: Relationship to Alcohol and Other Drug Use," *Journal of Substance Abuse*, 13, 5–16; Grief, J., and W. Hewitt (1998), "The Living Canvas: Health Issues in Tattooing, Body Piercing, and Branding," *Advances for Nurse Practitioners*, 12, 26–31; Roberti, Jonathon W., and Eric A. Storch (2005), "Psychosocial Adjustment of College Students With Tattoos and Piercings," *Journal of College Counseling* (Spring), 8 (1), 14–19.

70. Sirgy, M. Joseph, Dhruv Grewal, Tamara Mangleburg, and Jae-ok Park (1997), "Assessing the Predictive Validity of Two Methods of Measuring Self-Image Congruence," *Journal of the Academy of Marketing Science* (Summer), 25 (3), 229–241.

71. Sirgy, M. Joseph, and A. Coskun Samli (1985), "A Path Analytic Model of Store Loyalty Involving Self-Concept, Store Image, Geographic Loyalty, and Socioeconomic Status," *Journal of the Academy of Marketing Science* (Summer), 13 (3), 265–291.

72. Aaker (1999), 47.

73. Landon, E. Laird (1974), "Self Concept, Ideal Self Concept, and Consumer Purchase Intentions," *Journal of Consumer Research* (September), 1 (2), 44–51.

Chapter 7

1. This definition is based on a summary of several works in the social psychology and consumer behavior literatures, including Eagly, Alice, and Shelly Chaiken (1993), *The Psychology of Attitudes*, New York, Harcourt Brace; Cacioppo, John, Stephen Harkins, and Richard Petty (1981), "The Nature of Attitudes and Cognitive Responses and Their Relations to Behavior," in *Cognitive Responses in Persuasion*, Richard Petty, Thomas Ostrom, and Timothy C. Brock, eds., Hillsdale, NJ: Lawrence Erlbaum; Thurstone L. L. (1931), "The Measurement of Social Attitudes," in *Readings in Attitude Theory and Measurement*, M. Fishbein ed., New York, Wiley.

2. Katz, Daniel (1960), "The Functional Approach to the Study of Attitudes," *Public Opinion Quarterly*, 24 (2), 163–204.

3. Gibson, Heather, Cynthia Willming, and Andrew Holdnak (2003), "We're Gators. . . . Not Just Gator Fans: Serious Leisure and University of Florida Football," *Journal of Leisure Research*, 34 (4), 397–425.

4. Ray, Michael (1973), "Marketing Communications and the Hierarchy-of-Effects," in *New Models for Mass Communications*, P. Clarke, ed., Beverly Hills, CA, Sage, 1973, 147–176.

5. Krugman, Herbert (1965), "The Impact of Television Advertising: Learning Without Involvement," *Public Opinion Quarterly*, 29 (Fall), 349–356.

6. A recent example of the experiential nature of consumption may be found in Belk, Russell, Guliz Ger, and Soren Askegaard (2003), "The Fire of Desire: A Multisited Inquiry into Consumer Passion," *Journal of Consumer Research*, 30 (3), 326–351.

7. Fishbein, Martin, and Icek Ajzen (1975). *Belief, Attitude, Intention, and Behavior: An Introduction to Theory and Research*, Reading, MA, Addison-Wesley.

8. A number of researchers have addressed this issue including Alwitt, Linda F., and Ida E. Berger (1992), "Understanding the Link Between Environmental Attitudes and Consumer Product Usage: Measuring the Moderating Role of Attitude Strength," in *Advances in Consumer Research*, vol. 20, Leigh McAlister and Michael Rothschild, ed., Provo, UT, Association for Consumer Research, 1992), 189–194; Wicker, Allan (1969), "Attitudes versus Actions: The Relationship of Verbal and Overt Behavioral Responses to Attitude Objects," *Journal of Social Issues*, (Autumn): 25, 41–78.

9. Ajzen, Icek, and Martin Fishbein (1977), "Attitude–Behavior Relations: A Theoretical Analysis and Review of Empirical Research," *Psychological Bulletin* (September), 84 (5), 888–918.

10. Ryan, Michael J., and E. H. Bonfield (1980), "Fishbein's Intentions Model: A Test of External and Pragmatic Validity," *Journal of Marketing*, 44 (2), 82–95.

11. More on this model may be found in Notani, Art Sahni (1998), "Moderators of Perceived Behavioral Control's Predictiveness in the Theory of Reasoned Action," *Journal of Consumer Psychology*, 7 (3), 247–271. Also, an interesting presentation of the planned behavior model applied to food choice may be found in Conner, Mark T. (1993), "Understanding Determinants of Food Choice: Contributions from Attitude Research," *British Food Journal*, 95 (9), 27–32.

12. Mitchell, Andrew A. and Jerry Olson (1981), "Are Product Attribute Beliefs the Only Mediator of Advertising Effects on Brand Attitude?" *Journal of Marketing Research*, 18, 318–332.

13. Several studies have approached this issue including Scott MacKenzie and Richard Lutz (1989), "An Empirical Examination of the Structural Antecedents of Attitude towards the Ad in an Advertising Pretesting Context," *Journal of Marketing*, 53 (April), 48–65; Burton, Scot, and Donald Lichtenstein (1988), "The Effect of Ad Claims and Ad Context on Attitude towards the Advertisement," *Journal of Advertising*, 17 (1), 3–11.

14. Brown, Tom J., and Peter A. Dacin (1997), "The Company and the Product: Corporate Associations and Consumer Product Responses," *Journal of Marketing*, 61 (January), 68–84.

15. Sen, Sankar, and C.B. Bhattacharya (2001), "Does Doing Good Always Lead to Doing Better? Consumer Reactions to Corporate Social Responsibility," *Journal of Marketing Research*, 38 (May), 225–243.

16. Petty, Richard E., John T. Cacioppo, and David Schuman (1983), "Central and Peripheral Routes to Advertising Effectiveness: The Moderating Role of Involvement," *Journal of Consumer Research*, 10 (2), 135–146.

17. Celsi, Richard L., and Jerry C. Olson (1988), "The Role of Involvement in Attention and Comprehension Processes," *Journal of Consumer Research*, (September), 15 (2), 210–224; MacInnis, Deborah J., and C. Whan Park (1991), "The Differential Role of Characteristics of Music on High- and Low-Involvement Consumers' Processing of Ads," *Journal of Consumer Research*, (September), 18 (2), 161–173.

18. Heider, Fritz (1958), *The Psychology of Interpersonal Relations*, New York, John Wiley.

19. Russell, Cristel, and Barbara B. Stern (2006), "Consumers, Characters, and Products: A Balance Model of Sitcom Product Placement Effects," *Journal of Advertising*, 35 (1), 7–21.

20. Woodside, Arch (2004), "Advancing Means-End Chains by Incorporating Heider's Balance Theory and Fournier's Consumer-Brand Relationship Typology," *Psychology & Marketing*, 21 (4), 279–294.

21. Escalas, Jennifer Edson, and James R. Bettman (2005), "Self-Construal, Reference Groups, and Brand Meaning," *Journal of Consumer Research*, 32 (3), 378–389.

22. Sherif, Muzafer, and Carl Hovland (1961), *Social Judgment: Assimilation and Contrast Effects in Communication and Attitude Change*, New Haven, CT, Yale University Press.

23. Hoffman, Donna L., and Thomas P. Novak (1996), "Marketing in Hypermedia Computer-Mediated Environments: Conceptual Foundations," *Journal of Marketing*, 60 (3), 50–68.

24. This estimate based on information retrieved online on January 30, 2009 at **www.internetworldstats.com/stats.htm**.

25. Hoffman and Novak (1996).

26. Dudley, Sid C. (1999), "Consumer Attitudes Toward Nudity in Advertising," *Journal of Marketing Theory and Practice*, 7 (4), 89–96.

27. LaTour, Michael S. (1990), "Female Nudity in Print Advertising: An Analysis of Gender Differences in Arousal and Ad Response," *Psychology & Marketing*, 7 (1), 65–81.

28. Simpson, Penny M., Steve Horton, and Gene Brown (1996), "Male Nudity in Advertisements: A Modified Replication and Extension of Gender and Product Effects," *Journal of the Academy of Marketing Science*, 24 (3), 257–262.

29. Huang, Ming-Hui (2004), "Romantic Love and Sex: Their Relationship and Impacts on Ad Attitudes," *Psychology & Marketing*, 21 (1), 53–73.

30. Sternthal, Brian, and C. Samuel Craig (1973), "Humor in Advertising," *Journal of Marketing*, 37 (October), 12–18.

31. Krishnan, H. S., and D. Chakravarti (2003), "A Process Analysis of the Effects of Humorous Advertising Executions on Brand Claims Memory," *Journal of Consumer Psychology*, 13 (3), 230–245.

32. Zhang, Yong (1996), "The Effect of Humor in Advertising: An Individual-Difference Perspective," *Psychology & Marketing*, 13 (6), 531–545.

33. Cline, Thomas W., Moses B. Altsech, and James J. Kellaris (2003), "When Does Humor Enhance or Inhibit Ad Responses?" *Journal of Advertising*, 32 (3), 31–46.

34. Chattopadhyay, Amitava (1990), "Humor in Advertising: The Moderating Role of Prior Brand Evaluations," *Journal of Marketing Research*, 29 (November), 466–476.

35. Smith, Stephen M. (1993), "Does Humor in Advertising Enhance Systematic Processing," in *Advances in Consumer Research*, vol. 20, L. McAlister and M. Rothschild, eds., Provo, UT, Association of Consumer Research, 155–158.

36. LaTour, Michael S., and Herbert J. Rotfeld (1997), "There Are Threats and (Maybe) Fear-Caused Arousal: Theory and Confusions of Appeals to Fear and Fear Arousal Itself," *Journal of Advertising*, 3 (Fall), 45–59.

37. Keller, Punam Anand, and Lauren Goldberg Block (1996), "Increasing the Persuasiveness of Fear Appeals: The Effect of Arousal and Elaboration," *Journal of Consumer Research*, 22 (4), 448–459.

38. Mowen, John C., Eric G. Harris, and Sterling A. Bone (2004), "Personality Traits and Fear Response to Print Advertisements: Theory and an Empirical Study," *Psychology & Marketing*, 21 (11), 927–943.

39. Potter, Robert F., Michael S. LaTour, Kathryn A. Braun-LaTour, and Tom Reichert (2006), "The Impact of Program Context on Motivational System Activation and Subsequent Effects on Processing a Fear Appeal," *Journal of Advertising*, 35 (3): 67–80.

40. Tanner, John F., James B. Hunt, and David R. Eppright (1991), "The Protection Motivation Model: A Normative Model of Fear Appeals," *Journal of Marketing,* 55 (3), 36–45.

41. Duke, Charles R., Gregory M. Pickett, Les Carlson, and Stephen J. Grove (1993), "A Method for Evaluating the Ethics of Fear Appeals," *Journal of Public Policy & Marketing*, 1 (Spring), 120–130.

42. Sawyer, Alan G., and Daniel J. Howard (1991), "Effects of Omitting Conclusions in Advertisements to Involved and Uninvolved Audiences," *Journal of Marketing Research*, 28 (November), 467–474.

43. Wilkie, William L., and Paul W. Ferris (1973), "Comparison Advertising: Problems and Potential," *Journal of Marketing*, 39 (October), 7–15.

44. Miniard, Paul W., Michael J. Barone, Randall L. Rose, and Kenneth C. Manning (2006), "A Further Assessment of Indirect Advertising Claims of Superiority Overall All Competitors," *Journal of Advertising,* 35 (4), 53–64.

45. Haugtvedt, Curtis P., and Duance T. Wegener (1994), "Message Order Effects in Persuasion: An Attitude Strength Perspective," *Journal of Consumer Research*, 21 (June), 205–218.

46. Unnava, H. Rao, Robert E. Burnkrant, and Sunil Erevelles (1994), "Effects of Presentation Order and Communication Modality on Recall and Attitude," *Journal of Consumer Research*, 21 (December), 481–490.

47. Jain, S. P., and S. S. Posavac (2001), "Prepurchase Attribute Verifiability, Source Credibility, and Persuasion," *Journal of Consumer Psychology*, 11 (3), 169–180.

48. Homer, Pamela M., and Lynn R. Kahle (1990), "Source Expertise, Time of Source Identification, and Involvement in Persuasion," *Journal of Advertising*, 19 (1), 30–39.

49. Wilson, Elizabeth, and Daniel L. Sherrell (1993), "Source Effects in Communication and Persuasion Research: A Meta-Analysis of Effect Size," *Journal of the Academy of Marketing Science*, 21 (2), 101–112.

50. Wiener, Josh, and John C. Mowen (1985), "The Impact of Product Recalls on Consumer Perceptions," *The Journal of the Society of Consumer Affairs Professionals in Business*, (Spring), 18–21.

51. Lafferty, Barbara A., Ronald E. Goldsmith, and Stephen J. Newell (2002), "The Dual Credibility Model: The Influence of Corporate and Endorser Credibility on Attitudes and Purchase Intention," *Journal of Marketing Theory & Practice*, 10 (3), 1–12.

52. Till, Brian D., and Michael Busler (2000), "The Match-Up Hypothesis: Physical Attractiveness, Expertise, and the Role of Fit on Brand Attitude, Purchase Intent, and Brand Beliefs," *Journal of Advertising*, 3 (Fall), 1–13; Chaiken, Shelly (1979), "Communicator Physical Attractiveness and Persuasion," *Journal of Personality and Social Psychology*, 37 (August), 1387–1397.

53. Baker, Michael, and Gilbert Churchill (1977), "The Impact of Physically Attractive Models on Advertising Effectiveness," *Journal of Marketing Research*, 14 (November), 538–555.

54. Kang, Yoon-Soon and Paul M. Herr (2006), "Beauty and the Beholder: Toward an Integrative Model of Communication Source Effects," *Journal of Consumer Research*, 33 (1): 123–130.

55. Information gathered from Marketing Evaluations, Inc. website (January 8, 2008) at: **http://www.qscores.com**.

56. Lynch, James and Drue Schuler (1994), "The Matchup Effect of Spokesperson and Product Congruency: A Schema Theory Interpretation," *Psychology & Marketing*, 11 (September–October): 417–445; Kamins, Michael A. (1990), "An Investigation into the 'Match-Up' Hypothesis in Celebrity Advertising: When Beauty May Be Only Skin Deep," *Journal of Advertising*, 19 (1): 4–13.

57. **www.coca-colablak.com**, accessed December 10, 2007; "Welcome Black! Coca-Cola Blak Arrives in the United States," **http://www .thecoca-colacompany.com/press center/nr_20060315_americas_welcome_blak.html**, accessed December 11, 2007; Coke Thinks Coffee-Cola Is It; 'Coca-Cola Blak' Adds a Jolt of Joe," **http://www.msnbc.msn.com/ id/10334920**, accessed December 8, 2007; "Taste Test: Coke BlaK; It's Coke with Coffee, Double the Caffeine, and Half the Calories," ConsumerReports .org, March 2006, **http://www .consumerreports.org/cro/food/beverages/cola/taste-test-coke-blak-306/ overview/index.htm**, accessed December, 15, 2007; "U.S. Coffee Consumption Shows Impressive Growth," *Food & Drink Weekly,* February 16, 2004, **http://findarticles.com/p/articles/**

mi_m0EUY/is_6_10/ai_113524726, accessed December 16, 2007; "Coffee Drinkers and Their Habit," *Business-Week* on-line extra, October 10, 2005, http://www.businessweek.com/magazine/content/05_41/63954201.htm?chan=search, accessed December 12, 2007.

Chapter 8

1. Guimond, S., S. Brunot, A. Chatard, D. M. Garcia, D. Martinot, N. R. Branscombe, M. Desert, S. Haque, and V. Yzerbyt (2007), "Culture, Gender, and the Self: Variations and Impact of Social Comparison Processes," *Journal of Personality and Social Psychology*, 92 (June), 1118–1134.

2. Sung, Y., and S. F. Tinkham (2005), "Brand Personality Structures in the United States and Korea: Common and Culture-Specific Factors," *Journal of Consumer Psychology*, 15 (4), 334–350.

3. Ball, D. (2006), "Women in Italy Like to Clean but Shun The Quick and Easy," *Wall Street Journal*, April 25, A1.

4. McCracken, G. (1986), "Culture and Consumption: A Theoretical Account of the Structure and Movement of the Cultural Meaning of Consumer Goods," *Journal of Consumer Research*, 13, 71–84.

5. Lenartowicz, T., and K. Roth (1999), "A Framework for Culture Assessment," *Journal of International Business Studies*, 30, 781–798; Lenartowicz, T., and K. Roth (2001), "Culture Assessment Revisited: The Selection of Key Informants in IB Cross-Cultural Studies," 2001 Annual Meeting of the Academy of International Business.

6. Overby, J. W., R. B. Woodruff, and S. F. Gardial (2005), "The Influence of Culture on Consumers' Desired Value Perceptions: A Research Agenda," *Marketing Theory*, 5 (June), 139–163.

7. See Hofstede, Geert (2007), http://www.geert-hofstede.com/geert_hofstede_resources.shtml for an overview, accessed August 9, 2007.

8. For a concise review of Hofstede's value dimensions, see Soares, A. M., M. Farhangmehr, and A. Shoham (2007), "Hofstede's Dimensions of Culture in International Marketing Studies," *Journal of Business Research*, 60, 277–284.

9. Hirschman, E. C. (2003), "Men, Dogs, Guns and Cars," *Journal of Advertising*, 32 (Spring), 9–22.

10. Hofstede (2007).

11. Jung, J. M., and J. J. Kellaris (2006), "Responsiveness to Authority Appeals Among Young French and American Consumers," *Journal of Business Research*, 59 (June), 735–744.

12. Jung, J. M., and J. J. Kellaris (2004), "Cross-National Differences in Proneness to Scarcity Effects: The Moderating Roles of Familiarity, Uncertainty Avoidance and Need for Cognitive Closure," *Psychology & Marketing*, 21 (September), 739–753.

13. Erevelles, S., R. Abhik, and L. Yip (2001), "The Universality of the Signal Theory for Products and Services," *Journal of Business Research*, 52 (May), 175–187.

14. Hofstede, G. (2001), *Culture's Consequences*. Thousand Oaks, CA: Sage Publications.

15. Keysuk, K., and C. Oh (2002), "On Distributor Commitment in Marketing Channels for Industrial Products: Contrast Between the United States and Japan," *Journal of International Marketing*, 10, 72–107; Ryu, S., S. Kabadavi, and C. Chung (2007), "The Relationship Between Unilateral and Bilateral Control Mechanisms: The Contextual Effect of Long-Term Orientation," *Journal of Business Research*, 60 (July), 681–689.

16. Hofstede (2001).

17. Wang, C. L. (2007), "Guanxi vs. Relationship Marketing: Exploring Underlying Differences," *Industrial Marketing Management*, 36, 81–86.

18. Worthington, S. (2005), "Entering the Market for Financial Services in Transitional Economies," *International Journal of Bank Marketing*, 23, 381–396.

19. Byrne, P. M. (2007), "Thinking Beyond BRIC," *Logistics Management*, 46, 24–26.

20. For example, see Muller, T. E. (2000), "Targeting the CANZUS Baby-Boomer Explorer and Adventurer Market," *Journal of Vacation Marketing*, 6, 154–169.

21. Durkheim, E. (1895). The Rules of *Sociological Method*, Chicago: University of Chicago Press.

22. Laroche, M., Z. Yang, C. Kim, and M.O. Richard (2007), "How Culture Matters in Children's Purchase Influence: A Multi-Level Investigation," *Journal of the Academy of Marketing Science*, 35 (Winter), 113–126.

22a. Bokale, J. (2008), "Supermarkets Bolster Focus on Children's Ranges," Marketing, February 6, 1.

23. Chankon, K., M. Laroche, and M. Tomuk (2004), "The Chinese in Canada: A Study of Ethnic Change with Emphasis on Gender Roles," *Journal of Social Psychology,* 144 (February), 5–27.

24. Laroche, M., K. Chankon, M. Tomiuk, and D. Belisle (2005), "Similarities in Italian and Greek Multidimensional Ethnic Identity: Some Implications for Food Consumption," *Canadian Journal of Administrative Science*, 22, 143–167.

25. Bristol, T., and T. F. Mangleburg (2005), "Not Telling the Whole Story: Teen Deception in Purchasing," *Journal of the Academy of Marketing Science*, 33 (Winter), 79–95.

26. Bakir, A., G. M. Rose, and A. Shoham (2005), "Consumption Communication and Parental Control of Children's Viewing: A Multi-Rater Approach," *Journal of Marketing Theory and Practice*, 13 (Spring), 47–58; Carlson, L., and S. Grossbart (1988), "Parental Style and Consumer Socialization in Children," *Journal of Consumer Research*, 15 (June), 77–94.

27. Lueg, J. E., and R. Z. Finney (2007), "Interpersonal Communication in the Consumer Socialization Process: Scale Development and Validation," *Journal of Marketing Theory and Practice*, 15 (Winter), 25–39.

28. Business Wire (1999), "International Survey Shows That Coca-Cola and McDonald's are Teenagers' Favorite Brands," (2/8), www.encyclopedia.com/printable.aspx?id=1G1:53724844, accessed August 18, 2007.

29. Devaney, P. (2007), "Coca-Cola to Launch on Virtual World Second Life," *Marketing Week* (2/19), 6.

30. Muk, A., and B. J. Babin (2006), "U.S. Consumers Adoption—Non-Adoption of Mobile SMS Advertising," *Journal of Mobile Marketing*, 1 (June), 21–29.

31. Brand Strategy (2003), "Global Teen Culture—Does it Exist?" 167 (January), 37–38.

32. Parker, R. S., A. D. Schaefer, and C. M. Hermans (2006), "An Investigation Into Teens' Attitudes Towards Fast-Food Brands in General: A Cross-Cultural Analysis," *Journal of Foodservice Business Research*, 9 (4), 25–40.

33. Miller, C., F. Bram, J. Reardon, and I. Vida (2006), "Teenagers' Response to Self- and Other-Directed Anti-Smoking Messages," *International Journal of Market Research*, 49, 515–533.

34. Moschis, G. P., R. L. Moore, and R. B. Smith (1984), "The Impact of Family Communication on Adolescent Consumer Socialization," *Advances in Consumer Research*, 11, 314–319.

35. Clark, A. E., and Y. Loheac (2007), "It Wasn't Me, It Was Them! Social Influence in Risky Behavior by Adolescents," *Journal of Health Economics*, 26, 763–784; Kelly, K. J., M. D. Slater, and D. Karan (2002), "Image Advertisements' Influence on Adolescents' Perceptions of the Desirability of Beer and Cigarettes," *Journal of Public Policy & Marketing*, 21 (Fall), 295–304.

36. Mourali, M., M. Laroche, and F. Pons (2005), "Individual Orientation and Consumer Susceptibility to Interpersonal Influence," *Journal of Services Marketing*, 19, 164–173.

37. Matilla, A. S., and P. G. Patterson (2004), "The Impact of Culture on Consumers' Perceptions of Service Recovery Efforts," *Journal of Retailing*, 80, 196–207.

38. Fong, Mei (2007), "Tired of Laughter, Beijing Gets Rid of Bad Translations," *Wall Street Journal* (2/5), A1.

39. See Griffin, Babin, and Modianas (2000).

40. Dallimore, K. S., B. A. Sparks, and K. Butcher (2007), "The Influence of Angry Customer Outbursts on Service Providers' Facial Displays and Affective

States," *Journal of Services Marketing*, 10 (August), 78–92.

41. Wang, L. A., J. Baker, J. A. Wagner, and K. Wakefield (2007), "Can a Retail Web Site Be Social?" *Journal of Marketing*, 71 (July), 143–157; Qiu, L., and I. Bernbasat (2005), "Online Consumer Trust and Live Help Interfaces: The Effects of Text-to-Speech Voice and Three-Dimensional Avatars," *Journal of Human-Computer-Interaction*, 19, 75–94.

42. Maxa, R., and J. Levine (1999), "Jetiquette," *Forbes*, 163 (2/8), 169 ; Danbom, D. (2004), "American Idle," *Business Finance*, 10 (October), 64.

43. Kramer, T., S. Spolter-Weisfeld, and M. Thakker (2007), "The Effect of Cultural Orientation on Consumer Responses to Personalization," *Marketing Science*, 26 (March/April), 246–258.

44. Pigliasco, G. C. (2005), "Lost in Translation: From Omiyage to Souvenir: Beyond Aesthetics of the Japanese Ladies' Gaze in Hawaii," *Journal of Material Culture*, 10 (July), 177–196.

45. Sheth, J. N. (2007), "Rise of Chindia and Its Impact on World Marketing," presented at the 2007 Academy of Marketing Science World Marketing Congress, Verona, Italy, July 13.

46. Sheth (2007).

47. Mobile phone and population statistics from the CIA Factbook (2008); **https://www.cia.gov/library/publications/the-world-factbook/index.html**, accessed January 27, 2008.

47a. Strizhakova, Y., R. A. Coulter and L. Price (2008), "Branded Products as a Passport to Global Citizenship: Perspectives from Developed and Developing Countries," *Journal of International Marketing*, 16 (4), 57–85.

48. Sheth (2007).

49. See **www.transparency.org** for an overview of culture and corruption around the world.

50. DePaulo, Bella (2006), *Singled Out: How Singles Are Stereotyped, Stigmatized, and Ignored, and Still Live Happily Ever After*, New York: St. Martin's Press; Fowler III, Aubrey R. (2007), Dinner for One: A Grounded Theory of Grocery Shopping in the Single Person Household, Dissertation Proposal; U.S. Census Bureau (2006), *American Community Survey*, **http://factfinder.census.gov/ servlet/ADPTable?_bm=y&-geo_id=01000US&-ds_name=ACS_2005_EST_G00_&-_lang=en&-_caller=geoselect&-format=.**

Chapter 9

1. Park, C. Whan, and V. Parker Lessig (1977), "Students and Housewives: Differences in Susceptibility to Reference Group Influence," *Journal of Consumer Research*, 4 (September), 102–110.

2. Michener, H. Andrew, and Michelle P. Wasserman (1995), "Group Decision Making," in *Sociological Perspectives on Social Psychology*, Karen S. Cook, Gary Alan Fine, and James S. House, eds., Boston: Allyn and Bacon, 336–361.

3. Webley, Paul, and Ellen K. Nyhus (2006), "Parent's Influence on Children's Future Orientation and Saving," *Journal of Economic Psychology*, 27 (1), 140–149.

4. Muniz, Albert M., Jr., and Thomas C. O'Guinn (2001), "Brand Community," *Journal of Consumer Research*, 27 (4), 412–432.

5. Alexander, James H., John W. Schouten, and Harold F. Koening (2002), "Building Brand Community," *Journal of Marketing*, 66 (1), 38–54.

6. Lascu, Dana-Nicoleta, and George Zinkhan (1999), "Consumer Conformity: Review and Applications for Marketing Theory and Practice," *Journal of Marketing Theory and Practice*, 7 (3), 1–12.

7. Ross, Jill, and Ross Harradine (2004), "I'm Not Wearing That! Branding and Young Children," *Journal of Fashion Marketing and Management*, 8 (1), 11–26.

8. Smith, Karen H., and Mary Ann Stutts (2006), "The Influence of Individual Factors on the Effectiveness of Message Content in Antismoking Advertisements Aimed at Adolescents," *Journal of Consumer Affairs*, 40 (2), 261–293; Rosenberg, Mary (2007), "Anti-Smoking Ads Aimed at Peers," *The Wall Street Journal*, May 14, **http://query.nytimes.com/gst/fullpage.html?sec=health&res=9D06E5D8163FF934A25751C0A9649C8B63.**

9. Albers-Miller, Nancy (1999), "Consumer Misbehavior: Why People Buy Illicit Goods," *The Journal of Consumer Marketing*, 16 (3), 273–287.

10. Gergen, Kenneth J., and Mary Gergen (1981), *Social Psychology*, New York: Harcourt Brace Jovanovich.

11. French, J. R. P., and B. Raven (1959), "The Bases of Social Power," in D. Cartwright, ed., *Studies in Social Power*, Ann Arbor, MI: Institute for Social Research.

12. Park and Lessig (1977).

13. Bearden, William O., and Michael J. Etzel (1982), "Reference Group Influence on Product and Brand Purchase Decisions," *Journal of Consumer Research*, 9 (2), 183–194.

14. Park and Lessig (1977).

15. Bearden and Etzel (1982).

16. Bearden, William O., Richard G. Netemeyer, and Jesse E. Teel (1989), "Measurement of Consumer Susceptibility to Interpersonal Influence," *Journal of Consumer Research*, 15 (4): 473–481.

17. Batra, Rajeev, Pamela M. Homer, and Lynn R. Kahle (2001), "Values, Susceptibility to Normative Influence, and Attribute Importance Weights: A Nomological Perspective," *Journal of Consumer Research*, 11 (2), 115–128.

18. Wooten, David B., and Americus Reed II (2004), "Playing it Safe: Susceptibility to Normative Influence and Protective Self-Presentation," *Journal of Consumer Research*, 31 (3), 551–556.

19. Wooten, David B., and Randall L. Rose (1990), "Attention to Social Comparison Information: An Individual Difference Variable Affecting Consumer Conformity," *Journal of Consumer Research*, 16 (4), 461–471.

20. Clark, Ronald A., and Ronald E. Goldsmith (2006), "Global Innovativeness and Consumer Susceptibility to Interpersonal Influence," *Journal of Marketing Theory and Practice*, 14 (4), 275–285.

21. Wang, Cheng Lu, and Allan K. K. Chan (2001), "A Content Analysis of Connectedness vs. Separateness Themes Used in U.S. and P.R.C. Print Advertisements," *International Marketing Review*, 18 (2), 145–157; Wang, Cheng Lu, and John C. Mowen (1997), "The Separateness—Connectedness Self-Schema: Scale Development and Application to Message Construction," *Psychology & Marketing*, 14 (March), 185–207.

22. Wang and Mowen (1997).

23. Wang and Chan (2001).

24. Argo, Jennifer J., Darren W. Dahl, and Rajesh V. Manchanda (2005), "The Influence of a Mere Social Presence in a Retail Context," *Journal of Consumer Research*, 32 (2), 207–212.

25. Dahl, Darren W., Rajesh V. Manchanda, and Jennifer J. Argo (2001), "Embarrassment in Consumer Purchase: The Roles of Social Presence and Purchase Familiarity," *Journal of Consumer Research*, 28 (3), 473–481.

26. On-line content retrieved at Word of Mouth Marketing Association (WOMMA) website: **http://www.womma.org/wom101/04/.**

27. Brown, Tom J., Thomas E. Berry, Peter A. Dacin, and Richard F. Gunst (2005), "Spreading the Word: Investigating Antecedents of Consumers' Positive Word-of-Mouth Intentions and Behaviors in a Retailing Context," *Journal of the Academy of Marketing Science*, 33 (2), 123–138.

28. Chung, Cindy M. Y. (2006), "The Consumer as Advocate: Self-Relevance, Culture, and Word-of-Mouth," *Marketing Letters*, 17 (4), 269–284; Wangenheim, Florian v. (2005), "Postswitching Negative Word-of-Mouth," *Journal of Service Research*, 8 (1), 67–78.

29. Bone, Paula (1995), "Word-of-Mouth Effects on Short-Term and Long-Term Product Judgments," *Journal of Business Research*, 32 (3), 213–223.

30. Babin, Barry J., Yong-Ki Lee, Eun-Ju Kim, and Mitch Griffin (2005), "Modeling Consumer Satisfaction and Word-of-Mouth: Restaurant Patronage in Korea," *Journal of Services Marketing*, 19 (3), 133–139.

31. Godes, David, and Dina Mayzlin (2004), "Using Online Conversations to Study Word-of-Mouth Communication," *Marketing Science*, 23 (Fall), 545–560.

32. Horrigan, John, and Lee Rainie (2006), "The Internet's Growing Role in Life's Major Moments," *Pew Internet &*

American Life Project, http://www.pewinternet.org/topcs.asp?c=6.

33. On-line content retrieved at Word of Mouth Marketing Association (WOMMA) website: http://www.womma.org/wombat/blog/2006/06/.

34. Maclaran, Pauline, and Miriam Catterall (2002), "Researching the Social Web: Marketing Information from Virtual Communities," *Marketing Intelligence & Planning*, 20 (6), 319–326.

35. Horrigan, John, and Lee Rainie (2006), "The Internet's Growing Role in Life's Major Moments," *Pew Internet & American Life Project*, http://www.pewinternet.org/topcs.asp?c=6.

36. Lenhart, Amanda (2009), "*Pew Internet Project Data Memo*", online content retrieved at http://www.pewinternet.org/~/media//Files/Reports/2009/PIP_Adult_social_networking_data_memo_FINAL.pdf.pdf, accessed April 3, 2009.

37. Khermouch, Gary, and Jeff Green (2001), "Buzz Marketing: Suddenly this Stealth Strategy is Hot—But it's Fraught with Risk," *BusinessWeek*, (July 20), 50.

38. Kaikati, Andrew M., and Jack G. Kaikati (2004), "Stealth Marketing: How to Reach Consumers Surreptitiously," *California Management Review*, 46 (4), 6–22.

39. WOMMA, "Unethical Word-of-Mouth Marketing Strategies," online content retrieved at http://www.womma.org/wom101/06/.

40. Johnson, Mark (2005), "Target the Few to Reach the Many," *PR Week*, (October 4), S8–S11.

41. Solomon, Michael (1986), "The Missing Link: Surrogate Consumers in the Marketing Chain," *Journal of Marketing*, 50 (October), 208–218.

42. Rogers, Everett M. (1995), *Diffusion of Innovations*, 4th ed., New York: The Free Press.

43. Data retrieved from U.S. Census Bureau, www.factfinder.census.gov.

44. These estimates based on a Fox News report retrieved at http://www.foxnews.com/story/0,2933,271412,00.html.

45. Roberts, Sam (2007), "51% of Women are Now Living Without Spouse," *The New York Times* (January 16), 1.

46. "50 Million Children Lived With Married Parents in 2007", U.S. Census Bureau News, http://www.census.gov/Press-Release/www/releases/archives/marital_status_living_arrangements/012437.html, accessed April 3, 2009.

47. "Fertility of American Women 2006", U.S. Census Bureau Current Population Reports, August, 2008, http://www.census.gov/prod/2008pubs/p20-558.pdf, accessed April 3, 2009.

48. Koch, Wendy (2007), "Number of Single Men Adopting Fosters Kids Doubles; Historic Shift from When Kids Went Only to Married Couples," *USA Today* (June 15), 5A.

49. Wilkes, Robert E. (1995), "Household Life-Cycle Stages, Transitions, and Product Expenditures," *Journal of Consumer Research*, 22 (1), 27–41.

50. Chatzky, John (2007), "Your Adult Kids are Back. Now What?" *Money*, 36 (1), 32–35.

51. Chatzky, John (2007).

52. "A Generation Caught Between Two Others," *MSNBC News Report*, February 13, 2007, online content retrieved at http://www.msnbc.msn.com/id/17134636/, accessed April 3, 2009.

53. "Valuing The Invaluable: The Economic Value of Family Caregiving, 2008 Update," AARP Public Policy Institute, online content retrieve at: http://assets.aarp.org/rgcenter/il/i13_caregiving.pdf, accessed April 3, 2009.

54. Gentry, James W., Suraj Commuri, and Sunkyu Jun (2003), "Review of Literature on Gender in the Family," *Academy of Marketing Science Review*, 1.

55. Lee, Christina K. C., and Sharon E. Beatty (2002), "Family Structure and Influence in Family Decision Making," *Journal of Consumer Marketing*, 19 (1), 24–41.

56. Belch, Michael A., and Laura A. Willis (2002), "Family Decisions at the Turn of the Century: Has the Changing Structure of Households Impacted the Family Decision-Making Process?" *Journal of Consumer Behaviour*, 2 (2), 111–125.

57. Anonymous (2007), "Kid Power," *Chain Store Age*, 83 (3): 20.

58. Koetters, Michelle (2007), "Tweeners' Money Talks," *Knight Ridder Tribune Business News*, (May 14), 1.

59. Maich, Steve (2006), "The Little Kings and Queens of the Mall," *Maclean's*, 119 (25), 37.

60. This definition based on Scott Ward (1980), "Consumer Socialization," in Harold H. Kassarjian and Thomas S. Robertson, eds., *Perspectives in Consumer Behavior*, Glenview, IL: Scott, Foresman, 380.

61. Muniz, Albert M., Jr., and Hope Jensen Schau (2005), "Religiosity in the Abandoned Apple Newton Brand Community," Journal of Consumer Research, 31(March), 737–747; Schau, Hope Jensen, and Albert M. Muniz, Jr. (2006), "A Tale of Tales: The Apple Newton Narratives," Journal of Strategic Marketing, 13 (March), 19–33.

Chapter 10

1. Dhar, R., and S. M. Knowlis (1999), "The Effect of Time Pressure on Consumer Choice Deferral," *Journal of Consumer Research*, 25 (March), 369–384.

2. Kaplan, M. F., L. T. Wanshula, and M. P. Zanna (1993), "Time Pressure and Information Integration in Social Judgment: The Effect of Need for Structure," in *Human Judgment and Decision Making*, O. Svenson and

A. J. Maule, eds., New York: Plenum, 255–267.

3. Nowlis, S. M. (1995), "The Effect of Time Pressure on the Choice Between Brands that Differ in Quality, Price and Product Features," *Marketing Letters*, 6 (October), 287–296.

4. Suri, R., and K. B. Monroe (2003), "The Effects of Time Constrains on Consumers' Judgments of Prices and Products," *Journal of Consumer Research*, 30 (June), 92–104.

5. Wagner, J., and M. Mokhtari (2000), "The Moderating Effect on Household Apparel Expenditure," *Journal of Consumer Affairs*, 34 (2), 22–78.

6. Roslow, S., T. Li, and J. A. F. Nicholls (2000), "Impact of Situational Variables and Demographic Attributes in Two Seasons on Purchase Behaviour," *European Journal of Marketing*, 34 (9), 1167–1180.

7. *Prepared Foods* (2007), "Tea Totally," 176 (May), 33.

8. *Consumer Reports* (2004), "Wake Up to the Risks of Drowsy Driving," 69 (4), 23.

9. Michals, D. A. (1985), "Pitching Products by the Barometer," *BusinessWeek*, (July 8), 45.

10. Zhuang, G., A. S. Tsang, N. Zhou, F. Li, and J. A. Nicholls (2006), "Impacts of Situational Factors on Buying Decisions in Shopping Malls," *European Journal of Marketing*, 40, 17–43.

11. Robinson, H., F. Riley, O. Dall, R. Rettie, and G. Rolls-Willson "The Role of Situational Variables in Online Grocery Shopping in the UK," *Marketing Review*, 7 (Spring), 89–106.

12. Babin, B. J., W. R. Darden, and M. Griffin (1994), "Work and/or Fun: Measuring Hedonic and Utilitarian Shopping Value," *Journal of Consumer Research*, 20(4), 644–656.

13. Babin et al. (1994)

14. Babin, B. J., and J. S. Attaway (2000), "Atmospheric Affect as a Tool for Creating Value and Gaining Share of Customer," *Journal of Business Research*, 49, 91–99.

15. Darden, W. R., and B. J. Babin (1994), "Exploring the concept of affective quality: Expanding the concept of retail personality," *Journal of Business Research*, 29 (February), 101–109.

16. Ramanathan, S., and P. Williams (2007), "Immediate and Delayed Emotional Consequences of Indulgence: The Moderating Influence of Personality Type on Mixed Emotions," *Journal of Consumer Research*, 34, 212–223.

17. Childers, T. L., C. L. Carr, J. Peck, and S. Carson (2001), "Hedonic and Utilitarian Motivations for Online Shopping Behavior," *Journal of Retailing*, 77, 511–535.

18. Franken, I. H. A., and P. Muris (2006), "Gray's Impulsivity Dimension: A Distinction Between Reward Sensitivity and Rash Impulsiveness," *Personality & Individual Differences*, 40 (July),

1337–1347; Ramanathan and Williams (2007).

19. Dholakia, U. M. (2000), "Temptation and Resistance: An Integrated Model of Consumption Impulse Formation and Enactment," *Psychology & Marketing,* 17 (November), 955–982.

20. Kaufman-Scarborough, C., and J. Cohen (2004), "Unfolding Consumer Impulsivity: An Existential–Phenomenological Study of Consumers with Attention Deficit Disorder," *Psychology & Marketing,* 21 (August), 637–669.

21. Beatty, S. E., and E. M. Ferrell (1998), "Impulse Buying: Modeling its Precursors," *Journal of Retailing,* 74, 161–191.

22. Zhang, X., V. R. Prybutok, and D. Strutton (2007), "Modeling Influences on Impulse Purchasing Behaviors During Online Marketing Transactions," *Journal of Marketing Theory and Practice,* 15 (Winter), 79–89.

23. Babin, B.J., and W. R. Darden (1995), "Consumer Self-Regulation in a Retail Environment," *Journal of Retailing,* 71 (Spring), 47–70.

24. Herzenstein, M., S. S. Posavac, and J. J. Brakus (2007), "Adoption of New and Really New Products: The Effects of Self-Regulation Systems and Risk Salience," *Journal of Marketing Research,* 44 (May), 251–260.

25. Dholakia (2000); Babin and Darden (1995).

26. Darden and Babin (1994); Russell, J. A. and G. Pratt (1980), "A Description of the Affective Quality Attributable to Environments," *Journal of Personality and Social Pscyhology,* 38, 311–322.

27. Bitner, M. J. (1992), "Servicescapes: The Impact of the Physical Environment on Customers and Employees," *Journal of Marketing,* 56 (April), 57–71.

28. Koernig, S. K. (2003), "E-Scapes: The Electronic Physical Environment and Service Tangibility," *Psychology & Marketing,* 20, 151–167; Lee, Y. K., C. K. Lee, S. K. Lee, and B. J. Babin (2008), "Festivalscapes and Patrons' Emotions, Satisfaction, and Loyalty," *Journal of Business Research,* (in press).

29. Brady, M. K., C. M. Voorhees, J. J. Cronin, and B. L. Boudreau (2006), "The Good Guys Don't Always Win: The Effect of Valence on Service Perceptions and Consequences," *Journal of Services Marketing,* 20, 83–91.

30. Williams, G. (2004), "It's a Style Thing," *Entrepreneur,* 32 (March), 34; Iacbucci, D., and A. Ostrom (1993), "Gender Differences in the Impact of Core and Relational Aspects of Services on the Evaluation of Service Encounters," *Journal of Consumer Psychology,* 2, 257–286.

31. Haytko, D. L., and J. Baker (2004), "It's All at the Mall: Exploring Adolescent Girls' Experiences," *Journal of Retailing,* 80 (Spring), 67–83.

32. Babin, B. J., and J. C. Chebat (2004), "Perceived Appropriateness and Its Effect on Quality, Affect and Behavior," *Journal of Retailing and Consumer Services,* 11 (September): 287–298; Michon, R., J. C. Chebat, and L. W. Turley (2005), "Mall Atmospherics: the Interaction Effects of the Mall Environment on Shopping Behavior," *Journal of Business Research,* 58 (May), 576–583.

33. Orth, O. R., and A. Bourrain (2005), "Ambient Scent and Consumer Exploratory Behavior: A Causal Analysis," *Journal of Wine Research,* 16, 137–150.

34. Michon et al. 2005.

35. Turley, L. W., and J. C. Chebat (2002), "Linking Retail Strategy, Atmospheric Design and Shopping Behavior," *Journal of Marketing Management,* 18, 125–144; Milliman, R. E. (1986), "The Influence of Background Music on the Behavior of Restaurant Patrons," *Journal of Consumer Research,* 13 (September), 286–289; Babin and Chebat (2003).

36. Crowley, A. E. (1993), "The Two-Dimensional Impact of Color on Shopping," *Marketing Letters,* 4, 59–69; Bellizi, J., and R. E. Hite (1992), "Environmental Color, Consumer Feelings and Purchase Likelihood," *Psychology & Marketing,* 59 (Spring), 347–363; Babin, B. J., D. M. Hardesty, and T. A. Suter (2003), "Color and Shopping Intentions: The Intervening Effect of Price Fairness and Affect," *Journal of Business Research,* 56, 541–551.

37. Babin, Hardesty, and Suter (2003).

38. Cotlet, P., M. C. Lichtlé, and V. Plichon (2006), "The Role of Value in a Services: a Study in a Retail Environment," *Journal of Consumer Marketing,* 23, 219–227; Eroglu, S. A., K. Machleit, and T. F. Barr (2005), "Perceived Retail Crowding and Shopper Satisfaction: The Role of Shopping Values," *Journal of Business Research,* 58 (August), 1146–1153.

39. Sharma, A., and T. F. Stafford (2000), "The Effect of Retail Atmospherics on Customers' Perceptions of Salespeople and Customer Persuasion: An Empirical Investigation," *Journal of Business Research,* 49 (February), 183–191.

40. Babin and Chebat (2004).

41. Mangleburg, T. F., P. F. Doney, and T. Bristol (2004), "Shopping with Friends and Teen's Susceptibility to Interpersonal Influence," *Journal of Retailing,* 80 (Summer), 101–116.

42. Mandel, N., and E. J. Johnson (2002), "When Web Pages Influence Choice: Effects of Visual Primes on Experts and Novices," *Journal of Consumer Research,* 29 (September), 235–245.

43. Wang, L. C., J. Baker, J. Wagner, and K. Wakefield (2007), "Can a Web Site be Social?" *Journal of Marketing,* 71 (July), 143–157.

44. Heath, C., and J. B. Soll (1996), "Mental Budgeting and Consumer Decisions," *Journal of Consumer Research,* 23 (June), 40–52.

45. Michon, R., H. Yu, D. Smith, and J. C. Chebat (2007), "The Shopping Experience of Female Fashion Leaders," *International Journal of Retail and Distribution Management,* 35 (6), 488–501; Swinyard, W. R. (1992), "The Effects of Mood, Involvement, and Quality of Store Experience on Shopping Intentions," *Journal of Consumer Research,* 20 (September), 271–280.

46. Babin, B. J., and W. R. Darden (1996), "Good and Bad Shopping Vibes: Spending and Patronage Satisfaction," *Journal of Business Research,* 35 (March), 201–206.

47. Smith, J. W. (2004), "More than Stuff," *Marketing Management,* (March/April), 56.

Chapter 11

1. Xu, Alison Jing, and Robert W. Wyer, Jr. (2008), "The Effect of Mind-Sets on Consumer Decision Strategies," *Journal of Consumer Research,* forthcoming.

2. Bagozzi, Richard P., and Utpal Dholakia (1999), "Goal Setting and Goal Striving in Consumer Behavior," *Journal of Marketing,* 63 (Special Issue), 19–32.

3. Lawson, Robert (1997), "Consumer Decision Making Within a Goal-Driven Framework," *Psychology & Marketing,* 14 (5), 427–449.

4. Luce, Mary Frances, James R. Bettman, and John W. Payne (2001), "Tradeoff Difficulty: Determinants and Consequences for Consumer Decisions," *Monographs of the Journal of Consumer Research Series,* 1 (Spring); Menon, Kalyani, and Laurette Dube (2000), "Ensuring Satisfaction by Engineering Salesperson Response to Customer Emotions," *Journal of Retailing,* 76 (3), 285–307.

5. Mowen, John C. (1988), "Beyond Consumer Decision Making," *Journal of Consumer Marketing,* 5 (1), 15–25.

6. Anonymous (2003), "POP Sharpens Its Focus," *Brandweek,* 44 (24), 31–36.

7. Prasad, V. Kanti (1975), "Socioeconomic Product Risk and Patronage Preferences of Retail Shoppers," *Journal of Marketing,* 39 (July), 42–47; Dowling, Grahame R., and Richard Staelin (1994), "A Model of Perceived Risk and Intended Risk-Handling Activity," *Journal of Consumer Research,* 21 (1), 119–134.

8. This definition is based on Oliver, Richard (1997), *Satisfaction: A Behavioral Perspective on the Consumer,* New York: McGraw-Hill.

9. O'Brien, Louise, and Charles Jones (1995), "Do Rewards Really Create Loyalty?" *Harvard Business Review,* 73 (May/June), 75–82.

10. Keller, Kevin Lane (1998), *Strategic Brand Management: Building, Measuring, and Managing Brand Equity.* Upper Saddle River, NJ: Prentice Hall.

11. Aaker, David A. (1997), *Building Strong Brands*, New York: The Free Press, 21.
12. Olshavsky, Richard W., and Donald H. Granbois (1979), "Consumer Decision Making—Fact or Fiction?", *Journal of Consumer Research*, 6 (2), 93–100.
13. Moyer, Don (2007), "Satisficing," *Harvard Business Review*, 85 (4), 144; Schwartz, Barry, Andrew Ward, John Monterosso, Sonja Lyubomirsky, Katherine White, and Darrin R. Lehman (2002), "Maximizing versus Satisficing: Happiness Is a Matter of Choice," *Journal of Personality and Social Psychology*, 83 (5), 1178–1197.
14. Bruner, Gordon C., III, and Richard J. Pomazal (1988), "Problem Recognition: The Crucial First Stage of the Consumer Decision Process," *Journal of Consumer Marketing*, 5 (1), 51–63.
15. Sirgy, Jospeh M. (1983), Social Cognition and Consumer Behavior, New York: Praeger.
16. Beatty, Sharon, and Scott M. Smith (1987), "External Search Effort: An Investigation Across Several Product Categories," *Journal of Consumer Research*, 14 (1), 83–95.
17. Bloch, Peter H., Daniel L. Sherrell, and Nancy M. Ridgway (1986), "Consumer Search: An Extended Framework," *Journal of Consumer Research*, 13 (1), 119–126.
18. Lurie, Nicholas H. (2004), "Decision Making in Information-Rich Environments: The Role of Information Structure," *Journal of Consumer Research*, 30 (4), 473–487.
19. Punj, Girish, and Richard Brookes (2004), "Decision Constraints and Consideration Set Formation in Consumer Durables," *Psychology & Marketing*, 18 (8), 843–864; Shocker, Allan D., Moshe Ben-Akiva, Bruno Boccara, and Prakash Nedungadi (1991), "Consideration Set Influences on Consumer Decision Making and Choice: Issues, Models, and Suggestions," *Marketing Letters*, 2 (3), 181–197.
20. Donkers, Bas (2002), "Modeling Consideration Sets Across Time: The Relevance of Past Consideration," in American Marketing Association Conference Proceedings, vol. 13, Chicago: American Marketing Association, 322.
21. Hauser, John R., and Birger Wernerfelt (1990), "An Evaluation Cost Model of Consideration Sets," *Journal of Consumer Research*, 16 (4), 393–408.
22. Jarvis, Cheryl Burke (1998), "An Exploratory Investigation of Consumers' Evaluations of External Information Sources in Prepurchase Search," in Advances in Consumer Research, vol. 25, Joseph W. Alba and J. Wesley Hutchinson. eds.. Provo, UT: Association for Consumer Research.
23. Lichtenstein, D. R., N. M. Ridgway, and R. P. Netemeyer (1993), "Price Perceptions and Consumer Shopping Behavior," Journal of Marketing Research, 30, 234–245.

24. Bickart, Barbara, and Robert M. Schindler (2001), "Internet Forums as Influential Sources of Consumer Information," *Journal of Interactive Marketing*, 15 (3), 31–40.
25. Ratchford, Brian T., Myung-Soo Lee, and Debabrata Talukdar (2003), "The Impact of the Internet on Information Search for Automobiles," *Journal of Marketing Research*, 40 (2), 193–209.
26. Mathwick, Charla, and Edward Rigdon (2004), "Play, Flow, and the Online Search Experience," *Journal of Consumer Research*, 31 (2), 324–332.
27. Ariely, Dan (2000), "Controlling the Information Flow: Effects on Consumers' Decision Making and Preferences," *Journal of Consumer Research*, 27 (2), 233–248.
28. Mazursky, David, and Gideon Vinitzky (2005), "Modifying Consumer Search Processes in Enhanced On-Line Interfaces," *Journal of Business Research*, 58 (10), 1299–1309.
29. Beatty and Smith (1987).
30. Srinivasan, Narasimhan, and Brian T. Ratchford (1991), "An Empirical Test of a Model of External Search for Automobiles," *Journal of Consumer Research*, 18, 233–242; Johnson, Eric J., and Edward J. Russo (1984), "Product Familiarity and Learning New Information," *Journal of Consumer Research*, 11, 542–550; Moore, William L., and Donald R. Lehmann (1980), "Individual Differences in Search Behavior for a Nondurable," *Journal of Consumer Research*, 7, 296–307.
31. Moorthy, Sridhar, Brian T. Ratchford, and Debabrata Talukdar (1997), "Consumer Information Search Revisited: Theory and Empirical Analysis," *Journal of Consumer Research*, 23 (4), 263–277; also see Alba, Joseph W., and J. Wesley Hutchinson (1987), "Dimensions of Consumer Expertise," *Journal of Consumer Research*, 13 (4), 411–454.
32. Beatty and Smith (1987).
33. Dowling, G. R., and R. Staelin (1994), "A Model of Perceived Risk and Intended Risk-Handling Activity," *Journal of Consumer Research*, 21 (1),119–134; Dedler, Konrad, I. Gottschalk, and K. G. Grunert (1981), "Perceived Risk as a Hint for Better Information and Better Products," in Advances in Consumer Research, vol. 8, Kent Monroe, ed., Ann Arbor, MI: Association for Consumer Research, 391–397.
34. Mehta, Nitin, Surendra Rajiv, and Kannan Srinivasan (2003), "Price Uncertainty and Consumer Search: A Structural Model of Consideration Set Formation," *Marketing Science*, 22 (1), 58–84.
35. Beatty and Smith (1987),
36. Beatty and Smith (1987).
37. Capon, Noel, and Mariane Burke (1980), "Individual, Product Class, and Task-Related Factors in Consumer Information Processing," *Journal of*

Consumer Research, 7 (3), 314–326; Newman, Joseph, and Richard Staelin (1972), "Prepurchase Information Seeking for New Cars and Major Household Appliances," *Journal of Marketing Research,* 7 (August): 249–257.
38. Cobb, Cathy J., and Wayne D. Hoyer (1988), "Direct Observation of Search Behavior in the Purchase of Two Nondurable Products," *Psychology & Marketing,* 2 (3), 161–179; Newman and Staelin (1972).
39. Punj, Girish (1987), "Presearch Decision Making in Consumer Durable Purchases.", *Journal of Consumer Marketing,* 4 (1): 71-83.
40. Reynolds, Kristy E., Judith Anne Garretson Folse, and Michael A. Jones (2006), "Search Regret: Antecedents and Consequences," *Journal of Retailing,* 82 (4), 339–348.
41. Walsh, Bryan (2007), "Back to the Tap," *Time* (August 20), 56.
42. Devaney, Polly (2006), "America: As Tastes Change, Coca-Cola's Supremacy Drip, Drip, Drips Away," *Marketing Week* (April 6), 30.
43. White, Nicola M. (2007), "Tide Turning Against Flood of Empties," McClatchy—Tribune Business News (December 19).
44. Demirjian, Karoun (2007), "Food and Beverage Retailer Alliance Plans to Sue Chicago over Bottled-Water Tax," McClatchy—Tribune Business News (December 27).

Chapter 12

1. Futrell, Charles M. (2003), *ABCs of Relationship Selling,* 7th ed., Boston: McGraw-Hill.
2. Myers, James H., and Mark Alpert (1968), "Determinant Buying Attitudes: Meaning and Measurement," *Journal of Marketing,* (October), 13–20.
3. Williams, Terrell G. (2002), "Social Class Influences on Purchase Evaluation Criteria," *Journal of Consumer Marketing,* 19 (2/3), 249–276; Dhar, Ravi, and Klaus Wertenbroch (2000), "Consumer Choice Between Hedonic and Utilitarian Goods," *Journal of Marketing Research,* 37 (February), 60–71; Hirschman, Elizabeth C., and S. Krishnan (1981), "Subjective and Objective Criteria in Consumer Choice: An Examination of Retail Store Choice," *Journal of Consumer Affairs,* 15 (1), 115–127.
4. Schwartz, Barry (2004), "The Tyranny of Choice," *Scientific American,* 290 (4), 70–75.
5. Pham, Michel T., Joel B. Cohen, John W. Pracejus, and G. David Hughes (2001), "Affect Monitoring and the Primacy of Feelings in Judgment," *Journal of Consumer Research,* 28 (2), 167–188.
6. Gorn, Gerald, J., Marvin E. Goldberg, and Kunal Basu (1993), "Mood, Awareness, and Product Evaluation," *Journal of Consumer Psychology,* 2 (3): 237–256.

7. Bakamitsos, Georgios A. (2006), "A Cue Alone or a Probe to Think? The Dual Role of Affect in Product Evaluations," *Journal of Consumer Research*, 33 (December), 403–412.

8. Moreau, C. Page, Arthur B. Markman, and Donald R. Lehmann (2001), "What Is It? Categorization Flexibility and Consumers' Responses to Really New Products," *Journal of Consumer Research*, 27 (4), 489–498.

9. This discussion based on Alba, Joseph W., and J. Wesley Hutchinson (1987), "Dimensions of Consumer Expertise," *Journal of Consumer Research*, 13 (4), 411–454.

10. Johnson, Michael D., and Claes Fornell (1987), "The Nature and Methodological Implications of the Cognitive Representation of Products," *Journal of Consumer Research*, 14 (2), 214–228.

11. Viswanathan, Madhubalan, and Terry L. Childers (1999), "Understanding How Product Attributes Influence Product Categorization: Development and Validation of Fuzzy Set-Based Measures of Gradedness in Product Categories," *Journal of Marketing Research*, 36 (1), 75–94.

12. Sujan, Mita, and Christine Dekleva (1987), "Product Categorization and Inference Making: Some Implications for Comparative Advertising," *Journal of Consumer Research*, 14 (3), 372–378.

13. Dawar, Niraj, and Philip Parker (1994), "Marketing Universals: Consumers' Use of Brand Name, Price, Physical Appearance, and Retailer Reputation as Signals of Product Quality," *Journal of Marketing*, 58 (2), 81–95.

14. John, Deborah Roedder, and Mita Sujan (1990), "Age Differences in Product Categorization," *Journal of Consumer Research*, 16 (4), 452–460.

15. Alba and Hutchinson (1987).

16. Williams (2002).

17. Bergen, Mark, Shantanu Dutta, and Steven M. Shugan (1996), "Branded Variants: A Retail Perspective," *Journal of Marketing Research*, 33 (1), 9–19.

18. Fasolo, Barbara, Gary H. McClelland, and Peter M. Todd (2007), "Escaping the Tyranny of Choice: When Fewer Attributes Make Choice Easier," *Marketing Theory*, 7 (1), 13–26.

19. Mitra, Debanjan, and Peter N. Golder (2006), "How Does Objective Quality Affect Perceived Quality?," *Marketing Science*, 25 (3), 230–247.

20. Dawar and Parker (1994).

21. Miller, Elizabeth G., and Barbara E. Kahn (2006), "Shades of Meaning: The Effect of Color and Flavor Names on Consumer Choice," *Journal of Consumer Research*, 32 (1), 86–92.

22. Jacoby, J., D. E. Speller, and C. A. Kohn (1974), "Brand Choice Behavior as a Function of Information Load: Replication and Extension," *Journal of Consumer Research*, 1, 33–41; Malhotra, Naresh K. (1982), "Information Load and Consumer Decision Making," *Journal of Consumer Research*, 8, 419–430.

23. Fasolo et al. (2007).

24. Kivetz, Ran, and Itamar Simonson (2000), "The Effects of Incomplete Information on Consumer Choice," *Journal of Marketing Research*, 37 (4), 427–448.

25. Hair, Joseph F., Jr., Rolph Anderson, Ronald L. Tatham, and William C. Black, *Multivariate Data Analysis*, 5th ed., Upper Saddle River, NJ: Prentice Hall.

26. Wright, Peter (1975), "Consumer Choice Strategies: Simplifying Vs. Optimizing," *Journal of Marketing Research*, 12 (February), 60–67.

27. Hirschman and Krishnan (1981); Baker, Julie, A. Parasuraman, Dhruv Grewal, and Glenn B. Voss (2002), "The Influence of Multiple Store Environmental Cues on Perceived Merchandise Value and Purchase Intentions," *Journal of Retailing*, 66 (2), 120–142.

28. Seock, Yoo-Kyoung, and Jessie H. Chen-Yu (2007), "Website Evaluation Criteria Among U.S. College Student Consumers with Different Shopping Orientations and Internet Channel Usage," *International Journal of Consumer Studies*, 31 (3), 204–212; Kim, Soyoung, Reginald Williams, and Yulee Lee (2003), "Attitude Toward Online Shopping and Retail Website Quality: A Comparison of U.S. and Korean Consumers," *Journal of International Consumer Marketing*, 16 (1), 89–111.

29. Clucas, David (2006), "Digital Cameras Make Picture-Perfect Gifts," *Boulder County Business Report*, 25 (22), 24A; Blackman, Andrew (2004), "Watching the Web: Where Shoppers Rate Items," *Wall Street Journal* (May 2), 4; Mossberg, Walter S., and Katherine Boehret (2006), "The Mossberg Solution: Buying A Digital Camera: Our Annual Guide," *Wall Street Journal* (April 19), D1.

Chapter 13

1. Tatzel, Miriam (2003), "The Art of Buying: Coming to Terms with Money and Materialism," *Journal of Happiness Studies*, 4 (4), 405–435.

2. Woodruff, Robert B. (1997), "Customer Value: The Next Source for Competitive Advantage," *Journal of the Academy of Marketing Science*, 25 (2), 139–153.

3. McCracken, Grant (1986), "Culture and Consumption: A Theoretical Account of the Structure and Movement of the Cultural Meaning of Consumer Goods," *Journal of Consumer Research*, 13 (1), 71–84.

4. Wiener, Bernard (2000), "Attributional Thoughts about Consumer Behavior," *Journal of Consumer Research*, 27 (3): 382–387.

5. Havlena, William J., and Morris B. Holbrook (1986), "The Varieties of Consumption Experience: Comparing Two Typologies of Emotion in Consumer Behavior," *Journal of Consumer Research*, 13 (3), 394–403.

6. Holbrook, Morris B. (2006), "Consumption Experience, Customer Value, and Subjective Personal Introspection: An Illustrative Photographic Essay," *Journal of Business Research*, 59, 714–725; Hirschman, Elizabeth C., and Morris B. Holbrook (1983), "Hedonic Consumption: Emerging Concepts, Methods, and Propositions," *Journal of Marketing*, 46, 92–101.

7. Patterson, Paul G., and Richard G. Spreng (1997), "Modeling the Relationship Between Perceived Value, Satisfaction, and Repurchase Intentions in a Business-to-Business, Services Context: An Empirical Investigation," *International Journal of Industry Management*, 8 (5), 414–434.

8. www.theacsi.org, accessed October 17, 2007.

9. Online content retrieved at American Consumer Satisfaction Index website, www.theacsi.org, accessed May 18, 2009.

10. Slater, Stanley (1997), "Developing a Customer Value-Based Theory of the Firm," *Journal of the Academy of Marketing Science*, 25 (2), 162–167.

11. Woodruff (1997).

12. Holbrook, Morris B. (1986), "Emotion in the Consumption Experience: Toward a Model of the Human Consumer," in *The Role of Affect in Consumer Behavior: Emerging Theories and Applications*, Robert A. Peterson et al., eds., Lexington, MA: Heath, 17–52.

13. This definition based in part on Westbrook, Robert A., and Richard L. Oliver (1991), "The Dimensionality of Consumption Emotion Patterns and Consumer Satisfaction," *Journal of Consumer Research*, 18 (1), 84–91.

14. Babin, Barry J., and Mitch Griffin (1998), "The Nature of Satisfaction: An Updated Examination and Analysis," *Journal of Business Research*, 41, 127–136.

15. Babin and Griffin (1998).

16. Oliver, Richard L. (1983), "Measurement and Evaluation of Satisfaction Processes in Retail Settings," *Journal of Retailing*, 57 (Fall), 25–48.

17. Churchill, Gilbert A., Jr., and Carol Surprenant (1982), "An Investigation into the Determinants of Customer Satisfaction," *Journal of Marketing Research*, 19 (4), 491–504.

18. Zeithaml, Valarie A., Leonard L. Berry, and A. Parasuraman (1993), "The Nature and Determinants of Customer Expectations of Service," *Journal of the Academy of Marketing Science*, 21 (1), 1–12.

19. Tse, David K., and Peter C. Wilton (1988), "Models of Consumer Satisfaction Formation: An Extension," *Journal of Marketing Research*, 24 (2), 204–212; LaTour, Stephen A., and Nancy C. Peat (1979), "Conceptual and Methodological Issues in Consumer Satisfaction Research," in *Advances in Consumer Research*, vol. 6, William L. Wilkie, ed., Ann Arbor, MI: Association of Consumer Research.

20. Spreng, Richard A., and Thomas J. Page, Jr. (2001), "The Impact of Confidence in Expectations on Consumer Satisfaction," *Psychology & Marketing*, 18 (11), 1187–1204.

21. Hoch, Stephen J., and John Deighton (1989), "Managing What Consumers Learn from Experience," *Journal of Marketing*, 53 (2), 1–20.

22. Spreng and Page (2001).

23. For a discussion of this topic, see Carrilat, F. A., J. Fernando, and J. P. Mulki (2007), "The Validity of the SERVQUAL and SERVPREF Scales," *International Journal of Service Industry Management*, 18 (May), 472-490. Also see, Bebko, C., L. M. Sciulli, and R. K. Garg (2006), "Consumers' Level of Expectations for Services and the Role of Implicit Service Promises," *Services Marketing Quarterly*, 28, 1–23.

24. Peter, J. Paul, Gilbert A. Churchill, Jr., and Tom J. Brown (1993), "Caution in the Use of Difference Scores in Consumer Research," *Journal of Consumer Research*, 19 (4), 655–662.

25. Adapted from Babin and Griffin (1998).

26. Spreng, Richard A., Scott B. MacKenzie, and Richard W. Olshavsky (1996), "A Reexamination of the Determinants of Consumer Satisfaction," *Journal of Marketing*, 60 (3), 15–32.

27. Fournier, Susan, and David Glen Mick (1999), "Rediscovering Satisfaction," *Journal of Marketing*, 63 (4), 5–23.

28. Price, Linda L., Eric J. Arnould, and Patrick Tierney (1995), "Going to Extremes: Managing Service Encounters and Assessing Provider Performance," *Journal of Marketing*, 59 (April), 83–97.

29. Adams, J. Stacey (1965), "Inequity in Social Exchange," in *Advances in Experimental Social Psychology*, vol. 2, Richard Berkowitz, ed., New York: Academic Press, 267–299.

30. Oliver, Richard L., and John E. Swan (1989), "Consumer Perceptions of Interpersonal Equity and Satisfaction in Transactions: A Field Survey Approach," *Journal of Marketing Research*, 53 (2), 21–35.

31. Wiener, Bernard (2000), "Attributional Thoughts about Consumer Behavior," *Journal of Consumer Research*, 27 (3), 382–387.

32. Festinger, Leon (1957), *A Theory of Cognitive Dissonance*, Stanford, CA: Stanford University Press.

33. Sweeney, Jillian C., Douglas Hausknecht, and Geoffrey N. Soutar (2000), "Cognitive Dissonance After Purchase: A Multidimensional Scale," *Psychology & Marketing*, 17 (5), 369–387.

34. Jacoby, Jacob, Carol K. Berning, and Thomas F. Dietvorst (1977), "What About Disposition?" *Journal of Marketing*, 41 (2), 22–28.

35. Online content retrieved May 13, 2009, "Municipal Solid Waste in the United States: 2007 Facts and Figures," Environmental Protection Agency, website: http://www.epa.gov/epawaste/nonhaz/municipal/pubs/msw07-rpt.pdf.

36. Price, Linda L., Eric J. Arnould, and Carolyn Folkman Curasi (2000), "Older Consumers' Disposition of Special Possessions," *Journal of Consumer Research*, 27 (2), 179–182.

37. Lastovicka, John L., and Karen V. Fernandez (2005), "Three Paths to Disposition: The Movement of Meaningful Possessions to Strangers," *Journal of Consumer Research*, 31 (4), 813–823.

38. Coulter, Robin A., and Mark Ligas (2003), "To Retain or to Relinquish: Exploring the Disposition Practices of Packrats and Purgers," *Advances in Consumer Research*, 30, 38–43.

Chapter 14

1. Consumer Policy (2007), "Complain? Why Bother, It's the NHS," *Consumer Policy Review*, 17 (September/October), 221; Simos, P. (2005), "Seven Steps to Handle Complaints," *Restaurant Hospitality*, 89 (August), 36; Blodgett, J. G., D. H. Granbois, and R. G. Walters (1993), "The Effects of Perceived Justice on Complainants' Negative Word-of-Mouth Behavior and Repatronage Intentions," *Journal of Retailing*, 69 (Winter), 399–428.

2. Fornell, C., and B. Wernerfelt (1987), "Defensive Marketing Strategy by Customer Complaint Management," *Journal of Marketing Research*, 24, 337–346.

3. Voohees, C. M., M. K. Brady, and D. M. Horowitz (2006), "A Voice from the Silent Masses: An Exploratory and Comparative Analysis of Non-Complaining," *Journal of the Academy of Marketing Science*, 34 (September), 513–527.

4. Simos, P. (2005).

5. Voorhees et al. (2006).

6. Hart, C. A., J. L. Heskett, and E. W. Sasser (1990), "The Profitable Art of Service Recovery," *Harvard Business Review*, 68 (4), 148–56.

7. Romaniuk, J. (2007), "Word of Mouth and the Viewing of Television Programs," *Journal of Advertising Research*, 47 (December), 462–470.

8. www.consumerist.com/consumer/complaints, accessed October 25, 2007.

9. Benton, J. (2007), "Jumpin Jeep Ruin Lives, Destroy Property," www.consumeraffairs.com, October 23, accessed October 26, 2007.

10. Crain, K. (2004), "At CBS, Shades of Audi Debate," *Automotive News*, 79 (9/20), 12; Flint, J. (1988), "Hot Seat," *Forbes*, 142 (June), 199.

11. See www.snopes.com for more on this story, accessed October 26, 2007.

12. Griffin, M., B. J. Babin, and J. Attaway (1996), ""Anticipation of Injurious Consumption Outcomes and Its Impact on Consumer Attributions of Blame," *Journal of the Academy of Marketing Science*, 24 (Fall), 314–327.

13. Blodgett, J. G., D. H. Granbois, and R. G. Walters (1993), "The Effects of Perceived Justice on Complainants' Negative Word-of-Mouth Behavior and Repatronage Intentions," *Journal of Retailing*, 69 (Winter), 399–428.

14. Nyer, P. M., and M. Gopinath (2005), "Effects of Complaining Versus Negative WOM on Subsequent Changes in Satisfaction: The Role of Public Commitment," *Psychology & Marketing*, 22 (December), 937–953.

15. Lange, F., and M. Dahlen (2006), "Too Much Bad PR Can Make Ads Ineffective," *Journal of Advertising Research*, 46 (December), 528–542; Aaker, J., S. Fournier, and B. S. Adam (2004), "When Good Brands go Bad," *Journal of Consumer Research*, 31 (June), 1–16.

16. Lange and Dahlen (2006).

17. Pullig, C., R. C. Netemeyer, and A. Biswas (2006), "Attitude Basis Certainty and Challenge Alignment; A Case of Negative Publicity," *Journal of the Academy of Marketing Science*, 34 (Fall), 528–542.

18. Burnham, T. A., J. K. Frels, and V. Mahajan (2003), "Consumer Switching Costs: A Typology, Antecedents and Consequences," *Journal of the Academy of Marketing Science*, 31 (Spring), 109–126.

19. Burnham et al. (2003).

20. Antón, C., C. Camarero, and M. Carrero (2007), "The Mediating Effect of Satisfaction on Consumers' Switching Intention," *Psychology & Marketing*, 24 (June), 511–538.

21. Antón et al. (2007).

22. Jones, M. A., K. E. Reynolds, D. L. Mothersbaugh, and S. E. Beatty (2007), "The Positive and Negative Effects of Switching Costs on Relational Outcomes," *Journal of Services Research*, 9 (May), 335–355.

23. Balabanis, G., N. Reynolds, and A. Simintiras (2006), "Base of E-Store Loyalty: Perceived Switching Barriers and Satisfaction," *Journal of Business Research*, 59 (February), 214–224.

24. Babin, B. J., and J. S. Attaway (2000), "Atmospheric Affect as a Tool for Creating Value and Gaining Share of Customer," *Journal of Business Research*, 49 (August), 91–99.

25. Gourville, J. T. (2006), "Eager Sellers & Stony: Understanding the Psychology of New-Product Adoption," *Harvard Business Review*, 84 (June), 99–106.

26. Magi, A. W. (2003), "Share of Wallet in Retailing: The Effects of Consumer Satisfaction, Loyalty Cards and Shopper Characteristics," *Journal of Retailing*, 79 (Summer), 97–106.

27. Shin, Dong H., and Won Y. Kim (2007), "Mobile Number Portability on Customer Switching Behavior: In the Case of the Korean Mobile Market." *Info* 9, 38–54.

28. Wangenheim, F. V. (2005), "Postswitching Negative Word of Mouth," *Journal of Services Research*, 8, 67–78.

29. Chiu, H. C., Y. C. Hsieh, Y. C. Li, and L. Monle (2005), "Relationship Marketing and Consumer Switching

Behavior," *Journal of Business Research*, 58 (December), 1681–1689.

30. Babin and Attaway (2000).

31. Chiu et al. (2005).

32. Palmatier, R. W., R. P. Dant, D. Grewal, and K. R. Evans (2006), "Factors Influencing the Effectiveness of Relationship Marketing: A Meta-Analysis," *Journal of Marketing*, 70 (October), 136–153.

33. Hennig-Thurau, T. (2000), "Relationship Quality and Customer Retention through Strategic Communication of Customer Skills," *Journal of Marketing Management*, 16, 55–79.

34. For more information on these characteristics, see Boles, J. S., J. T. Johnson, and H. C. Barksdale, Jr. (2000), "How Salespeople Build Quality Relationships: A Replication and Extension," *Journal of Business Research,* 48 (April), 75–81. Macintosh, G. (2007), "Customer Orientation, Relationship Quality and Relational Benefits to the Firm," *Journal of Services Marketing*, 21, 150–157; Jones, D. L., M. Brenda, and J. Sim (2007), "A New Look at the Antecedents and Consequences of Relationship Quality in the Hotel Service Environment," *Services Marketing Quarterly*, 28, 15–31.

Chapter 15

1. Fullerton, R. A., and G. Punj (2004), "Repercussions of Promoting an Ideology of Consumption: Consumer Misbehavior," *Journal of Business Research*, (57), 1239–1249.

2. Fowler III, Aubry R., Barry J. Babin, and Amy K. Este (2005), "Burning for Fun or Money: Illicit Consumer Behavior in a Contemporary Context," paper presented at the *Academy of Marketing Science Annual Conference*, presented May 27, 2005, Tampa, FL.

3. Fullterton and Punj (2004).

4. Fowler et al. (2005).

5. Vitell, Scott J. (2003), "Consumer Ethics Research: Review, Synthesis and Suggestions for the Future," *Journal of Business Ethics*, 43 (1/2): (March), 33–47.

6. This definition based on: Babin, Barry J., and Laurie A. Babin (1996), "Effects of Moral Cognitions and Consumer Emotions on Shoplifting Intentions," *Psychology & Marketing*, 13 (December), 785–802.

7. Reidenbach, R. E., D. P. Robin, and L. Dawson (1991), "An Application and Extension of a Multidimensional Ethics Scale to Selected Marketing Practices and Marketing Groups," *Journal of the Academy of Marketing Science*, 19 (2), Spring, 83–92.

8. Vitell, Scott (2003), "Consumer Ethics Research: Review, Synthesis, and Suggestions for Future Research"

9. Hunt, Shelby, and Scott Vitell (1986), "A General Theory of Marketing Ethics," *Journal of Macromarketing*, 6 (1), Spring, 5–16.

10. This section is based on Fullerton and Punj (2004).

11. Merton, Robert (1968), *Social Theory and Social Structure*. New York: Free Press.

12. Hamilton, V. Lee, and David Rauma (1995), "Social Psychology of Deviance and Law," in Karen S. Cook, Gary A. Fine, and James S. House, eds., *Sociological Perspectives on Social Psychology*, Boston: Allyn and Bacon, 524–547,.

13. Information and statistics provided by the National Association for Shoplifting Prevention (NASP), a non-profit organization: **www.shoplifting prevention.org**, assessed June 9, 2009.

14. This section based in large part on Cox, Dena, Anthony D. Cox, and George P, Moschis (1990), "When Consumer Behavior Goes Bad: An Investigation of Adolescent Shoplifting," *Journal of Consumer Research*, 17 (2), September), 149–159.

15. Babin and Babin (1996); Webster, Cynthia (2000), "Exploring the Psychodynamics of Consumer Shoplifting Behavior," *American Marketing Association Conference Proceedings* (11), 360–365.

16. Babin, Barry J., and Mitch Griffin (1995), "A Closer Look at the Influence of Age on Consumer Ethics," *Advances in Consumer Research*, (22), 668–673.

17. Information obtained from BSA/IDC Global Software Piracy Study 2008, Business Software Alliance website: **http://global.bsa.org/globalpiracy2008/index.html**, accessed June 9, 2009.

18. Fowler et al. (2005).

19. Shropshire, Corilyn (2007), "Spam Floods Inboxes," *Knight Ridder Tribune Business News*, (Jan 23, 2007), 1; Anonymous (2007), "U.S. Branded 'Biggest Spam and Virus Host'," *Precision Marketing* (January 26), 9.

20. Herskovits, Beth (2006), "APA Shows Public How Psychology Fits Into Their Lives," *PR Week* (January 2), 19.

21. Information obtained from Fight Crime: Invest in Kids website: **http://www.fightcrime.org/releases.php?id=231**, accessed June 9, 2009.

22. Information obtained from Coalition Against Insurance Fraud website: **http://www.insurancefraud.org**, accessed June 9, 2009

23. Information obtained at Federal Trade Commission website, **http://www.ftc.gov/bcp/edu/microsites/idtheft/consumers/about-identity-theft.html**, accessed June 17, 2009

24. Dupre, Kathryne, Tim Jones, and Shirley Taylor (2001), "Dealing With the Difficult: Understanding Difficult Behaviors in a Service Encounter," *American Marketing Association Proceedings*, 173–180.

25. Bitner, Mary J., Bernard H. Booms, and Lois Mohr (1994), "Critical Service Encounters: The Employee's Viewpoint," *Journal of Marketing*, 58 (4), 95–106.

26. Harris, Lloyd, and Kate L. Reynolds (2003), "The Consequences of Dysfunctional Customer Behavior," *Journal*

of Service Research, 6 (2), November, 144–161.

27. Thorne, Scott (2006), "An Exploratory Investigation of the Characteristics of Consumer Fanaticism," *Qualitative Market Research*, 9, 51–72; Pimentel, Robert W., and Kristy E. Reynolds (2004), "A Model for Consumer Devotion: Affective Commitment with Proactive Sustaining Behaviors," *Academy of Marketing Science Review*, 1–45.; Wakefield, Kirk L., and Daniel L. Wann (2006), "An Examination of Dysfunctional Sports Fans: Method of Classification and Relationships with Problem Behaviors," *Journal of Leisure Research*, 38, 168–186; Hunt, Kenneth A., Terry Bristol, and R. Edward Bashaw (1999), "A Conceptual Approach to Classifying Sports Fans," *Journal of Services Marketing*, 13, 439–449.

28. Saporito, Bill (2004), "Why Fans and Players are Playing So Rough," *Time* (December 6), 30–35.

29. Wakefield and Wann (2006.

30. Reynolds, Kate L., and Lloyd C. Harris (2005), "When Service Failure Is Not Service Failure: An Exploration of the Forms and Motives of 'Illegitimate' Customer Complaining," *Journal of Services Marketing*, 19, 321–335.

31. Information obtained from Consumer Products Safety Commission website, **http://www.cpsc.gov**, accessed March 17, 2008.

32. Stoltman, Jeffrey, and Fed Morgan (1993), "Psychological Dimensions of Unsafe Product Usage," in Rajan Varadarajan and Bernard Jaworski, eds., *Marketing Theory and Applications*, 4th ed., Chicago: American Marketing Association.

33. National Safety Commission (2006), "Road Rage Leads to More Road Rage" (December 6), **http://www.nationalsafetycommisson.com**, accessed March 17, 2008

34. Crimmins, Jim, and Chris Callahan (2003), "Reducing Road Rage: The Role of Target Insight in Advertising for Social Change," *Journal of Advertising Research*, (December), 381–390.

35. Bone, Sterling A., and John C. Mowen (2006), "Identifying the Traits of Aggressive and Distracted Drivers: A Hierarchical Trait Model Approach," *Journal of Consumer Behaviour*, 5 (5), September–October, 454–465; also Hennessy, D. A., and D. L. Wiesenthal (1997), "The Relationship Between Traffic Congestion, Driver Stress, and Direct versus Indirect Coping Behaviors," *Ergonomics* (40), 348–361.

36. Information obtained from Mothers Against Drunk Drivers website: **http://www.madd.org/**, accessed June 17, 2009.

37. Information obtained from Centers for Disease Control website, **http://www.cdc.gov/MotorVehicleSafety/Impaired_Driving/impaired-drv_factsheet.html**, accessed June 17, 2009.

38. Information obtained from the "Under Your Influence" website, supported by

the National Highway Traffic Safety Administration, www.underyour influence.org/UnderageDrinkingFact .html, accessed June 17, 2009

39. MADD and Nationwide Insurance Survey, Conducted by Gallup (2005), "Drinking and Driving: Americans' Greatest Highway Safety Concern," http://www.madd.org/stats/10270, accessed March 17, 2008.

40. Statistics in this section based on Quinlan, Kyran P., Robert D. Brewer, Paul Siegel, David A. Sleet, Ali H. Mokdad, Ruth A. Shults, and Nicole Flowers (2005), "Alcohol Impaired Driving Among U.S. Adults 1993–2003," American Journal of Preventive Medicine, (May), 346–350.

41. Insurance Information Institute website: http://www.iii.org/media/ hottopics/insurance/cellphones/, accessed March 17, 2008

42. National Highway Traffic Safety Administration (2006), "An Overview of the 100 Car Naturalistic Study Findings," http://www-nrd.nhtsa.dot.gov/ pdf/nrd-12/100Car_ESV05summary .pdf, accessed March 17, 2008.

43. Joint research report sponsored by State Farm Insurance and The Center for Injury Research and Prevention at The Children's Hospital of Philadelphia (2006), "Driving Through the Eyes of Teens," http://www.chop.edu/ youngdrivers, accessed March 17, 2008

43a. Information obtained from the "Under Your Influence" website, supported by the National Highway Traffic Safety Administration, www.underyour influence.org/Underage DrinkingFact .html, accessed June 17, 2009

44. A summary of current legislative proposals can be found at the Insurance Information Institute website, http:// www.iii.org/media/hottopics/ insurance/cellphones/, accessed March 17, 2008.

45. This definition based on O'Guinn, Thomas C., and Ronald J. Faber (1989), "Compulsive Buying: A Phenomenological Exploration," Journal of Consumer Research, 16 (2), September, 147–157.

46. Nataraajan, Rajan, and Brent G. Goff (1992), "Manifestations of Compulsiveness in the Consumer-Marketplace Domain," Psychology & Marketing, 9, 31–44.

47. This definition based on Faber, Ronald, and Thomas O'Guinn (1992), "A Clinical Screener for Compulsive Buying," Journal of Consumer Research, 19 (3), December, 459–469.

48. Hirschman, Elizabeth C. (1992), "The Consciousness of Addiction: Toward a General Theory of Compulsive Consumption," Journal of Consumer Research, (September), 155–179; O'Guinn and Faber (1989); Dittmar, Helga (2005), "A New Look at Compulsive Buying: Self-Discrepancies and Materialistic Values as Predictors of Compulsive Buying Tendencies," Jour-

nal of Social and Clinical Psychology, (September), 832–859.

49. Roberts, James A., Chris Manolis, and John F. Tanner, Jr. (2006), "Adolescent Autonomy and the Impact of Family Structure on Materialism and Compulsive Buying," Journal of Marketing Theory and Practice, 14 (4), Fall, 301–314.

50. Roberts, James A. (1998), "Compulsive Buying Among College Students: An Investigation of its Antecedents, Consequences, and Implications for Public Policy," Journal of Consumer Affairs, 32 (2), Winter, 295–319; O'Guinn and Faber (1989).

51. Fossi, Caroline (2005), "Citadel Study Finds Compulsive Shoppers Have High Levels of Debt, Guilt" Knight Ridder Tribune Business News (May 3), 1.

52. Parker-Pope, Jessica (2005), "This is Your Brand at the Mall: Why Shopping Makes You Feel So Good," Wall Street Journal (December 6), D1.

53. Roberts (1998).

54. Koran, Lorrin M., Ronald J. Faber, Elias Aboujauode, Michael D. Large, and Richard T. Serpe (2006), "Estimated Prevalence of Compulsive Buying Behavior in the United States," The American Journal of Psychiatry, (October), 1806–1812.

55. Yanovski, Susan, and Billinda K. Dubbert (1993), "Association of Binge Eating Disorder and Psychiatric Comorbidity in Obese Subjects," The American Journal of Psychiatry, (October), 1472–1479.

56. National Institute for Alcohol Abuse and Alcoholism website, http://www .niaaa.nih.gov, accessed March 17, 2008

57. Information obtained from Mothers Against Drunk Drivers website: http:// www.madd.org/Under-21/College/ Statistics/AllStats.aspx#STAT_1800, accessed June 17, 2009

58. Piacentini, Maira G., and Emma N. Banister (2006), "Getting Hammered? . . . Students Coping with Alcohol," Journal of Consumer Behaviour, 5 (2), March–April, 145–156.

59. Wechsler H., J. E. Lee, M. Kuo, M. Seibring, T. F. Nelson, and H. P. Lee (2002), "Trends in College Binge Drinking During a Period of Increased Prevention Efforts: Findings from Four Harvard School of Public Health Study Surveys," Journal of American College Health, 50, 203–217; Presley, C. A., M. A. Leichliter, and P. W. Meilman (1998), Alcohol and Drugs on American College Campuses: A Report to College Presidents: Third in a Series, 1995, 1996, 1997, Carbondale, IL: Core Institute, Southern Illinois University.

60. Shim, Soyeon, and Jennifer Maggs (2005), "A Cognitive and Behavioral Hierarchical Decision-Making Model of College Students' Alcohol Consumption," Psychology & Marketing, 22 (8), August, 649–668.

61. Information obtained from Mothers Against Drunk Drivers website: http:// www.madd.org/Under-21/College/ Statistics.aspx

62. This definition based on Netemeyer, Richard G., Scot Burton, Leslie K. Cole, Donald A. Williamson, Nancy Zucker, Lisa Bertman, and Gretchen Diefenbach (1998), "Characteristics and Beliefs Associated with Probable Pathological Gambling: A Pilot Study with Implications for the National Gambling Impact and Policy Commission," Journal of Public Policy & Marketing, 17 (2), Fall, 147–160.

63. Balabanis, George (2002), "The Relationship Between Lottery-Ticket and Scratch-Card Buying Behaviour, Personality and Other Compulsive Behaviors," Journal of Consumer Behaviour, 2 (1), September, 7–22.

64. Statistics based on information found at National Council on Problem Gambling, http://www.npcgambling.org, accessed March 17, 2008.

65. McComb, J.L., and Hanson W.E. (2009), "Problem Gambling on College Campuses," NASPA Journal, 46 (1), pgs. 1–29.

66. Levens, Suzi, Anne-Marie Dyer, Cynthia Zubritsky, Kathryn Knott, and David W. Oslin (2005), "Gambling Among Older, Primary Care Patients," American Journal of Geriatric Psychiatry, 13, 69–76; also Loroz, Peggy Sue (2004), "Golden-Age Gambling: Psychological Benefits and Self-Concept Dynamics in Aging Consumers' Consumption Experiences," Psychology & Marketing, 25 (1), May, 323–350.

67. Kwak, Hyokjin, George M. Zinkhan, and Elizabeth P. Lester Roushanzamir (2004), "Compulsive Comorbidity and its Psychological Antecedents: A Cross-Cultural Comparison Between the U.S. and South Korea," The Journal of Consumer Marketing, 21, 418–434; Netemeyer, Richard G., Scot Burton, Leslie K. Cole, Donald A. Williamson, Nancy Zucker, Lisa Bertman, and Gretchen Diefenbach (1998), "Characteristics and Beliefs Associated with Probable Pathological Gambling: A Pilot Study with Implications for the National Gambling Impact and Policy Commission," Journal of Public Policy & Marketing, 17 (2), Fall, 147–160.

68. Partnership for a Drug Free America (2006), "Generation Rx: National Study Confirms Abuse of Prescription and Over-the-Counter Drugs," Partnership for a Drug Free America website, http://www.drugfree.org, accessed March 17, 2008.

69. The National Institute on Drug Abuse "Monitoring the Future" Study, 2008, online content retrieved at: www .drugabuse. Gov/pdf/infofacts/ HSYouthTrends08.pdf, accessed June 18, 2009.

70. "About Identity Theft—Deter, Detect, Defend Avoid ID Theft," The Federal Trade Commission, 2007, http://www .ftc.gov/ftc/privacy.shtm; Pitts, Byron,

"An Identity Theft Nightmare, Victim Still Battling His Creditors Four Years Later," CBS News, February 25, 2005, **http://www.cbsnews.com/ stories/2005/02/25/eveningnews/ consumer/main676597.shtml**; Sullivan, Bob, "Data Theft Affects 145,000 Nationwide, MSNBC, February 18, 2005, **http://www.msnbc.msn .com/id/6979897/**.

Chapter 16

1. This definition based on Laczniak, Gene R., and Patrick E. Murphy (2006), "Normative Perspectives for Ethical and Socially Responsible Marketing," *Journal of Macromarketing*, 26 (2), 154–177.

2. Karpatkin, Rhoda H. (1999), "Toward a Fair and Just Marketplace for All Consumers: The Responsibilities of Marketing Professionals," *Journal of Public Policy & Marketing*, 18 (1), 118–122.

3. Xia, Lan, Kent B. Monroe, and Jennifer L. Cox (2004), "The Price is Unfair! A Conceptual Framework of Price Fairness Perceptions," *Journal of Marketing*, 68 (October), 1–15; Campbell, Margaret C. (1999), "Perceptions of Price Fairness: Antecedents and Consequences," Journal of Marketing Research, 36 (May), 187–199.

4. Kotler, Philip (1972), "What Consumerism Means for Marketers," *Harvard Business Review*, 50 (May–June), 48–57.

4a. McShane, Larry (2009), "Bruce Springsteen Slams Tickmaster Over Working on a Dream Ticket Sales," *New York Daily News* (online), online content retrieved at: **http://www.nydailynews .com/gossip/2009/02/04/2009-02-04_ bruce_springsteen_slams_ticketmaster_ ove.html**, accessed June 19, 2009.

5. Smith, N. Craig, and Elizabeth Cooper-Martin (1997), "Ethics and Target Marketing: The Role of Product Harm and Consumer Vulnerability," *Journal of Marketing,* 61 (3), 1–20.

6. Sirgy, M. Joseph, J. S. Johar, and Tao Gao (2006), "Toward a Code of Ethics for Marketing Educators," *Journal of Business Ethics*, 63, 1–20.

7. This definition based on Brown, Tom J., and Peter A. Dacin (1997), "The Company and the Product: Corporate Associations and Consumer Product Responses," *Journal of Marketing*, 61 (1), 68–84.

8. Sen, Sankar, and C. B. Bhattacharya (2001), "Does Doing Good Always Lead to Doing Better? Consumer Reac-

tions to Corporate Social Responsibility," *Journal of Marketing Research*, 38 (2), 225–243.

9. Lantos, Geoffrey P. (2001), "The Boundaries of Strategic Corporate Social Responsibility," *Journal of Consumer Marketing*, 18 (7), 595–630.

10. These findings summarize several research works including Luo, Xueming, and C. B. Bhattacharya (2006), "Corporate Social Responsibility, Customer Satisfaction, and Market Value," *Journal of Marketing*, 70 (4): 1–18; Lichenstein, Donald R., Minette E. Drumwright, and Bridgette M. Braig (2004), "The Effect of Corporate Social Responsibility on Customer Donations to Corporate-Supported Nonprofits," *Journal of Marketing*, 68 (4), 16–32; Sen, Sankar, and C. B. Bhattacharya (2001), "Does Doing Good Always Lead to Doing Better Consumer Reactions to Corporate Social Responsibility," *Journal of Marketing Research*, 38 (2), 225–243; Brown, Tom J., and Peter A. Dacin (1997), "The Company and the Product: Corporate Associations and Consumer Product Responses," *Journal of Marketing*, 61 (1), 68–84.

11. Kotler (1972).

12. Federal Trade Commission website, **http://www.ftc.gov/bcp/conline/pubs/ buspubs/ad-faqs.shtm**, accessed March 17, 2008.

13. National Advertising Review Council website, **http://www.narcpartners .org/**, accessed March 17, 2008.

14. Online content retrieved from American Advertising Federation website, **http://www.aaf.org**, accessed March 17, 2008.

15. American Psychological Association (2004), "Television Advertising Leads to Unhealthy Habits in Children; Says APA Task Force" (February 23), **http:// www.apa.org/releases/childrenads .html**, accessed August 2007.

16. Children's Advertising Review Unit (2006), "Self Regulatory Program for Children's Advertising," *Council of Better Business Bureau.*

17. On-line information obtained from the Federal Trade Commission website: **http://www.ftc.gov/bcp/conline/pubs/ buspubs/coppa.shtm**, accessed March 17, 2008.

18. Fuller, Donald A., and Jacquelyn A. Ottman (2004), "Moderating Unintended Pollution: The Role of Sustainable Product Design," *Journal of Business Research*, 57, 1231–1238.

19. Fry, Marie-Louis, and Michael Jay Polonsky (2004), "Examining the

Unintended Consequences of Marketing," *Journal of Business Research*, 57, 1303–1306.

20. Tybout, Alice M., Brian Sternthal, and Bobby J. Calder (1988), "Information Availability as a Determinant of Multiple-Request Effectiveness," *Journal of Marketing Research*, 20 (August), 280–290; Mowen, John C. Mowen, and Robert Cialdini (1980), "On Implementing the Door-in-the-Face Compliance Strategy in a Marketing Context," *Journal of Marketing Research*, 17 (May), 253–258; Freedman, Jonathon L., and Scott C. Fraher (1966), "Compliance Without Pressure: The Foot-in-the-Door Technique," *Journal of Personality and Social Psychology*, 4 (August), 195–202.

21. Cialdini, Robert, and David Schroeder (1976), "Increasing Compliance by Legitimizing Paltry Contributions: When Even a Penny Helps," *Journal of Personality and Social Psychology*, 34 (October), 599–604.

22. WOMMA, "Unethical Word-of-Mouth Marketing Strategies," **http:// www.womma.org/wom101/06/**, accessed March 17, 2008.

23. Consumer Product Safety Commission website, **http://www.cpsc.gov/ about/about.html**, accessed March 17, 2008.

24. Freed, Joshua (2007), "RIAA: Expect More Download Suits," USAToday. com, **http://www.usatoday.com/tech/ news/2007-10-04-riaa-download-law suits_n.htm**, accessed 1/1/2008; Geisler, Markus, and Mali Pohlmann (2003), "The Anthropology of File-Sharing: Consuming Napster as a Gift," *Advances in Consumer Research*, 30 (1), 273–279; Jagger, Mick, and Keith Richards (1969), "You Can't Always Get What You Want," *Let It Bleed*, Decca/ABKCO; Langenderfer, Jeff, and Don Lloyd Cook (2001), "Copyright Policies and Issues Raised by *A&M Records v. Napster:* 'The Shot Heard 'Round the World' or 'Not with a Bang but a Whimper?' " *Journal of Public Policy & Marketing*, 20, 280–288; Mamudi, Sam (2003), "Record Industry Targets Downloaders," *Managing Intellectual Property* (July/August), 6; Menn, J. (2003), *All the Rave: The Rise and Fall of Shawn Fanning's Napster*, New York: Crown Business; Taylor, Chris (2003), "Downloader Dragnet," *Time* (August 4), 42; Wade, Jared (2004), "The Music Industry's War on Piracy," *Risk Management Magazine* (February), 11–15.

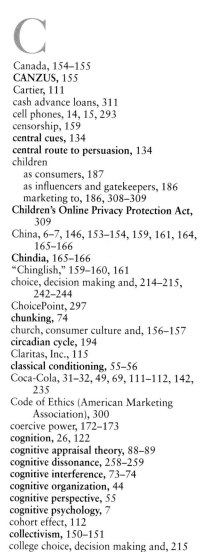

complaining behavior and, 268, 269
computer-mediated behaviors, 289
cybersquatting, 302
for decision making, 237–238
e-segments and, 38
fearfulness and, 210
morphing technology, 49
personality and consumer behavior, 108, 112, 116
interpretive research, 16–17
involuntary attention, 52
involvement, 53
    comprehension and, 67
    decision making and, 225
    motivation and, 85–88
iPhone (Apple), 221
Italy, 148–149

J

Japan, 133, 151
Jeep, 269
JMD (just meaningful difference), 50
JND (just noticeable difference), 48–50, 238–239
judgments, 238

K

Kellaris, James, 26
Kellogg's, 310
Kennedy, John F., 302
KFC, 75–76
Kindle, 11
knowledge, memory and, 70–71
knowledge function of attitudes, 122–123
Kohl's, 251
Kotler, Philip, 303

L

Lambert's Café, 204
laws, consumer safety, 307, 313–314
learning, 41–42. *see also* perception
left skewed distribution, 259–260
legitimate power, 172–173
Levitt, Theodore, 12, 302
lexicographic rules, 241, 243
liability, 313–314
lifestyles, 113
likeability, 66–67, 141
limited decision making, 219
locus, satisfaction and, 257
long-term memory, 75–76
long-term orientation, 152–153
loyalty. *see* brand loyalty
loyalty/card programs, 272, 276
lying, 79

M

macroeconomics, 6–7
Mall of America, 191
manners, 163
marketing communications, 238

marketing concept, 7–8, 301
marketing ethics, 298–316
    American Marketing Association Code of Ethics, 300
    consumerism and, 301–305
    corporate social responsibility and, 305–306
    ethics, defined, 299
    marketing ethics and marketing strategy, 299–301
    product liability and, 313–314
    public criticism of marketing, 307–313
    regulation of marketing activities, 307
marketing mix, 33, 302–304
"Marketing Myopia" *(Harvard Business Review),* 302
marketing strategy, 10–11, 10–16
    CB Idea Checklist for, 36–37
    consumer value and, 30–33
    marketing ethics and, 299–301
marketing tactics, 31
market mavens, 181–182
market orientation, 9
market segmentation, 33–35
marriage, 183–184, 250
masculinity, 151
Maslow, Abraham, 84
Maslow's hierarchy of needs, 84–85
matchup hypothesis, 141
materialism, 107
Maytag, 111
McDonald's, 11, 314
meaning
    comprehension and, 73–76
    culture and, 145–149
    meaningfulness, 141
    motivation and, 95–99
    satisfaction and, 255–256
    transference, 249
meaningful encoding, 74–75
meaning transference, 249
measurement, of satisfaction, 259–261
media, consumer culture and, 156–157
memory, 70–71
    emotional effect on memory, 95
    lying and, 79
    mood-congruent recall, 96
    multiple store theory of memory, 70–73
    sensory, 71–72
    workbench memory, 72–73
memory trace, 75
mental budgeting, 209
Mercedes, 76–77
Merchants of Cool, The (film), 100
mere exposure effect, 50–51
message congruity, 65
message effects, 137–141
messages, comprehension and, 66–69. *see also* communication
metric equivalence, 161
Microsoft, 11
middle-aged consumers, 185–186
Minnesota Motor Vehicle Department, 9
minority groups, growth of, 112
mobile phones. *see* cell phones
modeling, 158–159
moderating variables, 86
mood, 89–90, 209–210
mood-congruent judgments, 89–90
mood-congruent recall, 96
moral beliefs, 285–286

moral equity, 285
morals, 305
morphing technology, 49
motivation, 82–100
    decision making and, 215–216
    emotion, behavior and, 93–95
    emotion, meaning, and schema-based affect, 95–99
    emotion, measuring, 90–93
    emotion and value, 88–90
    hierarchy of needs and, 84–88
    human behavior and, 83–84
    of misbehavior, 286–287
    motivations, defined, 83
    of teenagers, 100
motivational research era, 105
Motorola, 15
Mountain Dew, 111
multiple store theory of memory, 71–72
multiple-trait approach, 106
music
    attitude and, 125
    comprehension and, 73
    computer-mediated behaviors and, 289
    fan clubs and, 175
    piracy, 315
    as situational influence, 205–206
    subliminal messages in, 48
    tempo of, 206
myspace.com, 116, 180

N

Napster, 315
National Highway and Traffic Safety Authority (NHTSA), 269
National Radio Company, 12
NCAA Men's Basketball Tournament, 194
need recognition, 220–221, 231
needs, 310–311
negative dimensions of emotion, 91–92
negative disconfirmation, 253
negative public publicity, 269
negative reinforcement, 57
negative word-of-mouth, 268–269
negligence, 313–314
Newton (Apple), 188
New Zealand, 154–155
niche marketing, 12–13
Nick at Night, 131
nodes, 76–77
nomothetic perspective, 106
noncompensatory rules, 241
nondurable goods, 247
"nonfamily," 184
nongenerosity, 107
nonlinear effect, 207
nonverbal communication, 161–162
nostalgia, 79–80
nuclear families, 183
numbers, comprehension and, 64

O

Odbert, Henry, 106
olfactory, 132, 205
Olympic Games (2008), 161
one-to-one marketing, 12

CB This book is closely organized to the consumer value framework (CVF). The heart of the framework is value! Things like internal and external influences help explain why consumers makes the decisions they make. These decisions then shape the value they receive from consumption – the process of converting a product into value. Based on the value received, the consumer builds relationships with service providers, retailers, brands and other marketing entities.

Key Terms

Utilitarian Value

Hedonic Value

Perception

Culture

Motivation

Situational Influence

Relationship Quality

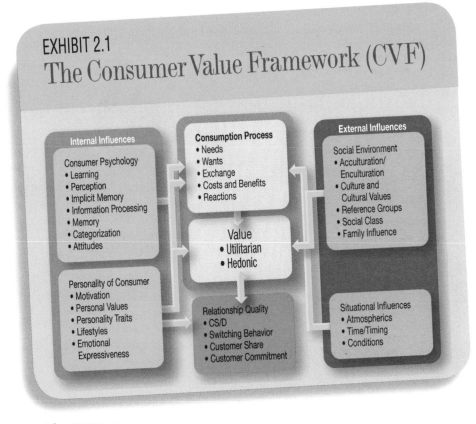

EXHIBIT 2.1
The Consumer Value Framework (CVF)

Internal Influences

Consumer Psychology
- Learning
- Perception
- Implicit Memory
- Information Processing
- Memory
- Categorization
- Attitudes

Personality of Consumer
- Motivation
- Personal Values
- Personality Traits
- Lifestyles
- Emotional Expressiveness

Consumption Process
- Needs
- Wants
- Exchange
- Costs and Benefits
- Reactions

Value
- Utilitarian
- Hedonic

Relationship Quality
- CS/D
- Switching Behavior
- Customer Share
- Customer Commitment

External Influences

Social Environment
- Acculturation/ Enculturation
- Culture and Cultural Values
- Reference Groups
- Social Class
- Family Influence

Situational Influences
- Atmospherics
- Time/Timing
- Conditions

The CVF in Action

1. **Value:**

   The consumer receives value from the gaming experience:
   - Utilitarian Value – to the extent that she is pursuing the task of actually making a profit from the experience.
   - Hedonic Value – to the extent that the gaming experience is exciting and gratifying.

2. **Relationship quality:**
   - The casino studies her behavior closely to help cultivate a mutually beneficial relationship where she becomes loyal based on the value received.

3. **Internal influences:**
   - A great deal of consumer psychology is involved and influences what activities she favors based on perceptions of the game attributes – for instance, which attributes increase the odds of winning?
   - Consumer personality also influences her actions. Some consumers may hold values that would leave them uncomfortable in a gaming environment. Emotional expressiveness is on display in a casino but one might need extra care about this around a poker table!

4. **External influences:**
   - The social environment including culture will determine the appropriateness of visiting a casino for each type of consumer.
   - The charged atmospherics frame all decision making while also enhancing the value of the experience itself.

5. **Consumption process:**
   - The decisions made while in the casino are a result of all the influences and manifest themselves in desires and the willingness to participate in exchange. Ultimately, the reactions lead to value and a potential willingness to return again and further a relationship with this marketing entity.

Visit **4ltrpress.cengage.com/cb** for additional study tools.

Loyalty rewards associate value with the desired behavior —such as using an AMEX card.

PART 1 IN REVIEW

Chapters 1-2

PART 1 Part 1 of *CB* allows the connection between the business world and actual consumer behavior to be understood. Consumer behavior is relevant to study to help understand what actions may lead certain businesses to be more successful than others. Part I provides this knowledge as an introduction and as an important backdrop to studying and actually using all consumer behavior theory.

Key Terms

Consumer Behavior

Value

Product Positioning

Consumption

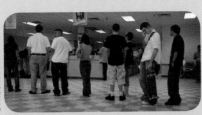

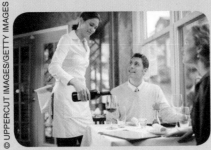

Why does the treatment of customers vary from setting to setting?

Competition plays a key role and this illustration demonstrates that competitive environments drive businesses to serve customers better.

EXHIBIT 1.1 **outlines the basic consumption process. It illustrates how consumption turns things into value. Ultimately, this a key to success in business.**

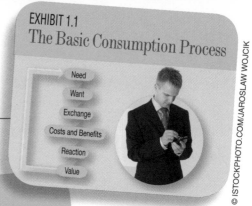

EXHIBIT 1.1

The Basic Consumption Process

Need
Want
Exchange
Costs and Benefits
Reaction
Value

EXHIBIT 2.2

The Value Equation

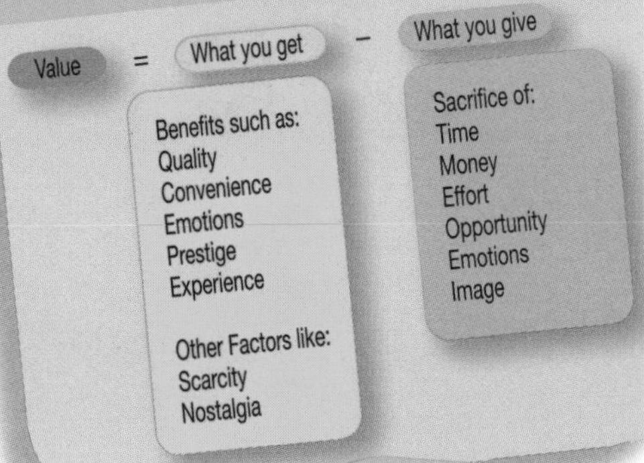

Value
=
What you get
–
What you give
Benefits such as:
Quality
Convenience
Emotions
Prestige
Experience
Other Factors like:
Scarcity
Nostalgia
Sacrifice of:
Time
Money
Effort
Opportunity
Emotions
Image

EXHIBIT 2.2 **gives an overview of how net value results. Many things can contribute positively to value and many things can contribute negatively. Ultimately, value is the result of weighing positive benefits against negative consequences.**

Value can be either utilitarian (meaning beneficial because some task is solved) or hedonic (meaning the experience itself is the benefit).

EXHIBIT 2.3

Consumption Activities Can Fall into Any of These Categories

		Utilitarian Value	
		Low	**High**
Hedonic Value	**Low**	Bad Positioning – slow "fast" food	Okay Positioning – fast, "fast" food
	High	Okay Positioning – restaurant w/ nice atmosphere but poor food	Superior Positioning – restaurant w/ great atmosphere and great food

EXHIBIT 2.7

A Perceptual Map for a Local Rock Music Radio Market

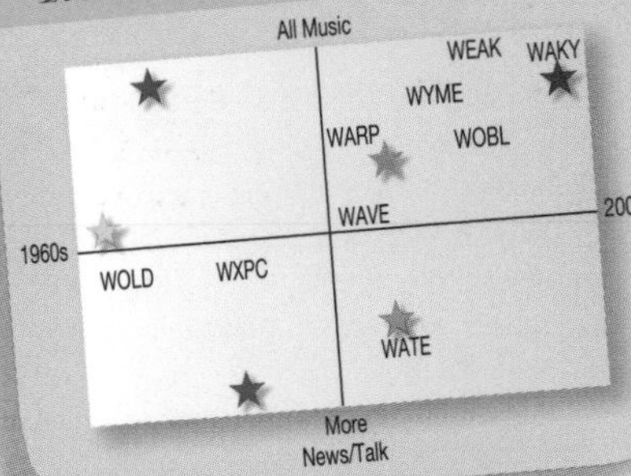

All Music
WEAK
WAKY
WYME
WARP
WOBL
WAVE
2000s
1960s
WOLD
WXPC
WATE
More
News/Talk

Perceptual maps are a critically important tool to understand market competition and market opportunities. The perceptual map shows where consumers "locate" one of a set of competitors.

Visit **4ltrpress.cengage.com/cb** for additional study tools.

PART 2 Part 2 of *CB* deals with intrapersonal influences on consumer behavior. The key issues pertaining to perception, learning and memory, motivation, personality, and attitude formation and change are discussed. The concepts listed below are very important! Remember, these issues most often work together in influencing consumer behavior!

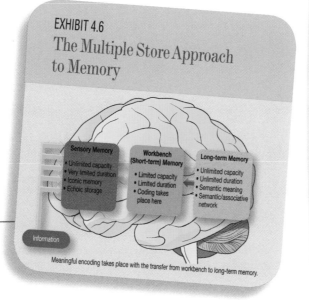

EXHIBIT 3.3
Sensing, Organizing, and Reacting

SENSING

ORGANIZING

REACTING

What will everyone else think?

Does this fit?

© DAVID STUART/DIGITAL VISION/GETTY IMAGES

EXHIBIT 3.3 highlights the basic phases of perception: sensing, organizing, and reacting. Perception is vital for consumer learning to occur. Consumers are exposed to thousands of stimuli daily, and their perceptions of the stimuli are subjective.

Key Terms

Perception

Memory

Motivation

Personality

Attitude

Compensatory Model

EXHIBIT 4.6 highlights the multiple store approach to memory. The three memory components, including sensory, workbench, and long-term play important roles in consumer learning, and they also influence the elements of perception.

EXHIBIT 4.6
The Multiple Store Approach to Memory

Sensory Memory	Workbench (Short-term) Memory	Long-term Memory
• Unlimited capacity	• Limited capacity	• Unlimited capacity
• Very limited duration	• Limited duration	• Unlimited duration
• Iconic memory	• Coding takes place here	• Semantic meaning
• Echoic storage		• Semantic/associative network

Information

Meaningful encoding takes place with the transfer from workbench to long-term memory.

Utilitarian Motivations Lead to	Hedonic Motivations Lead to
Choosing the most convenient place to have lunch	Going out to a trendy, new restaurant for dinner
Buying a tank of gas for the car	Driving the car fast on a curvy road even when not rushed
Choosing to shop with retailers that are seen as useful and easy to use	Choosing to shop with retailers that are seen as fun and exciting
Using air freshener to cover up a strange smell in the apartment	Using air freshener because one really likes the smell
Going gift shopping out of a sense of obligation to give a gift	Giving a gift to enjoy the giving process and the joy the recipient experiences when opening the gift

There are many ways to view the concept of motivation, but one easy and useful way to classify motivation is by matching motives with hedonic and utilitarian value.

Visit **4ltrpress.cengage.com/cb** for additional study tools.

The study of the personality is important because personality consists of the thoughts, emotions, intentions, and behaviors that consumers exhibit consistently. One major way to view the human personality from the trait approach is through the Five Factor Model. Consumers often buy products that they believe are consistent with their personalities.

Personality Trait	Description
Extroversion	Talkative, outgoing
Agreeableness	Kindhearted, sympathetic
Openness to Experience	Creative, open to new ideas, imaginative
Stability	Even-keeled, avoids mood swings
Conscientiousness	Precise, efficient, organized

Source: Based on McCrae, R. R., and P. T. Costa (2005), *Personality in Adulthood: A Five-Factor Theory Perspective*, 2nd ed., New York, Guilford.

ATO Model

$$A_o = \sum_{I=1}^{N} (b_i)(e_i)$$

A_o attitude toward the object in question (or A_{brand})

b_i strength of belief that the object possesses attribute i

e_i evaluation of the attractiveness or goodness of attribute i

N number of attributes and beliefs

Attitudes are a prominent part of "reasoned action." An attitude model can provide useful diagnostic information for firms looking to improve their competitive positioning in the marketplace by helping to become a more "reasonable" choice.

Don't forget that these intrapersonal influences most often work together in consumer behavior! Part 3 of the text deals with interpersonal influences such as culture and reference groups.

Visit **4ltrpress.cengage.com/cb** for additional study tools.

PART 3 Part 3 of *CB* focuses on factors in the external environment, meaning things that are not a characteristic of the consumer himself or herself, and how they influence value.

PART 3 IN REVIEW

Chapters 8-9

Key Terms

Culture

Core Societal Values (CSV)

Verbal Communication

Nonverbal Communication

Reference Groups

Normative Influence

Informational Influence

EXHIBIT 8.1
Culture, Meaning, and Value

Behavior	Meaning in United States	Alternate Meaning
Consumer age 14–18 consuming beer or wine in a restaurant	Unacceptable or even illegal in most areas.	Wine is part of a nice family meal in other areas, including much of western Europe.
People gathering to eat barbecue pork ribs	This menu is part of a pleasant social event.	Pork is not an acceptable food item among Hebrews and Muslims.
Supervisors and employees socializing together	Supervisors and coworkers can be friendly with each other.	Employees and supervisors should keep their distance away from work. An employee who acts too casually with a "senior" could incur a sanction.
Kissing	Purely a family or romantic activity.	In many nations, kissing is common when making a new acquaintance or greeting a friend.

In all cases, what a consumer consumes helps determine how accepted one is by other consumers in society. Likewise, the consumption act itself generally has no absolute meaning. Rather, culture embodies meaning. Consumer culture can be thought of as commonly held societal beliefs that define what is socially gratifying. Perhaps more simply, culture shapes value! Exhibit 8.1 provides examples of common behaviors that vary in meaning across cultures.

EXHIBIT 8.5
CSV Difference Scores Relative to American Consumers

	Power Distance	Individualism	Masculinity	Uncertainty Avoidance	Long-Term Orientation	Total Distance Score
Australia	−4	−1	−1	5	2	6.9
United Kingdom	−5	−2	4	−11	−4	13.5
Brazil	29	−53	−13	30	36	77.6
Russia	53	−52	−26	49	26	96.3
India	37	−43	−6	−6	32	65.7
China	40	−71	4	−6	89	121.8

EXHIBIT 8.5 demonstrates how CSV scores on each cultural value dimension can be used to represent how similar or different one culture is from another. In this case, each country is scored based on how different it is from U.S. culture.

Visit **4ltrpress.cengage.com/cb**
for additional study tools.

EXHIBIT 9.2 **illustrates how reference group influence can vary from one type of consumer decision to another. A reference group has significant relevance to a consumer and helps shape the value one receives by either conforming or not conforming with the group. Think about how reference groups influence choices in designer sunglasses and how popular brands like Ray-Ban and Oakley are over time.**

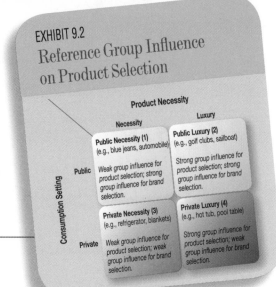

EXHIBIT 9.2
Reference Group Influence on Product Selection

	Product Necessity	
	Necessity	**Luxury**
Public	**Public Necessity (1)** (e.g., blue jeans, automobile) Weak group influence for product selection; strong group influence for brand selection.	**Public Luxury (2)** (e.g., golf clubs, sailboat) Strong group influence for product selection; strong group influence for brand selection.
Private	**Private Necessity (3)** (e.g., refrigerator, blankets) Weak group influence for product selection; weak group influence for brand selection.	**Private Luxury (4)** (e.g., hot tub, pool table) Strong group influence for product selection; weak group influence for brand selection.

Consumption Setting

Source: Adapted from William O. Bearden and Michael J. Etzel (1982), "Reference Group Influences on Product and Brand Purchase Decisions," *Journal of Consumer Research,* 9 (2), 183–194.

© ERIC CARR/ALAMY

Maybe Talk Isn't Cheap

Marketers are excited about the many opportunities that are available in cyberspace. One of the fastest-growing opportunities can be found with blogging. In fact, what was once considered as simply a way for consumers to express their opinions about various issues, products, or companies has become an important part of the modern marketing mix.

A number of web sites that allow companies to hire bloggers to write blogs about their products have been introduced. Sites such as **payperpost.com**, **sponsoredreviews.com**, and **reviewme.com** are growing in popularity. Although the requirements for each site vary, the basic idea is that bloggers are given the opportunity to blog about products or companies for pay. Advertisers tell bloggers what products or services they want included in the blog, and the blogger agrees to write about it. The arrangement can be a win–win situation for both the blogger and advertiser. Of course, this practice may be considered to be unethical by some. Nevertheless, this form of Internet promotion is rapidly becoming an important component of buzz marketing, and given the popularity of the Internet blog, it is likely that this practice will continue to grow in popularity.

Sources: Johnson, Carolyn Y. (2007), "Blogging for Dollars," *Knight Ridder Tribute Business News* (April 16), 1; Fernando, Angelo (2007), "Transparency Under Attack," *Communication World,* 24 (2), 9–11; Schwartz, Matthew (2007), "Can Paid Blog Reviews Pay Off?", *B to B,* 92 (2), 1–3; Frazier, Mya (2006), "Want to Build Up Blog Buzz? Starting Writing Checks for $8," *Advertising Age,* 77 (44): 3–4; Armstrong, Stephen (2006), "Bloggers for Hire," *New Statesman,* 135 (4807), 26–27.

WOM behavior is incredibly influential. The story at the left illustrates how technology is making WOM even more powerful. Many blogs like the ones described here allow consumers to tell their stories to the world. In this way, they pass on value information to other consumers.

PART 4 Part 4 of *CB* discusses the influence of situations on consumer behavior and also consumer decision making.

PART 4 IN REVIEW

Chapters 10-12

EXHIBIT 10.2
Shopping Activities and Shopping Value

High Hedonic Value

- Experiential—outshopping at a mall in a neighboring city

- Impulsive—deciding to buy four pairs of shoes at an unannounced sale

- Epistemic (ongoing)—visiting a wine store to taste new wines

- Epistemic (situational)—searching for warranty information about air conditioners

- Acquisitional—stopping at a convenience store for gas and a quart of milk

Low Utilitarian Value — High Utilitarian Value

Low Hedonic Value

Situations play an important role in influencing consumer behavior. Shoppers are often subjected to situational influencers that affect decision making and value. There are four main types of shopping activities that correspond to utilitarian and hedonic value.

Key Terms

Situational Influences

Decision Making Process

Consideration Set

Noncompensatory Rules

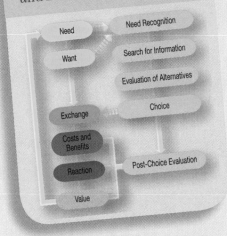

EXHIBIT 11.1
Basic Consumption Process and Decision Making

Need — Need Recognition

Want — Search for Information

Evaluation of Alternatives

Exchange — Choice

Costs and Benefits

Reaction — Post-Choice Evaluation

Value

The consideration set is very important to consumer behavior. The consideration set includes the alternatives that will actually be considered when a consumer makes a decision. This differs from the other sets pictured in Exhibit 11.5.

EXHIBIT 11.5
Consideration Set

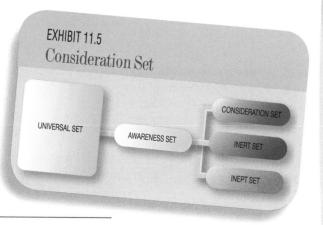

UNIVERSAL SET — AWARENESS SET — CONSIDERATION SET / INERT SET / INEPT SET

The decision making process consists of five major phases including need recognition, search for information, evaluation of alternatives, choice, and post-choice evaluation. This approach assumes a rational decision making perspective.

EXHIBIT 12.7
Noncompensatory Decision Approaches

Attribute	Importance	Chevy Aveo Belief Ratings	Ford Focus Belief Ratings	Honda Fit Belief Ratings	Hyundai Accent Belief Ratings
Gas mileage	10	5	7	9	8
Low price	9	8	6	7	10
Styling	8	9	8	4	4
Warranty	5	4	8	9	8
Service	6	5	6	7	3
Handling	7	6	5	3	3

Note: Belief ratings are performance judgments scaled from 1 = very poor to 9 = very good. Importance ratings are scaled so that 10 = most important, 9 = next most important, and so on.
Source: Wright, Peter (1975), "Consumer Choice Strategies: Simplifying Vs. Optimizing," *Journal of Marketing Research*, 12 (1), 60–67.

Consumers often use noncompensatory decision rules when making a choice. These rules set strict guidelines for product selection. The major types of noncompensatory rules are listed in Exhibit 12.7 and include the conjunctive rule, the disjunctive rule, the elimination-by-aspects rule, and the lexicographic rule.

Key Terms

Satisfaction

Relationship Quality

Moral Beliefs

Marketing Ethics

Consumers tend to be more satisfied with exchanges they find valuable, as value is at the heart of marketing transactions.

According to the Expectancy Disconfirmation approach, consumers compare their performance perceptions to their expectations to arrive at a level of satisfaction.

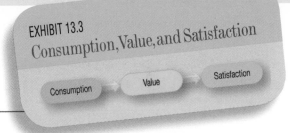

EXHIBIT 13.3
Consumption, Value, and Satisfaction

Consumption → Value → Satisfaction

EXHIBIT 13.5
Basic Disconfirmation Process

Expectations
Performance Perceptions
Disconfirmation → Satisfaction

Performance > Expectations = +Disconfirmation➡Satisfaction
Expectations > Performance = −Disconfirmation➡Dissatisfaction

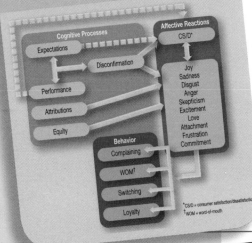

EXHIBIT 14.1
A More Detailed Look at Postconsumption Reactions

Cognitive Processes
Expectations
Disconfirmation
Performance
Attributions
Equity

Affective Reactions
CS/D*
Joy
Sadness
Disgust
Anger
Skepticism
Excitement
Love
Attachment
Frustration
Commitment

Behavior
Complaining
WOM†
Switching
Loyalty

*CS/D = consumer satisfaction/dissatisfaction
†WOM = word-of-mouth

Firms are interested in what happens after a consumer is satisfied or dissatisfied because they would like customers to return to do business again. Strong feelings influence many consumer behaviors.

Moral beliefs play a major role in ethical decision making. Ethical decision making then influences consumer misbehavior, which can take several forms.

EXHIBIT 15.1
Moral Beliefs, Ethical Decision Making, and Behavior

Moral Beliefs
• Moral equity
• Contractualism
• Relativism

Ethical Decision Making
• Deontology
• Teleology

Consumer Behavior/Misbehavior

CONSUMER MISBEHAVIOR	CONSUMER PROBLEM BEHAVIOR
• Shoplifting • Computer-mediated behaviors: illicit sharing of software and music, computer attacks, cyberbullying • Fraud • Abusive consumer behavior • Dysfunctional sports behaviors • Illegitimate complaining • Product misuse: aggressive driving, drunk driving, cell phone use	• Compulsive buying • Compulsive shopping • Eating disorders • Binge drinking • Problem gambling • Drug abuse

Several pieces of legislation are aimed at protecting consumers from marketer misbehavior.

Sherman Antitrust Act (1890)	Prohibits restraint of free trade
Federal Food and Drug Act (1906)	Prohibits misleading practices associated with food and drug marketing
Clayton Act (1914)	Restricts price discrimination, exclusive dealing, and tying contracts
Wheeler Lea Act (1938)	Provides FTC with jurisdiction over misleading or false advertising
Fair Packaging and Labeling Act (1966)	Marketers must present proper packaging and content information about products
Child Protection Act (1966)	Prohibits the marketing of dangerous toys
Truth In Lending Act (1968)	Lenders required to disclose complete costs associated with loans
Consumer Product Safety Act (1972)	Created Consumer Product Safety Commission
Children's Online Privacy Protection Act (1998)	Establishes rules governing online marketing practices aimed at children
Anticybersquatting Consumer Protection Act (1999)	Prohibits the act of cybersquatting
Consumer Telephone Records Act (2006)	Prohibits the sale of consumer cell phone records
Consumer Product Safety Improvement Act of 2008	Establishes product safety standards and other requirements for children's products
Credit Card Accountability, Responsibility, and Disclosure Act 2009	Amends Truth in Lending Act to establish fair and transparent practices relating to consumer credit
Helping Families Save Their Homes Act 2009	Prevents mortgage foreclosures and enhances mortgage availability

Visit **4ltrpress.cengage.com/cb**
for additional study tools.

Chapter Summary

LO1 Understand the meaning of *consumption* and *consumer behavior.*

Consumption represents the process by which goods, services, or ideas are used and transformed into value. The basic consumer behavior process includes steps that begin with consumer needs and finish with value. Consumer behavior, or CB as it is sometimes called, can be viewed either from the standpoint of human behavior or as a field of study. In terms of human behavior, consumer behavior is the set of value-seeking activities that take place as people go about addressing realized needs. Thus, consumer behavior captures the things that we do as we try to seek out, purchase, and use goods, products, services, and ideas. Consumer behavior as a field of study represents the study of consumers as they go about the consumption process. Thus, textbooks, trade literature, and research journals all direct their subject matter toward the behavior of consumers in an effort to develop consumer behavior theory.

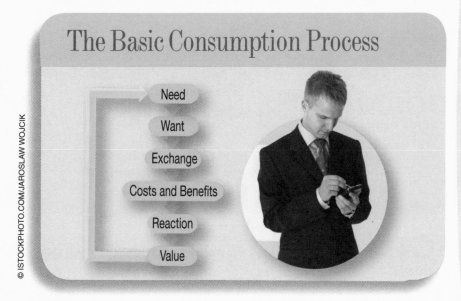

The Basic Consumption Process

Need
Want
Exchange
Costs and Benefits
Reaction
Value

© ISTOCKPHOTO.COM/JAROSLAW WOJCIK

LO2 Describe how consumers get treated differently in various types of exchange environments.

Two market characteristics help explain how customers are treated: competitiveness and dependence. In a competitive market, consumers do not have to put up with poor treatment because some other business will gladly provide a better alternative. Thus, competitive markets drive organizations toward a consumer orientation as a way of surviving in the marketplace. Similarly, a business that depends on repeat business also must emphasize the creation of valuable exchange relationships with its customers; otherwise, customers will simply go elsewhere the next time they desire that particular good or service.

Glossary Terms

anthropology study in which researchers interpret relationships between consumers and the things they purchase, the products they own, and the activities in which they participate

attribute a product feature that delivers a desired consumer benefit

benefits positive results of consumption

cognitive psychology study of the intricacies of mental reactions involved in information processing

consumer behavior set of value-seeking activities that take place as people go about addressing realized needs

consumer behavior as a field of study study of consumers as they go about the consumption process; the science of studying how consumers seek value in an effort to address real needs

consumer (customer) orientation way of doing business in which the actions and decision making of the institution prioritize consumer value and satisfaction above all other concerns

consumption process by which goods, services, or ideas are used and transformed into value

costs negative results of consumption

differentiated marketers firms that serve multiple market segments each with a unique product offering

economics study of production and consumption

ethnography qualitative approach to studying consumers that relies on interpretation of artifacts to draw conclusions about consumption

exchange acting out of the decision to give something up in return for something of greater value

interpretive research approach that seeks to explain the inner meanings and motivations associated with specific consumption experiences

market orientation organizational culture that embodies the importance of creating value for customers among all employees

marketing multitude of activities that facilitate *exchanges* between buyers and sellers, including production, pricing, promotion, distribution, and retailing, which are all focused on providing value for consumers

Visit **4ltrpress.cengage.com/cb** for additional study tools.

niche marketing plan wherein a firm specializes in serving one market segment with particularly unique demand

one-to-one marketing plan wherein a different product is offered for each individual customer so that each customer is treated as a segment of one

phenomenology qualitative approach to studying consumers that relies on interpretation of the lived experience associated with some aspect of consumption

product potentially valuable bundle of benefits

production orientation approach where innovation is geared primarily toward making the production process as efficient and economic as possible

psychology study of human reactions to their environment

qualitative research tools means for gathering data in a relatively unstructured way including case analysis, clinical interviews, and focus group interviews

quantitative research approach that addresses questions about consumer behavior using numerical measurement and analysis tools

relationship marketing activities based on the belief that the firm's performance is enhanced through repeat business

researcher dependent subjective data, which requires a researcher to interpret the meaning

resource-advantage theory theory that explains why companies succeed or fail; the firm goes about obtaining resources from consumers in return for the value the resources create

social psychology study that focuses on the thoughts, feelings, and behaviors that people have as they interact with other people

sociology the study of groups of people within a society with relevance for consumer behavior because a great deal of consumption takes place within group settings or is affected by group behavior

touchpoints direct contacts between the firm and a customer

undifferentiated marketing plan wherein the same basic product is offered to all customers

want way a consumer goes about addressing a recognized need

LO3 Explain the role of consumer behavior in business and society.

Consumer behavior is clearly important as an input to business/marketing strategy. The firm can build value only with an understanding of what exactly leads to a high-value experience. In addition, consumer behavior knowledge is necessary in understanding how customers view competing firms within a market. Consumer behavior also is important because it is a force that shapes society. In fact, consumer behavior helps form society in many ways. Trends such as the decreasing acceptability of smoking, the increasing acceptability of using mobile phones in social situations, as well as changes in general marketplace etiquette are all caused by consumers. Finally, knowledge of consumer behavior is important in making responsible decisions as a consumer. An educated consumer is a more effective consumer.

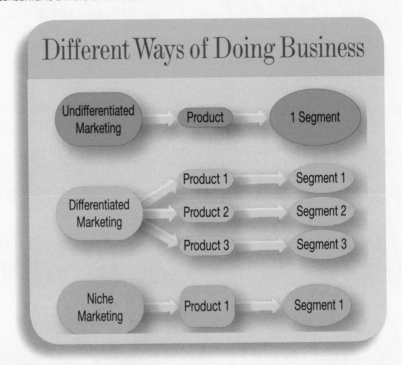

Different Ways of Doing Business

LO4 Be familiar with basic approaches to studying consumer behavior.

Many people with varied backgrounds study consumer behavior. Thus, consumer behavior is studied from many different perspectives involving many different research tools. An interpretative approach seeks to explain the inner meanings and motivations associated with specific consumption experiences. Interpretative research usually involves qualitative research tools as case analyses, clinical interviews, focus group interviews, and others where data are gathered in a relatively unstructured way. Quantitative research addresses questions about consumer behavior using numerical measurement and analysis tools. The measurement is usually structured, meaning the consumer will simply choose a response from among alternatives supplied by the researcher.

LO5 Describe why consumer behavior is so dynamic and how recent trends affect consumers.

Consumer behavior is ever changing. Several trends are shaping today's consumer climate. These include increasing internationalization of the marketplace, the rate of technological innovation, and changes in demographics that affect buying power and quality of life. Consumer research continues to evolve along with these changes.

Visit **4ltrpress.cengage.com/cb**
for additional study tools.

Chapter Summary

LO1 Describe the consumer value framework, including its basic components.

The Consumer Value Framework represents consumer behavior theory illustrating factors that shape consumption-related behaviors and ultimately determine the value associated with consumption. Value lies at the heart of the CVF. Value results from the consumption process, which represents the decision-making process of consumers seeking value. This process is influenced directly and indirectly by external and internal influences such as culture and psychology, respectively. When high value results, consumers may become loyal and build relationships with customers. The CVF is useful for organizing consumer behavior knowledge both in theory and in practice.

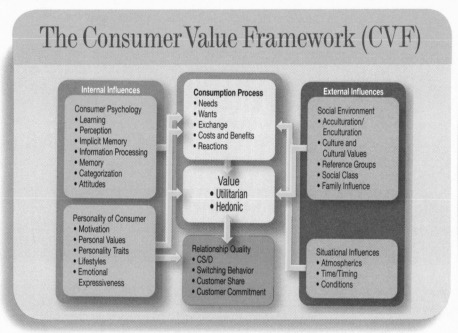

The Consumer Value Framework (CVF)

LO2 Define consumer value and compare and contrast two key types of value.

Value is a personal assessment of the net worth obtained from an activity. Value is what consumers ultimately pursue because valuable actions address motivations that manifest themselves in needs and desires. In this sense, value captures how much gratification a consumer receives from consumption. Activities and objects that lead to high utilitarian value do so because they help the consumer accomplish some task. Utilitarian value is how the consumer solves jobs that come along with being a consumer. The second type of value is hedonic value, which is the net worth obtained from the experience itself and the emotions associated with consumption. Hedonic value represents the immediate gratification that comes from some activity or experience. Hedonic value is very emotional and subjective in contrast to utilitarian value; however, the best consumption experiences offer some levels of both types of value.

Value = What you get − What you give

Visit **4ltrpress.cengage.com/cb**
for additional study tools.

Glossary Terms

affect feelings associated with objects or experienced during events

augmented product actual physical product purchased plus any services such as installation and warranties necessary to use the product and obtain its benefits

cognition thinking or mental processes that go on as we process and store things that can become knowledge

Consumer Value Framework (CVF) consumer behavior theory that illustrates factors that shape consumption-related behaviors and ultimately determine the value associated with consumption

corporate strategy way a firm is defined and its general goals

customer lifetime value (CLV) approximate worth of a customer to a company in economic terms; overall profitability of an individual consumer

Customer Relationship Management (CRM) systematic management information system that collects, maintains, and reports detailed information about customers to enable a more customer-oriented managerial approach

elasticity degree to which a consumer is sensitive to changes in some product characteristic

external influences social and cultural aspects of life as a consumer

hedonic value value derived from the immediate gratification that comes from some activity

ideal points combination of product characteristics that provide the most value to an individual consumer or market segment

individual differences characteristic traits of individuals, including personality and lifestyle

internal influences things that go on inside of the mind and heart of the consumer

market segmentation separation of a market into groups based on the different demand curves associated with each group

marketing mix combination of product, pricing, promotion, and distribution strategies used to implement a marketing strategy

marketing strategy way a company goes about creating value for customers

marketing tactics ways marketing management is implemented; involves price, promotion, product, and distribution decisions

perceptual map tool used to depict graphically the positioning of competing products

product differentiation marketplace condition in which consumers do not view all competing products as identical to one another

product positioning way a product is perceived by a consumer

relationship quality degree of connectedness between a consumer and a retailer, brand, or service provider

situational influences things unique to a time or place that can affect consumer decision making and the value received from consumption

social environment elements that specifically deal with the way other people influence consumer decision making and value

strategy planned way of doing something

target market identified segment or segments of a market that a company serves

total value concept business practice wherein companies operate with the understanding that products provide value in multiple ways

utilitarian value value derived from a product that helps the consumer with some task

value a personal assessment of the net worth obtained from an activity

LO3 Apply the concepts of marketing strategy and marketing tactics to describe the way firms go about creating value for consumers.

A marketing strategy is the way a company goes about creating value for customers. Thus, strategy and value go hand in hand. Marketing strategy is most effective when a firm adopts the total value concept. The total value concept is practiced when companies operate with the understanding that products provide value in multiple ways. Many products and brands, for instance, provide benefits that produce utilitarian value and some that provide hedonic value.

LO4 Explain the way market characteristics like market segmentation and product differentiation affect marketing strategy.

Market segmentation is the separation of a market into groups based on the different demand curves associated with each group. Product differentiation is a marketplace condition in which consumers do not view all competing products as identical to one another. Thus, if multiple segments are offered a unique product that closely matches their particular desires, all segments can receive high value. These characteristics affect the value consumers take from consumption. Individual market segments represent groups of consumers with similar tastes and thus receive value in much the same way as the other.

LO5 Analyze consumer markets using elementary perceptual maps.

Positioning refers to the way a product is perceived by a consumer. This can be represented by the amount and types of characteristic perceived. A standard marketing tool is a perceptual map. A perceptual map is used to depict the positioning of competing products graphically. Consumer ideal points also can be located on a perceptual map. Perceptual mapping can help marketers identify competitors, analyze the potential effect associated with changing the marketing mix, and spot opportunities in the marketplace.

LO6 Justify adopting the concept of consumers' lifetime value as an effective long-term orientation for many firms.

Customer Lifetime Value represents the approximate worth of a customer to a company in economic terms. Put another way, CLV is the overall profitability of an individual consumer. Thus, marketers can maximize the value they receive from exchange by concentrating their marketing efforts on consumers with high CLVs. From a business standpoint, firms that adopt the CLV as an important outcome are consumer-oriented in the long term.

The CB Idea Checklist

Question	Idea
What specific consumer needs and desires are involved?	
How is the product positioned? How is our position superior to competitors?	
How does the consumer actually receive value from this company?	
Where is this product consumed?	
Who is buying the product? Who is not buying the product?	
Why should a consumer buy this product? Why should a consumer avoid this product?	
When do consumers find the product the most valuable and least valuable?	
What are the key CVF elements involved in understanding the consumption process in this case?	
Is additional consumer research needed?	

Visit **4ltrpress.cengage.com/cb**
for additional study tools.

Chapter Summary

LO1 Understand the elements of consumer perception.

Perception can be thought of as a consumer's awareness and interpretation of reality. Perception essentially represents one's subjective reality. During the perceptual process, consumers are exposed to stimuli, devote attention to stimuli, and attempt to comprehend the stimuli. Exposure refers to the process of bringing some stimulus within the proximity of a consumer so that it can be sensed by one of the five human senses. Attention is the purposeful allocation of information processing capacity toward developing an understanding of some stimulus. Comprehension occurs when the consumer attempts to derive meaning from information that is received.

Objective and Subjective Reality Don't Always Match

Enough to Eat? May look like more than 500 grams

500 grams of food

Not Enough to Eat? May look like less than 500 grams

LO2 Know the phases in the consumer perception process.

Consumers develop perceptions through the perceptual process. The perceptual process consists of three stages: sensing some stimuli by seeing, hearing, smelling, tasting, or touching; organizing the input from these human senses; and reacting as a result of this organization. This perceptual process allows consumers to interpret stimuli.

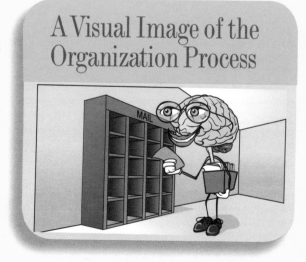

A Visual Image of the Organization Process

MAIL

Visit **4ltrpress.cengage.com/cb** for additional study tools.

Glossary Terms

absolute threshold level over which the strength of a stimulus must be greater so that it can be perceived

accommodation state that results when a stimulus shares some but not all of the characteristics that would lead it to fit neatly in an existing category and consumers must process exceptions to rules about the category

assimilation state that results when a stimulus has characteristics such that consumers readily recognize it as belonging to some specific category

attention purposeful allocation of information processing capacity toward developing an understanding of some stimulus

behaviorism approach to learning theory of learning that focuses on changes in behavior due to association without great concern for the cognitive mechanics of the learning process

classical conditioning change in behavior that occurs simply through associating some stimulus with another stimulus that naturally causes some reaction; a type of unintentional learning

cognitive organization process by which the human brain assembles sensory evidence into something recognizable

comprehension attempt to derive meaning from information

conditioned response response that results from exposure to a conditioned stimulus that was originally associated with the unconditioned stimulus

conditioned stimulus object or event that does not cause the desired response naturally but that can be conditioned to do so by pairing with an unconditioned stimulus

contrast state that results when a stimulus does not share enough in common with existing categories to allow categorization

discriminative stimuli stimuli that occur solely in the presence of a reinforcer

explicit memory memory that developed when the person was trying to remember the stimulus

exposure process of bringing some stimulus within proximity of a consumer so that the consumer can sense it with one of the five human senses

extinction process through which behaviors cease because of lack of reinforcement

implicit memory memory for things that a person did not try to remember

information processing perspective perspective that focuses on changes in thought and knowledge and how these precipitate behavioral changes

instrumental conditioning type of learning in which a behavioral response can be conditioned through reinforcement— either punishment or rewards associated with undesirable or desirable behavior

intentional learning process by which consumers set out to specifically learn information devoted to a certain subject

involuntary attention attention that is beyond the conscious control of a consumer

involvement the personal relevance toward, or interest in, a particular product

JMD just meaningful difference; smallest amount of change in a stimulus that would influence consumer consumption and choice

JND just noticeable difference; condition in which one stimulus is sufficiently stronger than another so that someone can actually notice that the two are not the same

learning change in behavior resulting from some interaction between a person and a stimulus

mere exposure effect effect that leads consumers to prefer a stimulus to which they've previously been exposed

negative reinforcement removal of harmful stimuli as a way of encouraging behavior

orientation reflex natural reflex that occurs as a response to something threatening

perception consumer's awareness and interpretation of reality

positive reinforcers reinforcers that take the form of a reward

preattentive effect that occurs without attention

product placements products that have been placed conspicuously in movies or television shows

punishers stimuli that decrease the likelihood that a behavior will persist

selective attention process of paying attention to only certain stimuli

selective distortion process by which consumers interpret information in ways that are biased by their previously held beliefs

LO3 Be able to apply the concept of the JND.

The JND (just noticeable difference) represents how much stronger one stimulus is relative to another so that someone can actually notice the two are not the same. The key to using the JND concept is to realize that when some positive change is made to a stimulus, the best strategy is usually to make the change in a big enough increment that consumers notice something has changed. When some negative change must be made, marketers may consider small incremental changes that are less likely to be noticed.

LO4 Apply the concepts of implicit and explicit memory.

Implicit memory is memory for things that a person did not try to remember. Thus, when someone learns something after only a simple exposure to a stimulus, implicit memory is the explanation. Preattentive processes like mere exposure can produce implicit memory. Information processing and cognitive learning result in explicit memory, wherein a consumer actively tries to remember the stimuli to which he or she has been exposed.

LO5 Know the ways in which a consumer's attention can be enhanced.

Attention is the purposeful allocation of information processing capacity toward developing an understanding of some stimulus. Consumer attention can be enhanced in a number of ways. These include the use of stronger stimuli, contrast, movement, and surprise.

LO6 Know the difference between intentional and unintentional learning.

Learning is a change in behavior. Learning takes place in one of two ways. Either consumers learn things without trying to do so or they actively expend some effort. The first approach corresponds more to a behavioral theory of learning, while the second approach corresponds more closely to an information processing, or cognitive learning, perspective. Learning without trying only requires that a consumer be exposed to a stimulus. In contrast, the information processing perspective requires an active learning and the ability to pay attention to information.

Discriminative Stimuli, Behavior, Reinforcer

DISCRIMINATIVE STIMULI → BEHAVIOR → REINFORCER

selective exposure process of screening out certain stimuli and purposely exposing oneself to other stimuli

sensation consumer's immediate response to a stimulus

shaping process through which a desired behavior is altered over time, in small increments

subliminal persuasion persuasion that results from subliminal processing

subliminal processing way that the human brain deals with very low-strength stimuli, so low that one cannot notice anything

unconditioned response response that occurs naturally as a result of exposure to an unconditioned stimulus

unconditioned stimulus stimulus with which a behavioral response is already associated

unintentional learning learning that occurs when behavior is modified through a consumer–stimulus interaction without any effortful allocation of cognitive processing capacity toward that stimulus

Weber's law law stating that a consumer's ability to detect differences between two levels of the stimulus decreases as the intensity of the initial stimulus increases

Visit **4ltrpress.cengage.com/cb** for additional study tools.

Chapter Summary

LO1 Understand the concept of comprehension and the factors that influence what gets comprehended.

Comprehension refers to the interpretation or understanding that a consumer develops about some attended stimulus. From an information processing perspective, comprehension results after a consumer has been exposed to and attends to some information. Several factors influence comprehension, including characteristics of the message, characteristics of the receiver, and characteristics of the environment.

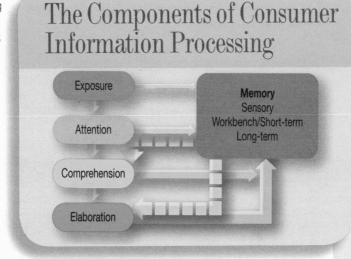

The Components of Consumer Information Processing

- Exposure
- Attention
- Comprehension
- Elaboration

Memory
Sensory
Workbench/Short-term
Long-term

LO2 Use the multiple store theory of memory to explain how knowledge, meaning, and value are inseparable.

The multiple store theory of memory explains how processing information involves three separate storage areas: sensory, workbench (short-term), and long-term memory. Everything sensed is recorded by sensory memory, but the record lasts too short a time to develop meaning. A small portion of this information is passed to the workbench, where already known concepts are retried from long-term memory and attached to new stimuli in a process known as meaningful encoding. All meaning is stored in an associative network residing in long-term memory. This network of knowledge links together concepts in a way that explains why things have value. Thus, value is rooted in meaning.

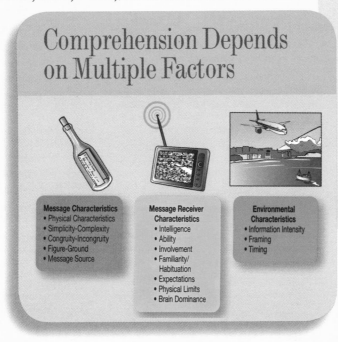

Comprehension Depends on Multiple Factors

Message Characteristics
- Physical Characteristics
- Simplicity-Complexity
- Congruity-Incongruity
- Figure-Ground
- Message Source

Message Receiver Characteristics
- Intelligence
- Ability
- Involvement
- Familiarity/Habituation
- Expectations
- Physical Limits
- Brain Dominance

Environmental Characteristics
- Information Intensity
- Framing
- Timing

Glossary Terms

adaptation level level of stimuli to which a consumer has become accustomed

associative network network of mental pathways linking all knowledge within memory; sometimes referred to as a semantic network

chunking process of grouping stimuli by meaning so that multiple stimuli can become one memory unit

cognitive interference notion that everything else that the consumer is exposed to while trying to remember something is also vying for processing capacity and thus interfering with memory and comprehension

comprehension attempt to derive meaning from information

counterarguments thoughts that contradict a message

credibility extent to which a source is considered to be both an expert in a given area and trustworthy

declarative network cognitive components that represent facts

dostats Russian word that can be roughly translated as acquiring things with great difficulty

dual coding coding that occurs when two different sensory traces are available to remember something

echoic storage storage of auditory information in sensory memory

elaboration extent to which a consumer continues processing a message even after an initial understanding is achieved

encoding process by which information is transferred from workbench memory to long-term memory for permanent storage

episodic memory memory for past events in one's life

exemplar concept within a schema that is the single best representative of some category; schema for something that really exists

expectations beliefs of what will happen in some situation

expertise amount of knowledge that a source is perceived to have about a subject

figure object that is intended to capture a person's attention, the focal part of any message

figure–ground distinction notion that each message can be separated into the focal point (figure) and the background (ground)

framing process wherein the very same information can take on different meanings from situation to situation or based on the way that information is presented

ground background in a message

habituation process by which continuous exposure to a stimulus affects the comprehension of, and response to, the stimulus

iconic storage storage of visual information in sensory memory and the idea that things are stored with a one-to-one representation with reality

information intensity amount of information available for a consumer to process within a given environment

likeability extent to which a consumer likes the message source

long-term memory repository for all information that a person has encountered

meaningful encoding coding that occurs when information from long-term memory is placed on the workbench and attached to the information on the workbench in a way that the information can be recalled and used later

memory psychological process by which knowledge is recorded

memory trace mental path by which some thought becomes active

message congruity extent to which a message is internally consistent and fits surrounding information

multiple store theory of memory theory that explains memory as utilizing three different storage areas within the human brain: sensory, workbench, and long-term

nodes concepts found in an associative network

nostalgia yearning to relive past events, which can also be positively associated with purchase behavior

paths representations of the association between nodes in an associative network

personal elaboration process by which a person imagines himself or herself somehow associating with a stimulus that is being processed

physical characteristics tangible attributes or the parts of the message that are sensed directly

LO3 Understand how consumers make associations with meaning as a key way to learn.

Consumers have alternatives for making associations with meaning. With meaningful encoding, consumers associate information in short-term memory with information in long-term memory. Chunking is one way that multiple stimuli can become a single memory unit. Chunking is related to meaningful encoding in that meaning can be used to facilitate this process. In other words, pieces of individual information are chunked together based on meaning. A group of randomly arranged letters is likely to be difficult to chunk. In this case, seven letters represent seven memory units. Arranged into a word, however, such as *meaning*, the seven memory units become one memory unit. Marketers who aid chunking are better able to convey information to consumers. Putting together associations with meaning is a key way to learn something.

LO4 Use the concept of associative networks to map relevant consumer knowledge.

An associative network, sometimes referred to as a semantic network, is the network of mental pathways linking all knowledge within memory. Associative networks can be drawn similarly to the way a road map would be constructed. All nodes are linked to all other nodes through a series of paths. Nodes with high strength tend to become conscious together based on their high strength of association.

LO5 Be able to apply the concept of a cognitive schema, including exemplars and prototypes, to understand how consumers react to new products.

A schema is the cognitive representation of a phenomenon that provides meaning to that entity. Thus, products and brands have schemata. To the extent that a new product or brand can share the same nodes or characteristics with an existing brand, consumers will more easily understand what the product does. Category exemplars and prototypes often provide the comparison standard for new brands.

priming context or environment that frames thoughts and therefore both value and meaning

prospect theory theory that suggests that a decision, or argument, can be framed in different ways and that the framing affects risk assessments consumers make

prototype schema that is the best representative of some category but that is not represented by an existing entity; conglomeration of the most associated characteristics of a category

repetition simple mechanism in which a thought is kept alive in short-term memory by mentally repeating the thought

response generation reconstruction of memory traces into a formed recollection of information

retrieval process by which information is transferred back into workbench memory for additional processing when needed

schema cognitive representation of a phenomenon that provides meaning to that entity

script schema representing an event

semantic coding type of coding wherein stimuli are converted to meaning that can be expressed verbally

sensory memory area in memory where a consumer stores things exposed to one of the five senses

social schema cognitive representation that gives a specific type of person meaning

social stereotype another word for social schema

spreading activation way cognitive activation spreads from one concept (or node) to another

support arguments thoughts that further support a message

tag small piece of coded information that helps with the retrieval of knowledge

trustworthiness how honest and unbiased the source is perceived to be

workbench memory storage area in the memory system where information is stored while it is being processed and encoded for later recall

Visit **4ltrpress.cengage.com/cb** for additional study tools.

Chapter Summary

LO1 Understand what initiates human behavior.

Human behavior, meaning the actions of a consumer, is initiated by the realization that something is needed to either maintain one's current status or to improve one's life status. Consumer motivations are the inner reasons or driving forces behind human actions as consumers are driven to address real needs. Needs are the first stage in the consumption process, which is in the center of the CVF.

LO2 Classify basic consumer motivations.

Consumer motivations can be classified a number of ways. Maslow's hierarchy of needs provides a classification mechanism by which consumer needs are prioritized. The most basic needs are physical, followed by needs for safety, belongingness, esteem and status, and self-actualization. Additionally, consumer motivations can be usefully divided into two groups: Utilitarian motivations drive the pursuit of utilitarian value, and hedonic motivations drive the pursuit of hedonic value.

An Illustration of Consumer Motivations According to Maslow's Hierarchy

Self-actualization—Learning a foreign language for fun

Esteem—Describing one's life on MySpace.com

Belongingness and love—Home and family

Safety and security—Gated apartment

Physiological needs—Dumpster dining (finding food in garbage)

Hedonic Value

Utilitarian Value

LO3 Describe consumer emotions and demonstrate how they help shape value.

Emotions are psychobiological reactions to human appraisals. Emotions are considered psychobiological because they involve psychological processing and physical responses. Emotions result from cognitive appraisals, and each emotion creates visceral responses so that they are tied to behavior in a very direct way. The close link between emotion and behavior means that marketing success is determined by the emotions that consumption

Glossary Terms

autobiographical memories cognitive representation of meaningful events in one's life

autonomic measures responses that are automatically recorded based on either automatic visceral reactions or neurological brain activity

bipolar situation wherein if one feels joy he or she cannot also experience sadness

cognitive appraisal theory school of thought proposing that specific types of appraisal thoughts can be linked to specific types of emotions

consumer affect feelings a consumer has about a particular product or activity

consumer involvement degree of personal relevance a consumer finds in pursuing value from a given act of consumption

emotional contagion extent to which an emotional display by one person influences the emotional state of a bystander

emotional effect on memory relatively superior recall for information presented with mild affective content compared to similar information presented in an affectively neutral way

emotional expressiveness extent to which a consumer shows outward behavioral signs and otherwise reacts obviously to emotional experiences

emotional intelligence awareness of the emotions experienced in a situation and the ability to control reactions to these emotions

emotional involvement type of deep personal interest that evokes strongly felt feelings simply from the thoughts or behavior associated with some object or activity

emotional labor effort put forth by service workers who have to overtly manage their own emotional displays as part of the requirements of the job

emotions psychobiological reactions to human appraisals

enduring involvement ongoing interest in some product or opportunity

flow extremely high emotional involvement in which a consumer is engrossed in an activity

hedonic motivation desire to experience something emotionally gratifying

homeostasis state of equilibrium wherein the body naturally reacts in a way so as to maintain a constant, normal bloodstream

Maslow's hierarchy of needs A theory of human motivation which describes consumers as addressing a finite set of prioritized needs

moderating variable variable that changes the nature of the relationship between two other variables

mood transient and general affective state

mood-congruent judgments evaluations in which the value of a target is influenced in a consistent way by one's mood

mood-congruent recall consumers will remember information better when the mood they are currently in matches the mood they were in when originally exposed to the information

motivations inner reasons or driving forces behind human actions as consumers are driven to address real needs

PAD self-report measure that asks respondents to rate feelings using semantic differential items. Acronym stands for pleasure–arousal–dominance.

product enthusiasts consumers with very high involvement in some product category

product involvement the personal relevance of a particular product category

psychobiological A response involving both psychological and physical human responses

schema-based affect emotions that become part of the meaning for a category (a schema)

self-improvement motivations motivations aimed at changing the current state to a level that is more ideal, not at simply maintaining the current state

shopping involvement personal relevance of shopping activities

situational involvement temporary interest in some imminent purchase situation

utilitarian motivation desire to acquire products that can be used to accomplish something

visceral responses certain feeling states that are tied to physical reactions/behavior in a very direct way

creates because consumers value positive emotional experiences. Emotions are particularly closely linked to hedonic value.

LO4 Apply different approaches to measuring consumer emotions.

Several different approaches for measuring emotion exist. Because of the visceral nature of emotions, autonomic measures can capture emotional experience by sensing changes in the body chemistry such as sweating or by sensing neurological activity. Unfortunately, such measures are usually obtrusive and interfere with the natural experience of emotion. Therefore, self-report approaches such as the PANAS and the PAD scale are popular for assessing consumer emotion. The PANAS assumes that positive and negative emotion can be experienced separately to some extent while the PAD scale assumes that emotions such as pleasure and displeasure are bipolar opposites.

LO5 Appreciate the fact that not all consumers express emotions in the same way.

Several individual difference characteristics influence the way consumers respond emotionally and react to emotions in consumption situation. For example, high levels of the personality trait neuroticism tend to lead to consumers experiencing relatively high levels of negative emotion. Additionally, in any given consumption situation, consumers are likely to vary in emotional involvement. Consumers with high emotional involvement can experience intense emotions during consumption and can even reach the level of a flow experience. Furthermore, consumers have different levels of emotional expressiveness. Although men and women tend to experience the same amounts of emotion, women tend to be more emotionally expressive.

LO6 Define the concept of schema-based affect.

Perhaps no concept better illustrates how emotion and cognition are wired together than schema-based affect. Schema-based affect represents the fact that emotions become part of the meaning for any category or thing. The feelings associated with a category are activated along with the activation of the schema. When a brand schema becomes associated with high levels of positive affect, the brand has high brand equity. Similarly, a brand that is associated with high levels of negative schema-based affect is probably in trouble.

Examples of Schema-Based Affect

Schema	Affect	Typical Consumer Reaction
Disney	Joyfulness, fun	Consumers have increased brand equity and lower price sensitivity for Disney products.
Individual countries (United Kingdom, France, United States, Japan, Israel, China)	Consumers may have slightly different affect associated with each country	Consumers are less favorable toward products manufactured in countries for which that consumer's schema evokes negative affect.
Telemarketing	Aggravation	Consumers often hang up quickly as a built-in avoidance response.
Baby	Tenderness, warmth	Products associated with babies are viewed more favorably.
Sports star	Excitement	Consumers may generalize excitement to products and services endorsed by the star.
Stereotypes	Each stereotype evokes slightly different affect	The affect associated with the stereotype can cause consumers to be more or less willing to approach and may alter information processing.

Visit **4ltrpress.cengage.com/cb**
for additional study tools.

Chapter Summary

LO1 Define personality and know how various approaches to studying personality can be applied to consumer behavior.

Personality can be defined as "the totality of thoughts, emotions, intentions, and behaviors that people exhibit consistently as they adapt to their environment." There are several different ways to study the human personality. Freud's psychoanalytic approach received considerable attention in the early days of consumer research. Trait theory, wherein researchers examine specific traits that relate to consumption, has also received much research attention. With this approach, consumer researchers have focused on both single-trait and multiple-trait perspectives. The five-factor model is a popular multiple-trait model. The personology approach combines both motivational theory and personality.

LO2 Discuss major traits that have been examined in consumer research.

Value consciousness refers to the tendency of consumers to be highly focused on receiving value in their purchases. Materialism refers to the extent to which material goods have importance in a consumer's life. Consumers who are relatively materialistic view possessions as a means to achieving happiness and symbols of success. Innovativeness refers to the degree to which an individual is open to new ideas and tends to be relatively early in adopting new products, services, or experiences. Innovativeness has been shown to relate to a number of consumer behaviors, including new product adoption, novelty seeking, information seeking, and online shopping. Complaint-proneness refers to the extent to which consumers tend to voice complaints about unsatisfactory product purchases. Consumers with a strong degree of complaint-proneness tend to be middle-aged, well-educated, upwardly mobile, and assertive. Competitiveness refers to the extent to which consumers strive to be better than others.

Five-Factor Model

Personality Trait	Description
Extroversion	Talkative, outgoing
Agreeableness	Kindhearted, sympathetic
Openness to Experience	Creative, open to new ideas, imaginative
Stability	Even-keeled, avoids mood swings
Conscientiousness	Precise, efficient, organized

Source: Based on McCrae, R. R., and P. T. Costa (2005), *Personality in Adulthood: A Five-Factor Theory Perspective*, 2nd ed., New York, Guilford.

Glossary Terms

aggregation approach approach to studying personality in which behavior is assessed at a number of points in time

AIO statements activity, interest, and opinion statements that are used in lifestyle studies

brand personality collection of human characteristics that can be associated with a brand

competitiveness enduring tendency to strive to be better than others

complaint proneness extent to which consumers tend to voice complaints about unsatisfactory product purchases

demographics observable, statistical aspects of populations such as age, gender, or income

ego component in psychoanalytic theory that attempts to balance the struggle between the superego and the id

five-factor model multiple-trait perspective that proposes that the human personality consists of five traits: agreeableness, extraversion, openness to experience (or creativity), conscientiousness, and neuroticism (or stability)

geodemographic techniques techniques that combine data on consumer expenditures and socioeconomic variables with geographic information in order to identify commonalities in consumption patterns of households in various regions

hierarchical approaches to personality approaches to personality inquiry that assume that personality traits exist at varying levels of abstraction

id the personality component in psychoanalytic theory that focuses on pleasure-seeking motives and immediate gratification

idiographic perspective approach to personality that focuses on understanding the complexity of each individual consumer

individual difference variables descriptions of how individual consumers differ according to specific trait patterns of behavior

innovativeness degree to which an individual is open to new ideas and tends to be relatively early in adopting new products, services, or experiences

lifestyles distinctive modes of living, including how people spend their time and money

materialism extent to which material goods have importance in a consumer's life

motivational research era era in consumer research that focused heavily on psychoanalytic approaches

multiple-trait approach approach in trait research wherein the focus remains on combinations of traits

nomothetic perspective variable-centered approach to personality that focuses on particular traits that exist across a number of people

personality totality of thoughts, emotions, intentions, and behaviors that a person exhibits consistently as he or she adapts to the environment

pleasure principle principle, found in psychoanalytic theory, that describes the factor that motivates pleasure-seeking behavior within the id

PRIZM popular geodemographic technique that stands for Potential Ratings Index by ZIP Market

psychoanalytic approach to personality approach to personality research, advocated by Sigmund Freud, that suggests personality results from a struggle between inner motives and societal pressures to follow rules and expectations

psychographics quantitative investigation of consumer lifestyles

reality principle the principle in psychoanalytic theory under which the ego attempts to satisfy the id within societal constraints

self-concept totality of thoughts and feelings that an individual has about himself or herself

self-congruency theory theory that proposes that much of consumer behavior can be explained by the congruence of a consumer's self-concept with the image of typical users of a focal product

self-esteem positivity of the self-concept that one holds

semiotics study of symbols and their meanings

single-trait approach approach in trait research wherein the focus is on one particular trait

superego component in psychoanalytic theory that works against the id by motivating behavior that matches the expectations and norms of society

symbolic interactionism perspective that proposes that consumers live in a symbolic environment and interpret the myriad of symbols around them and that members of a society agree on the meanings of symbols

LO3 Understand why lifestyles and psychographics are important to the study of consumer behavior.

Given that lifestyle concepts give marketers much valuable information about consumers, lifestyle studies have been popular with consumer researchers for many years. Purchase patterns are often influenced heavily by consumer lifestyles, and for this reason marketers often target consumers based on lifestyles. Psychographics, the quantitative investigation of consumer lifestyles, is well-suited to help marketers in this process. Both VALS and PRIZM represent important psychographic techniques. The great advantage of lifestyles and psychographics is the ability to capture information in a specific, relevant consumer context.

LO4 Comprehend the role of the self-concept in consumer behavior.

The self-concept, defined as "the totality of thoughts and feelings that an individual has about himself or herself," is another important topic in consumer behavior research. Consumers are motivated to act in accordance with their self-concepts, and for this reason, several product choices can be related to the self-concept. A consumer can hold a number of different concepts about the self, including the actual self, the ideal self, the social self, the ideal social self, the possible self, and the extended self.

LO5 Understand the concept of self-congruency and how it applies to consumer behavior issues.

Self-congruency theory helps to explain why a consumer is motivated to purchase products that match his or her self-concept. Consumers often desire to buy products that match their own self-concepts, and marketers segment markets based on the match between consumer self-concept and product attributes.

For consumers, body piercing and tattooing have become more popular than ever.

© ISTOCKPHOTO.COM/CHRIS GRAMLY

trait distinguishable characteristic that describes one's tendency to act in a relatively consistent manner

trait approach to personality approaches in personality research that focus on specific consumer traits as motivators of various consumer behaviors

VALS popular psychographic method in consumer research that divides consumers into groups based on resources and consumer behavior motivations

value consciousness the extent to which consumers tend to maximize what they receive from a transaction as compared to what they give

Visit **4ltrpress.cengage.com/cb** for additional study tools.

Chapter Summary

LO1 Define attitudes and describe attitude components.

Consumer attitudes are relatively enduring evaluations of objects, products, services, issues, or people. Attitudes have three components. The first component is a cognitive component. This component consists of the beliefs that consumers have about products and their features. The next component is the affective component. This component consists of the feelings that consumers have about the product and its features. The last component is a behavioral component, which describes how consumers act toward the object in question.

LO2 Describe the functions of attitudes.

Several functions of attitudes have been presented including the utilitarian, ego-defensive, value-expressive, and knowledge functions. The utilitarian function refers to the use of attitudes to gain something that is valued. The ego-defensive function refers to the use of attitudes to protect oneself from harm. The value-expressive function refers to the use of attitudes to express a consumer's core beliefs and ideologies. The knowledge function refers to the use of attitudes to simplify consumer decision making.

LO3 Understand how the hierarchy of effects concept applies to attitude theory.

The hierarchy of effects approach explains the process through which beliefs, affect, and behavior occurs. These hierarchies depend upon the consumer's buying situation. In a high-involvement context, consumer beliefs are formed, followed by affect, and finally by behavior. Low-involvement, experiential, and behavioral influence hierarchies are also quite frequent in consumer behavior.

Hierarchy of Effects

Purchase Context	Hierarchy of Effects
High involvement	Belief–affect–behavior
Low involvement	Belief–behavior–affect
Experiential	Affect–behavior–belief
Behavioral Influence	Behavior–belief–affect

LO4 Comprehend the major consumer attitude models.

Two major approaches to measuring consumer attitudes were presented in this chapter: the attitude-toward-the-object (ATO) and behavioral intentions models. The ATO model includes three key elements: salient beliefs, strength of beliefs, and evaluation of attributes. The behavioral intentions model includes two key elements: attitude toward a behavior and subjective norms. These models are commonly used by consumer

Visit **4ltrpress.cengage.com/cb**
for additional study tools.

Glossary Terms

ABC approach to attitudes approach that suggests that attitudes encompass one's **a**ffect, **b**ehavior, and **c**ognitions (or "beliefs") toward an object

attitude tracking effort of a marketer or researcher to track changes in consumer attitudes over time

attitude-behavior consistency extent to which a strong relationship exists between attitudes and actual behavior

attitude-toward-the-object model attitude model that considers three key elements including beliefs consumers have about salient attributes, the strength of the belief that an object possesses the attribute, and evaluation of the particular attribute

attitudes relatively enduring overall evaluations of objects, products, services, issues, or people

attribute feature of a product or object

balance theory theory that states that consumers are motivated to maintain perceived consistency in the relations found in a system

behavioral intentions model model, developed to improve upon the ATO model, that focuses on behavioral intentions, subjective norms, and attitude toward a particular behavior

central cues information presented in a message about the product itself, its attributes, or the consequences of its use

central route to persuasion path to persuasion found in ELM where the consumer has high involvement, motivation, and/or ability to process a message

compensatory model attitudinal model wherein low ratings for one attribute are compensated for by higher ratings on another

consistency principle principle that states that human beings prefer consistency among their beliefs, attitudes, and behaviors

counterarguments arguments that contradict a message

ego-defensive function of attitudes function of attitudes whereby attitudes work as defense mechanisms for consumers

elaboration likelihood model attitudinal change model that shows attitudes are changed based on differing levels of consumer involvement through either central or peripheral processing

functional theory of attitudes theory of attitudes that suggests that attitudes perform four basic functions

hierarchy of effects attitude approach that suggests that affect, behavior, and cognitions form in a sequential order

knowledge function of attitudes function of attitudes whereby attitudes allow consumers to simplify decision-making processes

matchup hypothesis hypothesis that states that a source feature is most effective when it is matched with relevant products

message effects how the appeal of a message and its construction affects persuasiveness

peripheral cues nonproduct-related information presented in a message

peripheral route to persuasion path to persuasion found in ELM where the consumer has low involvement, motivation, and/or ability to process a message

persuasion attempt to change attitudes

primacy effect effect that occurs when the information placed early in a message has the most impact

recency effect effect that occurs when the information placed late in a message has the most impact

social judgment theory theory that proposes that consumers compare incoming information to their existing attitudes about a particular object or issue and that attitude change depends upon how consistent the information is with the initial attitude

source effects characteristics of a source that impact the persuasiveness of a message

support arguments arguments that support a message

theory of planned action attitudinal measurement approach that expands upon the behavioral intentions model by including a perceived control component

utilitarian function of attitudes function of attitudes in which consumers use attitudes as ways to maximize rewards and minimize punishment

value-expressive function of attitudes function of attitudes whereby attitudes allow consumers to express their core values, self-concept, and beliefs to others

researchers who focus on understanding the elements that comprise consumer attitudes. The approaches are also useful for marketing managers who develop marketing campaigns.

ATO Model

$$A_o = \sum_{I=1}^{N} (b_i)(e_i)$$

A_o = attitude toward the object in question (or A_{brand})
b_i = strength of belief that the object possesses attribute i
e_i = evaluation of the attractiveness or goodness of attribute i
N = number of attributes and beliefs

LO5 Describe attitude change theories and their role in persuasion.

There were a number of major approaches to changing attitudes presented in this chapter. The first approach focuses on the ATO model. According to this approach, attitudes can be changed by changing the strength of beliefs about attributes, by adding new beliefs to the attitude equation, by changing the evaluation of attributes, or by altering the schema-based affect for the brand/object. The second approach was the behavioral influence approach, which focuses on changing behaviors directly. The third approach was the schema-based affect approach. This approach focuses on changing affect found in product schemas. The fourth approach was the balance theory approach. This approach suggests that consumers seek consistency in systems that are comprised of three elements: the observer, another person, and an object. Attitudes toward an object are affected by the perceived relations found with the system. The fifth approach was the elaboration likelihood model (ELM). The ELM suggests that persuasion occurs as the result of processing within one of two routes: a central route and a peripheral route. In high-involvement situations, the central route is activated, and in low-involvement situations, the peripheral route is activated. Attitude change is usually longer lasting when persuasion occurs in the central route. The sixth and final approach to attitude change was the social judgment theory approach. This theory suggests that an incoming message is compared to an initial attitudinal position and an assimilation or contrast effect occurs depending on the perceived closeness of the incoming message to the original attitude.

LO6 Understand how message and source effects influence persuasion.

Both source and message effects play important roles in persuasion. Message effects include issues related to the overall content and construction of the message. Sex appeals, humor appeals, and fear appeals are all used frequently by marketers. Source effects, or effects that are attributed to the spokesperson or company, are also important. Source effects include source credibility, source likeability, source attractiveness, and source meaningfulness.

Visit **4ltrpress.cengage.com/cb** for additional study tools.

Chapter Summary

LO1 Understand how culture provides the true meaning of objects and activities.

Culture is the set of commonly held societal beliefs that define what behaviors are socially gratifying among a societal group. These societal beliefs are sometimes referred to as core societal values (CSV), or cultural values. These beliefs frame everyday life and provide a reference point with which to judge behaviors. Acceptable behaviors become norms of the society, and when consumers act inconsistent with these norms, they face negative repercussions in the form of cultural sanctions. Culturally consistent behaviors are rewarded and are thus associated with greater value than culturally inconsistent behaviors.

LO2 Use the key dimensions of core societal values to understand the concept of cultural distance.

Five key CSV dimensions are discussed in the chapter: individualism–collectivism, power distance, masculinity–femininity, uncertainty avoidance, and long-term orientation. Societies that share similar CSV profiles, like the CANZUS nations, tend to have low cultural distance. In contrast, societies with very different profiles, such as most Arab nations, have high cultural distance. Chances are that high cultural distance means consumers in those different cultures find value in significantly different behaviors. Therefore, cultural distance may be at least as important as geographic distance when a company is facing a decision about serving a foreign market.

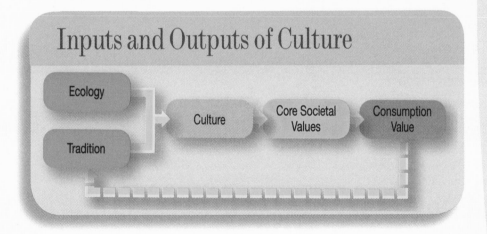

Inputs and Outputs of Culture

Ecology
Tradition
→ Culture → Core Societal Values → Consumption Value

LO3 Define acculturation and enculturation.

Acculturation and enculturation are two important consumer socialization processes. Acculturation is the process by which consumers come to learn a culture other than their natural, native culture. Enculturation is the process by which consumers learn their native culture. In both cases, the learning takes place through both formal and informal methods. Much of this learning occurs through the process of modeling. Modeling means that consumers try to mimic the behavior of others within the societal group. When the behavior is consistent with cultural norms, the rewards the consumers receive help to shape their overall pattern of behavior.

Visit **4ltrpress.cengage.com/cb** for additional study tools.

Glossary Terms

acculturation process by which consumers come to learn a culture other than their natural, native culture

body language nonverbal communication cues signaled by somatic responses

BRIC acronym that refers to the collective economies of Brazil, Russia, India, and China

CANZUS acronym that refers to the close similarity in values between Canada, Australia, New Zealand, and the United States

Chindia combined market and business potential of China and India

collectivism extent to which an individual's life is intertwined with a large cohesive group

consumer culture commonly held societal beliefs that define what is socially gratifying

consumer ethnocentrism belief among consumers that their ethnic group is superior to others and that the products that come from their native land are superior to other products

core societal values (CSV), or cultural values commonly agreed upon consensus about the most preferable ways of living within a society

cultural distance representation of how disparate one nation is from another in terms of their CSV

cultural norm rule that specifies the appropriate consumer behavior in a given situation within a specific culture

cultural sanction penalty associated with performing a nongratifying or culturally inconsistent behavior

dialects variations of a common language

ecological factors physical characteristics that describe the physical environment and habitat of a particular place

enculturation way a person learns his or her native culture

ethnic identification degree to which consumers feel a sense of belonging to the culture of their ethnic origins

etiquette customary mannerisms consumers use in common social situations

femininity sex role distinction within a group that emphasizes the prioritization of relational variables such as caring, conciliation, and community; CSV opposite of masculinity

glocalization idea that marketing strategy may be global but the implementation of that strategy at the marketing tactics level should be local

guanxi (pronounced gawn-zeye) Chinese term for a way of doing business in which parties must first invest time and resources in getting to know one another and becoming comfortable with one another before consummating any important deal

individualism extent to which people are expected to take care of themselves and their immediate families

long-term orientation values consistent with Confucian philosophy and a prioritization of future rewards over short-term benefits

masculinity sex role distinction within a group that values assertiveness and control; CSV opposite of femininity

metric equivalence statistical tests used to validate the way people use numbers to represent quantities across cultures

modeling process of imitating others' behavior; a form of observational learning

nonverbal communication information passed through some nonverbal act

power distance extent to which authority and privileges are divided among different groups within society and the extent to which these facts of life are accepted by the people within the society

purchasing power parity (PPP) total size of the consumer market in each country in terms of total buying power

quartet of institutions four groups responsible for communicating the CSVs through both formal and informal processes from one generation to another: family, school, church, and media

sex roles societal expectations for men and women among members of a cultural group

shaping socialization process by which consumers' behaviors slowly adapt to a culture through a series of rewards and sanctions

socialization learning through observation of and the active processing of information about lived, everyday experience

LO4 List fundamental elements of verbal and nonverbal communication.

Verbal communication refers to the transfer of information through the literal spoken or written word. One of the key elements of verbal communication is comprehension across languages. When communicating with consumers in a different language, the process of translation–back translation is important to make sure the intended message is really being communicated. Nonverbal communication refers to elements such as body language, etiquette, symbols, and the meaning of time and space, as well as the way a consumer signals agreement. High-context cultures depend heavily on nonverbal communication.

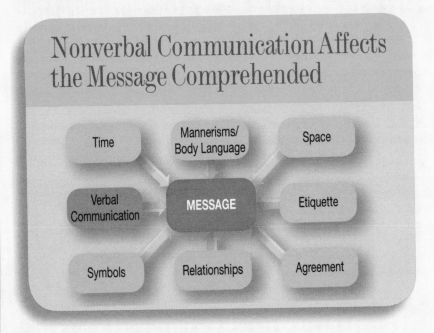

LO5 Discuss current emerging consumer markets and scan for opportunities.

New consumer markets have emerged over the last few years. The fall of communism, advances in technology, and the desire for firms to obtain low-cost labor have enabled consumers in places like China and Russia to participate more fully in the free-market economy. In fact, the acronym BRIC refers to the combined market power of consumers in Brazil, Russia, India, and China. Firms can have success marketing to these emerging consumer markets, but they must first understand each culture's CSV profile and the proper way to communicate with consumers in those markets.

subculture culture existing at a lower level than overall culture

tradition customs and accepted ways of everyday behavior in a given culture

translational equivalence two phrases share the same precise meaning in two different cultures

uncertainty avoidance extent to which a culture is uncomfortable with things that are ambiguous or unknown

verbal communication transfer of information through either the literal spoken or written word

world teen culture speculation that teenagers around the world are more similar to each other than to people from other generations in the same culture

Visit **4ltrpress.cengage.com/cb**
for additional study tools.

Chapter Summary

LO1 Understand the different types of reference groups that influence consumers and how reference groups influence value perceptions.

A number of different types of reference groups influence consumers. A primary group is a group that includes members who have frequent, direct contact. A secondary group is a group that has much less contact than in a primary group, but these groups still influence consumer behavior. A formal group is a group in which consumers formally become members. An informal group is a group that has no membership or application requirements and codes of conduct may be nonexistent. An aspirational group is a group in which a consumer desires to become a member. A dissociative group is a group that a consumer wants to avoid being perceived as belonging to. Belonging to groups can be quite valuable for consumers. The benefits associated with membership often outweigh the costs associated with membership. Also, hedonic value is often derived from belonging to groups and from participating in group activities. Group members often receive economic, or utilitarian, value from membership as well.

LO2 Describe the various types of social power that reference groups exert on members.

Social power refers to the ability of an individual or a group to alter the actions of others. Social power is divided into specific categories that include referent power, legitimate power, expert power, reward power, and coercive power. Referent power exists when a consumer wishes to model his or her behaviors after a group or another person. Here, the consumer imitates the behaviors and attitudes of the referent others because of their liking or admiration for that person or group of people. Legitimate power is exerted when one's position in a group determines the level of social power he or she can hold over group members. Expert power refers to the ability of a group or individual to influence a consumer due to his or her knowledge of, or experience with, a specific subject matter. Reward power exists when groups are able to reward members for compliance with expectations. Finally, coercive power exists when groups have the ability to sanction or punish members for noncompliance with group expectations.

Types of Social Power

Referent Power
Legitimate Power
Expert Power
Reward Power
Coercive Power

LO3 Comprehend the difference between informational, utilitarian, and value-expressive reference group influence.

The informational influence of groups refers to the ways in which consumers use the behaviors and attitudes of reference groups as information for making their own decisions. The utilitarian influence of groups refers to the ways in which consumers conform to group expectations in order to receive a reward or avoid punishment. The value-expressive influence of groups refers to the ways in which consumers internalize a group's values or the extent to which consumers join groups in order to express their own closely held values and beliefs.

Visit **4ltrpress.cengage.com/cb** for additional study tools.

Glossary Terms

aspirational group group in which a consumer desires to become a member

attention to social comparison information (ATSCI) individual difference variable that assesses the extent to which a consumer is concerned about how other people react to his or her behavior

boomerang kids young adults, between the ages of 18 and 34, who move back home with their parents after they graduate from college

brand community groups of consumers who develop relationships based on shared interests or product usage

buzz marketing marketing efforts that focus on generating excitement among consumers and that are spread from consumer to consumer

conformity result of group influence in which an individual yields to the attitudes and behaviors or others

connected self-schema self conceptualization of the extent to which a consumer perceives himself or herself as being an integral part of a group

consumer socialization the process through which young consumers develop attitudes and learn skills that help them function in the marketplace

diffusion process way in which new products are adopted and spread throughout a marketplace

dissociative group group to which a consumer does not want to belong

extended family three or more generations of family members

family household at least two people who are related by blood or marriage who occupy a housing unit

formal group group in which a consumer formally becomes a member

group influence ways in which group members influence attitudes, behaviors, and opinions of others within the group

guerrilla marketing marketing of a product using unconventional means

household decision making process by which decisions are made in household units

household life cycle (HLC) segmentation technique that acknowledges that changes in family composition and income alter household demand for products and services

informal group group that has no membership or application requirements and that may have no codes of conduct

informational influence ways in which a consumer uses the behaviors and attitudes of reference groups as information for making his or her own decisions

market maven consumer who spreads information about all types of products and services that are available in the marketplace

nuclear family a mother, a father, and a set of siblings

online social network a computer-mediated portal that allows consumers to post information about themselves, their hobbies, their interests, and products that they enjoy

opinion leader consumer who has a great deal of influence on the behavior of others relating to product adoption and purchase

peer pressure extent to which group members feel pressure to behave in accordance with group expectations

primary group group that includes members who have frequent, direct contact with one another

reference group individuals who have significant relevance for a consumer and who have an impact on the consumer's evaluations, aspirations, and behavior

sandwich generation consumers who must take care of both their own children and their aging parents

secondary group group to which a consumer belongs whose contact is less frequent than that found in a primary group

separated self-schema self conceptualization of the extent to which a consumer perceives himself or herself as distinct and separate from others

sex role orientation (SRO) family's set of beliefs regarding the ways in which household decisions are reached

social power ability of an individual or a group to alter the actions of others

stealth marketing guerrilla marketing tactic in which consumers do not realize that they are being targeted for a marketing message

surrogate consumer consumer who is hired by another to provide input into a purchase decision

LO4 Understand the importance of word-of-mouth communications in consumer behavior.

Word-of-mouth refers to information about products, services, and experiences that is transmitted from consumer to consumer. WOM is influential because consumers tend to believe other consumers more than they believe advertisements and explicit marketing messages from companies. Consumers tend to place more emphasis on negative WOM than on positive WOM. It is also important because in today's information age, WOM can be spread to millions of consumers very easily on the Internet via e-mail or on social networking websites.

LO5 Comprehend the role of household influence in consumer behavior.

The family unit is a very important primary reference group for consumers. Family members typically have a great deal of influence over one another's attitudes, thoughts, and behaviors. This is also true of "nonfamily" households. Because household members often have frequent, close contact with one another, they often have much influence on the behavior of one another. The role that each household member plays in the household decision-making process depends on the beliefs and sex orientation of each individual household.

Traditional Household Life Cycle Categories

	Under 35 Years	35 – 64 Years	Older than 64 Years
One-adult household	Bachelor 1	Bachelor 2	Bachelor 3
Two-adult household	Young Couple	Childless Couple	Older Couple
Two adults + children	Full Nest 1 (children < 6 years old) Full Nest 2 (children > 6 years old)	Delayed Full Nest (children < 6 years old) Full Nest 3 (children > 6 years old)	
One adult + children	Single Parent 1 (children < 6 years old) Single Parent 2 (children > 6 years old)	Single Parent 3	

Adapted from Mary C. Gilly and Ben M. Enis (1982), "Recycling the Family Lifecycle: A Proposal for Redefinition," in *Advances in Consumer Research*, Vol. 9, Andrew A. Mitchell, ed., Ann Arbor, MI: Association for Consumer Research, 271–276.

susceptibility to interpersonal influence individual difference variable that assesses a consumer's need to enhance his or her image with others by acquiring and using products, conforming to the expectations of others, and learning about products by observing others

utilitarian influence ways in which a consumer conforms to group expectations in order to receive a reward or avoid punishment

value-expressive influence ways in which a consumer internalizes a group's values or the extent to which a consumer joins groups in order to express his or her own closely held values and beliefs

viral marketing marketing method that uses online technologies to facilitate WOM by having consumers spread messages through their online conversations

word-of-mouth (WOM) information about products, services, and experiences that is transmitted from consumer to consumer

Visit **4ltrpress.cengage.com/cb** for additional study tools.

Chapter Summary

LO1 Understand how value varies with situations.

The value a consumer obtains from a purchase or consumption act varies based on the context in which the act takes place. These contextual effects are known as situational influences, meaning effects independent of enduring consumer, brand, or product characteristics. Contextual effects can involve things related to time, place, or antecedent conditions. They also can affect consumer information processing, shopping including purchase situations, and actual consumption. Situational influences change the desirability of consuming things and therefore change the value of these things. Situational influences can also override consumer brand preferences in many product categories.

LO2 Know the different ways that time affects consumer behavior.

The term *temporal factors* is sometimes used to refer to situational characteristics related to time. Time can affect consumer behavior by creating time pressure. A consumer facing time pressure may not be able to process information related to making the best choice. The time of year can affect consumer behavior through seasonality. Cyclical patterns of consumption exist for many products, like champagne, which is predominantly sold during the holidays. The time of day can also influence consumption significantly. For instance, most consumers do not want gumbo for breakfast. But, for lunch or dinner, gumbo is great!

LO3 Analyze shopping as a consumer activity using the different categories of shopping activities.

Shopping can be defined as the set of value-producing consumer activities that directly increase the likelihood that something will be purchased. Shopping activities are very strongly shaped by the sense of place and, therefore, are highly relevant to understanding how situations influence consumption. Shopping activities can be divided into four categories: acquisitional, epistemic, experiential, and impulsive. Each category is associated with a different orientation toward buying things and receiving shopping value.

Shopping Activities and Shopping Value

High Hedonic Value

- Experiential—outshopping at a mall in a neighboring city
- Impulsive—deciding to buy four pairs of shoes at an unannounced sale
- Epistemic (ongoing)— visiting a wine store to taste new wines
- Epistemic (situational)— searching for warranty information about air conditioners
- Acquisitional—stopping at a convenience store for gas and a quart of milk

Low Utilitarian Value · **High Utilitarian Value**

Low Hedonic Value

Visit **4ltrpress.cengage.com/cb** for additional study tools.

Glossary Terms

acquisitional shopping activities oriented toward a specific, intended purchase or purchases

action-oriented consumers with a high capacity to self-regulate their behavior

advertiming ad buys that include a schedule that runs the advertisement primarily at times when customers will be most receptive to the message

affective quality retail positioning that emphasizes a unique environment, exciting décor, friendly employees, and, in general, the feelings experienced in a retail place

antecedent conditions situational characteristics that a consumer brings to information processing

atmospherics emotional nature of an environment or the feelings created by the total aura of physical attributes that comprise a physical environment

background music music played below the audible threshold that would make it the center of attention

circadian cycle rhythm (level of energy) of the human body that varies with the time of day

congruity how consistent the elements of an environment are with one another

consumer self-regulation tendency for consumers to inhibit outside, or situational, influences from interfering with shopping intentions

crowding density of people and objects within a given space

epistemic shopping activities oriented toward acquiring knowledge about products

experiential shopping recreationally oriented activities designed to provide interest, excitement, relaxation, fun, or some other desired feeling

fit how appropriate the elements of a given environment are

foreground music music that becomes the focal point of attention and can have strong effects on a consumer's willingness to approach or avoid an environment

functional quality retail positioning that emphasizes tangible things like a wide selection of goods, low prices, guarantees, and knowledgeable employees

hedonic shopping value worth of an activity because the time spent doing the activity itself is personally gratifying

impulsive consumption consumption acts characterized by spontaneity, a diminished regard for consequences, and a need for self-fulfillment

impulsive shopping spontaneous activities characterized by a diminished regard for consequences, spontaneity, and a desire for immediate self-fulfillment

impulsivity personality trait that represents how sensitive a consumer is to immediate rewards

mental budgeting memory accounting for recent spending

nonlinear effect a plot of the effect by the amount of crowding, which does not make a straight line

olfactory refers to humans' physical and psychological processing of smells

outshopping shopping in a city or town to which consumers must travel rather than in their own hometowns

personal shopping value (PSV) overall subjective worth of a shopping activity considering all associated costs and benefits

retail personality way a retail store is defined in the mind of a shopper based on the combination of functional and affective qualities

seasonality regularly occurring conditions that vary with the time of year

servicescape physical environment in which consumer services are performed

shopping set of value-producing consumer activities that directly increase the likelihood that something will be purchased

situational influences things that influence consumers that are independent of enduring consumer, brand, or product characteristics

social environment the other customers and employees in a service or shopping environment

state-oriented consumers with a low capacity to self-regulate their behavior

temporal factors situational characteristics related to time

time pressure urgency to act based on some real or self-imposed deadline

unplanned shopping shopping activity that shares some, but not all, characteristics of truly impulsive consumer behavior; being characterized by situational memory, a utilitarian orientation, and feelings of spontaneity

utilitarian shopping value worth obtained because some shopping task or job is completed successfully

LO4 Distinguish the concepts of unplanned, impulse, and compulsive consumer behavior.

The line between unplanned and impulse is not always clear because some unplanned acts are impulsive and many impulsive acts are unplanned. Simple unplanned purchases usually lack any real emotional involvement or significant amounts of self-gratification. Additionally, unplanned purchases often involve only minimal negative consequences and thus fail to really qualify as having negative consequences at all. Compulsive acts are distinguished from impulsive acts by the relative degree of harmfulness associated with them. Impulsive acts are relatively harmless and, in fact, can have significant positive outcomes in terms of a consumer's emotional well-being. Compulsive acts, however, are associated with a consumer whose behavior is either self-detrimental or truly harmful to another consumer.

LO5 Use the concept of atmospherics to create consumer value.

A store's atmosphere can create value through facilitating either the task of shopping or the gratification of the shopping experience itself. Each retail or service place is characterized by a particular atmosphere. An atmosphere that greatly facilitates the shopping task can be designed. For example, convenience stores have redesigned their sales floors and taken out substantial numbers of product offerings. The result is that the consumer can complete the task of getting a needed product in less time. An atmosphere can also simply be more emotionally pleasant and therefore gratifying to be in. Some modern retail outlets are retail theaters with multiple opportunities for consumers to be entertained regardless of whether they purchase anything.

The Qualities of an Environment

- Knowledgable Employees
- Low Prices
- Wide Selection
- Convenient
  - Shopping
  - Parking
  - Payment
  - Hours
  - Location

Functional Quality

ATMOSPHERE

- Friendly Employees
- Colors
- Lights
- Music
- Odors
- Prestigious Brands
- Other Shoppers
  - Crowds
  - Ease of Movement

Affective Quality

LO6 Understand what is meant by antecedent conditions.

Antecedent conditions refer to situational characteristics that a consumer brings to a particular information processing, purchase, or consumption environment. Antecedent conditions include things like economic resources, mood, and other emotional perceptions such as fear. They can shape the value in a situation by framing the events that take place. A consumer in a good mood, for example, tends to look at things more favorably than a consumer in a bad mood.

Visit **4ltrpress.cengage.com/cb** for additional study tools.

Chapter Summary

LO1 Understand the activities involved in the consumer decision making process.

The consumer decision making process consists of five activities: (1) need recognition, (2) search for information, (3) evaluation of alternatives, (4) choice, and (5) post-choice evaluation. Consumers recognize needs when discrepancies are realized between actual and desired states. Consumers search for information from both internal and external sources. With internal search, consumers search their memories for appropriate solutions to problems. External searches consist of information-gathering activities that focus on friends, family, salespeople, advertising, and Internet-based information. Consumers evaluate alternatives based on the information that has been gathered and eventually make a decision.

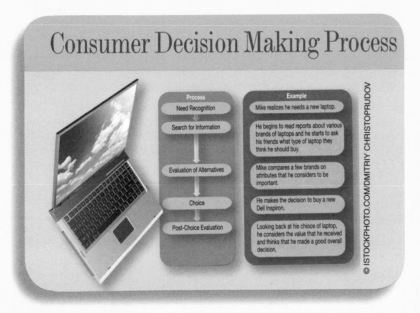

Consumer Decision Making Process

Process	Example
Need Recognition	Mike realizes he needs a new laptop.
Search for Information	He begins to read reports about various brands of laptops and he starts to ask his friends what type of laptop they think he should buy.
Evaluation of Alternatives	Mike compares a few brands on attributes that he considers to be important.
Choice	He makes the decision to buy a new Dell Inspiron.
Post-Choice Evaluation	Looking back at his choice of laptop, he considers the value that he received and thinks that he made a good overall decision.

© ISTOCKPHOTO.COM/DMITRIY CHRISTOPRUDOV

LO2 Describe the three major decision-making research perspectives.

The three major decision-making research perspectives are the rational decision-making perspective, the experiential decision-making perspective, and the behavioral influence decision-making perspective. The rational perspective assumes that consumers diligently gather information about purchases, carefully compare various brands of products on salient attributes, and make informed decisions regarding what brand to buy. This approach centers around the assumption that human beings are rational creatures who are careful with their decision making and behavior. The experiential decision-making perspective assumes that consumers often make purchases and reach decisions based on the affect, or feeling, attached to the product or behavior under consideration. The behavioral influence-making perspective assumes that consumer decisions are learned responses to environmental influences.

Glossary Terms

actual state consumer's perceived current state

awareness set set of alternatives of which a consumer is aware

behavioral influence decision-making perspective decision-making research perspective that assumes many consumer decisions are actually learned responses to environmental influences

brand inertia what occurs when a consumer simply buys a product repeatedly without any real attachment

brand loyalty deeply held commitment to rebuy a product or service regardless of situational influences that could lead to switching behavior

consideration set alternatives that are considered acceptable for further consideration in decision making

consumer search behavior behaviors that consumers engage in as they seek information that can be used to resolve a problem

desired state perceived state for which a consumer strives

experiential decision-making perspective assumes consumers often make purchases and reach decisions based on the affect, or feeling, attached to the product or behavior under consideration

extended decision making consumers move diligently through various problem-solving activities in search of the best information that will help them reach a decision

external search gathering of information from sources external to the consumer such as friends, family, salespeople, advertising, independent research reports, and the Internet

habitual decision making consumers generally do not seek information at all when a problem is recognized and select a product based on habit

inept set alternatives in the awareness set that are deemed to be unacceptable for further consideration

inert set alternatives in the awareness set about which consumers are indifferent or do not hold strong feelings

information overload situation in which consumers are presented with so much information that they cannot assimilate the variety of information presented

internal search retrieval of knowledge stored in memory about products, services, and experiences

limited decision making decision-making approach wherein consumers search very little for information and often reach decisions based largely on prior beliefs about products and their attributes

ongoing search search effort that is not necessarily focused on an upcoming purchase or decision but rather on staying up-to-date on the topic

perceived risk perception of the negative consequences that are likely to result from a course of action and the uncertainty of which course of action is best to take

prepurchase search search effort aimed at finding information to solve an immediate problem

price information that signals the amount of potential value contained in a product

quality perceived overall goodness or badness of some product

rational decision-making perspective assumes consumers diligently gather information about purchases, carefully compare various brands of products on salient attributes, and make informed decisions regarding what brand to buy

satisficing practice of using decision-making shortcuts to arrive at satisfactory, rather than optimal, decisions

search regret negative emotions that come from failed search processes

universal set total collection of all possible solutions to a consumer problem

Perspectives on Consumer Decision Making

Perspective	Description	Example
Rational perspective	Consumers are rational and they carefully arrive at decisions.	Zach carefully considers a number of options when buying a new car.
Experiential perspective	Decision making is often influenced by the feelings associated with consumption.	Marcie decides to go to a day spa for the pleasure and relaxation it provides.
Behavioral influence perspective	Decisions are responses to environmental influences.	The relaxing environment at the restaurant leads Jackie to stay and buy another drink.

LO3 Explain the three major types of decision-making approaches.

Decision-making approaches can be classified into extended decision making, limited decision making, and habitual (or "routine") decision making categories. With extended decision making, consumers search diligently for the best information that will help them reach a decision. They then assimilate the information that they have gathered and evaluate each alternative based on its potential to solve their problem. This process is usually lengthy and generally occurs when involvement is high and when there is a significant amount of purchase risk involved with the decision. With limited decision making, consumers spend little time searching for information and often reach decisions based largely on prior beliefs about products and their attributes. There is also little comparison between brands. Choice strategies are often based on simple decision rules that consumers develop. With habitual decision making, practically no information search takes place, and decisions are reached via habit.

LO4 Understand the importance of the consideration set in the decision-making process.

The consideration set is valuable because brands are placed in the set as consumers proceed through the decision-making process. For this reason, marketers find it valuable to understand the consideration set of their customers. Although the total universe of alternatives available for potentially satisfying a need may be quite large, only a small fraction of these options are generally included in the consideration set.

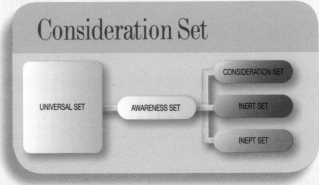

Consideration Set

LO5 Understand the factors that influence the amount of search performed by consumers.

Several factors influence the amount of search that consumers actually perform. Factors such as previous experience with a product, purchase involvement, perceived risk, time availability, attitudes toward shopping, personal factors, and situational pressures all have an impact on the information search effort.

Visit **4ltrpress.cengage.com/cb** for additional study tools.

Chapter Summary

LO1 Understand the difference between evaluative criteria and determinant criteria.

The attributes that consumers consider when evaluating alternative solutions to a problem are evaluative criteria. These criteria include features or benefits associated with a potential solution. Determinant criteria are the factors that have the biggest impact on actual consumer choice. Both evaluative and determinant criteria influence decision making.

LO2 Comprehend how value affects the evaluation of alternatives.

Value is at the heart of the alternative evaluation process. Consumers seek benefits that are associated with a potential solution to a problem. Benefits come from the features or characteristics of the alternatives under consideration. From the value perspective, consumers seek solutions that will deliver benefits while minimizing associated costs.

LO3 Explain the importance of product categorization in the evaluation of alternatives process.

Categorization is important because product categories provide the framework from which consumers evaluate alternative solutions to a problem. When new information about a viable alternative is presented, this information is compared to information that is stored as knowledge in a consumer's perceived product category. This information allows the consumer to make better inferences about the alternative solution.

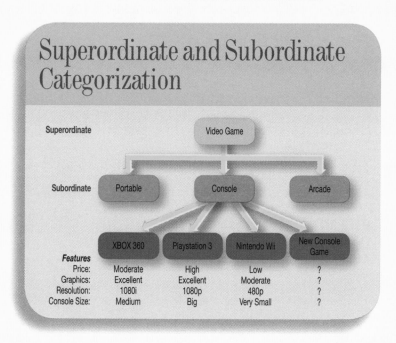

Superordinate and Subordinate Categorization

	Superordinate	Video Game		
Subordinate	Portable	Console	Arcade	

Features	XBOX 360	Playstation 3	Nintendo Wii	New Console Game
Price:	Moderate	High	Low	?
Graphics:	Excellent	Excellent	Moderate	?
Resolution:	1080i	1080p	480p	?
Console Size:	Medium	Big	Very Small	?

Glossary Terms

affect-based evaluation evaluative process wherein consumers evaluate products based on the overall feeling that is evoked by the alternative

attribute correlation perceived relationship between product features

attribute-based evaluation evaluative process wherein alternatives are evaluated across a set of attributes that are considered relevant to the purchase situation

benefit perceived favorable results derived from a particular feature

bounded rationality idea that consumers attempt to act rationally within their information processing constraints

compensatory rule decision-making rule that allows consumers to select products that may perform poorly on one criterion by compensating for the poor performance on one attribute by good performance on another

conjoint analysis technique used to develop an understanding of the attributes that guide consumer preferences by having consumers compare product preferences across varying levels of evaluative criteria and expected utility

conjunctive rule noncompensatory decision rule where the option selected must surpass a minimum cutoff across all relevant attributes

determinant criteria criteria that are most carefully considered and directly related to the actual choice that is made

disjunctive rule noncompensatory decision rule where the option selected surpasses a relatively high cutoff point on any attribute

elimination-by-aspects rule noncompensatory decision rule where the consumer begins evaluating options by first looking at the most important attribute and eliminating any option that does not meet a minimum cutoff point for that attribute and where subsequent evaluations proceed in order of importance until only one option remains

evaluative criteria attributes that consumers consider when reviewing alternative solutions to a problem

Visit **4ltrpress.cengage.com/cb**
for additional study tools.

feature performance characteristic of an object

judgments mental assessments of the presence of attributes and the consequences associated with those attributes

lexicographic rule noncompensatory decision rule where the option selected is thought to perform best on the most important attribute

noncompensatory rule decision-making rule in which strict guidelines are set prior to selection and any option that does not meet the guidelines is eliminated from consideration

perceptual attributes attributes that are visually apparent and easily recognizable

product categories mental representations of stored knowledge about groups of products

signal attribute that consumer uses to infer something about another attribute

underlying attributes attributes that are not readily apparent and can be learned only through experience or contact with the product

LO4 Distinguish between compensatory and noncompensatory rules that guide consumer choice.

The attitude-toward-the-object model is a compensatory model. This type of model allows an alternative to be selected even if it performs poorly on a specific attribute. Noncompensatory models focus on strict guidelines that are set before alternative evaluation. The major noncompensatory rules are the conjunctive, disjunctive, lexicographic, and elimination-by-aspects rule. The conjunctive rule is a rule in which an option that is selected must surpass a minimum cutoff across all relevant attributes. The disjunctive rule is used when an option that surpasses a relatively high cutoff point on any attribute is selected. The lexicographic rule leads the consumer to select the option that performs best on the most important attribute. The elimination-by-aspects rule is used when the consumer begins evaluating options by first looking at the most important attribute and eliminating any option that does not meet a minimum cutoff point for that attribute. The process continues as the consumer considers the next most important attribute and so on, until only one option is left to be chosen.

Noncompensatory Decision Approaches

Attribute	Importance	Chevy Aveo Belief Ratings	Ford Focus Belief Ratings	Honda Fit Belief Ratings	Hyundai Accent Belief Ratings
Gas mileage	10	5	7	9	8
Low price	9	8	6	7	10
Styling	8	9	8	4	4
Warranty	5	4	8	9	8
Service	6	5	6	7	3
Handling	7	6	5	3	3

Note: Belief ratings are performance judgments scaled from 1 = very poor to 9 = very good. Importance ratings are scaled so that 10 = most important, 9 = next most important, and so on.
Source: Wright, Peter (1975), "Consumer Choice Strategies: Simplifying Vs. Optimizing," *Journal of Marketing Research*, 12 (1), 60–67.

Visit **4ltrpress.cengage.com/cb** for additional study tools.

Chapter Summary

LO1 Gain an appreciation of the link from consumption to value to satisfaction.

Consumers only receive value from marketing efforts through consumption. Consumers consume products, services, and experiences and receive value in return. The value that they receive is related to their overall satisfaction, and consumers tend to be more satisfied with exchanges they find valuable. Accordingly, consumers focus first and foremost on the value that they receive from consumption.

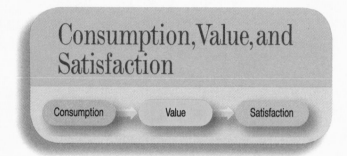

Consumption, Value, and Satisfaction

Consumption → Value → Satisfaction

LO2 Discuss the relative importance of satisfaction and value in consumer behavior.

One major goal of marketers is to create customer satisfaction. Consumer satisfaction itself is a mild, positive emotional state resulting from a favorable appraisal of a consumption outcome—in other words, a favorable satisfaction judgment. Satisfaction, in turn, affects a number of postconsumption behaviors such as word-of-mouth intentions, loyalty, and repeat purchase behavior and is clearly an important concept. Satisfaction and value are related, but not perfectly. In fact, some marketers provide customers with low satisfaction but still do remarkably well in the marketplace because they provide high value. Walmart is perhaps one of the best companies to illustrate this phenomenon. For this reason, even though satisfaction is important, value remains the most important key outcome for consumer behavior.

LO3 Know that emotions other than satisfaction can affect postconsumption behavior.

Emotions other than satisfaction result from appraisals of consumption outcomes. Some, like anger, are both negative and much stronger in motivating behavior following consumption. Others, like warmth, are controlling and can help build relationships. Even though satisfaction receives considerable attention, a fuller range of emotion is needed to fully account for consumption outcomes.

LO4 Use the expectancy disconfirmation, equity, and attribution theory approaches to explain consumers' postconsumption reactions.

The expectancy disconfirmation model proposes that consumers use expectations as benchmarks against which performance perceptions are judged. When performance perceptions are more positive than what was expected, positive disconfirmation is said to occur. When performance perceptions fall below expectations, negative disconfirmation

Glossary Terms

attribution theory theory that proposes that consumers look for the cause of particular consumption experiences when arriving at satisfaction judgments

cognitive dissonance an uncomfortable feeling that occurs when a consumer has lingering doubts about a decision that has occurred

confirmatory bias tendency for expectations to guide performance perceptions

consumer refuse any packaging that is no longer necessary for consumption to take place or, in some cases, the actual good that is no longer providing value to the consumer

consumer satisfaction mild, positive emotion resulting from a favorable appraisal of a consumption outcome

consumption frequency number of times a product is consumed

consumption process process in which consumers use the product, service, or experience that has been selected

desires level of a particular benefit that will lead to a valued end state

durable goods goods that are usually consumed over a long period of time

equity theory theory that proposes that people compare their own level of inputs and outcomes to those of another party in an exchange

expectancy/disconfirmation theory satisfaction formation theory that proposes that consumers use expectations as a benchmark against which performance perceptions are judged

expectations Preconsumption beliefs of what will occur during an exchange and consumption of a product

left skewed distribution of responses consistent with most respondents choosing responses such that the distribution is not evenly spread among responses but clustered toward the positive end of the scale

meaning transference process through which cultural meaning is transferred to a product and onto the consumer

Visit **4ltrpress.cengage.com/cb**
for additional study tools.

negative disconfirmation according to the expectancy disconfirmation approach, a perceived state wherein performance perceptions fall short of expectations

nondurable goods goods that are usually consumed quickly

positive disconfirmation according to the expectancy disconfirmation approach, a perceived state wherein performance perceptions exceed expectations

self-perception theory theory that states that consumers are motivated to act in accordance with their attitudes and behaviors

service quality overall goodness or badness of a service experience, which is often measured by SERVQUAL

SERVQUAL way of measuring service quality that captures consumers' disconfirmation of service expectations

occurs. The expectancy disconfirmation approach remains the dominant theory of viewing satisfaction processes today. Equity theory proposes that consumers consider the fairness of transactions by comparing their own outcomes and inputs to the outcomes and inputs of another party in the transaction. As long as the ratio of outcomes to inputs of each party are approximately equal or favor the consumer, satisfaction is likely to result. Attribution theory proposes that consumers consider the cause of events when making satisfaction judgments. When consumers make external attributions, they tend to be more dissatisfied with unpleasant experiences than when they make internal attributions.

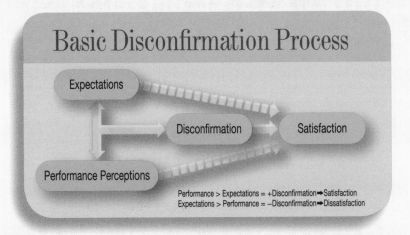

Basic Disconfirmation Process

Expectations → Disconfirmation → Satisfaction

Performance Perceptions

Performance > Expectations = +Disconfirmation → Satisfaction
Expectations > Performance = −Disconfirmation → Dissatisfaction

LO5 Understand problems with commonly applied satisfaction measures.

Marketers often express frustration with measuring satisfaction because the results may not be as useful or diagnostic as they may have hoped. One problem is that the typical ways of measuring, such as a four-item check box, end up providing very little information because consumers overwhelmingly report satisfaction. The result is data that are left skewed, in this instance meaning that the bulk of consumers have indicated that they are satisfied or very satisfied. A better way of satisfaction is to ask the question several different ways with at least some of those ways providing a wider range of possible responses.

LO6 Describe some ways that consumers dispose of products.

Disposal represents the final process in consumption. In this stage of the consumption process, consumers either permanently or temporarily get rid of products. There are many alternatives available to consumers to do this, including trashing, recycling, trading, donating, or reselling.

Visit **4ltrpress.cengage.com/cb**
for additional study tools.

Chapter Summary

LO1 List and define the behavioral outcomes of consumption.

Complaining behavior occurs when a consumer actively seeks out someone to share an opinion with regarding a negative consumption event. WOM behavior occurs when a consumer decides to complain or state an opinion publicly to other consumers about something that happened during a consumption experience with a specific company. When negative WOM reaches a large scale, such as when public media get involved, negative WOM becomes negative publicity. Switching behavior refers to times when a consumer chooses a competing choice, rather than repeating the previous purchase behavior in a given product category. Consumers can also exhibit loyalty-related behaviors. Loyal consumers tend to repeat consumption behavior over and over again.

LO2 Understand why consumers complain and know the ramifications of complaining behavior for a marketing firm.

Emotions influence whether or not a consumer complains, and negative approach emotions like anger are more likely to precede complaining behavior than are avoidance emotions like disgust or even milder negative emotions like dissatisfaction. Complaining should actually be encouraged because when a customer complains, the firm has a chance to recover and convert the complaining customer into a satisfied customer. Aside from this, complaints are an extremely valuable source of feedback for improving the product offering.

The Complainer versus the Noncomplainer and Negative Word-of-Mouth

© PHOTODISC RF/GETTY IMAGES/NEWSCOM

- More likely to become a satisfied customer
- More likely to return
- Tells others when company responds poorly
- Valuable source of information

© MARCIO EUGENIO/ SHUTTERSTOCK

- Unlikely to return
- May well tell others about experience
- Can become a satisfied customer if firm can take preemptive action despite the lack of a complaint

Glossary Terms

antiloyal consumers consumers who will do everything possible to avoid doing business with a particular marketer

competitive intensity number of firms competing for business within a specific category

complaining behavior action that occurs when a consumer actively seeks out someone to share an opinion with regarding a negative consumption event

consumer inertia situation in which a consumer tends to continue a pattern of behavior until some stronger force motivates him or her to change

customer commitment sense of attachment, dedication, and identification

customer share portion of resources allocated to one brand from among the set of competing brands

financial switching costs total economic resources that must be spent or invested as a consumer learns how to obtain value from a new product choice

loyalty card/program device that keeps track of the amount of purchasing a consumer has had with a given marketer once some level is reached

negative public publicity action that occurs when negative WOM spreads on a relatively large scale, possibly even involving media coverage

negative word-of-mouth (negative WOM) action that takes place when consumers pass on negative information about a company from one to another

positive WOM action that occurs when consumers spread information from one to another about positive consumption experiences with companies

procedural switching costs lost time and effort

relational switching cost emotional and psychological consequences of changing from one brand/retailer/service provider to another

relationship quality degree of connectedness between a consumer and a retailer

share of wallet customer share

switching times when a consumer chooses a competing choice, rather than the previously purchased choice, on the next purchase occasion

switching costs costs associated with changing from one choice (brand/retailer/service provider) to another

LO3 Use the concept of switching costs to understand why consumers do or do not repeat purchase behavior.

Switching costs involve the cost of changing from one brand/retailer/service provider to another. Switching costs can be procedural, financial, or relational. Any of these can motivate a consumer to continue making the same purchase decisions as in the past. This can occur even if the consumer is dissatisfied with this behavior. When switching costs are high and few competitors are available to a consumer, he or she can end up feeling captive and forced to continue to do business with a company even when he or she believes service is bad and feels dissatisfied. Some types of procedural switching costs in particular, such as loyalty cards or incompatible features, can alienate consumers.

Vulnerability to Defections Based on CS/D

CUSTOMERS	HIGH COMPETITIVE INTENSITY		LOW COMPETITIVE INTENSITY	
	SWITCHING COSTS		SWITCHING COSTS	
	Low	High	Low	High
Satisfied	Vulnerable	Low vulnerability	Low vulnerability	No vulnerability
Dissatisfied	Highly vulnerable	Vulnerable	Vulnerable	Low vulnerability

LO4 Describe each component of true consumer loyalty.

True consumer loyalty is more than just repeated behavior. Consumer loyalty can be described behaviorally by the concept of customer share, sometimes known as share of wallet. This is the percent of resources allocated to one from among a set of competing marketers. Over time, consumers may also begin to identify strongly with a brand and develop customer commitment. A committed customer will go out of his or her way and even pay more to continue doing business with a preferred brand, retailer, or service provider.

LO5 Understand the role that value plays in shaping loyalty and building consumer relationships.

Value is the result of consumption and as such plays a key role in determining how the consumer behaves following consumption. For functional goods and services, such as banking or auto repair, utilitarian value is particularly important in bringing consumers back and creating loyalty. For experiential goods and services, such as fine dining, hedonic value is relatively important in bringing consumers back and creating loyalty.

Visit **4ltrpress.cengage.com/cb** for additional study tools.

Chapter Summary

LO1 Understand the consumer misbehavior phenomenon and how it affects the exchange process.

Consumer misbehavior does indeed affect the exchange process. For fair exchanges to occur, the consumer, the marketer, and other consumers must trust each another. Abusive or threatening consumers can harm employees, other consumers, and even themselves. Consumers who misbehave also cause monetary harm to the entire marketing system. Insurance costs escalate, prices of consumer products soar, employees must be counseled, and new technologies must be added to retail outlets all because of consumer misbehavior. Computer-mediated misbehavior also causes disruptions in electronic commerce.

LO2 Describe the role of value in consumer misbehavior.

Value is at the heart of consumer misbehavior. However, with consumer misbehavior, value is maximized when a consumer performs illegal or illicit acts. Value, in this way, is a very selfish thing for the guilty party. Consumers attempt to obtain all the benefits they can while sacrificing very little, if any, costs.

LO3 Comprehend how consumers' moral beliefs and evaluations influence the choice to engage in consumer misbehavior.

The decision to engage in consumer misbehavior is largely affected by consumers' moral beliefs and evaluations. Moral beliefs consist of three parts: moral equity, contractualism, and relativism. These factors combine to determine the perceived ethicality or morality of behaviors. Evaluations consist of both deontological and teleological components. Deontological evaluations regard the inherent rightness or wrongness of a course of action, whereas teleological evaluations consist of an assessment of the goodness or badness of the consequences of the actions.

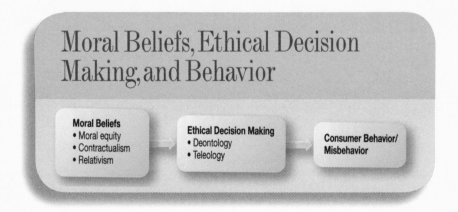

Moral Beliefs, Ethical Decision Making, and Behavior

Moral Beliefs
• Moral equity
• Contractualism
• Relativism

→

Ethical Decision Making
• Deontology
• Teleology

→

Consumer Behavior/ Misbehavior

Glossary Terms

addictive consumption physiological dependency on the consumption of a consumer product

anomie state that occurs when there is a disconnect between cultural goals and norms and the capacities of members of society to act within societal norms in effort to achieve those goals

binge drinking consumption of five or more drinks in a single drinking session for men and four or more drinks for women

binge eating consumption of large amounts of food while feeling a general loss of control over food intake

compulsive buying chronic, repetitive purchasing that is a response to negative events or feelings

compulsive consumption repetitive, excessive, and purposeful consumer behaviors that are performed as a response to tension, anxiety, or obtrusive thoughts

compulsive shopping repetitive shopping behaviors that are a response to negative events or feelings

consumer misbehavior behavior that violates generally accepted norms of conduct

consumer problem behavior consumer behavior that is deemed to be unacceptable but that is seemingly beyond the control of the consumer

contractualism beliefs about the violation of written (or unwritten) laws

culture jamming attempts to disrupt advertisements and marketing campaigns by altering the messages in some meaningful way

deontological evaluations evaluations regarding the inherent rightness or wrongness of specific actions

dysfunctional fan behavior abnormal functioning relating to sporting event consumption

moral beliefs beliefs about the perceived ethicality or morality of behaviors

moral equity beliefs regarding an act's fairness or justness

problem gambling obsession over the thought of gambling and the loss of control over gambling behavior and its consequences

relativism beliefs about the social acceptability of an act

retail borrowing practice of buying products with the sole intention of returning the products after they have been used

teleological evaluations consumers' assessment of the goodness or badness of the consequences of actions

LO4 Distinguish between consumer misbehavior and consumer problem behavior.

Consumer misbehavior can be distinguished from consumer problem behavior in terms of self-control. In most situations, a consumer can control consumer misbehavior; however, a consumer will experience great difficulty controlling problem behavior. This is particularly the case for addictive consumer behavior when a consumer becomes physically dependent on the consumption of a product.

Consumer Misbehavior and Problem Behavior

CONSUMER MISBEHAVIOR	CONSUMER PROBLEM BEHAVIOR
• Shoplifting • Computer-mediated behaviors: illicit sharing of software and music, computer attacks, cyberbullying • Fraud • Abusive consumer behavior • Dysfunctional sports behaviors • Illegitimate complaining • Product misuse: aggressive driving, drunk driving, cell phone use	• Compulsive buying • Compulsive shopping • Eating disorders • Binge drinking • Problem gambling • Drug abuse

LO5 Understand specific consumer misbehaviors and problem behaviors.

Consumer misbehaviors include shoplifting, computer-mediated attacks, fraud, abusive consumer behavior, dysfunctional sports fan behaviors, illegitimate complaining, and product misuse. Consumer problem behaviors include compulsive consumption (compulsive buying and shopping), binge eating, binge drinking, problem gambling, and drug addiction.

Visit **4ltrpress.cengage.com/cb**
for additional study tools.

Chapter Summary

LO1 Discuss marketing ethics and how marketing ethics guide the development of marketing programs.

Marketing ethics are societal and professional standards of right and fair practices that are expected of marketing managers. Marketing programs must be planned in ways that adhere to marketing ethics. Most firms have explicitly stated rules and codes of conduct for their employees and their activities in the marketplace. Most professional organizations also have these codes. These ethics provide a framework from which marketing decisions can be made.

LO2 Describe the consumerism movement and how the movement has affected marketing practice.

The consumerism movement gained momentum in the 1960s with the passage of the Consumer Bill of Rights. Since that time, consumer advocacy groups have exerted pressure on businesses to ensure that they are acting within the best interests of society. In part as a result of the consumerism movement, marketers began to acknowledge and accept what is referred to as the societal marketing concept, which states that marketing decision making should be made within a framework that considers the effects of marketing action on societal well-being.

The Marketing Mix and Business Ethics

TOOL	COMMON USE	UNETHICAL USE
Product	The development of a good, service, or experience that will satisfy consumers' needs.	Failure to disclose that product won't function properly without necessary component parts.
Place	The distribution of a marketing offer through various channels of delivery.	Limiting product availability in certain markets as a means of raising prices.
Price	The marketer's statement of value received from an offering that may be monetary or non-monetary.	Stating that a regular price is really a "sales" price. This practice is prohibited by law.
Promotion	Communicating an offering's value through techniques such as advertising, sales promotion, and word-of-mouth.	Promoting one item as being on sale and then informing the customer that the product is out of stock and that a more expensive item should be bought. This practice, known as "bait and switch," is illegal.

Glossary Terms

altruistic duties expectations placed upon a firm to give back to communities through philanthropic activities

Children's Online Privacy Protection Act act that was established to protect children's privacy in online environments

compensatory damages damages that are intended to cover costs incurred by a consumer due to an injury

Consumer Bill of Rights introduced by President John F. Kennedy in 1962, list of rights that includes the right to safety, the right to be informed, the right to redress and to be heard, and the right to choice

consumerism activities of various groups to voice concern for, and to protect, basic consumer rights

corporate social responsibility organization's activities and status related to its societal obligations

customer orientation practice of using sales techniques that focus on customer needs

deceptive advertising message that omits information that is important in influencing a consumer's buying behavior and is likely to mislead consumers acting "reasonably"

deficient products products that have little or no potential to create value of any type

desirable products products that deliver high utilitarian and hedonic value and that benefit both consumers and society in the long run

door-in-the-face technique ingratiation technique used in personal selling in which a salesperson begins with a major request and then follows with a series of smaller requests

equity theory theory of satisfaction in which a consumer compares the ratio of his or her own outcomes and inputs to the same ratio for another party in a transaction

ethical duties expectations placed on a firm to act within ethical boundaries

ethics standards or moral codes of conduct to which a person, group, or organization adheres

Visit **4ltrpress.cengage.com/cb** for additional study tools.

even-a-penny-will-help technique ingratiation technique in which a marketing message is sent that suggests that even the smallest donation, such as a penny or a dollar, will help a cause

foot-in-the-door technique ingratiation technique used in personal selling in which a salesperson begins with a small request and slowly leads up to one major request

"I'm working for you!" technique technique used by salespeople to create the perception that they are working as hard as possible to close a sale when they really are not doing so

ingratiation tactics that are used to become more attractive and likable to another person or party

marketing concept concept that states a firm should focus on consumer needs as a means of achieving long-term success

marketing ethics societal and professional standards of right and fair practices that are expected of marketing managers as they develop and implement marketing strategies

morals personal standards and beliefs used to guide individual action

negligence situation whereby an injured consumer attempts to show that a firm could foresee a potential injury might occur and then decided not to act on that knowledge

planned obsolescence act of planning the premature obsolescence of product models that perform adequately

pleasing products products that provide hedonic value for consumers but may be harmful in the long run

products liability extent to which businesses are held responsible for product-related injuries

puffery practice of making exaggerated claims about a product and its superiority

punitive damages damages that are sought to punish a company for behavior associated with an injury

sales orientation practice of using sales techniques that are aimed at satisfying the salesperson's own needs and motives for short-term sales success

salutary products products that are good for both consumers and society in the long run and that provide high utilitarian value, but no hedonic value

societal marketing concept marketing concept that states that marketers should consider not only the wants and needs of consumers but also the needs of society

LO3 Comprehend the role of corporate social responsibility in the field of marketing.

It is important for businesses today to focus on "doing well by doing good." Being socially responsible is one way in which businesses attempt to do well by doing the right things. Corporate social responsibility refers to an organization's activities and status related to its societal obligations. Due to increased pressure from various consumer and media groups, companies are finding that they must be socially responsible with their marketing programs.

LO4 Understand the various forms of regulation that affect marketing practice.

Federal, state, and local laws are in place to protect consumers from many forms of marketer misbehavior. Federal bodies, such as the Federal Trade Commission and the Food and Drug Administration, exist to monitor exchanges that take place between consumers and marketing organizations. Other groups, such as the Better Business Bureau, the American Association of Advertising Agencies, and the American Marketing Association, also play important roles in monitoring marketing activities. Although these groups attempt to bring fairness to the marketplace, ultimately it is up to the decision maker to ensure that his or her own actions, and the actions of his or her firm, fall within generally accepted business guidelines.

LO5 Comprehend the major areas of criticism to which marketers are subjected.

Several issues in marketing receive criticism from various groups. Issues such as deceptive advertising, marketing to children, marketing unsafe products, planning the obsolescence of current products, using manipulative sales tactics, and practicing stealth marketing campaigns are all considered questionable by various groups.

LO6 Understand how products liability issues can provide both positive and negative results for consumers.

Strict liability is the primary legal doctrine governing products liability cases in the United States today. Under strict liability, a consumer suing a company over a product injury need only show that an injury occurred and that a product was faulty. Generally, demonstrating a faulty product has not proved difficult. Policies such as this protect consumers by providing relatively consumer-friendly vehicles to pursue damages from companies for injuries. In this way, they help consumers. However, they also harm consumers by driving up the costs of many products and restricting the amount of products available to choose from.

stealth marketing marketing technique in which consumers do not realize that they are being targeted for a particular product promotion

strategic initiatives process of strategically engaging in socially responsible activities in order to increase the value of the firm

strict liability legal action against a firm whereby a consumer demonstrates in court that an injury occurred and that the product associated with the injury was faulty in some way

Visit **4ltrpress.cengage.com/cb** for additional study tools.